UNDERSTANDING

PAEDIATRIC ANAESTHESIA

FOURTH EDITION

UNDERSTANDING

PAEDIATRIC ANAESTHESIA

FOURTH EDITION

CHIEF EDITOR

Rebecca Jacob, DA, MD
Retired Professor and HOD
Christian Medical College
Vellore, Tamil Nadu

ASSOCIATE EDITOR

Vibhavari Naik, MD, DNB, Hon. Fellowship
(Paediatric Anaesthesia)
Senior Consultant Anaesthesiologist
Basavatarakam Indo-American Cancer Hospital
and Research Institute
Hyderabad, Telangana

Wolters Kluwer

Publishing Manager: Sangeetha P
Production Editor: Pooja Chauhan
Asst Manager-Manufacturing: Sumit Johry

3rd Floor, Tower B, Building No. 10, Phase II, DLF Cyber City, Gurugram, Haryana - 122002

First Edition, 2006 © B I Publications Pvt. Ltd.
Second Edition, 2008 © B I Publications Pvt. Ltd.
Third Edition, 2015 © Wolters Kluwer (I) Pvt. Ltd.
Fourth Edition, 2023 © Wolters Kluwer (I) Pvt. Ltd.

ISBN-13: 978-93-95736-49-7

Published by Wolters Kluwer (India) Pvt. Ltd., New Delhi

Compositor: B2K - Bytes 2 Knowledge
Printed and bound at SDR Printers, Trans Delhi Signature City, Ghaziabad (UP)

For product enquiry, please contact – Marketing Department (marketing@wolterskluwerindia.co.in) or log on to our website www.wolterskluwerindia.co.in.

Foreword

"Life begins at the end of your comfort zone."
N D Walsch

"Work hard in silence, let your success be your noise."
Anonymous

Providing safe anaesthesia, especially to very small and vulnerable children is a challenge for anaesthetists. The process of learning, training and providing safe perioperative care for children requires knowledge, understanding, dedication, passion and a big heart. Having been a practising anaesthetist for more than four decades, I hold the strong belief that providing anaesthesia for children is not just a job but also requires constant learning, sharpening of one's skills and developing the art of providing it. Guarding a child's life, taking charge of their care and handing them back safely to their family is a privilege, honour and immense responsibility. In this context, Dr. Rebecca Jacob, with her long and illustrious anaesthetic career, has been a passionate advocate for providing safe anaesthesia for children, regardless of where one works.

Dr Rebecca Jacob retired as a Professor and Head of Anaesthesia from Christian Medical College, Vellore, India. She edited and published the first edition of her multi-author book 'Understanding Paediatric Anaesthesia' in 2005 and a second and third edition followed. The tremendous interest and positive response to the book have spread across India, and overseas and have been translated into several Asian and European languages. Dr Jacob is a vocal advocate for keeping things simple and doing the job well. Her passion for paediatric anaesthesia with an emphasis on safety is palpable. Her love for teaching and regard for those who practice anaesthesia in primary- and secondary-tier hospitals across Asia is well known. Her approach is not only to publish a textbook but also to make the book informative, clinically oriented, practical and user-friendly. This updated fourth edition of the book is welcomed. The hard work gone into writing and editing it is a testimony to Rebecca's amazing energy, enthusiasm and perseverance.

Elsa Varghese
Former Professor, Kasturba Medical College Manipal
Former President, Indian Association of Paediatric Anaesthesiologists

Preface

Almost every practicing anaesthetist in India is required to anaesthetise a child sometime in his/her career, as 40% of India's population of more than 1.4 billion comprises children. Specialist paediatric anaesthetists and hospitals caring only for children are few and far between. Although the specialty of paediatric anaesthesia has gained popularity in recent times, with numerous hospitals offering fellowships in the field, universities recognising centres of excellence to grant a DM degree in the subject, and associations and societies being formed to promote interest in the field, it is important to note that this interest and training represents only the 'tip of the iceberg'. There are many anaesthetists who are called upon to anaesthetise children occasionally and in many hospitals a trained paediatric anaesthetist is often a luxury. Most trained anaesthetists are afraid to anaesthetise children especially neonates and infants because of perceived difficulty or fear of stepping into the unknown. Invariably, a paediatric anaesthetist is someone who demonstrates an interest in working with children, enjoys interacting with children or is simply assigned to administer anaesthesia to children on a specific day. Through this book titled *Understanding Paediatric Anaesthesia*, we have set out to demystify the problems associated with anaesthetising children in a simple and enjoyable manner.

The chapters in the previous editions of this book were contributed by a team of doctors from the Christian Medical College, Vellore. The first edition was noticed and adopted by the World Federation of Societies of Anaesthesiologists which was looking for a simple book on the subject. Dr. Cote and Dr. Thirlwell came on board as Consulting Editors for the second edition and the book was on its way for international acceptance. It has been translated into French, Spanish, Mandarin, Turkish and Bahasa Indonesii languages. The third edition was widely accepted but we felt, that over time, it needed updating. Dr. Vibhavari Naik has helped tremendously with the fourth edition as Associate Editor.

In the current edition, we have added a number of chapters on topics of current interest like safety and simulation. New chapters on endocrine diseases and gastric ultrasound also find a place. Other chapters have been updated and revamped while maintaining simplicity and readability, something that has made this book popular with students, the occasional paediatric anaesthetist and even seasoned paediatric anaesthetists who would like a quick browse through before dealing with a difficult case.

Rebecca Jacob

Acknowledgments

I would like to express my gratitude to my teachers, Dr. Valerie Major (India and Wales) and Dr. Ian Stevens (South Australia), who instilled in me a deep passion for my specialty.

I am immensely thankful to my parents and grandparents for their unwavering support and for teaching me the importance of questioning, seeking answers, and respecting myself and my work.

I am indebted to my loving husband and sons, who have provided me with love, support, and patience throughout the years. I am also grateful to my two amazing daughters-in-law and four grandchildren, who have completed our family.

I extend my heartfelt thanks to all the contributors who dedicated their time and efforts to bring this book to fruition. Your care and dedication have helped turn my dream into reality. A special appreciation goes to the contributors of the first three editions, whose inputs were invaluable. We have drawn extensively from their contributions in producing this edition, and we are truly grateful for their contribution.

To Dr. Vibhavari Naik, an exceptional Associate Editor, I am incredibly grateful for her diligence, hard work, love, time and patience. I also thank her husband and in-laws for their understanding and support extended to her during this venture.

I would like to acknowledge the publishing team at Wolters Kluwer (I), particularly Dr. Vandana Mittal and Ms. Pooja Chauhan. It has been a pleasure working with you professionals, and I appreciate your patience, guidance and understanding.

To all my students over the past 45 years, it has been a privilege to teach you and witness your growth. I am grateful to have you as both friends and colleagues.

Lastly, I dedicate this book to all our paediatric patients. It is our hope that this endeavour will contribute to creating a safer world for you.

Rebecca Jacob

About the Editors

Dr Rebecca Jacob is a former Professor and HOD of Anaesthesia at the Christian Medical College, Vellore. With over 40 years of experience as a postgraduate teacher and examiner in various universities, she has made significant contributions in the field of of Paediatric Anaesthesia. Dr. Jacob previously served as the Chair of the Paediatric Committee of the World Federation of Societies of Anaesthesiologists (WFSA). She actively participated in the WFSA's Subcommittees on Safety and Quality of Practice as well as Primary Trauma Care. A former President of the Indian Association of Paediatric Anaesthesiologists (IAPA) and the Asian Society of Paediatric Anaesthesiologists (ASPA), her passion for imparting knowledge and her special love for children motivated her to extend her efforts beyond the borders of our nation. She took on the responsibility of organising and conducting the Paediatric Anaesthesia Fellowship course for anaesthesiologists from Asian countries under the aegies of the WFSA. Additionally, she coordinated the Paediatric Perioperative Life Support courses under the aegies of ASPA. As a member of the Medical Advisory Council of Smile Train India, she actively strives to ensure safety and establish standardised protocols in anaesthesia for all children undergoing surgery. This book represents her endeavour to bridge the gap between theory and practice, to demystify the art of paediatric anaesthesia, and to make its practice enjoyable for anaesthesiologists while providing a safe and less daunting experience for the child.

Dr Vibhavari Naik has been working as a Senior Consultant Anaesthesiologist and Intensivist at the Basavatarakam Indo-American Cancer Hospital and Research Institute in Hyderabad, India, for more than 12 years. She completed her MD and DNB in Anaesthesiology at B.J. Medical College Pune in 2000 and subsequently underwent training under the guidance of Dr. Rebecca Jacob at Christian Medical College, Vellore, focusing on paediatric anaesthesiology. In 2018, she was honoured with an 'Honorary Fellowship in Paediatric Anaesthesiology' by the Indian Association of Paediatric Anaesthesiologists (IAPA). Dr. Naik has served as the Treasurer of IAPA, an Executive Committee member of the Asian Society of Paediatric Anaesthesiologists (ASPA), and currently holds the position of Secretary of ASPA. Her areas of interests include paediatric oncoanaesthesia and advanced vascular access for children. She has a passion for teaching and volunteers to provide training through various international societies such as the AHA, Smile Train, Vital Anaesthesia Simulation Training, WFSA SAFE Paediatric course and ASPA PPLS courses. Supported by a loving family both at home and at work, Dr. Naik embraces new responsibilities. This book represents her ongoing journey of learning from her mentor, Dr. Rebecca Jacob, who, in addition to teaching her about paediatric anaesthesia, has imparted valuable life lessons.

Contributors

Aanchal R Bharuka, DA, DNB, Fellowship in Obstetric Anaesthesia and Critical Care
Consultant Anaesthesiologist, Basavatarakam Indo-American Cancer Hospital and Research Institute, Hyderabad

Amar Nandhakumar, DA, MD, DNB Fellow in Obstetric Anaesthesia, Fellow in Hepatobiliary and Surgical Oncology Including Liver Transplant
Consultant Anesthesiologist, Kovai Medical Center and Hospital, Coimbatore

Amitha Varmma Aredath, MBBS, DA, DNB, EDAIC
Consultant Anaesthesiologist, Manipal Hospital, Yeshwanthpur, Bangalore

Amjad Maniar, MD, Fellowship in Regional Anaesthesia
Consultant, Axon Group Anaesthesia Associates, Bangalore

Anisha De, MD
Associate Professor, Unit of Paediatric Anaesthesia, Department of Paediatric Surgery, Institute of Child Health, Kolkata

Anita Shirley Joselyn, MD DA DNB, Fellowship in Paediatric Anaesthesia
Professor, Department of Anaesthesia, Christian Medical College and Hospital, Vellore

Ashok Dharmalingam, DA MD, DNB, FANZCA, Grad Dip Clin USG
Staff Specialist Anaesthetist, John Hunter Hospital and Calvary Mater Newcastle, NSW, Australia; Conjoint Lecturer, University of Newcastle, NSW, Australia

Aparna Williams, MBBS, MD
Professor, Department of Anesthesiology, Christian Medical College and Hospital, Vellore

Basanth Kumar Rayani, MBBS, DA, DNB, MBA
Chief Anaesthesiologist, Basavatarakam Indo-American Cancer Hospital and Research Institute, Hyderabad

Chris Maria Joseph, MD, PDF (Advanced Clinical Anaesthesia and Perioperative Medicine)
Assistant Professor, Department of Anaesthesia, Christian Medical College and Hospital, Vellore

David Wright, BMedSci, BMBS, FRCA, PGCME, FHEA
Consultant Anaesthetist and Director of Simulation, Hull University Teaching Hospitals NHS Trust, England

Ekta Rai, MRCA, MD, Paediatric Anaesthesia Fellowship (KKH Singapore)
Professor and Head, Christian Medical College, Vellore

Erlinda C. Oracion, MD, MBAH
Patient Safety Advocate and Paediatric Anesthesiologist; Chair, Safety and Quality of Practice Committee, World Federation of Society of Anaesthesiologists; Senior Consultant, Cardinal Santos Medical Center, San Juan; Rizal Medical Center, Pasig City, Metro Manila

Garima Sharma, DA, DNB
Consultant Anaesthesiologist, Cloudnine Hospital, Malleswaram, Bangalore

Gayatri Sasikumar, MBBS, DA, DNB (Anaesthesiology), Fellowship in Paediatric Anesthesia (BCCH, Vancouver)
Consultant Anaesthesiologist, Children's Airway and Swallowing Centre, Manipal Hospital, HAL Old Airport Road, Bangalore

Georgene Singh, MD, DNB, DM (Neuroanaesthesia)
Professor, Department of Neuroanaesthesia, Christian Medical College and Hospital, Vellore

Guiseppe A Marraro, MD
Assistant Professor, University of Milan, Italy; Director, Anesthesia and Intensive Care Department, Paediatric Intensive Care Unit, Fatebenefratelli & Ophthalmiatric University affiliated Hospital, Milan, Italy

Ilamurugu Kaliaperumal, MBBS, MD, DA, DNB, FANZCA, FFPMANZCA
Senior Staff Specialist in Anesthetics and Pain Medicine, Townsville University Hospital, Queensland, Australia

Karthikeyan Chandrasekaran, MBBS, DA, MD, DNB, FANZCA
Senior Staff Specialist in Anaesthesia, Queensland Health, Australia

Kristy Xinghan Fu, MBBS, MRCPC
Assistant Professor, Department of Paediatrics, National University Hospital, Singapore; National University of Singapore, Yong Loo Lin School of Medicine, Singapore

Lakshmi Kumar, MD
Professor and Head, Amrita Institute of Medical Sciences & Research Centre, Kochi

Mathews Thomas, MD, DA
Associate Professor Anaesthesia, Pushpagiri Medical College, Thiruvalla

Nithya Jayaraman Ponmudi, MBBS, DCH, MD Paediatrics
Assistant Physician, Christian Medical College, Vellore

Prarthana M Raj, MD, Fellowship in Regional Anaesthesia
Anaesthesia Specialist, Aster RV Hospital, Bangalore

Poornachand Anne, MD
Consultant Anaesthesiologist, Basavatarakam Indo-American Cancer Hospital and Research Institute, Hyderabad

Priya Nair, DA, DNB, EDAIC, FIPM
Consultant Anaesthesiologist and Pain Physician, Manipal Hospital, Hebbal, Bangalore

Purva Makani, DA(UK), FFARCS (Irel), MBA, MMed
Professor, Hull University Teaching Hospital, Hull Royal Infirmary, England

Raj Sahajanandan, MD, DNB, FRCA
Professor, Department of Anaesthesia, Christian Medical College, Vellore

Rakhee Goyal, MD, Fellowship (Honorary) Paediatric Anesthesia
Director Anesthesia, Madhukar Rainbow Children's Hospital, New Delhi

Ramammani Mariappan, MD, Dip NB, Fellow in NA, NCC (UFT, Toronto, Canada)
Professor, Department of Neuroanaesthesia, Christian Medical College, Vellore

Rebecca Jacob, DA, MD
Retired Professor and HOD, Christian Medical College, Vellore

Riya Sarah Abraham, MD, Postdoctoral Fellowship in Regional Anaesthesia and Trauma Critical Care
Assistant Professor, Department of Anaesthesiology, Christian Medical College and Hospital, Vellore

Sajan Philip George, DA, MD
Professor, Christian Medical College and Hospital, Vellore

Sajana Mukundan, DA, DNB
Senior Consultant, Manipal Hospital, Yeswanthpur, Bangalore

Sarah Hodges, MBChB, FRCA
Anesthesiologist, Director of Anesthsia & Critical Care, CURE Children's Hospital of Zimbabwe

Sarathkumar M.S., MBBS, MD, PDF
Academic Senior Resident, Postgraduate Institute of Medical Education and Research, Chandigarh

Smithamol P.B., DA, DNB
Associate Professor, Department of Anaesthesia, Christian Medical College and Hospital, Vellore

Smruthi S., MBBS, DNB
Registrar, Manipal Hospital, Yeshwanthpur, Bangalore

Subramanyam Mahankali, MD, DNB, FRCA (Lond)
Consultant and Lead Anaesthesiologist, Aster RV Hospital, Bangalore

Swapna Thampi, DA, MD, DNB, MMED, FANZCA
Senior Consultant, Department of Anaesthesia, National University Health System, Singapore; Assistant Professor, Department of Anaesthesia, National University of Singapore, Singapore

Venkatesan Thiruvenkatarajan, MD, DA, DNB, FANZCA
Clinical Associate Professor, Discipline of Acute Care Medicine, University of Adelaide; Senior Consultant Anaesthetist, The Queen Elizabeth Hospital, Adelaide, South Australia

Verghese T Cherian, MBBS, MD, FFARCSI
Julien F Biebuyck M.D. Endowed Professor in Anesthesia, Department of Anesthesiology & Perioperative Medicine, Penn State Hershey Medical Center, Hershey, Pennsylvania

Vibhavari Naik, MD, DNB, Hon. Fellowship (Paediatric Anaesthesia)
Senior Consultant Anaesthesiologist, Basavatarakam Indo-American Cancer Hospital and Research Institute, Hyderabad

Zipporah Gathuya, MBChB, MMED (Anaesthesia), MPH
Paediatric Anesthesiologist, Gertrude Children Hospital, Nairobi, Kenya

PUBLISHER'S ACKNOWLEDGMENTS

The publisher would like to thank the following reviewers for their valuable suggestions:

Faculty Reviewers

Adarsh E
Professor and Head, Department of Paediatrics, Rajarajeshwari Medical College and Hospital, Bangalore, Karnataka

Fulton Sebastian Dsouza
Professor and Head (Unit 1), Department of Paediatrics, St. Johns Medical College, Bangalore, Karnataka

Mallesh K
Head, Department of Paediatrics, Vanivilas Hospital, Bangalore Medical College and Research Institute, Bangalore, Karnataka

Manasa M
Assistant Professor, Department of Anaesthesia, Rajarajeswari Medical College & Hospital, Bangalore, Karnataka

KNV Prasad
Professor, Department of Paediatrics, Sri Devaraj Urs Medical College, Kolar, Karnataka

Sudha Reddy V R
Professor and Head, Department of Paediatrics, Sri Devaraj Urs Medical College, Kolar, Karnataka

Student Reviewers

Bindu T
Postgraduate Student, Sri Devaraj Urs Medical College, Kolar, Karnataka

Matta Saikiranmai
MD Paediatrics (2nd Year), Rajarajeswari Medical College and Hospital, Bangalore, Karnataka

Table of Contents at a Glance

Detailed Table of Contents

1 Principles of Paediatric Anaesthesia

Vibhavari Naik

Children are very special people and they need special care. Although paediatric anaesthesia is one of the most professionally challenging specialities, it is also one of the most personally satisfying medical disciplines in which to work. It demands precision and accuracy from the anaesthetist and surgeon, as well as a high degree of efficiency and teamwork from all doctors, nurses and technicians who form the operating-room team. In order to give anaesthesia to children, some basic principles as described in the following text have to be known and followed. At the same time, it is also important to understand the basic developmental physiology, the knowledge of which can help a paediatric anaesthetist to take vital decisions.

Developmental Physiology

Organogenesis occurs in the first 1–8 weeks of intrauterine life, organ function in the second trimester and weight gain in the third trimester. Maternal stress, drug ingestion (alcohol) or infection, especially during the first two trimesters, can cause congenital abnormalities.

Details of basic terminology and physiology are found in Chapter 4. Of importance and requiring special consideration are the following:

Preterm infants: These infants are susceptible to certain diseases such as hyaline membrane disease, hypoglycaemia, hypocalcaemia, hypomagnesaemia, thrombocytopenia, hyperbilirubinaemia, polycythaemia and viral infection.

Apnoea of prematurity is due to brainstem immaturity, a special feature of which is respiratory fatigue. This apnoea can occur up to 60 weeks post-conceptual age.

Term and post-term infants: They are also susceptible to hypoglycaemia, hyperbilirubinaemia, thrombocytopenia, birth trauma and meconium aspiration pneumonia but to a lesser extent than preterm infants.

Pre-Operative Evaluation

The main goals of pre-operative evaluation are as follows:

- To establish whether a child is fit or unfit for surgery
- To look for the presence of any disease which may require pre-operative treatment that could affect the course of anaesthesia
- To decide which anaesthetic regimen is optimal for the child
- To establish rapport with the child and the parents to allay their anxiety. If parents speak a different language, an interpreter must be sought

The pre-operative medical evaluation is divided into two parts – history and physical examination all of which must be documented.

History

- Obtain a concise overview of the child's development and milestones since birth including their vaccination status
- Get the antenatal and birth history
- Find out whether the child is a term or preterm and calculate the post-conceptual age if preterm

- Check for a history of allergy
- History of complex disease – rely on previous medical records
- History of current medication (including nutritional supplements)
- History pertinent to every system
- Maternal history, especially for diabetes, maternal medications, drug abuse and infections during pregnancy
- History of exposure to smoking at home (parents or grandparents) is associated with increased airway reactivity in children

Physical Examination

In all cases, 'LOOK, LISTEN and FEEL', that is, inspection, palpation, percussion and auscultation.

General Physical Examination

A general physical examination is to be done from **head to toe** and includes looking for the following:

- Head circumference
- Fusion of fontanelles
- Dilated veins over the head and trunk

The signs specific to each disease should be looked for. In addition, look for pallor, cyanosis, icterus, clubbing, jaundice, lymphadenopathy, signs of dehydration, malnutrition, parasitic manifestations, scars, sinuses, petechial haemorrhage and pruritus.

Systemic Examination

Systemic examination should include examination of the central nervous system, cardiovascular system, abdomen and respiratory system. The detailed examination should be as follows.

Central nervous system examination includes the following:

- Cranial nerve examination
- Sensory system
- Motor system
- Autonomic neuropathy
- Developmental milestones
- Alertness and eye contact

Cardiovascular system, *respiratory system* and *abdomen examination* should be done in the following manner:

- Inspection
- Palpation
- Percussion
- Auscultation

Finally, look for associated congenital anomalies.

The examination of a child is an 'examination of opportunity'; if the child is quiet, listen to the heart and lungs and feel the abdomen. When the child cries, examine the airway, extremities and skin colour.

At the end of pre-anaesthetic evaluation, parents should be counselled regarding the perioperative risks and consented. The anaesthetic plan should be shared and the perioperative concerns addressed. Communication with the child should be age-appropriate and in simple words regarding what to expect. Children cannot legally consent till 18 years of age in most countries. But their verbal assent (meaning that they agree to participate) should be taken and recorded.

Pre-Operative Preparation

Pre-operative preparation should be undertaken with clear instructions given to the parent, nursing staff and the older child, both verbally and in writing. This includes the following:

- Pre-operative fasting
- Pre-medication

Pre-Operative Fasting

It is now well-recognised that prolonged fasting is distressing for the child and the parent and may result in significant fluid depletion. Children given sugar-containing clear fluids 2 hours before the induction of anaesthesia decreases thirst, gastric volume and hunger compared to children who fasted overnight. (Clear fluids are those which you can 'see through' and include water, coconut water, fruit juices without pulp, etc.) Fried and fatty foods or meat may prolong gastric emptying and may require fasting of 8 or more hours. Therefore, there appears to be no need for withholding clear fluids for more than 2 hours. In OTs where the timing of surgery is difficult to predict, one may make the fasting for clear fluids 3 hours. Refer Chapter 7 for further details.

Pre-Medication

The objectives of pre-medication are as follows:

- To produce sedation, ease separation anxiety and facilitate induction of anaesthesia
- To facilitate analgesia and decrease the requirement for general anaesthetic drugs
- To block harmful vagal reflexes
- To decrease secretions in the respiratory tract

Pre-medication may delay the emergence and recovery particularly when long-acting drugs are used for short-lasting procedures. The non-pharmacological techniques may be used in such situations as detailed below.

Routes for Pre-Medication

Oral Route

The oral route is the preferred route and medications such as triclofos and midazolam are commercially available as syrups and are better accepted by children. Other medications such as ketamine and dexmedetomidine are not available as syrups and, in some centres, mixed with honey or sugar water to mask the bitter taste. The oral bioavailability may be low for some drugs (midazolam and dexmedetomidine) due to the first pass hepatic clearance and absorption through nasal mucosa may be better.

Intranasal Route

The intranasal route is less preferred than the oral route due to discomfort and nasal irritation. Commercially, midazolam is available as a nasal spray. Alternatively, atomisers can improve precision in delivery.

Intramuscular Route

This route is useful for children who are fractious or recalcitrant and refuse all other ways of induction. It is also helpful in children with severe developmental delay. This route is more predictable than the rectal or nasal route. Ketamine 6 mg/kg is commonly used (along with atropine or glycopyrrolate) and takes 15–20 minutes for action.

Sedatives

These drugs produce sedation, anxiolysis and amnesia. Post-operative emotional and behavioural disturbances are reduced. Infants less than 6–8 months do not require sedation as separation from parents at this age is not a problem. Sedatives should not be given to children with airway problems and CNS disease.

- **Midazolam:**
  - It is a benzodiazepine.
  - Routes of administration: Oral 0.5–1 mg/kg, intravenous 0.05 mg/kg, rectal 1 mg/kg or intranasal 0.1–0.2 mg/kg. Given *orally*, it acts within 15 minutes and does not produce deep sleep but permits easy separation from the parents.
- **Triclofos:** It is a non-barbiturate hypnotic drug. In a dose of 75 mg/kg, it produces good anxiolysis and smooth induction. However, it takes about 30 minutes to act and has a long duration of action. It has a good anti-sialagogue effect and produces a higher gastric pH.
- **Dexmedetomidine:** It is an alpha-2 agonist and has sedative, anxiolytic, analgesic and anti-sialagogue activity. It is given intranasal (2–3 mcg/kg) and the onset of action in 15–30 minutes. The bioavailability from the oral route is low (<20%) and hence not preferred.

Analgesics

- **Fentanyl**: It is a narcotic drug which may be given in an intravenous dose of 1–5 mcg/kg. The disadvantages associated with its use are that it causes respiratory depression, nausea and vomiting and pruritis.
- **Ketamine**: It is an N-methyl-D-aspartate (NMDA) antagonist that may be given by different routes. These routes and doses are given below:
  - *Oral*: The dose is 6 mg/kg.
  - *Nasal*: The dose is 3 mg/kg.
  - *Intramuscular*: In a low dose of 3–4 mg/kg, it is used for analgesia and ease of separation of the child. In high doses of 8–10 mg/kg, it is used for anaesthesia.
  - *Intravenous*: The dose of ketamine is 1–2 mg/kg. The main advantage of using ketamine is the rapid onset of action and stable cardiovascular and respiratory responses. However, the main disadvantages associated with its

use are bitter taste, prolonged recovery and hypersalivation if not administered with an anti-sialagogue.

Midazolam should be combined with ketamine to reduce the hallucinations and emergence of delirium associated with it.

Anticholinergics

Examples are atropine, hyoscine and glycopyrrolate. They block vagal reflexes and decrease respiratory secretions and are therefore given to children with difficult airways to minimise coughing and breath-holding. They prevent bradycardia during instrumentation of the airway, following succinylcholine and the use of halothane. Their use pre-operatively is optional except in cases that have a propensity for bradycardia as in squint surgery. Care must be exerted when using atropine pre-medication in hot summers or in non-airconditioned rooms as it may increase body temperature further.

Pre-Induction

Equipment to be kept ready includes the following:

- S – suction
- O – oxygen
- A – airway
- P – pharmacy (drugs)
- M – monitors
- E – end-tidal carbon dioxide

The list can be easily remembered by the pneumonic S-O-A-P +ME.

Anaesthesia

Once the OT is prepared details of the anaesthetic plan may be discussed with the team.

Induction

There are various ways to induce a child for anaesthesia. Remember 'children do not like needles', especially when in the hands of masked strangers!

Parental Presence

The presence of parents during the induction of anaesthesia is desirable if it will help the child to be more cooperative and will allay their anxieties. Studies suggest that children are more secure when their parents are present. The groups of patients who seem to benefit most from parental presence are as follows:

- Children more than 4 years of age
- Children with parents who are not anxious
- Children who tend to be anxious

Parents should be informed about what to anticipate in terms of what they may observe during induction (eyes rolling up, noises from throat, excitement) and they must comply when asked to leave the induction room.

Occasionally, parents may interfere with induction through disruptive behaviour and may cause discomfort to the anaesthetist. One should exercise one's option to deny these parents access to the induction area since their presence is not the parent's right. The parental presence will be of no benefit to the neonate or infant.

It is better not to have parents present in the case of a 'full stomach' or if a difficult airway is anticipated.

Non-Pharmacological Techniques of Induction

Playing the child's favourite music and/or video on a mobile phone helps to distract the child. It also reduces pain and anxiety with cannulation when used along with local anaesthetic cream. Another popular technique is to ask the child to blow a balloon through a scented mask, which can be simulated for inhalational induction.

Pharmacological Techniques of Induction

The following types of induction techniques can be used. Inhalational and intravenous are the most commonly used:

- Inhalational induction
- Intravenous induction

Inhalational Induction

This is the most common technique. If the child is already asleep, a '*steal induction*' can be done by administration of oxygen and nitrous oxide with a mask held gently near the face. After 2–3 minutes, incremental doses of halothane/sevoflurane are introduced until the child is anaesthetised.

If the child is not asleep, he may be coaxed into accepting a clear perfumed mask with oxygen and nitrous oxide for 2–3 minutes followed by incremental doses of halothane/sevoflurane. Recalcitrant children may require 8% sevoflurane or 5% halothane with oxygen, nitrous oxide and restraint. This is rather traumatic for the parents and the child and is not generally recommended. Halothane and sevoflurane are both non-irritant and since blood gas solubility is less for the latter, sevoflurane induction is faster. The time from loss of eye-lash reflex to correct depth for cannulation is around 2.5 minutes for sevoflurane in nitrous oxide and oxygen and 90 seconds when additionally intranasal dexmedetomidine is used for pre-medication. Isoflurane is an irritant and not recommended for induction.

In recent times, the use of nitrous oxide and its effect on the environment has been highlighted. Most anaesthetists prefer to use oxygen and air with the inhalational agent for both induction and maintenance. It is better to use a clear mask because it is less intimidating to the child and he/she does not feel suffocated. It also helps the anaesthetist to visualise exhaled humidity, secretions, vomitus or cyanosis.

Intravenous Induction

This route is preferred for those who already have IV access in place, with a full stomach, trauma, older children and those with a known propensity for malignant hyperthermia.

Since children do not like needles, we should try to make it as quick and painless as possible. A cream made of a eutectic mixture of local anaesthetic agents (EMLA) can be applied on the dorsum of the hand. However, it takes 45–60 minutes for effectiveness and it may cause venoconstriction, making it more difficult to see the vein. *Iontophoresis* produces anaesthesia by transdermal delivery of local anaesthetic by means of a low-level electric current.

The advantages of intravenous induction include the following:

- Rapid onset
- Elimination of face masks and the feeling of suffocation
- Reduced risk of laryngospasm
- Decreased risk of the excitement phase

Drugs used for intravenous induction are as follows:

- Thiopentone 6–7 mg/kg
- Propofol 2.5–3 mg/kg
- Ketamine 1–2 mg/kg

Intravenous injection of propofol is painful, and pre- or co-administration of preservative-free lignocaine may be done.

Problems That Can Occur During Induction

- **Airway obstruction:** There are various ways to correct this which include jaw thrust, inserting an oral or nasal airway, or placing a rolled towel under the shoulders in case of infants.
- **Laryngospasm:** This usually occurs during light planes of anaesthesia, when there are secretions/blood at the vocal cords. Treatment consists of giving 100% oxygen with a tight mask seal, positive airway pressure, forward pressure on the angle of the jaw, deepening the plane of anaesthesia, and, if persistent, propofol or thiopentone may be given. Succinylcholine 0.2–0.5 mg/kg (with atropine) may have to be given as the last resort.
- **Bronchospasm:** The best treatment for this is prevention. A deep plane of anaesthesia is critical before the instrumentation of the airway. In case it occurs, deepen anaesthesia. Halothane is a good bronchodilator. Bronchodilators, nebulisers and steroids may be given.
- **Hypovolaemia** (prior to induction): This can be seen in patients with intestinal obstruction, bowel perforation, trauma and a bleeding tonsil. The fluid deficit should be corrected rapidly, and it is good to induce with ketamine as it does not produce vasodilatation or hypotension.
- **Vomiting and aspiration:** If a nasogastric tube is already in place, apply suction to it and leave it open. Pre-oxygenation followed by rapid sequence induction and intubation with Sellick's manoeuvre may be carried out in the older child. The tracheal cartilages are soft and compressible in the younger child, may distort the airway and prove ineffective.

Maintenance of Anaesthesia

Similar to the induction of anaesthesia, the maintenance of anaesthesia may be inhalational or intravenous. Volatile-based inhalational maintenance is the commonest though recently TIVA (total intravenous anaesthesia) is becoming popular. The details can be referred to in Chapter 3. The ventilation during maintenance can be spontaneous (short procedures) or controlled with the use of muscle relaxants. During controlled ventilation, the airway can be maintained with the use of one of the following – endotracheal tube, laryngeal mask airway, oropharyngeal/nasopharyngeal airway or face mask.

Maintenance of General Anaesthesia

The main goals are as follows:

- Adequate anaesthesia and good operating conditions for surgery
- Maintain physiological homeostasis, respiration and airway at all times
- Maintain adequate circulating blood volume

Inhaled Anaesthetic Agents

They help to provide anaesthesia and good operating conditions. The agents used are as follows:

- **Nitrous oxide:** This agent causes minimal respiratory depression. It has a low blood gas solubility; hence, its uptake and elimination are rapid. It should be avoided in patients who have bone marrow depression and those who have had bone marrow transplants. It should also be avoided in long abdominal surgeries, neurosurgeries, middle ear surgeries and in those with pulmonary blebs or cysts.
- **Halothane:** This agent has a sweet smell and is non-irritant. Despite the fact that it has a higher blood gas solubility, it has a rapid induction due to a lack of side effects such as coughing and breath-holding. In order to achieve rapid equilibrium with blood and tissues, the inspiratory concentration of halothane is increased to an extent greater than the final concentration required to maintain anaesthesia. This allows the loss of consciousness quickly. This is over-pressuring and it helps to shorten the second stage. Halothane may, however, cause myocardial depression if controlled respirations are initiated without rapidly reducing the inspired concentrations. Arrhythmias may also occur with hypercarbia, light anaesthesia and exogenous adrenaline.
- **Sevoflurane:** This agent is also a non-irritant. It has a low blood gas solubility of 0.69 and hence a rapid uptake. Fresh gas flows below 1 litre should be avoided due to nephrotoxicity. It is very expensive but has less myocardial depression compared to halothane.

Isoflurane and Desflurane can be used for the maintenance of anaesthesia but should not be used for induction due to the respiratory irritant properties.

Parenteral Agents and Neuromuscular Blockade

Narcotics and ketamine may be used to provide analgesia (refer to Chapters 3, 11, 12, 47 and Appendix 1).

There are a few important facts to remember in the neonatal age group:

- There is immaturity in the neuromuscular system.
- There is a longer elimination half-life.
- There are fewer fatigue-resistant muscles in the diaphragm.
- Closing volume is within the tidal volume.

Always remember to compare the pre-op and post-op muscle tone and also the depth of respiration and the vigour of crying. Bilateral hip flexion against gravity has been reported to be equivalent to a 5-second head lift in the adult and is a sign of adequate reversal.

Special Considerations During Maintenance

There are a few essential differences between adults and children which must be revisited during the maintenance of anaesthesia and the post-operative period. This is especially important in very little babies, very ill babies and those undergoing long and complicated procedures.

Fluids

Isotonic fluids are usually used intraoperatively, the reason being that most volume losses in this situation are isotonic. Large volumes of hypotonic solution like D5W are not recommended as it may rapidly diminish serum osmolality.

This results in electrolyte instability (high glucose and low sodium) and undesirable fluid shifts. Ideally, 1–2% dextrose in a balanced salt solution should be used as a maintenance fluid in all small babies. Neonates may require more dextrose. Plasma volume expansion necessary in response to diminished vascular tone under anaesthesia is difficult to achieve with isotonic fluids; hence, colloids may have to be used. In the preterm and very small neonate, albumin or fresh frozen plasma (if need to treat a coagulopathy) may be used. An increase in antidiuretic hormones and other stress hormones increases water retention in excess of sodium and this leads to dilutional hyponatraemia.

Hyperglycemia due to intravenous glucose administration in the intraoperative setting can be potentially harmful if at any time during anaesthesia, there is a possibility of hypoxia and cerebral ischaemia. Anaerobic metabolism produces large quantities of lactic acid. This reduces the pH of the brain which in turn increases cerebral damage.

Neonates, severely malnourished children and those previously on intravenous alimentation may benefit from maintenance glucose-containing fluids as a supplement to balanced salt solution for third space and blood losses. It is therefore important to monitor serum glucose levels in prematures, neonates, infants and any child who is malnourished, fasting for a long period or undergoing long surgery.

Metabolic

Some intraoperative 'sinking spells' and cardiac arrests are related to metabolic events, especially hypocalcaemia or hypoglycaemia.

Hypocalcaemia is when serum calcium levels are less than 8.0 mg/dl.

Administration of calcium gluconate 25–30 mg/kg over 2–3 minutes raises serum calcium levels. A continuous infusion of calcium gluconate 100–400 mg/kg/day may also be given (refer to Chapter 4).

Hypoglycaemia is defined as serum glucose <30 mg/100 ml on the first day of life and <45 mg/100 ml after 24 hours. Treatment consists of giving 3–4 mg/kg/min of dextrose and titrating according to the sugar values (refer to Chapters 4 and 7).

Hyperglycaemia is when glucose is >150 mg/100 ml. Glucose infusion should be stopped if it is greater than 250–300 mg/100 ml and insulin started at a dosage of 0.05–0.2 μ/kg/hr titrated to achieve normoglycaemia (refer to Chapters 4 and 7).

Thermoregulation (Refer to Chapter 4)

Neonates and infants are prone to hypothermia because of a large ratio of body surface to weight. They have a limited ability to cope with cold stress. Heat is lost by conduction, convection, radiation and evaporation. Heat loss should be minimised by warming mattresses, humidification of inspired gases, warming of fluids and using plastic wrap to decrease water loss through the skin.

Core temperature and peripheral temperature must always be measured for neonates, infants and children undergoing major surgery. A rise in both temperatures denotes hyperthermia and a fall denotes hypothermia. However, a fall in peripheral temperature with a normal core temperature denotes poor perfusion and requires volume replacement.

The temperature should be measured continuously and may be measured at the following sites: the axilla, skin, oesophagus and tympanic membrane and should be kept between 36 and 37°C. Hypothermia slows awakening and recovery and produces hypoxaemia through shivering (increased oxygen consumption), which can lead to metabolic acidosis. Do not extubate if the temperature is less than 35°C. Hypothermia predisposes to decreased coagulation and increased risk of bleeding.

What is commonly not known is that hypovolaemia is frequently related to hyperthermia with peripheral vasoconstriction attempting to conserve heat and decrease evaporation.

Hypotension and Bradycardia During Surgery

Bradycardia is defined as a pulse rate that drops by at least 40% or so and a blood pressure that drops approximately the same (absolute numbers are not given as they vary for different age groups). The major causes of bradycardia/hypotension are hypoxia, anaesthetic overdose, hypovolaemia, vagal reflexes, anaphylaxis, hyperkalaemia and air embolism. The sudden appearance of hypoxia and desaturation should be considered due to the patient's condition and not due to a fault in the monitors. **Always believe the monitors**.

Hypotension and bradycardia require the anaesthetist to

- turn off the anaesthetics,
- ventilate with 100% oxygen (check the endotracheal tube),
- give a bolus of fluid or blood,
- give IV adrenaline 5–10 μg/kg and repeat if necessary,
- notify the surgeons (who may have already heard your monitors) and
- institute CPR. Then look for the cause!

Monitoring During Surgery

The purpose of monitoring is to detect potential problems. It is not a substitute for close observation of the patient by the anaesthetist. According to the American Society of Anesthesiologists (ASA) guidelines, oxygenation should be checked by pulse oximetry and by measuring the inspired oxygen fraction (FiO_2). Ventilation should be monitored with end-tidal carbon dioxide ($EtCO_2$) and ventilator alarms should be used. Circulation should be monitored with an ECG, heart rate and blood pressure monitoring. The temperature should be monitored continuously.

Routine monitoring is denoted as (R) and special monitoring is denoted as (S) in the following text.

Cardiovascular Monitoring

- **Heart rate (R):** It can be measured by an ECG, a precordial or an oesophageal stethoscope attached by a tube to the anaesthesiologist's ear.
- **Blood pressure monitoring (R):** Non-invasive blood pressure monitoring can be used routinely as anaesthetics decrease blood pressure more in infants and children than in adults. Continuous blood pressure monitoring (arterial line) (S) should be done in situations where large fluid shifts and blood loss is expected.
- **Central venous pressure (S):** This should be used in major cases where blood and fluid losses may be considerable. It should be measured continuously as small blood and fluid losses significantly decrease the atrial filling pressure of children.
- **Pulmonary arterial pressure and cardiac output (S):** Not routinely measured in children.

Respiratory Monitoring

- **Blood gases and pH (S):** Monitoring of oxygenation is especially important in preterm infants less than 60 weeks' post-conceptual age who are susceptible to retinopathy of prematurity (ROP). To reduce the likelihood of ROP, the PaO_2 should be maintained between the normal range of 50–70 mmHg.
- **Pulse oximetry (R):** It accurately reflects the oxygen saturation (SaO_2) of infants and children of all ages when SaO_2 is above 70%. The SaO_2 should be kept above 95% except in preterm infants where it should be kept between 87 and 92% to reduce the likelihood of ROP. It is valuable in detecting hypoxia and hyperoxia in infants.
- **End-tidal gases (R):** Monitoring end-tidal gases gives early warning of changes in inspired oxygen, expired carbon dioxide and anaesthetic concentrations. It is an important adjunct in the detection of malignant hyperthermia. There are two types of analysers – side stream and main stream. Side stream analysers are usually preferred in children as they are of light weight.

Temperature Monitoring (R)

The temperature should be measured to monitor hypo or hyperthermia in neonates, infants and children undergoing major surgery.

Skin temperature is a measure of tissue perfusion. If tissue perfusion is adequate, the patient is warm all the way to the fingers and toes. Capillary refill is also a good indicator of peripheral perfusion as is urine output (S). It should be greater than 1 ml/kg/hr.

POCUS in Paediatric Anaesthesia

The increasing availability of ultrasound and increasing familiarity of the anaesthesiologists with the point-of-care ultrasound (POCUS) has increased the use of ultrasound in perioperative crisis situations. Apart from use in regional anaesthesia (refer to Chapter 14) and its role in identifying aspiration risk by gastric ultrasound (refer to Chapter 15), it has other perioperative applications:

- Endotracheal tube size and position verification
- An aid to vascular access
- To assess the volume status

- Identification of type of shock – hypovolemic, distributive, cardiogenic and obstructive
- Identification of lung pathology – pleural effusion, pneumothorax and consolidation
- Identification of cardiac pathology – pericardial effusion, valvular and ventricular function

POCUS requires training and practice to develop expertise and paediatric anaesthesiologists should learn this new skill to improve perioperative care in children.

Emergence and Recovery

There are three stages of emergence or recovery:

1. **First stage**: This is the immediate recovery and it occurs in 10–15 minutes. This includes the resumption of respiration, return of airway reflexes, stabilisation of haemodynamics and return of consciousness. It begins in the operating room and ends in the post-anaesthesia care or intensive care units.
2. **Second stage**: This is the intermediate recovery. It takes minutes to hours after surgery and involves the return of coordination and the return of sensorium. It usually occurs in the PACU.
3. **Third stage**: This may take hours to days and involves the return of normal baseline function (both motor and mental) and occurs in the ward or at home.

Complications During Recovery

Complications are more often seen in premature babies, children with upper respiratory tract infections, airway surgery or complex airway problems. Some complications are related to the drugs used such as sevoflurane (emergence delirium), narcotics (respiratory depression) and ketamine (delirium and increased salivation); others are related to surgery such as pain and hypovolaemia.

The commonly seen complications include the following:

- Emergence delirium
- Pain
- Nausea and vomiting
- Bronchospasm
- Laryngospasm
- Hypoventilation
- Aspiration
- Hypotension or hypertension
- Post-operative bleeding

The incidence of emergence of delirium/agitation during recovery is as high as 50% in literature and is distressing to the parents as well as caregivers. Pain and other causes of agitation (hypoxia, hypercarbia, hypotension, hypoglycaemia or a full bladder) should be ruled out before labelling it as emergence delirium. The use of propofol-based anaesthesia over sevoflurane has demonstrated lower emergence agitation. Dexmedetomidine 1 mcg/kg intravenously is useful as prophylaxis when administered before extubation and also can be used to treat emergency agitation after it develops.

Conclusion

Sound knowledge of basic anatomy, physiology, pharmacology and physics, a good rapport with the surgeon and the rest of the team with a genuine love for children can make anaesthetising children a real pleasure.

SUGGESTED READINGS

1. Cote CJ. Practice of Paediatric Anaesthesia. In: Practice of Anaesthesia for Infants and Children, 6th edn. Cote CJ, Lerman J, Anderson BJ (eds). WB Saunders, Philadelphia, 2019; pp. 1–7.
2. Marciniak B. Growth and Development. In: Practice of Anaesthesia for Infants and Children, 6th edn. Cote CJ, Lerman J, Anderson BJ, (eds). WB Saunders, Philadelphia, 2019; pp. 8–24.
3. Ghazal EA, Vadi MG, Mason LJ, et al. Preoperative Evaluation, Premedication and Induction of Anaesthesia. In: Practice of Anaesthesia for Infants and Children, 6th edn. Cote CJ, Lerman J, Anderson BJ (eds). WB Saunders, Philadelphia, 2019; pp. 35–68.
4. Lerman J, Sampathi V, Watt S. Induction Maintenance and Emergence. In: Paediatric Anaesthesia, 5th edn. Gregory GA, Andropoulus DB (eds). Churchill Livingstone, Philadelphia, 2012; pp. 330–360.
5. Davis PJ, Motoyama EK, Cladis FP. Special Characteristics of Pediatric Anesthesia. In: Smith's Anesthesia for Infants and Children, 10th edn. Davis PJ, Cladis FP (eds). Elsevier, Philadelphia 2022; pp. 2–10.

2 PAEDIATRIC ANAESTHETIC EQUIPMENT

Rebecca Jacob • Aparna Williams

Equipment for paediatric anaesthesia is expected to be smaller than that used in adults, and the requirements for this equipment are also essentially different. The ideal characteristics of paediatric anaesthesia equipment are as follows:

- Have minimal resistance to airflow
- Have minimal dead space
- Are light weight
- Are easy to use and reliable
- Able to conserve heat and moisture

Paediatric airway equipment will be discussed under the following headings:

1. Face masks
2. Airways: Oral and nasal
3. Endotracheal tubes (ETTs)
4. Laryngoscope blades
5. Supraglottic airway devices such as laryngeal mask airways (LMAs) and I-gel
6. Paediatric breathing systems and their functional characteristics
    - Ayre's T-piece
    - Closed circuit
    - Bains circuit
7. Paediatric difficult airway cart

Face Masks

An ideal face mask should have the following characteristics:

- It should have a good fit without obstructing the nares.
- It should accommodate the oropharyngeal and nasopharyngeal airways during ventilation.
- Dead space should be minimal.
- It should be transparent for detecting cyanosis, humidification during expiration and vomiting.
- It should be comfortable for the patient and the anaesthetist.

The commonly used paediatric masks are as follows:

- Anatomical face mask
- Transparent plastic mask
- Rendell-Baker–Soucek mask (RBS mask)
- Masks for special purposes

Anatomical Face Mask

The anatomical face mask has a body made of rubber that can be widened or narrowed to fit the face. It also has an inflatable pad around the rim to ensure optimal fit (Fig. 2.1). Different sizes of anatomical face mask are given in Table 2.1.

Figure 2.1 Anatomical face masks.

Table 2.1 Sizes of Anatomical Face Masks

Patient	Size
Infant	0
Small child	1
Bigger child	2

Transparent Face Mask

A transparent face mask is similar to the anatomical face mask but its body is made of clear plastic (Fig. 2.2). The inflatable pad comes in different colours and may be scented. The available sizes are given in Table 2.2.

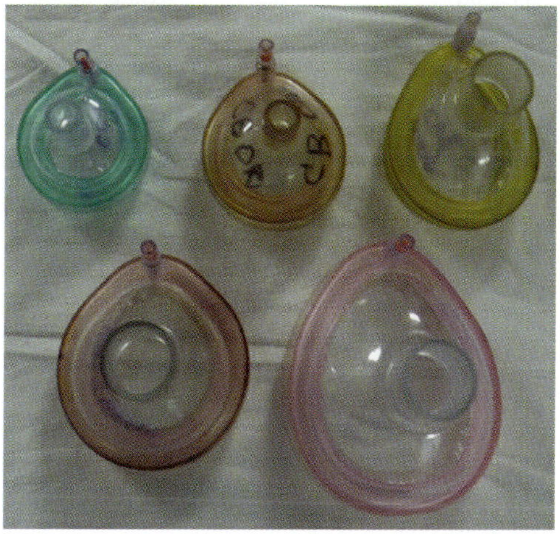

Figure 2.2 Transparent face masks with inflatable cuffs.

Table 2.2 Sizes of Transparent Face Masks

Patient	Size
Pre-term	00
Infant	0
Small child	1
Bigger child	2

Rendell-Baker–Soucek Mask

(Fig. 2.3)

The RBS mask was designed specifically for children under the age of 10 years. It is available in black and silicone versions. The advantages of this mask are a low dead space, and less effort is required while holding the mask without leak. The available sizes are given in Table 2.3.

Masks for Introduction of the Laryngobronchoscope

These masks are designed like anatomical face masks with an inflatable cuff. However an opening in the body permits the introduction of a fibreoptic laryngobronchoscope (e.g. Patil-Syracuse mask for use with fibreoptic scope; Fig. 2.4).

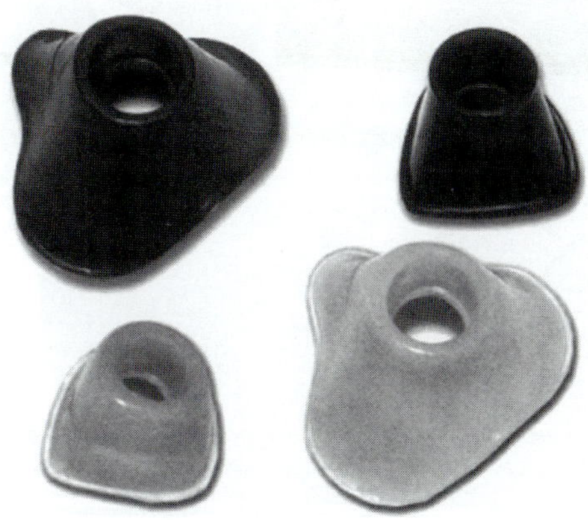

Figure 2.3 Rendell-Baker-Soucek mask.

Table 2.3 Rendell-Baker-Soucek Masks

Patient	Size	Dead Space (cumm)
Preterm	0	3
Infants up to 1 yr	1	4
Small children (1–3 yrs)	2	8
Children (4–10 yrs)	3	12

Figure 2.4 Patil Syracuse mask.

Airways

The airways used in paediatric anaesthesia are nasopharyngeal or oropharyngeal (Fig. 2.5).

Nasopharyngeal Airway (NPA)

- NPAs should provide a conduit for gas flow between the tongue and the posterior pharyngeal wall.

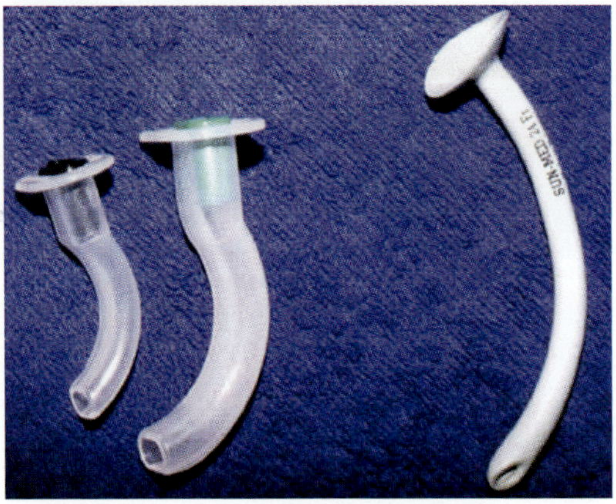

Figure 2.5 Nasopharyngeal and oropharyngeal airways.

- The ideal NPA should be soft with a rounded tip so as to prevent trauma, and a flange to prevent it from slipping into the nose.
- The length of the NPA should approximate the distance from the tip of the nose to the tragus of the ear.
- It is not used commonly because of trauma to adenoids, epistaxis or laryngospasm.

Oropharyngeal Airway (OPA)

The commonly used oropharyngeal airway is the Guedel airway. It is available in black rubber and PVC versions. The PVC airways are colour-coded (Fig. 2.6).

The sizes available are given in Table 2.4.

The appropriate size is approximately the distance from the angle of the mouth to the angle of the mandible. If it is too long, it occludes the inlet of the glottis and/or goes into the oesophagus. If it is too short, it only reaches the mid tongue (Fig. 2.7).

Figure 2.6 Guedel's oropharyngeal airways in different sizes.

Table 2.4 Details of Guedel Oropharyngeal Airways

Patient	Size	Length (in cm)	Colour
Pre-term	000	3.5	Pink/clear
Term baby	00	4.5	Blue
Infant	0	5.5	Black
Small child	1	6.5	White
Bigger child	2	7.5	Green

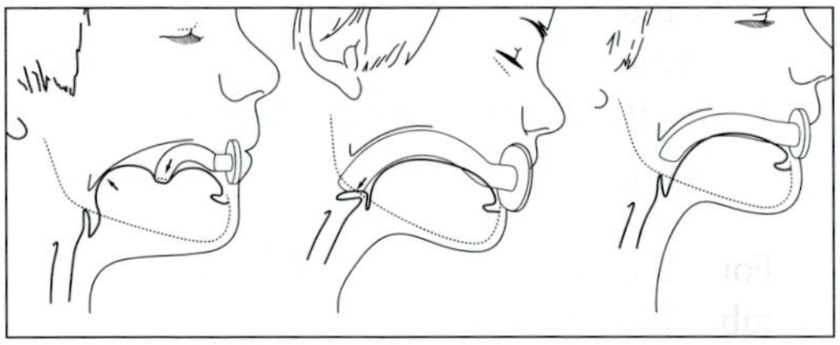

Figure 2.7 Sizing and position of oropharyngeal airways – Too short, too long and just the right length of oropharyngeal airways. (Reproduced with permission from Wheeler M, Cote CJ, Todres ID. In: A Practice of Anesthesia for Infants and Children, 3rd ed. 2001; 91).

Endotracheal Tube

1. While selecting an ETT, several points need to be considered:
   - It should be large enough to allow spontaneous or controlled ventilation but not so large as to damage the trachea.
   - It should be made of non-inflammatory material.
   - It should be implant tested.
   - It should not be easily kinkable.
   - It should be easily sterilised unless disposable.
   - The cuff leak pressure should be between 15 and 30 cm of water.
2. Situations where cuffed ETTs are recommended are as follows:
   - Patients with a high risk of aspiration as in bowel obstruction
   - Laparoscopic surgery
   - To occlude a tracheo-oesophageal fistula
   - Critical care, especially in severe lung disease where mechanical ventilation is needed.
   - Sophisticated lung function tests
   - Airway burns

3. Selection of the size of the ETT (uncuffed tubes – cuffed tubes would be ½ a size smaller)
   - The diameter of the distal joint of the index finger of the child or lumen of the external nares is approximately equal to the size of the ETT required for the child.
   - There are many formulae for calculating tube sizes. The most commonly used is Penlington's formula which takes the patients' age into account. Separate formulae are used for children less than 6 years and children greater than 6 years:
     Age less than 6 years: Age in years/3 + 3.5
     Age greater than 6 years: Age in years/4 + 4.5
4. Formula for measuring the ideal length of the tube: The ideal length of the tube is measured from the teeth to mid-trachea and the formulae are as follows:
   - Age/2 + 12 for an *oral tube*
   - Age/2 + 15 for a *nasal tube*
5. Anatomical considerations while selecting the ETT
   - In adults, the region of the vocal cords is the narrowest part of the larynx and is not circular in shape. However, in children, the cricoid cartilage is the narrowest part of the airway and is circular in shape. Therefore, large tubes will produce ischaemia of the tracheal mucosa at the level of the cricoid cartilage.
   - In adults, 1 mm oedema may cause only 4% increase in resistance and 44% reduction in the cross-sectional area. But in infants, 1 mm oedema results in 75% reduction in the cross-sectional area and 16% increase in resistance.
   - A small difference in radius will make a big difference in flow through the ETT, thereby increasing the airway resistance and work of breathing. The following equation relates the flow to the pressure difference and radius:
     Flow (Q) = (3.14 × *P* × *R*4)/8 *nl* (Hagen–Poiseuille equation)
     P, pressure difference; *R*, radius; *n*, viscosity; *l*, length.
6. The available versions of ETT are as follows:
   - Red rubber tube (not used now)

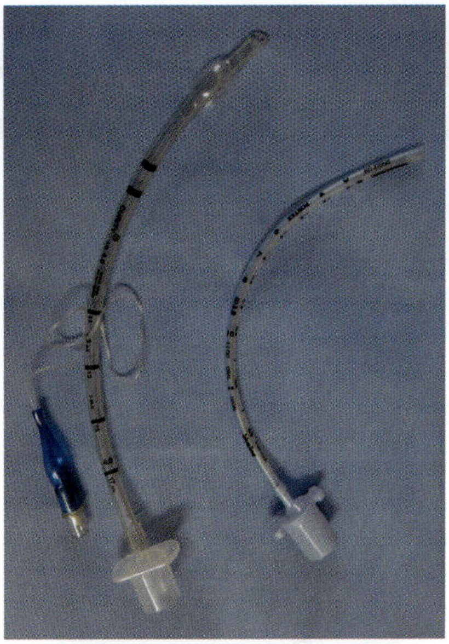

Figure 2.8 Cuffed and uncuffed endotracheal tubes.

   - Polyvinyl chloride in both uncuffed and cuffed versions (**Fig. 2.8**)
   - Microcuffed endotracheal tubes: ETTs with micro thin-walled, high-volume, low-pressure polyurethane cuffs with no 'step' between the tube and the cuff: They have a short cuff length with adequate multiple depth markings above the cuff so that the cuff is not inflated in the subglottic region. The bevel is also short, reducing the chances of endobronchial intubation, and there is no Murphy eye (**Fig. 2.9a** shows the entire tube and **Fig. 2.9b** shows the patient end of the tube)
   - Flexible wire-reinforced tubes that are essentially non-kinkable (**Fig. 2.10**)
   - Preformed ETT – The Ring–Adair–Elwyn (RAE) preformed ETT (**Fig. 2.11**): The distal ends of the tubes are bevelled on the left, with one opening on the right side opposite the bevel and one above the bevel on the left side. These openings provided ventilation of both lungs even when the tracheal tube is inserted into the right main stem bronchus. The *RAE orotracheal tube* was specifically designed for use with the Ring modification of the tongue retractor blade for a mouth gag and is used extensively in cleft palate and other oral surgery.

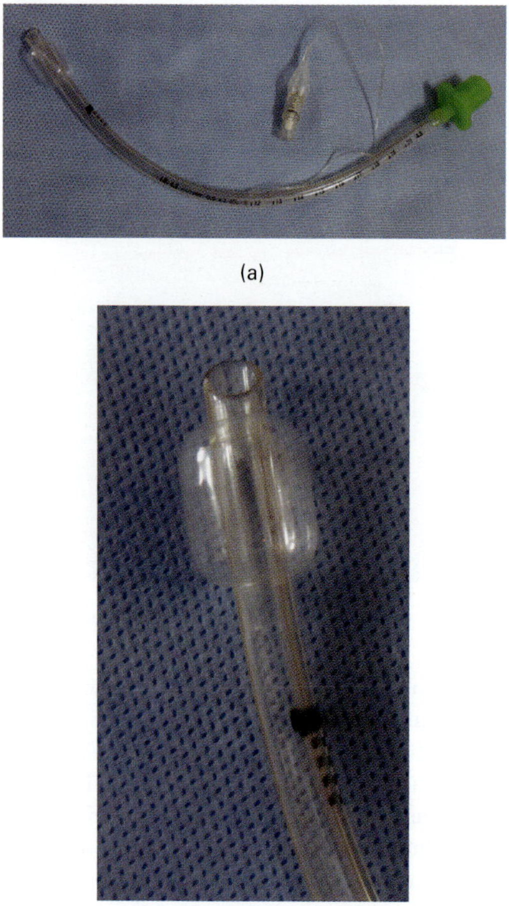

(a)

(b)

Figure 2.9 (a) The microcuffed tube in its entirety. (b) The patient end of the tube. Note the short bevel, short thin-walled cuff and multiple depth markings at the patient end of the tube. The machine end of the tube is standard. The pilot balloon of the cuff is also seen in subpart (a).

Figure 2.10 Flexometallic armoured tube.

The tracheal tube lies between the retractor blade and the tongue. The bend in the tube ensures that the machine end of the tube lies along the chin without obstructing the view at the surgical field.

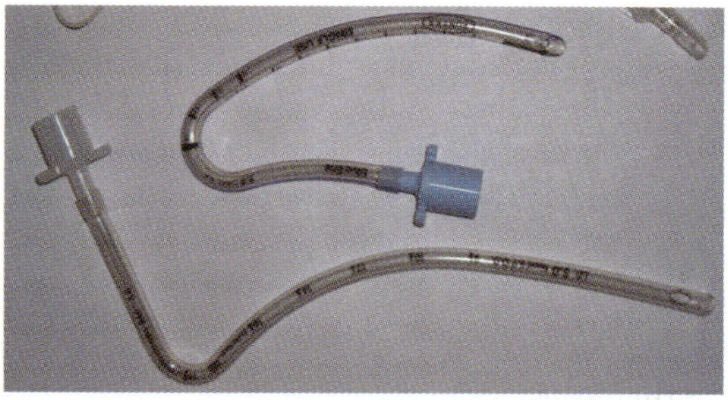

Figure 2.11 Preformed Ring–Adair–Elwyn tubes – oral (seen above) and nasal (seen below).

The *RAE nasotracheal tube* is moulded so that the distal end of the tube lies on the forehead.

One of the major disadvantages is that the RAE tracheal tubes have pre-determined lengths, and endobronchial intubation can sometimes be a problem.

Supraglottic Airway Devices

Supraglottic airway devices are new in the 'airway armamentarium' of the anaesthetist. They are often used routinely in anaesthetic procedures but can also be life-saving as an airway rescue device.

Laryngeal Mask Airways

Laryngeal mask airways (LMAs) are commonly used to manage the airways of infants and children for short surgical procedures. The LMA classic consists of a mask with a silicone inflatable cuff that seals the perimeter of the larynx and a wide bored tube that connects it with the anaesthesia circuit.

The available sizes for paediatric patients are given in Table 2.5.

Table 2.5 Sizes of Laryngeal Mask Airway (LMA) Available for Paediatric Patients

Size of LMA	Length (cm)	Patient Weight (kg)	Volume for Cuff Inflation (ml)
1	8	<5	2–4
1.5	10	5–10	4–6
2	11	6.5–25	5–10
2.5	12.5	20–30	12–15

Complications

Studies have shown that, like the ETT, inflation of the cuff for a longer period of time can produce ischaemic injury to the pharynx and larynx. Laryngospasm can occur if the LMA is inserted during the light plane of anaesthesia. Since the epiglottis is floppy and large in children, it can get folded under the LMA and produce obstruction. It may also get injured while inserting a bougie or an ETT through the LMA.

Versions of LMA available for paediatric patients are as follows:

- **Classic** (Fig. 2.12)
- **Flexible or metal-reinforced stem** (Fig. 2.13a)
- **Proseal LMA:** The stem is floppy and easier to insert with an introducer. It has a built-in bite block and a parallel tube open at the tip which can be used for suction or passage of an NG tube (Fig. 2.13b)
- **LMA Supreme:** It is similar to the proseal with a parallel tube open at the tip. However, the stem is stiff and has a preformed curve (like the ILMA) for ease of insertion (Fig. 2.13c)
- **Intubating LMA (ILMA):** It has a curved metal-reinforced stem. It is not available in smaller sizes (Fig. 2.13d). Note that the epiglottis bars have been replaced by a moveable flap for ease of passage of an ETT (Fig. 2.13e).

I-gel

- The I-gel airway (Intersurgical; Fig. 2.14) is another supraglottic airway device that can be used in children for maintaining the airway during routine surgical procedures. It can be used with spontaneous or intermittent positive pressure ventilation.
- The significant difference between the LMA and the I-gel is that the I-gel has a preformed silicone cushion which provides a 'fit' around the glottis – not an inflatable cuff like the LMA.
- Studies have shown that haemodynamic parameters, ease of insertion, and post-operative complications are comparable between the LMA, proseal LMA and the I-gel.
- Sizes available for children: The sizes available for paediatric patients are given in Table 2.6.

Table 2.6 Sizes of I-gel Airway Available for the Paediatric Patients

Description	Size	Patient Weight (kg)
Neonates	1.0	2–5
Infants	1.5	5–10
Small children	2.0	10–25
Large children	2.5	25–35

Other Supraglottic Airway Devices

The AirQ-Intubating Laryngeal Airway (AirQ-ILA) (Cookgas LCC, USA) is available in paediatric sizes (1, 1.5, and 2.0) and can facilitate endotracheal intubation. The other devices include the King Laryngeal Tube family devices (King Systems, Indiana) and the Cobra Perilaryngeal Airway (Engineered Medical Systems, Indiana) (Fig. 2.15). This supraglottic airway device has not gained much popularity. The combitube and easy tube can be used in older children as rescue devices for failed oxygenation.

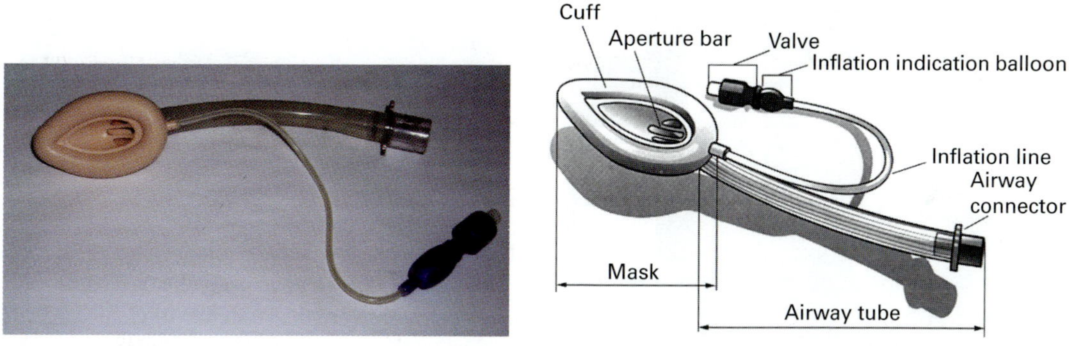

(a) (b)

Figure 2.12 (a) The laryngeal mask airway (LMA) classic. (b) Components of the LMA classic.

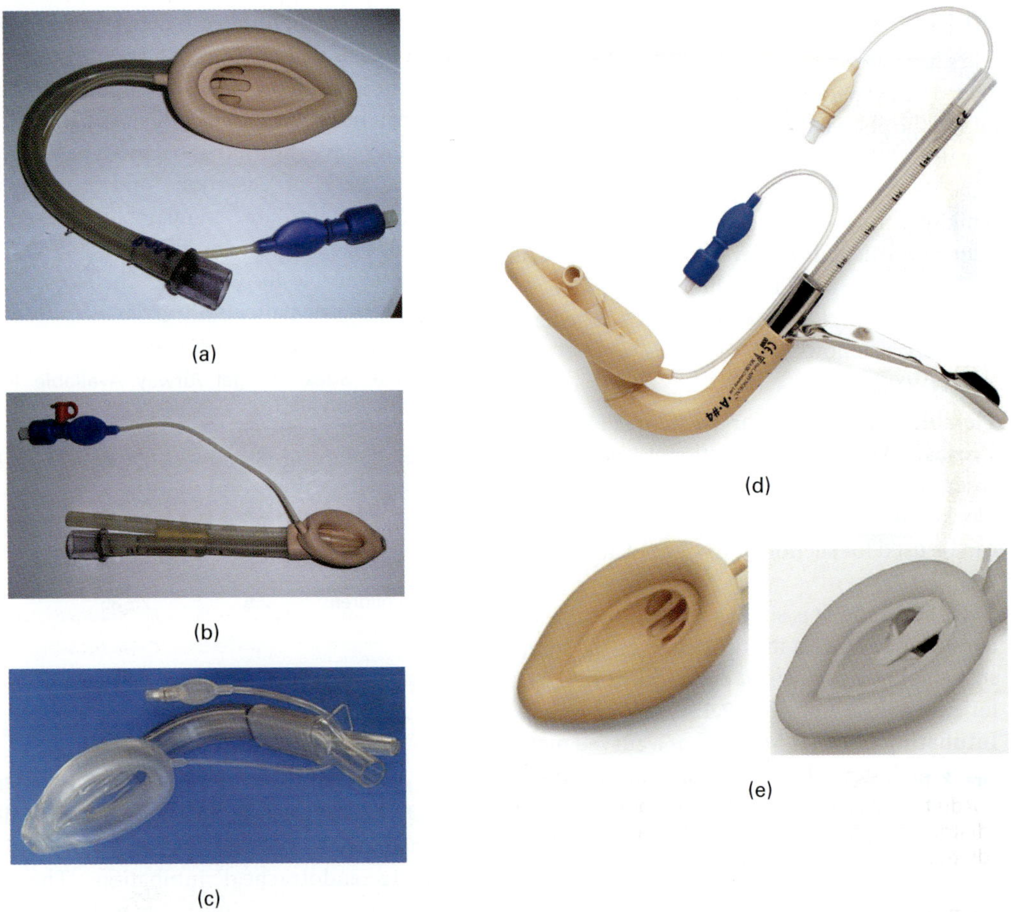

Figure 2.13 Different types of laryngeal mask airways (LMAs). (a) LMA flexible wire reinforced. (b) LMA Proseal. (c) LMA Supreme. (d) Intubating LMA. (e) Comparison of LMA Classic with epiglottic bars and intubating LMA (ILMA) with movable flange.

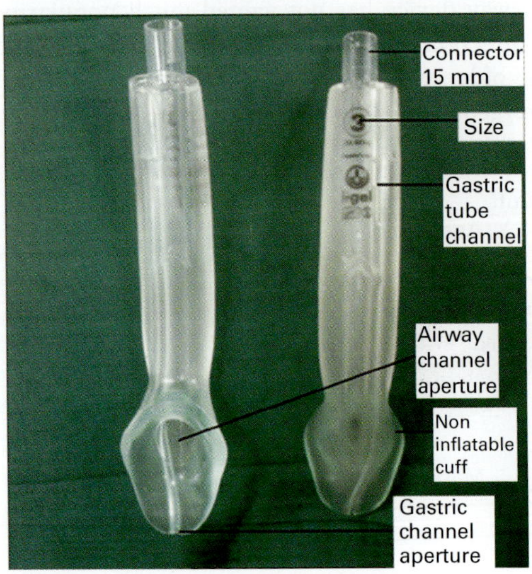

Figure 2.14 I-gel (Intersurgical).

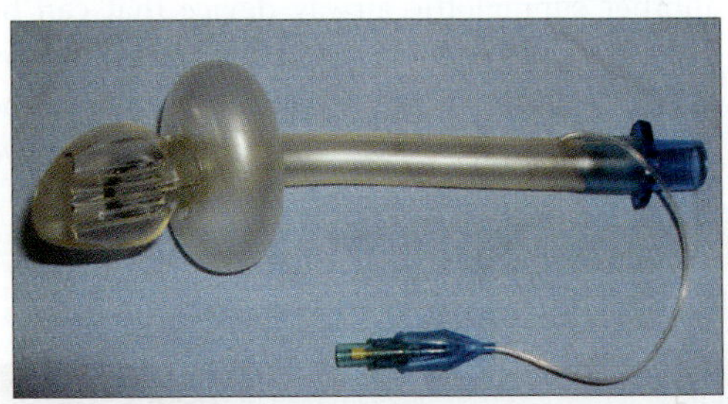

Figure 2.15 Cobra perilaryngeal airway.

Laryngoscope

The laryngoscope has a blade and a handle (Fig. 2.16). The laryngoscope blades commonly used in children are the straight Miller, Seward and Oxford or the curved Macintosh blades.

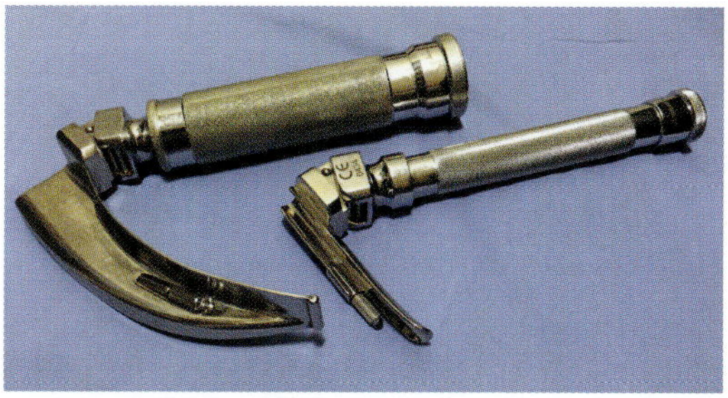

(a)

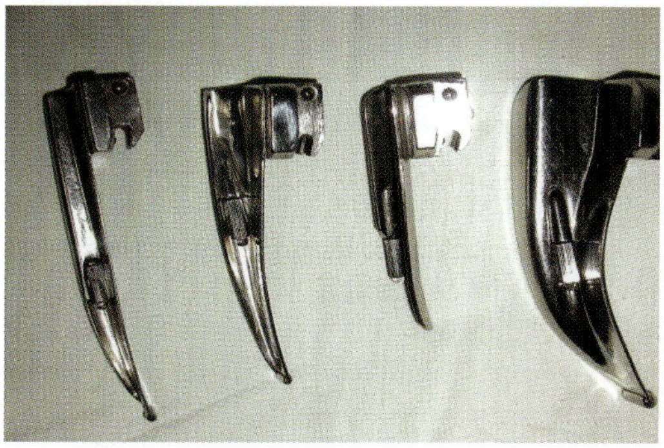

(b)

Figure 2.16 Laryngoscopes – adult and paediatric. (a) Adult Macintosh blade laryngoscope with paediatric straight blade laryngoscope. (b) Various paediatric laryngoscope blades.

While using the Macintosh blade, the tip of the blade is placed in the vallecula and traction is applied to lift the epiglottis to visualise the laryngeal opening.

The available sizes of a Macintosh blade are given in Table 2.7.

Table 2.7 Sizes of Macintosh Blades

Patient	Size	Length (mm)
Neonate	0	83
Infant	1	97
Child	2	104
Larger children	2.5	–

While using a straight blade, the epiglottis may be lifted to view the laryngeal inlet. Since the posterior surface of the epiglottis is innervated by the vagus, traction on the epiglottis can produce bradycardia and laryngospasm. (This is seen more commonly in the spontaneously breathing patient under light anaesthesia.)

The available sizes of Miller blades are shown in Table 2.8.

Table 2.8 Sizes of Miller Laryngoscope Blade

Patient	Size	Length (mm)
Premature	00	62
Neonate	0	76
Infant	1	102
Child	2	152
A ½ size is available for small infants		

Magill Forceps

Magill forceps is available in two paediatric sizes (Fig. 2.17). It is an angulated forceps which should be found on every anaesthetist's intubation tray. It is useful in 'feeding' the ETT into the glottis, especially during nasotracheal intubation. It is used to insert a throat pack and can be used to remove foreign bodies such as loose teeth from the oral cavity.

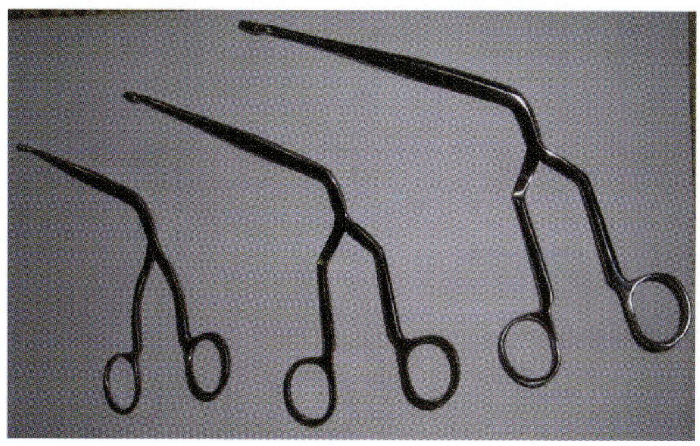

Figure 2.17 Magill forceps.

Stylets

Stylets are long, thin bendable rods that can be inserted into the ETT prior to intubation and curved into a hockey stick shape to facilitate intubation (Fig. 2.18). Care must be taken to see that the stylet reaches the tip of the tube but does not protrude out. If it does not reach the tip of the tube the tube will bend during intubation; if it sticks out it will cause trauma to the glottis, vocal cords and tracheal mucosa.

Bougies

A bougie is a straight, semi-rigid stylet-like device with a preformed curved tip used to facilitate

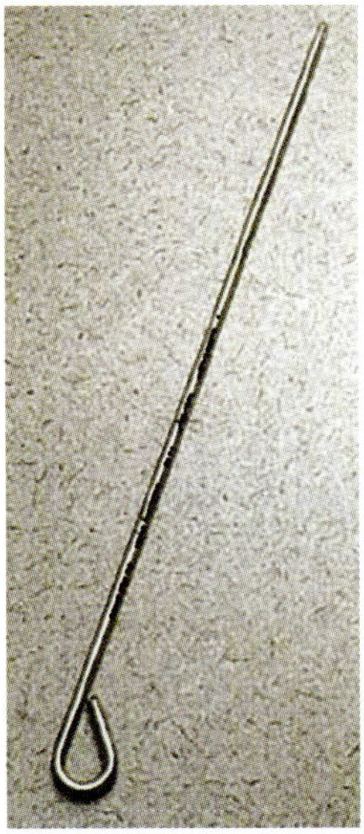

Figure 2.18 Stylet.

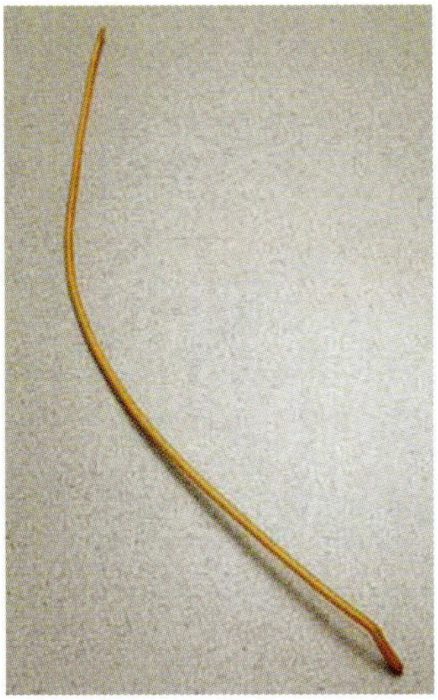

Figure 2.19 Bougie.

intubation (Fig. 2.19). The bougie may be introduced between the vocal cords. While maintaining the laryngoscope and bougie in position, an assistant may thread the ETT over the bougie into the trachea.

Special Instruments

The special instruments discussed are as follows:

- Video laryngoscope
- Optical stylets and rigid fibreoptic intubating endoscopes
- Rigid bronchoscope
- Fibreoptic laryngo/bronchoscope

Video Laryngoscopes

Video laryngoscopes (VLs) are used for oral intubation and require some mouth opening. They can be used for intubation in conditions with limited neck movement, airway swelling, airway masses, obese children and those with anatomical abnormalities. VLs can also be used to visualise airway abnormalities immediately below the vocal cords. They can provide the glottic view for other team members and not just the laryngoscopist, but the view with most scopes is limited to the midline while traditional classic laryngoscopy gives a much broader view of the mouth.

Depending on the type of blade used, the video laryngoscopes can be divided into three types: traditional (Storz C-MAC, Truview), hyperangulated (C-MAC D blade, Glidescope AVL) and channelled types (AirTraq, King Vision; Fig. 2.20). The most commonly available video laryngoscopes for use in children are AirTraq optical laryngoscope, Glidescope (Verathan Medical), C Mac (Karl Storz), Truview PCD paediatric VLS (Truphatek), Pentax-AWS (Pentax Corporation) and the McGrath Series 5 (LMA North America). All of them are not easy to use. There is a definite learning curve to the successful use of video laryngoscopes. Often, the glottis is well visualised but advancing the tube can be a problem. If the VL blade is inserted too deep the ETT can hinge on the arytenoid. The VL blade should be withdrawn, and the ETT should be rotated counter-clockwise to overcome this problem. In non-channelled VLs, the intubation guide/stylet should be pre-formed to the curvature of the VL blade for easy insertion of the ETT. The ETT cuff may be damaged when a cuffed ETT is used with a channelled VL.

A good view with the VL may be obscured by secretions (worth giving glycopyrrolate as a pre-medication) or blood. Fogging is another problem which is overcome in part by the flow of oxygen over the lens as with the Truview scope.

(a)

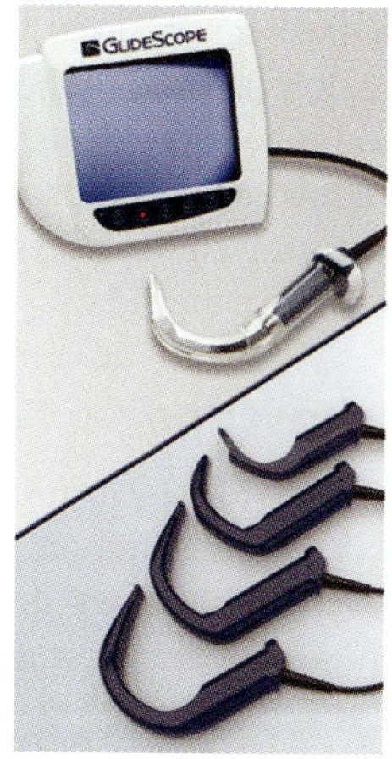

(b)

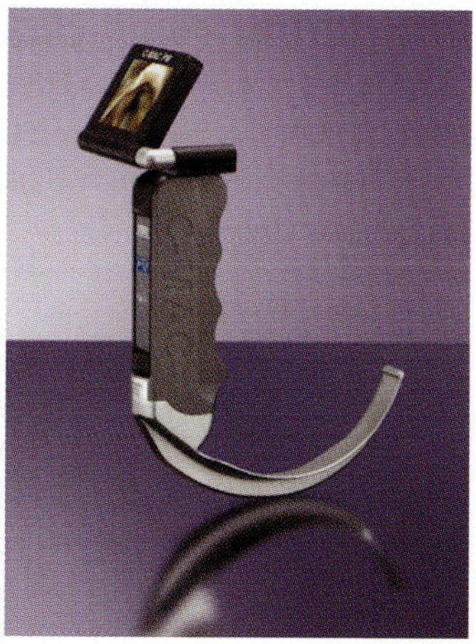

(c)

(d)

Figure 2.20 (a) Airtraq. (b) Glidescope. (c) C-Mac. (d) Truscope.

Optical Stylets and Rigid Fibreoptic Intubating Endoscopes

Lighted (optical) stylets are also available where the tip of the light wand is seen glowing in the cricopharyngeal region indicating a correct placement of the tube (**Fig. 2.21**).

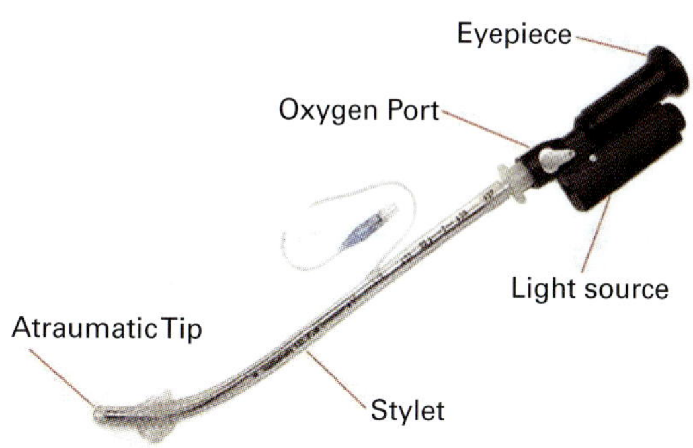

Figure 2.21 Lighted optical stylet.

Optical intubating endoscopes can also be used for indirect laryngoscopy. The Shikani optical stylet (Clarus Medical) is malleable and has a fixed eyepiece. The two rigid fibreoptic paediatric intubating endoscopes include the Brambrink and the Bonfils optical scope (Karl Storz). The Bonfils scope is a rigid fibreoptic device with a swivelling eyepiece. These devices require a retromolar insertion technique to view the glottis. The fibreoptic lighted intubation stylet (Anaesthesia

Medical Specialities) can be used for a tube with an ID of 3.5 mm. It is inserted in the midline orally. The endotracheal tube is preloaded on this equipment, and they allow easy assembly. They appear to have a shorter learning curve. However, fogging or secretions may obscure the view.

Rigid Bronchoscope

Rigid bronchoscopes (Fig. 2.22) are also ventilating bronchoscopes, having a side port for connection to the anaesthesia circuit. They may be used for diagnostic purposes but are most commonly used for retrieving foreign objects. Ventilation may be spontaneous or controlled. However, controlled ventilation has to be interrupted during suction or removal of the foreign body during this manoeuvre (refer to Chapter 23).

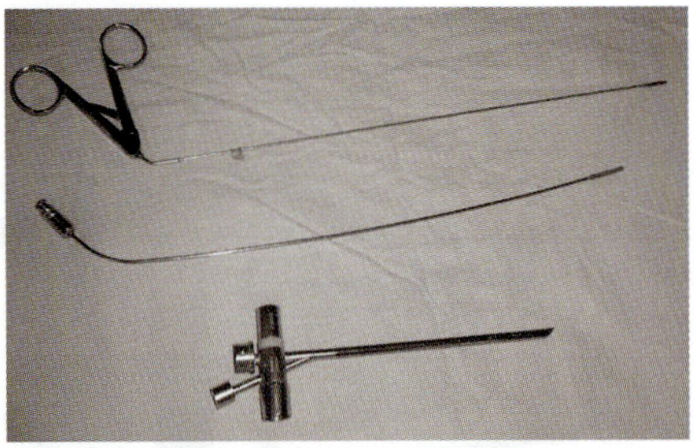

Figure 2.22 Rigid bronchoscope with suction and tissue holding forceps.

Fibreoptic Laryngo/Bronchoscope

Fibreoptic laryngo/bronchoscope (FOB) contains a fibreoptics system that transmits the image from the tip of the instrument to an eyepiece or a video camera at the proximal end (Fig. 2.23).

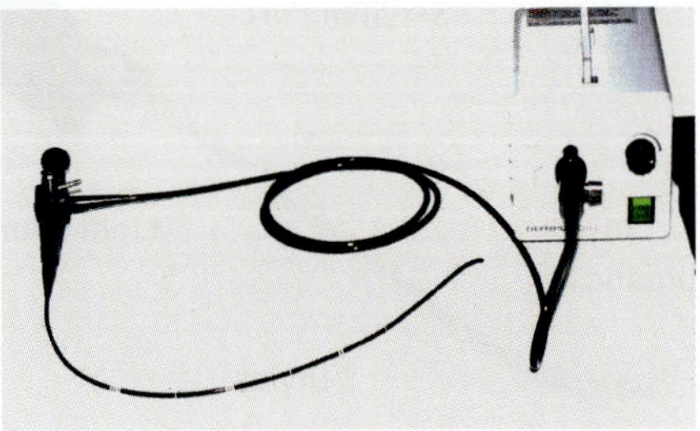

Figure 2.23 Fibreoptic bronchoscope.

Using Bowden cables, connected to a lever at the handpiece, the tip can be manipulated to navigate the instrument around corners. Most flexible scopes also carry a suctioning channel (which can also be used to instil medication such as local anaesthetics). However, this channel may be absent in the smallest paediatric sizes. The FOB is longer and thinner than a rigid bronchoscope.

Flexible fibreoptic intubation is the gold standard for the management of difficult intubation. It is particularly useful in children with limited mouth opening as in temporomandibular joint ankylosis.

The smallest flexible FOBs have an OD of 2.2 mm to allow intubation with an ETT 3.0 mm ID. For ease of intubation, it is important to use an ETT whose ID is 0.5–1.0 mm larger than the OD of the flexible FOS being used. The FOS with a suction channel has a minimal OD of 2.8 mm. For more details, refer to Chapter 19.

Circuits

The commonly used circuits are as follows:

- Jackson-Rees modification of Ayre's T piece (Fig. 2.24)
- Bain's circuit (Fig. 2.25)
- Circle system (Fig. 2.26)
- Emergency resuscitation self-inflating bag and mask (Fig. 2.27)

Jackson–Rees Modification of Ayre's T Piece (Mapleson F System) (Fig. 2.24 a,b)

It is used for children less than 25 kg.

Its components include the following:

- Ayre's T piece
- Corrugated tube between T piece and reservoir bag
- Reservoir bag with or without airway pressure limiting (APL) valve
- Angle connector and face mask

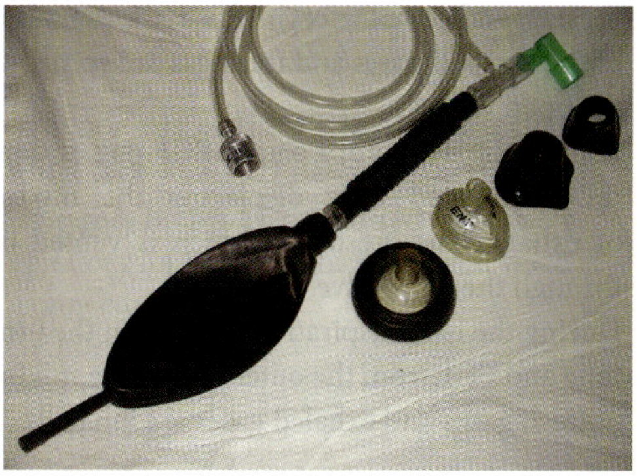

(a)

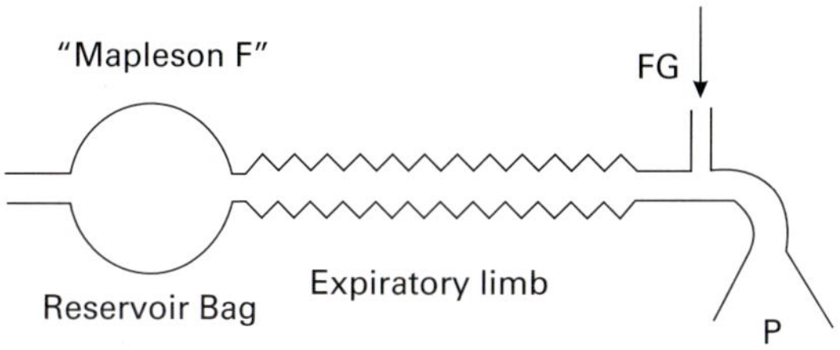

(b)

Figure 2.24 (a) Ayre's T piece with Jackson–Rees modification. (b) Diagrammatic representation of Mapleson F (the expiratory limb consists of a corrugated tube attached to a reservoir bag). FG, fresh gas; P, patient.

Functional Analysis of Mapleson F System

In this analysis, the terms used include FGF – fresh gas flow, RR – respiratory rate, TV – tidal volume and IPPV – intermittent positive pressure ventilation.

Mapleson F System During Spontaneous Ventilation

The breathing system should be filled with fresh gas before it is connected to the patient. When the patient inspires, FG (Fresh Gas) from the reservoir bag and corrugated tube flows to the patient.

During exhalation, there is a continuous FG into the system at the patient end. The exhaled gases get mixed with FG as it flows into the corrugated tube and reservoir bag. Once the system is full, the excess gas is vented to the atmosphere through the 'tail'/valve situated at the reservoir bag.

During the expiratory pause, FGF continues to flow and fill the proximal part of the corrugated tube while the mixed gas is vented through the 'tail'/valve.

During the next inspiration, the patient breathes the fresh gas as well as the mixed gas (dead space gas and expired gas) from the corrugated tube and reservoir bag.

Factors that Influence the Composition of Inspired Mixture

- FGF, RR expiratory pause, TV, the length of the corrugated tube, CO_2 production in the body
- CO_2 rises if FGF is low, RR is high with a short expiratory pause, the corrugated tube is short or absent, if equipment placed between the FGF and the patient increases the dead space and if the patient's basal metabolic rate is high as with a fever. FGF should be 1.5–2 times the minute volume to minimise rebreathing

Mapleson F System During Controlled Ventilation

- The expiratory valve is partially closed so that it opens only after sufficient pressure has developed in the system.
- During inspiration, FGF from machine, corrugated tube and reservoir bag enters the patient.
- During exhalation, exhaled gases get mixed with the FG that is flowing into the system at the patient end.
- During the expiratory pause, FG continues to enter the system and pushes the mixed gas towards the reservoir bag.
- During the next inspiration, the patient gets ventilated with the gases in the corrugated tube, i.e. mixture of fresh, alveolar and dead space gases. As the pressure in the system increases, the expiratory valve opens and the content of the reservoir bag is discharged to the atmosphere.
- Factors that influence the composition of mixture in the corrugated tube from which the patient gets ventilated are the same factors for the spontaneous respiration, the only difference being that these parameters can be totally controlled by an anaesthesiologist. They are not patient dependent.

Advantages of Mapleson F System

- The system is simple, inexpensive, easy to assemble and can be easily disinfected.

- Some components are difficult to clean.
- Resistance is high in this system, so work of breathing is high during spontaneous breathing.

Special Devices with Circle System

There are special devices with the circle system to decrease the dead space and resistance.

- Divided airway adaptor dead space is only 0.5 ml, whereas in a conventional circle system the dead space is about 40 ml
- Circulators

Emergency Resuscitation

For emergency resuscitation, a self-inflating bag with a one-way valve at the patient end can be used with a mask or endotracheal tube. (**Fig. 2.27**). An oxygen reservoir bag at the other end helps to increase inspired oxygen concentration. It is available in neonatal and paediatric sizes.

Figure 2.27 Self-inflating resuscitation bag with oxygen reservoir.

Crash Cart or Emergency Trolley

Definition: A crash cart is a portable trolley that is used while resuscitating a patient during an emergency as in a cardiac or respiratory arrest or in the management of a difficult airway. It contains all the equipment and drugs required for resuscitation.

It should be mobile with heavy duty wheels. It should be well labelled with easily accessible shelves and drawers to carry essential equipment, drugs and fluids (see Chapter 16).

Note: A portable defibrillator or one on a wheeled trolley should be available near the crash cart.

Note: A difficult airway cart should also have a variety of tools to aid intubation such as a fibreoptics laryngo/bronchoscope or video laryngoscopes (refer above).

SUGGESTED READINGS

1. Fisher DM. Anaesthesia equipment for Pediatrics. In: Paediatric Anaesthesia, 4th edn. Gregory GA, ed. Churchill Livingstone, Philadelphia, 2002; pp. 191–216.
2. Dorsch JA, Dorsch SE. Understanding Anaesthesia Equipment, 4th edn. Lippincott Williams and Wilkins, Philadelphia, 2006.
3. Hatch DJ. Paediatric anaesthetic equipment. *Br J Anaesth* 1985; 57:672–684.
4. Ring WH. Modification of the Crowe-Davis gag. *Anesthesiology* 1963; 24:740–741.
5. Ring WH, Adair JC, Elwyn RA. A new pediatric endotracheal tube. *Anesth Analg* 1975; 54:273–274.
6. Blum RH, Cote CJ. Pediatric equipment. In: A Practice of Anesthesia for Infants and Children, 4th edn. Cote CJ, Lerman J, Todres ID, eds. Saunders Elsevier, Philadelphia, 2009; pp. 1099–1126.
7. Fiadjoe JE, Feldman JM, Cohen DE. Equipment. In: Smith's Anesthesia for Infants and Children. Davis PJ, Cladis FP, Motoyama EK, eds. Elsevier Mosby, Philadelphia, 2011; pp. 293–321.

3

Pharmacokinetics and Pharmacodynamics of Anaesthetic Drugs in Paediatrics

Subramanyam Mahankali • Prarthana M Raj

Definitions

The definitions provided below will aid in a better understanding of the concepts of pharmacokinetics and pharmacodynamics of the anaesthetic drugs in paediatric age group.

- **Pharmacokinetics** describes the absorption, distribution, metabolism and elimination of drugs. Another way of describing it is what the body does to the drugs.
- **Pharmacodynamics** describes the effects of drugs on the body. It is the relationship between the concentration at the effector site (usually plasma concentration) and the biological effect of the drug.
- **Phase I metabolism** refers to the biotransformation to render drugs more water soluble (to prepare for elimination) by means of oxidation, reduction, or hydrolysis.
- **Phase II metabolism** is the biotransformation to render the drug more water soluble (to prepare for elimination) through conjugation reactions such as glucuronidation, sulfation and acetylation.
- **Bioavailability** describes the extent (and rate) of uptake of an active drug into the body given by any route other than intravenous (IV). It is expressed as a percentage when compared to IV administration of the same drug. If an orally administered drug is poorly absorbed or has a high first-pass metabolism, it will have a low bioavailability.
- **First-pass metabolism** usually refers to the metabolic change, which takes place in the liver after oral administration. A high first-pass metabolism will reduce the bioavailability of a drug, for example, morphine, midazolam and propranolol.

  Sublingual or rectal administration can bypass the liver and hence increase the drug bioavailability.

  Some drugs undergo first-pass metabolism in the gut mucosa, for example, methyldopa.
- **p*K*** is the pH at which 50% of the drug is ionised.
- **Volume of distribution (V_d)** is a theoretical term to quantify the distribution of a drug. It is the volume in which the amount of drug would need to be uniformly distributed to produce the observed blood concentration.
  Therefore, V_d × Drug concentration in blood = Total amount of drug in the body.
- **Context-sensitive half-time (CSHT)** is a pharmacokinetic concept that is used to describe the time it takes for the plasma concentration of a drug to decrease by 50% after continuous infusion of the drug for a certain duration of time.
- **TIVA** is the total IV anaesthetic, where no volatile anaesthetic gases such as sevoflurane and desflurane are used.
- **TCI** stands for target-controlled infusion. It is a method of administering medication through a specialised computer microprocessor chip-controlled IV infusion pump in a way that is tailored to the individual characteristics of the patient, such as weight, age, and gender, with the goal of achieving a desired effect at the effector site.

Introduction

The importance of age-appropriate pharmacotherapy was recognised more than 100 years ago when Dr Abraham Jacobi, the father of American paediatrics, wrote 'Paediatrics does not deal with miniature men and women, with reduced doses and same class of disease in smaller bodies, but... each has its own independent range and horizon'. Many drugs have not been thoroughly studied in children. As clinical paediatric studies pose financial and ethical challenges, data are frequently extrapolated from adults. Thus, while administering drugs to children, extra care should be taken and it is very important to understand the developmental pharmacology of neonates, infants and children.

Pharmacokinetics and pharmacodynamics are two important concepts in the field of medicine that describe how drugs move through and affect the body. Pharmacokinetics explains what happens to a drug in the body, whereas pharmacodynamics describes the actions produced by the drug on the body. Therefore, the effects of a drug result from a combination of its pharmacokinetic and pharmacodynamic characteristics in that individual. Many aspects of pharmacodynamics and pharmacokinetics differ between the adult and the paediatric population. Children exhibit different pharmacokinetics from adults because of their altered protein binding, larger volume of distribution (V_d), smaller proportion of fat and muscle stores, and immature renal and hepatic function.

Failure to appreciate these differences can result in preventable morbidity or even mortality.

The dual processes of pharmacokinetics and pharmacodynamics of drugs administered to patients in general are illustrated in **Figure 3.1**.

Pharmacokinetics

Pharmacokinetics describes what happens to drugs once they are administered. It refers to the way that drugs are absorbed, distributed, metabolised and eliminated from the body. This is described in detail in the following text.

Absorption of Drugs

In children, a variety of routes of administration of drugs are used.

Oral (Enteral) Administration

The efficacy of orally administered drugs depends on the rate and extent of absorption from the gastrointestinal tract (mainly the small intestine), physicochemical nature of the drug, nature of gastrointestinal juices, rate of gastrointestinal emptying, intestinal motility, bowel length, and absorptive surface area and gut blood flow. All these factors vary with age especially affected in the neonate.

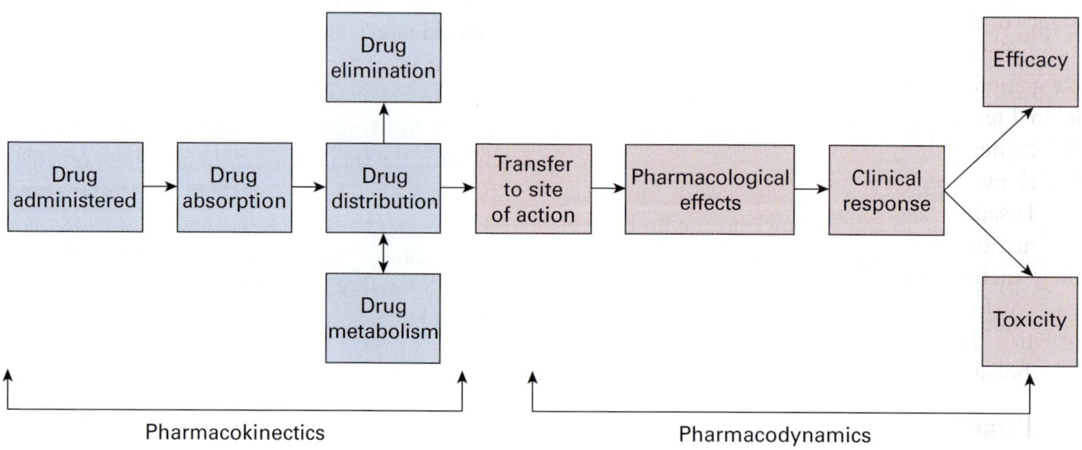

Figure 3.1 The fate of a drug once administered depends on the distribution, metabolism and elimination. This is influenced by the pattern of pharmacokinetics and pharmacodynamics of the drug.

Gastric pH: The gastric pH, which is 6–8 at birth, decreases to 1–2 within 24 hours as the body starts producing gastric acid and finally reaches adult levels of 1.5–3.5 between 6 months and 3 years of age. Premedication drugs such as morphine, pentobarbital or atropine do not alter the volume of gastric juice but glycopyrrolate does reduce the volume of gastric juice by a third and increases the pH of 68% gastric samples to above 2.5.

Gastrointestinal secretions: A decreased basal acid output and the total volume of gastric secretions are seen in the neonate. Bile acid secretion being less in the neonate may reduce the absorption of lipid-soluble drugs. Reduced gastric acid secretion increases bioavailability of acid-labile drugs (e.g. penicillin) and decreases bioavailability of weakly acidic drugs (e.g. phenobarbital).

Gastrointestinal motility: The rate of gastric emptying varies during the neonatal period but can be markedly increased in the first week of life. Long-chain fatty acids (as found in certain neonatal formula feeds) can delay gastric emptying, and this must be remembered while determining the fasting status of neonates appearing for surgery. It also increases the time taken to reach therapeutic concentrations when enteral drugs are given to infants <3 months.

Processes of both passive and active transport are fully mature in infants by approximately 4 months of age. Intestinal enzymatic changes in the neonate such as low activity levels of cytochrome P4501A1 (CYP1A1) can alter the bioavailability of drugs.

Infants with surgically removed bowel, congenital atretic bowel or the ones who have jejunal feeding tubes may have specific absorptive defects depending on the segment and length of the bowel involved.

Disadvantages of the oral route include emesis, destruction of the drug by digestive enzymes or their metabolism prior to absorption, and presence of food or other drugs, which cause irregularities in absorption and hepatic first-pass metabolism.

Oral Transmucosal Drug or Nasal Administration

This route of administration of drugs bypasses the liver and hence the hepatic first-pass metabolism and causes a rapid onset of drug action, for example, sublingual – nitroglycerin and nasal – midazolam, fentanyl, dexmedetomidine and ketamine.

Parenteral

Intramuscular injection (IM): The rate of systemic absorption of drugs after IM administration is more rapid and predictable than after oral or rectal administration due to high density of skeletal muscle capillaries in infants than older children. Reduced skeletal muscle blood flow and inefficient muscular contractions (responsible for drug dispersion) can theoretically reduce the rate of IM absorption of drugs in neonates.

Subcutaneous injection: In this route, the drug is deposited in the layer beneath the dermis of the skin. As subcutaneous tissue is poor in blood supply, the absorption is slow and sustained. This route is used for morphine delivery for acute post-operative or palliative cancer pain and insulin delivery in children with Type 1 diabetes mellitus. The commonly used sites for subcutaneous injection in children are – anterolateral thigh, abdomen (avoiding area around umbilicus) and lateral arm for single dose and chest for subcutaneous canula insertion.

Intravenous injection: Drugs injected intravenously act almost immediately. However, some drug may be lost due to its adsorption to the glass or plastic infusion system. Its effects may be delayed if the infusion rate is slow. This can result in an inaccurate inference regarding the patient's requirement for a higher or lower dosage of medication.

Transdermal

Drug delivery through the skin to achieve a systemic effect of a drug is commonly known as transdermal drug delivery systems (TDDS) and differs from the traditional topical drug delivery. The drug is stored in the TDDS either in a reservoir or impregnated into the fabric of the patch. On applying the TDDS to the skin, a drug concentration gradient is developed, and the drug starts to move down the gradient. A second drug reservoir is established in the stratum corneum. As the drug moves further into the skin, it is absorbed into the local capillary vasculature and is then transported into the systemic circulation. As a result of this absorption process, there is a delay between the TDDS application and the development of a desired minimum effective concentration. This delay varies between drugs. The transdermal drug delivery system offers numerous benefits, including the restriction of hepatic first-pass metabolism, improvement of therapeutic efficacy and sustained maintenance of plasma drug concentration levels. The drugs presently used in this method include fentanyl, buprenorphine, hyoscine, clonidine, nitroglycerin and some hormones.

Enhanced percutaneous absorption of drugs is noted in infancy, which is due to the presence of a thinner stratum corneum in the preterm neonate and a greater extent of cutaneous perfusion and hydration of the epidermis throughout childhood. Neonates have a large ratio of body surface area to body mass. There is a potential for drug overdose in neonates by this route.

Rectal

Drugs are given rectally to avoid some of the problems of orally administered drugs. This route should be avoided in immunosuppressed patients or in those undergoing chemotherapy. Drugs administered in the anal canal below the ano-rectal or dentate line bypass the liver after absorption, while drugs inserted above this line are absorbed via the superior rectal vein and undergo first-pass hepatic metabolism. Because hepatic metabolism is immature in neonates and infants, rectal-drug bioavailability in drugs undergoing extensive first-pass metabolism is higher. Rectal formulations, on the other hand, may be expelled more quickly in young children due to more frequent high-amplitude pulsatile contractions. Absorption of rectally administered drugs is thus slow and erratic and depends on whether the drugs are given in the form of suppositories, rectal capsules or enemas. The commonly used drugs by rectal route include paracetamol and diclofenac sodium. Other drugs that have been used include thiopentone, methohexital, diazepam, atropine and acetaminophen.

Intrapulmonary/Inhalational

A fundamentally different pattern of uptake is seen for an inhaled drug in that it crosses the alveolar membrane into the blood along its partial pressure gradient. This produces an exponential wash-in, until at equilibrium (i.e. the partial pressure in blood equals that in the inspired and expired gas) no further net uptake occurs.

A clinical effect requires sufficient uptake to exert an adequate partial pressure in the body tissues; it is achieved most rapidly by

- high fractional concentration of the inhaled drug.
- high minute ventilation.
- low blood–gas partition coefficient.

Irrespective of the route of administration of drug (IV or inhalational), the expected anaesthetic effect occurs only when the concentration of the drug at the receptor site reaches the target concentration to produce anaesthesia.

The intrapulmonary route of drug administration can be particularly useful in neonates and children for several reasons:

Faster onset of action: Inhalation allows medications to be delivered directly to the lungs, where they can quickly enter the bloodstream and start to work, leading to a rapid onset of action. This can be particularly important in neonates and children with respiratory distress or acute respiratory conditions, where rapid relief of symptoms is critical.

Reduced systemic side effects: Intrapulmonary delivery can result in lower systemic side effects compared to oral or injectable routes of administration, as medications delivered directly to the lungs may have less exposure to other parts of the body. This can be particularly important in neonates and children, who may be more susceptible to side effects from medications.

Improved compliance: Inhaled medications can be easier for children to take than oral medications, as they do not require swallowing pills or liquids. This can improve compliance with treatment and may result in better outcomes.

Targeted treatment: Inhalation allows medications to be delivered directly to the site of action in the lungs, allowing for targeted treatment of respiratory conditions such as asthma, cystic fibrosis and bronchiolitis. In children with respiratory distress syndrome (RDS), surfactants can be delivered directly to the lungs. The intrapulmonary administration allows for targeted treatment of RDS and can lead to a rapid improvement in respiratory function.

Though the goal is to achieve a predominantly local effect, systemic exposure does occur. Developmental changes in the architecture of the lung and its ventilatory capacity (e.g. minute ventilation, vital capacity and respiratory rate) can alter patterns of drug deposition and hence systemic absorption after intrapulmonary administration of drug.

Uptake and Distribution of Drugs Other Than Inhalational Agents

Absorption of drug from the site of administration and distribution to the effector site depends on cardiac output, tissue perfusion and blood tissue partition coefficient of the drug. Age-dependent changes influence the apparent volume of distribution (V_d) of drugs. The two important factors which are responsible for plasma concentration of free drug are volume of distribution and plasma protein binding.

Volume of distribution: The relatively larger extracellular and total body water spaces in neonates and infants compared to adults, coupled with adipose tissue that has a higher ratio of water to lipid, result in lower plasma concentrations of these drugs.

Plasma protein binding: The primary binding proteins are albumin (for acidic drugs) and α_1-acid glycoprotein (for basic drugs). Foetal albumin has a lower binding affinity and capacity for drugs like weak acids (salicylates). Substances such as free fatty acids, bilirubin, sulpha and maternal steroids can displace a drug from albumin-binding sites and increase the free fraction of the drug in the neonate. Serum albumin concentrations reach adult levels by 5 months of age. However, albumin only accounts for a small fraction of drug binding. Another protein of significance is α_1-acid glycoprotein. A reduced amount of this protein is probably responsible for a significant proportion of unbound drug in infants. Drugs such as diazepam, propranolol and lignocaine are less highly bound to α_1-acid glycoprotein in children than in adults.

A reduction in the quantity of total plasma proteins (including albumin) in the neonate increases the free fraction of drug. This decreased binding of drugs to proteins, coupled with an incompletely developed blood–brain barrier, can lead to accumulation of drugs such as barbiturates and morphine in the central nervous system (CNS) of neonates.

Metabolism

Metabolism through biotransformation to more polar forms is required for many drugs before they can be eliminated. Two types of drug biotransformation can occur: phase I and phase II reactions. Although the liver is the primary site for biotransformation, other organs are also involved, including the lungs and kidneys.

Development of Phase I and Phase II Enzymes

Phase I reactions (oxidation, reduction and hydrolysis) are cytochrome P-450 dependent. The activity of many cytochrome P-450 isoforms including CYP3A4, CYP2C and CYP1A2 is markedly decreased in the first 2 months of life. The clearance of intravenously administered midazolam from plasma is primarily a function of hepatic CYP3A4 and CYP3A5 activity, and the level of activity increases during the first 3 months of life. Most phase I enzymes function at adult levels by 6 months of life.

Phase II reactions involve conjugation with acetate, glycine, sulphate and glucuronic acid. It is seen that some phase II pathways (e.g. sulfonation) are mature at birth while others (e.g. glucuronidation) are not. All phase II enzymes mature by 1 year of age. Individual isoforms of glucuronosyltransferase (UGT) have unique maturational profiles. Levels of UGT2B7 (responsible for glucuronidation of morphine) are markedly diminished in the first 2 months of life. Glucuronidation of acetaminophen (a substrate for UGT1A6) and salicylates is decreased in newborns. A compensatory pathway (glycine pathway) for metabolism of salicylates makes their elimination half-life only slightly longer in neonates.

Both phase I and phase II reactions can be induced by barbiturates. The rate of drug metabolism is also determined by other factors such as intrinsic rate of the process and hepatic blood flow. In general, the half-lives of medications that are eliminated by the liver are prolonged in neonates, decreased in children 4–10 years of age and reached adult values in adolescents.

Excretion

The neonatal kidney receives only 5–6% of cardiac output compared to adults who receive 20–25% of cardiac output. Term neonates have a full complement of glomeruli while preterm neonates do not have a full number of glomeruli. The glomerular filtration rate (GFR) is approximately 2–4 ml per minute per 1.73 m^2 in term neonates. This increases rapidly over the first 2 weeks of life and reaches adult values by 8–12 months of age. Tubular secretion is immature at birth and reaches adult values during the first year of life. Renal drug clearance is also affected by the renal extraction ratio and by the glomerular pore size. Slightly acidic urine at birth (pH 6–6.5) decreases the elimination of weak acids. If the kidney is the primary route of drug elimination, the neonate's reduced renal function can delay the drug elimination and clinicians must individualise therapy in an age-appropriate fashion.

A concise overview of the physiological factors that affect the pharmacokinetics of drugs as described above is given in **Figure 3.2**.

Other Important Factors

Some other important factors, mentioned below, also need to be considered when dealing with pharmacokinetics.

Volume of Distribution

Premature and full-term infants have a much greater proportion of body weight in the form of

Absorption

- Age-dependent changes in the structure and function of gastrointestinal tract (GIT) affect oral absorption.
- The first-pass hepatic metabolism is a problem that is avoided in oral transmucosal drug administration.
- The skin thickness is similar in infants and adults, but the extent of perfusion and hydration diminishes from infancy to adulthood.
- Rectal absorption of drugs is erratic and the first-pass hepatic metabolism occurs in drugs administered above the ano-rectal line.

↓

Distribution

- Age-dependent changes in body composition influence the apparent volume of distribution of drugs
- In the first 6 months of life, infants have an expanded total body water and extracellular water, as compared with older infants and adults.
- Reduced levels of foetal albumin and α_1-acid glycoprotein contribute to the increased free fraction of drug.

↓

Metabolism

- The activity of many cytochrome P-450 (CYP) isoforms and a single glucuronosyl transferase isoform is markedly decreased during the first 2 months of life.
- The acquisition of adult activity over time is enzyme and isoform specific.
- Compensatory pathways can help in drug metabolism.
- Both phase I and phase II metabolic reactions mature by 1 year of age.

↓

Excretion

- The processes of glomerular filtration and active tubular secretion approximate adult activity by 6–12 months of age.

Figure 3.2 Physiological factors that affect the pharmacokinetics of drugs during their absorption, distribution, metabolism and excretion.

water than do older children and adults. Water-soluble medications will have a greater volume of distribution in these small patients, suggesting the need for a higher initial (loading) dose, based on weight, to achieve the desired serum level and clinical response.

Age-Related Body Water Compartments

Table 3.1 gives an overview of the age-related distribution of body water.

Table 3.1 Distribution of Body Water

Component	Premature	Neonate	Infant	Adult
ECF	50	35	30	20
ICF	30	40	40	40
Plasma	5	5	5	5
Total	85	80	75	65

Numbers as % body weight. ECF, extracelluar fluid; ICF, intracellular fluid.

Protein Binding

The degree of protein binding is usually less in premature and full-term infants than in adults or older children because of the infants' lower total protein and albumin. Lower protein binding results in higher free plasma levels of the drug, thus providing a greater amount of free drug leading to greater pharmacological effect.

Fat and Muscle Content

Premature and full-term neonates have a smaller proportion of body weight in the form of fat and muscle mass. Therefore, those drugs that depend on redistribution into muscle and fat have a high initial peak blood level, and they may have a more sustained blood level resulting in prolonged undesirable clinical effects, for example, prolonged sedation with barbiturates and respiratory depression with narcotics. So, a lower dose may be required.

Central Nervous System

Drugs can penetrate the CNS of neonates more easily than that of adults either because the neonatal blood–brain barrier is more permeable due to incomplete myelination or because the cerebral blood flow is slower and the drugs have a longer time to dissociate from plasma proteins. The blood–brain barrier in neonates is also more easily disrupted by hypoxia and acidosis than it is in adults.

Cardiovascular System

The incidence of bradycardia, hypotension and cardiac arrest during induction is higher in infants and small children than in adults. This has been attributed to an increased sensitivity of the cardiovascular system (CVS) to potent agents.

Bioavailability

Bioavailability describes the extent (and rate) of uptake of an active drug into the body when given by any route other than IV. It is expressed as a percentage when compared to IV administration of the same drug. If an orally administered drug is poorly absorbed or has a high first-pass metabolism, it will have a low bioavailability (Fig. 3.3).

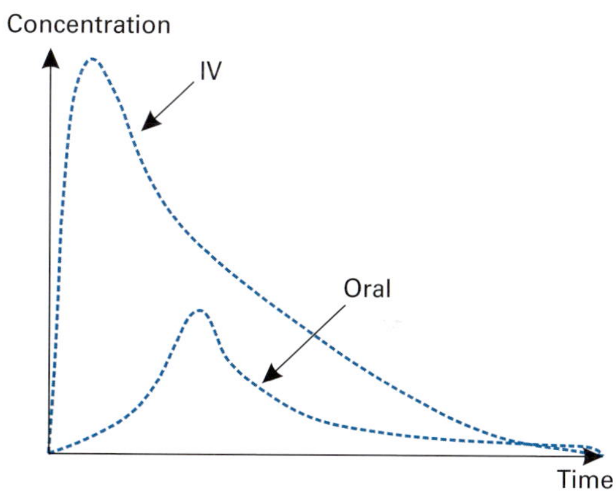

Figure 3.3 Oral bioavailability. Same dose administered IV and orally on separate occasions. Oral bioavailability = area under curve oral/area under curve IV.

Compartment Models

Drugs are not distributed uniformly throughout the body. The speed with which a drug reaches a particular tissue is largely dependent on its local blood flow. For analytical convenience, similar tissue types are often grouped together into various 'compartments' depending on their blood supply.

Compartment models are based on the body behaving as if it is divided into several hypothetical interlinked spaces or compartments.

It is important to note that pharmacokinetic compartments are mathematical models and do not correspond to actual tissues; they are a concept helping us to understand and describe the changes in plasma concentration with time, and so help to predict and compare pharmacokinetic profiles. **Figures 3.4–3.6A**, illustrate one-, two- and three-compartment models, respectively.

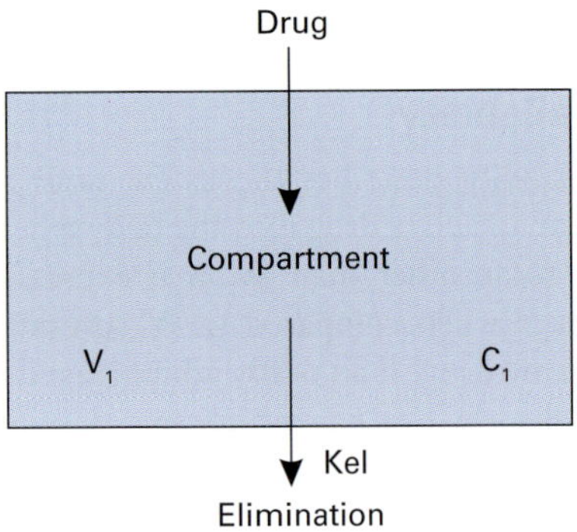

Figure 3.4 One-compartment model.

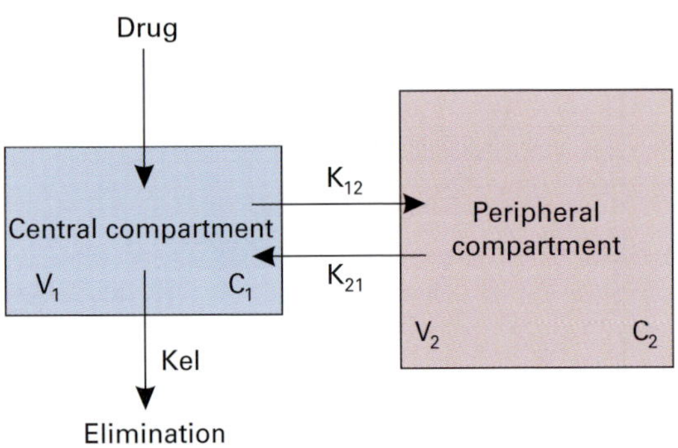

Figure 3.5 Two-compartment model.

One-Compartment Model

The simplest model is a one-compartment model. In this, all tissues are represented as a single composite compartment. A drug of dose (D) administered to the compartment is considered to get evenly distributed throughout. The plasma concentration (*C*) of the drug is measured to calculate the volume (*V*) of this hypothetical compartment. The plasma acting like a 'window' through which the compartment can be 'viewed'. The elimination rate constant (*K*el) defines the overall rate of removal of drug from this single compartment and is a combination of all the modes of elimination for that drug.

Two-Compartment Model

The one-compartment model is too simple to describe accurately the behaviour of most drugs, and this single compartment is therefore divided into central and peripheral compartments. Again, the plasma is the 'window' to the compartments and is not necessarily equivalent to the central compartment. The central compartment is the intermediary compartment through which the drug reaches the peripheral 'target' compartment. Many drugs, including thiopentone, show a good approximation to this model.

Three-Compartment Model

Some drugs, such as propofol, require further compartments to be added to allow accurate pharmacokinetic predictions. In this model, a third, deep peripheral compartment is added, and this communicates with the central compartment but at a much slower rate.

The three-compartment model is the most complex pharmacokinetic model and considers three compartments in the body. The first compartment is the central compartment, as in the two-compartment model, with the addition of two peripheral compartments. The second peripheral compartment is a deep peripheral compartment that distributes the drug slowly and consists of poorly perfused tissues such as skin and fat. The third peripheral compartment is a shallow peripheral compartment, which distributes the drug more rapidly and consists of less-vascularised tissues such as muscle. The three-compartment model is useful for drugs that exhibit prolonged distribution or elimination phases, such as propofol, which is commonly used as an anaesthetic agent.

Any model is an approximation, but by increasing the number of compartments, the correlation with the real situation can be improved. However, the size of the improvements diminishes as the number of compartments increases.

Following an IV bolus, anaesthesia agents typically exhibit a three-phase exponential decrease in plasma concentration, which is analysed in the three-compartment model depicted in **Figure 3.6B**. Initially, the drug distributes to the central compartment (V1), consisting of plasma and well-perfused organs

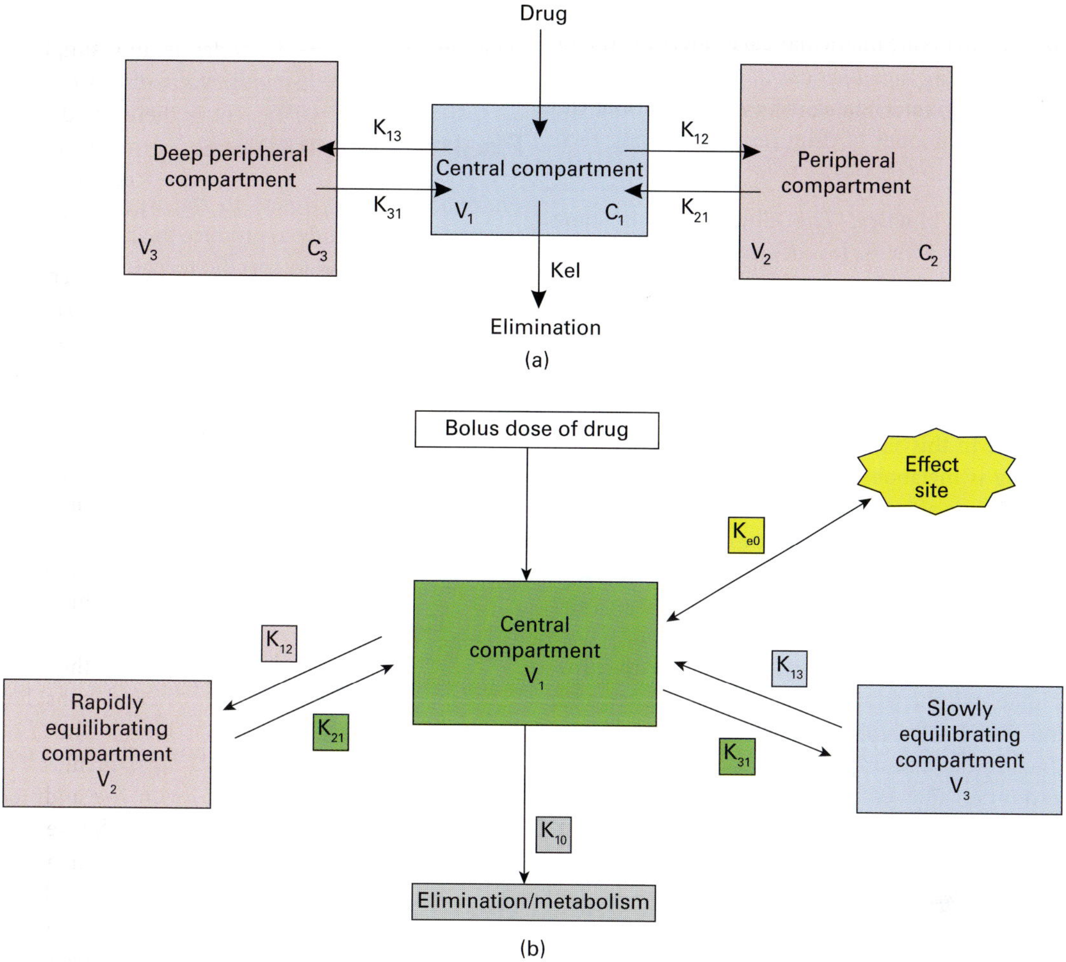

Figure 3.6 (a and b) Three-compartment model.

such as the heart, brain, kidney, liver and lungs. V1 receives 75% of cardiac output and constitutes 10% of total body mass. Afterward, the drug disseminates to other compartments. The peripheral compartment (V2) is rapidly perfused by the drug from the central compartment and includes less-irrigated tissues like muscle mass. V2 is highly significant as it prolongs the retention of drugs with high lipid solubility, leading to delayed recovery and respiratory depression even after infusion has ceased. The slow peripheral compartment (V3) consists of poorly irrigated tissues like the skin or fat and experiences the slowest drug distribution among all three compartments. These three compartments exist in equilibrium, known as 'steady-state' or 'equilibrium'. The distribution of the drug occurs in the central compartment V1 and two compartments that equilibrate rapidly, V2 and slowly, V3, with their rates determined by the rate constants K12 and K13. The drug also moves back into V1, as described by the rate constants K21 and K31, while clearance is described by the rate constant K10. Hypnotic and analgesic drugs affect the central nervous system, not the plasma, and their onset of action may be delayed due to limited diffusion into the central nervous system, as determined by the rate constant Ke0.

Elimination

First-order kinetics: Most drugs are cleared from the body with first-order exponential rates in which a constant fraction or constant proportion of drug is removed per unit of time. Because the proportion of drug cleared remains constant, the higher the concentration, the greater the amount of drug removed from the body.

Half-life is a first-order kinetic process because the same proportion or fraction of the drug is removed during equal periods of time. As described earlier, the greater the starting concentration, the greater the amount of drug removed during each half-life.

Zero-order kinetics: The elimination of some drugs occurs with the loss of a *constant amount per time rather than a constant fraction per time.* Zero-order (also known as Michaelis–Menten) kinetics may be designated saturation kinetics because such processes occur when excess amounts of drug saturate the capacity of metabolic enzymes or transport systems. In this situation, only a constant amount of drug is metabolised or transported per unit of time. This is affected more in the paediatric population because of their immature organs.

Certain drugs administered to neonates exhibit zero-order kinetics at therapeutic doses and may accumulate to excessive concentrations. These include thiopental, theophylline, diazepam, furosemide and phenytoin. Some drugs (e.g. phenytoin and ethyl alcohol) may exhibit mixed-order kinetics (i.e. first-order at low concentrations and zero-order after enzymes are saturated at higher concentrations). For these drugs, a small increment in dose may cause disproportionately large increments in serum concentrations (**Fig 3.7**).

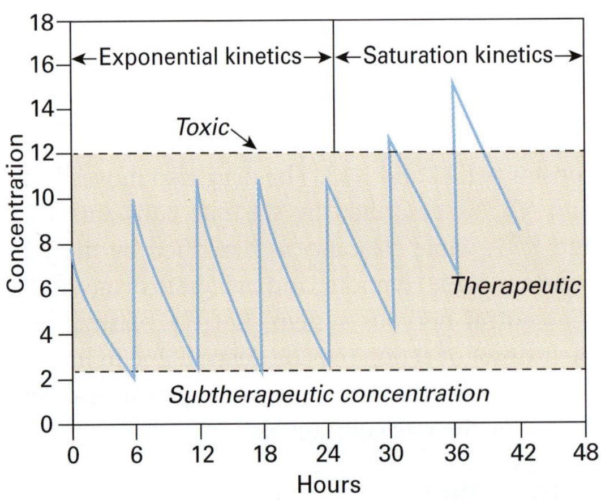

Figure 3.7 Transition from exponential to saturation kinetics. During every-6-hour dosing, concentrations during the first 24 hours reflect exponential kinetics with a half-life of 3 hours followed by a change to saturation kinetics at 24 hours with elimination of 1.0 mg/hr, leading to drug accumulation to toxic concentrations.

The principles above mentioned can be used to adjust drug doses rationally to achieve more effective drug concentrations at the site of action.

Pharmacodynamics

Pharmacodynamics refers to the way that drugs interact with the body to produce their effects. This can involve binding to specific receptors, blocking certain enzymes or pathways, or altering the function of certain organs or tissues. In simple terms, this is often expressed by the phrase '*what the drug does in the body*'.

Potency refers to the amount of drug required to produce a particular effect, usually measured as the dose needed to produce a specific response. A highly potent drug requires a smaller dose to produce the same effect as a less potent drug. **Efficacy**, on the other hand, refers to the maximum effect that a drug can produce, regardless of the dose. It is a measure of how well a drug can produce a desired effect. In summary, potency is a measure of the dose required to produce a particular effect, while efficacy is a measure of how well a drug can produce a desired effect.

There are several pharmacological terms that use a representative sample of the total population to describe the response which is applicable to the same extent as in adults. For example,

- **ED50:** Dose causing the specified effect in 50% of the sample population
- **LD50:** Dose causing a lethal effect in 50% of the sample population
- **Therapeutic index (TI):** The TI is a measure of the safety of a drug and is defined as the ratio of the dose that produces a toxic effect in 50% of individuals (TD50) to the dose that produces a therapeutic effect in 50% of individuals (ED50).

Drugs produce their effect because of their physicochemical properties, activity at receptors, inhibition of enzyme systems or influence on nucleic acid synthesis. Examples of these are given in the following text.

Physical Properties

Some drugs act on the body through their physical properties rather than their chemical properties. These drugs can have various mechanisms of action, including altering surface tension, modifying osmotic pressure or creating a physical barrier. An antacid neutralises acid in the gastric juice and is given frequently to reduce the likelihood of acid aspiration pneumonitis after inhalation of gastric contents. Stored blood is prevented from coagulating by sodium hydrogen citrate. This chelates calcium ions and may cause hypocalcaemia after a massive blood transfusion.

Action on Receptors

Many drugs act on the body through a receptor mechanism, which involves binding to specific receptors on the surface of cells or within the cell. Receptors are proteins that are responsible for transmitting signals between cells and are involved in a wide range of physiological processes. They bind selectively with endogenous compounds or drugs, resulting in changes within the cell. Most of the drugs we use to produce their effect by acting on specific receptors; for example, adrenaline and noradrenaline work on alpha- and beta-receptors, midazolam on benzodiazepine receptors and morphine on opioid receptors.

An *agonist* is a compound which binds to the receptor and changes the intracellular function and produces a maximal response.

A *partial agonist* is a compound which binds to the receptor and causes a change in the intracellular function like an agonist but produces less than maximal response.

An *antagonist* is a compound which combines selectively with the receptor but may produce no effect. It may interact with the receptor in a competitive (reversible) or non-competitive (irreversible) fashion.

An *agonist-antagonist* or *mixed agonist/antagonist* is used to refer to a drug which under some conditions behaves as an agonist, while under other conditions, behaves as an antagonist. This includes receptor ligands that act as agonists for some receptor types and antagonists for others or agonists in some tissues while antagonists in others.

Action on Enzymes

The other common way drugs act is by inhibiting the action of an enzyme or competing for its endogenous substrate. Drugs such as captopril (angiotensin-converting enzyme), aminophylline (phosphodiesterase) and edrophonium (acetylcholinesterase) produce their effect by reversible inhibition of the enzymes whereas drugs such as omeprazole (gastric hydrogen-potassium ATPase), aspirin (cyclooxygenase) and organophosphorus compounds (acetylcholinesterase) cause irreversible enzyme inhibition by forming a stable chemical bond between drug and enzyme, resulting in prolonged or permanent inactivity. The enzymes on which the drugs act are given in brackets.

Action on Nucleic Acid Synthesis

Drugs may act via receptors on the cell nucleus influencing protein synthesis by stimulating the production of messenger RNA. Consequently, drugs acting in this manner, for example, corticosteroids, have a slow speed of onset.

Age-Related Pharmacodynamic Changes in Children

True age-related pharmacodynamic changes may be qualitative and quantitative and may apply to both therapeutic and adverse effects. Pharmacodynamics in children can differ from those in adults due to differences in physiology, development and maturation. Here are some examples of age-related pharmacodynamic changes in children:

- **Absorption:** Children may have differences in gastrointestinal motility, gastric acid secretion and the size of the small intestine, which can affect drug absorption.
- **Distribution:** Children have a higher body water content and lower body fat content than adults, which can affect drug distribution. Additionally, protein binding may be lower in neonates, leading to higher concentrations of free drugs.
- **Metabolism:** Children have a different capacity for drug metabolism due to differences in liver and renal function. Enzyme activity may also change as children grow and develop.
- **Receptor sensitivity:** Receptor sensitivity may differ in children due to developmental changes in receptor expression and function.

- **Elimination:** Children have a higher GFR than adults, which can lead to faster drug elimination. However, renal function may be impaired in premature infants.

Understanding age-related pharmacodynamic changes in children is important for determining appropriate dosing, identifying potential drug interactions and minimising the risk of adverse effects. Paediatric pharmacodynamics can be influenced by a variety of factors, including age, weight, developmental stage and underlying medical conditions. As a result, dosing in children often requires careful consideration and monitoring.

Pharmacokinetics and Pharmacodynamics of Individual Drugs

The following categories of drugs will be discussed:

- IV induction agents
- Narcotics
- Neuromuscular blocking drugs
- Local anaesthetics
- Inhalational agents

Intravenous Induction Agents

The following IV induction agents will be discussed here: thiopentone, benzodiazepines, ketamine and propofol.

Thiopentone

Thiopentone requirements for induction of anaesthesia reveal an inverse relation with age. A significantly larger volume of distribution in the infant makes the ED-50 of thiopentone in infants significantly greater (7 mg/kg) than that in adults (4 mg/kg). This larger dose increases the store of drugs in the body and prolongs the drug's half-life. In neonates, due to their low body fat and muscle content, less thiopentone is distributed to these tissues, so the concentration in the CNS may remain high and delay awakening. The requirement for thiopentone is highest in the early neonatal period and reaches the adult level by 1–4 years.

Benzodiazepines

The premature and the mature infant at term eliminate diazepam at a slower rate than adults do. Differences in metabolism as described earlier alter the way in which neonates and infants reduce the plasma concentration of drugs. Neonates hydroxylate and N-demethylate diazepam less well than adults or children. This prolongs the elimination half-life of diazepam (75 ± 38 hours in preterm infants as compared to 18 ± 3 hours in children) and thus prolongs its effect.

Ketamine

In infants less than 3 months of age, the V_d is like that in older infants but the elimination half-life is prolonged. Hence, clearance is reduced in younger infants. Reduced metabolism and renal excretion in the young infant are the likely causes.

Propofol

Propofol has been used in children in the induction and maintenance of general anaesthesia. In a study done by Murat et al.,[1] 12 children aged between 1 and 3 years were given a single dose of propofol 4 mg/kg; an average V_d of 9.5 ± 3.7 l/kg with an average total body clearance of 53 ± 13 ml/min/kg was reported. Younger children demonstrated a larger V_d with a similar rate of clearance.

TIVA in Children

When induction and maintenance of general anaesthesia are by IV infusion, this is referred to as total intravenous anaesthesia (TIVA). TIVA has grown rapidly in popularity over the last three decades in both adult and paediatric anaesthesia. There are several reasons why the TIVA is becoming a popular technique:

- **Precise dosing and control:** TIVA allows for precise control of drug delivery, which can be particularly important in situations where small changes in drug concentration can have a significant impact on the patient's response.
- **Reduced side effects:** The TIVA can reduce the risk of side effects associated with inhaled anaesthetics, such as respiratory irritation or

bronchospasm, reduced nausea and vomiting and decreased post-operative delirium.

- **Rapid onset and recovery:** The TIVA can allow for a more rapid onset of anaesthesia and recovery than inhaled anaesthetics.
- **Reduced pollution:** The use of inhaled anaesthetics can contribute to environmental pollution. TIVA eliminates the need for inhaled agents, which can reduce the environmental impact of anaesthesia administration.
- **Organ-specific effects,** such as reduced airway reactivity with improved post-operative ciliary function, lower heart rate and reduced level of stress hormones, maintained cerebrovascular reactivity and preserved middle ear pressure; confer significant advantages in specific clinical settings.

This rapid increase in popularity is also due to the widespread availability of drugs with favourable pharmacological properties like propofol and remifentanil and the development of new concepts in pharmacokinetic-pharmacodynamic modelling, as well as advances in computer technology that have allowed the development of sophisticated anaesthetic delivery systems.

It is important to know the pharmacokinetic principles underpinning TIVA to be able to achieve and maintain an appropriate concentration of an IV anaesthetic or analgesic drug in the patient's plasma and brain. Anaesthesia may be induced and maintained either using manual dosing, where the anaesthetist determines the bolus dose(s) and infusion rate(s) used or using a target-controlled infusion (TCI) pump where the anaesthetist enters the desired 'target' to be achieved in the patient's plasma or brain.

What is the difference between TIVA and TCI?

In reality, both terms are used interchangeably but there is a difference. TIVA means the total IV anaesthetic, where no volatile anaesthetic gases such as sevoflurane and desflurane are used. While it can be given using a TCI pump, this is not necessary and it can be given through a simple ml/hour pump or even bolused by hand.

TCI stands for target-controlled infusion. It is a method of administering medication through a specialised computer microprocessor chip-controlled IV infusion pump in a way that is tailored to the individual characteristics of the patient, such as weight, age and gender, with the goal of achieving a desired effect at the effector site. In the case of IV anaesthetic agents, TCI infusions are used to achieve and maintain a specific concentration of the medication in the bloodstream that is predicted to produce the desired effect at the effector site.

TCI infusions use a mathematical model to predict the concentration of the medication in the bloodstream or effector site. In the context of anaesthesia, the effector site refers to the site in the body where the medication being administered produces its intended effect. In the case of IV anaesthetic agents, such as propofol or remifentanil, the effector site is typically the brain, where the medications produce their desired effect of inducing anaesthesia and providing pain relief.

What drugs are used for TIVA?

Anaesthetic drugs with a fast onset/ fast recovery are best suited for the TCI. The most common are propofol and remifentanil, although other drugs like alfentanil, sufentanil and dexmedetomidine can also be used. Propofol available in 2% concentration should be used in children to reduce the lipid load.

Propofol is the most used drug for the TCI because it has several properties that make it an effective choice for this technique. First, propofol has a rapid onset of action, meaning it starts to work quickly after it is administered. This allows for more precise control of the sedative effect during the TCI since the desired level of sedation can be achieved more quickly and maintained more consistently. Second, propofol has a relatively short duration of action, which means that it is rapidly metabolised and eliminated from the body once the infusion is stopped. This allows for a faster recovery time and less risk of residual sedation. Third, propofol has a wide margin of safety, meaning that it can be used at a range of doses without causing significant harm to the patient. This makes it a good choice for the TCI since the infusion rate can be adjusted based on the patient's individual needs and response to the medication.

Basic Infusion Pharmacokinetics

When a drug such as propofol is administered as a bolus, the blood concentration rises to a peak and then falls as the drug is redistributed into other tissue compartments and eliminated from the body (**Figs 3.8–3.11** illustrate changes in the plasma concentration of propofol following a single bolus, intermittent bolus, continuous infusion and

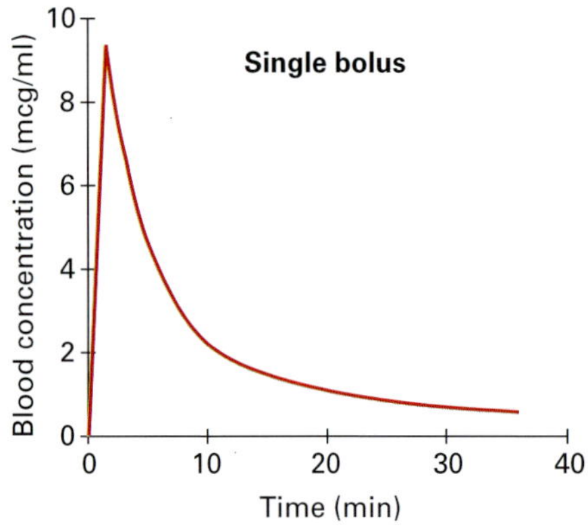

Figure 3.8 Plasma concentration of propofol after a single bolus.

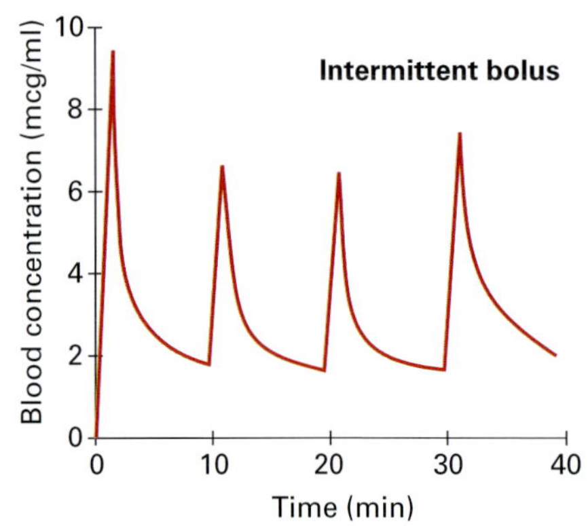

Figure 3.9 Plasma concentration of propofol following intermittent bolus.

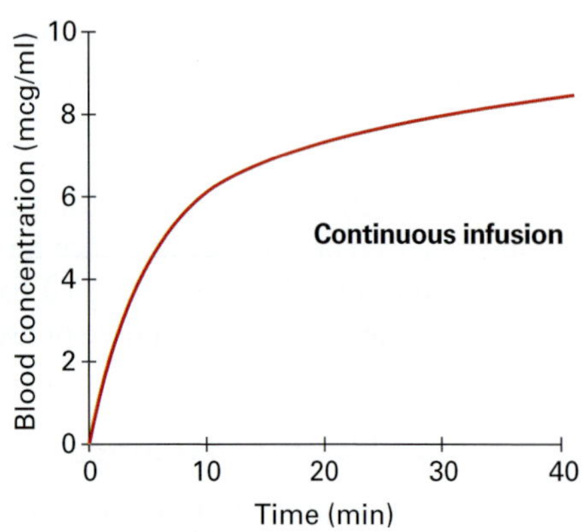

Figure 3.10 Plasma concentration of propofol following a continuous infusion.

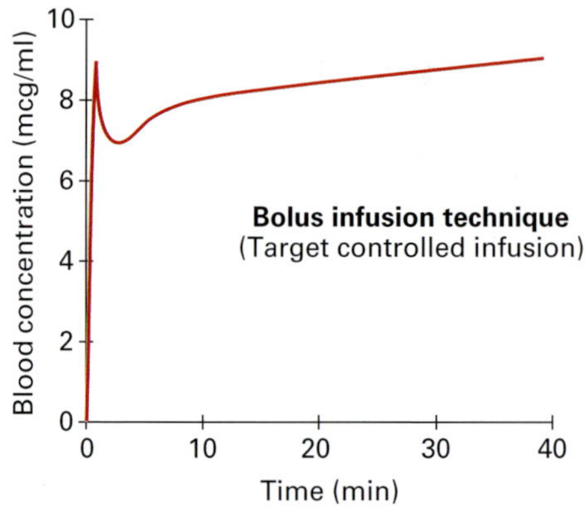

Figure 3.11 Plasma concentration following a bolus and continuous infusion of propofol.

bolus-infusion technique). If the bolus is followed by an infusion, the infusion will help maintain the plasma concentration as the drug is redistributed to other tissues and cleared. An infusion on its own will result in a slow increase in the blood concentration, reaching a steady-state after approximately five elimination half-lives, when redistribution to other organs has ceased and clearance equals the rate of drug administration.

Context-Sensitive Half-Time

The CSHT is a pharmacokinetic concept that is used to describe the time it takes for the plasma concentration of a drug to decrease by 50% after continuous infusion of the drug for a certain duration of time. The CSHT is an important concept in anaesthesia, as it helps to predict how long it will take for a patient to recover from the effects of a drug after the infusion is stopped.

The CSHT of a drug can vary depending on the duration of the infusion and the pharmacokinetic properties of the drug. For example, drugs with a short elimination half-life will have a shorter CSHT than drugs with a longer elimination half-life. Additionally, the CSHT may increase with longer durations of infusion since the drug may accumulate in the body over time (**Fig. 3.12**).

By understanding the CSHT of a drug, an anaesthesiologist can adjust the infusion rate of the drug to achieve the desired level of sedation or anaesthesia and can predict how long it will take for the patient to recover from the effects of the drug after the infusion is stopped.

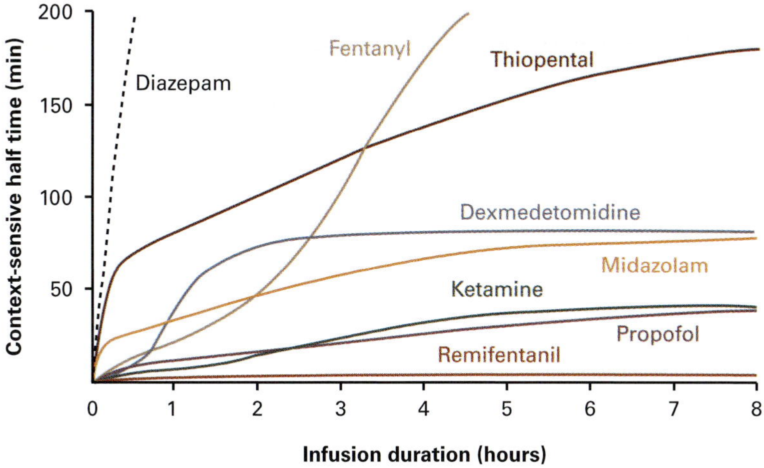

Figure 3.12 Graph depicting context-sensitive half-times of different IV agents.

Basic Principles of TCI Pumps

A typical TCI system consists of three main components: a user interface incorporating a display and method to input data, and a microprocessor to run the pharmacokinetic modelling software and to control the third component, namely the infusion device.

Early TCI devices did not cater for the paediatric population. Numerous paediatric TCI models have been developed but two are widely available: the Paedfusor and Kataria. Paedfusor uses age and weight as covariates; it can be used between 5 and 61 kg, and 1–16 years of age. Kataria can be used from 3 to 16 years of age and works with a minimum weight of 15 kg. Recently a universal Eleveld model that uses allometric scaling has been launched that can be used in children as small as 27 weeks post-conceptual age and 0.65 kg.

Manual infusion regimens for children, as seen in Tables 3.2 and 3.3, are markedly different when compared with adult regimens. The former, McFarlan and colleagues, based on the Kataria

Table 3.2 McFarlan Propofol Manual Infusion Scheme Based on the Kataria p*K* Parameter Estimates for Children Between the Ages of 3–11 Years

Induction Dose	Maintenance Dose				
	0–15 Minutes	15–30 Minutes	30–60 Minutes	1–2 Hours	2–4 Hours
2.5 mg/kg	15 mg/kg/hr	13	11	10	9
	250 mcg/kg/hr	215	185	165	150

Table 3.3 Steur Propofol Manual Infusion Scheme Adapted from Clinical Observations in Children <3 Years of Age

Age	Induction Dose	Maintenance Infusion					
		0–10 Minutes	10–20 Minutes	20–30 Minutes	30–40 Minutes	40–100 Minutes	>100 Minutes
<3 months	3–5 mg/kg	25	20	15	10	5	2.5
3–6 months	3–5 mg/kg	20	15	10	5	5	2.5
6–12 months	3–5 mg/kg	15	10	5	5	5	2.5
1–3 years	3–5 mg/kg	12	9	6	6	6	6

Table 3.4 Propofol TCI Models Available for Use in Children

TCI Model	Target Cp Value Common for all Models	Input Data Required to Setup	Notes
Schnider	Propofol (sole agent) 4–8 mcg/ml	Age, height, gender, weight	Designed for adults, can be used in children > 5 years. Best suitable for effect site targeting
Marsh		Weight, age (not used in calculation)	Suitable ideally for age > 16, weight >61 kg Best suitable for plasma site targeting
Kataria	Propofol + adjunct (e.g., regional anaesthesia or opioids) 3–4 mcg/ml	Age, weight	Suitable for ages 3–16 years, weight 15–61 kg
Paedfusor		Age, weight	Suitable for ages 1–16 years, weight 5–61 kg
Eleveld		Age, weight, and gender	Suitable for broad population ranging from neonates to elderly

TCI, target-controlled infusion.

pharmacokinetic data for 3–11 year olds. The latter (Table 3.3), Steur and colleagues, proposed more recently for children under 3 years of age. Currently available TCI models for use in children are shown in Table 3.4. It should be noted that paediatric TCI works on plasma site concentration (Cp) rather than effect site concentration prediction (Ce).

Narcotics

Even premature infants are known to perceive pain. To keep children pain-free, narcotics are used regularly. The more commonly used narcotics in children are morphine, pethidine and fentanyl. More details are provided in Chapter 47.

Morphine

Studies have demonstrated that morphine depresses the newborn's respiration more than pethidine. Pharmacokinetic studies of morphine also show that infants less than 1 week of age demonstrate longer elimination half-life compared to older infants.

Pethidine

Though pethidine is more lipid-soluble than morphine, there is reduced CNS uptake and sensitivity to pethidine. It produces only 1/10 the respiratory depression and less sedation than morphine. The activity of pethidine may be less because the opioid receptors of the brain are more primitive and do not recognise structural analogues.

Fentanyl

In the neonate, fentanyl clearance seems comparable to that of the older child or the adult, while in the premature infant fentanyl clearance is markedly reduced.

Neuromuscular Blocking Drugs

Clinically, most neuromuscular blocking drugs are studied under anaesthesia as the children are first anaesthetised and then the drugs are given. Infants have a much greater potentiation and reduction in dose requirements than older children (sevoflurane decreases the dose requirement of non-depolarising muscle relaxants by 70% if administered for 90 minutes in school-aged children and 40 minutes in infants).

Depolarising Muscle Relaxants

More succinylcholine is needed in infants than in older children or adults when calculated on a weight basis. Succinylcholine is rapidly distributed throughout the ECF because of its relatively small molecular size. The infant's blood volume and ECF volume are significantly greater than those of a child's or an adult's on a weight basis. Therefore, the recommended dose is twice that of adults (2 mg/kg). However, the rate of succinylcholine hydrolysis may be slower in the preterm infant than in the older child due to his/her immature liver.

Non-Depolarising Muscle Relaxants

There is substantial evidence to suggest that the neuromuscular junction in neonates is three times more sensitive to non-depolarising muscle relaxants (NDMRs) than that of adults. However, this sensitivity is balanced by an almost identical increase in the volume of distribution (because of the large ECF) so the required dose is unaffected. However, because of a prolonged elimination time, doses of additional relaxants should be reduced and given less frequently. Children of all ages are more resistant than adults to pancuronium. Vecuronium and rocuronium are longer acting in infants and should be less preferred over NDMRs with predictable and favourable kinetics. Atracurium is the preferred NDMR in neonates and infants due to predictable elimination – Hofmann elimination – which is devoid of liver and kidney function. The histamine release associated with atracurium may cause rash, bronchospasm, tachycardia and hypotension. The newer NDMR cis-atracurium has less propensity for histamine release but is longer in duration than atracurium by 5–15 minutes in infants. It has not received FDA approval for use in neonates.

Anticholinesterases

Neuromuscular blockade in children is antagonised much faster and by much smaller doses of anticholinesterases as compared to adults. Both cholinesterase and pseudo-cholinesterase levels are reduced in premature and term newborns. Adult levels are not reached until 1 year of age. Despite the reduced pseudo-cholinesterase levels, newborns are more resistant to succinylcholine than adults are.

Local Anaesthetic Agents

Local anaesthetics are used in children as a topical application or subcutaneous injection for needle procedures, neuraxial blockade and peripheral nerve blockade. Uptake into the nerves from perineural injection sites competes with uptake into the central circulation. Animal models indicate that less than 2–3% of an injected dose ever enters the nerve and within 30 minutes of injection more than 90% of an injected dose is taken up into the systemic circulation. This is significant as all the amino amides including bupivacaine, levobupivacaine, lignocaine and ropivacaine show diminished clearance in neonates with maturation over the first 3–8 months of age. Limited information suggests that the amino esters, which are metabolised by plasma esterases, have a very rapid clearance even in neonates.

Most drugs in paediatric dosing are usually on a weight-scaled basis. However, it has been found that neonates have a shorter block duration and require a much larger (fourfold) weight-scaled dose to achieve a similar dermatomal level when given as a subarachnoid block or achieve a peripheral nerve block like an adult. This is not only due to a higher weight-scaled volume of the cerebrospinal fluid (CSF) but there may also be age-related differences in pharmacodynamic responses, myelination, spacing of nodes of Ranvier, tissue barrier and other factors. Another important factor is the dependence of minimal blocking concentration on the length of nerve exposed to local anaesthetic. The minimal blocking concentration decreases dramatically as the length of the nerve exposed to the local anaesthetic is increased. Adults, therefore, need less drug to produce the desired blockade as they have a greater length of nerve exposed to the drug.

The implication of the above is that the TI of local anaesthetics in infants may be so narrow that the maximum safe infusion rates of the amino amides are too low to provide sole analgesia for the most major surgery of the thorax, abdomen or pelvis. Thus, infants require higher weight-scaled infusion rates than adults to achieve blockade but they can safely receive only a lower weight-scaled infusion rate than adults from the viewpoint of toxicity. To provide adequate safe analgesia, other agents such as opioids, clonidine or ketamine may be used in the epidural space to provide synergistic analgesia. Another approach is to use a single stereoisomer such as ropivacaine and levobupivacaine to decrease the likelihood of cardiac toxicity.

Inhalational Agents

The use of inhalational anaesthetics in children has been the mainstay of anaesthetic practice for the last 150 years. The potency of an inhaled anaesthetic is determined by its minimum alveolar concentration (MAC). The requirement for inhalational agents varies inversely with age. MAC is lower in preterm infants than in term infants and increases with post-conceptual age. Age-related changes in MAC imply that the same alveolar concentration will produce different levels of anaesthesia in children of different ages.

Age-related iso-MAC charts for isoflurane, sevoflurane and desflurane in the clinically useful MAC range (0.6 ± 1.6) and nomogram to estimate age-related MAC are available to help one administer the right amount of anaesthetic at the extremes of age.

A lower requirement of inhalational anaesthetics in preterms is due to an immature CNS, increased circulating progesterone and increased endorphins.

Factors Affecting F_E/F_I Ratio

F_E/F_I is the ratio of the end-tidal anaesthetic concentration to the inspired anaesthetic concentration, which is a measure of how rapidly gas equilibrates between lung and tissue. Factors influencing the uptake of the drug from the lung and distribution to tissues are inspired anaesthetic concentration, alveolar ventilation, functional residual capacity (FRC), cardiac output, the solubility of the anaesthetic agent and alveolar to the venous partial pressure gradient. Paediatric considerations of these will be discussed in detail.

F_I or Inspired Anaesthetic Concentration

The higher the anaesthetic concentration, the more quickly F_E moves towards F_I.

Changes in Ventilation and FRC

The greater the minute ventilation, as in infants and children, the more rapid the rise occurs (assuming a constant cardiac output). The smaller the FRC, the faster the F_E/F_I increases. The FRC in infants is smaller than that in adults but the tidal volume per kg body weight is the same as that of adults. The more rapid respiratory rate, though, increases the minute ventilation in the young.

Right-to-Left Shunting of Blood

Right-to-left shunting of blood is often present in neonates and infants; it slows down the induction of anaesthesia because the blood concentration of anaesthetics rises more slowly in them.

Blood/Gas Partition Coefficients and Anaesthetic Solubility

The F_E/F_I of an insoluble gas such as sevoflurane or nitrous oxide rises rapidly while with a more soluble gas such as halothane it rises more slowly. In general, however, inhaled anaesthetic agents are less soluble in the blood of paediatric patients. For example, the blood/gas partition coefficients of halothane and isoflurane are 18% lower in neonates than in young adults (20–40%) and in children (1–7 years) are 12% less than in young adults. This difference, which accounts for the more rapid rise of F_E/F_I in neonates, is due in part to lower albumin concentration and thus low blood/gas partition coefficient.

During anaesthesia, the blood–gas partition coefficient can drop by approximately 10% due to haemodilution with crystalloid and reduction in haematocrit.

Blood Tissue Partition

Anaesthetic solubility in the brain, heart and liver increases by approximately 50% between the newborn period and the middle age and is probably due to a decrease in water and an increase in lipid content with age.

Partial Pressure of Anaesthetics

Because the blood flow per unit tissue mass is greater in neonates, the level of anaesthetic in the tissue increases more rapidly and the induction of anaesthesia is more rapid.

Increased Cardiac Output

It reduces the rate of rise of alveolar concentration of anaesthetic because more anaesthetic is removed per unit of time. The cardiac output of neonates per kg is normally twice that of adults. However, F_E/F_I rises more rapidly because much of the neonates' and infants' cardiac output is directed to the vessel-rich tissues, which then get saturated sooner.

Induction Characteristics

The most used induction agent in paediatrics more recently is sevoflurane. The primary criterion to assure a rapid induction is the 'wash-in' curve in the first minute or two of anaesthesia. During the first couple of minutes of an inhalational induction, the alveolar-to-inspired concentration ratio of these potent inhaled anaesthetics reaches about 0.33. When the wash-in of halothane and sevoflurane was compared in the first few minutes, 5% inspired halothane achieved an alveolar concentration of 1.65% or 1.65 MAC whereas 8% sevoflurane achieved a concentration of 2.64, just in excess of 1 MAC. Although both anaesthetics provide for a rapid loss of eyelash reflex (1/3 faster with 8% sevoflurane than 5% halothane with single breath induction), the depth of anaesthesia achieved with sevoflurane is less than that of halothane because of the reduced MAC multiple in sevoflurane. It is also suggested that if sevoflurane is introduced slowly as is the practice with halothane, a protracted excitement phase is seen before an adequate depth of anaesthesia is achieved.

Sevoflurane can therefore be administered in a higher concentration of 6–8% to begin with and brought down rapidly once the baby is asleep.

The MAC for sevoflurane remains constant in the first 6 months of life, while that for halothane is less in the newborn than it is in the 6-month-old. Thus, an anaesthetic overdose with sevoflurane, in the newborn, is less likely.

A comparison of the anaesthetic characteristics of halothane and sevoflurane is seen in **Table 3.5**.

Table 3.5 Halothane Versus Sevoflurane

Clinical Sign	Halothane	Sevoflurane
Loss of eyelash reflex	Slower than sevoflurane	Rapid
Depth of anaesthesia	Greater	Less than halothane
Respiratory system	Reduces tidal volume Increases respiratory rate	Reduces tidal volume Can induce apnoea
Assisted ventilation	May not need	Necessary
Cardiovascular system	Maintains heart rate Reduces blood pressure	Increases heart rate Maintains blood pressure

Metabolism

Inhalational agents are apparently metabolised to a lesser degree by paediatric patients in comparison to adults. Infants can bio-transform halothane but do so to a lesser extent than adults. As further evidence for this is the low incidence of halothane-induced hepatitis in the paediatric age group despite having repeated anaesthetics with halothane.

Around 5% of inhaled sevoflurane is metabolised by cytochrome P450 producing hexafluoroisopropanol (CF3-CHOH-CF3) and inorganic fluoride ions. A plasma fluoride ion concentration of 50 μmol/l is quoted as the threshold for renal toxicity. Sevoflurane metabolism does produce levels above this threshold. The potentially hepatotoxic hexafluoroisopropanolol is rapidly conjugated before it can cause damage. Other degradation compounds have been seen in vitro but are not of significance. What is important, though, are the isolated reports of extreme heat and flammability occurring in breathing circuits using desiccated carbon dioxide absorbent.

Predictability

Established pharmacokinetic and pharmacodynamic data are derived from averaged population studies. When based on these, even the most sophisticated dosage schemes for IV drugs will produce substantial variation in response between individuals, in both the blood–brain concentration (pharmacokinetics) and the subsequent effects (pharmacodynamics).

In contrast, for inhalational anaesthetic agents, although pharmacodynamic variability will still occur, pharmacokinetic behaviour will be far more predictable, because of the physics of gas/vapour solution in a liquid. Indeed, at equilibrium, the partial pressure of an inhalational agent in the blood (and other tissues) will precisely be equal to that in the inhaled gas mixture. Furthermore, the end-tidal partial pressure of an inhalational agent can be measured in real-time, providing a value very close to that in arterial blood.

An Ideal Inhalational Agent Should Have the Following Characteristics

- Rapid onset and elimination
- Pleasant to smell
- Minimal respiratory irritant properties
- Should not cause myocardial and respiratory depression
- Should have little effect on cardiovascular and cerebral blood flow
- Should cause reduced cerebral and coronary oxygen consumption
- Minimal interaction with catecholamines
- Should not be metabolised to toxic compounds
- Should not trigger malignant hyperthermia

Sadly, none of the agents we have at present fulfil all the criteria though sevoflurane does seem to come close.

Individual Inhalational Agents

The following are the advantages and disadvantages of the inhalational agents:

1. **Halothane**
   - Advantages
     - Pleasant to smell
     - Airway-related problems are less
     - Cheaper
   - Disadvantages
     - Potent myocardial depressant
     - Potentiates the arrhythmogenic action of adrenaline
2. **Isoflurane**
   - Advantages
     - Less myocardial depression
     - Preservation of heart rate
     - Greater reduction of cerebral metabolic oxygen requirement
   - Disadvantages
     - Noxious stimuli
     - Airway irritability
3. **Desflurane**
   - Advantages
     - Rapid induction
     - Blood–gas partition coefficient like nitrous oxide
   - Disadvantages
     - Airway irritability
     - Hypertension
4. **Sevoflurane**
   - Advantages
     - Non-irritating odour
     - Low blood–gas partition coefficient
     - Rapid and smooth induction
     - Less cardiovascular effects
   - Disadvantages
     - Expensive
     - Emergence agitation and delirium has been reported in older children requiring sedatives and prolonging the hospital stay
5. **Nitrous oxide:** It is to be used with caution in the neonate due to potential problems of hypoxia-induced apnoea, hypotension, increased pulmonary vascular resistance and paradoxical gas embolism associated with its use. N_2O-causing de-nitrogenation of the lungs may produce significant alveolar collapse and V-Q mismatch. A compensatory central sympathetic stimulation in the presence of N_2O-induced myocardial depression is lacking in neonates, making them more at risk for hypotension.

REFERENCE

1. Murat I, Billard V, Vernois J, et al. Pharmacokinetics of propofol after a single dose in children aged 13 years with minor burns. *Anesthesiology* 1996; 84: 526–532.

SUGGESTED READINGS

1. Meretoja O. Update on muscle relaxants. *Ped Anaesth* 2004; 14:384–386.
2. Bersde C. Local anaesthetics in infants and children: an update. *Ped Anaesth* 2004; 14:387–393.
3. Kearns GL, Susan M, Abdel-Rahman, et al. Developmental pharmacology – drug disposition, action and therapy in infants and children. *New Engl J Med* 2003; 349:1157–1167. A review.
4. Stoelting RK. Pharmacology and Physiology in Anaesthetic Practice, 3rd edn. Lippincott – Raven, Philadelphia, 1999; pp. 1–35.
5. Gregory GA. Pharmacology. In: Pediatric Anaesthesia. Gregory GA (ed). Churchill Livingstone, New York, 1994; pp. 13–47.
6. Jonmarker C, Westrin P, Larsson S, Werner O. Thiopental requirements for induction of anaesthesia in children. *Anesthesiology* 1987; 67:104.
7. Lake CL. Paediatric Cardiac Anaesthesia. Appleton and Lange, East Narwolk, CN 1988.
8. Gormley SMC, Crean PM. Basic principles of anaesthesia for neonates and infants. *BJA/CEPD Rev* 2001; 5:130–133.
9. Lerman J. Inhalational anaesthetics. *Ped Anaesth* 2004; 14:380–383.
10. Cravero J, Surgenor S, Whalen K. Emergence agitation in paediatric patients after sevoflurane anaesthesia and no surgery: a comparison with halothane. *Ped Anaesth* 2000; 10:419–424.
11. Davis PJ, Bosenberg A, Davidson A, et al. Pharmacology of pediatric anesthesia. In: Smith's Anesthesia for Infants and Children. Davis PJ, Cladis FP,

Motoyama EK (eds). Elsevier, Mosby, Philadelphia, 2011; pp. 179–261.

12. Kumar R. Context sensitive half-life. RK.MD. 2017. Available from: https://rk.md/2017/context-sensitive-half-time
13. Anderson BJ, Bagshaw O. Practicalities of total intravenous anesthesia and target-controlled infusion in children. *Anesthesiology* 2019; 131(1): 164–185.
14. Chan V, Skowno J. A practical approach to propofol-based total intravenous anaesthesia (TIVA) in children. Paediatr Anaesth. 2018.

4 Neonates are Different

Mathews Thomas Kodippara • Rebecca Jacob • Anisha De

It may be obvious that children are not little adults, infants are not little children and neonates are not little infants. There are essential differences between adults, infants and neonates and physiological changes do not occur in a linear manner. In dealing with neonates, one has to understand that though there is an obligate miniaturisation, there is also a transitional physiology with developing physiological systems and a high gene impact on pathophysiological processes and diseases. In the following chapter, a system-wise review of the special characteristics seen in premature babies and infants and their anaesthetic implications is described.

Essential Terms

- **Neonate:** Defined as a baby within the first 44 weeks of post-conceptual age
- **Early neonate:** First 7 days
- **Late neonate:** From 7 to 28 days
- **Newborn:** Baby within the first 24 hours of birth
- **Infant:** Child up to 1 year of age.
- **Premature:** If born before 37 weeks of gestation
- **Mature:** If born >37 weeks of gestation
- **Postmature:** If gestational age >42 weeks
- **Post-conceptual age (PCA):** It is the gestational age plus post-natal age. This may reveal that an otherwise 'normal' infant is actually <44 weeks and is therefore at risk for retinopathy of prematurity or is <46 weeks and is at risk for post-operative apnoea.

A premature baby may be

- Low birth weight (LBW): <2500 g
- Very low birth weights (VLBWs): <1500 g
- Extremely low birth weights: <1000 g

Size of Neonates

The size of neonates is the most striking difference between adults and neonates (**Fig. 4.1**). Their weight is 1/20, length is 1/3 and surface area is 1/9 of the adult. The head of a newborn is 25% of the body length. His torso is long and his limbs are short. His surface/volume ratio is 70 times greater than that of the adult.

Respiratory System: Development and Physiology

The foetal lung develops from an outpouching of the foregut at 24 days of gestation. During foetal life, it is filled with an ultrafiltrate of plasma. By 24 weeks of gestation, type 2 pneumocytes produce granules containing the precursor of surfactant and by about 28 weeks the surfactant, the lipoprotein, begins to appear in the alveolar lining cells.

During gestation, the sphingomyelin level is constant while the surfactant production is accompanied by the appearance of the phospholipid lecithin. The estimation of the levels of these substances in the amniotic fluid helps to assess foetal maturity. A lecithin/sphingomyelin ratio of >2 indicates a low risk of respiratory distress syndrome (RDS) while a lecithin/sphingomyelin ratio of <2 indicates a very high risk of RDS. This information is important when induction of labour is considered.

In utero, foetal lungs do not participate in gas exchange. This is taken care of by the mother via the placental blood flow. The average blood gas values are listed in **Table 4.1**.

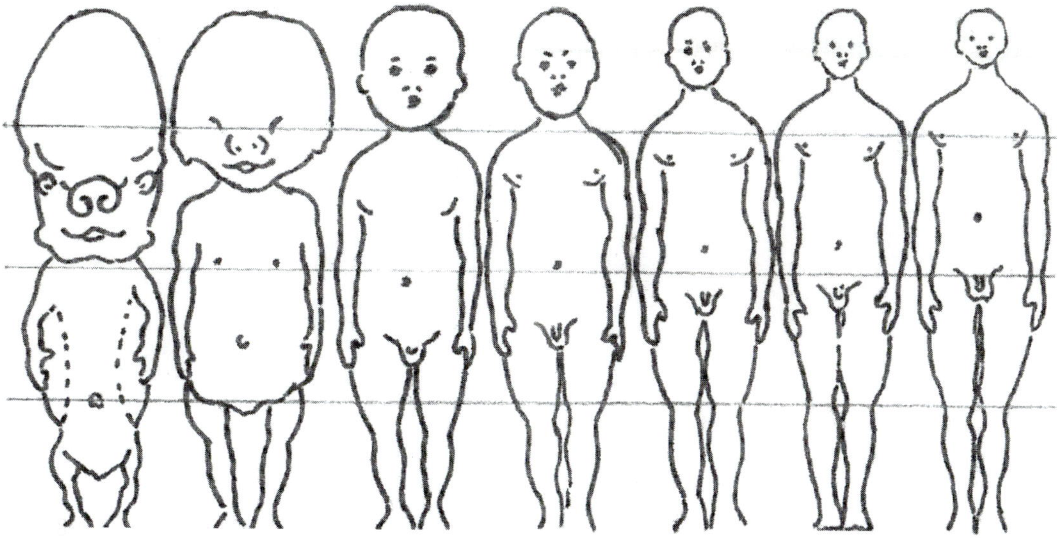

Figure 4.1 Neonates with a disproportionately large head and trunk.

Table 4.1 Arterial Blood Gas Values

Subject	Age	PCO_2 (mmHg)	PO_2 (mmHg)	pH
Newborn (term)	10 min	48	50	7.20
Newborn (term)	1 hr	35	70	7.35
Newborn (term)	1 wk	35	75	7.40
In utero	Third trimester	35–55	20–35	7.2–7.5

PCO_2, partial pressure of carbon dioxide; PO_2, partial pressure of oxygen.

Neonatal PO_2 is very low, and the following factors contribute to the same:

- Parenchymal shunts (e.g., areas of atelectasis)
- Cardiac shunts (e.g., patent ductus arteriosus [PDA])
- Anatomical shunts (e.g., arteriovenous shunts)

However, many factors in utero and perinatally prevent hypoxia; these include the following:

- Higher haemoglobin (Hb) levels: Haematocrit (Hct) 60% and Hb 18–19 g/dl at birth
- Role of foetal haemoglobin (HbF): 70–90% of Hb at birth is HbF
- Hb saturation curve shifted to give up O_2 to the tissues at lower partial pressures (15 mmHg because of simultaneous uptake of CO_2: refer under HbF)
- Greater blood volume 80 ml/kg at birth. Twenty percent more in the pre-term infant
- Greater cardiac output/surface area

Anatomy of the Respiratory Tract

The Upper Airway

The neonate has a proportionately large head and a small neck with poor muscle control hence the head tends to remain in the flexed position and is more prone to upper airway obstruction. This naturally flexed head precludes the use of a pillow under the head. Instead, the child needs a shoulder roll to align the airway for better laryngeal visualisation. He is an obligatory nose breather (remember this when you pass a nasogastric tube). Nasal obstruction is hazardous. The characteristics of the neonatal upper airway are shown in **Figure 4.2**.

Major differences from the adult airway include the following:

1. **Supraglottic part**
   - Narrow nares
   - Angle of the jaw is more obtuse
   - Large tongue
   - Non-ossified palate
   - Epiglottis is large, floppy, omega shaped and more cephalad

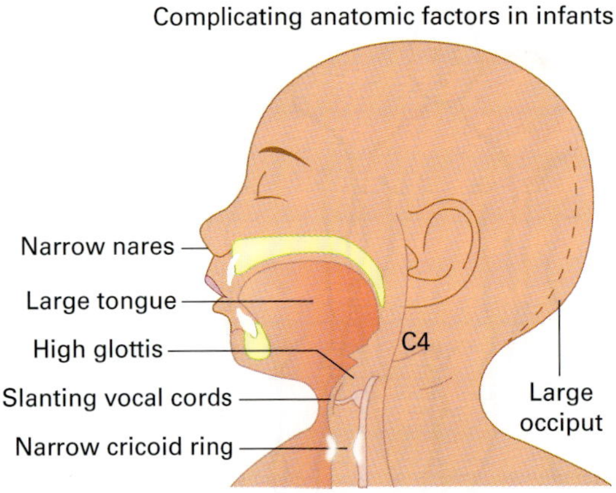

Figure 4.2 Characteristics of the head and upper airway in a neonate.

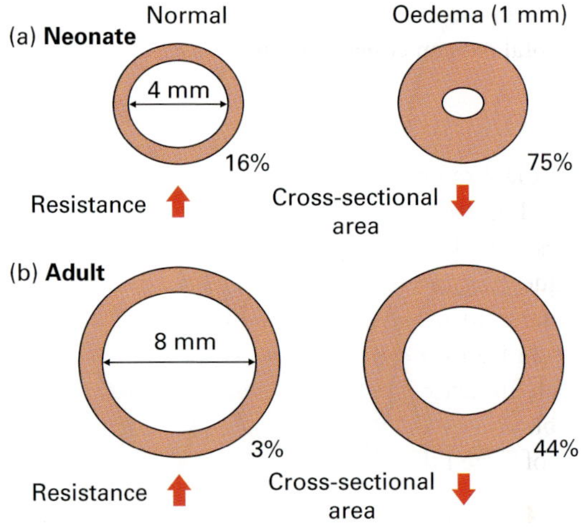

Figure 4.3 Implications of laryngeal oedema in (a) the neonate and (b) the adult.

- Larynx is more anterior and cephalad (C3: newborn, C4-5 at 6 years, C5-6 in the adult)
- Pliable laryngeal cartilages

2. **Subglottic part**
   - Narrow cricoid
   - Tracheal length 2–5 cm (average 4 cm)
   - Angulation of bronchi – more horizontal
   - High diaphragm
   - Horizontal ribs with a very pliable rib cage
   - Decreased number of alveoli

The cricoid ring (the only complete ring) is the narrowest part of the trachea. The same sized tube fits both the nose and the cricoid. The cricoid is circular; therefore, the tube is a good fit and there is usually no need for a cuff. In adults, the narrowest part of the larynx is at the level of the vocal cords. It is irregular and requires a cuff for a good seal. The use of the newer generation microcuffed tube in neonates is still debatable.

The resistance of the flow of air is inversely proportional to the fifth power of radius in the upper airway and to the fourth power in bronchioles beyond the fifth level. A tight-fitting tube or a conventional cuffed tube can produce mucosal oedema, especially in the subglottic or cricoid ring area. Consider that the trachea in the adult is 20 mm in diameter. One millimetre oedema will cause 19% reduction in the cross-sectional area. Compare with a child having 4 mm diameter at cricoid. One millimetre oedema will cause 60–70% reduction in the cross-sectional area. Thus, it is better to leave a mild 'leak' than to have a tight-fitting endotracheal tube, which may cause mucosal oedema. Cricoid ulceration may lead to subglottic stenosis (Fig. 4.3).

The neonatal larynx is more reactive to irritants and mechanical stimulants. Unlike older children, neonates lack protective reflexes like coughing. Hence, when stimulated, they develop breath-holding, laryngospasm and even bradycardia.

The Lower Airway

The newborn has between 20 and 50 million terminal airspaces. The adult level of 300 million alveoli is reached by a process of alveolar multiplication. Subsequent lung growth is by an increase in alveolar size. The lung volume in infants is disproportionately small in relation to body size. However, their metabolic rate is nearly twice that of the adult and therefore ventilatory requirement per unit lung volume is increased. The calibre of the airways is relatively narrow and hence the airway resistance is increased. Elastic tissue in the lungs is poorly developed and the lung compliance is less. This results in airway closure during the normal tidal ventilation. Decreased compliance results in ventilatory units with short time constants; that is, the time for filling the alveoli and respiratory gas exchange is very short due to the early airway closure. Consequently, infants can only maintain adequate alveolar ventilation by maintaining a high respiratory rate. The work of breathing is increased due to the increase in the resistance and decrease in the compliance. This results in a 15% increase in the total oxygen consumption.

The Diaphragm

The diaphragm has two types of muscle fibres. Type I muscle fibres are high oxidative muscle fibres which may be considered slow twitch, fatigue-resistant marathon muscle fibres. They help to maintain prolonged muscular activity. Type II muscle fibres are low oxidative fast twitch fibres which are active for short periods of time but are unable to sustain prolonged activity. The proportion of Type I fibres is given in **Table 4.2**.

Table 4.2 Proportion of Type I Fibres

Muscle	Premature	Neonate	Mature
Diaphragm	10%	25–30%	55%
Intercostal	20%	40%	65%

The pre-term infant spends 50–60% of his time in rapid eye movement (REM) sleep during which intercostal muscle activity is inhibited and paradoxical movement of the soft chest wall occurs. This is compensated, to a certain extent, by the diaphragm.

Mechanics of Respiration

Mechanics of respiration, in infants, is different from adults and less efficient as

- The intercostals muscles are weak.
- The sternum and thoracic cage are soft and compliant and permit indrawing (paradoxical movement) in case of excessive inspiratory effort or reduced pulmonary compliance.
- The diaphragm is high and its movement is piston like. It is the most important muscle of respiration. However, diaphragmatic splinting, as in the case of distension of the stomach or intestinal obstruction, is detrimental to respiration (**Fig. 4.4**).
- The ribs are more horizontal and do not have the bucket handle movement of the adult. Therefore, there is less anteroposterior and lateral thoracic expansion (**Fig. 4.5**).

Control of Ventilation

The control of respiration, which involves biochemical and reflex mechanisms, is well developed in the healthy full-term neonate. The higher centres are immature and very sensitive to respiratory depressants. This is more so in ex-premature infants below 52 weeks post-conceptual age.

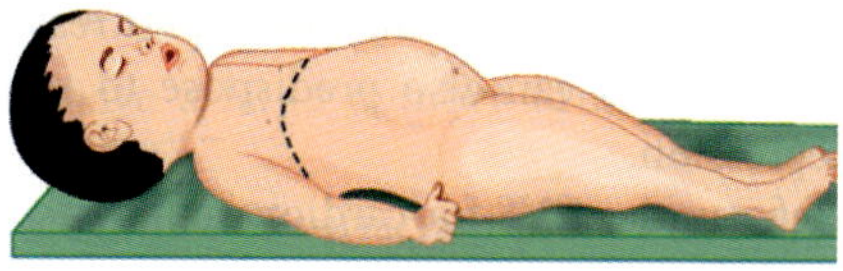

Figure 4.4 Respiratory mechanics.

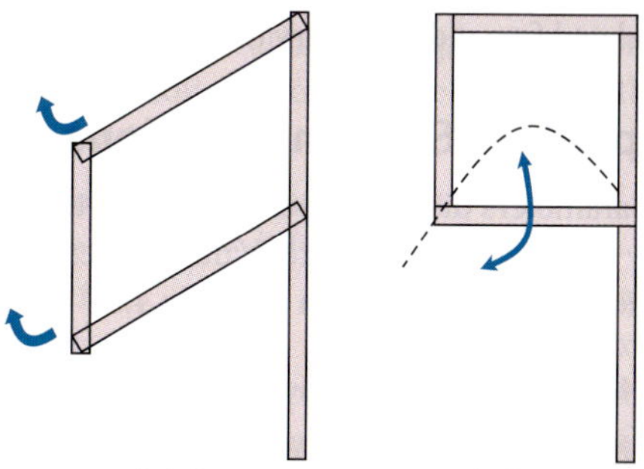

Figure 4.5 Comparison of respiratory mechanics in the child and adult. Note the 'bucket handle movement' in the adult compared to the 'piston' movement and high diaphragm in the infant.

Response to CO_2

Respiratory rate (RR) is increased with increasing $FiCO_2$. Ventilation relative to body mass is greater for any given $PaCO_2$ reflecting a higher metabolic rate. The CO_2 response curve is shifted to the left and therefore increased ventilation begins at lower levels of CO_2. This is suppressed by halothane. The response to increase in $FiCO_2$ is not well sustained in the pre-term infant and the slope of the CO_2 response curve is decreased in infants displaying episodes of apnoea.

Response to O_2

In a neutral thermal environment, hypoxaemia produces a biphasic response in pre-term and newborn infants with initial hyperventilation which occurs in 30 seconds (peripheral chemoreceptor response). Over 5 minutes, there is ventilatory depression. As the infants grow older, the biphasic response is lost and increased ventilation as a response to hypoxia is sustained. This response is abolished by hypothermia and there is only respiratory depression.

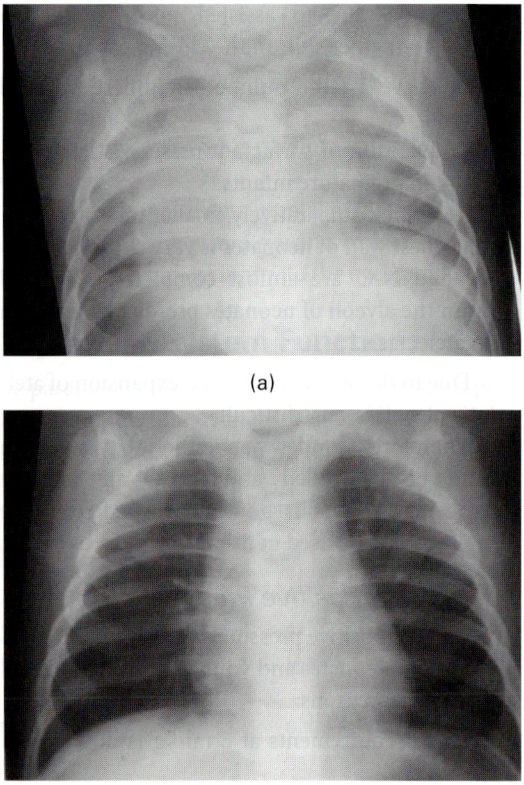

(a)

(b)

Figure 4.7 Normal chest X-ray. (a) Normal expiration and (b) normal inspiration.

1 year old. As the child grows, the liver goes up and the right dome rises to the adult position.

Changes during ventilation are marked (**Fig. 4.7**). During expiration, intrapulmonary shadows are accentuated and lung field translucency decreases. Tracheal calibre and size of retropharyngeal space vary with the phase of respiration. The costophrenic angles are shallow and diaphragmatic movements are less obvious. The heart size increases to occupy approximately 45% of the transverse diameter. The increase in supra cardiac thymic shadow is variable.

Anaesthetic Implications of Respiratory Physiology

- Due to high alveolar minute ventilation, the induction and emergence from inhalational anaesthesia are relatively rapid in neonates and infants.
- Due to decreased FRC in relation to the minute ventilation, the physiological reserve of oxygen is less. Therefore, adequate pre-oxygenation is important to prevent the rapid desaturation during periods of apnoea.
- There should be minimal apparatus DS, minimal resistance and minimal bulk of the apparatus.
- The respiratory response to hypoxia is temperature dependent and hence the importance of maintaining the body temperature.
- Care must be taken to avoid inadvertent gastric insufflation during mask ventilation. This will embarrass respiration due to its effect on the diaphragm.
- Nasal instrumentation should be done with utmost care. Neonates are obligatory nose breathers and any damage/obstruction will compromise respiration.
- Size of an endotracheal tube (ETT) should not be too narrow (increased resistance) or too wide (mucosal injury).

Circulatory System

Foetal circulation undergoes changes after birth, and the following discussion gives an overview of the same.

Transitional Circulation

The amniotic fluid which is produced by the baby's urine (100–200 ml/day) and tracheal secretion (200–400 ml/day) is isotonic. This fluid and the maternal circulation function as an extracellular compartment for the foetus. Fluid shifts in the mother are reflected in the foetus. Changes that occur include the following.

- At birth, the lung is filled with 20–30 ml of isotonic fluid per kg. With his first breath, this fluid shifts into the pulmonary interstitial space and thence into the intravascular space, thus providing a bolus of essentially protein-free fluid.

  The plasma oncotic pressure is lower due to low albumin levels – 19 g/l at 26–28 weeks as compared to 31 g/l in the 40-week term neonate.
- Changes at birth occur at the four main shunts: the placenta, the foramen ovale (FO), ductus venosus (DV) and ductus arteriosus (DA).
- The pulmonary vascular resistance (PVR) is high before birth because the lungs are relatively collapsed, filled with fluid and the pulmonary vasculature is constricted. At birth, the alveoli

within the pulmonary system change from being fluid filled to being air filled. O_2 tension increases and CO_2 tension falls, all of which contribute to a massive decrease in PVR, an increase in pulmonary blood flow and an increase in the oxygenation of the blood. Placental blood flow stops when the umbilical cord is clamped; this further leads to increase in the systemic vascular resistance. The left atrial pressure exceeds that of the right and the FO closes functionally. The increase in oxygenation results in closure of the DA and the neonatal circulation is established.

- The physiological closure of the smooth muscle of the PDA starts with the first breath and an increasing PaO_2. This is complete in 10–15 hours with fibrous closure occurring in 2–3 weeks. The PDA may remain open due to the action of PGE_2, low Ca^{2+}, decreased glucose and increased pulmonary artery pressure.
- Anatomical closure of the FO takes about 6 weeks. In the first few weeks of life, the neonate has a transitional circulation where he may revert to the foetal pattern with a patent FO and PDA. This occurs most commonly in the presence of hypoxia, acidosis, hypothermia, hypoglycaemia, hypocalcaemia and overhydration. Thus, all intravenous lines should be free of air bubbles even in the setting of a normal echocardiogram.

Neonates when exposed to hypoxia respond with

- Pulmonary vasoconstriction: This could result in the PDA reopening leading to a large right-to-left shunt
- Systemic vasoconstriction (not vasodilatation as develops in adults)
- Severe bradycardia
- Fall In cardiac output

Foetal Haemoglobin

With a P_{50} of 20 mmHg, foetal haemoglobin (HbF) has a greater affinity for O_2 than adult Hb, which has a P_{50} of 27 mmHg. It can therefore carry more O_2 at a lower PO_2. This is because HbF has less 2,3 diphosphoglycerate (DPG) and is relatively insensitive to 2,3 DPG which in itself lowers the O_2 affinity of the Hb molecule. It might be thought that the increased affinity of the HbF for O_2 would hinder the release of O_2 in the tissues, but the

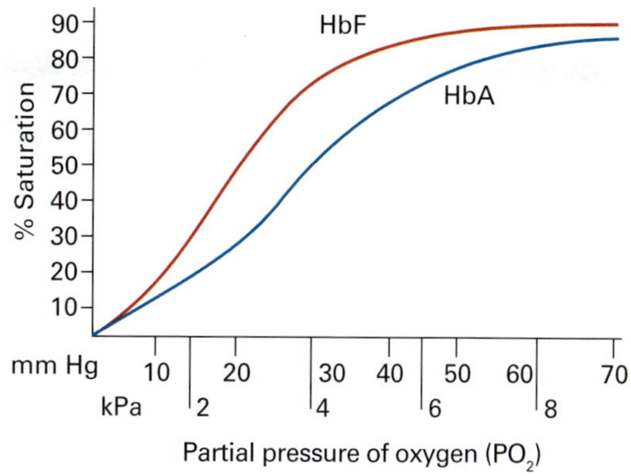

Figure 4.8 A comparison of oxygen dissociation curves with foetal haemoglobin (HbF) and adult haemoglobin (HbA).

simultaneous uptake of CO_2 shifts the dissociation curve to the right. As the tissue O_2 tension is so low (15 mmHg) and because the dissociation curve is so steep at 15 mmHg, adequate O_2 delivery to the tissues is ensured. At birth, approximately 70–80% of the total Hb is HbF. HbF is completely replaced by adult Hb by 3–4 months of age. A comparison of the oxygen dissociation curves of HbF and HbA is shown in **Figure 4.8**. Physiological anaemia of infancy reaches a low point (9–11 g/dl) by 2–3 months of age. By this time, HbA largely replaces HbF and oxygen delivery to the tissues now improves.

Myocardial Performance

At birth, the right ventricular muscle wall is thicker than that of the left ventricle. The ECG shows an axis of +180° during the first week of life. By 3–6 months, the adult pattern of left ventricular preponderance with an ECG axis of +90° is established.

The neonates' myocardium contains 30% less contractile tissue and more connective tissue than that of the older child. Thus, ventricles of the neonate are less compliant and contractile and he cannot increase his stroke volume. The sympathetic innervation of his myocardium is incomplete and stores of adrenaline are inadequate. Vagal influences predominate and bradycardia is common. There is centralisation of blood volume and the peripheral vascular response to catecholamines is reduced. Therefore, the ability of the neonate to increase stroke volume is very limited and cardiac output is primarily rate dependent. As the neonate has poor control of his capacitance vessels and his baroreceptors are inactive, he finds it difficult to maintain an adequate cardiac output in the presence of hypovolaemia. Hence, the neonate is unable to compensate for dehydration or blood loss and it is imperative that fluid deficits be accurately assessed and corrected promptly.

The neonate is volume dependent and volume intolerant.

Blood Volume at Birth

This is variable depending on the volume of placental transfusion: 90–100 ml/kg (60–70 ml/kg in adult). Delay in clamping the cord can increase the blood volume by up to 20% and can lead to haemodynamic decompensation. Foetal asphyxia on the other hand can lead to vasoconstriction, pooling of the blood in the placenta and severe hypovolaemia.

The total blood volume varies as given below:

- Newborn = 90–100 ml/kg
- 1–2 years = 75–80 ml/kg
- 2–16 years = 70–75 ml/kg

Haematocrit

Haemoglobin levels drop after birth and physiological anaemia occurs in infants up to 3 months of age (**Fig. 4.9**). This is more markedly seen in pre-term infants and can be as low as 10 g/dl between 8 and 12 weeks of age. The rapidity with which Hb levels decline varies inversely with gestational age, the decline being more rapid and greater in premature infants. This fall is caused by decreased erythropoietin activity (due to increased O_2 availability at birth) and a decrease in the survival time of RBCs (70 days in the neonate and 120 days in the adult). (Also refer to section on HbF.)

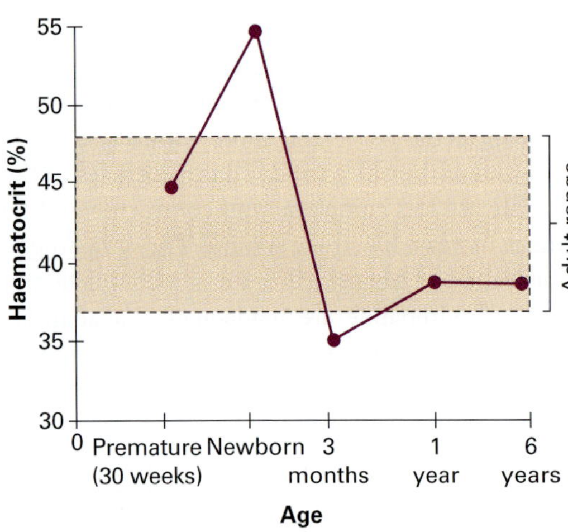

Figure 4.9 Haematocrit variations with age.

Blood Replacement Volume

Blood loss can be replaced by using the following formula:

Blood to be transfused (in ml)/Maximum allowable blood loss =

$$\text{Volume (ml)} = \frac{\text{Initial Hb} - \text{Final Hb}}{\text{Initial Hb}} \times \text{Neonates blood volume/Estimated blood volume (EBV)}$$

While replacing blood loss, it is good to remember that:

1. Haemoglobin concentration of whole blood = 10–13 g/dl (approximately)
2. Haemoglobin concentration of packed red cells = 18–23 g/dl (approximately)
3. EBV in a term neonate is 90 ml/kg and in a preterm is 100 ml/kg (approximately)
4. Hct in a newborn is 45–65% (depending on the gestational age)
5. Final Hb is the lowest tolerated Hb for that baby

Cardiac Output

Cardiac output is in the range of 350–400 ml/kg/min in utero, dropping to 150–200 ml/kg/min after 1 week and 70 ml/kg/min in the adult.

Blood Pressure

Blood pressure is variable. At birth the systolic blood pressure is 50–65 mmHg, going up by 10 mmHg/week (approximately). It may be 10 mmHg higher if there is delay in clamping the cord. This returns to normal in 4 hours.

The systolic blood pressure is a good indicator of blood volume and can be used as a guide to blood replacements during anaesthesia. Up to 9 months of age, blood pressure is higher in the legs. After this, it is reversed.

Hypertension in Neonates

The probable causes of *hypertension* in neonates include the following:

- Renal disease
- Coarctation of the aorta
- Pulse reflux (AR, PDA)

- CNS disease, poisoning
- Endocrine – pituitary, adrenal, thyroid
- Essential hypertension

Heart Rate

Heart rate is variable but should not be less than 100/min. In an infant, a normal sinus rhythm up to 200/min is acceptable (normally 100–170 beats/min in the neonate). In the pre-school child, the heart rate is normally up to 100/min.

Sinus arrhythmias are common. Any other irregular rhythms are abnormal. Bradycardia is usually a sign of hypoxaemia and should be treated primarily with ventilation and 100% oxygen. Bradycardia during manipulation of the upper airway occurs more commonly than in adults.

Cardiac Arrest

A heart rate of less than 85 beats/min in the neonate should be considered as an arrest. Serious dysrhythmias are rare and usually secondary to hypoxia, acidosis and hypovolaemia. Most arrests occur in asystole. Ventricular fibrillation occurs with electrolyte imbalance or congenital heart disease.

Anaesthetic Implications

- The heart rate should be kept to the higher side since the cardiac output is rate dependent.
- Avoid factors that increase the chances of reversion to transitional circulation.
- Avoid air bubbles in the intravenous lines while administering drugs.
- Systolic blood pressure is a good indicator of blood volume and can be used as a guide to blood replacement during anaesthesia.

A basic understanding of the accurate ***age-specific*** *normal values of all biological parameters such as heart rate and blood pressure is crucial.*

Nervous System

The nervous system of neonates is characterised by anatomical and functional immaturity. At birth, the brain is only 10% of the total body weight. It doubles in size at 6 months and trebles by 1 year. The blood–brain barrier is poorly developed. Similarly, the neuromuscular junction is immature at birth. Till 12 weeks of age, sensitivity to acetylcholine is along the whole length of the nerve. Sensitivity to d-tubocurarine is increased and suxamethonium is decreased. And *Yes! Neonates do feel pain.* Pain pathways develop very early and by the third trimester the pathways between the thalamus and somatosensory cortex are functional.

Cerebral Circulation

A major cause of neonatal death is intraventricular haemorrhage. The anatomy of the circulation over the basal ganglia is unusual with short thin-walled and poorly supported capillaries opening at right angles into the branches of the internal cerebral vein which in turn opens into the veins of Galen, again at right angles.

There is a potential for venous obstruction, and great surges of arterial pressure may cause rupture of the capillaries with intraventricular haemorrhage. Such surges of pressure may be caused by neonatal asphyxia, apnoea, osmotic effects of large boluses of 8.4% sodium bicarbonate, 10% dextrose, hypertension caused by inadequate analgesia or by the stimulus of awake intubations.

Anaesthesia and the Developing Brain – Neuronal Apoptosis

Over the last decade, much research has been conducted on the effect of anaesthetics on the developing brain. Volatile anaesthetics, ketamine and propofol cause neuronal apoptosis and changes to the dendritic morphology in rodents and primates. These effects occur at particular periods of neurodevelopment. Translating laboratory data and animal studies to clinically significant terms is difficult because animal studies use higher doses of IV anaesthetics and longer duration of exposure to volatile anaesthetics. Another area of uncertainty is the exact period of vulnerability, although data suggests that the vulnerable period in humans may be from late pregnancy up to the third year of life.

Some studies have shown that premature infants who undergo laparotomy and neonates who have major surgery have poor neurodevelopmental outcomes. However, surgery itself results in inflammatory and humeral stress and is associated with metabolic, haemodynamic and respiratory events that can affect neuronal development. These confounding factors make it difficult to definitely ascribe anaesthesia exposure to poor neurological outcomes.

Although animal data suggests the harmful effect of anaesthetics on the developing brain, it is still not clear if it translates to clinically relevant neuro-behavioural outcomes.

Thermal Regulation

Hypothermia is defined as follows:

- **Mild**: 35–36.3°C
- **Moderate**: 32–34.9°C
- **Severe**: <32°C

Temperature Control

Temperature control is a balance between heat loss and heat production.

Heat loss is due to the following factors:

- Decreased thermal mass
- Decreased insulating tissue
- Increased body surface area (BSA) to weight ratio

And due to processes, such as

- radiation,
- conduction,
- convection and
- evaporation through lungs and skin.

Heat production is by shivering and metabolism of brown fat. *Shivering is almost non-existent in the infant.* Infants rely primarily on non-shivering thermogenesis to generate heat. This mechanism, which also increases O_2 consumption, is largely centred in the brown adipose tissue (2–6% of the term infant's body weight) located around the scapulae, in the mediastinum and around the kidneys and the adrenal glands. The cells of the brown fat have many mitochondria, fat vacuoles and a rich blood and autonomic nerve supply. Noradrenaline released at the sympathetic nerve endings increases metabolic activity in the brown fat, i.e. hydrolysis of triglycerides to fatty acids and glycerol. This in turn increases oxygen consumption and heat production. The stimulus to increase metabolic activity in brown fat is exposure to cold. This response is lost under anaesthesia. Brown fat deposits decline during the first few weeks of extrauterine life. The VLBW neonates have very little brown fat.

General anaesthesia can precipitate hypothermia by reduction in metabolism, heat redistribution due to peripheral vasodilatation and central inhibition of thermoregulation.

Neutral Temperature

Neutral temperature is defined as the ambient temperature that results in the least oxygen consumption. The thermoneutral range where oxygen consumption is minimal varies with age. It is 34°C in the pre-term neonate, 32°C in the term neonate and 28°C in the adult (**Table 4.4**).

Table 4.4 Neutral (NT) and Critical Temperatures (CT) for Different Age Groups

Age	NT (°C)	CT (°C)
Pre-term	34	28
Term	32	23
Adults	28	1

Critical Temperature

Critical temperature is that ambient temperature below which an unclothed, unanaesthetised individual cannot maintain a normal core body temperature. Below this temperature, hypothermia sets in (**Table 4.4**).

Hypothermia (temperature loss) predisposes to

- metabolic acidosis,
- increased oxygen uptake,
- right-to-left shunting,
- respiratory depression and hypoventilation,
- depressed conscious state and delayed recovery from anaesthesia,
- prolonged action of drugs,
- difficulty in assessing hypovolaemia,
- decreased surfactant,
- dysrhythmias and cardiac depression,
- increased morbidity and surgical wound infections and
- coagulopathies and increased blood transfusions.

Ideally, premature infants should be plastic or foil wrapped and kept in a warm (euthermic) humid, still atmosphere with an ambient operating room (OR) temperature between 25°C and 28°C.

Neonatal Fluid, Electrolyte and Metabolic Homeostasis

Initial fluid requirements are low due to pulmonary interstitial fluid shifts coincident with birth and an expanding circulatory fluid volume.

The requirement in the first 2 days of life is about 90 and 75 ml/kg, respectively. The distribution of water in the various body compartments varies with the neonate's age, the premature baby having the highest percentage of extracellular fluid (Table 4.5).

Table 4.5 Distribution of Body Water as Percentage of Total Body Weight

Compartment (% of TBW)	Premature	Neonate	Infant	Adult
ECF	50	35	30	20
ICF	30	40	40	40
Plasma	5	5	5	5
Total	85	80	75	65

Renal Functions

Renal function only matures by 18 months of age.

At birth

- Glomerular filtration is low
- Tubular reabsorption is poor with inability to concentrate urine
- There is hormonal immaturity and imbalance
- High water turnover and liability to dehydration
- They are obligatory salt losers
- Drug elimination is decreased
- Serum levels of protein and urea are low

Renal blood flow may be compromised if intra-abdominal pressure rises, as after an omphalocele repair.

Insensible Water Loss

Insensible water loss is much greater in the pre-term VLBW infant. Losses are mainly due to evaporation from BSA. Other insensible water losses are due to increased respiratory exchange, radiant warmers and phototherapy. A 26–28 weeks' VLBW baby may have a mean evaporative loss of 82 ml/kg/day during his first day of life compared to a term baby's 10 ml/kg/day.

Water and Sodium

Glomerular filtration rate and urine concentrating power (tubular function) are poor in the neonate. This is more so in the premature baby who is less able to conserve sodium. The lack of renal responsiveness to the water and sodium load could be due to high levels of various hormones such as aldosterone, vasopressin, angiotensin II and atrial natriuretic hormone as well as due to the immaturity of the kidney. Water retention and hyponatraemia may be associated with vasopressin release during CPAP. Intracerebral haemorrhage and pneumothorax are also associated with acute imbalances in neonatal water homeostasis. Both hyper and hypotonic solutions can cause rapid cerebral fluid shifts. Overhydration can cause pulmonary oedema, persistent PDA and congestive heart failure.

The term 'neonate' requires 2–3 mEq/kg/day of sodium. The pre-term infants require much more, that is, 5 mEq/kg/day in <30 weeks' gestation and 4 mEq/kg/day in 30–35 weeks' gestation. This supplementation should continue for at least 2 weeks. It is interesting to note that growth seems to be related to sodium supplementation, and the milk of mothers of pre-term infants contains more sodium than the milk of the mother of a term infant.

Serum Potassium

The serum levels give only a rough estimate of the potassium content of the body as 98% of potassium is in the cells. Acidosis is associated with hyperkalaemia and alkalosis is associated with hypokalaemia. Many drugs and medications can cause changes in the serum potassium. In case of oliguria, anuria, shock, acidosis and renal failure all potassium containing intravenous fluids should be stopped and replaced with normal saline.

Very fresh whole blood contains less free potassium and is preferable to stored blood. The mother would be a good source of fresh blood for the neonate.

Maintenance potassium is 2–3 mEq/kg/day during infancy.

Serum Calcium

Hypocalcaemia is *most common in the premature neonates in the first 48 hours of life*. It also occurs in the sick and asphyxiated neonate. It is associated with alkalosis (caused by vigorous bicarbonate therapy or hyperventilation) which decreases the ionised calcium concentration as does infusions of albumin and citrated blood products.

They have lower serum protein concentrations and more unbound or 'free' calcium. The total body reserves of calcium are low in the pre-term infant. The daily maintenance requirement of calcium is 240–400 mg/kg (higher requirements in premature infant).

Hypocalcaemia is defined as serum total calcium <8 mg/dl (2 mmol/L) in full terms and <7 mg/dl (1.75mmol/L) in preterms. An ionic calcium of <4 mg/dl (1 mmol/L) is hypocalcaemia in both terms and preterms. Symptomatic newborns should be treated with 10–20 mg of elemental calcium (1–2 ml/kg/dose of 10% Ca gluconate) slowly over 10 minutes with cardiac monitoring. This should be followed by a continuous infusion of 50–75 mg/kg/d or 1–3 mg/kg/hr elemental calcium.

Do remember that correction of hypocalcaemia may be ineffective in presence of hypomagnesemia.

Calculation of Fluid and Electrolyte Requirements

These should be simple, understandable and practical in order to avoid mistakes that can have dire consequences in small children and neonates.

Howland in 1911 measured energy consumption in children and concluded that children under 1 year of age (3–10 kg) metabolise 100 kcal/day and older children metabolise 75 kcal/day while adults metabolise only 35 kcal/day. In 1957, Holliday and Segar reviewed data which correlated caloric requirements with basal metabolism and active energy needs. They concluded that infants in hospital required half their calories for basal metabolism and half for growth

They also suggested that metabolism of 1 calorie produces 0.2 ml of water and consumes 1.2 ml of water. Therefore, calorie and water consumption are considered equal. A 1-year-old child weighing 0.10 kg requires 100 kcal/kg/day of energy and 100 ml/kg/day (24 hours) of water. Transpose this to an hourly basis and the following will be the requirements of fluid:

- Infants weighing 0–10 kg, fluid requirement is 4 ml/kg/hr
- Children weighing 10–20 kg, fluid requirement is 40 ml + 2 ml/kg/hr above 10 kg
- For infants weighing >20 kg, fluid requirement is 60 ml + 1 ml/kg/hr above 20 kg.

It has been suggested that the basal metabolism decreases profoundly under anaesthesia, and therefore the caloric requirement also decreases. The fluid requirement, however, seems to be more than caloric requirement. One formula suggested for perioperative fluid and calorie therapy is as follows (also refer under blood glucose):

Calorie requirements = 1.5 × weight (kg) + 5 = maintenance calories per hour (kcal/hr)

Fluid requirements = 2.5 ml × weight (kg) + 10 = maintenance fluid per hour (ml/hr)

Sodium requirement = 0.045 × weight (kg) + 0.16 = maintenance sodium per hour (mEq/hr)

Potassium requirement = 0.03 × weight (kg) + 0.10 = maintenance potassium per hour (mEq/hr)

Maintenance of Blood Glucose

A relatively higher proportion of brain weight to body weight increases brain sugar requirements in neonates. Term neonates need 3–5 mg/kg/min glucose while preterms require 5–6 mg/kg/min to maintain normoglycaemia.

Hypoglycaemia is defined as blood glucose levels of <40 mg/dl. It is found most commonly in VLBW babies and in babies with diabetic mothers. Management includes an initial bolus of 2.5–5 ml/kg 10% dextrose, followed by a maintenance dose of 5–8 mg/kg/min (full term) and 8–10 mg/kg/min (preterm) with periodic monitoring. In the absence of intravenous routes, buccal dextrose gel can be used to control severe hypoglycaemia.

Hyperglycaemia is defined as blood glucose levels of over 125–140 mg/dl. It is usually iatrogenic, and the resulting hyperosmolar state can cause intraventricular haemorrhage and osmotic diuresis resulting in dehydration and hyponatraemia.

With regard to energy, it is important to consider the following factors in the neonate as he/she has

- increased metabolic requirements,
- decreased body reserves of carbohydrates,
- poor liver function and
- an increased tendency to go into hypoglycaemia.

Suggested Maintenance and Replacement Solutions

Five percent dextrose solution, which provides 20% of calories that are metabolised, is recommended along with saline of 0.2–0.9% as a maintenance solution. This amount of dextrose results in decreased catabolism of endogenous protein and a lower renal solute load. Full-strength Ringer's lactate or 0.9% normal saline may be used as a replacement solution.

VLBW babies have poor body fat and glycogen stores, a high metabolic rate and oxygen consumption. They may be given 10% dextrose at the rate of 6 ml/kg/hr (10 mg/kg/min). However, with the stress of surgery and additional glucose sources such as banked blood, this quantum of dextrose may overwhelm their renal threshold and cause an osmotic diuresis.

It has been noted that *hypoglycaemia is rare in older infants* even after prolonged fasting. The brain, heart and intestine may suffer greater damage during ischaemic events when glucose infusions are used. So, glucose-free balanced salt solutions or solutions containing 1% glucose are being preferred in operating rooms, though this requires much closer monitoring of blood glucose levels perioperatively.

Total Parenteral Nutrition

If a neonate is on total parenteral nutrition (TPN), it should not be stopped abruptly for surgery. Abrupt termination of TPN could cause hypoglycaemia because of the high level of circulating insulin. Glucose requirements during surgery should be met with 10% dextrose. The TPN fluid should not be used as an extracellular fluid replacement either, as it is grossly hypertonic.

Monitoring During the Perioperative Period

A precordial or oesophageal stethoscope and the *anaesthetist's eyes and hands,* to look for cyanosis, feel the pulse and temperature, listen for the heart and breath sounds, are irreplaceable.

ECG – Watch out for arrhythmias!

SaO_2 – Arterial desaturation is more frequent in neonates than in older children as explained above. The oxyhaemoglobin dissociation curve depends on the proportion of HbF to adult Hb. Since the neonate at 3 weeks has about 70% HbF, keeping the Hb saturated at 85–95% (SaO_2) will maintain the PaO_2 at the desirable range of 60–80 mmHg.

Blood Pressure Monitoring

Systolic pressure reflects circulating blood volume. Its accurate determination serves as a guide to blood replacement. Intra-arterial monitoring may be done for major cases. Non-invasive blood pressure is reasonably accurate, but avoid cycling devices more often than at 3–4 minutes intervals to avoid limb ischaemia.

Serial Arterial Blood Gases, Glucose, Calcium and Electrolytes

These are worth monitoring in the very sick neonate or in a neonate undergoing major surgery, remembering that frequent estimations can lead to anaemia and hypovolaemia.

Temperature

Monitor both core and peripheral temperatures. Rising core and peripheral temperatures denote hyperthermia and a fall in both denotes hypothermia. A falling peripheral temperature with a near-normal core temperature denotes poor perfusion – *give more fluids!*

Induction of Anaesthesia and Maintenance

Awake or paralysed intubation – one must choose the safest approach depending on one's own familiarity with neonatal intubations. There is evidence that awake intubation in the unparalysed, unanaesthetised neonate can cause acute arterial hypertension which can give rise to an increase in the intracranial pressure and can cause intraventricular haemorrhage, particularly in the premature and asphyxiated newborn. In addition, even in the pre-oxygenated neonate, awake intubation may be associated with trauma, apnoea, obstructed breathing, desaturation and bradycardia. With agents such as halothane, respiration must be quickly controlled to avoid apnoea and bradycardia. Although, with the newer inhalation agents, such complications are less frequent, higher mean alveolar concentrations (MACs) may still cause myocardial depression.

Indications for Awake Intubation

- Apnoea or severe respiratory distress
- Moribund or haemodynamically unstable
- Upper airway anomalies where the ability to achieve intubation is in doubt
- Untrained personnel

Succinyl choline – 1.5–2.0 mg/kg by the IV route or 4 mg/kg may be used intramuscularly.

If an IV induction is planned, thiopentone 1–5 mg/kg may be used.

Anaesthetic Requirements

In neonates, induction as well as emergence from anaesthesia is rapid. The MAC for babies 0–1 month of age is 25% less than that for those 1–6 months of age; after 6 months of age, MAC decreases.

Induction and emergence from inhalational anaesthetics are very rapid because of the following reasons:

- High ratio of alveolar ventilation to FRC
- High respiratory rate
- Higher heart rate and cardiac output

A greater proportion of vessel-rich tissues means that the ratio of end-tidal to inspired concentration (Fe/Fi) more rapidly approaches unity and high myocardial concentrations are reached earlier causing hypotension and bradycardia

Transportation

Post-transportation neonatal mortality in India approximates 15–36%. Hence, special precautions should be taken to minimise the distance transferred and time to transfer. Neonates should always be accompanied by expert medical and nursing personnel. The transport should be in incubators or isolettes with heaters, uninterrupted monitoring and continuation of ongoing fluids, drug infusions and respiratory support.

Pain Management

Multimodal analgesia tailored and individualised to the baby's requirements with consideration to their birth weight and maturity is the general recommendation. They include non-pharmacological methods (kangaroo care, facilitated tucking, non-nutritive sucking or massage). Pharmacological methods include local or topical anaesthetics, titrated and lower doses of opioids (fentanyl or morphine), and non-opioids (acetaminophen) should be used with greater caution. USG-guided blocks (caudal) can be considered in selected cases.

Behavioural Issues

Neonates are mainly trust seekers and have emerging motor and sensory abilities. Unlike older children, they seldom show separation anxiety and less regressive and negative behaviour. Hence, providing positive sensory stimulations and a safe environment is usually sufficient to soothe and calm them.

Acknowledging that neonates are different, dealing with them appropriately with empathy and compassion, proper optimisation and preparation of the baby and caregiver, and providing a warm, safe, adequately manned environment are essential to successful perioperative management.

SUGGESTED READINGS

1. Short A, Stevens K. Basic science relevant to practical paediatric anaesthesia: Update in anaesthesia. https://resources.wfsahq.org.
2. Jacob R. What's special about neonates – a review. *Ind J Anaesth* 1998: 42:11–32.
3. Anaesthesia for premature infants. In: Principles of Paediatric Anaesthesia, 4th Edition. Gregory GA (ed). Churchill Livingstone, Philadelphia, 2002; pp. 345–368.
4. Siedman L. Anaesthesia for ex premature infants. In: Principles of Paediatric Anaesthesia, 4th edn. Gregory GA, ed. Churchill Livingstone, Philadelphia, 2002; pp. 369–380.
5. Spaeth JP, Lam JE. The extremely premature infant (Micropremie) and common neonatal emergencies. In: Cote CJ, Lerman J, Anderson BJ, eds. 6th edn. Saunders Elsevier, Philadelphia, 2019; pp. 841–867.
6. Neonatology for Anaesthesiologists.. In: Smith's Anesthesia for Infants and Children. Davis PJ, Cladis FP, eds. 9th edn. Elsevier Mosby, Philadelphia, 2017; pp. 513–570.
7. McCann ME, et al. Clinical research approaches to studying pediatric anesthetic neurotoxicity. *Neurotoxicology* 2009, 30:766–771.
8. Sun L. Early childhood general anesthesia exposure and neurocognitive development. *BJA* 2010; 105(S1):161–168.
9. Davidson AJ. Anesthesia and neurotoxicity to the developing brain: The clinical relevance. *Ped Anesth* 2011; 21:716–721.
10. Boyer TJ, Kritzmire SM. Neonatal Anesthesia. In: StatPearls [Internet]. Treasure Island (FL): StatPearls Publishing; 2022.
11. Lerman J (editor). Neonatal Anesthesia. 1st edition. NY: Springers 2015.

5 NEONATAL RESUSCITATION

Garima Sharma • Nithya Jayaraman Ponmudi

Resuscitation of a newborn infant is in many ways different from resuscitating an older child or an adult. About 10% of all neonates need some form of active resuscitation at birth and approximately 1% need intensive resuscitative measures to restore cardiorespiratory function.

Birth asphyxia accounts for a fifth of all neonatal deaths worldwide, and simple resuscitative measures can decrease morbidity and mortality due to birth asphyxia.

One may anticipate the need for resuscitation when certain risk factors are present during pregnancy and labour. These include antepartum factors, such as pregnancy-induced hypertension, hypertension, previous neonatal deaths, intrauterine growth retardation, anaemia, diabetes and twins. Intrapartum risk factors include prematurity, antepartum haemorrhage, operative delivery, breech, premature rupture of membranes, foetal distress, narcotic administration, anaesthesia and meconium passage in utero. However, in 50% of instances, asphyxia occurs unexpectedly. Thus, it is most important to be prepared for resuscitation at all times.

Successful neonatal resuscitation efforts depend on critical actions that must occur in rapid succession to maximise the chances of survival.

Major Concepts

The primary goal of neonatal care at birth is to facilitate the transition to the external world. The guidelines apply to the newly born baby who is transitioning from the fluid-filled womb to the air-filled room. Initial lung expansion at birth requires higher ventilation pressures than later in infancy. Failure to expand alveolar spaces adequately may result in hypoxaemia and asphyxia. Asphyxia leads to progressive hypoxia, hypercapnia, hypoperfusion and acidosis.

The consequences of hypoxia and acidosis are pulmonary vasoconstriction, the opening of the ductus arteriosus, right-to-left shunting, myocardial dysfunction, poor cardiac output, metabolic acidosis and organ system damage.

There can be two types of apnoea – primary or secondary requiring resuscitation. In both primary and secondary apnoea, there is bradycardia. During primary apnoea the neonate will respond to tactile stimulation by re-initiation of breathing. However, if the asphyxia continues, the neonate begins irregular gasping respiratory efforts that then slowly decrease in frequency and eventually cease. This is secondary apnoea which requires oxygen, ventilation, chest compression, and medications.

Preparation for Resuscitation

Preparation for resuscitation involves having not only at least one trained person but also proper equipment. **Box 5.1** indicates some of the essential equipment needed at all deliveries for neonatal resuscitation. Universal precautions and strict asepsis should also be maintained.

Cord Management

After an uncomplicated term or late preterm birth, it is reasonable to delay cord clamping for 30 seconds, until after the baby is placed on the mother, dried, and assessed for breathing, tone and activity. Delay in clamping the cord could

Box 5.1 List of Equipment Required for Neonatal Resuscitation

- Self-inflating bag (newborn size)
- Face mask (0 and 1 size)
- Mucous extractor/suction apparatus
- Source of warmth
- Oxygen
- Gloves, warm linen and clock
- Laryngoscope with straight blade (0 and 1 size)
- Endotracheal (ET) tubes (sizes 2.0. 2.5, 3.0, 3.5 and 4 mm ID)
- Nasogastric tubes (sizes 6 and 8 Fr)
- Disposable syringes (1, 2 and 10 ml)
- Disposable needles (no. 23 and 24)
- Stethoscope
- Adhesive tape
- Drugs – Normal saline, naloxone and epinephrine (1:10,000)

increase haemoglobin and prevent hypotension. However, milking the cord can increase blood volume and may even cause ventricular haemorrhage in prematures less than 28 weeks of gestation.

Technique of Resuscitation

Neonatal resuscitation involves a series of quick steps which involve ongoing evaluation and resuscitation of the newborn baby.

Evaluation

All newborn infants need to be rapidly assessed for

- respiration,
- heart rate and
- colour/oxygen saturation

The presence of meconium and a quick assessment of the infant's muscle tone and period of gestation are also important. Apgar scores that are traditionally used in fact have no role in neonatal resuscitation. Sequential actions are taken based on the evaluation of the infant's condition at birth and the infant's response to resuscitative efforts.

Respiration

Respiration is evaluated by observing the chest and it is classified as spontaneous, vigorous, apnoeic or gasping. Most newborn infants are able to establish regular respiration with good colour and a heart rate above 100 beats per minute (bpm) after initial respiratory efforts. Gasping or apnoea indicates the need for ventilation.

Heart Rate

It is monitored by auscultation over the precordium with a stethoscope (preferred method) or palpation of umbilical cord pulse counted for 6 seconds and multiplied by 10. The heart rate should normally be above 100 bpm. Pulse oximetry and electrocardiography (ECG) remain important adjuncts to provide continuous heart rate assessment in babies needing resuscitation.

Colour/Oxygen Saturation

The infant's colour may be categorised as centrally cyanosed, peripherally cyanosed, pale or pink. A healthy neonate will appear pink without oxygen though acrocyanosis is common initially. Central cyanosis is usually noticed over the face, trunk and mucosa. Pallor may be due to hypotension, severe anaemia, hypothermia or acidosis.

The International Liaison Committee on Resuscitation (ILCOR) guidelines (2020) recommend the use of a pulse oximeter in the immediate neonatal period since the clinical assessment of skin colour correlates poorly with oxygen saturation at this time. Target preductal saturations after birth are seen in **Table 5.1**.

Table 5.1 Target Preductal Saturations After Birth

Time (min)	Oxygen Saturation
1	60–65%
2	65–70%
3	70–75%
4	75–80%
5	80–85%
10	85–95%

From Aziz K, Lee HC, Escobedo MB, et al. Part 5: Neonatal resuscitation: 2020 American Heart Association Guidelines for Cardiopulmonary Resuscitation and Emergency Cardiovascular Care. *Circulation* 2020; 142(2):S524–S550.

Temperature

The temperature should be measured and recorded after birth and monitored as a measure of quality. The temperature of newly born babies should be maintained between 36.5 and 37.5°C. Hypothermia (<36°C) should be prevented as it is associated with increased neonatal mortality and morbidity, especially in very preterm (<33 weeks) and very-low-birth-weight babies (<1500 g), who are at increased risk for hypothermia.

Thus, there are four categories of action during initial neonatal resuscitation–TABC. The TABC of resuscitation involves maintenance of temperature, airway, breathing and circulation.

The algorithm for resuscitation is given in **Figure 5.1**.

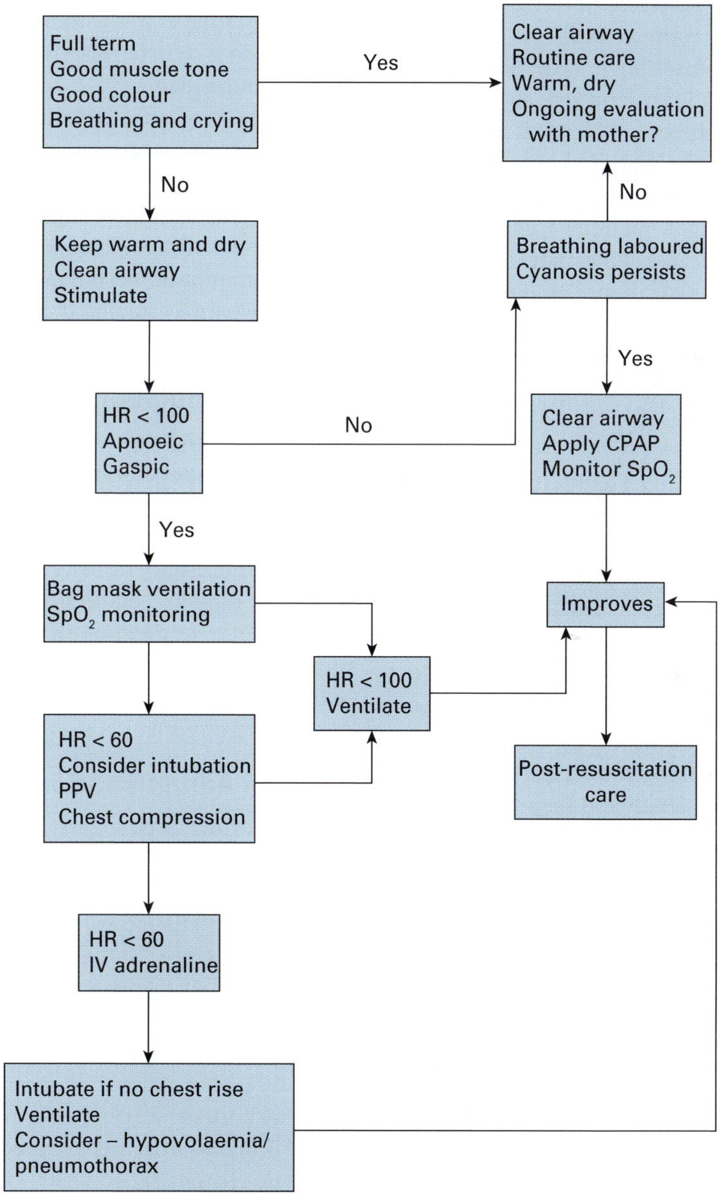

Figure 5.1 Neonatal resuscitation chart. CPAP, continuous positive airway pressure; HR, heart rate; IV, intravenous; PPV, positive pressure ventilation. Modified from Aziz K, Lee HC, Escobedo MB, et al. Part 5: Neonatal resuscitation: 2020 American Heart Association Guidelines for Cardiopulmonary Resuscitation and Emergency Cardiovascular Care. *Circulation* 2020; 142(2):S524–S550.

Initial Steps

The initial steps of neonatal resuscitation are as important as other aspects. These include preventing heat loss, positioning, suctioning, evaluation and tactile stimulation.

Prevention of Heat Loss

The infant should be placed under a radiant heat source (a radiant warmer, bulb or heater) with a pre-warmed mattress/linen. The baby is dried thoroughly, the wet linen removed, and the baby is wrapped in warm sheets and blankets. After drying, the baby may also be placed skin-to-skin on the mother's chest or abdomen to maintain warmth. Very-low-birth weight preterm babies are more prone to heat loss because of their larger body surface area and immature skin. Hence, additional heating methods are recommended such as plastic wrap (food or medical grade, heat-resistant plastic) to cover the baby or the use of an exothermic mattress.

Positioning

The baby is best positioned on his back or side with the head in a neutral or slightly extended position, using a 1-inch shoulder roll, with sideways turning of the head, if possible.

Suctioning

Healthy, vigorous, newly born infants generally do not require suctioning after delivery. Secretions may be wiped from the nose and mouth with gauze or a towel. If suctioning is necessary, clear secretions first from the mouth and then from the nose with a bulb syringe or suction catheter (8 or 10 Fr). Suction pressure should not exceed 80–100 mmHg. Aggressive pharyngeal suctioning can cause laryngeal spasm and vagal bradycardia and delay the onset of spontaneous breathing.

Clearing the Airway of Meconium

When the amniotic fluid is meconium-stained, intrapartum suctioning of the mouth, pharynx and nose is not recommended.

Some *depressed* infants will have meconium in the trachea despite such suctioning, necessitating tracheal suctioning after delivery. If the infant has absent or depressed respiration, hypotonia or bradycardia, direct laryngoscopy is performed immediately after birth for suctioning of residual meconium from the hypopharynx (under direct vision) and intubation/suction of the trachea. Tracheal suctioning of the vigorous infant with meconium-stained fluid does not improve the outcome and may cause complications.

Warmth can be provided by a radiant heater but drying and stimulation generally should be delayed in such infants. Tracheal suctioning is done by applying suction directly to the endotracheal (ET) tube as it is withdrawn from the airway. Suction via a catheter inserted into the ET tube is not recommended.

Intubation and suctioning are continued until the quantum of meconium recovered is minimal. However, if the infant's heart rate or respiration is severely depressed, it may be necessary to start positive pressure ventilation despite the presence of a small amount of meconium in the airway. Later, when the baby is stabilised, gastric lavage may be done to remove the swallowed meconium.

Tactile Stimulation

The stimulation provided by drying and suctioning usually is adequate to initiate effective respiration in most newly born infants. Additional tactile stimulation is provided by a flick of the soles or rubbing the back, done once or twice, along with the use of free-flow oxygen. Tactile stimulation may initiate spontaneous respiration in infants who are in primary apnoea but if they do not respond to these efforts, the infant is in secondary apnoea and positive pressure ventilation would be required.

Oxygen Administration

There is evidence to suggest that survival is better when resuscitation is started with room air rather than 100% oxygen. Hence, it is recommended to start resuscitation with room air or blended oxygen (40–60%). The oxygen concentration can be decreased or increased as per preductal oxygen saturation. If the baby's heart rate remains <60 bpm after 90 seconds of resuscitation with room air or 40% oxygen, increase the concentration of oxygen to 100% until recovery of a normal heart rate.

All these initial steps should be completed in about 60 seconds.

If asphyxia persists as in secondary apnoea, the following steps should be established:

- ventilation,
- chest compression and
- medications.

Ventilation

Most neonates can be effectively resuscitated with bag and mask ventilation. Intermittent positive pressure ventilation (IPPV) is indicated for babies with apnoea, gasping respiration, bradycardia with a heart rate below 100 bpm, and persistent central cyanosis despite the use of 100% oxygen.

The initial breaths need to be delivered with a pressure of 30–40 cm H_2O and thereafter at 15–20 cm H_2O. The optimal rate of providing positive pressure ventilation is 40–60 breaths per minute done at a count of a squeeze – two – three – squeeze. The bag is squeezed only with fingertips and not with the whole hand.

The adequacy of ventilation is measured by a rise in heart rate and, less reliably, chest expansion. Peak inflation pressures of up to 30 cm H_2O in term newborns and 20–25 cm H_2O in preterm newborns are usually sufficient to inflate the lungs.

Inadequate response to ventilation may be due to the following reasons:

- Poor seal between mask and face for which the mask needs to be reapplied
- Airway obstruction (reposition the neck, clear secretions and open the infant's mouth)
- Inadequate inflation pressure
- Inadequate oxygen: Check the oxygen delivery system including the oxygen supply and connection of the tubing

An orogastric catheter may need to be inserted to deflate the stomach when resuscitation with bag and mask ventilation is continued for over 2 minutes. For this a 6–8 Fr sized tube is passed and gastric contents aspirated; then the outer end is left open.

After 30 seconds of ventilation, breathing and heart rate should be assessed. If spontaneous regular respiration is present and the heart rate is above 100 bpm, IPPV may be withdrawn. If respiration is inadequate or the heart rate is below 100 bpm, IPPV is continued by bag and mask or through an ET tube. If the heart rate is below 60 bpm, IPPV is continued with chest compressions and ET intubation. Figure 5.2 shows the position of neonate during face mask ventilation.

Resuscitation Bag

The resuscitation bag used in neonates usually has a volume of 240 ml to deliver a tidal volume of 5–8 ml/kg. The self-inflating bag has an air and oxygen inlet, patient outlet and valve assembly. It requires an oxygen source and a reservoir and has safety features such as a pressure-release valve (when pressure exceeds 30–35 cm H_2O) and a pressure gauge (also see Chapter 2).

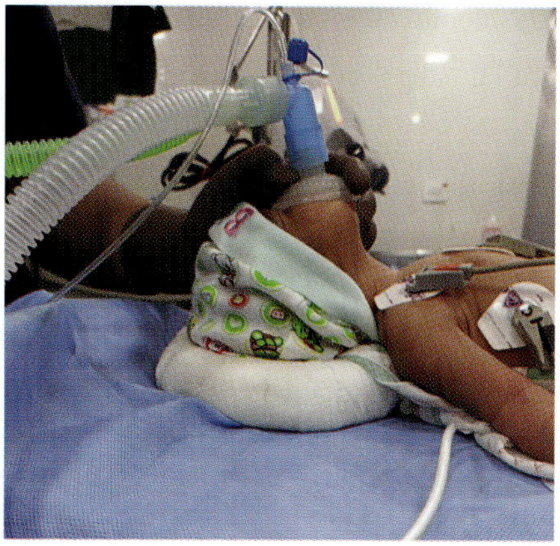

Figure 5.2 Position of the neonate during face mask ventilation.

Face Masks

Face masks should form a seal around the mouth and nose without covering the eyes and preferably have cushioned edges. The usual mask sizes are 0 and 1 and are round or anatomically shaped. It is important to test the equipment prior to use by blocking the patient outlet in the palm of the operator's hand and compressing the bag to check the adequacy of pressure, working of the pop-off valve, and the presence and working of the valve assembly.

Two important **contraindications** to bag and mask ventilation are as follows:

1. Thick meconium-stained liquor before tracheal suction
2. Diaphragmatic hernia

Endotracheal Intubation

Indications for ET intubation are as follows:

- Ineffective or prolonged bag and mask ventilation
- With chest compression
- When tracheal suctioning is required for thick meconium
- Electively in diaphragmatic hernia
- Electively in extremely low-birth weight babies
- For administration of medications

The depth of insertion of the ET tube (for orotracheal intubation) can be calculated using the formula: 'baby's weight in kg plus 6 cm': this is the depth at the lip in cm.

Oral intubation is done using a laryngoscope with a straight blade (size 0 for preterm and size 1 for term infants, Table 5.2). The infant is placed on a flat surface with the head in the midline and the neck slightly extended. The operator stands at the head end of the infant holding the laryngoscope in the left hand, stabilising the infant's head with the right hand. The blade of the laryngoscope is slid over the tongue and the tip is introduced into the vallecula or onto the epiglottis. The blade is then lifted to visualise the vocal cords and the ET tube is introduced. Cricoid pressure may be required.

Table 5.2 Selection of ET Size

Tube Size (ID mm)	Weight (g)	Gest Age (wk)
2.5	<1,000	<28
3.0	1,000–2,000	28–34
3.5	2,000–3,000	35–38
3.5–4.0	>3,000	>38

ET, endotracheal tube; ID, internal diameter.

Confirmation of ET tube placement is done by auscultating for equal breath sounds in the axillae, absence of breath sounds over the stomach, watching the rise of the chest with each ventilation, absence of gastric inflation, and noting improvement in heart rate, colour and activity of the infant. Final confirmation is by chest radiograph with the ET tube tip at T-2.

Three actions to be done after intubation are to note the cm mark on the tube at the level of the upper lip, secure the tube to the infant's face and shorten the outer end of the tube 4 cm from the lip margin. Potential complications of intubation are hypoxia, bradycardia, apnoea, pneumothorax, soft-tissue injury and infection.

Hypoxia during intubation can be minimised by providing free-flow oxygen and limiting each intubation attempt to 20 seconds.

Use of CPAP

The use of CPAP in preterm infants in the delivery room reduces the rates of intubation, mechanical ventilation, surfactant use and duration of ventilation. CPAP should be used in preterm babies who are breathing spontaneously and have respiratory distress. There is no evidence to support or refute the use of CPAP in the delivery room in the term baby with respiratory distress.

Laryngeal Mask Airway

A laryngeal mask is recommended during resuscitation of term and preterm neonates at 34 weeks or more of gestation when either effective ventilation is not achieved by face mask ventilation or tracheal intubation is not successful or feasible. During chest compressions, the use of a laryngeal mask has not been evaluated. Figure 5.3 shows the newborn with laryngeal mask airway (LMA).

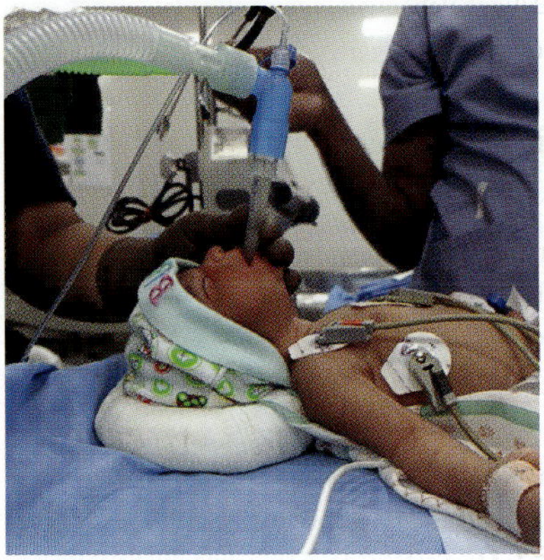

Figure 5.3 Newborn with LMA.

Chest Compression

Chest compression is indicated if, after 30 seconds of the bag and mask ventilation with 100% oxygen, the heart rate remains below 60 bpm. Chest compression must always be accompanied by ventilation with 100% oxygen.

Compression Technique

The techniques employed are the two-thumb–encircling hands technique or the two-finger technique (see Chapter 28).

The two-thumbs–encircling hands technique is the preferred method. The two thumbs are placed on the sternum, superimposed or adjacent to each other, with fingers encircling the chest and supporting the back. Alternatively, two fingers are placed on the sternum at right angles to the chest with the other hand supporting the back (the two-finger technique).

The pressure required is one-third of the anteroposterior diameter of the chest, applied over the lower third of the sternum between the nipple and the xiphisternum. Chest compressions should be delivered smoothly and produce a palpable pulse. During chest compression, the thumbs and fingers should not be lifted from the sternum. The rate required is 3 chest compressions to 1 ventilation (3:1), with 90 chest compressions to 30 ventilations in 1 minute. The heart rate is assessed every 30 seconds and chest compressions are continued until the heart rate exceeds 60 bpm.

Chest compressions run the risk of broken ribs and pneumothoraces. Precautions to be observed include avoiding pressure on the ribs, xiphisternum and abdomen.

Medications

Drugs are rarely needed in neonatal resuscitation. The bradycardia encountered is usually due to inadequate lung inflation or hypoxia; bradycardia usually improves with adequate ventilation. Medications are required only if the heart rate remains below 60 bpm despite adequate ventilation with 100% oxygen and chest compression.

Routes of Administration

The preferred route for the administration of drugs is the umbilical vein since it can be easily accessed. All drugs and volume expanders can be administered through this route. A 5 Fr catheter is passed just below the skin level and a free flow of blood should be obtained before administering drugs. The intraosseous route may be a reasonable alternative, determined by the local availability of equipment, training and experience.

Other routes are peripheral veins and intratracheal instillation.

Drugs that may be used in neonatal resuscitation are epinephrine (adrenaline), volume expanders, sodium bicarbonate, naloxone and dopamine.

Volume Expanders

When blood loss is suspected in a newly born infant who responds poorly to resuscitation (ventilation, chest compressions and/or epinephrine), it may be reasonable to administer a volume expander without delay. Normal saline (0.9% sodium chloride) is the crystalloid fluid of choice. Uncrossmatched type O, Rh-negative blood (or crossmatched, if immediately available) is preferred when blood loss is substantial. An initial volume of 10 ml/kg over 5–10 minutes may be reasonable and may be repeated if there is an inadequate response. The recommended route is intravenous, with the intraosseous route being an alternative.

With volume expansion, there is less pallor, correction of metabolic acidosis, and blood pressure and peripheral pulses improve. If signs of hypovolaemia persist, volume expanders can be repeated.

Naloxone

Naloxone is not recommended as part of the initial resuscitation for newborns with respiratory depression in the delivery room. For the clinical situation of a newborn with respiratory depression after maternal opiate exposure, the focus needs to remain on effective ventilation and airway support for the persistently apnoeic newborn.

Epinephrine (Adrenaline)

The indications for use of epinephrine are a heart rate below 60 per minute despite 30 seconds of IPPV and chest compressions, or if there is asystole. The standard formulation of epinephrine is a 1:1,000 preparation. This is diluted 10 times to a 1:10,000 solution, and 0.01–0.03 mg/kg (0.1–0.3 ml/kg) is preferably administered by the intravenous route as a rapid bolus. While vascular access is being established, a higher dose (0.05–0.1 mg/kg of 1:10,000 dilution) of epinephrine can be administered through the ET tube. It has inotropic and chronotropic effects and the heart rate increases to above 100 per minute within 30 seconds. If bradycardia persists, epinephrine may be repeated after 3–5 minutes.

Sodium Bicarbonate

It has no role in brief arrests, and its use must be preceded, accompanied and followed by ventilation. The use of sodium bicarbonate is only indicated in cases of prolonged arrest that do not respond to other therapy. Routine use of bicarbonate cannot be recommended; its hyperosmolarity and CO_2-generating properties can in fact be detrimental.

Table 5.3 APGAR Score

Score	0 points	1 point	2 points
Appearance (skin color)	Cyanotic / Pale all over	Peripheral cyanosis only	Pink
Pulse (heart rate)	0	<100	100–140
Grimace (reflex irritability)	No response to stimulation	Grimace or weak cry when stimulated	Cry when stimulated
Activity (tone)	Floppy	Some flexion	Well flexed and resisting extension
Respiration	Apneic	Slow, irregular breathing	Strong cry

Drugs such as atropine, dexamethasone, calcium, nikethamide (coramine) and dextrose have no role in neonatal resuscitation.

Procedures After Resuscitation

It is important to document the condition of the baby at birth and the response to resuscitation. The Apgar score at 1 and 5 minutes helps in quantifying this information and is useful for ongoing clinical care, communication and medicolegal purposes (**Table 5.3**). This may be recorded thereafter every 5 minutes until the baby is stable. It is also useful to give a narrative description of the sequence of events with timings and interventions performed.

After adequate ventilation and circulation have been established, the newborn infant should be monitored and supportive care provided as clinically indicated.

The parents and family of the newborn infant should be counselled about the procedures undertaken and the course of action after resuscitative efforts have been completed.

In certain situations, such as extreme prematurity and lethal congenital malformations, the option of non-initiation or discontinuation of resuscitation after initial assessment may be considered. The opinion of the family, local guidelines, resources and data on the outcome of such babies would influence these decisions.

Asystole for more than 10 minutes despite all resuscitative measures is very unlikely to result in survival or survival without disability. Similarly, if there is no breathing after 20 minutes or only gasping after 30 minutes of ventilation, resuscitative efforts may be discontinued. The family should be counselled and provided emotional support.

SUGGESTED READINGS

1. Niermeyer S, Kattwinkel J, Reempts PV, et al. International Guidelines for Neonatal Resuscitation: An Excerpt from the Guidelines 2000 for Cardiopulmonary Resuscitation and Emergency Cardiovascular Care: International Consensus on Science. *Pediatrics* 2000; 106:e29.
2. Management of Newborn Problems: A Guide for Doctors, Nurses and Midwives: A WHO publication of the Integrated Management of Pregnancy and Childbirth (IMPAC) Series Basic Newborn Resuscitation: A Practical Guide. WHO/RH/MSM/98.1.
3. Søreide E, Morrison L, Hillman K, et al. The formula for survival in resuscitation. *Resuscitation* 2013; 84:1487–1493.
4. Cheng A, Magid DJ, Auerbach M, et al. Part 6: Resuscitation education science: 2020 American Heart Association Guidelines for Cardiopulmonary Resuscitation and Emergency Cardiovascular Care. *Circulation* 2020;142(2):S551–S579.
5. Berg KM, Cheng A, Panchal AR, et al. On behalf of the Adult Basic and Advanced Life Support, Pediatric Basic and Advanced Life Support, Neonatal Life Support, and Resuscitation Education Science Writing Groups. Part 7: Systems of care: 2020 American Heart Association Guidelines for Cardiopulmonary Resuscitation and Emergency Cardiovascular Care. *Circulation* 2020; 142(2):S580–S604.
6. International Liaison Committee on Resuscitation. Continuous evidence evaluation guidance and templates. Available from: https://www.ilcor.org/documents/continuous-evidence-evaluation-guidance-and-templates. (accessed 31 December 2019).
7. Aziz K, Lee HC, Escobedo MB, et al. Part 5: Neonatal resuscitation: 2020 American Heart Association Guidelines for Cardiopulmonary Resuscitation and Emergency Cardiovascular Care. *Circulation* 2020; 142(2):S524–S550.

6 NEONATAL SURGICAL EMERGENCIES

Rebecca Jacob • Anita Shirley Joselyn

The challenge of administering anaesthesia to a neonate as compared to an older child or an adult lies in the immaturity of organ systems and the resultant physiology and pharmacology. Neonates differ in hepatic and renal maturity, body compositions and protein binding. These differences combined with a lower cardiac therapeutic index mandate that all medications be carefully titrated to effect. Neonates are less able to maintain normal homeostasis and are thus vulnerable to stress. They are more vulnerable to hypoxia, hypotension, hypothermia, hypo- or hyperglycaemia and hypocalcaemia (refer to Chapter 4).

Pre-operative evaluation should include a maternal and perinatal history which could provide important clues to diagnosis, for example, the correlation between maternal polyhydramnios and neonatal tracheo-oesophageal fistula (TOF). Remember that the presence of one anomaly mandates a search for others. Especially look out for congenital heart disease!

Almost all neonatal surgical emergencies are 'urgencies' and not emergencies. They can afford to wait for at least 24–48 hours while the baby is stabilised and allows for better foetal to neonatal transition.

Neonatal surgical emergencies commonly seen in the first week of life are as follows:

- Congenital diaphragmatic hernia (CDH)
- Tracheo-oesophageal fistula (TOF)
- Congenital lobar emphysema or lung cysts
- Anorectal malformation for diversion colostomy
- Omphalocele and gastroschisis
- Intestinal obstruction
- Meningomyelocele

In the second week and later are:

- Necrotising enterocolitis (NEC)
- Hernia

Congenital Diaphragmatic Hernia

Incidence: 1 in 4,000–5,000 live births

Occurrence: At 10–13 weeks' gestation

Mortality rate: 40–60%

Pathophysiology

A failure in the closure of the diaphragm permits the abdominal contents to herniate into the thorax. The herniated bowel acts as a space-occupying lesion (mass effect) that causes lung compression, prevents normal lung development and causes pulmonary vascular changes and cardiac malposition. This occurs more commonly on the left side, with 80% occurring through the posterolateral foramen of Bochdalek and few through the anterolateral foramen of Morgagni and occasionally through the oesophageal hiatus (**Figs 6.1–6.4**).

Lung hypoplasia is usually ipsilateral but may occasionally be bilateral. These lungs have smaller bronchi, less bronchial branching, with decreased alveolar surface area, and abnormal pulmonary vasculature. Arteriolar smooth muscle is thickened and extends to the capillary level of the alveoli. This impairs pulmonary function by increasing

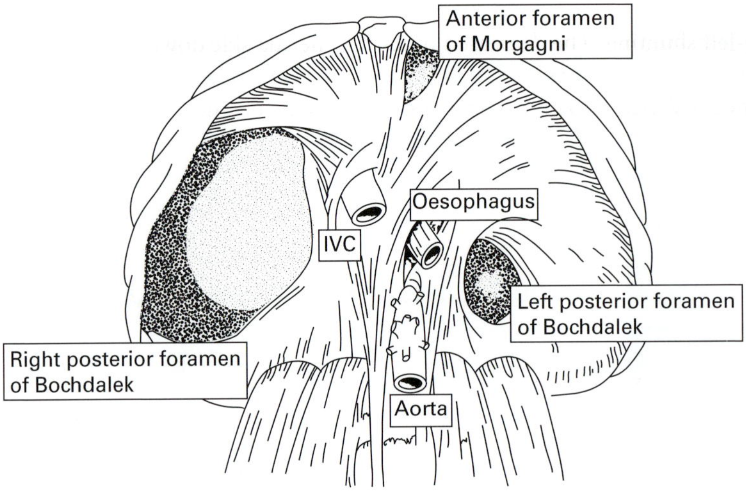

Figure 6.1 Abnormal anatomy of the diaphragm in case of congenital diaphragmatic hernia. IVC, inferior vena cava.

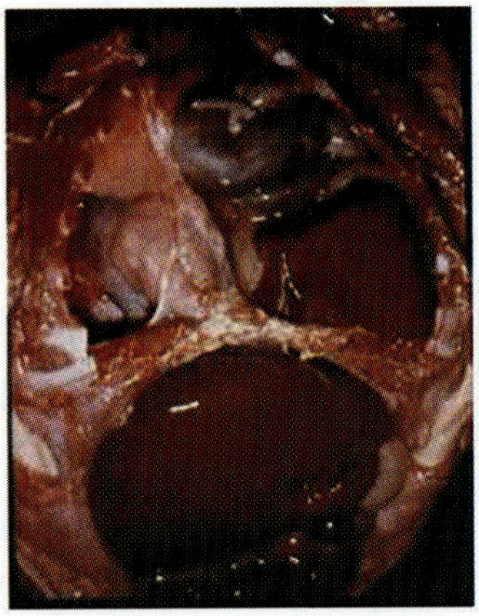

Figure 6.2 Left-sided congenital diaphragmatic hernia. Note the intrathoracic spleen, bowel and appendix.

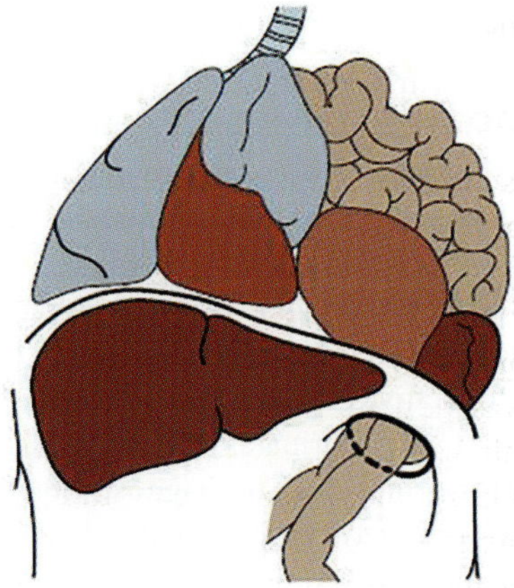

Figure 6.3 Left-sided congenital diaphragmatic hernia with intrathoracic bowel and spleen.

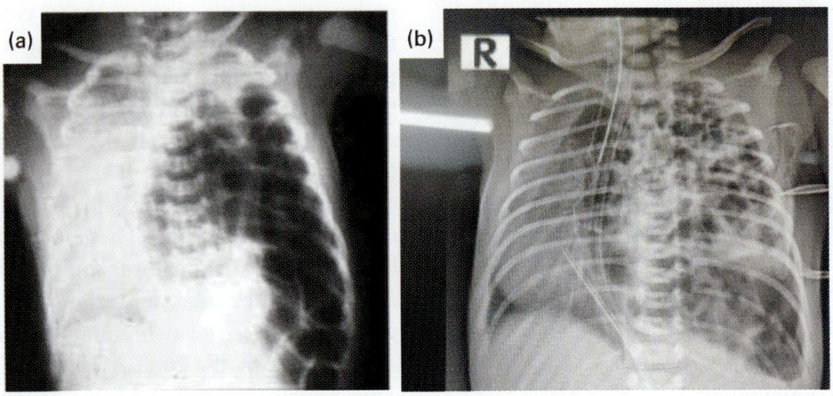

Figure 6.4 (a and b) Images of congenital diaphragmatic hernia (CDH) chest X-ray. Note abdominal contents in the chest with a shift of the mediastinum.

pulmonary artery pressure, which may cause further right-to-left shunting. The decreased functional lung volume and increase in pulmonary vascular resistance (PVR) lead to post-natal hypoxaemia, acidosis and, in severe cases, right heart failure. Pulmonary vasoconstriction is worsened by hypoxaemia and acidosis which in turn exacerbates respiratory distress and cyanosis. *The degree of lung hypoplasia and pulmonary hypertension depends on the time during gestation when the hernia occurred being more severe if the hernia occurs early in gestation.*

Other cardiac abnormalities and malrotation may be associated. Kinking or obstruction of the inferior vena cava (IVC) can decrease the preload and thus the cardiac output. Severe cases may even present in shock.

The presentation and outcome depend on the degree of lung hypoplasia and associated cardiac abnormalities.

Diagnosis

CDH is often diagnosed prenatally by ultrasonography or foetal MRI.

Clinical Features

After birth, the infants develop severe respiratory distress as the bowel in the chest distends with swallowed air, which further compresses the ipsilateral lung shifting the mediastinum and compressing the contralateral lung.

The neonate presents with

- Severe respiratory distress – dyspnoea, tachypnoea, cyanosis and severe chest retraction
- Increased anteroposterior diameter of the chest with a relatively scaphoid-shaped abdomen
- Apex beat shifted along with the mediastinum
- Poor air entry and bowel sounds in the chest on auscultation
- Hypoxia/acidosis

Chest X-ray shows air-filled viscera in the chest and mediastinal shift (**Fig. 6.4**).

Management

Initial management should stress the importance of stabilising the patient before attempting repair.

Management includes the following:

- Nasogastric (NG) tube to decompress the stomach
- Positioning the neonate semi-recumbent with hernia side down
- **Do not mask ventilate**! This will cause distension of the stomach and severe respiratory compromise
- Secure the airway with an endotracheal tube (ETT), sedate and ventilate to maintain normocarbia, and prevent hypoventilation and acidosis which worsen pulmonary hypertension
- Monitor airway pressures – a sudden increase could indicate a pneumothorax (barotrauma). Be aware that vigorous ventilation with high inspiratory pressures may cause barotrauma
- Vasopressors may be required to keep up the systemic vascular resistance, thereby also helping to decrease the right-to-left shunt
- Maintain body temperature
- Monitor and correct arterial blood gas and electrolytes. Avoid acidosis and hypercarbia. Alkalosis (respiratory or metabolic) helps to improve pulmonary flow
- Remember that acid and Na excretion require mature kidneys

The CDH Euro Consortium suggested the following as indicators that the neonate is stable for surgery:

- Normal mean arterial pressure (MAP) for gestation
- Preductal SpO_2 between 85% and 95% on FiO_2 < 50%
- Lactate <3 mmol/L
- Urine output (UOP) > 1 ml/kg/hr

Ventilation Strategies

Ventilation strategies have changed in the recent past. Instead of maintaining a respiratory alkalosis, a strategy of permissive hypercapnia with $PaCO_2$ of 45–55 mmHg, a pH greater than 7.3 with peak inspiratory pressures of 25 cm H_2O has been suggested. The goal is to maintain pre-ductal saturations of 85–95%. Post-ductal saturations are ignored in the absence of significant metabolic acidosis (pH < 7.2 or PCO_2 > 65 mmHg). Decreased barotrauma may be the reason for improved survival.

Neonates who require a peak airway pressure of over 25 cm of H_2O may be tried on high-frequency oscillatory ventilation (HFOV), which provides high respiratory rates at low tidal volumes. HFOV appears to improve oxygenation and ventilation with reduced barotrauma. Theoretically, a higher oxygen tension will improve pulmonary blood flow, while lower peak inspiratory pressure prevents barotrauma.

Inhaled nitric oxide (iNO) may prove useful in treating pulmonary hypertension. NO is an endogenous regulator of vascular tone, and iNO can act as a selective pulmonary vasodilator. However, vasodilatation may occasionally worsen the condition. Oral sildenafil, administered preoperatively, at a dose of 0.5–1 mg/kg per dose, can be beneficial for children with pulmonary hypertension. However, it is advised to delay its use in cases of extreme prematurity until retinal vascularity is established.

In the very sick neonate, extracorporeal membrane oxygenation (ECMO) has been tried with varying success. The cost of the set-up and the difficulty in instituting and maintaining the treatment are prohibitive.

Surgical Management

Surgical repair is via a trans-abdominal subcostal incision on the affected side. The bowel and other abdominal contents are replaced in the abdomen and the diaphragmatic defect is closed. A muscle flap or synthetic mesh may be required for abdominal closure. More recently, thoracoscopic repair of CDH is performed. Contraindications for a thoracoscopic repair include right-sided CDH with herniation of the liver, which causes difficulty in reducing the contents, big left-sided defect with the liver as content and primary pulmonary hypertension (PPH) resistant to treatment.

Anaesthetic Challenges

Anaesthetic challenges include potential hypoxia and hypotension from distension of the stomach and bowel, hypoxaemia from primary pulmonary hypoplasia and systemic hypotension caused by kinking of major blood vessels, particularly those of the liver during reduction of hernia and abdominal closure. Primary pulmonary hypertension and right ventricular failure may occur. Poor cardiac output may require ionotropic support. Hypocalcaemia may occur after transfusion of blood products and will need correction to maintain optimal cardiac function.

The provision of adequate analgesia to blunt the stress response minimises sudden increases in PVR with resultant right-to-left shunting.

IV access for maintenance of a constant circulating volume is essential. It is preferable to use upper limb veins as increased intra-abdominal pressure may cause lower limb venous congestion. Very often, the neonate presents with an *umbilical vein and artery* catheterised by the neonatologist. It is very important that these two lines are protected during surgery. Ensure careful control of ventilation, monitor airway pressures, and maintain oxygenation, normothermia, and fluid and electrolyte balance as described above.

A sudden elevation in peak inspiratory pressures, a decrease in lung compliance or sudden hypotension may indicate a pneumothorax. It usually occurs in the ipsilateral lung but can also occur in the contralateral lung, and the surgeon should be prepared for immediate chest tube placement.

Prior to induction confirm that the NG tube is in place, aspirated and left open.

Anaesthesia

The type of anaesthetic agents used depends on the cardiovascular status of the patients, type of ventilation and preference of the anaesthetist. Fentanyl provides cardiac stability; low doses of halogenated inhalational anaesthetics along with a muscle relaxant such as atracurium or vecuronium are often used. If ventilation has been a problem, HFOV may have to be shifted to the operating room in selected cases.

Since CDH patients are often sedated during their stabilisation period, they may develop a resistance to the sedatives and require higher doses of narcotics and benzodiazepines.

The use of N_2O may compromise the ability to close the abdomen by over-distending the bowel and is therefore not recommended as a part of anaesthesia management.

Thoracoscopic CDH repair (**Fig. 6.5**) has added concerns due to carbon dioxide insufflation. There may be decreased lung compliance and increased resistance to ventilation. An extra source of carbon dioxide can cause a greater incidence of hypoxia and hypercarbia in the intraoperative period. In addition, the venous return to the heart can be compromised worsening the neonates' haemodynamic status and cardiac output. Large volumes of unhumidified carbon dioxide can

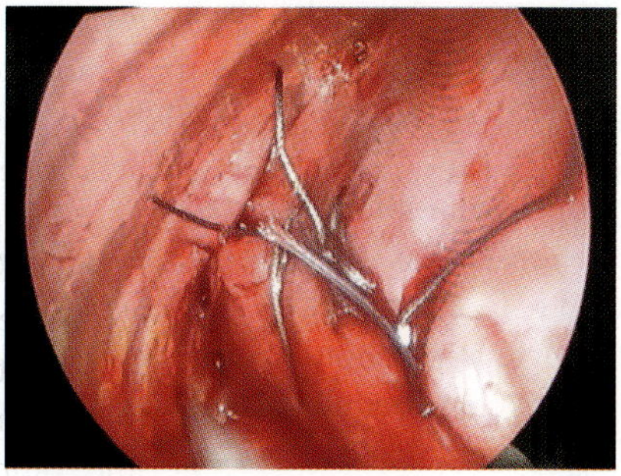

Figure 6.5 Thoracoscopic repair of congenital diaphragmatic hernia with sutures seen on the diaphragm.

cause significant hypothermia. The insufflation pressure should be limited to 4–6 mmHg. Ventilatory strategy during thoracoscopic repair must include using pressure-controlled ventilation with peak airway pressures between 20 and 25 cm H_2O, a respiratory rate of 40–60 times/minute, an inhaled oxygen concentration (FiO_2) to maintain preductal saturation of 85–95%, inspiratory/expiratory ratio (I:E ratio) of 1:1–1.5, positive end expiratory pressure (PEEP) of 5–6 mmHg, $PaCO_2$ values of 50–70 mmHg and pH of 7.25 or above. Dopamine or dobutamine should be considered to maintain haemodynamic stability in addition to IV fluids (see Chapter 24).

Post-operative ventilation is planned and FiO_2 is adjusted to maintain a PaO_2 of >150 mmHg and preductal saturation of 85–95%,. The infant is slowly weaned from oxygen over 48–72 hours to avoid the '*honeymoon phenomenon*' characterised by an early smooth course followed by a sudden development of pulmonary vasoconstriction and potentially lethal pulmonary hypertension.

CDH – Points to Think About

- Not an emergency. Medical stabilisation is important prior to surgical correction.
- Do not mask ventilate! Intubate and ventilate gently to avoid pneumothorax.
- Consider pneumothorax if there is a sudden increase in peak inspiratory pressure, decrease in lung compliance or hypoventilation.
- Mortality depends on lung immaturity and pulmonary hypertension.
- Avoid acidosis and hypoxia which make pulmonary hypertension worse.
- Both hypoxia and hyperoxaemia need to be avoided in the neonate with CDH.
- Cardiovascular status should be monitored and hypotension treated aggressively.

Tracheo-Oesophageal Fistula

TOF occurs in 1:3,000 live births, and 50% of these patients have associated congenital anomalies.

Associated Anomalies

The associated anomalies include the following:

1. **VATER**
    - **V**ertebral anomalies or ventricular septal defect
    - **A**nal atresia
    - **TOF**
    - **E**sophageal (Oesophageal) atresia
    - **R**adial aplasia and renal anomalies
2. **VACTERL**
    - **C**ardiac and **l**imb anomalies in addition to the above

Pathology

There are five major varieties of TOF. Type C (upper-end blind with lower-end communicating) is the most common (**Fig. 6.6C**). The fistula commonly occurs in the posterior muscular part of the trachea, just above the carina.

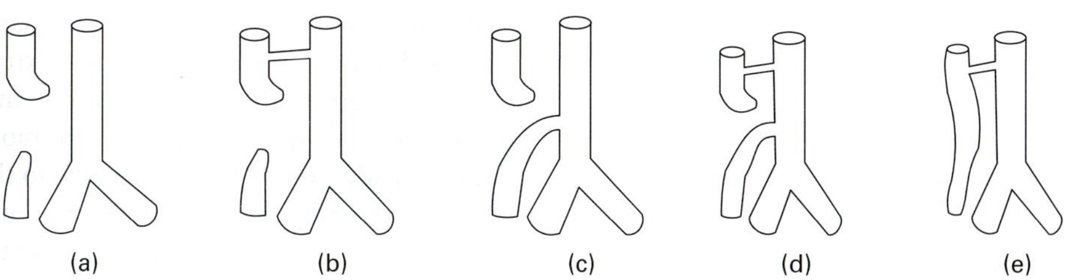

Figure 6.6 (a–e) Tracheo-oesophageal fistula (TOF) classification. Type C is the most common.

Diagnosis

Antenatally – Maternal polyhydramnios and absence of the stomach bubble on ultrasound. **Postnatally** – The abnormality presents with the 3 Cs of oesophageal atresia: choking, coughing and cyanosis. The baby appears 'mucousy' and the passage of an NG tube meets with obstruction.

Investigations

Chest X-ray (**Fig. 6.7**) shows the catheter coiled up in the blind proximal pouch. Air from the fistula is visible in the bowel in all except Type A where there is no communication between the oesophagus and the airway. An X-ray may also show signs of aspiration pneumonia.

Barium is contraindicated due to the risk of aspiration.

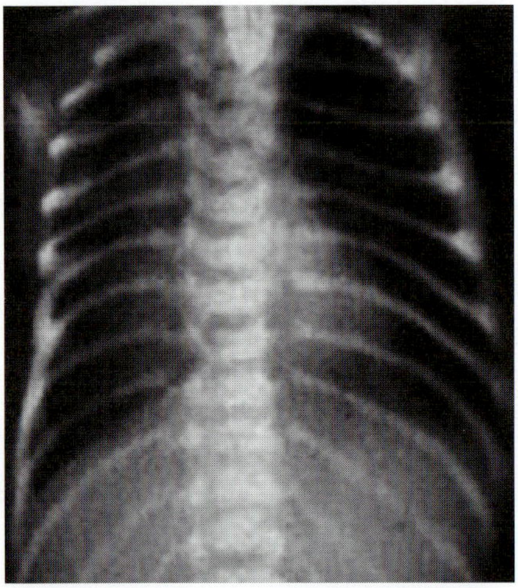

Figure 6.7 X-ray showing an nasogastric (NG) tube coiled in the upper oesophageal pouch.

Pre-Operative Management

The following are essential for a favourable outcome:

- Emergency surgery is not essential and 24–48 hours' stabilisation allows for full assessment including cardiac assessment, better transition from the foetal to the neonatal state and treatment of pulmonary pathology (atelectasis and/or pneumonitis)
- The oesophageal pouch should be kept free of secretions, by inserting a tube into the pouch and applying intermittent suction with a syringe
- Position the child: 30° head up to prevent aspiration
- Regular chest physiotherapy should be encouraged
- Appropriate antibiotics started
- If the child has pneumonia, this should be treated before surgery
- Electrolyte levels should be checked as they may be deranged from the inadequate replacement of large amounts of saliva/secretions which may have been sucked out
- Gastrostomy may be performed under local anaesthesia to decompress the stomach and provide nutrition if surgery is delayed
- A pre-surgical bronchoscopy with a rigid or flexible bronchoscope may be done to assess the presence, type, size and location of the fistula (**Fig. 6.8**), the presence of a proximal fistula or bronchial cleft or tracheomalacia. It could also help to decide on the technique of intubation and timing of extubation. A guide wire may be inserted into the fistulous tract for easy recognition of the tract during surgery (**Fig. 6.9**). A laryngeal mask airway (LMA) may be used as a conduit for doing fibreoptic bronchoscopy with a flexible bronchoscope.

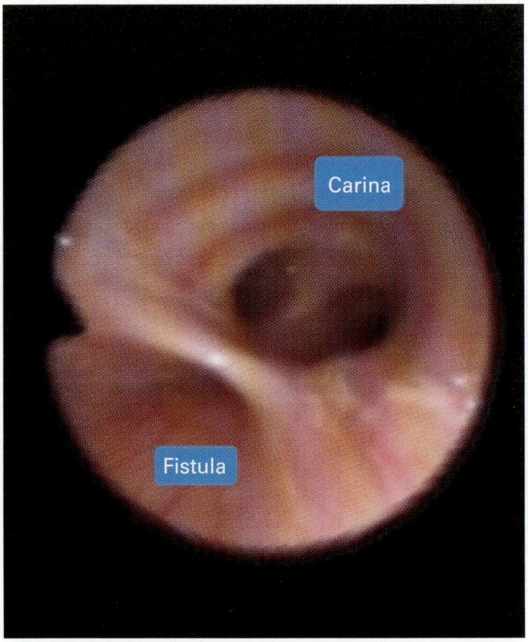

Figure 6.8 Flexible bronchoscopic view of the trachea showing carina and fistula proximal to the carina.

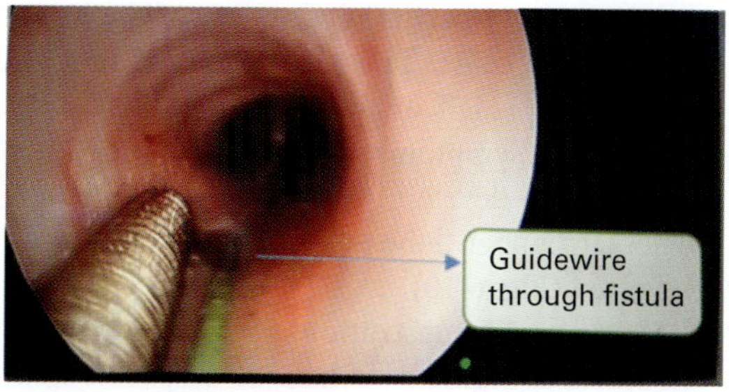

Figure 6.9 Flexible bronchoscopic view of the trachea with a guidewire (green coloured) inserted through fistula tract.

Anaesthetic Challenges

Primarily involves securing the airway and providing adequate ventilation. Awake intubation is frequently advocated to avoid controlled ventilation and probable overdistension of the stomach via the fistula with consequent aspiration or respiratory compromise. However, awake intubation is not advisable as it can predispose the baby to develop intraventricular haemorrhage. So, intubation is done only after induction of anaesthesia. The child may be induced with an intravenous induction agent such as a bolus of propofol 0.5 mg/kg or an inhalational agent like sevoflurane, and the vocal cords sprayed with 2% lidocaine (maximum dose: 3–4 mg/kg). Maintenance is on spontaneous ventilation with O_2/sevoflurane. A muscle relaxant is used only after assessing whether gentle ventilation produces adequate chest movement without inappropriate abdominal distension, and the trachea is intubated. A muscle relaxant is not used for intubation if there is any doubt as to the ability to ventilate or if there is ventilatory gas loss in the stomach. The child is then intubated under deep anaesthesia while breathing spontaneously where due to the negative intrathoracic pressure, gases preferentially enter the lungs rather than the TOF. The ETT is passed into one main bronchus, the chest auscultated, and the tube withdrawn into the trachea to a position just above the carina, that is, just when auscultation shows bilateral breath sounds. The goal is to place the tip of the ETT beyond the origin of the TOF but above the carina. The final position of the tip of the ETT can also be confirmed with FOB scope if smaller sizes are available.

Another option for induction/intubation is sedation with minimal midazolam 25–50 mcg/kg plus fentanyl 0.5–1 mcg/kg in titrated doses along with topical lignocaine spray. This may be followed by awake-sedated intubation.

If there is a major air leak through the fistula, consider passing a Fogarty catheter into it under vision (fibreoptic) so as to occlude the TOF. This is often difficult and passing the Fogarty through a rigid scope via the gastrostomy may be an easier option.

Surgical Repair

Surgical repair is performed in the left lateral position, extrapleurally, through a right thoracotomy. The fistula is usually found where the azygous vein passes over the trachea to enter the superior vena cava. The azygous vein is divided, the fistula isolated and the tracheal end sutured. The proximal oesophageal pouch is identified and dissected superiorly to provide adequate length for primary anastomosis, which is done over a size 10 NG tube. If this length is insufficient, the surgeon settles for an oesophagostomy and gastrostomy and waits until the child grows bigger for definitive surgery like a gastric 'pull-up' or oesophageal reconstruction.

Occasionally, when inadequate ventilation and gastric dilatation become a problem, an emergency transpleural ligation of the TOF with a reoperation 8–10 days later to divide the fistula and repair the atresia has been advocated.

Thoracoscopic TOF repair is more commonly performed nowadays. There are no contraindications for a thoracoscopic repair. It depends primarily on the expertise of the surgeon.

TOF: Points to Think About

- Note that a change in the insertion distance of the ETT of as little as 1–2 mm may determine whether one is ventilating both lungs, one lung or the fistula.

- Beware the loss of 'lower' lung ventilation – a chest stethoscope fixed near the left axilla helps to detect endobronchial intubation.
- Hypoxaemia can occur if the ETT slips out or into the fistula.
- Beware of the enthusiastic assistant retracting the lung and the underlying heart and great vessels – this can cause dramatic hypotension and bradycardia and inadequate ventilation. In these instances, 'hand ventilation' may be preferred.
- Continuous communication with the surgeon throughout the procedure is essential.
- Post-operative ventilation should be considered if the neonate is small (premature), if he/she has aspirated pre-op, if the anastomosis is under tension or if intravenous narcotics such as morphine or fentanyl are considered for post-op analgesia.
- Post-operative analgesia may be provided with intravenous narcotics or an epidural or paravertebral block placed during the anaesthetic and continued post-op (see Chapters 13, 14 and 16.)

Congenital Lung Cysts or Lobar Emphysema

Four major congenital cystic lesions of the lung share similar embryological and clinical characteristics. They are as follows:

- **Congenital lobar emphysema**: It is defined as a hyperinflation of one or more pulmonary lobes due to a partial obstruction of the bronchus, which causes pressure symptoms on adjacent organs. Half of the patients present with respiratory symptoms at birth while the other half tend to develop them by 6 months of age. The left upper lobe is the most commonly involved (**Fig. 6.10**).
- **Pulmonary sequestration**: It is a condition in which a segment or lobe of dysplastic lung tissue exists with no communication with the normal lung or tracheobronchial tree. It may be intralobar or extralobar and is supplied by an anomalous vascular system, commonly from the systemic circulation. The tissue is nonfunctional.
- **Congenital cystic adenomatoid malformation** (CCAM): It is also referred to as congenital pulmonary airway malformation. This is a benign lung lesion that appears before birth as a cyst or mass in the chest made up of abnormal lung tissue that does not function properly but continues to grow (**Fig. 6.11**).
- **Bronchogenic pulmonary cysts:** They are foregut-derived malformations of the respiratory tract. If they occur early in gestation, they are usually located in the mediastinum. Later in gestation, they are found in the lung tissue. However, they may be found anywhere along the development of the foregut in an ectopic site.

The **location** of cysts may thus be

- Central
  - Anterior mediastinum

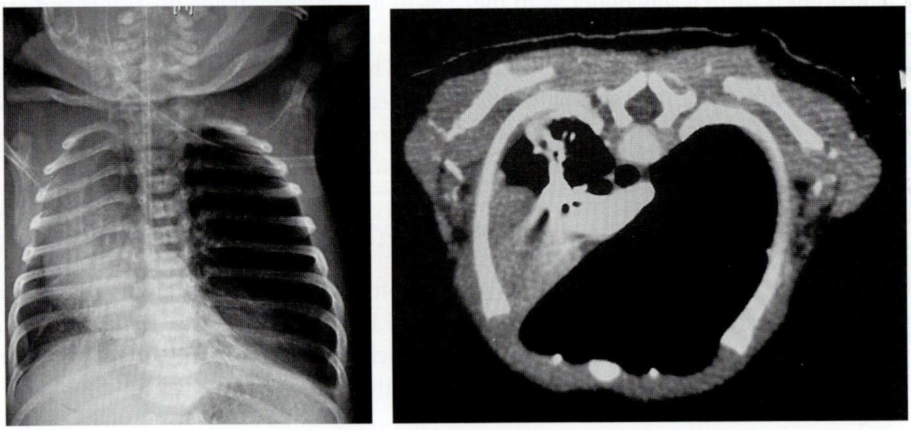

Figure 6.10 Chest X-ray and CT scan of a neonate with congenital lobar emphysema of the left upper lobe. There is a significant shift of the mediastinum to the opposite side.

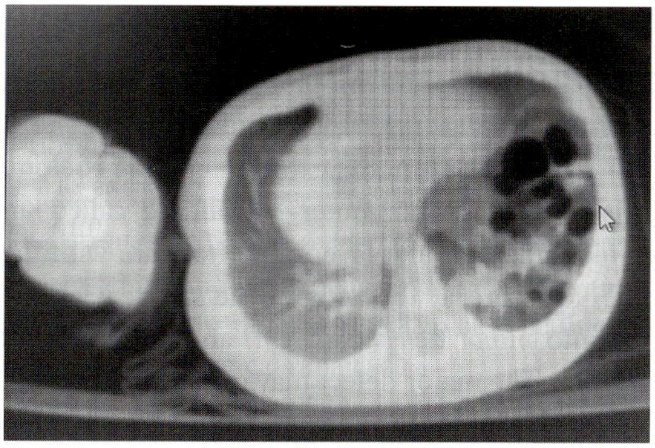

Figure 6.11 CT scan picture showing left lung lower lobe CCAM. CCAM, Congenital cystic adenomatoid malformation.

  - At Carina
  - At Hilum
- Paratracheal
- Lung parenchyma

The presentation of cystic lung lesions includes the following:

- Obstruction by mass effect – mediastinum
- Obstruction to air flow–fixed or ball valve effect with hyperinflation of the lung beyond it
- Chronic respiratory infection or abscess formation
- Rupture with haemorrhage or bronchopleural fistula formation

Diagnosis

It is by common presenting symptoms of recurrent respiratory infections, tachypnoea and respiratory distress. Chest X-ray and computed tomography (CT scan) are key imaging modalities used for diagnosis.

Treatment

Thoracotomy or thoracoscopic resection of the affected lobe of the lung.

Anaesthesia

Induction

A crying struggling child can increase the amount of air trapping. Positive pressure ventilation can also increase air trapping. Therefore, the preferred mode for induction and maintenance of anaesthesia is a well sedated child maintained on spontaneous respiration until the thorax is opened.

Mode of Induction – awake (sedation) or inhalational

- If assisted ventilation is required, keep peak inspiratory pressure low
- Alternatively sedation and IV ketamine may be used. Total intravenous anaesthesia (TIVA) may be considered

Maintenance

- High-frequency oscillatory ventilation with low airway pressures is especially useful.
- Local infiltration of the surgical incision site or intercostal blocks can provide analgesia.
- Avoid the use of nitrous oxide as this will cause the air-filled cyst to enlarge.
- Selective endobronchial blocking is useful especially if the cyst is fluid-filled, infected or linked to the bronchial tree.
- One-lung ventilation is often required. The options available for providing one-lung ventilation in a neonate are very limited and are restricted to the use of single-lumen ETT on the contralateral side of surgery or the use of Fogarty embolectomy catheter (3.0 Fr) on the operative side (**Fig. 6.12**).

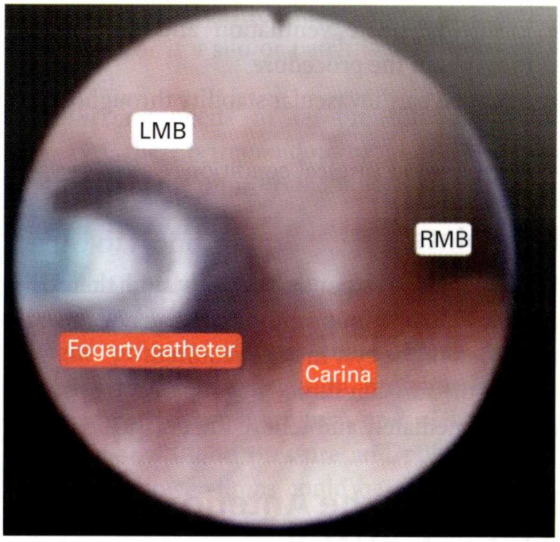

Figure 6.12 Flexible bronchoscopic view of carina through ETT. The bulb of Fogarty size 3 catheter was seen in the left main bronchus. LMB, left main bronchus; RMB, right main bronchus.

25 cm H_2O. Treatment is to reopen the wound, and aggressive hydration and inotropic support (higher doses of dopamine and dobutamine will be required due to the neonate's inability to augment inotropes).

Other effects of raised intra-abdominal pressure include decreased organ perfusion and therefore organ function. Intra-abdominal pressure >15 mmHg decreases renal blood flow and therefore affects fluid and salt homeostasis. Pressures above 20 mmHg reduce splanchnic blood flow and slows hepatic metabolism. Visceral ischaemia leads to prolonged ileus, metabolic acidosis, NEC and sepsis.

Avoid nitrous oxide as it can increase distension of the bowel. Administer adequate muscle relaxants, in spite of which primary closure may be impossible. In this case, a prosthetic pouch (silo), to cover and contain the bowel extra-abdominally, may be used and the size of the pouch reduced subsequently in stages. This allows the abdominal cavity to gradually accommodate the increased mass without severely compromising ventilation or organ perfusion. This procedure may be done in the neonatal intensive care unit (NICU) or in the operating room.

The criteria to be used as guidelines to assess abdominal pressure for safe closure are as follows:

- Intragastric pressure < 20 cm H_2O
- Intravesical pressure < 20 cm H_2O
- End-tidal CO_2 < 50 mmHg
- Maximum ventilatory pressure ≤ 35 cm H_2O

Post-Operative Management

- Post-op ventilation should be considered electively in cases of large defects.
- Compromised hepatic function may markedly affect drug metabolism, especially that of opioids.
- One should also be aware of concomitant congenital abnormalities.
- Enteral nutrition is often delayed because of raised intra-abdominal pressure or because of gastrointestinal (GI) pathology such as atresia and NEC or intra-abdominal sepsis. In these cases, parenteral nutrition is advised.

Other GI emergencies include the following:

- Obstruction
- Compromised intestinal blood supply
- Combination of both

Intestinal Obstruction

The incidence of intestinal obstruction is 1:1,500 and its causes include the following:

- Duodenal or ileal atresia (these are often associated with other anomalies)
- Malrotation with midgut volvulus
- Peritoneal bands where blood supply may be compromised
- Intra-abdominal herniae
- Meconium ileus
- Intussusception (most common after the second month)

Upper Gastrointestinal Tract Obstruction

Midgut volvulus is the most common form of presentation.

Clinical Features

- The neonate presents in the first 24 hours with a tender distended abdomen, bilious vomiting, dehydration, sodium loss, hypochloraemia, metabolic alkalosis and increasing haemodynamic instability.
- Acidosis and the presence of bloody stools are ominous signs.
- Bowel ischaemia and gangrene may be expected.
- Aspiration could be a serious complication.
- Maternal polyhydramnios could give a clue to its presence.

Investigations

- An X-ray may show a 'double bubble' sign in duodenal atresia.
- Diagnosis of volvulus can be confirmed by upper GI ultrasound.

Anaesthetic Management

Mortality for midgut volvulus is as high as 18–25%. Management should start straightaway with aggressive correction of the fluid and electrolyte abnormalities with good peripheral access.

Surgery is urgent in these cases as this is a true emergency. Do not waste time trying to get arterial access, though it is good if one is available. Full stomach precautions to protect the airway and general principles should be followed, as in the case of all sick neonates.

Surgical Management

Surgical repair of the volvulus involves reduction of the volvulus, division of fixation (Ladd) bands between the abnormally located caecum, duodenum and jejunum and widening of the base of the mesentery. Extensive bowel resection may be required in case of bowel gangrene.

Lower Gastrointestinal Obstruction

Obstruction of the lower GIT presents later, usually within 2–7 days (except imperforate anus, which may present at birth). The child presents with abdominal distension and failure to pass faeces or meconium.

There is dehydration which occurs due to sequestration of fluid and electrolytes in the bowel. Vomiting is late. Acidosis is a complicating factor.

Anaesthetic Management

- Delay surgery except with intussusception where vascularity is compromised.
- Correct electrolyte imbalance and dehydration, which may require up to 30–40 ml/kg of colloid.
- Check haematocrit – polycythaemia may be present due to dehydration.
- Protect the airway.
- Avoid N_2O to prevent further distension of the bowel.

Necrotising Enterocolitis

NEC is best described by Kosloske's triad of

- Intestinal ischaemia – necrosis of the bowel leading to perforation and sepsis
- Colonisation of pathogenic bacteria
- Excess protein substrate in the intestinal lumen

Aetiology

- Prenatal asphyxia
- Umbilical artery catheterisation
- Hyperosmolar feeds
- Exchange transfusions
- PDA (patent ductus arteriosus) with decreased blood supply to the bowel

Clinical Presentation

The baby presents with abdominal distension (dilated and distended bowel and pneumoperitoneum; Fig. 6.15), bilious vomiting, ileus, bloody stools, peritonitis, septicaemia, hyper or hypothermia, acidosis, shock, coagulopathy, oliguria and jaundice, episodes of apnoea and bradycardia.

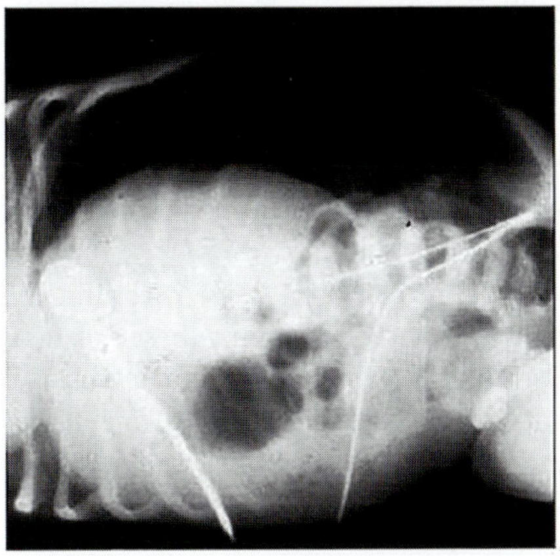

Figure 6.15 Lateral decubitus X-ray showing pneumoperitoneum and dilated bowel.

Lateral decubitus X-rays (Fig. 6.15) show

- fixed dilated intestinal loops,
- pneumatosis intestinalis,
- portal vein air,
- ascites and
- pneumoperitoneum

Both complete blood count and electrolytes may be significantly altered and disseminated intravascular coagulation may also be present

Medical Management

- Gut rest – stop feeds/gastric decompression with an NG tube
- Treat infection with antibiotics
- Nutrition – IV, not oral
- Correct the metabolic acidosis, hypovolaemia and coagulopathy
- Respiratory distress would require ventilation
- Administer platelets, fresh frozen plasma (FFP) and blood (RBC) as indicated

Surgical Management

Surgical management is only required in neonates with evidence of perforation, abdominal mass or abdominal wall erythema. Surgery consists of resection of diseased bowel, stomal formation or primary anastomosis and peritoneal lavage.

Anaesthetic Management

Anaesthetic management focuses on continued resuscitation with fluids and inotropes, blood and blood products, antibiotics and post-op ventilation. An opioid-based anaesthetic is best tolerated.

However, the outcome is poor with a mortality of 10–30%.

A good neonatal intensive care unit and an anaesthetist trained in handling these sick neonates with continuing experience in maintaining skills such as airway management and line placement are essential in ensuring a good outcome for these patients.

SUGGESTED READINGS

1. Ross F, McFadyen G, Budac S, et al. Anaesthesia for Thoracic Surgery. In: Paediatric Anaesthesia, 6th edition. Gregory GA (ed). New Jersey: John Wiley & Sons Ltd 2020; pp. 607–626.
2. Sun LS, Saraiya NR, Philipp J, et al. Anaesthesia for Abdominal Surgery. In: Paediatric Anaesthesia, 6th edition. Gregory GA (ed). New Jersey: John Wiley & Sons Ltd 2020; pp. 793–813.
3. Hammer GB. Anesthesia for Thoracic Surgery. In: A Practice of Anesthesia for Infants and Children, 6th edition. Cote CJ, Lerman J, Anderson BJ (eds). Saunders Elsevier, Philadelphia 2019; pp. 1622–1668.
4. Boat AC, Sadhasivam S. Congenital Diaphragmatic Hernia. In: Clinical Pediatric Anesthesia – A Case Based Handbook. Goldschneider KR, Davidson AJ, Wittkugel EP, Skinner A (eds). Oxford University Press, New York 2012; pp. 551–560.
5. Wheeler M. Neonatal Surgical Emergencies. In: ASA Refresher Course Lectures. American Society of Anesthesiologists 2003; 165:1–7.
6. Rankin L. Tracheoesophageal Fistula Repair. In: Clinical Pediatric Anesthesia – A Case Based Handbook. Goldschneider KR, Davidson AJ, Wittkugel EP, Skinner A (eds). Oxford University Press, New York 2012; pp. 529–540.
7. Stoddart P. Omphalocele and Gastroschisis Repair. In: Clinical Pediatric Anesthesia – A Case Based Handbook. Goldschneider KR, Davidson AJ, Wittkugel EP, Skinner A (eds). Oxford University Press, New York 2012; pp. 541–550.
8. Leininger K, Chiu K. Anesthetic Considerations. In: Congenital Diaphragmatic Hernia. StatPearls, Treasure Island (FL) 2022.
9. Liu H, Le C, Chen J, et al. Anesthetic management of thoracoscopic procedures in neonates: A retrospective analysis of 45 cases. *Transl Pediatr* 2021; 10(8):2035–2043. doi: 10.21037/tp-21-265. PMID: 34584873; PMCID: PMC8429869.
10. Snoek KG, Reiss IK, Greenough A, et al. Standardized Postnatal Management of Infants with Congenital Diaphragmatic Hernia in Europe: The CDH EURO Consortium Consensus - 2015 Update. *Neonatology*. 2016; 110(1):66–74.

7 Fluid Management in the Paediatric Patients

Sajan Philip George • Anita Shirley Joselyn

The approach to fluid management in infants and children is different to that in adults, although recent changes in practice mean that the differences in approach are now less pronounced. Our understanding of the fluid requirements and the effect of the hypotonic fluids in children has helped to modify our practice to ensure a safe anaesthetic for children.

Fluid requirements in children correlate with their increased metabolism and therefore their maintenance requirements are much higher than those in adults. Water and electrolytes in the fluids correct deficits and maintain cardiac output, which will ensure adequate oxygen delivery. In the operating room, the fluid requirements may rapidly change, necessitating frequent assessment and modifications. The composition of fluid compartments, especially the extracellular fluid (ECF) and intracellular fluid (ICF) compartments, varies with age. The plasma compartment as a percentage of body weight, however, remains constant (**Table 7.1**; **Fig. 7.1**).

Table 7.1 Fluid Compartments (% of Body Weight) and Volume Changes with Age

Component	Premature	Neonates	Infant	Adult
Extracellular fluid	50	35	30	20
Intracellular fluid	30	40	40	40
Plasma	5	5	5	5
Total	85	80	75	65

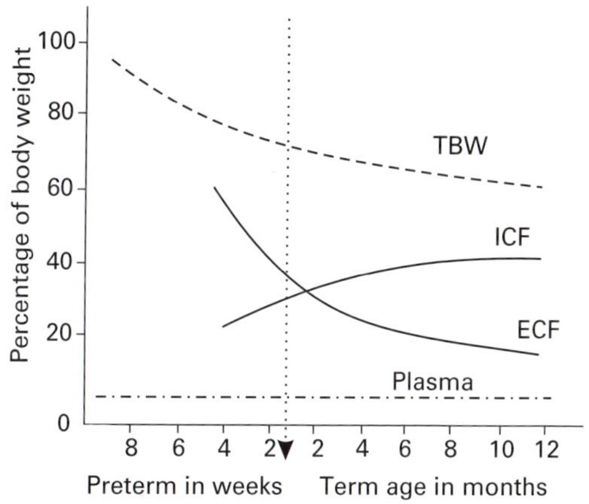

Figure 7.1 Fluid compartment changes with age. Note that the plasma volume remains constant in proportion to the body weight. ECF, extracellular fluid; ICF, intracellular fluid; TBW, total body water.

Fluids are administered for the following purposes:

- **Resuscitation:** Correction of pre-existing hypovolaemia/dehydration (depending on the weather or medical conditions)
- **Maintenance:** Maintaining body functions at a basal rate and is required for four basic reasons:
  - Evaporation from the skin, an essential part of thermoregulation
  - Excretion of waste products from the kidney and the stool
  - Water loss from the respiratory tract
  - Growth
- **Replacement:** Ongoing losses due to evaporation from the surgical wound, humidification of inspired gases, blood loss, hyperthermia and third

space losses (leakage into the tissues) during the intra-operative and post-operative period

Fluid Compartments

The ECF compartment in prematures and infants is much larger than in adults. The intravascular blood or plasma volume and the interstitial fluid form the *functional ECF compartment* with the same electrolyte composition but separated from each other by vascular endothelium. The major difference between these two compartments is that plasma contains protein. Fluid moves freely between the intravascular and interstitium dependent only on mechanical forces such as hydrostatic pressure and oncotic pressure. Movement of fluid in and out of the ICF on the other hand requires energy and is associated with corresponding electrolyte shifts. The intravascular compartment, whose 'size' we monitor by haemodynamic changes of heart rate, blood pressure and central venous pressure, is actually an extension of the large ECF which helps to maintain the intravascular volume as far as possible. When symptoms of hypovolaemia become obvious, it indicates that the large 'buffer compartment' of the ECF is also depleted and cannot replenish the contracted vascular volume.

Incomplete development of the myocardium and immature sympathetic nervous system in young children and babies makes these children more sensitive to hypovolaemia. Myocardial contractility, ventricular compliance and vascular tone are lower and less variable making tachycardia the primary compensatory mechanism during volume depletion. Cardiac output decreases when the limits of tachycardia are reached. Anaesthetic 'depression' further accentuates hypovolaemia and may limit the compensatory sympathetic response and thus the tachycardia. Therefore, the maintenance of effective vascular volume (with replenishment of the ECF) is essential to maintain circulatory function and vital organ perfusion.

Determining Fluid Requirements

Howland in 1911 measured energy consumption in children and concluded that children under 1 year of age (3–10 kg) metabolise 100 kcal/day and older children 75 kcal/day, while adults metabolise only 35 kcal/day.

In 1957, Holliday and Segar reviewed data which correlated calorie requirements with basal metabolism and active energy needs. They concluded that infants in hospital required half their calories for basal metabolism and half for growth. In the infant, the growth requirement is more than that in the older child. Therefore, they suggested that the caloric requirement is

0–10 kg = 100 kcal/kg/day

10–20 kg = 1,000 kcal + 50 cal for each kg over 10 kg but less than 20 kg

20 kg and up = 1,500 kcal + 20 cal for each kg over 20 kg

Metabolism of 1 calorie produces 0.2 ml of water and consumes 1.2 ml of water, so calorie and water consumption are considered equal. For example, a 1-year-old child weighing 10 kg requires 100 kcal/kg/day of energy and 100 ml/kg/day of water.

On transposing this calculation to an hourly basis, total volume/day divided by 24 hours:

0–10 kg = 4 ml/kg/hr of fluid

10–20 kg = 40 ml + 2 ml/kg/hr, above 10 kg but <20 kg

>20 kg = 60 ml + 1 ml/kg/hr >20 kg

This is the commonly used 4/2/1 formula for pre-operative fluid therapy. Fever increases the caloric requirement by 10–12% for every degree centigrade rise in temperature above normal.

Pre-Operative Assessment

Pre-operative assessment of fluid status is a very important part of fluid management and is an essential part of the pre-anaesthesia assessment. Clinically, severity of dehydration is assessed as given in **Table 7.2**.

Four investigations that confirm the type of dehydration are as follows:

1. Serum osmolarity and serum sodium
2. Acid–base status, serum pH and base deficit
3. Serum potassium and correlate with pH
4. Urine output (rule out acute tubular necrosis)

Table 7.2 Clinical Features of Dehydration

Symptoms and Signs	Mild	Moderate	Severe
Weight loss	3–5%	6–9%	>10%
General condition	Alert, restless	Thirsty, lethargic	Cold, sweaty
Pulse	Normal rate, volume	Rapid, weak	Rapid, feeble
Respiration	Normal	Deep, rapid	Deep, rapid
Anterior fontanellae	Normal	Sunken	Very sunken
Systolic pressure	Normal	Normal/low	Low, unrecordable
Skin turgor	Normal	Decreased	Markedly decreased
Eyes	Normal	Sunken, dry	Grossly sunken
Mucous membrane	Moist	Dry	Very dry
Urine output	Adequate	Less, dark coloured	Oliguria, anuria
Capillary refill	Normal	<2 sec	>3 sec
Estimated deficit	30–50 ml/kg	60–90 ml/kg	100 ml/kg

The above investigations will indicate the type of dehydration:

- **Hyponatraemic** (serum osmolarity < 270 mOsm/l, serum Na < 130 mEq/l), children on low sodium containing fluids like Isolyte P or 5% dextrose
- **Isonatraemic** (serum osmolarity 270–300 mOsm/l, serum Na 130–150 mEq/l)
- **Hypernatraemic** (serum osmolarity > 310 mOsm/l, serum Na > 150 mEq/l)

Physiological Compensatory Mechanisms

Various mechanisms in the body attempt to compensate for fluid losses and help maintain circulation. These may be temporary or definitive.

Temporary compensatory mechanisms include production of endogenous vasopressors (such as antidiuretic hormone, angiotensin II and catecholamines), transcapillary refill with fluids shifting from the interstitial compartment to the vascular compartment and ADH causing reabsorption of water from the distal renal tubule. This last mechanism may result in hyponatraemia.

The *definitive compensatory mechanisms* are through the renal system. Twenty-five percent of the cardiac output passes through the kidney. When there are sodium and water deficits, there is almost complete re-absorption of the glomerular filtrate by the distal and collecting tubule seen clinically as a reduction in urine output and an increase in specific gravity. A low blood volume, low blood pressure or a low Na in the distal tubule results in the activation of the renin–angiotensin–aldosterone system, which ensures the re-absorption of Na and water to restore a normovolaemic state and a normal serum Na.

Stress Response in Sick Children

Part of the stress response to illness is the secretion of ADH, as mentioned above, causing water retention by the kidney. In extreme cases, this water retention can lead to cerebral oedema, resulting in confusion, seizures and death. A marker of this problem is hyponatraemia. Children have healthy brains with less space within their cranial vaults for retained water and become symptomatic with sodium levels much higher than the levels at which adults experience symptoms and signs. For this reason, overhydration of sick children with hypotonic fluids such as 4% dextrose and 0.18% NaCl should be avoided as the 'extra' water in these fluids adds to the volume retained by the kidney (this fluid has been removed from many paediatric hospitals because of this problem). Alternative fluids that can be used include 5% dextrose and 0.45% saline, 0.9% saline and Ringer's lactate.

Note: Ringer's lactate contains calcium and may lead to harmful precipitation when administered with some drugs (e.g. ceftriaxone) or blood products.

necessary if the haemoglobin is greater than 10 g/dl and that it is almost always indicated when it is less than 6 g/dl. Although the task force did not consider transfusion in neonates, infants or children, the guidelines still have some applicability for the paediatric practitioner. The exception to this general practice is for neonates and the premature, who have a high concentration of foetal haemoglobin which limits oxygen delivery to tissues. In patients younger than 3 months of age, in whom foetal haemoglobin concentrations may still be high, the anaesthesiologist may consider achieving haemoglobin levels greater than 10 g/dl, especially if the patient is ill, or has apnoea of prematurity. In addition, physiologic anaemia, with a haemoglobin of about 9–11 g/dl, occurs at 8–12 weeks of age in term infants. Preterm infants have a lower, earlier nadir than term babies. Infants with severe cardiopulmonary disease are generally maintained at a haematocrit of 40–45% and at 30–35% if cardiopulmonary disease is not present but major surgery is planned. On the other hand, healthy older children who typically lack cardiac and vascular disease may be able to tolerate even lower haemoglobin levels. Therefore, *guidelines for the necessity of transfusion in children must consider the postnatal age, the specific situation, concomitant illness, the vital signs, adequacy of oxygenation and volume of blood loss.*

According to the Association of Anaesthetists of Great Britain and Ireland (AAGBI) guidelines 2016 for the use of blood components, for almost all children over the age of 3 months, a 'restrictive' approach for transfusion is appropriate. For neonates and children with congenital heart diseases, a higher transfusion threshold can be considered. However, these thresholds are not clearly defined. In the restrictive approach, most clinical trials consider a transfusion trigger of 7.0 or 8.0 g/dl; whereas, in the liberal approach, it is 9.0 or 10.0 g/dl. Most trials also show that the benefit outweigh the risks in a lower trigger such as 6.0–7.0 g/dl as long as there is no ongoing bleeding and patient is haemodynamically stable.

A study on perioperative RBC transfusion in *neonates and infants* called the NECTARINE trial shows an increase in mortality and morbidity in neonates and infants exposed to perioperative RBC transfusions. This trial recommends a transfusion trigger of 10.0–13.0 g/dl, 9.5–12.5 g/dl and 8.5–11.0 g/dl *in the first, second and third week of life,* respectively.

If blood loss is anticipated, it is important to understand the developmental differences in blood volume (**Table 8.1**).

Table 8.1 Expected Blood Volumes (EBV) in Children at Different Ages

Age	EBV (ml/kg)
Preterm	90–100
Full term	80–90
3 mon to 1 yr	70–80
>1 yr	70

Although the infant has a larger blood volume per kilogram than older children, a similar volume of blood lost in an infant generally represents a greater percentage of the patient's blood volume. Knowledge of the patient's circulating blood volume and a baseline haematocrit will allow the clinician to calculate the maximum allowable blood loss (MABL):

$$\text{MABL} = \frac{(\text{Hct starting} - \text{Hct minimum})}{\text{Hct starting}} \times \text{estimated blood volume}$$

The target haemoglobin will vary among patients and clinical circumstances. Because methods of estimating intraoperative blood loss lack precision, it is best to follow serial Hgb/Hct in the perioperative period. These numbers must be evaluated in the clinical context. The measured haemoglobin may be high in a patient who has not been adequately volume resuscitated. On the other hand, aggressive crystalloid replacement may erroneously indicate the need for blood transfusion despite minimal decrement in red cell mass.

A more recent publication from the *American Association of Blood Banks* (AABB) put forward several recommendations for RBC transfusion. Although the recommendations did not address paediatric patients, there are some lessons to be learned. The AABB recommends adhering to a restrictive transfusion strategy (7–8 g/dl) in hospitalised, stable patients. In post-operative surgical patients, transfusion should be considered at a haemoglobin concentration of 8 g/dl or less or for symptoms related to anaemia such as chest pain, orthostatic hypotension or tachycardia unresponsive to fluid resuscitation, or congestive heart failure. Comparable symptoms in an infant that may indicate the need for transfusion include persistent tachypnoea or tachycardia, the need for oxygen therapy or ventilator support, or apnoea and bradycardia unresponsive to methylxanthines.

Once the threshold for transfusion has been reached, how much blood is necessary?

$$\text{Amount of blood to transfuse} = \frac{(\text{Hct desired} - \text{Hct present})}{\text{Hct blood product to transfuse}} \times \text{estimated blood volume}$$

The haematocrit of PRBCs is 60–70%, and for whole blood, it is approximately 35–40%. *Transfusion of PRBCs 10–15 ml/kg will increase haemoglobin 2–3 g/dl.* If a patient requires less than a full unit to reach the desired haematocrit, it may be prudent to transfuse to a higher haematocrit to provide some margin for additional blood loss and to minimise the likelihood of exposure to additional units. Because of the need for small volume transfusion for infants, blood banks may prepare small volume aliquots using a closed system to conserve resources and to minimise the risks of bacterial contamination and of exposure to multiple donors. PRBCs should be ABO compatible but, because of the small plasma volume, do not need to be ABO identical. Rh– females should not receive Rh+ PRBCs to avoid Rh sensitisation.

Whole Blood

Whole blood provides red cells, non-labile coagulation factors and platelets (factors V and VIII are present in lesser amounts, and platelets are rapidly affected by refrigeration). Whole blood may be used in the form of fresh whole blood or modified whole blood. Fresh whole blood is whole blood stored either at room temperature for less than 24 hours or at 4°C for less than a 48-hour period. Whole blood which has undergone leukoreduction and also inactivation of the platelet component is modified whole blood.

The use of whole blood is now replaced with component therapy and the use of crystalloids. The use of whole blood is now reserved for uncommon indications like massive haemorrhage/trauma, exchange transfusion and when there is continued bleeding even after transfusion of four or more units of PRBCs. It is used as a part of damage control resuscitation in areas where it is available. It is indicated in life-threatening massive haemorrhage when there is a symptomatic decrease in oxygen-carrying capacity, and a need for volume expansion, coagulation factors and platelets. Because of the potential presence of isoagglutinins directed against recipient A and/or B antigens in the plasma of whole blood, transfusion of *ABO identical* whole blood is necessary. The use of whole blood is contraindicated in patients with chronic anaemia and cardiac failure due to the risk of volume overload.

Fresh Frozen Plasma

Indications for transfusion of fresh frozen plasma (FFP) include correction of coagulopathy associated with massive blood transfusion, correction of acquired coagulation factor deficiencies, correction of prolonged prothrombin time (PT >1.5 INR), emergency reversal of coumadin (may also respond to vitamin K in non-emergency situations) and specific factor deficiencies when a recombinant factor is not available. FFP contains all factors with factors V and VIII diminishing most rapidly with storage. Thawed FFP may be used for up to 5 days with decreased levels of factors V, VII, VIII and protein S. The dose is usually 15–20 ml/kg, which should increase coagulation factor levels by about 20% for about 5 hours. The usual rate of transfusion is 10–20 ml/kg/hr. Massive blood transfusion in the paediatric patient will result in clinically significant clotting factor deficiency when more than one blood volume has been lost. Early transfusion of FFP and platelets, as part of a massive transfusion protocol, may help prevent coagulopathy. Recent studies in trauma patients with significant bleeding suggest a 1:1:1 ratio of PRBCs, FFP and platelet pheresis units as soon as transfusion begins.

FFP transfusion may not be indicated when INR (International Normalised Ratio) is <1.8 in a non-bleeding, stable patient. Irrespective of the INR, pre-procedure FFP transfusion is not required in minor procedures like peripherally inserted central catheter (PICC) line insertion, bone marrow aspiration, thoracocentesis, paracentesis, etc. In congenital coagulation factor deficiency, after a haematology consult, FFP may be considered if factor concentrate is not available.

FFP must be ABO compatible with the recipient's blood. Rh compatibility is not required.

A major concern of FFP administration is *citrate toxicity* resulting in hypocalcaemia and hypotension. FFP contains more citrate per unit volume than other blood components. This effect is even more profound in the setting of reduced hepatic blood flow and/or function and in neonates because of their reduced ability to metabolise citrate. Neonates may also experience profound hypotension in response to hypocalcaemia due to their immature myocardium. It is recommended that FFP should not be given at a rate of greater than 1 ml/kg/min in the absence of exogenous calcium administration.

Platelets

The indications for platelet transfusion are similar for older infants, children and adults. Platelets may be administered prophylactically prior to major invasive procedures and major surgeries if the platelet count is less than 50×10^9/l or if there is a known defect in platelet function. Platelets are not indicated if platelet count is greater than 100×10^9/l. Prophylactic platelet transfusion for minor surgeries and minor invasive procedures is indicated when the platelet count is $<20 \times 10^9$/l. When the platelet count is between 50 and 100×10^9/l, the decision to transfuse platelets should be based on clinical judgement and on the current situation such as the presence of microvascular bleeding or the high likelihood of platelet dysfunction after cardiopulmonary bypass. For stable term and preterm neonates without other risk factors, the transfusion threshold is a platelet count of $<25 \times 10^9$/l, as higher thresholds showed a higher risk of intraventricular haemorrhage. The threshold is 50×10^9/l for neonates with risk factors such as bleeding, coagulopathies, and surgical prophylaxis, and it is 100×10^9/l for those with major bleeding or requiring major surgery (e.g., neurosurgery). Although infants may bleed at a higher platelet count than older patients because of diminished levels of circulating coagulation factors, most platelet transfusions in infants are given for a platelet count of less than 50×10^9/l in the presence of bleeding. Once the platelet count has dropped to this level, it is likely that approximately 'one platelet dose' (6 units for an adult and 10–20 ml/kg for a child) will be required for each blood volume replaced. A transfusion rate of 10–20 ml/kg/hr is recommended.

Apart from the above indications, medications like aspirin and other non-steroidal anti-inflammatory drugs, dipyridamole, platelet P2Y12 blockers, glycoprotein IIa/IIIb inhibitors, etc., and certain conditions such as renal failure, may cause platelet dysfunction. This may interfere with surgical haemostasis. Hence, we can transfuse platelets in these cases prophylactically to maintain a higher platelet concentration.

Although a rare complication in paediatric cardiac surgery, heparin-induced thrombocytopenia is not an indication for platelet transfusion.

Platelets may be derived from a single unit of blood, that is, random donor platelets which provide 5.5×10^{10} platelets in 50–70 ml of plasma at a concentration that is two to four times greater than in the circulation or from a single donor (i.e. apheresis platelets). The apheresis product provides platelets equivalent to six units of random donor platelets in 200–400 ml of plasma. Platelets are stored at 20–24°C with gentle continuous agitation for a maximum of 7 days from the collection date. *Platelets contain ABO antigens, but not Rh antigens*, on their surface. ABO-matched platelets should be used whenever possible to limit immune destruction by the recipient. Because of the small volume of RBCs in the plasma, transfusion of Rh-mismatched platelets can lead to alloimmunisation. If the administration of platelets from an Rh+ donor to an Rh– female of childbearing age becomes necessary, Rh immune globulin is recommended to minimise the potential for haemolytic disease of the newborn with future pregnancies.

Platelet doses of 10 ml/kg can be expected to increase platelet count by $50–100 \times 10^9$/l. Platelets must be infused through a 170–260 μ filter. Microaggregate filters (20–40 μ) should not be used as they will remove most of the platelets. Platelets are preferably not transfused in tubing used for

PRBCs, as they adhere to the fibrin captured by the filter. It is not recommended that platelets be infused through fluid-warming devices. However, data that show a detrimental effect of these devices on platelets are scarce.

Cryoprecipitate

Cryoprecipitate provides factors VIII and XIII, von Willebrand factor and fibrinogen. It may be used for patients with congenital hypofibrinogenaemia (if fibrinogen concentrate is not available), acquired hypofibrinogenaemia secondary to bleeding, disseminated intravascular coagulation or liver dysfunction, haemophilia A in the absence of factor concentrate and von Willebrand disease unresponsive to desmopressin acetate (DDAVP). It is also used in severe hypofibrinogenaemia of <1.5 g/l. Dosage in paediatric patients is generally 5–10 ml/kg for body weight up to 15 kg. For weight over 15 kg, a maximum of 10 units of adult dose can be used (each unit volume is 5–15 ml).

If *fibrinogen concentrate* is available, it can be used at a dose of 70 mg/kg. It is manufactured from plasma and does not require a group screening.

Prothrombin Complex Concentrate

It is a balanced concentrate containing either three-factor (II, low VII, IX, X and proteins C&S) or four-factor (II, high VII, IX, X and proteins C&S) human plasma-derived products. It is mainly used in adults; paediatric use is limited. It is indicated in an urgent reversal of vitamin K-based anticoagulants (warfarin) when INR is >1.5 and the patient is bleeding or has to undergo an urgent or major surgical procedure. Non-urgent reversal of warfarin is usually managed with vitamin K alone. The dose of prothrombin complex concentrate (PCC) used is 25–50 IU/kg for children weighing <40 kg. It is administered along with vitamin K. It is transfused at a rate of 1 ml/minute for the initial 15 minutes and subsequently increased to not more than 3 ml/minute.

Massive Transfusion

Rapid and massive transfusion is not unusual in children undergoing craniofacial, liver transplant, trauma, and some cardiovascular and orthopaedic surgeries. Massive transfusion is defined as 100% of the total blood volume transfused over a 24-hour period or 50% of the total blood volume over a 12-hour period. Massive transfusion protocol recommends the use of PRBCs, plasma and platelets in the ratio 1:1:1 unit, with increased use of plasma and less use of crystalloids in the first 24 hours. The underlying cause of bleeding should be concomitantly managed.

Transfusion of large quantities of blood components can affect coagulation, potassium and calcium concentrations, acid–base balance, oxygen-carrying capacity and body temperature.

Large volume transfusion increases the likelihood of *hypothermia*. The paediatric patient has a high underlying risk of hypothermia due to the large surface area to weight ratio. Forced air warming, maintaining a high ambient room temperature and humidification of inhaled gases may help to keep the child normothermic, but if transfusion of cold blood products is involved, fluid-warming devices must be used. Devices used in the adult population may be adapted for paediatric use.

Conventional fluid warmers utilise a coiled system of tubing traversing warming plates. This type of warmer is adequate for blood administration at slower rates. One must remember that the priming volume of such an administration set is high in relation to the smallest patients' blood volume. When priming with crystalloid, it is prudent to disconnect from the patient and discard the primed crystalloid prior to transfusion so as to avoid an unintentional crystalloid bolus. Conventional warmers of this type have high resistance to flow and require a pressure bag or manual assistance in order to administer blood rapidly. Manual assistance via 22- or 24-gauge IV catheters is most efficient, with rapid withdrawal and injection of fluids utilising a 10 ml syringe in lieu of another size syringe or manual compression of a pressure pump chamber included in some adult blood administration tubing sets. Newer generation heating plate-type warmers such as the Ranger (Arizant Healthcare, Eden Prarie, MN, USA) are able to deliver fluids more rapidly than their conventional counterparts with the use of specialised high-flow disposables.

Other means of warming blood products prior to administration include devices that incorporate counter current heat exchange (tube within a tube of hot water) such as the Hot Line (Level-1

Technologies, Rockland, MA, USA) and the Level-1 infusion system. The FMS 2000 (Belmont Industries, Belmont Inc, Billerica, MA, USA) utilises magnetic induction for heating of fluids and is most useful in anticipated cases of massive transfusion with multiple blood products. Recent military advances have resulted in the development of alternative means of heating rapidly infused fluids such as the rapid infusion warmer (Rocky Research, Boulder City, NV, USA), which uses an exothermic reaction between ammonia and salt and can use battery power. Although these new technological devices have not been studied for use in children, they can be adapted for smaller patients. A very important adaptation is the assurance of air removal, especially in warming devices that utilise delivery under pressure. A seemingly small volume of air, when delivered to a child, may result in haemodynamically significant venous air embolus or even delivery of air to the systemic circulation via a patent foramen ovale, which is more prevalent in children than in adults.

Transfusion-related *hyperkalaemia* has resulted in fatal cardiac dysrhythmias in children more frequently than in adults, with the highest prevalence being in the age group of 1–5 years, due to a rapid rise in serum potassium when potassium-rich blood is combined with the relatively small blood volume of a child. Blood components with the highest potassium concentration include units approaching their expiry date, irradiated units and whole blood. Hence, it depends on the storage age, blood type, volume transfused in 12 hours and modification of the units, that is, leukoreduced, irradiated, washed and supernatant reduced. The incidence of transfusion-associated hyperkalaemia is much less when a normal infusion rate (10–15 ml/kg) is followed, whereas it is often linked with massive transfusion or exchange transfusion. Therefore, the AABB recommends that PRBC transfusion to smaller infants, particularly neonates, should be limited to units less than 5 days old (the typical shelf life of a unit of PRBCs is 42 days). The 1-day mortality rate in transfusion-associated hyperkalaemia was found to be 20%, and patients with multiple comorbidities were at a higher risk. Washing of erythrocytes effectively lowers the potassium concentration and should be utilised when newer PRBC units are not available or irradiation of the unit is necessary.

Most blood banks have a protocol for the emergency release of blood products. Group O Rh-negative blood can be safely used without the need for cross-matching in such situations.

Recent advances show that the use of recombinant factor VIIa, FFP, cryoprecipitate, fibrinogen concentrate and PCC can help in preventing coagulopathies. The use of antifibrinolytics such as tranexamic acid has also proved to be helpful.

Complications of Blood Transfusion

The more common complications of blood component transfusion are as follows:

- Hyperkalaemia
- Hypocalcaemia and citrate toxicity
- Hypothermia
- Acid–base imbalance
- Acute respiratory distress syndrome
- Deep vein thrombosis (in platelet transfusion)
- Multi-organ failure and death in critically ill patients

The incidence of transfusion-associated complications has evolved over time as donor exclusion and testing have decreased infectious risk. The more uncommon complications are:

Infectious complications

HIV infection	1:1,900,000
HCV infection	1:1,700,000
HBV infection	1:1,000,000
Human T lymphotrophic virus infection	1:2,700,000
Bacterial contamination of RBCs	1:50,000

Non-infectious complications

Fatal haemolysis	1:500,000
Transfusion-related acute lung injury	1:10,000
Transfusion-associated circulatory overload	1:1,000
Febrile non-haemolytic reaction	1:100
Allergic (urticarial)	1:100
Delayed haemolysis	1:1,600

Transfusion Reactions

The majority of non-infectious transfusion-related deaths result from ABO incompatibility. The most common site of physician error resulting in fatal haemolytic transfusion reaction is the operating room. Clerical error is the cause of many of these deaths. Because of this, meticulous observation of blood-checking protocols is necessary, and transfusion of any blood product, even autologous blood, should not be considered risk-free.

Infants do not develop antibodies to ABO antigens in the first 4 months of life. As a result, they are at a low risk of developing a major haemolytic transfusion reaction. They may, however, have circulating maternal antibodies. In addition, Rh (D) antigen is very immunogenic and sensitisation has been reported in infants. Transfusion of O-negative RBCs, AB-negative platelets and FFP to all infants less than 4 months of age is a safe option and is practised by many blood banks. An alternative is to provide type-specific blood, if maternal antibodies are not detectable, in order to conserve O group blood which may be in short supply.

Infections

The largest overall infection risk in transfusion is bacterial transmission with platelet administration (1:2,000 with sepsis occurring in 1:75,000). Platelets are stored at room temperature for up to 7 days from the date of collection. The bacterial infectious risk increases with the age of the product and the number of donor units. Testing for bacterial contamination is available. In addition, it is highly recommended that once the seal of any blood product is broken (i.e. with onset of transfusion), any remainder of that unit should be discarded after 4 hours. Exposure to room temperature and contamination which naturally occurs once a unit is punctured for transfusion allows bacterial proliferation and a higher risk of transmission to the recipient if continued after the 4-hour limit.

Transfusion-Associated Graft-vs-Host Disease (TA-GVHD)

Because of the parents' desire to minimise perceived risks of transfusion and paediatric providers' interest in family-centred care, directed donation of blood may be offered to parents. Transfusion of blood from first-degree relatives or to immunocompromised patients may lead to transfusion-associated graft-vs-host disease (TA-GVHD). This occurs because donor lymphocytes are not recognised as foreign by the recipient. Donor lymphocytes then proliferate and can attack recipient tissue. Symptoms typically begin 8–10 days after transfusion and include rash, fever, enterocolitis with watery diarrhoea, elevated liver function tests (LFTs) and pancytopenia. This serious and often fatal complication can be avoided by irradiation of blood prior to transfusion. Other groups requiring irradiated blood include preterm infants, stem cell or bone marrow transplant recipients, and patients with congenital immunodeficiencies, haematologic malignancies or solid tumours in addition to those receiving blood from a first-degree relative. Of note, leucocyte reduction technologies (i.e. filtration), though reducing the number of transfused lymphocytes, do not eliminate the risk of TA-GVHD.

Combining Strategies to Minimise Homologous Blood Use

Posterior spinal fusion is a procedure with risk for significant blood loss. Transfusion of bank blood is common. However, there are many potential opportunities to combine strategies to minimise the need for bank blood.

Autologous pre-donation is an option in the paediatric population, although some adjustments need to be made for smaller teens and children. Considering the reduced blood volume, it may be necessary to remove less than a full unit of blood. Whole blood collection bags contain 50 ml of preservative for an intended total of 500 ml once 450 ml of blood have been withdrawn.

Utilising the MABL formula can assist in determining how much blood can safely be removed from a patient:

$$\text{MABL} = \frac{(\text{Hct starting} - \text{Hct lowest acceptable pre-operatively})}{\text{Hct starting}} \times \text{Estimated blood volume}$$

(e.g. for a 30 kg patient, with a pre-operative haematocrit of 33, whose blood volume is 2,250 ml, if one decides that 30 is the lowest acceptable haematocrit with which to start the operation, the amount to be withdrawn is 33–30/33 × 2,250 or 204 ml, a significant amount less than a standard whole blood unit of 450 ml).

If the autologous donation is done far enough in advance of the planned surgery (at least 6 weeks), erythropoietin (EPO) may be used to allow repeated donations, but the likelihood of cooperation with multiple blood draws and injection of EPO diminishes in general in the very young.

Directed donation, especially from parents, is a popular request before major elective surgery. If the blood from a first-degree relative is irradiated, there should be no additional risk in this situation. Some have suggested that those donors who give frequently and are therefore tested frequently may present less infectious risk, but this has not been proved.

After induction of anaesthesia, whole blood can be removed and replaced with colloid or crystalloid. Normovolaemic haemodilution allows the patient to lose more dilute blood during the operation. The blood can then be replaced with the autologous whole blood with active platelets and coagulation factors towards the completion of the procedure. Care must be taken to minimise bacterial contamination, to avoid coagulation by using a system with the appropriate preservative/anticoagulant and to remove the desired volume of blood by weighing the bag as blood is withdrawn.

For spinal fusion surgery, surgical factors influence blood loss. Positioning of the patient with the abdomen free from external compression can decrease the collateral blood flow through Batson's plexus and decrease intraoperative blood loss. Infiltration of the skin and subcutaneous tissue with a dilute solution of local anaesthetic containing adrenaline can decrease blood loss during opening. The skill of the surgical team in this and other major operations is also crucial.

Deliberate hypotension can also decrease surgical blood loss. It should, however, be used with caution when using haemodilution because the combination may lead to impaired oxygen delivery to tissues. This risk is difficult to monitor because our indicators of end-organ wellness are rather crude and tend to reveal tissue hypoxia only after it has occurred.

Cell salvage can be utilised intraoperatively to re-infuse shed blood. It is best used for large volume blood loss since the size of the equipment limits the use of this technology for smaller patients. Pharmacologic adjuvants such as epsilon aminocaproic acid (Amicar) and tranexamic acid have been safely used in children but studies have shown inconsistent benefits.

SUGGESTED READINGS

1. Technical Manual, 18th edition. Mark K. Fung (ed). AABB 2014.
2. Cote CJ, Lerman J, Anderson BJ. Strategies for blood product management, reducing transfusions, and massive blood transfusion. In: A Practice of Anesthesia for Infants and Children, 6th edn. Cote CJ, Lerman J, Todres ID, eds. Saunders Elsevier, Philadelphia, 2019; pp. 1212–1336.
3. Dressler AM, Finck CM, Carroll CL, Bonnani CC, Spinella PC. Use of a massive blood transfusion protocol with hemostatic resuscitation for severe intra operative bleeding in a child. *J Pediatr Surg* 2010; 45:1530–1533.
4. Riskin DJ, et al. Massive transfusion protocols: The role of aggressive resuscitation versus product ratio in mortality reduction. *J Am Coll Surg* 2009; 209:198–205.
5. Spinella PC, Holcomb JR. Resuscitation and transfusion principles for traumatic haemorrhagic shock. *Blood Rev* 2009; 23:231–240.
6. Mo YD, Bahar B, Jacquot C. Intrauterine, neonatal and pediatric transfusion therapy. *Ann Blood* 2022; 7:13.
7. Zhou H, Lan J, Zhu H, et al. Evaluation for perioperative blood transfusion during major abdominal procedures in a pediatric population: A Retrospective Observation Cohort Study. *Transfus Med Hemother* 2020; 47:68–74.
8. Klein AA, Arnold P, Bingham RN, et al. AAGBI guidelines: The use of blood components and their alternatives 2016. *Anaesthesia* 2016; 71:829–842.
9. Durandy Y. Use of blood products in pediatric cardiac surgery. *Artif Organs* 2015; 39(1):21–27.
10. Fuchs A. Peri-operative red blood cell transfusion in neonates and infants: Neonate and Children audit of Anaesthesia pRactice IN Europe (NECTARINE). *Eur J Anaesthesiol* 2022; 39:252–260.
11. Yamada C, Edelson MF, Lee AC, et al. Transfusion-associated hyperkalemia in pediatric population: Prevalance, risk factors, survival, infusion rate and RBC unit features. *Transfusion* 2021; 61: 1093–1101.

12. Evangelista ME, Gaffley M, Neff LP. Massive transfusion protocols for pediatric patients: Current perspectives. *J Blood Med* 2020; 11:163–172.
13. S Blain, N Paterson. Paediatric massive transfusion, *BJA Educ* 2016; 16:269–275.
14. Barcelona SL, Thompson AA, Coté CJ. Intraoperative pediatric blood transfusion therapy: A review of common issues. Part II: Transfusion therapy, special considerations, and reduction of allogenic blood transfusion. *Ped Anesth* 2005; 15:814–830.

9 Laboratory Investigations in Paediatrics – What, When and Why

Rebecca Jacob

The main purpose of pre-operative investigations is to provide additional and prognostic information to supplement the clinical history of the patient establishing a baseline measurement for later reference. They provide information that confirms or questions the current clinical management. They help to guide perioperative therapy and could predict post-operative complications, thus helping to reduce the morbidity of surgery.

Pre-operative investigations also provide opportunistic screening that is unrelated to surgery. However, studies on adults have shown that most abnormalities found on pre-operative lab tests are clinically unimportant so much so that many clinicians do not follow-up the results they have routinely ordered. Those that are important can usually be predicted from a complete history and physical examination. Many studies have compared the yield from indicated (warranted from history, i.e. risk group) versus unindicated (unwarranted) pre-operative testing. Few unindicated tests yield beneficial changes in pre-operative care. In fact, the more tests ordered, the higher the possibility of an abnormal result with a greater likelihood of the physician pursuing a borderline false positive. For example, Roizen et al. in a retrospective study on chest radiographs in 66 patients found that 386 extra chest X-rays were ordered without the indication of need and only one abnormality of elevated hemidiaphragm with phrenic nerve palsy was seen. On the other hand, three lung 'shadows' led to three sets of invasive procedures including one thoracotomy with no discovery of disease! They, therefore, say that the primary problem with ordering a battery of tests for all patients is that the lab tests are not very good screening devices for disease; their results are costly to pursue, they add new risks to the patient, increase medico-legal risk to the physician and render operating rooms (ORs) inefficient!

The American Society of Anaesthesiologists (ASA) in their published guidelines on pre-anaesthetic evaluation conclude: '*Routine pre-operative tests (i.e. tests intended to discover a disease or disorder in an asymptomatic patient) do not make an important contribution to the process of perioperative assessment and management of the patient by the anaesthesiologist*'.

A typical example of this is the review by O'Connor and Drasner. They found that out of 486 patients, 5 cases were cancelled due to abnormal testing (**Table 9.1**) and 48 cancelled due to medical reasons.

Therefore, it is imperative that benefit/risk strategies for testing guidelines are developed in keeping with good history taking and clinical examination taking into account the complexity of the surgery/procedure being undertaken.

In 2003, The National Institute of Clinical Excellence published guidelines for routine testing in adults. Eleven tests were considered as routine, which include plain chest X-ray, 12-lead ECG, full blood count (FBC), tests of haemostasis, serum urea, creatinine and electrolytes, random glucose, urine analysis (UA), blood gases, lung function tests, pregnancy tests and sickle cell haemoglobin (Hb) tests. There is no mention of liver function test other than tests of haemostasis.

In the light of the above, let us now look at the commonly ordered laboratory tests and their relevance in children.

Table 9.1 Details of Patients Whose Surgery Was Cancelled Due to Abnormal Laboratory Tests

Age	Clinical Presentation	Investigation	Treatment	Outcome
21 months	Clinically healthy	Hb 9.4 g/dl	Iron therapy	Surgery 1 month later
2 months	34-Week gestation, clinically healthy	Hb 8.0 g/dl	Iron to 10.5 g/dl	Surgery 2 months later
3 months	Clinically healthy	UA-, WBC+ Trace Bacteria	No suprapubic aspiration	Surgery postponed Emergency incarcerated hernia
3 months	Clinically healthy	UA multiple organisms	On antibiotics	Surgery 2 months later. Still clinically healthy
7 years	Clinically healthy	Prolonged PTT	Detailed testing	T&A 5 months later. Still prolonged PTT

PTT, prothrombin time; T&A, tonsillectomy and adenoidectomy; UA, urine analysis; WBC, white blood cell.

Haemoglobin

The primary purpose of perioperative Hb testing is to identify an underlying disease process, which may increase perioperative morbidity and mortality. It is also useful in estimating allowable blood loss during major surgery. Most of the published data come from the west. While interpreting the data, one sees that the data that come from institutions working with poor and migrant populations would appear to be similar to that from developing countries. Again, one cannot generalise the data as the influence of urban development and education plays a major role in nutritional anaemia.

Anaemia

Anaemia is defined as an Hb concentration that is <2 standard deviations below the mean for the normal population. It is one of the most common medical conditions encountered by the anaesthetist. In India, malnutrition and worm infestation are the most common causes of chronic anaemia in children. It has been suggested that the limited capacity of blood to transport oxygen to the tissues in anaemic patients may be directly related to anaesthetic morbidity and mortality increasing the cardiac workload and increasing the incidence of intraoperative hypoxia (consensus conference on perop red cell transfusion, JAMA 1988). Two compensatory mechanisms offset the limited capacity of the anaemic blood to transport oxygen to the tissues: a rightward shift of the oxyhaemoglobin dissociation curve and an increase in the cardiac output. The magnitude of the compensatory changes depends on the severity of the anaemia. However, the cardiac output only increases when the Hb is <9 g/l, and many children with chronic anaemia as in renal disease deny any symptoms of anaemia. It has also been suggested that anaesthetists cannot reliably identify those outpatients who are anaemic.

Healthy children of 3 years of age and older scheduled for minor surgery need not be tested for anaemias. There is no evidence to suggest that mild or moderate anaemia contributes to perioperative morbidity; these cases are generally of short duration, blood loss negligible and the cost per analysis an issue of concern.

Routine pre-op Hb testing rarely influences the conduct of anaesthesia (deferral or outcome) for minor surgical procedures but when a patient presents with a low Hb, the anaesthetist is in a dilemma as to whether to proceed or not. Historically, an Hb level of 10 g/l has been the cut-off for safe anaesthesia and surgery although there is no consensus and no absolute guidelines on the issue. In neonates and infants, on the other hand, there is evidence that there is a high incidence of cardiac arrests with an Hb <10 g/l, so much so that Hb testing in them is justified. Anaemia in the neonatal period could be due to recent blood loss, isoimmunisation, congenital haemolytic anaemia or congenital infection. Anaemia, first detected at 3–6 months after birth, suggests a congenital disorder of Hb synthesis or structure.

Recommendations for Hb Estimation

For all the reasons discussed in the preceding text, it is recommended that Hb estimations should only be done in neonates and infants for anything other than minor surgery and in older children who will undergo surgical procedures with a potential for blood loss, those with clinically suggestive chronic illness or haemoglobinopathies, former preterm infants or those under 6 months of age. *Refer also to Chapter 8.*

White Blood Cell Counts

White blood cell (WBC) counts help in early identification of an infectious process. In the study by O'Connor and Drasner[1], 13 out of 486 children had abnormal WBC counts. One was apparently due to otitis media. Twelve were unexplained and did not have it followed up or the surgery cancelled. Thus, the investigation had no bearing on the management! We suggest that routine WBC count is unnecessary unless it is definitely indicated by history and clinical examination, for example, immunosuppressed children for transplantation, or will change the course of therapy like cancellation of cardiac surgery.

Chest X-Ray

Before the late 1970s, chest X-ray was a routine pre-operative requirement for elective surgery. After various studies showed that very few clinically important abnormalities were revealed by X-ray, the American Academy of Paediatrics recommended the elimination of this requirement. This change has reduced radiation exposure in children and saves both time and money. However, there is a codicil to this in developing countries. We see a lot more of tuberculosis, bronchiectasis, lung abscess and hydatid cyst of the lung than in the west. So a good clinical history and clinical examination with a high index of suspicion may mandate a chest X-ray even in a patient for minor surgery like a lymph node biopsy.

Renal Function Tests

Renal function tests include UA as well as measurement of serum levels of urea, creatinine and electrolytes.

Urine Analysis

The UA includes measurement of specific gravity and dipstick readings for LN (leucocyte/nitrite). The LN measures leukocyte esterase and nitrite, which are markers for WBC and bacteria, respectively. If positive, follow-up with microscopic examination for WBC, casts and RBCs. If indicated by clinical markers, look for protein and myoglobin. Difficulty in urine collection and interpretation with little influence on surgical management/outcome suggests that *routine UA testing adds little to the pre-op evaluation of the healthy child.*

Urea and Creatinine

Blood urea nitrogen (BUN) is a breakdown product of protein, and its level varies directly with the protein intake. Its level increases in clinical conditions such as gastrointestinal bleeding, sepsis, dehydration and corticosteroid administration and falls in cases of starvation, malnutrition, muscle wasting and liver disease. The BUN increases sharply in cases of acute renal failure and more slowly in cases of chronic renal failure. Interpretation of BUN values must thus rely on a change over time rather than on absolute values, considering concomitant conditions.

Creatinine is the breakdown product of muscle. Its level rises by 1–2 mg/dl/day but this is cleared by the kidney. Values higher than 2 mg/dl/day may be seen in rhabdomyolysis. Its absolute value and along with change over time is a much more reliable indicator of the underlying renal function than BUN levels. Creatinine clearance as measured from the urine is a better indicator of renal function.

Serum Electrolytes

Serum electrolytes reflect renal and hormonal status. Hyperkalaemia may warn of impending arrhythmias and the need for caution with the use of blood and blood products. Hyponatraemia has been implicated in increased seizure activity. Hypocalcaemia is seen in renal failure. HCO_3 levels help to ascertain the acid/base status.

It is important to do the above tests both in cases of suspected renal impairment or when a major surgery is planned, in which muscle and tissue trauma along with blood replacement and massive fluid shifts are expected. It is also wise to have baseline values of renal function tests (RFTs) when the use of contrast media is planned, as contrast media can precipitate or worsen renal failure.

Blood Sugar

Hypoglycaemia may be seen in neonates and preemies. Other than in these patients' routine blood sugar estimation is not necessary unless indicated by history and clinical findings.

Liver Function Tests

Liver function tests are not done routinely. However, they are useful in detecting hypoalbuminaemia, which will influence drug and fluid therapy.

Tests of Haemostasis

These are only indicated if there is a strong clinical or family history of bleeding, major surgery or contemplation of neuraxial regional blockade or regional catheter placement.

Lung Function Tests

Lung function tests are expensive. Also, it is very difficult to perform and interpret lung function tests in very young children. Children over 6 years (school-going) may be able to do spirometry tests. These tests should only be done, if indicated, in children with spine deformities, those undergoing spinal surgery, or those requiring thoracotomy for lung or mediastinal surgery.

Blood Gas Analysis

Blood gas analysis is only to be undertaken if definitely indicated by history, clinical findings or in those cases with respiratory disease coming for lung or cardiac surgery.

A room air pulse oximeter saturation is extremely helpful. A baseline saturation of 95% or less is suggestive of clinically important pulmonary or cardiac compromise and should be further investigated.

Advanced Radiological Investigations

Advanced radiological investigations include a CT scan or an MRI; these are done only if definitely indicated by history or clinical findings or if the surgery contemplated warrants.

Conclusion

An operation represents physiological stress. The magnitude of the physiological stress increases with the invasiveness of the procedure. Therefore, we need to assess the need for laboratory investigations in relation to the severity of surgery.

The following grades indicate the severity of surgery with clinical examples and the laboratory investigations are recommended:

- **Grade 1. Minor:** For example,
  - Circumcision and MRI
  - No investigations required
- **Grade 2. Intermediate:** For example,
  - Herniotomy – Hb
  - Tonsillectomy – Hb, platelets, bleeding time, prothrombin time and activated partial thromboplastin time
  - Repair of cleft lip and cleft palate – Hb
- **Grade 3. Major:** For example,
  - Augmentation cystoplasty – Hb, platelets, cross-matching, urea, electrolytes, creatinine and UA
  - Excision hepatoma – Hb, cross-matching, liver function tests, urea, electrolytes, creatinine, UA, random blood glucose and haemostasis tests – platelets, bleeding time, prothrombin time and activated partial thromboplastin time
- **Grade 4. Major + surgery:** For example,
  - Thoracotomy – lung surgery, neurosurgery, cardiac surgery, Hb, cross-matching, chest X-ray, urea, creatinine, UA, haemostasis tests, lung function tests for thoracotomy (in older children), arterial blood gases and pulse oximetry

Recommendations for Pre-Op Lab Testing

Grade 1 or 2 surgery: Pre-operative laboratory investigations are not recommended *unless indicated by history and clinical findings.*

Grade 3 or 4 surgery: Table 9.2 shows the investigations that are routinely asked for (+) and not asked for (–); others may be asked for depending on history and clinical findings (+/-).

Table 9.2 Recommendations for Pre-Operative Lab Testing

Investigations	<6 months	6 months to 1 year	1–5 years	5–12 years	12–16 years
Chest X-ray	–	–	–	–	–
ECG	–	–	–	–	–
FBC	+	+	+	+	+
Haemostasis	±	±	±	±	±
RFT	+	+	+	+	+
RBS	+	+	–	–	–
UA	+	+	+	+	+

Routinely asked for (+) and not asked for (–); others may be asked for depending on history and clinical findings (±).
FBC, full blood count; RBS, random blood sugar; RFT, renal function test; UA, urine analysis.

REFERENCE

1. O'Connor ME, Drasner K. Preoperative laboratory testing of children undergoing elective surgery. *Anaesth Anal* 1990; 70:176.

SUGGESTED READINGS

1. Preoperative tests – the use of routine preoperative tests for elective surgery: National Institute of Clinical Excellence, NICE June 2003 Guidelines. Developed by National Collaborating Center for Acute Care. Available at: https://pubmed.ncbi.nlm.nih.gov/21089235/ (accessed on 01 July 2023).
2. Carlisle J, Langham J, Thomas G. Guidelines for routine preoperative testing (Ed 1). *BJA* 2004; 93:495–497.
3. Munro J, Booth A, Nicholl J. Routine preoperative testing: a systematic review of the evidence. *Health Technol Assess* 1997; 1(12):i–iv;1–62.
4. American Society of Anesthesiologists. Statement on routine Preoperative laboratory and diagnostic screening. American Society of Anesthesiologists 1993. Available from: http://www.asahq.org/Standards/28.html. (accessed 01 March 2022)
5. American Society of Anesthesiologists. Practice advisory for pre-anaesthetic evaluation: a report by the American Society of Anesthesiologists Task Force on Preanesthesia Evaluation. *Anesthesiology* 2002; 96(2):485–496.
6. NHS Executive. Clinical guidelines using clinical guidelines to improve patient care within the NHS. 1996. London, NHS Executive.
7. Steward DJ. Screening test before surgery in children. *Can J Anaesth* 1991; 38:693.
8. Marcello PW, Roberts PL. 'Routine' preoperative. Which studies in which patients? *Surg Clin North Am* 1996; 76(1):11–23.

10 Vascular Access in Children

Anne Poornachand • Vibhavari Naik

Vascular access in children is particularly challenging because of their smaller size and limited cooperation. Parental presence can further add to the difficulty if they are anxious. However, vascular access is an essential and integral part of perioperative care. Assessment and planning for vascular access should begin with pre-anaesthesia evaluation. This chapter covers the types and techniques of vascular access.

Pain during cannulation as well as anxiety needs to be addressed. Sucrose and non-nutritive sucking can help neonates. The distraction of the older child with toys, balloons or mobile phone cartoon videos can ease the vascular access procedure. Pre-application of local anaesthetic creams (lignocaine and prilocaine or tetracaine) helps reduce the needle prick pain. Application of an occlusive dressing (Fig. 10.1) at least 45 minutes prior to puncture is desirable. General anaesthesia may be required for some advanced access procedures.

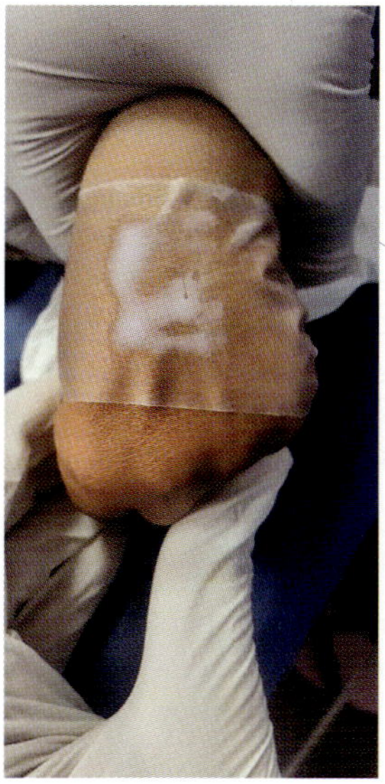

Figure 10.1 Occlusive dressing with a eutectic mixture of lignocaine and prilocaine on the desired cannula puncture site.

Types of Vascular Access

Vascular access can be venous or arterial. Figure 10.2 depicts the types of vascular access and the most used sites. Venous access can be further classified as peripheral or central venous access based on the location of the tip of a catheter. It is considered central if the tip of the catheter lies at the cavoatrial junction or in the inferior vena cava. Alternatively, based on the duration of catheter dwell time, vascular access is classified as short, intermediate and long term. The infusate characteristics that preclude the use of peripheral venous administration and require central venous access are shown in Table 10.1.

Table 10.1 Infusate Characteristics that Require Central Vein for Administration

Osmolarity of solution (mOsm/L)	>600 to 750
pH of infusate	<5 or >9
Dextrose concentration	>10%
Irritant and vesicant drugs	Require central vein
Tonicity of solution	Hypertonic solution

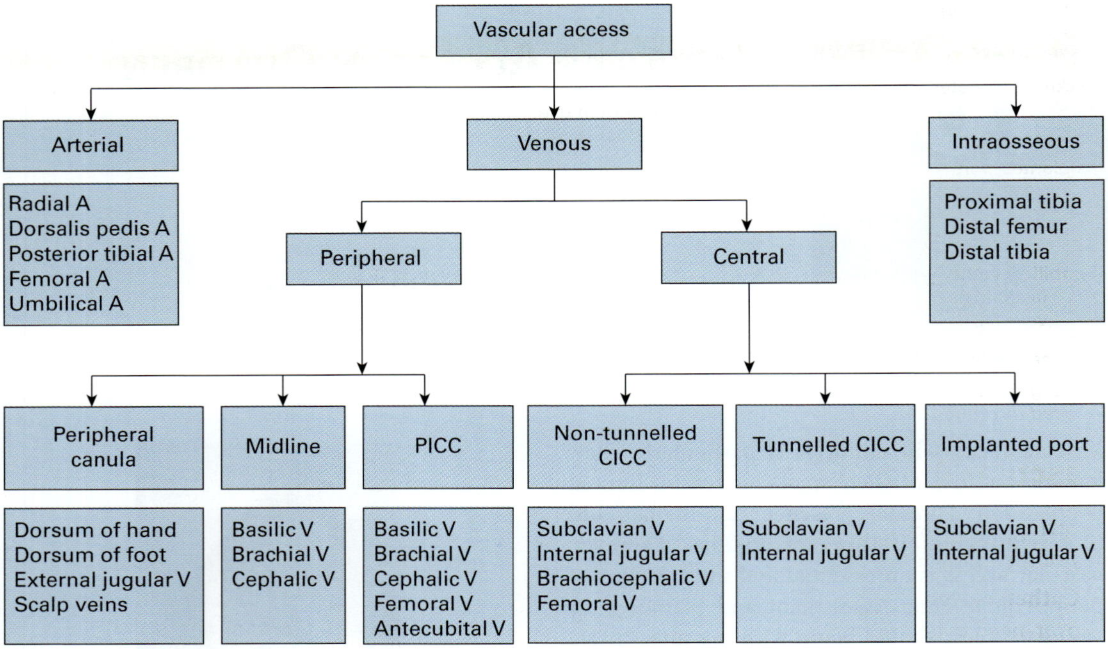

Figure 10.2 Types of vascular access and most used sites. A, artery; CICC, centrally inserted central catheter; PICC, peripherally inserted central catheter; V, vein.

Aseptic Precautions

Aseptic precautions must be followed during the insertion of intravascular catheters. It starts with hand hygiene of the personnel involved. Hand hygiene is best achieved with soap and water or alternately with a chlorhexidine-alcohol-based solution. Clean gloves are sufficient for peripheral cannula placement. Sterile gloves, skin paint with an antiseptic solution and a sterile towel are required for arterial line placement. Maximum sterile barrier precautions with sterile gloves and full-body sterile drapes are recommended during the placement of central venous catheters. The skin of the patient can be prepared with chlorhexidine, alcohol 70% or povidone-iodine. For infants <2 months of age where the safety of chlorhexidine has not been established, 70% alcohol may be used. During the access to these devices, an aseptic non-touch technique is advised. Hubs should be cleaned with a 2% chlorhexidine or 70% alcohol wipe for 30 seconds and allowed to dry before access. Flushing of catheters helps maintain patency. **Table 10.2** describes the flushing recommendations for each vascular access.

Table 10.2 Flushing and Locking Protocols for Various Vascular Access Devices in Paediatric Patients

Vascular Access	Flushing and Locking Protocol#
Peripheral line	A flushing volume of a minimum 1 ml of 0.9% normal saline before and after each access or every 8 hours (nurses shift change) when not in use.
Midline and PICC 3 Fr and larger	A minimum of 2 ml of 0.9% normal saline is used for flushing before and after each access or every 12 hours when not used. Locking is done with 1 U/ml heparin in NICU location. About 10 U/ml heparin is used as a locking solution outside NICU.
PICC 1 Fr and 2 Fr	Patency is maintained with continuous infusion of 0.5 U/ml heparin at 0.5–1 ml/hr.
Non-tunnelled CICC	Flushing is done with a minimum of 2 ml of 0.9% normal saline before and after each use or every 12 hours if not in use. Locking is done with 10 U/ml heparin. About 1 U/ml heparin is used in the NICU location.

(Contd.)

Table 10.2 (*Contd.*)

Vascular Access	Flushing and Locking Protocol#
Hickman catheter	Flushing is done with a minimum of 2 ml of 0.9% normal saline before and after each use or every 12 hours if not in use. Locking done with 1 U/ml heparin in NICU or 10 U/ml heparin outside NICU.
Implanted port	A minimum of 3 ml of 0.9% normal saline is used for flushing before and after each use or every 12 hours when the port is accessed but not in use. Locking with 10U/ml heparin when accessed. For monthly locks when de-accessed 100 U/ml heparin is used.
Umbilical catheters (arterial and venous)	Flushing is done with continuous infusion of 0.5 U/ml heparin at 0.5 ml/hr.

CICC, centrally inserted central catheter; NICU, neonatal intensive care unit; PICC, peripherally inserted central catheter.

As a general rule, the flushing volume should be at least double the volume of the device. Patients with heparin-induced thrombocytopenia should not be given heparin.

Vascular Access Techniques

Securing a catheter in the vessel can be done using any of the following techniques:

- **Catheter-over-needle:** Integrated catheter-over-needle is inserted in the vessel and the catheter slides inside while the needle is removed
- **Seldinger technique:** A needle is first placed in the vessel. A guidewire is then passed through the needle, the needle removed and the catheter threaded over the guide wire
- **Modified Seldinger technique:** Similar to the Seldinger technique, but a dilator sheath is placed over the guidewire through which the catheter is placed, and the sheath is removed.

The modified Seldinger is the safest technique and is used for advanced catheter placements like PICCs, the Seldinger technique for CICCs and catheter-over-needle for peripheral venous cannulation. The cost increases as the complexity of the technique increases.

Role of Ultrasound in Vascular Access

Over the last decade, ultrasound use has increased in peri-operative care including its use in vascular access. Ultrasound can be used in all vascular cannulations (arterial, venous – peripheral and central veins). The American Institute of Ultrasound in Medicine (AIUM) (2019) detailed practice parameters for the use of ultrasound in vascular access.

- Screening and identifying the most suitable vein: RaCeVA and RaPeVA protocols are described for CICCs and PICCs, respectively. Elaboration of these protocols is out of the scope of this chapter.
- Determination of catheter size based on vein size: catheter external diameter should not occupy > 33–45% of vein diameter.
- During the placement: Confirmation of needle and guidewire placement, catheter tip navigation and location confirmation.
- After placement: To rule out complications.

A high-frequency linear array transducer (5–18 Hz) with a smaller footprint (25 mm) also called a hockey stick probe is preferred in children. Venepuncture may be done as transverse or longitudinal (probe relation to the vessel) and 'in plane' or 'out of plane' (needle relation to probe). Though the 'in plane' has the advantage of a complete needle view, it lacks the spatial orientation of the surrounding critical structures. 'In plane' is preferred for brachiocephalic vein puncture whereas 'out of plane' is preferred for PICC lines. Figure 10.3 depicts the transverse 'out of plane', longitudinal 'in plane' and transverse in-plane techniques for internal jugular vein (IJV) cannulation. The artery can be differentiated from

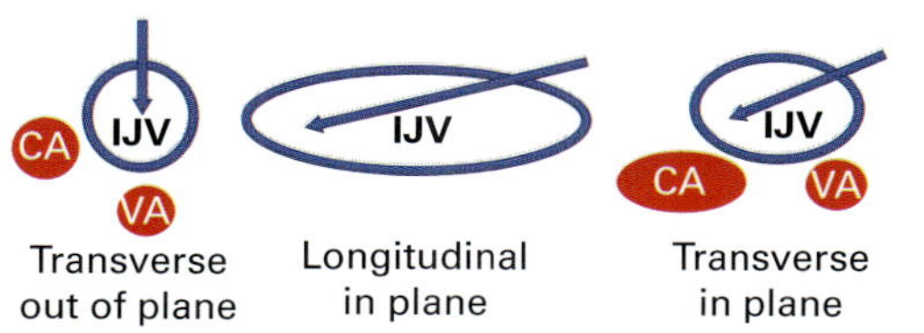

Figure 10.3 Ultrasound approaches to cannulation – transverse out of plane, longitudinal in plane, transverse in plane. CA, carotid artery; IJV, internal jugular vein; VA, vertebral artery.

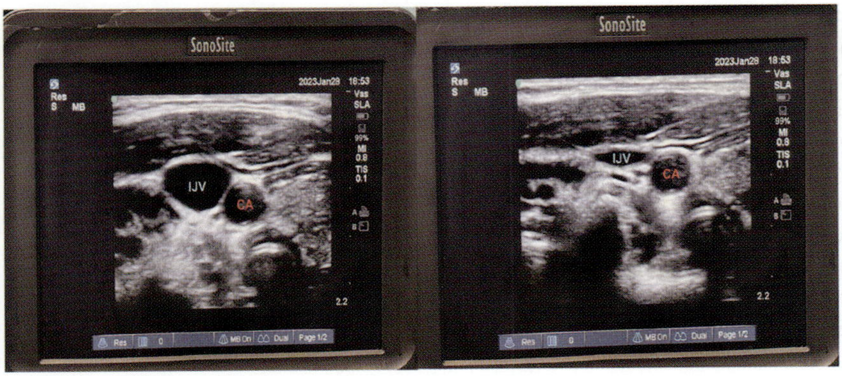

Figure 10.4 Ultrasound differentiation of artery and vein showing vein compressibility. *Upon application of pressure with a transducer, the vein is easily compressible (right side of the image), whereas the artery is non-compressible. Arterial pulsations become more prominent on external compression.* CA, carotid artery; IJV, internal jugular vein.

a vein on ultrasound by the presence of pulsatility, non-compressibility, pulsatile flow on colour doppler and no respiratory variations as compared to the vein (**Fig. 10.4**). Downside to use of ultrasound is the availability and operator expertise.

Arterial Access

Arterial cannulations are done for sick children requiring haemodynamic monitoring (invasive blood pressure monitoring or cardiac output monitoring) and those requiring repeated blood gas measurements. The preferred sites for arterial cannulation in children are the radial artery, dorsalis pedis artery and posterior tibial artery. Other alternatives are the femoral and axillary sites. Brachial arteries should preferably be avoided for cannulation in children due to lack of collateral flow posing a risk for limb ischemia. The role of modified Allen's test before radial artery cannulation is controversial and hence not universally practised. The Seldinger technique is preferred for safe access in infants and younger children. Arterial cannulation may be done using the palpation technique, but ultrasound guidance is preferred. Ultrasound additionally offers the advantage of calculating the arterial diameter and choosing an appropriate catheter size. The size of the arterial cannula for a radial artery may alternatively be selected on the age and weight of the patient as shown in **Table 10.3**. Infection at the insertion site and coagulopathy are contraindications.

Table 10.3 Selection of Arterial Line Based on Age and Weight of the Child

Weight and Age of the Child	Radial Arterial Line
Infants <5 kg	24G
Infants 5–10 kg	22G/24G
Children 10–25 kg	22G
Children >25 kg	20G/22G

Umbilical artery catheterisation is done in sick preterm neonates for blood gas measurements, repeated blood sampling and arterial blood pressure monitoring. The procedure must be done under strict aseptic precautions with sterile body drapes. A 3.5 Fr catheter for babies <1500 g or a 5 Fr catheter for babies >1500 g is selected. Umbilical arteries are thick-walled and have small lumens. The origin of celiac, mesenteric and renal arteries corresponds to T12-L1 vertebra level, and hence catheter tip position should be avoided at this location to avoid occlusion or thrombosis of these branches of the aorta. Two positions for the tip of the umbilical artery catheter are recommended, high and low – above and below the origin of the renal artery, respectively. A high position of the tip of the umbilical artery catheter corresponds to T6-T9 vertebra on X-ray and a low position corresponds to L4-L5 on X-ray. The high position is preferred as it has fewer complications. Shukla's or Wright's formula may be used to calculate the length of the catheter for a high position. Alternatively, shoulder umbilical length nomograms are available for both high and low positions.

Catheters with side holes have shown the risk of aortic thrombosis; hence, catheters with holes at the tip are preferred. Apart from cord infection, intra-abdominal infection is a contraindication for umbilical artery catheterisation. It is recommended not to keep the catheter in place for >5 days to avoid infections and thrombotic complications.

All the components of the pressure monitoring system should be handled in a sterile manner and all the components of the transducer system including the flushing system should be replaced at a 96-hour interval.

Peripheral Venous Access

Peripheral venous cannulation is the commonest venous access secured. The most accessed site is the dorsum of the hand. Lower limb cannulations are generally avoided as they interfere with the mobility of the child. The antecubital vein is best avoided for the risk of inadvertent arterial cannulation. In neonates and early infancy, scalp veins may be accessed if routine sites are not available. The external jugular vein is another site in older children which allows wide bore access but loose skin, a collapsible vein, and narrow-angle for cannula insertion make it relatively difficult. External jugular cannulation can be made easy by bending the cannula 10–15 degrees as shown in **Figure 10.5a**.

Various techniques are available to make the peripheral veins more prominent or visible.

1. **Tourniquet application:** The application of a tourniquet and tapping makes veins more prominent. The tourniquet pressure should only occlude the venous return and not the arterial flow. For neonates and infants, compression with the index finger and middle finger while maintaining the skin stretch with the thumb is practised (**Fig. 10.6**).
2. **Transillumination technique:** Thinner skin in children <2 years allows easy visibility of veins using this technique. Light-emitting diodes are preferred over regular lights as they have greater transillumination power and a lesser risk of burns due to heat (**Fig. 10. 7**).

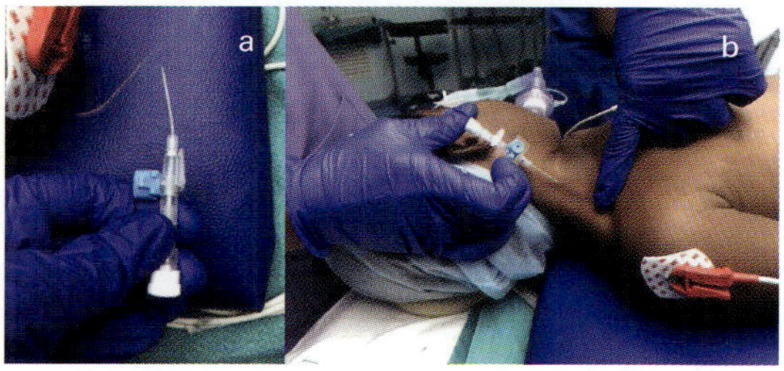

Figure 10.5 (a) Peripheral cannula bent (10–15 degrees) for (b) external jugular vein cannulation.

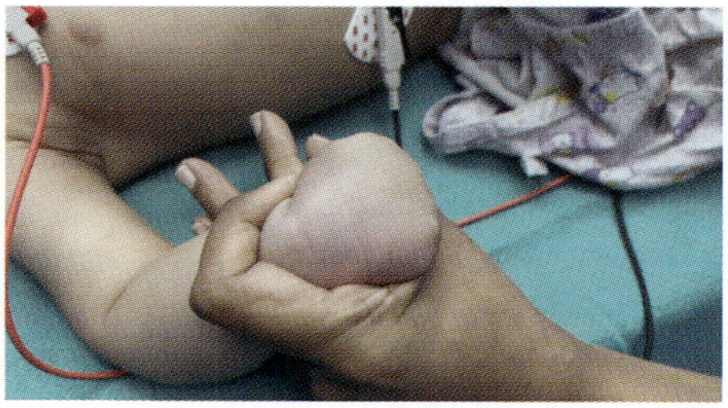

Figure 10.6 Hand position for dorsal vein cannulation in neonates and infants.

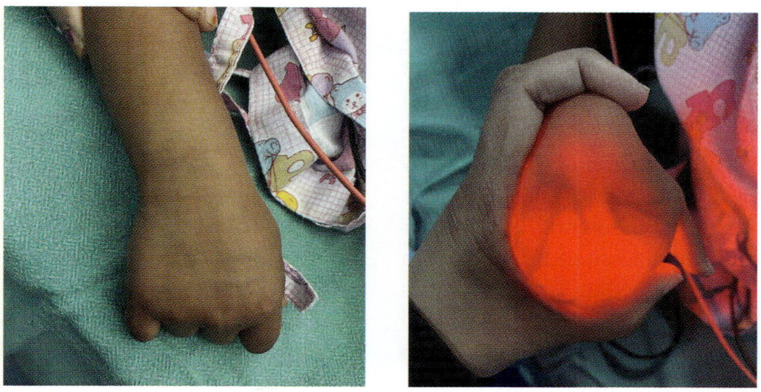

Figure 10.7 Transillumination technique: veins are seen as dark lines.

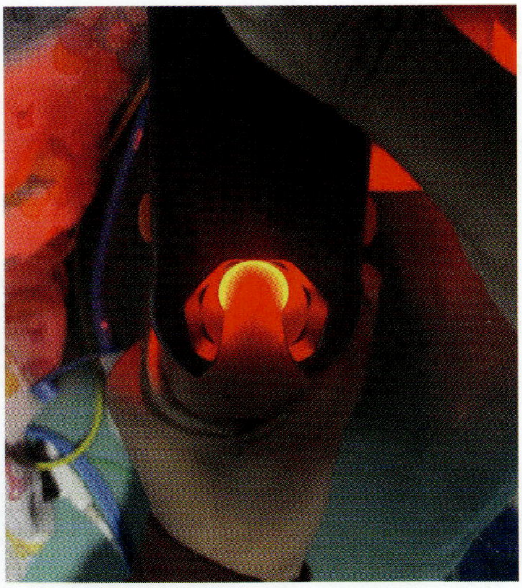

Figure 10.8 Near-infrared technique delineating vein as dark linear structure in the centre of the illuminated area.

3. **Near-infrared devices:** This technique is particularly useful when the veins are not prominent on visualisation and palpation. With the application of infrared light in darker ambient surroundings, the haemoglobin in the blood absorbs the infrared light, thereby delineating the vessel (**Fig. 10.8**). This technique is suitable for superficial peripheral veins.
4. **Ultrasonography:** When equipment and expertise are available, ultrasound can be used for difficult peripheral venous cannulation. This technique is suitable for deeper peripheral veins as in obese children.

Technique of peripheral venous cannulation: The smallest cannula required for the treatment should be chosen. The vein is stabilised by stretching the skin and the cannula is inserted at an angle of 10–25 degrees till a back flash of blood is seen in the hub. A saline drop in the hub of the needle lowers the surface tension and allows early flashback in narrow calibre veins. Once the back flash is seen, the angle of the cannula is further dropped and the catheter is advanced into the vein with the removal of the needle. The cannula is secured with transparent tapes, and an additional splint is applied to the limb in younger children to prevent dislodgement of the cannula. Care must be taken to avoid compromising the blood supply due to the tight application of the splint.

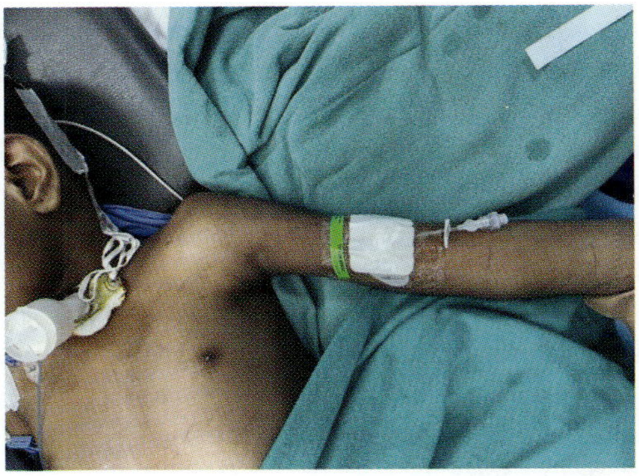

Figure 10.9 A midline catheter is placed in the left arm vein.

Midline Access

Midline access catheters are 6–12 cm long. They are usually peripheral venous access cannulated in the deeper midarm or forearm veins under ultrasound guidance (**Fig. 10.9**). Though underutilised they are particularly useful in situations where the child would need peripheral access for a longer duration (prolonged antibiotic therapy or daily sedation for radiotherapy treatment). Regular peripheral cannula would last 3–5 days whereas the midlines last for 2–3 weeks when handled carefully.

Peripherally Inserted Central Venous Access

Peripherally inserted central catheters (PICC) are catheters accessed through a peripheral vein with the tip positioned at the cavoatrial junction. They provide long-term access and are relatively safe to perform in a coagulopathic or thrombocytopenic patient. Most accessed veins in infants and children are the arm veins: the basilic, brachial and cephalic veins. The femoral vein is an alternate access, and the tip of the catheter may be left in the inferior vena cava. The best vein for cannulation is selected after a RaPeVA screening. Venepuncture is preferably done in the midarm under ultrasound guidance and the catheter advanced using a modified Seldinger technique. In the neonate, the cubital or saphenous vein may be accessed using an epicutaneo-caval catheter. PICC lines are available as open end or closed end. Open-end PICCs are valve-less whereas close-end PICCs are called Groshong catheters with a slit-like valve near the

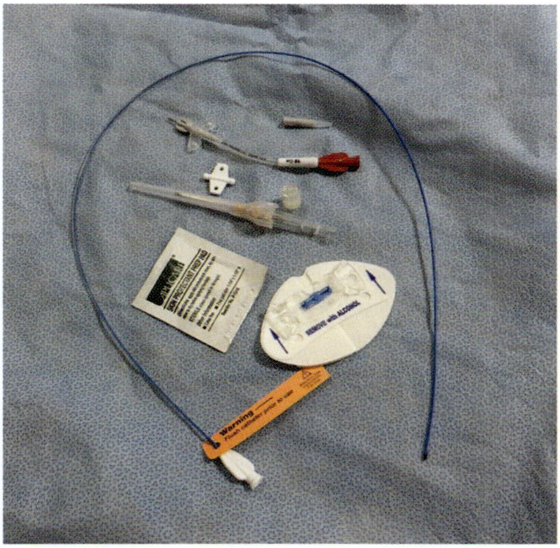

Figure 10.10 Close-ended peripherally inserted central line kit.

catheter end. The latter claim to have fewer occlusion rates. **Figure 10.10** depicts the Groshong catheter placement kit.

Central Venous Access with Non-Tunnelled Catheters

These are routinely done in ICU patients or as a part of venous access in children undergoing major surgery. Local skin infection is an absolute contraindication. Coagulopathy and thrombocytopenia are relative contraindications. Commonly accessed veins are the internal jugular, subclavian and femoral vein. The size of the catheter may be selected based on the age and weight of the child as shown in **Table 10.4**. The anticipated catheter length can be calculated by measuring the distance between the point of insertion to the sternal angle.

Table 10.4 Selection of Central Venous Catheter (CVC) Based on Age and Weight of the Child

Age and Weight of the Child	CVC – Length and size
Infants <5 kg	5 cm, 3 Fr
Infants 5–10 kg	8 cm, 4 Fr
Children 10–25 kg	12 cm, 5 Fr
Children >25 kg	15 cm, 7 Fr

Internal Jugular Vein Cannulation Technique

Two techniques are described: the landmark-based approach and the ultrasound-guided technique. Ultrasound-guided venepuncture and navigation are recommended over landmark technique as it is associated with a higher success rate and lower complication rate. In a landmark-based approach, the needle is inserted at the medial edge of the sternomastoid at the level of the thyroid cartilage and advanced towards the ipsilateral nipple. Slight head rotation to the opposite side and a slight Trendelenburg position will make the vein calibre larger and easier to access. IJV is a low pressure easily collapsible vein making it susceptible to double puncture with a risk of injury to the carotid, pleura and vertebral artery.

Subclavian Vein Cannulation Technique

The child is positioned with a small towel fold between the shoulder blades and a slight Trendelenburg position. Ultrasound-guided infraclavicular subclavian cannulation has been described but is challenging as the clavicle overlaps the vein. In landmark-based technique, the needle, with a saline-loaded syringe attached, is inserted at the junction of the medial two-thirds and lateral one-third of the clavicle (infraclavicular) and advanced below the clavicle towards the suprasternal notch. Once blood is freely aspirated and checked for venous/inadvertent arterial puncture, the modified Seldinger technique is followed. Alternatively in neonates and infants, the brachiocephalic vein is a good choice under ultrasound guidance.

Brachiocephalic Vein Cannulation Technique

The brachiocephalic vein can be identified using a linear transducer (hockey stick probe) placed at the lower neck near the sternoclavicular junction, tilting the probe towards the patient's feet in the frontal plane. The pleura can be seen posterior to the vein as a white glistening structure showing pleural sliding movements. Venepuncture is done in an in-plane orientation followed by

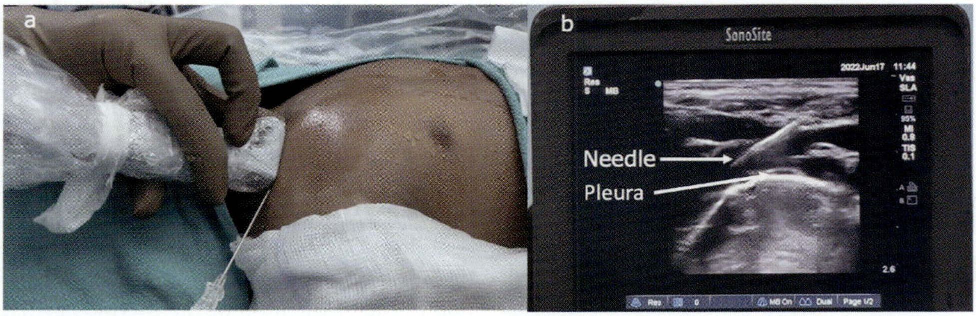

Figure 10.11 Ultrasound-guided brachiocephalic vein cannulation.

catheter placement using the Seldinger technique (**Fig. 10.11**).

Femoral Vein Cannulation Technique

The lower limb of the child is externally rotated at the hip and slightly flexed in the knee. The femoral artery is palpated and needle entry is made medial to the palpating finger 1 cm below the inguinal crease. Ultrasound-guided puncture improves the ease of cannulation. Catheter placement is done following the Seldinger technique. Keeping the entry site clean is a challenge especially for female babies.

Tunnelled Cuffed Central Catheters

Tunnelled catheters are long-term, large-bore central venous access used for chemotherapy, bone marrow transplant procedures and plasmapheresis. Broviac and Hickman catheters are tunnelled catheters made of silicone, which makes them less thrombogenic. Broviac catheters are available from 2.7 to 6.6 Fr as single-lumen catheters and are used for infants and younger children. Hickman catheters are available from 7 to 12.5 Fr as single-, double-, or triple-lumen and are used for older children and adolescents. Placement is done under strict aseptic precautions with full-body sterile draping. The internal jugular or the subclavian vein is accessed via the modified Seldinger technique and the tip of the catheter is positioned at the cavoatrial junction. A tunnelling rod is used to tunnel the catheter to the ipsilateral infraclavicular area, which is the preferred exit site (**Fig. 10.12**).

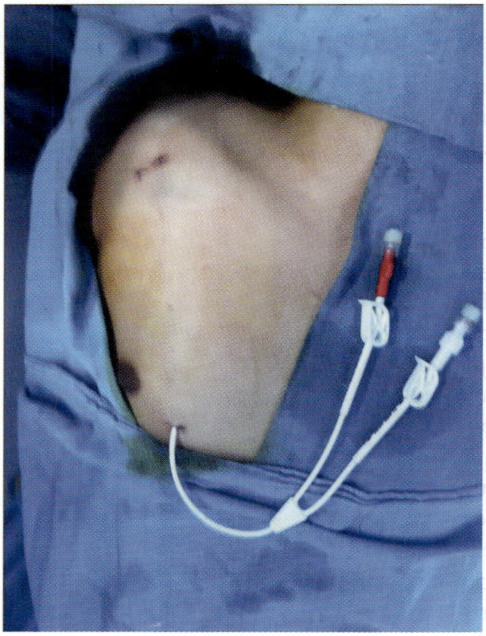

Figure 10.12 Hickman tunnelled catheter.

These catheters are characterised by a Dacron cuff, which should be positioned subcutaneously 4–5 cm close to the exit site. Sterile dressings are done at the venepuncture and exit sites. The Dacron cuff allows for the growth of tissue onto it which later provides stability to the catheter and serves as a barrier to infection.

Proper care in the handling these devices is essential to prevent bloodstream infections and catheter blockades. The catheter hub must be accessed in a non-touch sterile manner, cleaned with 2% chlorhexidine or 70% alcohol wipe for 30 seconds and allowed to dry. Clamping of the catheter is done over the protective sleeve provided.

Catheters that have been inserted recently can be removed by gentle traction alone whereas the older catheters need cut down of fibrous tissue around the Dacron cuff. Pressure needs to be applied over the vein puncture site to stop the bleeding. Skin closure with sutures and a sterile dressing are required.

Implanted Port

A port is a totally implantable vascular access device, which can serve as a long-term vascular access. Over the last decade, they have been used increasingly in children requiring chemotherapy, repeated transfusions as in thalassemia, and long-term nutritional support. Anaesthesiologists should familiarise themselves with accessing this device for perioperative care.

Ports should be accessed following strict aseptic precautions (**Fig. 10.13**). The Port site should be inspected before use for erythema, swelling, induration or tenderness, which may indicate infection or extravasation of the drug because of the incorrect needle placement or needle displacement. Age-appropriate cleaning solutions must be used to clean the skin over the port site and a non-coring needle is inserted into the silicone diaphragm after stabilising the port body with the thumb and index finger of the operator's left hand. The correct position of the needle is confirmed by the loss of resistance while inserting it and the free backflow of blood on aspiration. Flushing of the ports is recommended before and after each use with 0.9% normal saline. The flushing technique of push–stop–push–stop creates turbulence to allow cleansing of the catheter, which is then clamped under positive pressure, while the last 0.5 ml of flush is being pushed. This prevents the backflow of blood into the catheter while disconnecting the syringe and is called locking. Heparin 10 U/ml may be used as a lock solution. Newer ports are MRI compatible and can withstand high pressure generated in the catheter during CT contrast injections. The patient's port card should be verified before use for these indications.

Intraosseous Access

Bone marrow has a network of non-collapsible veins, which can be accessed in emergency situations like cardiac arrest when regular venous access is difficult to obtain. This route is used for the administration of fluid, drug, blood products and blood sampling. Common sites for needle insertion are the proximal tibia (most preferred) followed by the distal femur, distal tibia, proximal humerus, iliac crest, and sternum. This route is particularly helpful in children <6 years due to their thinner bone cortex and larger marrow but can be used in older children too. Needle placement is done following aseptic precautions after local anaesthetic infiltration. Special intraosseous needles are available, in the absence of which a bone marrow aspiration needle (**Fig. 10.14**) or a paediatric epidural needle can be used. Needle insertion points are 2 cm caudal and medial to the tibial tuberosity for proximal tibial access, and 1–3 cm proximal to the intercondylar line of the distal femur in the anterior midline for distal femoral access. A 10- to 15-degree tilt of the needle during

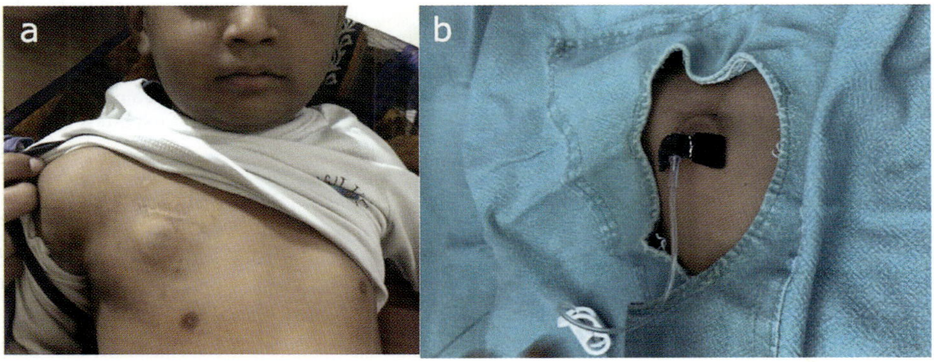

Figure 10.13 (a and b) The implanted port under the skin on the anterior chest wall accessed using a Huber needle.

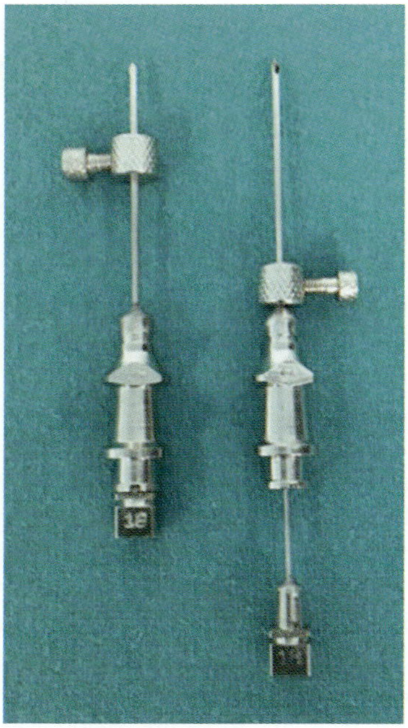

Figure 10.14 Bone marrow aspiration needle is used as an intraosseous needle for emergency access.

insertion (caudal tilt for proximal tibial access and cranial tilt for distal femoral access) should be taken to avoid damage to the growth plate. Contraindications to intraosseous access are local skin infections and bone diseases. An intraosseous needle is removed at the earliest once stable venous access is established.

Umbilical Venous Access

Used in resuscitation of neonates when accessing a peripheral line is difficult. It can also be used as a central line during the first 10 days of life. Infection of the umbilical cord or intra-abdominal infections are contraindications for the procedure. The procedure should be done under strict aseptic precautions. The thin-walled umbilical vein is identified after stabilising the cord stump with tape. The vein is dilated with artery forceps and an umbilical catheter (3.5 Fr if <3.5 kg; 5 Fr if >3.5 kg) or a 5-Fr infant feeding tube is passed beyond 4–5 cm till a good backflow is noticed. Newer antibiotic-coated polyurethane catheters have demonstrated a reduced rate of complications. To use it as a central line, the tip of the catheter should be at the junction of the inferior vena cava and the right atrium, which is confirmed on X-ray. Recently point-of-care ultrasound has demonstrated improved accuracy in catheter tip placement and could become the standard of care in future.

Table 10.5 summarises the advantages and disadvantages of different vascular access devices.

Table 10.5 Summary of Different Vascular Access Devices

Vascular Access	Dwell Time	Advantages	Disadvantages
Peripheral line	Short term Usually, 3–5 days	Ease of access Less expensive Fewer complications	Short-term access Not suitable for hyperosmolar solutions and irritant drugs
Midline	Intermediate term 2–4 weeks	Intermediate term access, avoids repeated peripheral cannula placements for patients requiring longer duration treatments	Costly, needs expertise and ultrasound
PICC	Long term Few weeks to months	Central line for practical purpose, safer in coagulopathic patients	Need training, ultrasound expertise, expensive
Non-tunnelled CICC	Short term Up to 2 weeks	Short-term access for patients requiring vasopressors in ICU, major surgeries	Bloodstream infections
Tunnelled catheters	Long term Few months	Less infections compared to non-tunnelled counterparts, large bore allows bone marrow transplant and plasmapheresis	Expensive, expertise needed, requires fluoroscopy, done under GA preferably

(Contd.)

Table 10.5 (*Contd.*)

Vascular Access	Dwell Time	Advantages	Disadvantages
Implanted ports	Long term Months to few years	Long-term access with least infection rate, cosmetically better, allows activities like swimming, showering, etc.	Most expensive, GA required, need expertise, fluoroscopy required
Intraosseous	Short term Few hours to few days	Useful in emergencies with difficult IV access	Needs training, risk of osteomyelitis
Arterial line	Short term Few days	Accurate blood pressure measurement, frequent ABG sampling	Arterial thrombosis
Umbilical vein	Short term Few days	Neonatal resuscitation, first 10 days of life, used as central line	Needs training, false tract and infections

ABG, arterial blood gas; CICC, centrally inserted central catheter; GA, general anaesthesia; ICU, intensive care unit; IV, intravenous; PICC, peripherally inserted central catheter ABG, arterial blood gas.

Complications of Vascular Access

1. **Complications related to peripheral venous access**
   - *Early:* bleeding and hematomas
   - *Late:* thrombophlebitis and extravasation can occur when hyperosmolar and vesicant drugs are infused through a peripheral vein
2. **Complications of central venous access**
   - *Early:* intraprocedural arrhythmias, air embolism, pneumothorax, arterial puncture, hematomas, nerve plexus injury and primary malposition of tip of a catheter
   - *Late:* bloodstream infections, catheter occlusion, fibrin sheath formation, intravascular thrombosis and secondary malposition of catheter tip which can happen during violent coughing, catheter fractures, catheter pinch-off syndromes and port body fractures
3. **Complications of arterial access**
   - *Early:* bleeding and hematomas
   - *Late:* thrombosis, distal ischemia and aneurysm
4. **Complications of intraosseous access**
   - *Early:* hematoma, extravasation and bone fracture
   - *Late:* osteomyelitis, cellulitis and compartment syndrome
5. **Complications of umbilical access**
   - *Early:* false tract, vessel perforation and malposition
   - *Late:* vessel thrombosis and infection

SUGGESTED READINGS

1. Naik V, Rayani B. Vascular access for infants and children. In: Principles and practice of paediatric anaesthesia, Dhayagude S et al. India: Jaypee brothers publishers; 1st ed 2016; 473–484.
2. Rayani BK, Anne P. Long term vascular access. In: Onco-Anaesthesia, Critical care and cancer pain. White falcon publishing; 2022; 341–357.
3. Naik VM, Rao KS, Rayani BK, et al. Long-term venous access devices and anaesthesiologists. *Update Anaesth* 2019; 33: 62–69.
4. Naik VM, Mantha SSP, Rayani BK. Vascular access in children. *Indian J Anaesth* 2019; 63(9): 737–745.
5. Moore C, Kollpainter R, Andrews L, et al. AIUM Practice parameter for the use of ultrasound to guide vascular access procedures. *J Ultrasound Med* 2019; 38:E4–E18.
6. Spencer TR, Pittiruti M. Rapid Central Vein Assessment (RaCeVA): A systematic standardised approach for ultrasound assessment before central venous catheterisation. *J Vasc Access* 2019; 20(3):239–249.
7. Pittiruti M, Scoppettuolo G. The GAVeCeLT manual of PICC and MIDLINE. Italy: Edra S.p.A, 2017; p53–54.
8. Gomella T, Cunningham M, Eyal FG, et al. Arterial access: umbilical artery catheterisation. In: Neonatology: Management, Procedures, On-call problems, Diseases, and Drugs 7e. McGraw Hill; 2013.
9. Bodenham Chair A, Babu S, Bennett J, et al. Association of Anaesthetists of Great Britain and Ireland: Safe vascular access 2016; 71:573–585.
10. Dawson RB. PICC zone Insertion Method. *J Assoc Vasc Access* 2011; 16(3):156–165.

11 ANAESTHESIA IN NON-OPERATING ROOM SETTINGS

Karthikeyan Chandrasekaran • Ashok Dharmalingam

Providing anaesthesia outside the operating room is a challenging aspect of anaesthesia delivery. We now recognise the need for the treatment of pain and emotional stress in children undergoing treatment. Providing anaesthesia services outside the OR has increased in recent times partly due to the increase in this segment of the population and partly due to the increase in the number and types of interventions available in various medical specialities.

Anaesthesia may be required for various diagnostic or therapeutic procedures in children who

- have painful and frightening procedures/illnesses.
- are confused, combative and developmentally delayed.
- are suffering from neurologic or neuromuscular disorders and are unable to lie still.

The goal of providing anaesthesia is to make the procedure as non-threatening and comfortable as safely possible so that there is a reduction of psychological trauma for the child and the parents while ensuring the success of the procedure.

This chapter aims to highlight some of the key principles to be undertaken while delivering the services with utmost safety and quality.

History

The concept of providing anaesthetic services in non-traditional settings was first provided by Crawford Long of Athens, Georgia, in 1842 when he anaesthetised an 8-year-old with sulphuric ether to amputate the boy's toe. Over the years, anaesthetic drugs and techniques have been refined to be used for a variety of investigations and procedures as described in the following sections.

General Considerations

The reluctance to provide anaesthesia in an unfamiliar environment can be eliminated by understanding the patients' clinical and psychological problems.

Check whether the patient is an outpatient and needs to be street-fit at the end of the procedure or whether he is already admitted or can be admitted to the hospital.

Clarification of the *details of the procedure* with a proceduralist – like how it is performed, duration, requirement for breath holding, anticoagulation and pain relief – helps in formulating the anaesthetic plan.

Special mention is required for children with behavioural abnormalities and intellectual disabilities, as one needs to adapt and tailor the type of anaesthesia accordingly.

Equipment

The safety standards for the conduct of anaesthesia can be maintained by checking the following:

1. Anaesthesia machine
   - Suction and oxygen sources
   - Availability of pulse oximeter, BP monitoring, ECG and a capnograph (desirable)
2. Standard defibrillation and resuscitation equipment

3. Emergency drugs in case of anaphylaxis with contrast dyes
4. Adequate illumination

An anaesthesia machine is mandatory. Box 11.1 highlights some of the other essential equipment.

If one is expected to provide anaesthesia in more than one location, it is a good idea to have a 'Travelling cart' with appropriate supplies ready to go to different locations as an alternative to stocking all locations.

Box 11.1 Equipment Required for Providing Anaesthesia in 'Distant Locations'

1. Oxygen supply (preferably central piped source) and backup E-cylinder oxygen supply
2. Suction apparatus
3. Waste gas scavenging (where anesthetic gases are used
4. Equipment
   a. Self-inflating hand resuscitator bag to deliver positive pressure ventilation
   b. Adequate anesthesia drugs, supplies, and equipment for each case
   c. Monitoring equipment to allow for "Standards for Basic Anesthetic Monitoring"
5. Sufficient electrical outlets
6. Adequate illumination with additional battery-powered backup lighting
7. Sufficient space to accommodate patient, personnel, and equipment
8. Emergency cart with defibrillator, drugs, and other equipment to provide CPR
9. Staff trained to support the anesthesiologist and two-way communication capabilities to request assistance
10. Observance of all building and safety codes and facility standards

CPR, cardiopulmonary resuscitation.

NPO Guidelines

Table 11.1 presents the NPO guidelines for conscious and deep sedation.

Table 11.1 NPO Guidelines Prior to the Procedure

Age	Solids and Milk	Clear Liquids
>6 months	6 hr	2–3 hr
<6 months	4 hr if breastfed	2 hr

Emergencies and Recovery

It is important for the anaesthetist to know where help and assistance are available in case of an emergency. Post-anaesthesia care unit is an ideal place for the recovery of the patient. Ensure the support staff is appropriately trained and adequate in number.

However, if this unit is at a distance then one needs to ensure that the patient is fully awake and stable prior to his/her transfer to the unit or the ward and that oxygen and monitoring are available for transport.

Modes of Management

In all these settings, the following two modes of management may be used:

- Sedation/anaesthesia (both general and regional) by anaesthetists outside the OR
- Conscious sedation and analgesia by non-anaesthetists

If the latter is the only alternative as in the case of a shortage of trained anaesthetists, the anaesthesia department can contribute to the safety of paediatric sedation by participating in the development of institutional guidelines that can be followed by different departments with backup and support provided by the department of anaesthesia.

It is important to remember that various studies have shown that:

- All sedatives and narcotics can cause problems even in recommended doses.
- All areas using sedation have reported adverse effects (e.g. dental procedures, electroencephalogram [EEG] and magnetic resonance imaging [MRI]).
- Children between 0 and 5 years of age are comparatively at a greater risk.
- Respiratory depression, obstruction and apnoea are the most common complications followed by haemodynamic and cardiac events.
- Adverse effects are related to multiple drugs, inadequate monitoring, inadequate practitioner skills and premature discharge of the patient.

Definition of Sedation

The Joint Commission on Accreditation of Healthcare Organisation (JCAHO) regulations contain recommendations made by the American Society of Anesthesiologists (ASA). ASA's efforts in developing guidelines for sedation have recently been reviewed. The revised standards include new language pertaining to the definition of the continuum of sedation/anaesthesia (**Fig. 11.1**). They define four levels of sedation and anaesthesia as shown in **Figure 11.1** and **Table 11.2**.

Guidelines

General guidelines (ASA and JCAHO) for both conscious and deep sedation have several points in common:

- Equipment requirements include (onsite and available) a positive pressure oxygen delivery system that can administer at least 90% oxygen for at least 60 minutes. An emergency kit containing emergency drugs, laryngoscopes and endotracheal tubes as well as monitors and a suction device.
- Documentation for the sedation should include a pre-sedation health evaluation, informed consent, records of medication given, vital signs, recovery parameters and instructions at discharge to the responsible persons.
- For 'Conscious Sedation', there must be an additional person to monitor the child's condition.
- Potential risks of sedation should be clearly understood. These are airway obstruction, hypoventilation, apnoea and cardiopulmonary impairment.

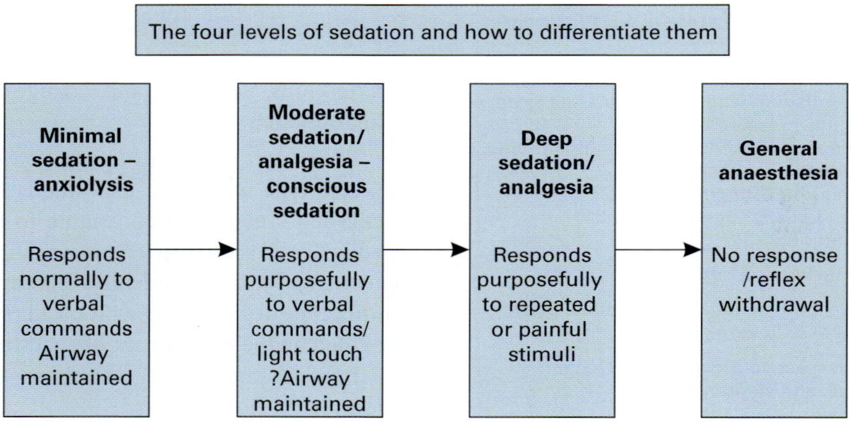

Figure 11.1 Four levels of sedation.

Table 11.2 Four Levels of Sedation

	Minimal Sedation Anxiolysis	Moderate Sedation/ Analgesia ("Conscious Sedation")	Deep Sedation/ Analgesia	General Anaesthesia
Responsiveness	Normal response to verbal stimulation	Purposeful response to verbal or tactile stimulation	Purposeful response following repeated or painful stimulation	Unarousable even with painful stimulus
Airway	Unaffected	No intervention required	Intervention may be required	Intervention often required
Spontaneous ventilation	Unaffected	Adequate	May be inadequate	Frequently inadequate
Cardiovascular function	Unaffected	Usually maintained	Usually maintained	May be impaired

Approved by the ASA House of Delegates on October 13, 1999, and last amended on October 23, 2019.

Procedural Sedation

The goals of procedural sedation are similar to those of anaesthesia for surgical procedures. The major goals are as follows:

1. Eliminating or minimising pain and anxiety
2. Avoiding emotional trauma
3. Controlling patient movement (behaviour) to ensure the adequacy of the test and/or a successful result
4. Assuring patient safety by maintaining respiratory, cardiovascular and autonomic stability
5. Returning the children to their normal state of function when the sedation or anaesthesia is completed

Advantages

The child lies still and pain-free during the entire procedure, making it much easier for the specialist clinician to successfully do the procedure in the minimum time required, thus making the whole process efficient and cost-effective.

It could also involve the parents in an intervention on their child, enhance the cooperation of both the child and parent and limit the child's fear of future procedures.

The following procedures are usually done outside the operating room:

- Diagnostic and therapeutic imaging areas. CT Scanner/MRI room/barium studies
- GI endoscopy, endoscopic retrograde cholangiopancreatography (ERCP)
- Radiotherapy – planning and treatment
- Lithotripsy
- Cardiac catheterisation – diagnostic and therapeutic
- Interventional neuroradiology
- Bone marrow aspiration and lumbar puncture for intrathecal chemotherapy
- Kidney biopsy or biopsy of anterior mediastinal mass under ultrasound guidance
- Electroconvulsive therapy

Awareness of complications that may occur during sedation is important. **Table 11.3** represents actions taken to prevent or deal with the occurrence.

Table 11.3 Red Flags in Sedation

System	Consideration
Apnoea (respiratory)	Strong clinical history, documented evidence or routine use of apnoea monitor – increases the respiratory risk and the need for post-op monitoring area.
Airway	Craniofacial defects with potential 'difficult airway' requires planning and availability of a difficult airway cart and trained help. Intubation or extubation may be considered in operating room.
Respiratory	Recent (< 8 weeks) pneumonia, bronchitis, asthma may require general anaesthesia (GA) with endotracheal tube. Check the availability of ICU for post-op care.
Cardiac	Unstable conditions especially cyanosis, depressed myocardial function, significant stenosis or regurgitation will require cardiology consultation and ICU for post-op care.
Gastrointestinal	Active gastroesophageal reflux and vomiting risk may warrant GA, with endotracheal intubation and rapid sequence intubation.
Neuromuscular	Children with muscular or mitochondrial disorders may present with hypotonia and lack of head control needing respiratory support. May also need post-procedure ICU monitoring.
Neurological and tremors	Behaviour disorders and intellectual disability need special planning with their regular medication dosing and appropriate carer support. Some tremors may not be ablated with sedation. May require GA.
Allergy	Sedation protocol should always be checked for any cross-allergic contraindications
Prior failed sedation	Causative analysis of previous failed sedation – may warrant changes to the principles of sedation. May require GA.

Anaesthetic Considerations at Specific Locations

Anaesthesia may be given in a radiology department, cardiac catheter lab, endoscopy room, outpatient department or oncology department.

Radiology Suite

The radiology suite includes an MRI scan, CT scan, digital subtraction angiography (DSA) room and ultrasound room.

The hazards of the environment include the following:

- Limited access to the patient
- Possibility of radiation exposure
- Dark cold rooms
- Hostile environment for electronic monitoring
- The anaesthetist may be alone

Special Safety Precautions in the radiology suite include the use of radiation shields for both the patient (as in covering the rest of the body while the arm is being X-rayed) and the caregiver. Also remember that contrast dyes are known to produce anaphylactic reactions. So take precautions while giving the dye; monitor the patient and have resuscitation equipment and drugs ready in case of need.

Magnetic Resonance Imaging

The following difficulties are encountered while giving anaesthesia in MRI rooms:

- Remote isolated location – cylindrical large bore magnet in MRI surrounds the body limiting access.
- Ferromagnetic objects may be hurled towards the scanner creating a lethal projectile.
- Large metal objects as well as glittering makeup interferes with the quality of the image.
- Electronic instruments may not function normally close to the magnet.
- Implantable ferromagnetic devices such as aneurysmal clips, surgical clips, pacemakers and cochlear implants are hazardous (check pre-procedure).
- Hypothermia
- Suboptimal lighting may lead to unrecognised airway obstruction, cyanosis, circuit disconnections and exhaustion of gas cylinders.
- Noise exposure – Allowable limit in a 1.5 Tesla MRI is 95 dB 2 hr/day.

Equipment

Most anaesthetic equipment can be modified or constructed to suit the MRI room. The equipment can be made of nickel, aluminium, stainless steel, tantalum and titanium instead of ferrous metals. The other option is to bolt the equipment to the wall or leave them outside the scanning room with long tubing and extensions leading to and from the patient.

MRI-compatible anaesthesia machines with ventilators are now available. For monitoring SpO_2, fibreoptic systems or cordless multichannel monitors with a parallel display in the viewing room are also available. It is prudent to use a respiratory belt and video camera.

Anaesthetic Management

This includes the following:

- In babies less than 6 months, 'feed and swaddle' technique can be used for non-painful procedures like brain MRI.
  - Monitored anaesthesia care: Syrup triclofos, oral midazolam, dexmedetomidine or ketamine.
- General anaesthesia: Inhalational induction – more likely (or requested) in the paediatric population. Maintenance either with intravenous or with an inhalational agent – laryngeal mask airway (LMA) spontaneous ventilation using Mapleson D circuit. Occasionally, intubation and intermittent positive pressure ventilation (IPPV) may be required.
- 'MRI anaesthesia supervised deep sedation service' – Anaesthesia is induced outside the MRI room using propofol 1–2 mg/kg or sevoflurane/halothane, if the IV is not initially placed. The child is stabilised, nasal cannula is placed, and propofol or dexmedetomidine infusion is started and titrated to a level of deep sedation. Once the child is stable, he/she is transferred to the MRI room.

Cardiac Catheterisation Laboratory

Children undergoing cardiac catheterisation are often a greater challenge for the anaesthetist as more complex procedures are done on patients with significant physiological impairment far away from the protective OR environment (refer to Chapter 26).

To provide safe anaesthesia, one must ensure:

- Adequate facilities – adequacy of room lighting, electrical outlets, inotropes, infusion pumps and access to the patient
- Close communication with the cardiologist
- Patient's current clinical, probable anatomical lesion and functional status to be checked and confirmed

A simple checklist to determine the significance of a child's heart disease:

1. **Anatomy**
    - Probable cardiac lesion
    - Presence of intracardiac shunts – magnitude and direction of flow, causes of variations in shunting
    - Presence of obstructive/valvular lesions – magnitude, dynamic versus fixed obstruction
    - Previous palliative/corrective surgery – the response to anaesthetics, the success of repair, the course in hospital
2. **Pathophysiology**
    - Heart failure
        - Based on clinical examination
        - Adequacy of current cardiac output by echocardiography
    - Known cardiac rhythm disturbances
    - Recent changes in exercise tolerance
3. **Pharmacology**
    - Medications – electrolytes, digoxin level
    - Allergy
    - Known useful or ineffective medications, especially anti-arrhythmics

Requirements

- Anaesthesia machine with basic monitoring – pulse oximetry, ECG, non-invasive blood pressure
- Emergency drugs with infusion pumps, defibrillators – resuscitation cart

Mode of Anaesthesia

Cardiologists prefer the patients to be breathing on room air spontaneously as this causes the least disturbance of haemodynamic values, saturations and the least effect on calculations of cardiac output shunt fraction and vascular resistances.

Monitored sedation with intravenous agents such as propofol may be used as an infusion. The child may be allowed to breathe room air (better for assessing normal oximetry in the various samples) or be given supplementary oxygen by mask or nasal prongs, if required.

General anaesthesia, either via LMA, endotracheal tube or mask, with the combination of inhalational (halothane/sevoflurane), intravenous agents (ketamine, propofol and midazolam) and opioids (fentanyl), may be used instead.

Local infiltration at the cannulation site is advantageous and reduces the anaesthetic/sedative requirement.

One must anticipate intra-procedure and post-procedure complications (especially with therapeutic procedures) and haemodynamic fluctuations. Dysrhythmias are often seen. Blood loss from puncture sites or from repeated sampling must be watched for and compensated. Less commonly seen complications are blood vessel/heart rupture, anaphylactic reactions to contrast media, seizures and embolic/thrombotic events.

Post-procedure management should be in a post-anaesthesia care unit (PACU) for at least 30 minutes. Discomfort at the femoral cannulation site can be treated with opioids and nonsteroidal anti-inflammatory drugs (NSAIDS).

Endoscopy

Upper GI endoscopy and oesophageal dilatation can be done under deep sedation with a combination of midazolam, ketamine and glycopyrrolate. However, this is associated with loss of airway reflexes and runs the risk of aspiration. If there is any h/o regurgitation, it is safer to secure the airway with an endotracheal tube.

ERCP is mostly done under general endotracheal anaesthesia. A motionless patient is a prerequisite to minimise the post-procedural biliary leak.

In all cases, close monitoring is imperative.

Radiation Oncology

Radiosensitive tumours require multiple, short radiation treatments. Challenges for the anaesthetists are maintaining the child very still for a very short duration at each treatment session – planning sessions take longer. The anaesthetist cannot remain inside the room during the treatment. Hence, adequate depth of anaesthesia and monitoring with a camera should be ensured (refer to Chapter 44).

Intravenous ketamine or propofol is preferred for treatments. Rectal methohexitone 25–35 mg/kg has also been used. GA with a volatile agent through a face mask followed by a short period of insufflation can also be used. Planning may require a full general anaesthetic (GA).

The need of the hour in India is to develop a structured and systematic approach to quality improvement and a culture that supports its implementation. Each institution or individual should be aware of the usefulness of conducting audits, analysing the results and initiating solutions to improve safety, getting started and sustaining the effort.

SUGGESTED READINGS

1. Holzman RS, Mason KP. Anesthesia and Sedation Outside the Operating Room. In: Pediatric Anesthesia, 5th edition. Gregory GA, Andropoulos DB (eds). Wiley Blackwell, Chichester, West Sussex 2012; pp. 919–944.
2. Sedation outside the OR suite: Sleeping beauty. *IARS 2004 Review Course Lectures.*
3. Kaplan RF. *ASA Annual Refresher Course Lectures* 2003; p. 266.
4. Mason KP, Holzman RS. Anesthesia and Sedation for Pediatric Procedures Outside the Operating Room. In: Smith's Anesthesia for Infants and Children. Davis PJ, Cladis FP, Motoyama EK (eds). Elsevier Mosby, Philadelphia 2011; pp. 1041–1058.
5. Tran L, Squires J, Vera C, Blasiole B. Anaesthesia and Sedation for Out-of-Operating Room Procedures. In: Smith's Anesthesia for Infants and Children. Davis PJ, Cladis FP (eds). Elsevier, Philadelphia 2022; pp. 1148–1167.
6. Landrigan-Oscar M, Cravero. JP Pediatric Sedation. In: Smith's Anesthesia for Infants and Children. Davis PJ, Cladis FP (eds). Elsevier, Philadelphia 2022; pp. 1168–1183.
7. Mahmoud M, Holzman RS, Mason. KP Anesthesia and Sedation Outside the Operating Room. In: Gregory's Pediatric Anesthesia, 6th edition. Andropoulos DB, Gregory GA (eds). Wiley-Blackwell, USA 2012; pp. 1012–1040.

Appendix

Commonly Used Drugs in Remote Locations (for further reference on drugs, see Appendix I)

Benzodiazepines

Diazepam:

Dose: Oral 0.1–0.3 mg/kg; bitter to taste, to be had with cola.

IV 0.1–0.3 mg/kg (max 10 mg)

IM and rectal are not recommended due to erratic absorption

Peak effect: IV 1–2 minutes; oral 60 minutes

Duration: IV 2–6 hours, dose-related elimination T1/2 20–40 hours

Adverse reactions: Respiratory depression and apnoea, ataxia and paradoxic excitation

Antagonist: Flumazenil 10 mcg over 15 seconds every 1–2 minutes up to 1 mg; observe at least for 2 hours for re-sedation

Midazolam:

Dose: Oral 0.25–0.75 mg; IV 0.05–0.15 mg/kg

Peak effect: Oral 10–30 minutes; IV 3–5 minutes

Causes retrograde and anterograde amnesia

Uses: USG-guided renal biopsy, GI endoscopy, ECT, radiotherapy, etc.

Triclofos sodium:

Dose: Oral/Rectal 25–100 mg/kg up to 1 g/dose (max 2 g in two divided doses)

Peak action: 30–60 minutes

Metabolite trichloroethanol is responsible for most of the sedative effects.

Caution: It can potentiate respiratory depression with opioids. It can also cause hyperbilirubinaemia and metabolic acidosis in a newborn.

Fentanyl:

Potent synthetic opioid; it can be used with midazolam for severe painful procedures.

Dose: Oral transmucosal 5–15 mcg/kg (>2 years of age or >10 kg); IV up to 2–3 mcg/kg in titrated doses.

Onset: Oral 15–30 minutes and peak 10–15 minutes following completion

Duration: Oral 2–3 hours; IV 30–45 minutes

Adverse effects: Bradycardia, respiratory depression, urinary retention, chest wall and glottic rigidity

Ketamine:

Produces dissociative anaesthesia and sedation while maintaining spontaneous respiration

Dose: Oral 4–6 mg/kg with atropine 0.02–0.03 mg/kg

IV 0.25–1 mg/kg with atropine 0.01–0.02 mg/kg

IM 1–2 mg/kg with atropine 0.02 mg/kg/glycopyrrolate 0.01 mg/kg is a good mucolytic and produces less tachycardia than atropine

Concomitant administration of midazolam 0.025 mg–0.05 mg/kg improves the level of sedation and reduces hallucinations.

Onset: IV <1 minute, IM 2–5 minutes (peak 20 minutes), oral/rectal >5 minutes (peak 30 minutes)

Duration: IV 15 minutes, IM/oral/rectal 30–120 minutes

Adverse reactions: Emergence hallucinations (up to 12%)

Stimulation of salivary and tracheobronchial secretions

Paradoxical hypotension in critically ill patients

Loss of protective reflexes

Uses: Upper GI endoscopy, CT scan

Contraindications: Head injury with LOC, increased ICP, open globe injury, hypertension, psychosis

Propofol:

Widely used for short-term sedation due to its short half-life

Uses: CT scan, MRI, central venous pressure (CVP) catheterisation

Dose range: IV 0.05–0.2 mg/kg/min infusion, bolus 2 mg/kg

Peak action: <30 seconds

Duration: 8–10 minutes

Adverse reactions: Pain on injection, apnoea, anaphylactic reactions, metabolic acidosis (PRIS syndrome)

Recent guidelines by ASA for use of propofol are as follows:

- Propofol causes loss of airway reflexes even in sedative doses.
- Propofol is considered under deep sedation as general anaesthesia.

Dexmedetomidine ($\alpha 2$ agonist) has been increasingly used in recent times for short procedures such as MRI and CT scan.

Dose: IV loading dose is 2–3 mcg/kg BW over 10 minutes followed by 1–2 mcg/hr as an infusionOnset: <6 minutes and half-life is 2 hours

Intranasal 2.5 mcg/kg

Onset: 15–20 minutes and offset time 55–100 minutes

Contraindications: Congenital cardiac abnormalities

Local anaesthetics:

- EMLA (eutectic mixture of local anaesthetic) cream – 2.5% prilocaine and 2.5% lidocaine mixture
  Uses: IV cannulations, skin incisions, lumbar punctures and circumcision
- TAC – Tetracaine 1%, adrenaline 1:4000, cocaine 4% mixture
  Useful as topical instillation in repair of open skin lacerations in the OPD

Nitrous oxide used in concentrations <50% is a useful mild, anxiolytic sedative agent which causes analgesia. Verbal contact must be maintained with the patient.

12 Anaesthesia for Short Painful Procedures

Zipporah Gathuya

This chapter has been included in this book on the request of doctors with very little paediatric anaesthesia experience doing community-based medicine in smaller hospitals where cases like those described in the following text are present often. Most of what is written in this chapter is from the personal experience of the author.

Examples of cases are as follows:

- Abscess
- Change of dressing for burns – minor and major
- Removal of stitches
- Removal of foreign bodies in the nose, ear, etc.
- Intravenous access
- Lumbar puncture for diagnosis and therapeutic
- Minor suturing
  - Cleaning of wounds and debridement
  - Bone marrow aspiration

The main issue with these procedures is that

- the patients and their parents are fairly anxious.
- fasting protocols are rarely enforced.
- there are discussions about whether or not these patients should always have an IV started or not.
- every patient must be treated as an individual.
- ex-prematures, obese children, syndromic children and those with obstructive sleep apnoea should not be considered for outpatient procedures with inexperienced caregivers.

Pre-Operative Evaluation

The patient must be evaluated adequately and thoroughly (refer to Chapter 1). Often, these children have never been to a doctor before. The present condition may be precipitated by another condition, for example, a seizure causing a fall with a resulting laceration that now requires suturing.

History of previous anaesthetics, allergies, fasting status and concurrent medical illnesses is important even for the smallest of procedures.

For repeat procedures, such as a change of dressing of burns, it is important to review the previous anaesthetic charts. Of concern should be the mode of anaesthesia and any complications. Previous anaesthetic experiences greatly influence subsequent exposures in terms of parents' and patients' cooperation and anxiety. Having the same anaesthesia provider helps a lot, especially if the previous experience was good.

A thorough physical examination, particularly an airway assessment, must be done, especially at the first encounter.

Note: All sedative drugs have been implicated in critical anaesthetic events and must, therefore, be used with extreme caution.

Intraoperative Management (Refer Chapter 1)

Basic monitoring, at least pulse oximetry, must be instituted as early as possible, preferably before induction. Several drugs may be used for these short painful procedures (refer to Chapters 3, 11, 47 and Appendix 1). These include the following.

Ketamine

Intramuscular ketamine is often used for short painful procedures such as lancing an abscess.

Ketamine should always be used with a drying agent such as atropine or glycopyrrolate.

It produces dissociative anaesthesia and sedation while maintaining spontaneous respiration.

Dose:

- *Oral:* 4–6 mg/kg with atropine 0.02–0.03 mg/kg
- *Intravenous:* 0.25–1 mg/kg with atropine 0.01–0.02 mg/kg
- *Intramuscular:* 1–2 mg/kg with atropine 0.02 mg/kg or glycopyrrolate 0.01 mg/kg. Glycopyrrolate is a good mucolytic and produces less tachycardia than atropine.

Concomitant administration of midazolam 0.025 mg – 0.05 mg/kg improves the level of sedation and reduces hallucinations.

Onset:

- IV <1 minute, IM 2–5 minutes (peak 20 minutes), oral/rectal >5 minutes (peak 30 minutes)

Duration:

- IV 15 minutes, IM/oral/rectal: 30–120 minutes

Adverse reactions:

- Emergence hallucinations (up to 12%)
- Stimulation of salivary and tracheobronchial secretions
- Paradoxical hypotension in critically ill patients
- Loss of protective reflexes

Intranasal Fentanyl

This may be used at doses of 1.5 mcg/kg to a maximum of 0.5 ml/nare. The onset of action for this is 10 minutes, and the duration of action is about 20 minutes. It has the equivalent of IV morphine and has little or no side-effects.

Dexmedetomidine

It is a hypnotic sedative. Given intranasally at 0.5–2 mcg/kg has an onset of action of 25 minutes and a duration of action of 85 minutes, making it give prolonged sedation compared to other agents. It, however, has very little or no respiratory or haemodynamic compromise.

General Anaesthesia

It may be intravenous or inhalational. Attempts at deep general anaesthesia, especially with inhalational agents, require some training in airway management. General anaesthesia should only be used by persons with some experience of anaesthesia, airway management with pulse oximetry and cardiovascular monitoring.

Induction mainly depends on whether there is an IV in place or not. For children without an IV, an inhalational induction with either halothane or sevoflurane is the way to go. For those with an IV, short-acting agents such as propofol may be used. Ketamine, thiopentone and midazolam may all be used.

The airway management depends on various factors including the procedure being performed, site, duration and position. For most short painful procedures, face mask may be sufficient or laryngeal mask airways (LMAs) may be used.

Maintenance is usually with oxygen with or without nitrous oxide and a volatile anaesthetic if the procedure outlasts the duration of the IV anaesthetic used.

Pain control must be meticulous as though some procedures are painless, others can be very painful. Very often, paracetamol either orally or as a suppository will suffice. For more details on pain management, refer to Chapter 47. For drugs and their doses, refer to Appendix I.

Recovery from Anaesthesia

At this point, the main challenges that may be encountered include vomiting and aspiration, especially if the fasting protocol was not observed. Always place the child in the lateral position after anaesthesia so as to encourage gravity-assisted drainage of sputum and vomitus.

Children must be continuously monitored as they recover from anaesthesia/sedation until they are fully awake.

Airway problems may include bronchospasm or laryngospasm. These must be dealt with as with any other anaesthetic (refer to Chapter 16).

Extreme somnolence may be due to too high a dose of sedatives, exhaustion or electrolyte imbalance. Wait and watch and give oxygen if necessary. Admission to the hospital may be warranted for observation.

Comprehensive discharge criteria must be in place and used to minimise incidences of discharge of patients who are not ready.

SUGGESTED READINGS

1. Tran L, Squires J, Vera C, et al. Anesthesia and Sedation for Out-of-Operating Room Procedures. In: Smith's Anesthesia for Infants and Children, 10th edition. Davis PJ, Cladis FP (eds). Elsevier, Philadelphia 2022; pp. 1148–1167.
2. Cravero JP, Landrigan-Ossar ML. Anesthesia Outside the Operating Room. In: Practice of Anaesthesia for Infants and Children, 6th edition. Cote CJ, Lerman J, Anderson BJ (eds). WB Saunders, Philadelphia 2019; pp. 1077–1094.
3. Homma Y, Norii T, Kanazawa T, et al. A mini-review of procedural sedation and analgesia in the emergency department. *Acute Med Surg* 2020; 7(1):e574.

13 Practical Paediatric Regional Anaesthesia

Sajana Mukundan • Rebecca Jacob

The scope of regional anaesthesia in children has widened with the increased understanding of anatomy, physiology and perception of pain in children. The use of peripheral nerve stimulators (PNSs) and ultrasound-guided nerve blocks has made regional anaesthesia safer in this age group.

How Are Blocks Different in Children?

The anatomy and physiology of children are different from that of adults and therefore the technique of placing regional blocks in them is also different.

Anatomy

Target nerves, in children, are smaller and closer to other anatomic structures and the skin than in older patients. The surface landmarks cannot be regarded as simple downscaling of adult landmarks. Also, the 'feel' of a needle going through a ligament or fascia is much less distinct in children than in the older patient. Therefore, it is important to be able to predict the depth at which the needle will reach the target nerve, the epidural or subarachnoid space (see below under central neuraxial blockade). All these factors lead to an increased risk of injury to the nerve and the surrounding structures.

Myelination of the peripheral nerves is an ongoing process in children and varies between children and also between individual nerves. Hence, there is early onset of sensory and motor blocks with risk of longer lasting motor block. Epidural fat is more gelatinous and less fibrous in infants than in the adult. This favours the spread of local anaesthetic and the passage of epidural catheters.

Physiology

The increased cardiac output in children results in increased systemic absorption of local anaesthetics leading to risk of local anaesthesia toxicity. Clinically, significant decreases in blood pressure related to sympathectomy from central neuraxial blockade are rare in children less than 5 years of age. This is probably related to decreased venous capacitance of the lower limb and the immaturity of the sympathetic system. Thus, preloading with fluids prior to a subarachnoid or an epidural block in children is unnecessary.

Pharmacology

Refer to Chapter 3 where pharmacology of local anaesthetic agents is described under individual drugs.

Patient Cooperation

Children rarely cooperate with adults, especially strangers carrying needles. Hence, most regional techniques, except subarachnoid blocks (SABs) in premature neonates, are performed in the deeply sedated state or in an anaesthetised child who cannot report paraesthesia. Therefore, in children, identification of the peripheral nerve must involve objective signs. Here, the nerve stimulator or ultrasound is invaluable.

Test Doses

Test doses with lignocaine are not very useful as the child cannot complain of circumoral numbness with IV or heaviness of the leg with a lignocaine sub-arachnoid block (SAB). The use of adrenaline in diagnosing intravascular placement is also controversial, especially as the child is under anaesthesia with inhalational agents. It has been suggested that > 25% increase in T-wave amplitude on the ECG and >10% increase in heart rate may be the signs to watch for.

Indications

- **Perioperative analgesia**: Regional anaesthesia provides good perioperative analgesia, thus reducing the requirement of general anaesthesia. It diminishes the potential risk associated with deeper planes of anaesthesia which would be necessary if analgesia were inadequate. It also ensures a smooth pain-free awakening. In short cases, it can help avoid airway instrumentation and provide faster comfortable wakeup times in the operating room (OR) with quicker discharge and thus 'turnaround time' in the post-anaesthesia care unit (PACU). However, it must be remembered that most blocks take up to 20 minutes to maximum blockade and full general anaesthetic levels must be maintained for that time. If after that the volatile anaesthetic cannot be reduced, it must be assumed that the block is not working and alternate plans must be made to provide analgesia.
- **Post-operative analgesia**: Regional anaesthesia provides optimal post-operative analgesia as part of a balanced multimodal approach to pain management, which includes paracetamol, non-pharmacological support and occasional use of opioids. Since even a single dose of opioids can cause vomiting, they should be avoided, if possible.
- Regional anaesthesia helps in the management of non-surgical pain such as that seen in cancer, sickle cell disease, fracture femur or reflex sympathetic dystrophy.
- It helps relieve spasms associated with paraplegia or reduce undesirable reflexes associated with the anal sphincter or testicles which may cause laryngospasm.
- It can also help immobilise the limb for several hours after the suturing of tendons and nerves.
- It may be used as the sole anaesthetic in premature infants who have a high incidence of apnoea, especially after a general anaesthetic.

Contraindications to the use of regional blockade in children:

- Lack of parental consent
- Infection at the site of injection
- Coagulopathy
- Anatomical anomalies
- Untreated hypovolaemia
- Poorly controlled seizures and neurological diseases (central neuraxial)
- Difficult airway (relative)

Requirements for Regional Anaesthesia

The basic requirements for a regional block in a child include the following:

- The anaesthetist should be adequately trained and skilled in performing regional anaesthesia in paediatrics.
- As most blocks are provided under anaesthesia, trained personnel should be available to maintain anaesthesia and monitor the child while the block is placed

  A well-equipped operating or procedure room with equipment and drugs appropriate to the paediatric block requirement
- Supportive surgical and nursing colleagues. Surgeons will have to accept longer induction times and exert more care in certain situations such as the application of a bandage or plaster on a leg after a caudal epidural has been placed where ischaemia will not present as pain (a tight plaster cast will cause ischaemia which will present as pain and cold cyanosed toes). A caudal anaesthetic will obtund pain and early signs of ischaemia will thus be lost. Therefore, the presence of a caudal in these cases calls for good nursing care and extremely alert surgeons. The PACU and ward nurses are, therefore, an essential part of the team.
- Information and instructions should be provided to the PACU, pain management teams and parents. This should include the extent of motor and sensory loss and its implications,

especially the protection of a numb or 'sleepy' limb. The treating team should also be able to diagnose early signs of compartment syndrome in the presence of regional blocks.

General Principles

- Blocks should only be undertaken after thoroughly examining the child
- Obtaining informed consent from the parents and in cases of older children discussing the block with them
- Checking the anaesthetic machine, means of oxygenation and ventilation
- Monitoring of pulse oximetry, blood pressure and ECG
- IV access ensured prior to placement of the block
- Ensuring that all aseptic precautions will be undertaken while performing the block
- For all peripheral nerve blocks, the drugs used are lignocaine 0.5–1% to a maximum of 5 mg/kg body weight if used without adrenaline and 7 mg/kg body weight if used with adrenaline or bupivacaine 0.2–0.25% to a maximum of 2 mg/kg body weight or ropivacaine 0.2% maximum of 2 mg/kg
- Careful aspiration should be performed before giving the drug to rule out intravascular injection, and the drug should be given slowly with frequent aspirations
- Availability of equipment and drugs for resuscitation of local anaesthetic systemic toxicity should be ensured

Types of Blocks

The following types of regional blocks are commonly used in children:

- Topical blocks
- Infiltration blocks
- Peripheral nerve blocks
- Central neuraxial blocks

Topical Blocks

It is important to remember that by removing sensation (i.e., anaesthetising the skin) so that the child does not feel the needle will not decrease his fear of the needle! So be gentle and kind when starting an IV after topical anaesthesia.

Indications

- To anaesthetise the skin and intact mucous membranes

Cautions

- Known sensitivity to prilocaine (eutectic mixture of local anaesthetics [EMLA])

Drugs/Dose

- Enough to have a good contact with the surface

Technique/Mode of Action

EMLA is a combination of lignocaine 2.5% and prilocaine 2.5% oil-in-water emulsion cream that can penetrate intact skin to a depth of 5 mm. The white cream requires 1 hour for its action. So, it should be applied to the skin and covered with an occlusive dressing for 1 hour prior to the procedure.

Topical analgesia (lignocaine 4%) has also been used for analgesia of mucous membranes (e.g., following tonsillectomy and circumcision) and for analgesia of exposed muscle and nerve (e.g., in cases of inguinal herniorrhaphy). Oropharyngeal and intratracheal lignocaine are often used for dentistry and bronchoscopy.

Infiltration Blocks

Infiltration nerve blocks of somatic nerves in the surgical field can also provide perioperative pain relief (Fig. 13.1).

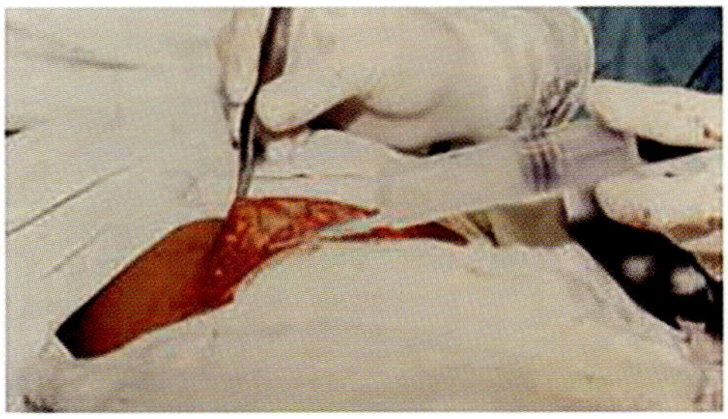

Figure 13.1 Infiltration block.

Peripheral Nerve Block

Peripheral nerve blocks can be performed using a *landmark-based technique*. Here, the nerve is approached using relevant landmarks. Its position is confirmed when paraesthesia is elicited. This can be uncomfortable and is not always accurate. In cases where paraesthesia may not be elicited as in children under general anaesthesia, the nerve may even be damaged.

Nerve Stimulator–Based Technique

The *nerve stimulator–based technique* (also using appropriate landmarks) uses small amounts of DC current applied to the nerve so as to elicit a motor response in the muscles supplied by the motor component of the nerve, thus providing objective evidence of proximity to the nerve. More recently, *ultrasound-guided* (USG) *nerve blocks* have gained popularity with nerve stimulator–based techniques often playing a role only in situations where ultrasound machines are not available. The concomitant use of both techniques is helpful in teaching novices the USG-guided technique and is especially useful in obese patients where it may improve block efficiency and efficacy.

Physiology and Physics of Nerve Stimulation

When a stimulus of sufficient strength is applied to a motor nerve, it depolarises the membrane to set off an action potential which is then propagated along the nerve to the muscle it supplies leading to its contraction. The ability of a current stimulus to elicit a muscular contraction depends on the strength of the current, the type of neuron, the proximity of the needle to the nerve and the electrical impedance of the surrounding tissues. The duration of current applied to elicit a response varies according to the type of nerve, with the motor Aα requiring the least time (100 μs) compared to the sensory C (>400 μs) or Aδ fibres (170 μs). Hence, a motor response is elicited even before the subject feels pain if the current applied is of a shorter duration. The *threshold current* is the minimum current required to elicit a motor response. It decreases as the stimulating needle approaches closer to the nerve. It must be remembered, however, that the electrical impedance of the surrounding tissue affects the threshold current. A highly conducting tissue around the nerve disperses the current away from the nerve increasing the threshold current whereas in a tissue with high impedance like fat the threshold current is reduced.

Equipment

The Nerve Stimulator

The present generation of nerve stimulators is designed to be a constant current generator to compensate for the wide range of impedances encountered clinically. The current output can range from 0.01 to 5 mA. The current output is controlled by a dial on the PNS, a foot operated pedal or a remote-controlled knob.

The nerve stimulator equipment (**Fig. 13.2**) consists of the electrical stimulator, the conducting wires, the electrode and the needle. The cathode end of the stimulator is always connected to the needle while the skin electrode is connected to the anode. The electrical impedance at the skin electrode interface should be minimised, and this necessitates the use of high-quality electrodes.

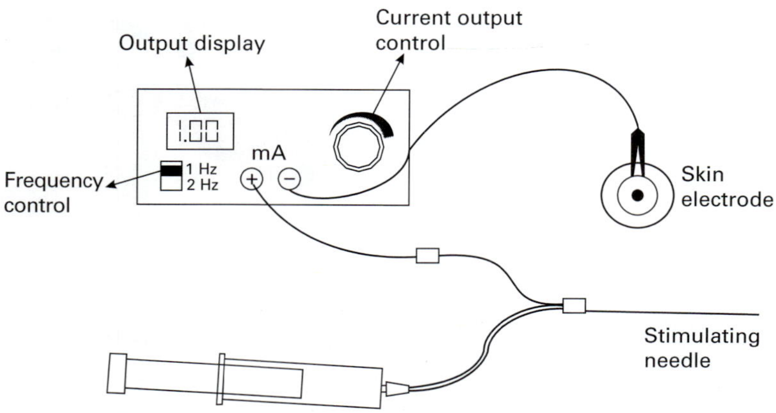

Figure 13.2 Setting up a nerve stimulator.

Stimulating Needle

A needle that is insulated completely except for the tip is preferable to the non-insulated needle as the insulation prevents the dispersion of the current into the surrounding tissue and reduces the threshold current. A needle of appropriate length depending on the probable depth of the neural structure to be identified is selected. Short bevel needles have been shown to reduce impalement of the nerve. It is preferable to use needles with depth markings for easy identification and documentation.

Practical Considerations for Use of the Nerve Stimulation Technique

Before the start of the procedure, the nerve stimulator and the connecting cables should be checked. The initial current intensity should be set at 1 mA for superficial nerve blocks and 1.5 mA for deep nerve blocks. The current duration of 0.1 ms is appropriate for motor nerve stimulation. A frequency of 1–2 Hz is selected as higher frequencies, though giving frequent feedbacks, would be uncomfortable. Lower frequencies can result in nerve injury between impulses.

The needle is inserted based on the anatomical landmarks used traditionally for the nerve block. As the needle advances towards the nerve, an appropriate motor response is sought. For deeper nerves, this may necessitate increase in current to up to 3 mA. However, such a response should be sought at a safe distance from the nerve. Once the sought-after muscle response is obtained, the current intensity amplitude is gradually reduced and the needle is advanced further slowly until the desired motor response is achieved with a current of 0.35–0.5 mA at 0.1 ms stimulus duration. A test dose of local anaesthetic abolishes the muscle twitch. Muscular twitch response at very low current 0.2 mA or less indicates intraneural placement. Absence of muscular twitch response even at high amplitude of current, however, does not rule out intraneural placement of the needle.

Peripheral Nerve Blocks

Commonly done nerve blocks in children are described under the following headings:

- Nerve blocks of the head and neck
- Nerve blocks of the thorax and abdomen
- Nerve blocks of the lower limb
- Nerve blocks of the upper limb

Nerve Blocks of the Head and Neck

Infraorbital Nerve Block

Anatomy

The infraorbital nerve (Fig. 13.3) is the termination of the second division of the trigeminal nerve, which is purely sensory to the lower eyelid, the lateral inferior portion of the nose and its vestibule, the upper lip and the mucosa of the upper lip. The nerve emerges onto the face through the infraorbital foramen of the maxilla before dividing into its four terminal branches.

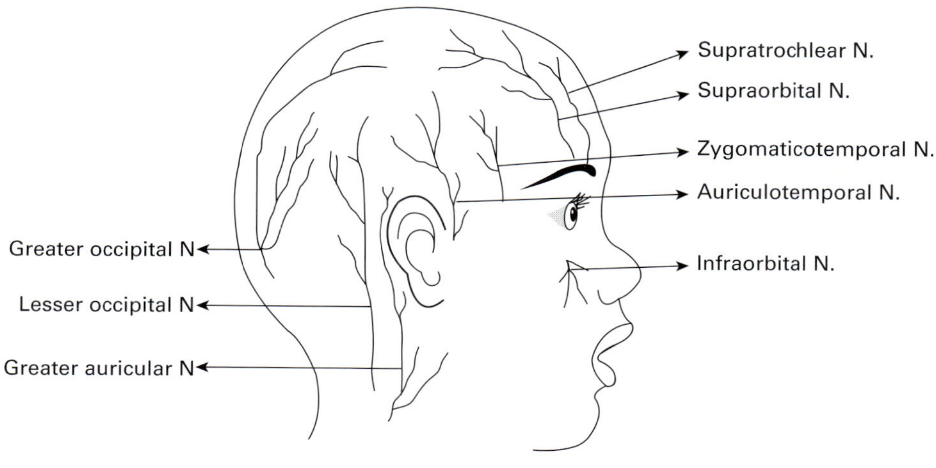

Figure 13.3 Nerve blocks of the face.

Indication

- Cleft lip surgery, surgery of the upper lip, rhinoplasty, surgery on the side of nose and skin of lower eyelids

Drugs/Dosages

- Bupivacaine 0.25–0.5%, ropivacaine 0.2%, lignocaine 1–2% with or without adrenaline and 0.25–1 ml per side depending on the size of the patient

Technique

Palpate the infraorbital foramen 0.5 cm from the mid-point of the lower orbital margin (mid-point of the inferior orbital margin corresponds to approximately the middle of the pupil, if the eyeball is central).

Intraoral route – Using a 25 or 27G 1.5″ needle, enter the alveolus above the incisor tooth aiming towards the finger of the non-dominant hand locating the infraorbital notch externally. Feel the needle come close to but not into the palpating finger. Inject enough local anaesthetic to feel a wheal rise.

Percutaneous route – Using a 26–27G needle, puncture the skin near the palpating finger, touch bone of notch and withdraw the needle slightly so that injection is not intraosseous. Inject the same amount as above.

Both intraoral and extraoral techniques can be given bilaterally.

Complications and Precaution

If an intraoral approach is used, it must be done prior to surgery to avoid disruption of repair. Complications of both approaches include ecchymosis, swelling and damage to the orbit.

Supraorbital/Supratrochlear Nerve Block

Anatomy

The supraorbital and supratrochlear nerves are the terminal branches of the frontal nerve which is the largest branch of the ophthalmic division of the trigeminal nerve.

Indications

- Bicoronal flaps and craniofacial surgery

Drugs/Dosages

- Bupivacaine 0.25–0.5%, ropivacaine 0.2%, lignocaine 1–2% with or without adrenaline and 0.5–3 ml per side depending on the size of the patient

Technique

For supraorbital nerve block, palpate the superior orbital notch/foramen. Place the needle below the eyebrow and direct the needle medially and cephalad. Raise a skin wheal. The needle is further directed towards the midline and a second injection is administered. Bilateral block is usually done.

Auriculotemporal Nerve Block

Anatomy

The nerve is a branch of mandibular division of the trigeminal nerve and the sensory fibres travel along with the superficial temporal artery in the infratemporal fossa providing sensation to the tragus and helix of the ear and the temple.

Indications

- Craniotomy for temporo-parietal incisions

Drugs/Dosages

- Bupivacaine 0.25–0.5%, ropivacaine 0.2%, lignocaine 1–2% with or without adrenaline and 0.5–3 ml per side depending on the size of the patient

Technique

A subcutaneous injection is given at the mid-point of the line joining the pinna and the angle of the eye.

Greater Auricular Nerve Block

Anatomy

The greater auricular nerve is a branch of the superficial cervical plexus. It wraps around the belly of the sternocleidomastoid muscle at the level of the cricoid cartilage, McKinney's point, before providing sensory innervation to the mastoid area and external ear.

Indication

- Analgesia in otoplasty and tympano-mastoid. These surgeries are often associated with nausea and vomiting. By providing good analgesia with a regional block, the incidence of post-operative nausea and vomiting can be reduced.

Drugs/Dosages

- Bupivacaine 0.25–0.5%, ropivacaine 0.2%, lignocaine 1–2% with or without adrenaline, and 0.5–3 ml per side depending on the size of the patient

Technique

Draw a line from the superior margin of the cricoid cartilage to the posterior border of the sternocleidomastoid, McKinney's point. Give 2–3 ml of the drug at this point.

Complication

- If too deep, deep cervical plexus block will result with Horner's syndrome, phrenic nerve palsy and/or central neuroaxial block.

Greater Occipital Nerve Block

Anatomy

Arises from the medial division of the posterior rami of C2, C3 nerve roots, becomes superficial at the level of the superior nuchal line, and travels cephalad along with the occipital artery. Innervates the skin of the posterior scalp up to the vertex.

Indications

- Occipital neuralgia and posterior fossa surgery

Drugs/Dosages

- Bupivacaine 0.25–0.5%, ropivacaine 0.2%, lignocaine 1–2% with or without adrenaline and 0.5–3 ml per side depending on the size of the patient

Technique

Place the patient in the prone position with the head flexed forward. Draw a line from the occipital protuberance to the mastoid. A needle is inserted at the junction of medial one-third and lateral two-thirds. Inject local anaesthetic in a fan-like distribution at this site.

Thorax and Abdomen

Intercostal Nerve Block (Fig. 13.4)

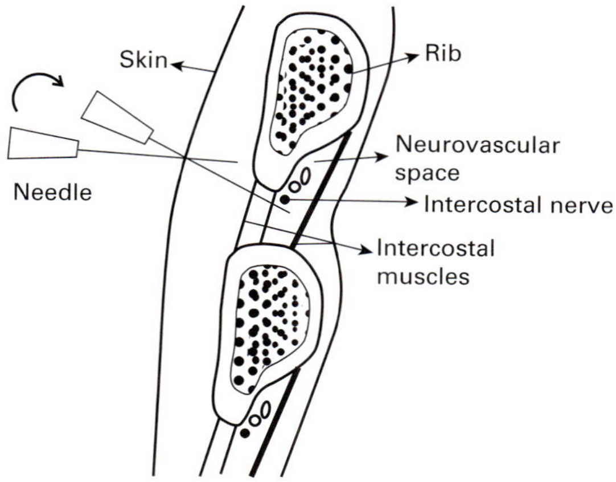

Figure 13.4 Intercostal nerve block.

Anatomy

The intercostal nerves derive from the ventral rami of the 1st to 12th thoracic nerves. They emerge from the intervertebral foramina and lie in the groove along the inner aspect of the lower border of the rib in between the external and the internal intercostal muscles superficially, and the innermost intercostals on the deeper plane. Each intercostal nerve divides into the following four branches:

- The grey rami communicantes to the sympathetic ganglia
- The posterior cutaneous branch which supplies the paravertebral area
- The lateral cutaneous branch which arises anterior to the mid-axillary line and sends branches both anteriorly and posteriorly
- The anterior cutaneous branch which supplies the anterior chest and abdomen

Indications

- Post-operative pain relief, analgesia in case of rib fracture

Drugs/Dosages

- Bupivacaine 0.25, ropivacaine 0.2%, lignocaine 1% with or without adrenaline 0.5–1 ml

of complications. The interscalene approach is rarely used in paediatrics due to lack of indications and increased complications. The other approaches to the brachial plexus should be done under ultrasound guidance to prevent complications like pneumothorax, neural injury and hematoma formation.

Axillary Approach to Brachial Plexus Block

Anatomy

The medial, lateral and posterior cords of the brachial plexus surround the axillary artery while the axillary vein lies on its medial side. All these structures are enclosed in a fascial sheath.

Indications

- Surgery on arm, forearm and hand

Drugs/Dosages

- Bupivacaine 0.25%, ropivacaine 0.2% and lignocaine 1% with adrenaline at 0.5 ml/kg up to 40 ml

Technique

The axillary artery is palpated at its highest point with the arm abducted and externally rotated (**Fig. 13.14**). A short bevel needle is inserted (with the other hand) slightly lateral and towards the artery until the 'pop' of entering the sheath is felt and the needle begins to pulsate. The entire volume of drug may be injected at this point with pressure applied distally directly on the artery or with a tourniquet. This prevents distal spread of the drug. If a nerve stimulator is used, look for twitching of the fingers. The indicators as to which nerve is being stimulated are as follows:

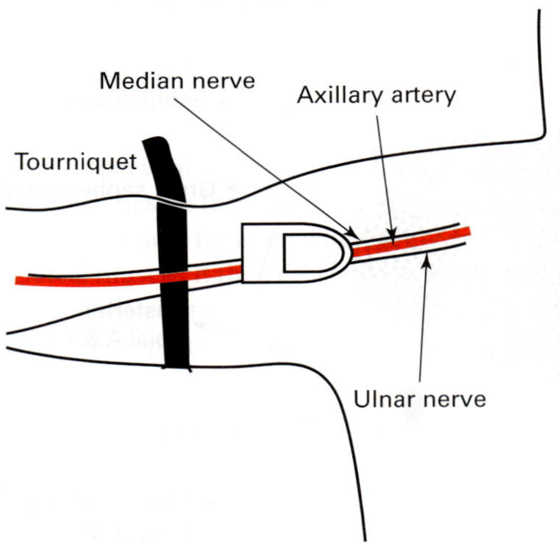

Figure 13.14 Brachial plexus block by the axillary approach. Note tourniquet distal to the point of injection.

- **Median nerve** – flexion of the index and middle fingers
- **Radial nerve** – extension of the wrist and fingers
- **Ulnar nerve** – flexion of the little and ring finger and adduction of the thumb

Caution

The brachial plexus is superficial in children. Avoid with supracondylar fractures or other fractures associated with nerve injuries and risk of compartment syndrome because of the need for frequent neurological evaluation.

Central Neuraxial Blockade

The commonest central neuraxial block used in children is the 'single shot' caudal epidural block. Spinal anaesthesia is rarely used though it is still often used in premature babies for hernia repair or circumcision. Lumbar and thoracic epidurals are becoming popular with the advent of smaller epidural needles and catheters. They provide good analgesia during surgery and well into the postoperative period.

Anatomy and Physiology

In neonates and infants, the anatomy and physiology are very different from adults. The caudal extent of the dura and spinal cord is approximately two vertebral spaces lower in infants than in adults. The conus medullaris is located at L3 vertebra and reaches the final L1 position only at 1 year of age (**Fig. 13.15**). Therefore, lumbar punctures for SAB in neonates and infants should only be performed between L4-5 and L5-S1 interspaces to avoid injury to the spinal cord.

The angle of approach to the epidural space is slightly more perpendicular to the plane of the back than in the older child or adult. The distance from the skin to the subarachnoid space is approximately 1.4 cm in neonates and increases with age.

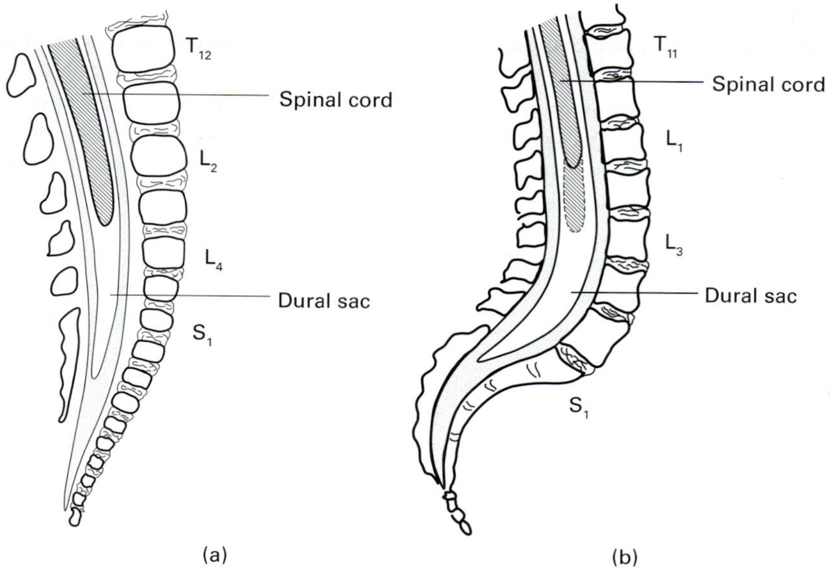

Figure 13.15 (a and b) (a) Neonatal caudal space – the spinal cord is lower and the spine less curved as compared to the adult sacrum and caudal epidural space (b). (Reproduced with permission from Polaner DM, Suresh S, Cote CJ. In: A Practice of Anesthesia for Infants and Children, 3rd edn, 2001; 642)

The ligamentum flavum is much thinner and less dense in infants and children making its penetration by the epidural needle more difficult to detect with a greater risk of dural puncture. The vertebral laminae are poorly calcified at this age and a paramedian approach 'walking the needle off' the lamina should not be attempted. Stick to a midline approach. The sacrum is narrower and flatter than in the adult and it is easier to puncture the dura from the caudal canal. Note that a sacral dimple may signify a spina bifida occulta, and dural puncture is more likely.

Cerebrospinal fluid (CSF) volume as a percentage of body weight is greater in infants accounting for the relatively high dose required to produce surgical anaesthesia with a SAB. The CSF turnover rate is high accounting for the short duration of the SAB.

Contraindications

Altered anatomy as in spina bifida or meningomyelocele (though SAB has been used for its repair), raised intracranial pressure or hydrocephalus, infection at the site of injection or sepsis, coagulopathy or uncorrected hypovolaemia.

Caudal Epidural Analgesia

Anatomy

The sacral hiatus is often found at the apex of an equilateral triangle, the base of which is formed by a line joining the posterior–superior iliac spines. However, this is not always the case as there are often congenital anomalies with regard to the sacrum. Palpate the sacral spines in the midline and continue palpating in a caudal direction until the sacral hiatus is reached. Moving the finger in a lateral to medial direction will detect the two sacral cornuae as bony ridges. Palpating from below upwards could lead to mistaken identification of the space between the sacrum and the coccyx as the sacral hiatus.

Indications

- Usually used for surgeries below the diaphragm, especially in sacral, lower lumbar areas and lower limbs.

Drugs/Dosages

Modified Armitage formula: 0.5 ml/kg – sacral, 0.75 ml/kg – T10, 1.0 ml/kg – lower thoracic (up to T6), 1.25 ml/kg – mid-thoracic.

Takasaki's formula: Volume (ml) = 0.05 ml/kg/dermatome to be blocked.

Technique (Fig. 13.16)

The patient is placed in the lateral position with the thighs flexed at right angles to the hip. The sacral hiatus is identified and the 22G short bevel needle inserted at an angle of 60°–90° at its apex until a distinct pop is felt. At this point, the sacrococcygeal membrane is best felt by the needle and is the deepest part of the sacral canal so that the entire bevel of the needle is within the canal. A needle with a longer bevel may be partly outside the canal or may traumatise a vessel or periosteum as it is pushed in. The needle is stabilised, careful aspiration for blood and CSF done. The drug may now be given at this point in small aliquots with repeated aspiration with a careful watch on the ECG. Some authors suggest decreasing the angle of entry to 30°–45° and advancing a few millimetres. This may be necessary in the smaller infant who has a shallower canal or when using a longer bevel needle to ensure that the whole bevel is inside the canal (beware of dural puncture with the longer bevel and this technique). It is easier to do the block with a saline-filled 2 ml syringe with a small air bubble entrapped in it attached to the needle. This is easier to hold like a pen and the position of the needle tip may be tested straightaway. Free flow of saline without a change in the shape of the air bubble confirms correct placement in the caudal epidural space.

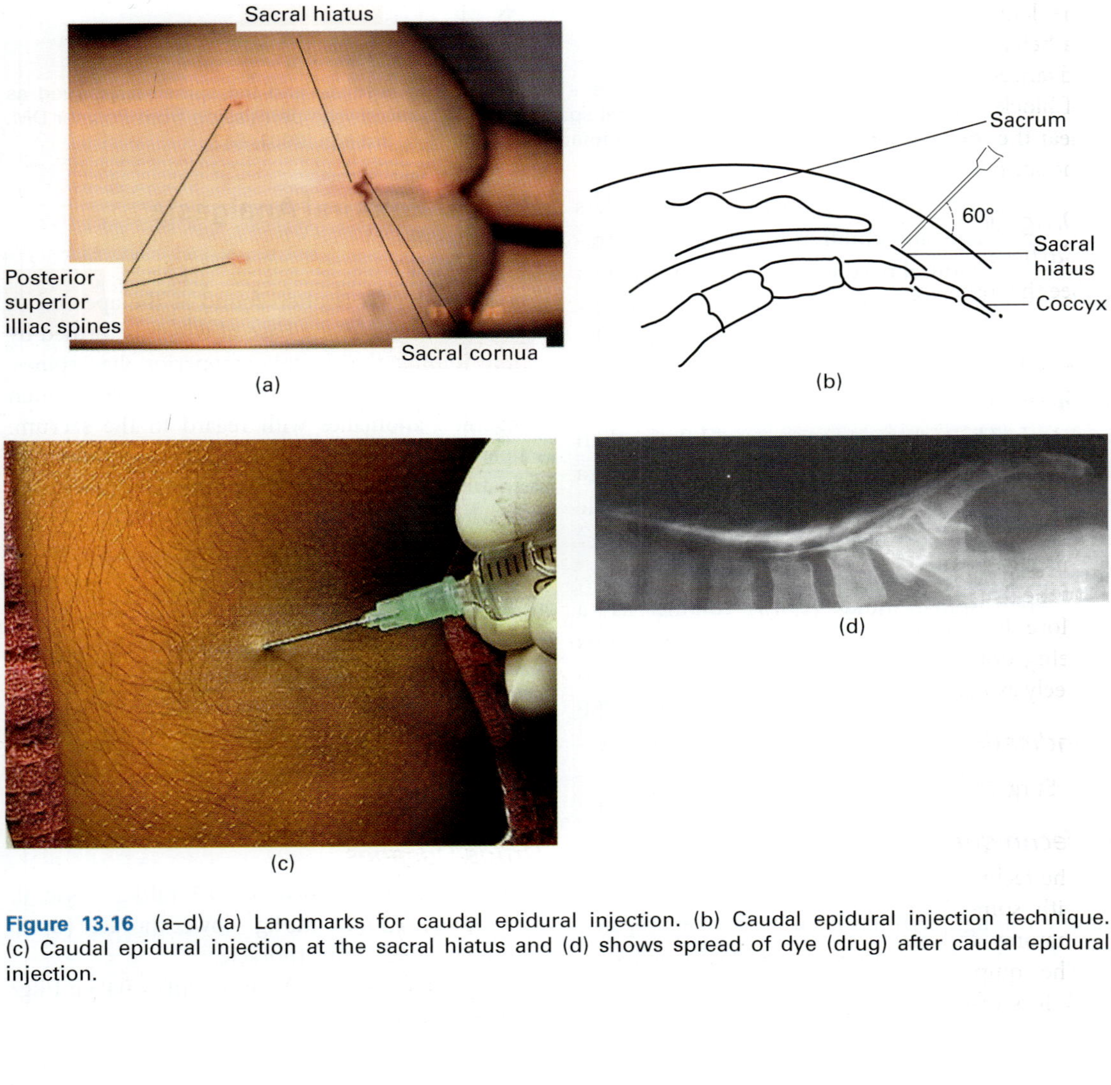

Figure 13.16 (a–d) (a) Landmarks for caudal epidural injection. (b) Caudal epidural injection technique. (c) Caudal epidural injection at the sacral hiatus and (d) shows spread of dye (drug) after caudal epidural injection.

Complications and Precautions

The most common reason for a failed block is the local anaesthetic being placed too low with the coccyx being mistaken for a sacral hiatus.

Intravascular, subperiosteal, subarachnoid, rectal puncture and nerve injury have all been described.

Continuous Caudal Epidural

Indications are similar to the 'single shot' but is used when the patient will benefit from prolonged analgesia. The procedure is the same as described above but the needle used is larger. It could be a Crawford needle or a large IV cannula or a paediatric Touhy needle. In all cases, check that the catheter will pass through it easily and the length of the needle with reference to the catheter. Once the needle is in place, the catheter is advanced 2–3 cm or more depending on the level of block required. The catheter tip is placed at or near the mid-point of the dermatomes involved in the surgical incision.

Drug Dosages and Tunnelling of Catheters

See the following text.

Lumbar and Thoracic Continuous Epidural Block

Advantages include exclusion of the insertion site from the diaper area with less risk of contamination with stool or urine, closer proximity to the desired tip location with less chance of curling or misplacement of the catheter and a lower volume of the drug required for a higher dermatomal level. More lumbar and thoracic epidural blocks are being done now that paediatric epidural kits are freely available.

Indications

- Surgery on thorax, abdomen and lower limbs

Technique

The technique is similar to that used in adults but with some important differences mainly in the anatomy and physiology (see the preceding text). The equipment required is shown in **Figure 13.17**. A loss-of-resistance technique is used; however, saline and not air should be used as fatal venous air embolism is more common in infants. The catheter is placed so that the tip lies at or near the dermatomes involving the surgical incision. It is important to secure the catheter well. This may be done by tunnelling the catheter out to a point 2–3 cm away from the point of entry. Reinforce the hub/catheter connection and dress the catheter so that the skin–catheter junction is visible. It is best not to disconnect and give the drug as this will introduce infection. Use a bacterial filter and run an infusion rather than using intermittent injections (**Fig. 13.18**).

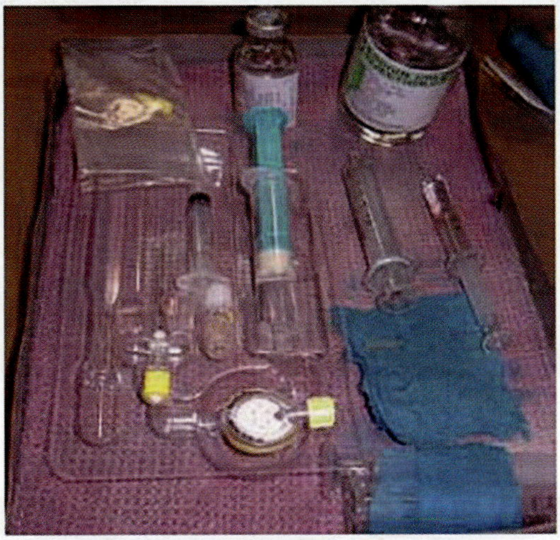

Figure 13.17 Equipment for continuous epidural block.

Drug/Dosages

Calculate the dose carefully to avoid administration of potentially toxic doses. We use 0.2% bupivacaine for the initial bolus followed by an infusion of 0.1% bupivacaine with 1 μgm of fentanyl. An initial bolus of 0.04 ml/kg/segment may be given followed by a maximum of 0.4 ml/kg/hr in children over 6 months of age and 0.1–0.2 ml/kg/hr in infants below 6 months.

Complications

- Problems with technique: Dural puncture (with headache especially in the older child), subarachnoid and intravascular puncture and infection.
- Retrieving the catheter in case of a spica cast is a problem.

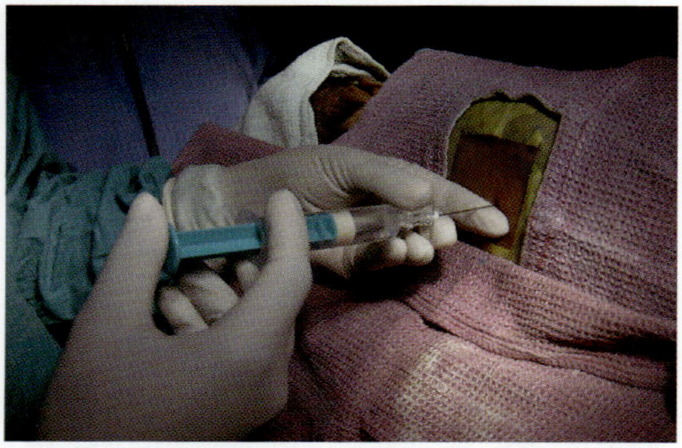

(a)

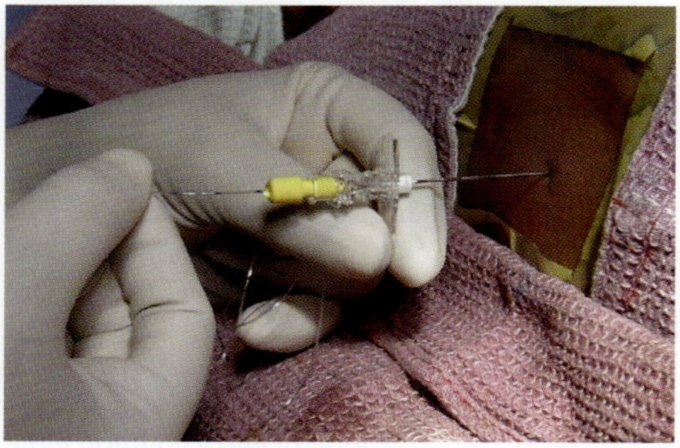

(b)

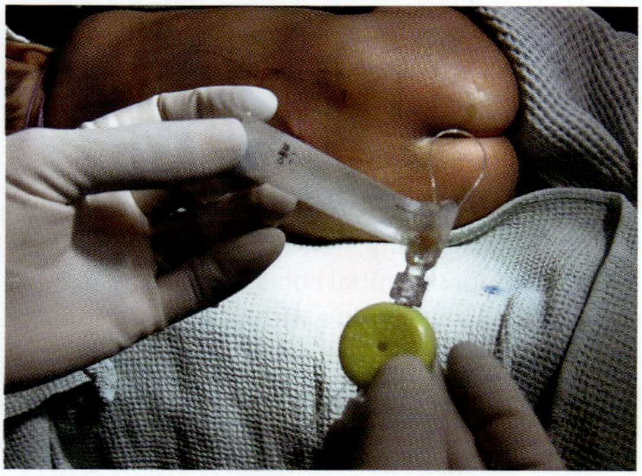

(c)

Figure 13.18 **(a–c)** (a) Epidural technique, (b) threading of the catheter and (c) fixing the filter.

Problems with the Drug and Dose

Allergy to local anaesthetic, overdose and drug toxicity, motor blockade, respiratory compromise especially with high blocks, urinary retention, itching and nausea and vomiting especially with opioids.

Problems with Equipment

- Catheter blocks, kinking, knotting or breaking and infusion pump malfunction

Precautions

- Need to maintain a clean dressing area in case of young infants.

Subarachnoid Blocks

Anatomy

See the preceding text.

Indications

- Surgery on the lower abdomen and lower limbs in preterm or ex-preterms who are at a high risk for post-op apnoea.

Drug/Dosage

- 0.2 mg/kg of 0.5% hyperbaric bupivacaine

Technique

With the child in the lateral or sitting position with the head extended, the back is cleaned and a small amount of local anaesthetic is infiltrated over L4-5 or L5-S1 (EMLA cream may be applied earlier). The lumbar puncture (LP) is performed with a 22G styleted paediatric spinal needle (CSF may take an unduly long time to flow in smaller needles) and the drug injected after aspiration.

Precautions

Perform the block at L4-5 or L5-S1 as the spinal cord ends at L3. When positioning the baby, ensure that the neck is extended as flexion may lead to airway obstruction. After doing the block, do not raise the lower part of the baby (as you would to place the cautery plate under the buttocks) so as to avoid a high block. Do not sedate the baby as this may produce apnoea. Most babies will go to sleep with a pacifier after the block.

Safety

All the techniques described in the preceding text are reasonably safe in the proper hands though not without some inherent risks. Just because we can perform a block, it does not necessarily mean that the patient requires it or it is the best choice for that individual child. Optimum analgesia is achieved by the proper administration of analgesics before, during and after the procedure along with the regional block. Emotional support to the child and his parents is also important.

SUGGESTED READINGS

1. Suresh S, Polaner DM, Coté CJ. 42 - Regional Anesthesia. In: A Practice of Anesthesia for Infants and Children, 6th edition. Coté CJ, Lerman J, Anderson BJ (eds).. Elsevier, Philadelphia 2019; pp. 941–87.e9.
2. Ecoffey C. Pediatric Regional Anesthesia. In: Gregory's Pediatric Anesthesia. Andropoulos DB, Gregory GA (eds) 2020. https://doi.org/10.1002/9781119371533.ch20
3. Suresh S, Voronov P. Head and neck blocks in children: An anatomical and procedural review. *Paediatr Anaesth* 2006; 16(9):910–918. doi: 10.1111/j.1460-9592.2006.02018.x. PMID: 16918651.
4. Byun S, Pather N. Pediatric regional anesthesia: A review of the relevance of surface anatomy and landmarks used for peripheral nerve blockades in infants and children. *Clin Anat* 2019; 32(6):803–823. doi: 10.1002/ca.23406. Epub 2019 May 24. PMID: 31087337.
5. Lang RS, Hall-Burton D, Praslick A, et al. Regional Anesthesia. In: Smith's Anesthesia for Infants and Children, 10th edition. Davis PJ, Cladis FP (eds). Elsevier, Inc., Philadelphia 2021; pp. 519–577.e8.
6. Roberts S. Peripheral Nerve Blocks for Children - NYSORA: @NYSORA; 2023 (updated 25 May 2023). Available from: https://www.nysora.com/topics/sub-specialties/pediatric-anesthesia/peripheral-nerve-blocks-children/

When the voltage is removed, it contracts back into its original thickness. A rapid application and removal of an electric current generate ultrasound waves.

Ultrasound transducers come in a variety of shapes and frequencies. The shape of the probe determines its field of view and the frequency determines how deep the sound waves penetrate and the resolution of the image.

Ultrasound probes (Fig. 14.2): Most ultrasound-guided regional anaesthetic blocks in children can be performed using high-frequency, linear ultrasound probes. These probes are available in variable frequencies based on their manufacturer and are multipurpose in their use. Some manufacturers offer smaller probes that are designed specifically for paediatric usage. These probes have a smaller footprint and are lightweight, allowing for better ergonomics when used on smaller patients. Paediatric probes are available as linear high-frequency probes with smaller width or as curved low-frequency probes.

4. **Keyboard:** The keyboard serves as an interface between the user and the machine. Apart from keys for alphabet inputs, it contains various dials and sliders to adjust the settings of the machine.

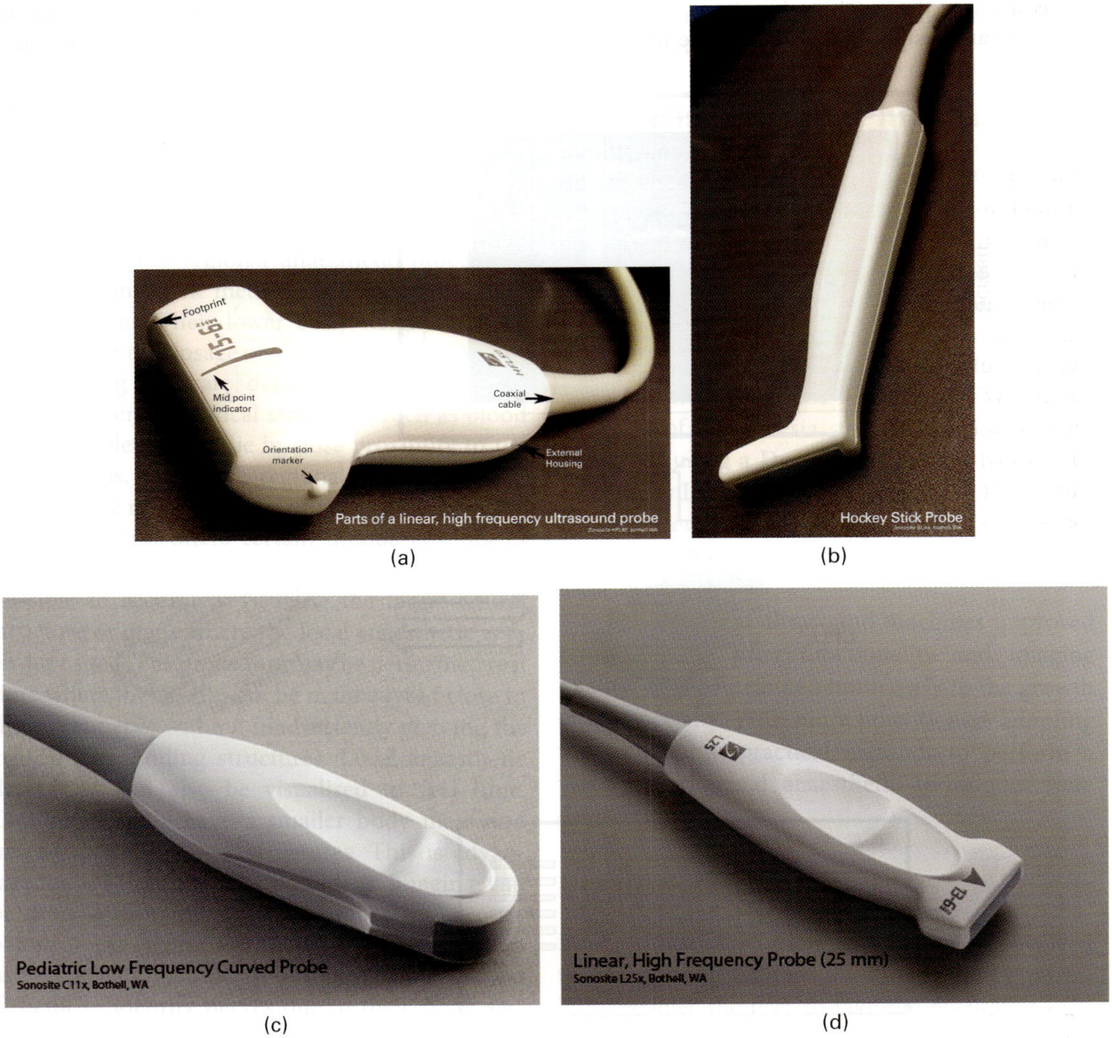

Figure 14.2 (a–d) Adult and paediatric probes.

Practical Considerations

Probe Grips

A common beginner's error is to hold the probe higher up, close to where the cable is attached. Holding the probe in this position does not allow the user to make fine adjustments and may contribute to hand fatigue. A more efficient way of holding the probe is depicted in Figure 14.3. The probe is held, close to the base in the non-dominant hand of the user. The little finger and hypothenar eminence rest upon the patient. This grip allows greater dexterity to perform probe movements while minimising fatigue during prolonged procedures.

Probe Movements

Image generation and optimisation is a crucial step in ultrasound-guided regional anaesthesia (USGRA). The quality images of the area to be scanned are not generated by merely placing the probe on the surface but are the result of various manoeuvres with the probe that enhance the primary image. Generating the best possible image helps to closely identify the structures within the area. Probe movements are a dynamic and ongoing process while performing the block. After generation of an optimal image, the probe will need further fine adjustment when the needle is inserted into the patient to ensure that both the needle and the target structure are visualised together in real time. This is an important concept, often overlooked by novices who keep the probe in a fixed position and are averse to moving it.

Figure 14.4 depicts some important movements of the probe to generate optimal images.

In-Plane Needling Technique

In-plane refers to the needling technique where the needle is inserted along the length of the ultrasound probe. Inserting the needle in this manner aligns the entire length of the beam with the shaft of the needle (Fig. 14.5). The resulting image should depict the shaft of the needle and its tip in its entirety. The advantage of using this approach for a nerve block is that the needle tip can easily be visualised, thereby improving precision. The disadvantage is that the needle visibility is dependent on the angle of insertion of the needle and the path to the target structure may not be the shortest.

Out-of-Plane Needling Technique

The out-of-plane approach involves insertion of the needle, usually at the midpoint of the probe where the needle eventually cuts across the ultrasound beam. The image formed is a cross-section of the needle tip/shaft (Fig. 14.6). The path to the target is usually the shortest with this approach. However, needle visibility is not often the best and one must rely on indirect markers such as tissue movement and hydro dissection to confirm where the needle tip is.

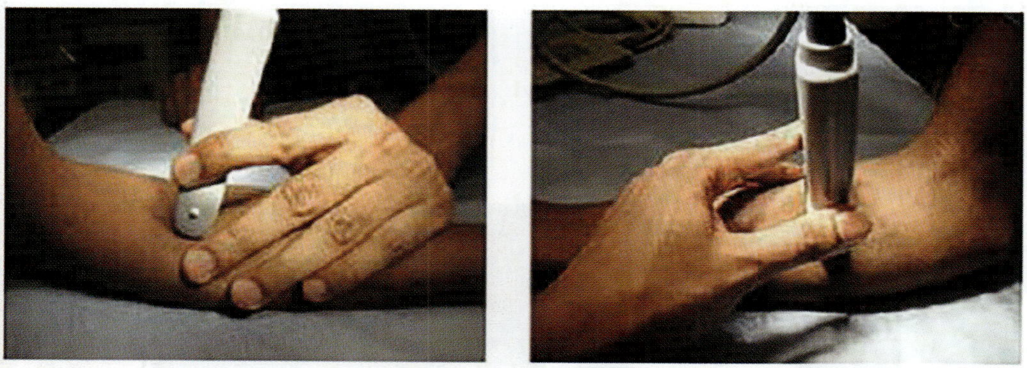

Figure 14.3 Probe grips: The probe is held close to the base primarily by the index finger and the thumb. The remaining fingers rest upon the patient. Note that there is enough place to move the probe in either direction and adequate space for needle insertion and visualisation.

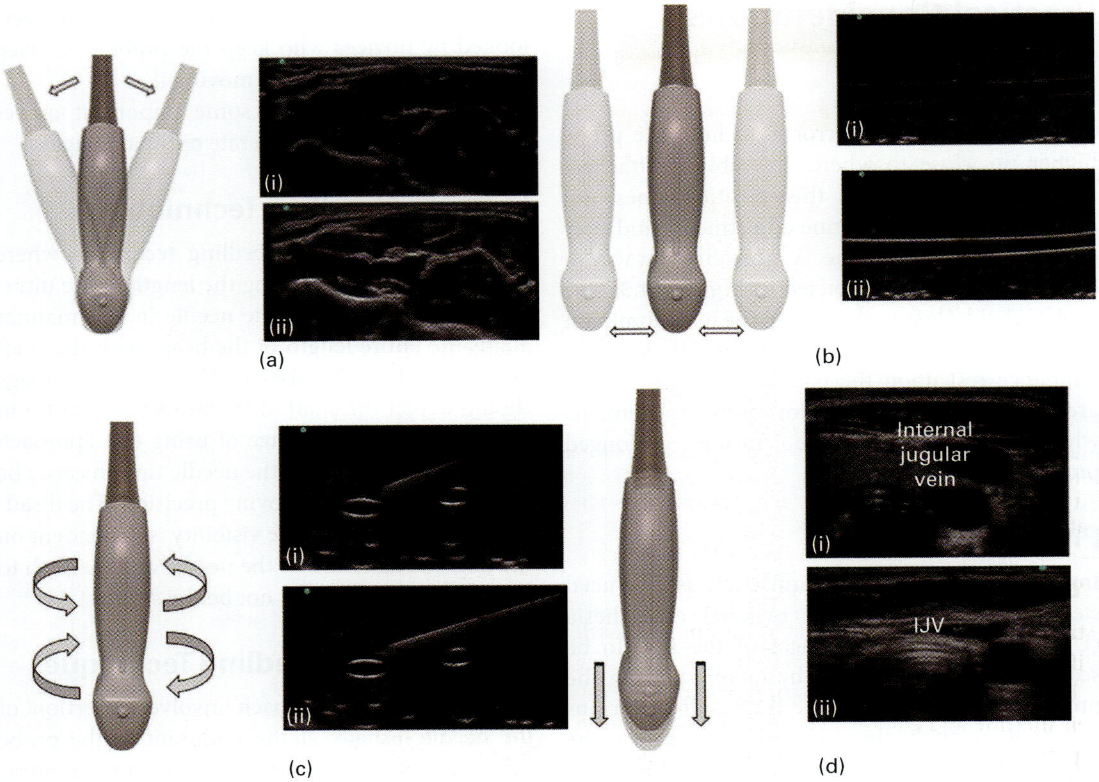

Figure 14.4 (a–d) Probe movements. (a) *Tilting:* Figure (i) shows the median nerve when the probe is placed directly on the skin without any optimisation movements. Figure (ii) shows how the image is enhanced by tilting the probe and overcoming anisotropy. (b) *Sliding:* Figure (i) shows how a structure can be aligned and imaged with greater clarity by sliding the probe towards it after initial recognition. (c) *Rotation:* Figure (i) shows how only part of the needle is being imaged. Figure (ii) The rotation manoeuvre aligns the beam with the shaft of the needle, thereby showing it in its entirety. (d) *Pressure:* (i), (ii) Gentle downwards pressure onto the patient's skin provides complete contact of the probe's footprint, thereby minimising air artifacts and enhancing picture quality. Pressure also may compress overlying tissues and bring the target structures apparently closer. Lastly, pressure may be used to compress and identify veins and distinguish them from non-compressible arteries. IJV, internal jugular vein.

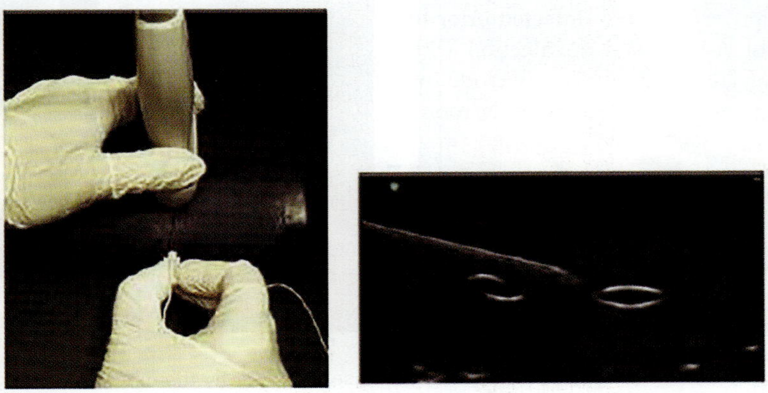

Figure 14.5 In-plane technique. Note how the needle is inserted precisely in line with the probe. The resulting ultrasound image shows in the entire shaft and the tip of the needle approaching the target. The probe is continuously adjusted during the block to maintain similar needle characteristics.

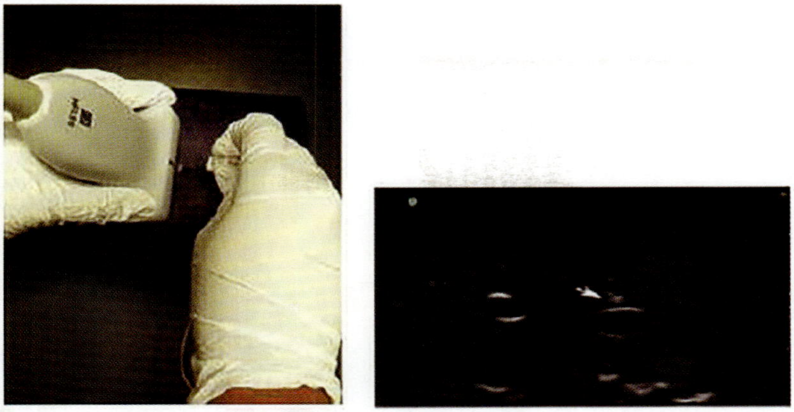

Figure 14.6 Out-of-plane technique. The needle is inserted at the midpoint of the probe at the marker which indicates the same. The resulting image shows the needle as a hyperechoic dot close to the target. It is important that the needle does not traverse far across the beam of the probe as this would display a cross-section of the shaft, rather than the needle tip.

Probe Sterility

Ultrasound probes are reusable equipment with a lifespan of several years. These probes are likely to be used on several thousand patients during their lifetime and can be a vehicle for transmission of pathogens between patients. Nerve blocks and continuous catheter techniques must be considered as sterile procedures at all times, and strict asepsis must be followed.

Asepsis can be maintained by using antimicrobial solutions on the patient, by strict scrubbing of hands by the procedurist and by using sterile disposable equipment and needles. The ultrasound probe, however, must be sterilised or isolated in a different manner.

Most manufacturers will provide information as to how a probe can be disinfected prior to use. Many do not recommend disinfection with alcohol-containing solutions as this may erode the probe in the long run. In a busy operating room, repeated attempts to sterilise the probe may prove impractical. Barrier methods to isolate the probe with sterile films are the most popular way to ensure asepsis.

There are several commercial plastic barrier sheaths available that isolate the probe and the cable. Other methods include placing a sterile tegaderm film over the probe footprint carefully, and another film is wrapped around the probe where it is gripped. This, however, will not cover the cable.

Another method is to insert the probe into a sterile glove and secure it with sterilised rubber bands or with improvised rubber bands made by cutting the fingers off a glove. The cable and the body of the probe are then wrapped with sterile drape cut to the appropriate size. This provides a makeshift barrier and is cost effective (Fig. 14.7). However, it must be noted that materials like rubber (latex) and silicone attenuate the ultrasound beam. There may be a slight degradation of the image when gloves are used as a barrier. Most of the time, this degradation is unnoticeable.

There is some concern about the coupling medium used to aid imaging. Conventional ultrasound jelly is not sterile and must not be used once asepsis is attained. Sterile ultrasound jelly is available in single-use packs and these can be made use of. If sterile ultrasound jelly is not available, an alternative is to use povidone iodine or even normal saline to ensure proper probe–patient contact. It is recommended that normal saline be used as a coupling medium when neuraxial blocks are attempted with ultrasound.

General Considerations

The concepts of USGRA in children are similar to those in adults, but with certain subtle differences based on the size of the child.

Younger children have smaller and more superficial nervous structures. This provides for

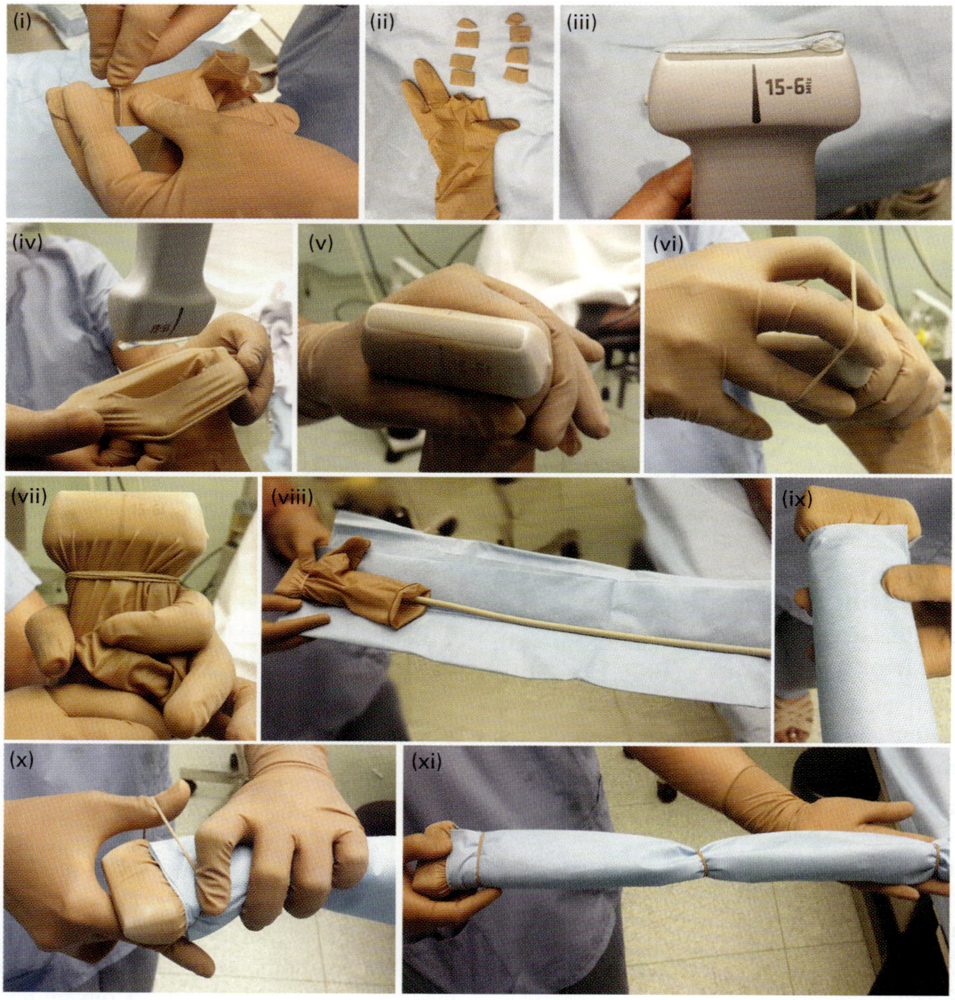

Figure 14.7 Our technique for sterile draping of an ultrasound probe. (i), (ii) The fingers of a glove are cut off into 1 inch bands. (iii) Ultrasound jelly is applied generously onto the probe. (iv) The probe with jelly is inserted into a glove. (v) No air bubbles should be present in the interface between glove and probe. (vi), (vii) The previously cut rubber bands from the fingers are used to hold the glove in position on the probe to prevent slippage. (viii) The bodies of the probe and cable are placed onto a sterile sheet. (ix) The sheet is carefully wrapped around the probe and cable to cover all exposed surfaces. (x), (xi) The sheet is held in place with additional rubber bands.

certain advantages and disadvantages. Superficial structures are usually imaged more easily and with greater clarity. In the same manner, critical structures such as the pleura also appear very superficial. Vascular structures are easily compressible with the weight of the ultrasound probe and care must be taken to visually isolate these structures before intervention. Larger probes may not form an appropriate footprint on the child leading to creation of air artefacts. Smaller nerves may require precise needling and can test the skill of the practitioner.

Local Anaesthetic Volumes

Though ultrasound usage seemingly appears to reduce the volume of local anaesthetic needed for a block, this has not been convincingly proven in all regional anaesthetic procedures in adults, with some blocks often requiring traditional volumes. In children, local anaesthetic dosages are based on weight, and therefore only very small volumes may be available for a practitioner to inject. Because of the highly variable weights of children, the correct volumes must be individually calculated for every patient. Hydrodissection with normal saline or dextrose solutions may be helpful to identify the correct plane of injection when very low volumes are required, thereby ensuring that the local anaesthetic is deposited at the correct site. Fascial plane blocks which rely on larger volumes for spread are another area where the clinician must be cautious. Spreading across extensive muscle surfaces enhances intravascular absorption. Fascial plane blocks have been shown to exhibit high levels of local anaesthetic in the plasma in adults. Reassuringly, this does not always contribute to a clinical picture of toxicity. We urge the clinician practising these blocks to pay special attention to the concentration and volume of the local anaesthetic as well as the site of injection before embarking on regional anaesthesia in the paediatric population.

Individual Nerve Blocks

The individual blocks are described in the following order: those of the upper limb, trunk and lower limb.

Blocks of the Upper Limb

Brachial plexus blocks are used to provide analgesia or surgical anaesthesia to the upper limb. The four conventional approaches to the brachial plexus are the interscalene, supraclavicular, infraclavicular and axillary. In addition, blockade of the terminal branches of the brachial plexus may also be useful for providing analgesia. Traditionally, the axillary approach to the brachial plexus has been the most widely used, perhaps due to its distance from critical structures, as compared to the other approaches. With the advent of ultrasound, the other approaches have gained popularity.

Interscalene Block (Fig. 14.8)

The interscalene block provides analgesia for surgeries involving the shoulder and most of the arm above the elbow (except the inner medial part). The technique under ultrasound involves deposition of the local anaesthetic solution close to the roots or proximal trunks of the brachial plexus. Typical coverage involves C5/6/7, with little or no spread below these levels.

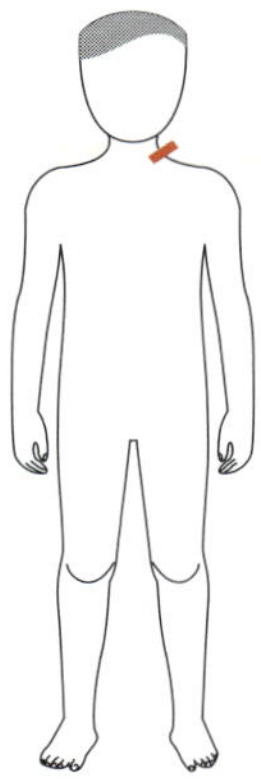

(a)

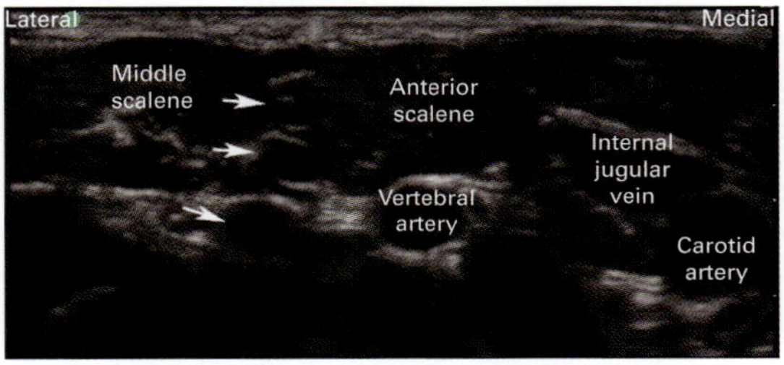

(b)

Figure 14.8 (a and b) Interscalene block.

Evidence for the interscalene block under ultrasound in children is limited to correspondence and isolated case reports. This is likely due to lack of application by anaesthetists rather than problems with the technique.

Equipment

High-frequency linear ultrasound probe, 25–50 mm short bevel needle, local anaesthetic.

Sonoanatomy and Scanning Technique

The ultrasound probe is placed transversely in close approximation to the side of the neck at the level of the cricoid cartilage. The trachea is identified in the midline as a large hypoechoic structure surrounded by the thyroid gland, which appears distinctly homogenous when free of pathology. Lateral to these structures lie the common carotid artery and the internal jugular vein. The vein and artery can be distinguished from one another by checking flow characteristics using the colour Doppler mode on the ultrasound machine. Excessive pressure on the neck can collapse the internal jugular vein in younger children. Superficial to these vessels lies the sternocleidomastoid muscle. The anterior scalene muscle is circular in appearance and lies lateral to the neck vessels and just under the lateral border of the sternocleidomastoid. Further lateral lies the middle scalene muscle. The roots or trunks of the brachial plexus are seen to emerge from between the scalene muscles as distinct hypoechoic structures.

The interscalene block can be performed either 'in-plane' or 'out-of-plane', with appropriate care taken with each approach. The 'in-plane' approach is preferably done with a lateral-to-medial approach. The long thoracic nerve and the dorsal scapular nerve can lie within the middle scalene muscle, and injury to these nerves during an interscalene block under ultrasound has been reported in adults.

Supraclavicular Block (Fig. 14.9)

The supraclavicular block is indicated for arm, elbow, forearm and hand surgery. It is a popular method of upper limb blockade in adults and is

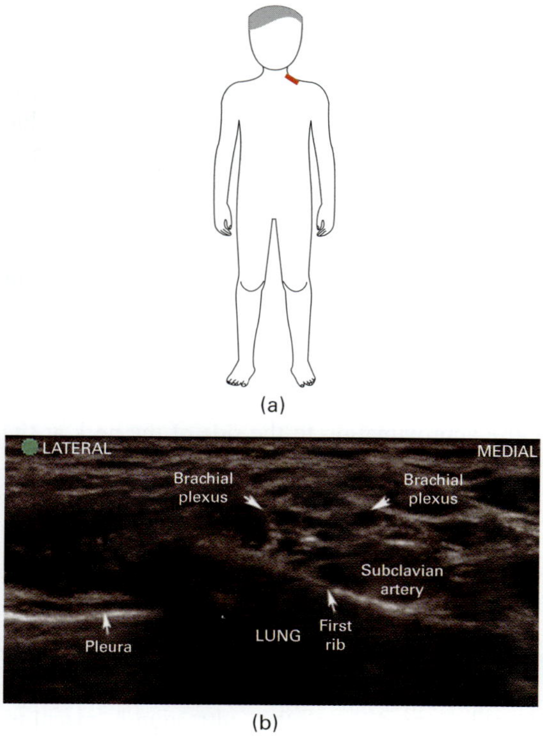

Figure 14.9 (a and b) Supraclavicular block.

extensively practiced under ultrasound guidance. Nevertheless, ultrasound does not eliminate the possibility of complications, including pneumothorax and vascular puncture occurring. There are a few reports of its usage in paediatrics. Some authors have used this technique in children as young as 6 months of age. Pneumothorax is a real possibility due to the proximity of the pleura in this region, and this approach has long been cautioned against when conventional techniques were applied. Meticulous technique and constant visualisation of the needle and critical structures can help in preventing a pneumothorax from occurring, but it may be prudent for the practitioner to have significant experience with ultrasound before venturing into this approach in young children.

Sonoanatomy and Scanning Technique

The probe is placed in a coronal oblique plane, above the clavicle. The probe is moved medial till the subclavian artery is identified. The brachial plexus at this level is arranged around the subclavian artery as a cluster of hypoechoic structures. When correctly imaged, the first rib, a hyperechoic line, appears to lie below the artery. The pleura lies in close proximity to the rib and is identified as a bright hyperechoic line that shows reflective artefacts.

Injection Technique

The plexus is approached 'in-plane' from the lateral to the medial direction. Needle visualisation is critical to ensure safety and accuracy during this block. Local anaesthetic is deposited at the 'corner pocket', which is the area bordered by the subclavian artery medially, the first rib inferiorly and the divisions of the brachial plexus superolaterally. A single injection may suffice, but if required, the needle can be redirected superiorly to ensure spread around the plexus.

Infraclavicular Block (Fig. 14.10)

The infraclavicular block targets the cords (posterior, lateral and medial) of the brachial plexus below the clavicle. This block provides effective analgesia for surgeries on the lower end of the humerus, elbow, forearm and hand. Due to its location, it appears to be a favourable location for placement

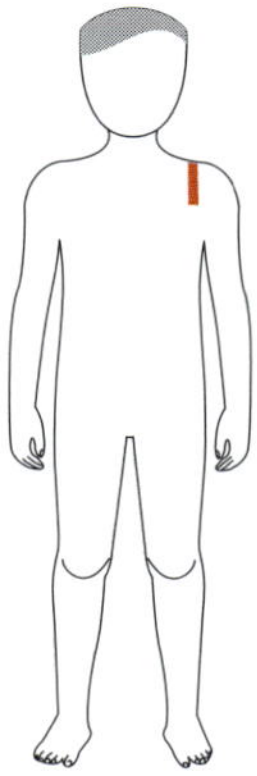

(a)

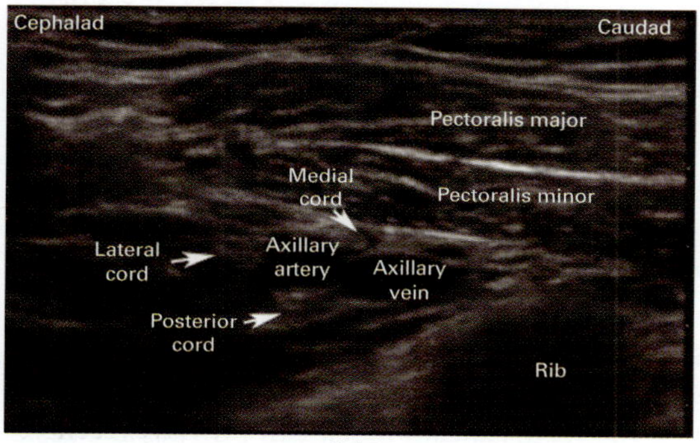

(b)

Figure 14.10 (a and b) Infraclavicular block.

of continuous catheters as the risk of dislodgement is minimal.

Patient Position

Supine with the arm abducted.

Sonoanatomy and Scanning Technique

The probe is placed in a parasagittal plane at the lateral one-third of the clavicle. The cords of the brachial plexus lie in close relation to the axillary artery in this region, and visualisation of the axillary artery and vein is required. The pectoralis major and minor muscles are seen superior to the axillary artery and vein and are distinctly separated by a hyperechoic perimysium. The pleura lies further inferior and medially and can be identified as a shimmering hyperechoic structure that moves with respiration when the probe is moved further medially. Individual variation in the cord position is often seen.

The posterior cord usually lies posterior to the axillary artery. Though the posterior cord is the largest of the three cords, it is often obscured by the posterior acoustic artefact of the axillary artery. Many practitioners therefore advocate injecting at a 6 o'clock position in relation to the artery for coverage of this block when visualisation is inappropriate. The posterior cord may also be seen at 7–8 o'clock position as a normal variation and the procedurist is encouraged to look for the cord in unusual locations rather than assume its location posterior to the artery.

The lateral cord is hyperechoic, well seen and lies between 9 and 12 o'clock positions in relation to the artery. The medial cord lies between 1 and 5 o'clock positions and may often be unseen because of the proximity of the vein.

Injection Technique

Both 'in-plane' and 'out-of-plane' techniques have been described in paediatrics. Of particular interest is whether a single-point injection is sufficient or if all three cords need to be individually targeted. The posterior cord injection is usually performed first, as this will prevent the neurovascular complex from displacing inferiorly (thereby making the subsequent injections deeper). Single-point injection techniques involve targeting the posterior cord and creating a local anaesthetic fill that subsequently envelops the lateral and medial cords ('U'-shaped fill).

Axillary Block (Fig. 14.11)

The axillary block is perhaps the most popular of the brachial plexus approaches when performed by conventional methods. This is due to the simplicity of the technique and the distance from critical structures such as the pleura or the arteries of the neck.

Position

The patient's arm is abducted and extended at the elbow.

Sonoanatomy and Scanning Technique

The ultrasound probe is placed in a sagittal plane in the anterior axillary fold, thereby providing a cross-section of the axillary vessels. The probe may eventually be moved caudad and cephalad to achieve a clearer view of the nerves. The nerves are typically arranged around the artery, but variants may commonly be encountered.

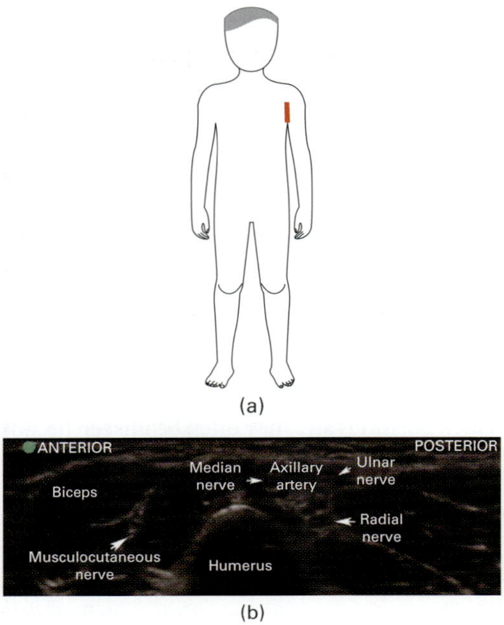

Figure 14.11 (a and b) Axillary block.

- **Musculocutaneous nerve:** This nerve is situated between the biceps and the coracobrachialis muscles. However, visualisation of this nerve may not always be possible in children.
- **Median nerve:** This nerve lies between the biceps muscle and the axillary artery, but this position can be variable.
- **Ulnar nerve:** This nerve usually lies medial and superficial to the artery.
- **Radial nerve:** This nerve is the largest of the nerves seen in the axilla. It is usually seen between 4 and 6 o'clock positions in relation to the artery. Visualisation may sometimes be confounded by scanning too distal. As the transducer is moved away from the axilla, the nerve is seen moving deeper as it spirals around the posterior aspect of the humerus under cover of the lateral head of the triceps. Therefore, it is useful that the actual position of the radial nerve be demonstrated by scanning proximal and distal in a to-and-fro manner, before attempting a 'blind' injection posterior to the axillary artery.

Abdominal Wall Blocks

Rectus Sheath Block (Fig. 14.12)

The rectus sheath block was first described in adults as early as in 1899. Ferguson et al. demonstrated

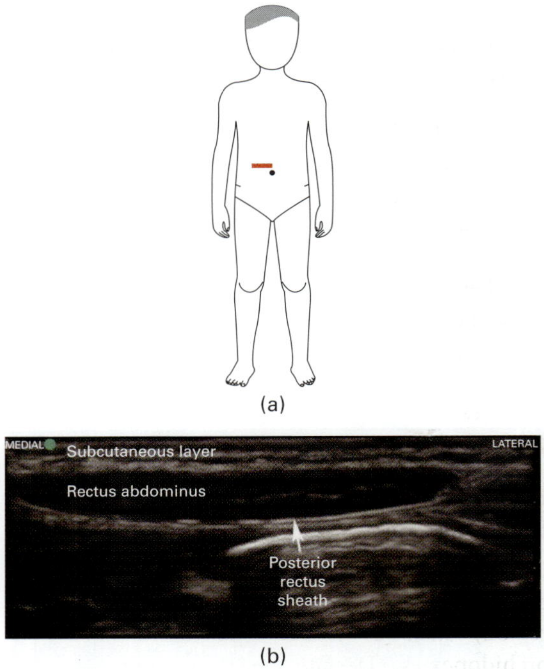

Figure 14.12 (a and b) Block of the rectus sheath.

that the rectus sheath block can provide analgesia for umbilical hernia repair in children. This technique has eventually become increasingly popular and is used to provide analgesia for umbilical and epigastric hernia repair, laparoscopic surgery and other small midline incisions.

Position

The position of the patient is supine.

Scanning Technique and Sonoanatomy

Analgesia around the umbilical area can be attained by performing the block at a level close to the umbilicus. Incisions that are higher will require the block to be given at a supraumblical zone. The probe can initially be placed along the midline of the anterior abdominal wall to identify the linea alba. As the probe is moved laterally, the belly of the rectus abdominis muscle comes into view and the hyperechoic anterior and posterior rectus sheath is identified. The fascia transversalis lies below the posterior rectus sheath and these two structures are usually seen as parallel hyperechoic lines. The peritoneum and abdominal contents can also be seen further posterior. When the probe is moved further lateral, the aponeurosis of the external oblique, internal oblique and transversus abdominis muscles are seen to converge towards the rectus abdominis.

Injection Technique

The area of local anaesthetic deposition is between the belly of the rectus muscle and the posterior rectus sheath. The target area can be approached either 'in-plane' or 'out-of-plane'. Care should be taken to ensure that the injectate is not intramuscular. Correct deposition below the muscular plane ensures cephalad and caudad spread of the local anaesthetic solution, thereby providing more extensive analgesia. The block needs to be performed bilaterally.

Ilioinguinal – Iliohypogastric Nerve Block (Fig. 14.13)

Ilioinguinal/iliohypogastric blocks can be performed for surgeries around the inguinal region, such as inguinal hernia repairs and orchidopexies. Despite being a fairly popular regional block, accurate deposition of the local anaesthetic solution has been erratic with the conventional landmark technique.

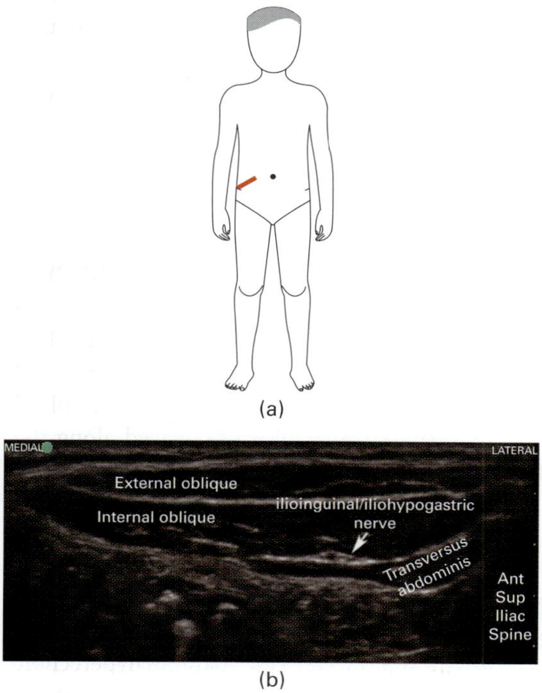

Figure 14.13 (a and b) Ilioinguinal/iliohypogastric block.

Position

The position of the patient is supine.

Scanning Technique and Sonoanatomy

The probe is placed transversely on the anterior abdominal wall with the edge resting on the anterior superior iliac spine of the side to be blocked. Often, a slight adjustment cephalad or probe rotation towards the umbilicus needs to be made to improve visibility. The three muscles of the abdominal wall (external oblique, internal oblique and transversus abdominis) are identified. The external oblique is usually very thin in this area. The ilioinguinal nerve arises from the first lumbar nerve and pierces the transversus abdominis muscle above the iliac crest. It then lies lateral to the iliohypogastric nerve between the internal oblique and the transversus abdominis muscles. Further caudad, the nerve pierces the internal oblique muscle and divides into filaments. Hence, it is preferable that the block be performed as cephalad as can be visualised. The ilioinguinal/iliohypogastric nerves are accompanied by a branch of the deep circumflex iliac artery which runs parallel. Pulsations of this vessel can be identified using the colour Doppler imaging and may serve as a marker when identification of the nerves is difficult.

Injection Technique

The block may be performed 'in-plane' or 'out-of-plane'. Care should be taken to avoid puncturing the accompanying artery. Intramuscular injection is common and hydrodissection with saline or dextrose may be needed to ensure that the needle is within the correct fascial plane.

Transversus Abdominis Plane Block (Fig. 14.14)

The transversus abdominis plane (TAP) block is a recently described abdominal wall block that has been popularised by ultrasound. First described by Rafi in 2001 as a landmark technique, it came into repute after the description of the block under ultrasound was done by Peter Hebbard. This block provides analgesia to the somatic component of the anterior abdominal wall. It does not provide visceral analgesia. Hence, it is appropriate to use this block as part of a multimodal analgesic regimen. The (posterior) TAP block provides analgesia for surgeries at the level of the umbilicus and

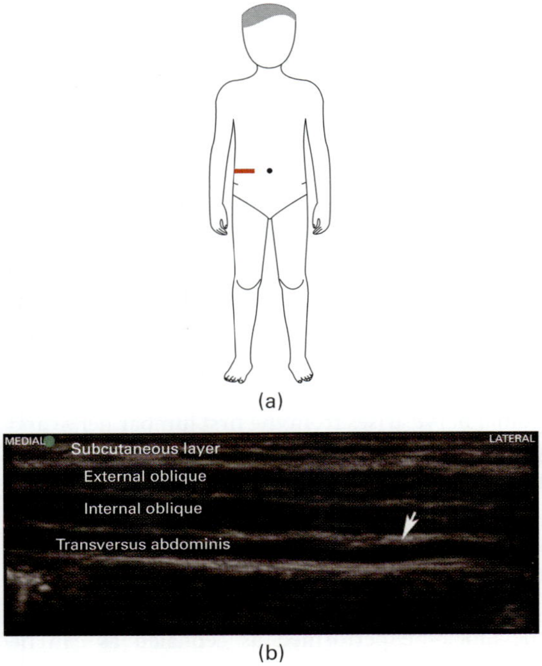

Figure 14.14 (a and b) Transversus abdominis plane block.

below (T10-L1). In larger children and for surgeries above the umbilicus, a variation of the posterior TAP block known as the subcostal TAP block may be performed. This will provide analgesia that cover the dermatomes between T7 and T10.

Position

The position of the patient is supine.

Sonoanatomy and Scanning Technique for Posterior TAP Block

The posterior TAP block aims to block the lower thoracic intercostal nerves that traverse the anterior abdominal wall. These nerves travel on the anterior surface of the quadratus lumborum and then in between the internal oblique and the transversus abdominis muscle. The block should provide somatic analgesia between T10 and L1, but this is dependent on block performance and the eventual spread of the local anaesthetic solution. This block is performed at the anterior-midaxillary line, between the iliac crest and the costal margin. The probe is placed transversely on the anterior abdominal wall and moved further lateral from the lateral edge of the rectus abdominis muscle. Beyond the aponeurotic sheaths, the external oblique, internal oblique and transversus abdominis muscles are clearly made out as distinct layers. Below the thin transversus abdominis muscle lies the peritoneum, and the motility of the bowels can be well made out. The probe is moved further lateral till it rests on the mid-axillary line.

Injection Technique for Posterior TAP Block

For a moderately sized child, a 10-cm short bevelled needle is used. The needle entry point is decided in such a way that the path of the needle lies parallel to the probe. This ensures excellent needle visibility. The needle is guided through the external and internal oblique until the posterior fascia of the latter is pierced. A distinct 'pop' is felt as the needle enters the plane between the internal oblique and the transversus abdominis muscle. Gentle hydrodissection is done to confirm that the needle does not lie intramuscular. As the drug is injected, the layer between the internal oblique and the transversus abdominis can be seen to separate. The TAP block must be performed bilaterally for midline incisions.

Sonoanatomy and Scanning Technique for Subcostal TAP Block (Fig. 14.15)

The linear high-frequency probe is placed on the upper abdomen, close to the xiphisternum in the midline. The direction of the probe follows the direction of the subcostal margin. In the midline, the linea alba and the rectus abdominis muscles are identified. As the probe is moved laterally along the subcostal margin, the transversus abdominis muscle is seen to lie below the rectus abdominis. Note that this arrangement is different from the scan performed for a posterior TAP block. As the probe progresses laterally, the usual arrangement of the abdominal muscles (external oblique/internal oblique/transversus abdominis) is obtained.

Injection Technique for Subcostal TAP Block

A short bevelled needle (50–100 cm) is used. The needle is inserted in a medial-to-lateral direction. The needle is guided to a point just under the lateral edge of the rectus abdominis muscle just above the transversus abdominis. This point allows for easy access into the right plane for the injection of local anesthesia (LA).

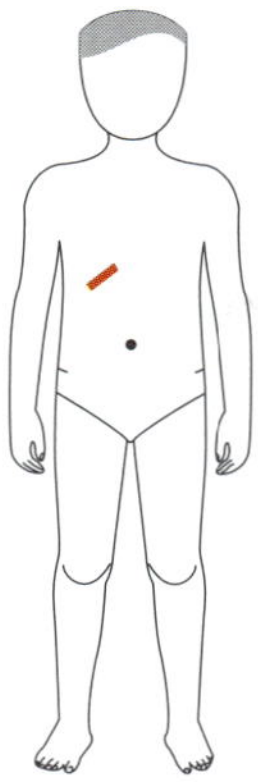

(a)

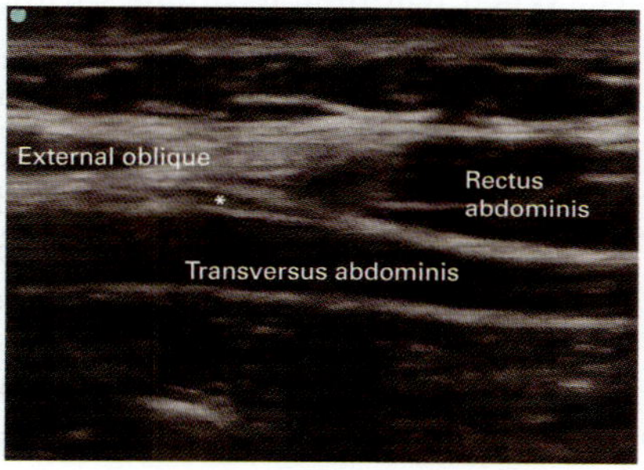

(b)

Figure 14.15 (a and b) Subcostal transversus abdominis plane block.

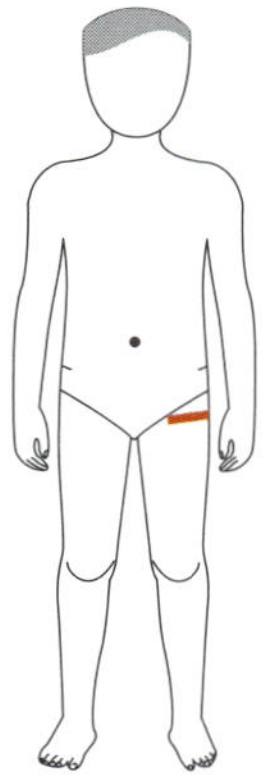

(a)

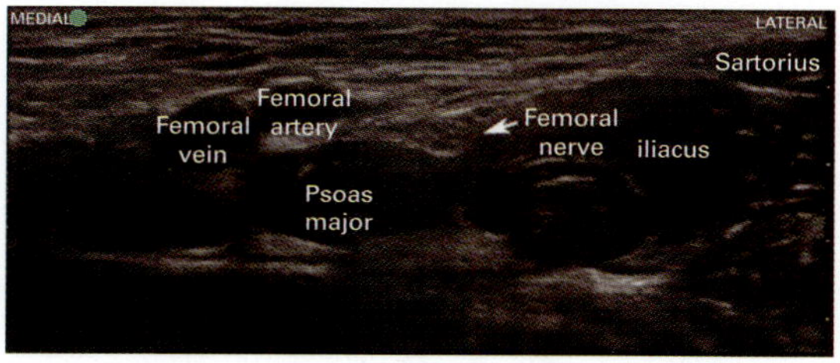

(b)

Figure 14.16 (a and b) Femoral nerve block.

Lower Limb Blocks

Femoral Nerve Block (Fig. 14.16)

The femoral nerve block is a simple and effective nerve block that provides analgesia to the anterior thigh and knee. The usage of ultrasound further simplifies this block.

Position

The position of the patient is supine.

Sonoanatomy and Scanning Technique

The femoral artery is the classical landmark for this block when performed with conventional methods or with ultrasound. The ultrasound probe is placed transversely along the inguinal crease and the pulsatile, non-compressible femoral artery is identified. The femoral vein lies medial or postero-medial to the artery and is compressible. The femoral nerve is a hyperechoic structure that varies in shape (triangular, flat, oval) and lies lateral to the femoral artery. Multiple hyperechoicfascial layers seen just below the skin are the fascia lata. The fascia iliaca is a more distinct single layer seen enclosing the femoral nerve. The iliacus muscle lies posterior to the nerve. Often, the circumflex branch of the femoral artery is seen running over the nerve.

Injection Technique

The nerve is approached, either 'in-plane' or 'out-of-plane'. A distinct 'pop' is felt as the needle pierces the fascia iliaca. Once within the fascia iliaca, the local anaesthetic may be injected.

Popliteal Sciatic Nerve Block (Fig. 14.17)

The sciatic nerve can be blocked at various levels during its course down the leg. The simplest of the many approaches to the sciatic nerve is to intercept it close to the popliteal fossa. This is the only point in its course that it lies in close proximity to large vascular structures (the popliteal artery and vein). The superficial course in this region also makes this a simple block to perform. The popliteal sciatic nerve block is an effective technique to provide analgesia to the entire leg, except for the skin on the medial side which is supplied by the saphenous nerve. It is useful, especially on surgeries around the ankle and foot.

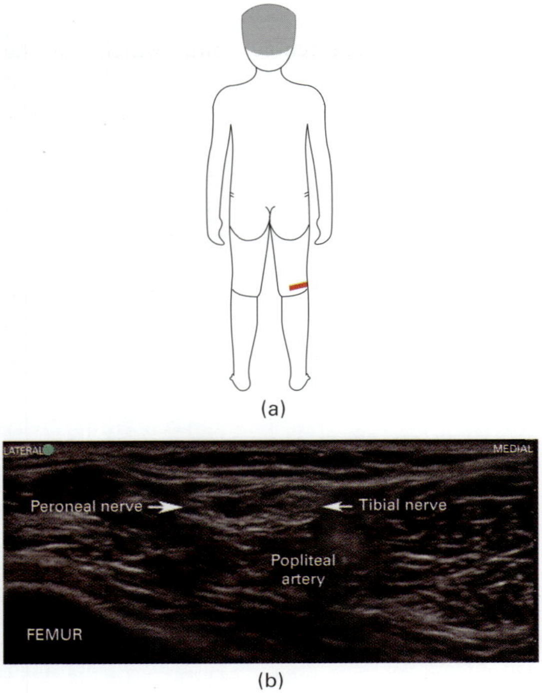

Figure 14.17 (a and b) Popliteal sciatic nerve block.

Position

The position of the patient is supine, lateral and prone.

Sonoanatomy and Scanning Technique

The linear probe is placed at the popliteal crease and the popliteal artery and vein are identified. The probe is tilted slightly caudad and moved cephalad. A hyperechoic, oval structure is seen superficial to the artery. In most cases, this is the tibial nerve. When the probe is moved further cephalad, a smaller hyperechoic structure is seen to join the tibial nerve. This is the peroneal nerve. If the split cannot be demonstrated, then the probe is moved further caudad to examine if the division is distal. The sciatic nerve is bounded by the rectus femoris laterally and the semi-tendinosus/ semi-membranosus muscles medially.

Injection Technique

The nerve can be approached in supine, lateral and prone positions. The block can be performed at the bifurcation, or the peroneal and tibial nerves can be blocked individually. This has been shown to speed up the onset of the block. This location is also suitable for catheter insertion.

Caudal Block (Figs 14.18 and 14.19)

The caudal epidural block is one of the most commonly performed regional anaesthetic procedures in children undergoing surgeries below the level of the umbilicus. The reasons for its popularity can be attributed to its simple technique and high success rates providing high-quality analgesia. The inclusion of ultrasound to further improve this technique has been a recent advance. Ultrasound allows identification of the point-of-needle insertion when anatomical landmarks cannot be palpated. In the same manner, congenital defects in the spine, such as spina bifida, may be identified. When real-time techniques with ultrasound are incorporated, tracking of the needle tip to the correct location, as well as visualisation of the local anaesthetic spread to the required level may be done, thereby achieving far greater precision and control over the block. However, imaging of the caudal space and the spine requires a high degree of competency and skill, and not all of the above-mentioned advantages can be achieved by the novice practitioner.

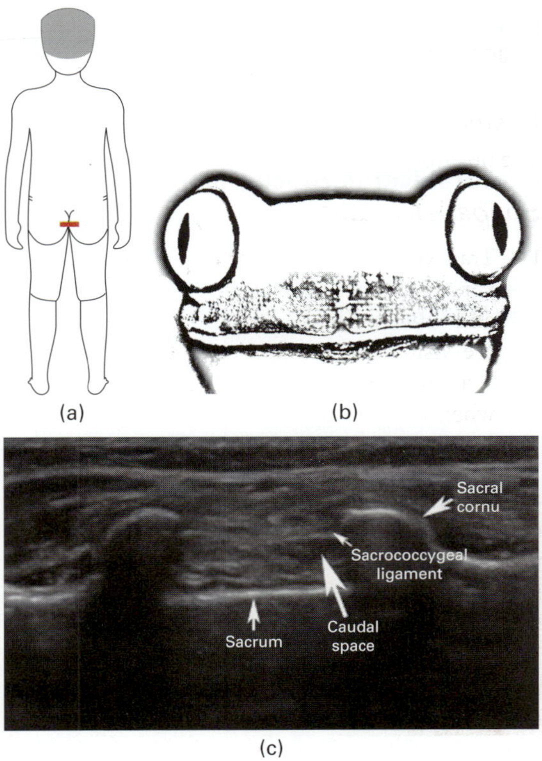

Figure 14.18 (a–c) Caudal epidural space – transverse view.

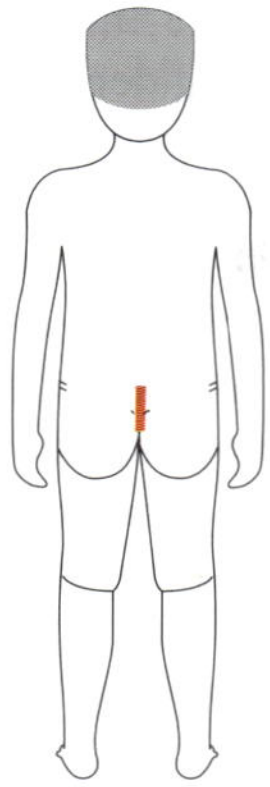

(a)

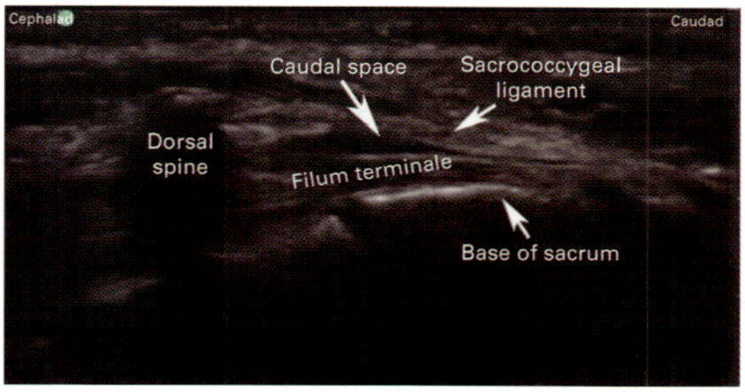

(b)

Figure 14.19 (a and b) Caudal epidural space – longitudinal view.

Position

The position of the patient is lateral and prone.

Sonoanatomy and Scanning Technique

1. Transverse scan: The probe is placed transversely at the level of the coccyx in the midline and traced cephalad till the sacral cornua are visualised. These are distinct hypoechoic structures which resemble the eyes of a frog when viewed from the front. Between the two cornua is the sacrococcygeal ligament which is hyperechoic. Below the ligament is a brighter, hyperechoic rim, which is the sacrum. Between the sacrococcygeal ligament and the sacrum lies a thin hypoechoic space. This is the caudal epidural space.
2. The probe is then turned longitudinally in the same area and the structures are viewed in the long axis. Locating the sacral cornua by the transverse scan provides an indication to where the needle entry point will be. The sacrococcygeal ligament is seen as a hyperechoic band which covers the sacral hiatus. The caudal space is seen as a darker hypoechoic area below it. The filum terminale is seen anterior to the caudal space.

Injection Technique

The block may be performed in the transverse view as an 'out-of-plane' procedure or 'in-plane' when imaged in the longitudinal view. The longitudinal view has the advantage of seeing the needle in its entirety as well as tracing the spread of the local anaesthetic as it travels cephalad in the caudal epidural space. It is unnecessary to advance the needle further once it has entered the caudal space. Catheters placed through this route may also be imaged in real time and the catheter tip can be accurately deployed at the desired level (**Fig. 14.20**).

Newer Fascial Plane Blocks and Their Application in Paediatrics

In the past decade, an entirely new array of fascial plane blocks, developed with the assistance of ultrasound, has entered regional anaesthesia literature. Most of these blocks are confined to the trunk. Furthermore, several variants of these newer blocks have been proposed leading to confusion regarding the correct terminology, application and effect.

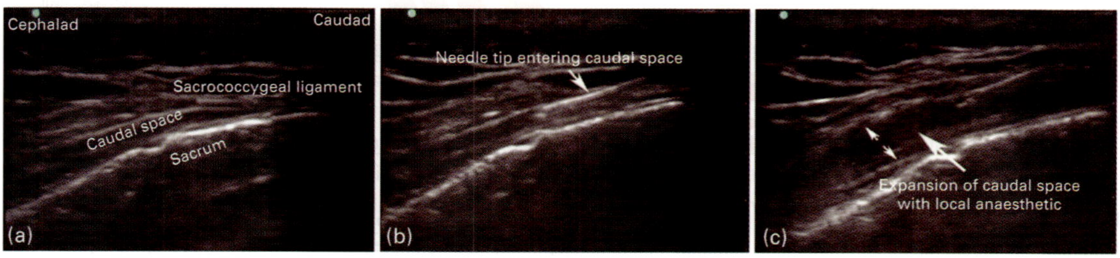

Figure 14.20 Caudal epidural block is being performed in a 10-year-old child with a tibial fracture. The caudal space appears well defined. The needle is placed just past the sacrococcygeal ligament. Local anaesthetic injection is smooth and immediately travels cephalad. As this is an older child, note the fused sacral elements.

thoracolumbar fascia. Drug spread to the paravertebral space will provide extensive analgesia of the abdomen, occasionally up to T6 on the side that was blocked.

Complications of Ultrasound-Guided Regional Anaesthesia

Regional anaesthesia nerve blocks can have some potential complications in paediatric patients. While these techniques are generally considered safe, it is important to be aware of the risks and care must be taken to avoid them. Each nerve block site may carry a risk of unique complications. Some of the complications associated with regional anaesthesia nerve blocks in paediatrics include the following:

- **Local anaesthesia systemic toxicity (LAST):** Excessive doses of local anaesthetics can lead to toxicity and can cause symptoms such as seizures, cardiovascular collapse, respiratory depression and even death. Incorrect calculation of the LA dose based on body weight and multiple nerve blocks (or fascial plane blocks) requiring greater volume and inadvertent intravascular injection can all result in systemic toxicity. Nerve blocks conducted under general anaesthesia or deep sedation, which is the norm in paediatrics, may hide the subtle signs of an overdose. LAST therapy has been revolutionised with the usage of 20% intravenous lipid emulsion (Intralipid, Fresenius Kabi). Management of LAST is depicted in Figure 14.22.
- **Nerve injury:** In rare cases, the needle or the catheter used to administer the local anaesthetic can damage the nerve, leading to permanent injury or paralysis. The use of highly concentrated local anaesthetic solutions is also best avoided in young children considering their neurotoxic potential.

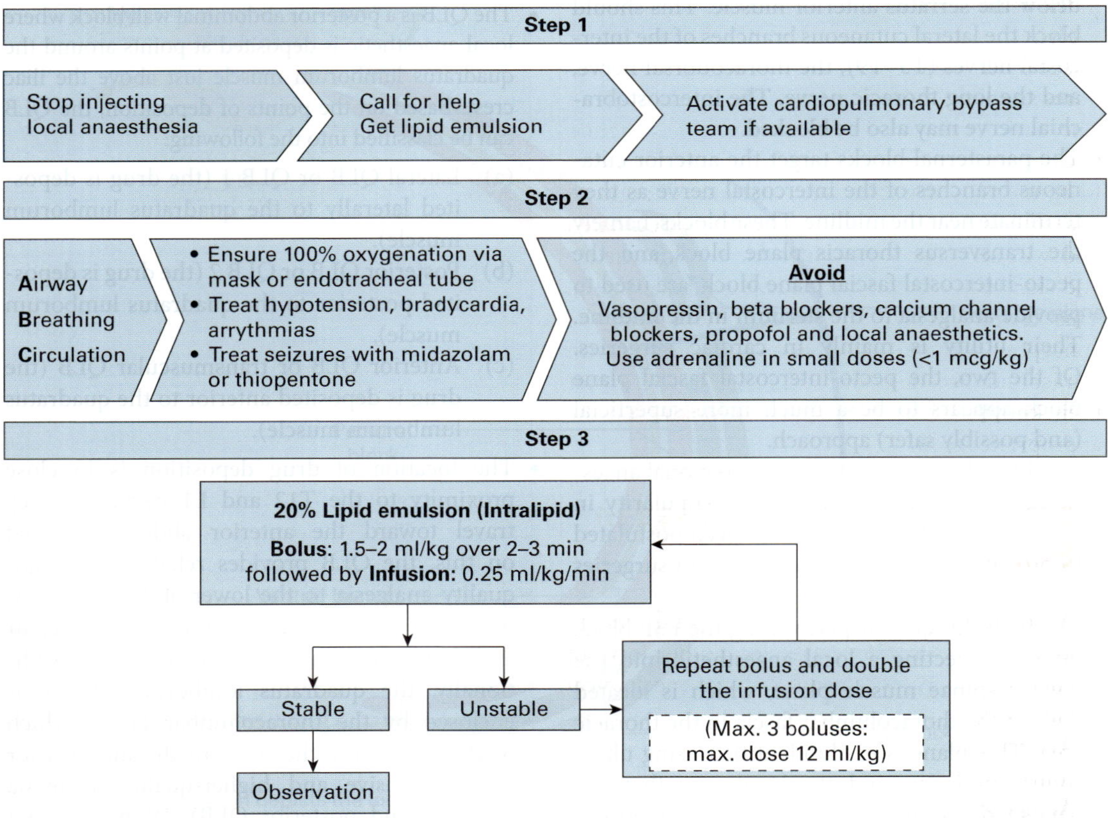

Figure 14.22 Management of local anaesthetic systemic toxicity. Adapted with permission from LAST Guidelines. Academy of Regional Anesthesia (AORA), India.

- **Infection:** Any invasive procedure carries a risk of infection, and regional anaesthesia nerve blocks are no exception. The current data in adults on single-shot nerve blocks are reassuring. However, nerve block catheters carry a high rate of colonisation, which could translate into a clinical infection, especially in the immunocompromised.
- **Hematoma:** Small arteries and veins in younger children may occasionally remain unidentified and come in the path of the needle. This can lead to hematoma formation, which can be easily tackled by applying pressure. Hematomas that leave transient patches on the skin can often cause concern to the child's caregivers. Reassurance in this situation is best done to allay any fears.

Conclusion

Ultrasound for regional anaesthesia is an exciting new advance in the speciality that promises more in the years to come. This technology is constantly evolving with manufacturers developing better image quality and enhancements that make procedures simpler for the user and safer for the patient. The basic concept of visualisation of a structure and its surroundings is here to stay and appears to be the way forward. Older methods of regional anaesthesia, however, are yet to be deemed outdated and will serve as a reminder for the knowledge and skill required to practice regional anaesthesia. This chapter serves as an introduction to the concept of regional anaesthesia in paediatrics with ultrasound. Readers are encouraged to further their knowledge on the subject by looking up the appropriate resources.

Common Terminology Used in USGRA

- **Absorption:** The loss of ultrasound energy as a result of its conversion to another form of energy such as heat or intracellular mechanical vibration.
- **Acoustic impedance:** The resistance to sound transmission through a medium.
- **Acoustic intensity:** The concentration of energy in a sound beam; the amount of acoustic power transmitted per unit area.
- **Amplitude:** The strength of a sound signal.
- **Anechoic:** Ultrasound characteristic where there is no reflection of ultrasound beams resulting in a black image such as that seen in blood vessels.
- **Anisotropy:** A different resulting echogenicity of soft tissues, such as tendons and nerves, when the angle of the transducer is changed.
- **Artefacts:** Display distortions, additions or errors that can adversely affect ultrasound image acquisition or interpretation.
- **Attenuation:** The loss of ultrasound energy when the wave travels deep into the tissues due to absorption, reflection and scattering of sound energy.
- **Axial resolution:** The ability to distinguish two structures as separate when the structures are lying close to each other along the same axis as the ultrasound path.
- **Cycle:** The combination of one rarefaction and one compression equals one cycle.
- **Diffuse reflection:** The reflection that comes off a reflector with an irregular surface.
- **Doppler effect:** A change in the frequency of sound as a result of motion between the sound source and the receiver; a positive shift occurs when the source and receiver are approaching each other and a negative shift occurs when they are moving away from each other.
- **Dynamic range:** The ratio of the maximum level of a given parameter to its minimum level; in ultrasound, the dynamic range defines a range of echo intensities that are displayed as a gradient of grey values (minimum value in black and maximum value in white pixels in the final image).
- **Echogenicity:** The degree of brightness of a structure displayed on ultrasound; this is influenced by the amount of beam returning to the transducer (reflection) after encountering the target structure.
- **Frequency:** The number of cycles per second; frequency is the inverse of wavelength; the higher the frequency, the shorter the wavelength.
- **Hyperechoic:** The image characteristic of a structure that is highly reflective resulting in a brighter displayed image compared to the surrounding structures; bone and pleura are examples of hyperechoic structures.
- **Hypoechoic:** The image characteristic of a structure that is less reflective than the surrounding

structure resulting in a darker displayed image compared to the surrounding structures; fluid-filled structures, for example vessels and cyst, are hypoechoic.
- **Interface:** The boundary between two tissue media with different acoustic impedances.
- **Lateral resolution:** The ability of the system to distinguish two structures as separate when the structures are lying side by side.
- **Longitudinal wave:** Movement of particles in the same direction as the direction of the wave propagation.
- **Period:** The amount of time required to complete one cycle.
- **Pulse repetition period:** The time from the start of one pulse to the start of the next pulse.
- **Pulse duration:** The time measured from the start of one pulse to the end of the same pulse.
- **Reflection:** Mirror-like redirection and return of a propagating sound wave towards the transducer that follows a standard law of reflection; for example, specular reflection results in the reflected angle being equal to the incident angle of the energy propagation.
- **Refraction:** A change in the direction of wave propagation when travelling from one medium to another with different propagation speeds according to Snell's Law of Refraction.
- **Resolution:** The ability to distinguish between two structures that lie close to one another.
- **Scattering:** A process by which the ultrasound is forced to deviate from a straight-line reflection and trajectory due to small, localised non-uniformities in the tissue.
- **Specular reflection:** The reflection that comes off a smooth reflector (e.g. a mirror).
- **Transverse wave:** Movement of particles perpendicular to the direction of the wave propagation.

SUGGESTED READINGS

1. Macfarlane AJR, et al. Regional anaesthesia: awake or asleep? *Anaesthesia* 2008; 63(11):1259–1260.
2. Kapral S, et al. Ultrasound-guided supraclavicular approach for regional anesthesia of the brachial plexus. *Anesth Analg* 1994; 78(3):507–513.
3. Casati A, et al. Effects of ultrasound guidance on the minimum effective anaesthetic volume required to block the femoral nerve. *Br J Anaesth* 2007; 98(6):823–827.
4. Duggan E, et al. Minimum effective volume of local anesthetic for ultrasound-guided supraclavicular brachial plexus block. *Reg Anesth Pain Med* 2009; 34(3):215–218.
5. Fredrickson MJ. Ultrasound-assisted interscalene catheter placement in a child. *Anaesth Intensive Care* 2007; 35(5):807–808.
6. De Jose Maria B, et al. Ultrasound-guided supraclavicular vs infraclavicular brachial plexus blocks in children. *Paediatr Anaesth* 2008; 18(9):838–844.
7. Yang CW, et al. Ultrasound-guided supraclavicular brachial plexus block in pediatric patients – A report of four cases. *Korean J Anesthesiol* 2010; 59:S90–S94.
8. Amiri HR, Espandar R. Upper extremity surgery in younger children under ultrasound-guided supraclavicular brachial plexus block: a case series. *J Child Orthop* 2010; 4(4):315–319.
9. Soares LG, et al. Eight ball, corner pocket: the optimal needle position for ultrasound-guided supraclavicular block. *Reg Anesth Pain Med* 2007; 32(1):94–95.
10. Marhofer P, et al. Ultrasound guidance for infraclavicular brachial plexus anaesthesia in children. *Anaesthesia* 2004; 59(7):642–646.
11. Ponde VC, Diwan S. Does ultrasound guidance improve the success rate of infraclavicular brachial plexus block when compared with nerve stimulation in children with radial club hands? *Anesth Analg* 2009; 108(6):1967–1970.
12. Weintraud M, et al. Ilioinguinal/iliohypogastric blocks in children: where do we administer the local anesthetic without direct visualization? *Anesth Analg* 2008; 106(1):89–93.
13. Haroon-Mowahed Y, Cheen Ng S, Barnett S, et al. Ultrasound in paediatric anaesthesia - A comprehensive review. *Ultrasound* 2021; 29(2):112–122. doi: 10.1177/1742271X20939260. Epub 2020 Jul 23. PMID: 33995558; PMCID: PMC8083139.
14. Ranganathan P, Ellison M, Lee J, et al. Role of ultrasound in pediatric anesthesia. *J Anesthesia Perioperative Med* 2018; 5:259–266. Doi:10.24015/JAPM.2018.0094.
15. Tsui B, Suresh S. Ultrasound imaging for regional anesthesia in infants, children, and adolescents: A review of current literature and its application in the practice of extremity and trunk blocks. *Anesthesiology* 2010; 112:473–492.
16. Chin KJ, Versyck B, Elsharkawy H, et al. Anatomical basis of fascial plane blocks. *Regional Anesthesia Pain Med* 2021; 46:581–599.

15

Principles of Ultrasonography and Assessment of Gastric Emptying

Garima Sharma

Compliance with fasting guidelines prior to surgery is considered essential to avoid the risk of pulmonary aspiration. Fasting in the paediatric age group is often associated with unpredictable delays in operating room schedules, which may lead to complications such as hypoglycaemia, dehydration, patient discomfort and parental dissatisfaction. On the other hand, perioperative aspiration of gastric contents is a serious complication of anaesthesia associated with high morbidity and mortality. Also, fasting guidelines do not guarantee complete gastric emptying, and there may be a need to objectively assess the gastric content and estimate volume as in cases of oesophageal and gastrointestinal pathology, raised intracranial pressure, emergency surgeries, etc. In this scenario, gastric ultrasound examination is finding a place as a point-of-care tool for aspiration risk assessment. It can determine the nature of the content (empty, clear fluid and thick fluid/solid), and when clear fluid is present, its volume can be estimated.

Basic Principles of B-Mode Ultrasound

Modern medical ultrasound is performed primarily using a pulse-echo approach with a brightness-mode (B-mode) display. This involves transmitting small pulses of ultrasound echo from a transducer into the body. As the ultrasound waves penetrate body tissues of different acoustic impedances along the path of transmission, some are reflected back to the transducer (echo signals) and some continue to penetrate deeper. The echo signals returned from many sequential coplanar pulses are processed and combined to generate an image. Thus, an ultrasound transducer works both as a speaker (generating sound waves) and a microphone (receiving sound waves). The ultrasound pulse is, in fact, quite short. It traverses a straight path referred to as an ultrasound beam. The direction of ultrasound propagation along the beamline is called the axial direction, and the direction in the image plane perpendicular to the axial is called the lateral direction. Usually, only a small fraction of the ultrasound pulse returns as a reflected echo after reaching a body tissue interface, while the remainder of the pulse continues along the beamline to greater tissue depths.

Generation of Ultrasound Pulses

Ultrasound transducers (or probes) contain multiple piezoelectric crystals, which are interconnected electronically and vibrate in response to an applied electric current. This phenomenon called the piezoelectric effect was originally described by the Curie's in 1880. Later, they also demonstrated the reverse piezoelectric effect, i.e., electricity applied to the quartz resulting in quartz vibration. These vibrating mechanical sound waves create alternating areas of compression and rarefaction when propagating through body tissues. Sound waves can be described in terms of their frequency (measured in cycles per second or hertz), wavelength (measured in millimetres) and amplitude (measured in decibels).

Ultrasound Wavelength and Frequency

The wavelength and frequency of the ultrasound are inversely related, i.e., the ultrasound of high frequency has a short wavelength and vice versa. Ultrasound waves have frequencies that exceed the upper limit for audible human hearing, i.e., greater than 20 kHz. Medical ultrasound devices use sound waves in the range of 1–20 MHz. Proper selection of transducer frequency is an important concept for providing optimal image resolution in diagnostic and procedural ultrasound. High-frequency ultrasound waves (short wavelength) generate images of high axial resolution. Increasing the number of waves of compression and rarefaction for a given distance can more accurately discriminate between two separate structures along the axial plane of wave propagation. High-frequency waves are more attenuated than low-frequency waves for a given distance; thus, they are suitable for imaging mainly superficial structures.

Conversely, low-frequency waves (long wavelength) offer images of lower resolution but can penetrate deeper structures due to a lower degree of attenuation. For this reason, it is best to use high-frequency transducers (up to 10–15 MHz range) to image superficial structures (such as for paediatric gastric ultrasound and stellate ganglion blocks) and low-frequency transducers (typically 2–5 MHz) for imaging the lumbar neuraxial structures that are deep in most adults.

Probe for Paediatric Ultrasound

A high-frequency transducer probe (4–15 MHz) is used in paediatric patients for gastric ultrasound because of the relatively superficial position of the antrum in these patients.

Gastric Ultrasound

Point-of-care ultrasound can determine the nature and volume of gastric contents when nil per oral (NPO) status is unknown or uncertain in the immediate pre-operative or pre-anaesthetic period. As such, it may be useful to anaesthesiologists, emergency physicians or intensivists who are initiating sedation, anaesthesia or airway management.

The evaluation of gastric content shares the following characteristics with other point-of-care ultrasound uses:

- It is performed at the patient's bedside by the clinicians treating the patient.
- It intends to answer a well-defined diagnostic question intended to guide clinical care.
- The exam is focused and goal-directed, therefore limited in scope and target structures.
- The findings are easily recognisable.
- The exam is easily learned and quickly performed.

Imaging of the Antrum

The way in which the stomach regulates the emptying of food to optimise digestion and absorption is complex. The function of the proximal stomach is generally recognised as a storage facility relaxing to accommodate food which is then passed down into the antrum where it is ground down into particles <1 mm in size before emptying into the small intestine. Several techniques have been used to provide insights into the mechanisms regulating this process. Ultrasonographic imaging of the antrum can be used to provide information relating to the volume or area of the distal stomach both in the fasted state and postprandially, thereby providing information about the distension of the whole stomach.

The use of ultrasound to assess the antrum is appealing in both the clinical and research setting due to the ease and simplicity with which it can be applied, especially in favour of other imaging modalities that are more expensive and time consuming.

Point-of-Care Ultrasound

Scanning Technique

The stomach can be imaged with the patient in the supine, sitting, semi-sitting, or right lateral decubitus (RLD) position. The best position depends on the section of the stomach to be imaged and affects sonographic findings. Several studies suggest that the distal parts of the stomach (antrum and body) are better evaluated in a semi-sitting or RLD position. Owing to a gravitational shift, a greater proportion of gastric content will move towards the more dependent areas of the stomach in these two positions. This may be especially important to evaluate gastric content in low-volume states in which gastric fluid may only be visible in a sitting position. However, scanning in critically ill patients may only be feasible in the supine position.

A high-frequency linear transducer probe (4–15 MHz) with standard abdominal settings or small part settings is most useful in paediatric patients. It provides the necessary penetration to identify the relevant anatomic landmarks. The epigastrium is scanned in a sagittal plane sweeping the transducer from the left to the right subcostal margins (**Fig. 15.1**).

Gastric Antrum

Several studies suggest that the antrum is the gastric region that is most amenable to sonographic examination. It is the gastric portion most consistently identified (98–100% of cases). It is found superficially between the left lobe of the liver anteriorly and the pancreas posteriorly in a sagittal or parasagittal scanning plane in the epigastrium. Important vascular landmarks including both the aorta or inferior vena cava and either the superior mesenteric artery or vein have been used to standardise a scanning plane through the antrum (**Fig. 15.2**). Not only is the antrum highly amenable to ultrasound imaging, its evaluation accurately reflects the content of the entire organ.

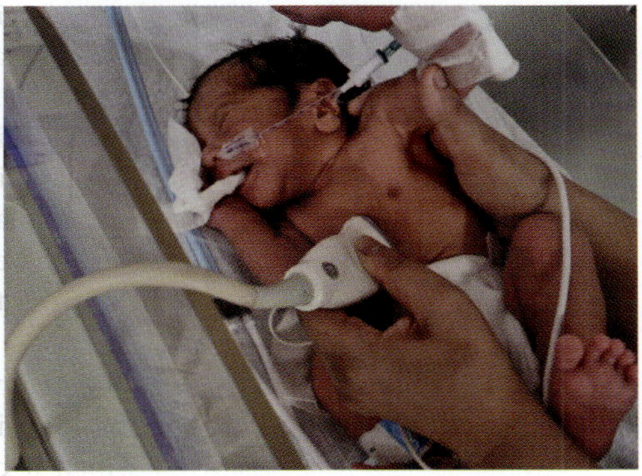

Figure 15.1 Probe placement and patient positioning.

Gastric Volume

The cross-sectional area (CSA) of the antrum can be measured using the free tracing tool method (**Figs 15.2** and **15.3**). Once the gastric antrum is identified, a still image of it is taken, and the cross-sectional area of the antrum in the RLD position (right lateral CSA) is measured by gastric volume (GV) (ml) = [27 + (14.6 × right lateral CSA)] – (1.28 × age) (**Figs 15.2** and **15.3**). This mathematical model is based on gastroscopic fluid assessment and is often used in adults. In paediatric patients, a mathematical model is suggested by Schmitz as follows:

GV (ml/kg) = [0.009 × antral right lateral CSA (mm^2)] – 1.36

Gastric contents may also be visualised, whether it is empty or has clear liquids or solids.

In an empty stomach, the antrum appears flat with juxtaposed anterior and posterior walls. In a sagittal plane, it is round to ovoid and has

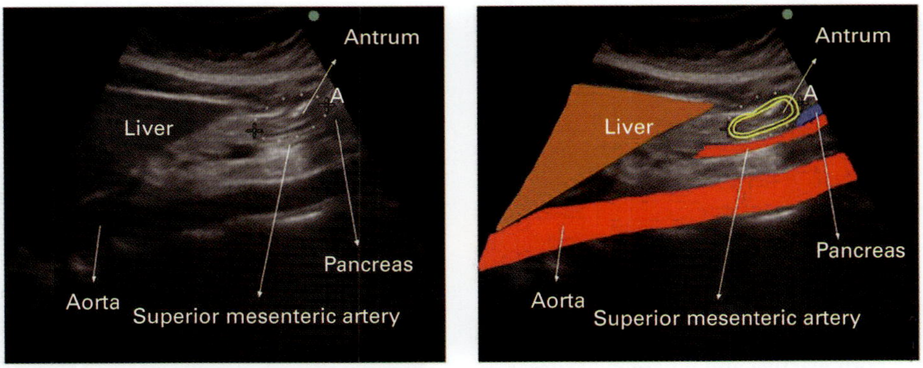

Figure 15.2 A still image of the antrum when the probe is positioned as in **Figure 15.1** and cross-sectional area calculation using the free tracing tool.

been compared with a 'target' or 'bull's eye' pattern (**Fig. 15.4**).

Baseline gastric secretions, water and apple juice appear hypoechoic or anechoic. With increasing volume, the antrum becomes round and distended. Air or gas bubbles appear as multiple mobile punctuate echoes, giving the appearance of a 'starry night' (**Fig. 15.5**).

Milk, thick fluids or suspensions have increased echogenicity. After a solid meal, a 'frosted-glass' pattern has been described as caused by a substantial amount of air mixed with the food bolus during the chewing and swallowing processes (**Fig. 15.6**). The air/solid mixture creates multiple ring-down artefacts on the anterior gastric wall, which typically 'blur' the posterior wall of the antrum. After some time, the air is displaced and the solid content can be better appreciated with a mixed echogenicity (**Fig. 15.7**). After oral intake of any type, peristaltic gastric contractions occur. They are noted easily in the ultrasound and can be lumen occlusive or non-occlusive.

Summary

Pre-operative fasting guidelines for a neonate suggest 4 hours of fasting for breast milk and 6 hours of fasting for formula feeds whereas in babies on solids, they suggest 6 hours of fasting for solids. Paediatric patients presenting for elective surgery have often been exposed to excessive fasting times or surreptitious feeding by the mothers.

Recent pre-operative fasting guidelines in children emphasise that prolonged fasting should be avoided because it is associated with perioperative dehydration, irritability, hypoglycaemia, and hypotension and suggest that carbohydrate-rich fluids before surgery reduce thirst, hunger, feelings of weakness and post-operative insulin resistance. However, many caregivers are reticent to give fluids within a short period prior to surgery.

The ability to assess gastric content and gastric distension is of particular relevance in patients in whom a delay in gastric emptying is expected such as those with trauma, raised intracranial pressure, etc. It is quite common for these patients to present for both elective and emergency surgeries. For elective surgeries even after fasting for more than 6 hours, they may have significant volume or even solids in cases of severely delayed gastric emptying. Thus, 'point-of-care' gastric ultrasound can be a very useful tool in identifying patients at risk of aspiration and also in those patients in which fasting times are doubtful.

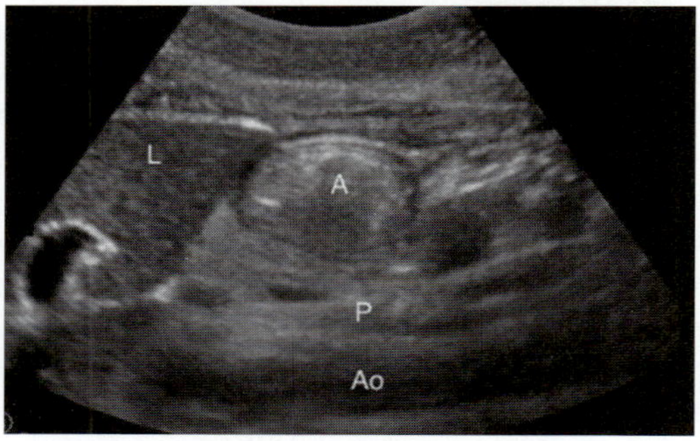

Figure 15.3 Sonographic image of the antrum with solids as the content seen as frosted glass appearance. A, Antrum; Ao, Aorta; L, Liver; P, Pancreas.

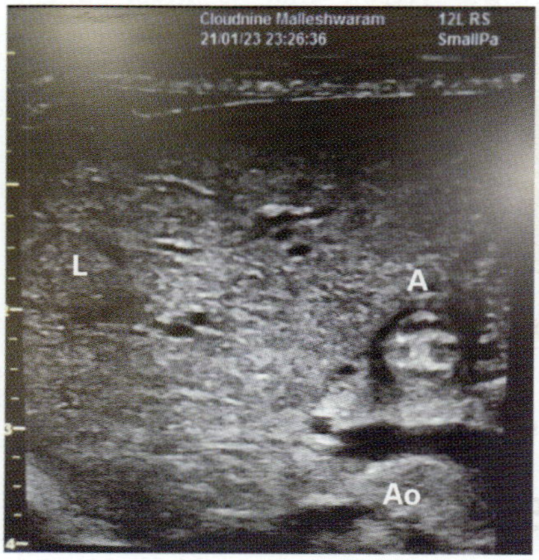

Figure 15.4 Appearance of an empty antrum. A, antrum; Ao, aorta; L, liver.

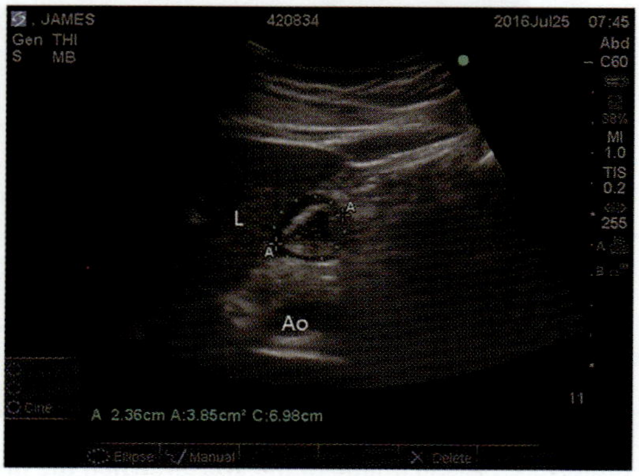

Figure 15.5 Antrum with clear liquids. A, antrum; Ao, aorta; L, liver.

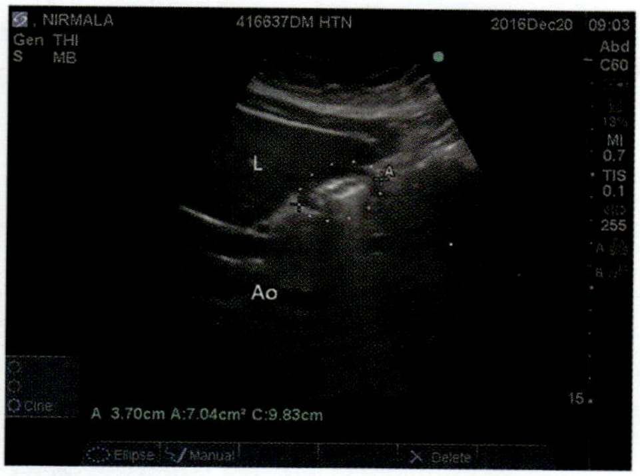

Figure 15.6 Antrum with solids immediately after ingestion. Ao, aorta.

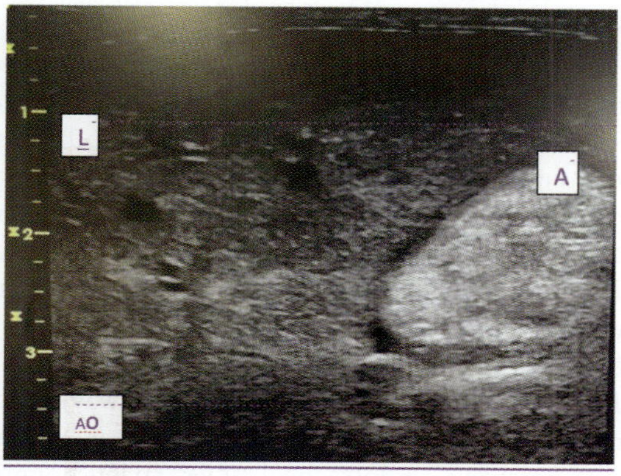

Figure 15.7 Antrum with solids ingested after 60 minutes.

SUGGESTED READINGS

1. Ng A, Smith G. Gastroesophageal reflux and aspiration of gastric contents in anesthetic practice. *Anesth Anal* 2001; 93:494–513.
2. Middleton W, Kurtz A, Hertzberg B. Practical Physics. In: Ultrasound, the Requisites, 2nd edition. Mosby, St Louis, MO 2004; pp. 3–27.
3. Perlas A, Davis L, Khan M, et al.. Gastric sonography in the fasted surgical patient: A prospective descriptive study. *Anesth Anal* 2011; 113:93–97.
4. Perlas A, Chan V, Lupu C, et al. Ultrasound assessment of gastric content and volume. *Anesthesiology* 2009; 111(1):82–89.
5. Bouvet L, Mazoit JX, Chassard D, et al. Clinical assessment of the ultrasonographic measurement of antral area for estimating preoperative gastric content and volume. *Anesthesiology* 2011; 114:1086–1092.
6. Perlas A, Mitsakakis N, Liu L, et al. Validation of a mathematical model for ultrasound assessment of gastric volume by gastroscopic examination. *Anesth Analg* 2013; 116:357–363.
7. Bouvet L, Chassard D. Contribution of ultrasonography for the preoperative assessment of gastric contents. *Ann Fr Anesth Reanim* 2014; 4:240–247.
8. Spencer AO, Walker AM, Yeung AK, et al. Ultrasound assessment of gastric volume in the fasted pediatric patient undergoing upper gastrointestinal endoscopy: Development of a predictive model using endoscopically suctioned volumes. *Paediatr Anaesth* 2015; 25:301–308.
9. Schmitz A, Thomas S, Melanie F, et al. Ultrasonographic gastric antral area and gastric contents volume in children. *Paediatr Anaesth* 2012; 22: 144–149.
10. 10. Song IK, Kim HJ, Lee JH, et al. Ultrasound assessment of gastric volume in children after drinking carbohydrate-containing fluids. *Br J Anaesth* 2016; 116(4):513–517.

16 POST-ANAESTHESIA CARE

Anita Shirley Joselyn • Chris Maria Jacob

The transition of the patient from a state of general anaesthesia to the pre-operative baseline state occurs in stages. The first stage, which involves the rapid return of protective airway reflexes necessary for cardiorespiratory stability, usually begins in the operating room and ends in the post-anaesthesia care unit (PACU) where the return of coordination and complete wakefulness usually occurs. Indeed, the development of the PACU resulted from the recognition that there are many common and potentially devastating complications that may occur during the emergence and recovery from anaesthesia. Children are more likely than adults to experience problems in the post-operative period. Different from those of adults and knowledge of such problems will result in better post-operative care.

Planning of recovery ideally begins before the operation. Pre-operative education with videos, dolls, colouring books and visits to the operating room may make the perioperative period less threatening to the child.

Set-Up in the PACU

Even though many paediatric patients are recovered in a set-up principally oriented to the care of adults, ideally the PACU must have personnel, equipment and procedures which are oriented to the special needs of children. In general, it is recommended that the PACU be located adjacent to the operating room to permit rapid transport of patients to and from the operating room and to allow ready access for surgeons and anaesthetists. It must also allow access to the radiology suite and laboratory.

It is recommended to have two beds allocated to each operating room. Each bed space should be provided with oxygen, suction, blood pressure cuffs, pulse oximetry and other equipment mentioned in **Box 16.1**. It is advisable to have a separate emergency cart/'Crash Cart' for resuscitation (**Box 16.2**). A 'Crash cart' is a multi-drawer-wheeled cabinet with the essential medications and tools that are required in an emergency situation (**Fig. 16.1**). This cart should have basic airway equipment like masks, airways, Magill forceps, supraglottic airways, endotracheal tubes, stylet, bougie, airway exchange catheter, laryngoscopes, IV access

Box 16.1 List of Routine Equipment at the Patient's Bedside

- O_2 supply with a flow regulator
- Self-inflating resuscitation bag
- Jackson Rees circuit, Ayres T piece
- Oral airways (sizes 00, 0, 1–5)
- Face masks (sizes 0, 1, 2, 3) and oxygen hoods
- Suction apparatus with appropriate suction catheters (6–14 Fr) and Yankauer suction tip
- Blood pressure cuffs (age appropriate)
- ECG monitor
- Thermometers
- SpO_2 monitor
- Infant and paediatric stethoscope
- Arterial blood gas kit
- Gloves

Table 17.2 Basis of Decision to Anaesthetise or Not

Do	Don't Do
• The child has a runny nose	• Parents confirm fever, malaise, cough and poor appetite
• No other symptoms 'much better'	• Ill appearing, lethargic
• Active happy child	• Purulent nasal discharge
• Clear rhinorrhoea	• Wheezing and rales
• Clear lungs	• Child <1 year, expreemie
• Older child	• Other factors – H/o reactive airway disease, major operation, ET required
• Experienced anaesthetist available	
• Social issues – a hardship for parents to be away from work and travel a great distance	

ET, endotracheal tube.

Management of Anaesthesia

The assessment and anaesthetic management of a child with URI is described in **Figure 17.1**.

Mode of Anaesthesia

The mode of anaesthesia in the concerned child undergoing the specific procedure is at the discretion of the individual anaesthetist. Management is directed at minimising secretions (a premedication with atropine is helpful) and avoiding stimulation of a potentially sensitive airway. Propofol is preferred for induction over ketamine and thiopentone. Amongst inhalational agents, sevoflurane has the highest bronchodilator properties followed by halothane than isoflurane. Desflurane being an airway irritant should be avoided. For muscle relaxation, vecuronium is preferred over atracurium which may cause bronchoconstriction secondary to histamine release.

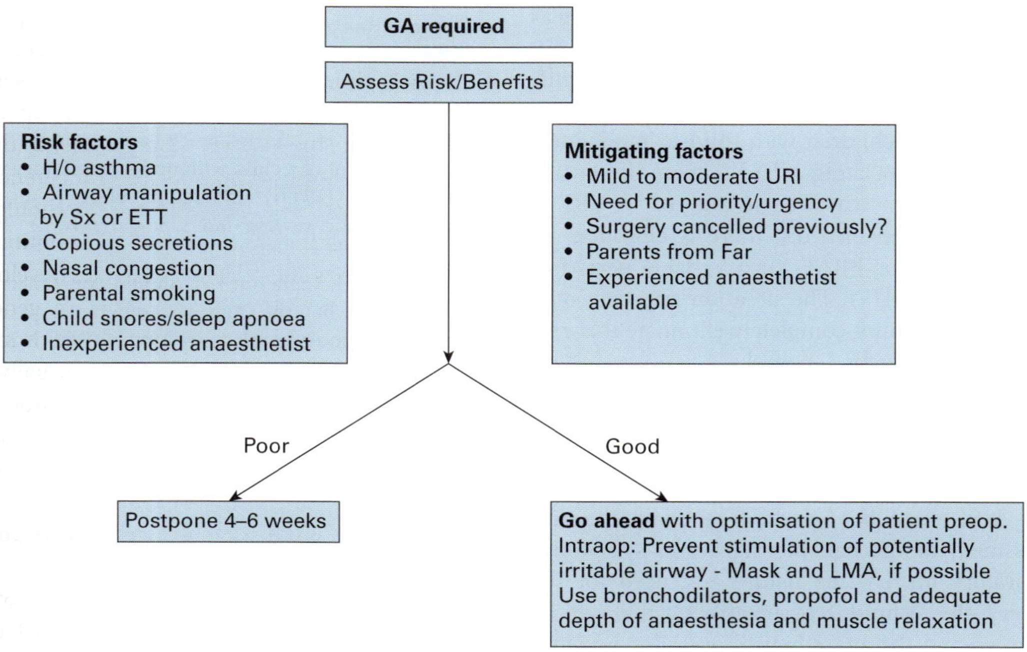

Figure 17.1 Assessment and anaesthetic management of a child with URI requiring general anaesthesia. ETT, endotracheal tube; LMA, laryngeal mask airway; URI, upper respiratory tract infection.

Generally, a face mask or an LMA is to be preferred over an ETT to reduce the instrumentation of the airway. If intubation is necessary, increasing the depth of anaesthesia with early use of muscle relaxants will provide early airway control to reduce the risk of laryngospasm. After intubation, it is worth suctioning secretions from the tracheobronchial tree under deep anaesthesia. IV atropine decreases the effects of increased acetylcholine on airways, such as increased secretions, bronchospasm and increased microvascular permeability. If bronchospasm occurs, it should be treated with an inhaled β_2-agonist such as salbutamol/albuterol. Atelectasis should be prevented by ventilating with adequate tidal volume intraoperatively, use of vital capacity manoeuvres, use of 3–5 cm water positive end-expiratory pressure as well as by adequate hydration. Humidification and hydration help to minimise drying and inspissation of secretions by dry anaesthetic and carrier gases and help to maintain adequate ciliary clearance mechanisms. Monitoring of oxygen saturation is mandatory intraoperatively as well as post-operatively in the post-anaesthesia care unit.

Anaesthesia is generally safe, without significant morbidity and usually has no mortality in the majority of children with mild-to-moderately active URI. Associating a bad outcome of anaesthesia with any trivial symptom of a URI is not always justifiable. Yes, there is definitely an increased risk for PRAE for a variable period of 2–6 weeks post-URI. The situation improves over time, but we cannot completely eliminate that risk always by waiting for 4–6 weeks.

Conclusion

In conclusion, the decision to anaesthetise a child with URI must be based on a comprehensive assessment of the patient's signs and symptoms, respiratory history, the nature and need for the surgery, the technique of anaesthesia that will be provided and the anaesthetist's overall experience and comfort in handling a child with URI. Prevention of stimulation of a potentially reactive airway, use of bronchodilators like salbutamol, induction with propofol and adequate suppression of airway reflexes with an optimal depth of anaesthesia have all been advocated for successfully dealing with a child with URI for anaesthesia and surgery.

There is a need to develop and fulfil discharge criteria from the recovery room as well as from day care surgery. A high index of suspicion should be maintained for problems in the perioperative period. Above all good judgement, vigilance and clinical experience play an important role while anaesthetising such children.

SUGGESTED READINGS

1. Parnis SJ, Barker DS, Van der Walt JH. Clinical predictors of anaesthetic complications in children with respiratory tract infections. *Paediatr Anaesth* 2001; 1:29–40.
2. Tait AR, Malviya S, Voepel-Lewis T, et al. Risk factors for perioperative adverse respiratory events in children with upper respiratory tract infections. *Anesthesiology* 2001; 95:299–306.
3. Tait AR, Malviya S. Anaesthesia for the child with upper respiratory tract infection: still a dilemma? *Anesth Analg* 2005; 100:59–65.
4. Parameswara G. Anesthetic concerns in patients with hyper reactive airways. *Karnataka Anaesth J* 2015; 1(1):8–16.
5. Lema GF et. al. Evidence-based perioperative management of a child with upper respiratory tract infections (URTIs) undergoing elective surgery: A systematic review. *Intl J Surg Open* 12. 2018; 17–24.
6. Cohen MM, Cameron CB. Should you cancel the operation when the child has an upper respiratory tract infection? *Anesth Analg* 1991; 71:282–288.
7. Cote CJ. The upper respiratory tract infection (URI) dilemma: Fear of complication or litigation? *Anesthesiology* 2001; 95:283–285.
8. Magnusson L, Spahn DR. New concepts of atelectasis during general anaesthesia. *Br J Anaesth* 2003; 91(1):61–72.
9. Von Ungern-Sternberg B, Boda K, Chambers NA, et al. Risk assessment for respiratory complications in paediatric anaesthesia: a prospective cohort study. *Lancet* 2010; 376:773–783.
10. Samol NB, Wittkugel EP. Upper Respiratory Infection. In: Clinical Pediatric Anesthesia: A Case-Based Handbook. Goldschneider KR, Davidson AJ, Wittkugel EP, Skinner AV (eds). Oxford University Press, New York 2012; pp. 22–31.

18 'Tight Bag' or 'High Airway Pressures' (Mechanical Obstruction, Laryngospasm and Bronchospasm)

Rebecca Jacob

'Tight Bag' or 'the airway pressures are high' is a frightening situation for any anaesthetist. The most common causes are discussed in a case-based manner.

Problem 1: Mechanical

A 6-month-old baby with a cleft lip presents for cheiloplasty. Mask ventilation is difficult as there is a leak around the mask. Fresh gas flows are increased and it is easier to ventilate. A muscle relaxant is given and the baby is easily intubated with a snug-fitting tube. *The reservoir bag is now full and tight, and the baby is difficult to ventilate.*

The probable *causes* of this situation are as follows:

- High fresh gas flows – no leak – there is a snug-fitting tube
- Oxygen 'flush' is stuck
- Secretions partially blocking the tube
- Tube is too deep – touching the carina or down one lung. It often happens with a Ring-Adair-Elwyn (RAE) tube
- Bronchospasm – light anaesthesia and atracurium
- Aspiration
- Air in the stomach with splinting of the diaphragm – difficulty with mask ventilation and high flows

Management

Management includes the following:

- Check air entry bilaterally (in both axillae)
- Shorten the tube if carinal or down one lung
- Check $EtCO_2$ trace
- Decrease the fresh gas flows
- Check the 'flush' valve
- If there are coarse rales – suck out the secretions
- Introduce a naso or orogastric tube and 'suck 'out the stomach
- Treat bronchospasm
- Always have a self-inflating resuscitator bag available in case of machine problems

Problem 2: Laryngospasm

A healthy 2-year-old girl weighing 10 kg presents for the repair of a unilateral cleft palate. Her lip was repaired without complications at the age of 6 months. For the prior several days, the patient has had a slight runny nose and occasional dry cough which has now resolved. She is otherwise well. No premedication is considered.

She cries during an inhalational induction with O_2, N_2O and sevoflurane. Soon after induction, a pulse oximeter, ECG and BP cuff are placed and the assistant looks for IV access. The child develops rocking movements of the chest, with minimal bag movements and poor fogging of the mask. She begins to desaturate. *She has developed partial laryngospasm.* With a jaw thrust, chin lift, head extension and 100% O_2 by mask with continuous positive airway pressure (CPAP), the saturation increases. The IV is secured, anaesthesia is deepened with propofol and the child is intubated without difficulty.

Anaesthesia is maintained with O_2/N_2O/sevoflurane supplemented with fentanyl/dexamethasone and ondansetron, and surgery proceeds.

Extubation

At the end of the surgery, the laryngoscopy reveals that there is no bleeding and all secretions are sucked out. The patient is placed on her side and extubated 'deep'. The airway is patent and she is transferred to the post-anaesthesia care unit (PACU). En route, she develops stridor followed by silence and rocking chest movements. CPAP is applied without benefit and the child becomes cyanotic. *The child has developed complete laryngospasm*! She is quickly transferred to PACU, oxygen is applied with propofol 1 mg/kg IV administered, and intermittent positive pressure ventilation (IPPV) is resumed followed by spontaneous respiration. As the propofol wears off, the stridor recurs and lignocaine 1.5 mg/kg IV is considered but before the drug reaches the patient, the IV becomes dislodged and the patient starts to desaturate. A jaw thrust is given with the application of pressure on the styloid process bilaterally. Succinylcholine 4 mg/kg is drawn up in the meantime and injected lingually. The airway begins to open up and another IV is placed. The heart rate drops precipitously and atropine 0.01 mg/kg is required to bring it up. The child's throat and pharynx are sucked, thus clearing the airway, and she is gently ventilated until she starts breathing spontaneously.

Laryngospasm – Lessons to Be Learned

Laryngospasm is a closure of the glottis due to reflex constriction of the laryngeal muscles. It is an exaggeration of a protective reflex that prevents aspiration of foreign objects into the tracheobronchial tree resulting in complete or partial closure of the glottis with impedance or total obstruction of airflow to the lungs. Often the spasm breaks spontaneously but if not, it can lead to severe hypoxemia, negative pressure pulmonary oedema, cardiac dysrhythmias, cardiac arrest and ultimately death.

The laryngospasm reflex is controlled by the extrinsic and intrinsic muscles of the larynx that are innervated by the internal branch of the superior laryngeal nerve which is itself a branch of the vagus. The abnormal excitation of the pathway often occurs by stimulation during light anaesthesia and is most commonly seen during induction and emergence.

Who Is at Risk for Laryngospasm?

- Small babies and young children
- Those who have had a recent upper respiratory tract infection (URI)
- Asthmatics
- Gastro-oesophageal reflux disease
- Those with choking episodes during sleep
- Parents who smoke
- Strong family history of asthma and atopy
- Airway surgery associated with bleeding into the airway

In addition, during anaesthesia certain factors predispose to laryngospasm:

- Child crying during induction – increased secretions
- Use of ketamine
- Inhalational induction
- Deep intubation without muscle relaxants
- Deep extubation
- Light plane of anaesthesia

Classification of Laryngospasm

1. **Partial laryngospasm:**
   - A high-pitched inspiratory stridor
   - Rocking or paradoxical chest movement
   - With a significant mismatch between the patient's respiratory efforts and the bag movement.
2. **Complete laryngospasm:**
   - SILENCE, no stridor, no breath sounds,
   - Rocking movement of the chest wall,
   - No bag movement, no $EtCO_2$ trace
   - No ventilation possible.
3. **Apnoea:** Silence with no chest movements.

Prevention

Start an IV early and secure well; spray cords with lignocaine – this is controversial as spraying under light planes of anaesthesia may itself be a stimulus for laryngospasm. *Awake extubation ensures that the patient will not have laryngospasm while emerging from anaesthesia.*

Management of Partial Laryngospasm

- Optimise head and airway position (Head tilt, jaw thrust and good mask seal)
- CPAP with 100% oxygen

- Minimise stimulation
- Deepen anaesthetic
  - A sub-hypnotic dose of propofol 0.5 mg/kg IV has the advantage of rapid onset of action, within 30–45 seconds. Its side effects are transient apnoea and hypotension. It can be used for burn victims where succinylcholine is contraindicated
  - Midazolam, 0.03 mg/kg for post-extubation laryngospasm
  - Suxamethonium 1–2 mg/kg IV with atropine 0.02 mg/kg (to prevent bradycardia) or 4 mg/kg IM (where onset is 3–4 minutes and duration is 20 minutes)
- Suction of airway, if needed

Management of Complete Laryngospasm or Partial with Decompensation

- Start as for incomplete spasm
- 'Laryngospasm notch pressure' or 'flutter bag' (see below)
- IV present – propofol, succinylcholine and atropine (see above)
- If there is no IV in place give IM or lingual succinylcholine and atropine
- Intubate if needed (always keep regular endotracheal tubes [ETTs] of an appropriate size when using RAE or flexometallic tubes)
- Look out for negative pressure pulmonary oedema

Description of Manoeuvres

- **Laryngospasm notch:** It is an anatomical entity which is bounded anteriorly by the ascending ramus of the mandible adjacent to the condyle, posteriorly by the mastoid process and cephalad by the base of the skull. **Larson's manoeuvre** is a bilateral firm digital pressure on the styloid process behind the posterior ramus of the mandible. It is essentially a vigorous jaw thrust with pressure between the posterior ramus of the mandible and anterior to the mastoid process, that is, into the laryngospasm notch. It appears to 'break' the laryngospasm, but the mechanism is poorly understood. One should not persist with this technique if a result is not obtained immediately. Resort to pharmacological means.
- **Jaw thrust:** Pull of the mandible forward which is a painful stimulus. It pulls the geniohyoid muscles on the stretch to pull the paraglottic region forward.
- **CPAP:** Continuous positive airway pressure can be maintained with a tight-fitting mask and (partial) closure of the valve on the reservoir bag while maintaining a fresh gas flow of oxygen. This distends the hypopharynx and helps break the laryngospasm.
- **Fluttering of the bag:** Rapid squeezing of the bag in a staccato rhythm apparently pushes oxygen through partially opened cords.

Beware of ventilating with a closed glottis – the oxygen will go into the stomach distending it and splinting the diaphragm making further ventilation difficult. Ventilating against a closed glottis distending the stomach leads to regurgitation when the patient is 'light'. So aspirate , that is, 'suck out' the stomach before extubation.

Problem 3: Bronchospasm

A 15 kg, 4-year-old boy presents for cleft palate surgery. A known asthmatic, he has had four acute episodes in the last 12 months and was treated with nebulised salbutamol and oral prednisolone. Presently, he is on twice daily inhaled fluticasone and thrice daily inhaled salbutamol. He has no h/o recent URTI and no features of atopy. His chest is clear. He is premedicated with two puffs of salbutamol and paracetamol.

Anaesthesia is induced with sevoflurane/O_2/N_2O with FiO_2 0.3. After IV cannulation propofol 20 mg is given, he is intubated with a 5 mm oral RAE uncuffed tube while breathing spontaneously. Fentanyl 2 mcg/kg and dexamethasone 0.15 mg/kg are given.

The patient is positioned and surgery starts. The gag is placed and the SpO_2 falls from 98% to 81% and tidal volume (TV) from 120 to 70 ml. There is no coughing or straining, but there are some intercostal retractions and a bilateral expiratory wheeze is heard. *The tube may have been pushed in and is now stimulating the carina.* The surgeon is informed and the gag is released and the endotracheal tube withdrawn slightly. FiO_2 is increased as is the sevoflurane to 4%. Air entry improves.

Do we proceed???

A trial of replacement of the gag is decided upon.

The tube is 'shortened' by withdrawing slightly and the gag is placed more carefully. The infiltration (with adrenaline) appears to help the ventilation and wheeze improves with the improvement of airway pressures. Sevoflurane is decreased to 2% and FiO_2 to 0.4 and surgery proceeds. Towards the end of the procedure, the SpO_2 falls again. There is no rash and BP is unchanged.

TV and saturation drop to 60 ml and 80%, respectively. Hand ventilation requires an airway pressure of 35 cm of water to adequately ventilate the lungs. Auscultation reveals bilateral expiratory wheeze. $EtCO_2$ shows upsloping of the plateau phase. It rises to 58 mmHg. A diagnosis of bronchospasm is made.

The respiratory rate is reduced to ten breaths a minute with an I:E ratio of 1:4. Sevoflurane is increased to 4% and FiO_2 to 1. Saturations come up to 93%. Suction in the ETT is negative. Four puffs of salbutamol are given in the ETT. Dexamethasone is given IV. The airway resistance normalises and inflation pressures, capnography trace and SpO_2 return to normal with an FiO_2 of 0.4.

The surgery is quickly completed and haemostasis is ensured. The child is extubated 'deep'.

In PACU, the saturation drops to 92% on room air but responds well to oxygen supplementation with a mask. He has a cough with a mild wheeze as he recovers but it settles with salbutamol nebulisation every 30 minutes over a period of 2 hours. After a normal chest X-ray, he is sent to the ward on supplementary oxygen. He is continued on his regular medications along with 3 days of oral prednisolone.

Bronchospasm – Lessons to Be Learned

Bronchospasm is caused by an increase in bronchial smooth muscle tone associated with increased airflow obstruction. In healthy subjects, the smooth muscle tone is regulated by the vagus. In asthma, there is a greater sensitivity to external stimuli.

1. Causes of **obstruction of small airways** (associated with bronchospasm):
   - Aspiration
   - Asthma
   - Infection – viral bronchiolitis, pneumonia
   - Chronic lung disease of prematurity
   - Transient infant wheeze
2. **Obstruction of large airways** is associated with
   - Airway and vascular malformations
   - Inhaled foreign body
   - Mediastinal cysts and masses

The causes of intraoperative wheezing are as follows:

1. **Mechanical:** Airway manipulation such as laryngoscopy under light anaesthesia, stimulation of carina or bronchus under light anaesthesia and bronchospasm after aspiration

   Other mechanical causes of airway obstruction – kinking of and secretions in the ETT, obstructive masses and foreign body aspiration
2. **Non-immunological anaphylaxis:** Anaphylactoid reaction
3. **Immunologically mediated anaphylaxis**

   For 2 and 3, see Chapter 42

Who is more likely to develop bronchospasm?

- Any child with a history of wheezing more than 3 times in the last 12 months.

Wheezing is a high-pitched musical whistle heard in *expiration*. This may occur as a result of obstruction to large or small airways. However, severe obstruction as in status asthmaticus may present as a silent chest.

- Any child who has wheezing with exercise
- Nocturnal dry cough
- Recent upper respiratory infection (URI) <2 weeks
- H/o hay fever
- Eczema – present or past
- Nasal polyposis

Pre-operative preparation to reduce the risk of bronchospasm:

- Nebulised β-2 agonist 10–30 minutes before surgery, for example, salbutamol 2.5 mg if the child is less than 20 kg and 5 mg if the child weighs more than 20 kg. If the child is used to a spacer, it may be used for salbutamol and ipratropium.
- Ipratropium bromide may be nebulised or used with a spacer as preparation for anaesthesia. A dose of 250 mcg/dose if body weight is <20 kg

or 500 mcg if >20 kg body weight may be given every 20–30 minutes.

- For children with rhinorrhoea, a topical nasal spray like oxymetazoline 0.05% 2–3 sprays per nostril may be used pre-induction.

Management of Persistent Wheezing During Anaesthesia

- Deepen the anaesthesia with a bolus of propofol (1 mg/kg) or sevoflurane. Ketamine may also be used.
- Check air entry bilaterally and shorten the tube by withdrawing it slightly, as necessary.
  - Supplemental oxygen to maintain SpO_2 >92%.
- Exclude mechanical causes by passing a suction catheter through the ETT and establishing suction.

Drugs that are used in the management of persistent wheezing are as follows:

1. β-2 agonists: Salbutamol
   - Through the inspiratory limb of the breathing circuit or directly to the ETT or supraglottic device – 1 puff = 100 mcg. In severe cases, it can be given as a continuous intravenous infusion of 1–5 mcg/kg/min after a loading dose of 15 mcg/kg given over 10 minutes
   - Nebulised 0.5% solution (5 mg/ml) diluted 0.5 ml in 4 ml or undiluted
   - Terbutaline 5–10 mcg/kg subcutaneously, maximum 0.4 mg given every 15 - 20 mins, maximum thrice
2. Ipratropium is an antagonist at the muscarinic cholinergic receptors. It causes bronchial smooth muscle dilatation and also reduces salivary and mucous gland secretions. It is given in the dose of 0.25–0.5 mg nebulised over 20 minutes and can be repeated a maximum of three times. Alternating ipratropium with salbutamol is more effective than either drug alone.
3. Adrenaline 1–2 mcg/kg IV. Ask the surgeon to infiltrate quickly
4. Systemic corticosteroids help decrease bronchial oedema and bronchial mucous production
   - Oral prednisolone 0.5–1 mg/kg (maximum 50 mg) once daily
   - Hydrocortisone 2–4 mg/kg (maximum 100 mg) 6 hourly
     - Steroids *work more slowly than β-2 agonists*
     - They *enhance and prolong the action of β-2 agonists within 1 hour*
     - Their *anti-inflammatory effect takes 4–6 hours*
5. Lignocaine 1.5 mg/kg IV reduces the airway response to instrumentation and drug-induced bronchospasm. *Lignocaine can itself increase the airway tone.*
6. In children over 5 years IV magnesium sulphate 75 mg/kg (maximum 2.5 g) over 20 minutes while monitoring the ECG. To be used in poorly controlled asthma
7. Drugs that help maintain bronchodilation during anaesthesia include inhalational agents such as halothane and sevoflurane, propofol and ketamine. However, ketamine increases post-operative nausea and vomiting, induces hallucinations and has a longer recovery time.

Theophyllines – aminophylline and diprophylline – are not advised as they cause cardiac dysrhythmias

Antibiotics are not advocated.

If the patient cannot cooperate or anaphylaxis is thought to be the cause of bronchospasm, the drugs can be given IM or subcutaneously as in the case of adrenaline.

Post-Extubation Croup

Post-extubation croup can also cause airway obstruction. This is best treated with nebulised adrenaline and systemic steroids.

Ventilation Strategies During IPPV

The aim of ventilation strategies during IPPV is to minimise the risk of dynamic hyperinflation that can lead to barotrauma (pneumothorax), raised intrathoracic pressure with severe hypotension and cardiac arrest. A slow respiratory rate with an increase in the I:E (inspiratory to expiratory) ratio and permissive hypercapnia is aimed for. Suggested initial ventilatory settings are a TV of 8–10 ml/kg and a respiratory rate of 12–16/min (<5 years) and 10–12/min (>5 years). The I:E ratio should be 1:4 and positive end-expiratory pressure (PEEP) of 0–4 cm H_2O. The driving pressure (inspiratory plateau pressure – PEEP) of 25–30 cm H_2O (<5 years) and 30–35 cm H_2O (>5 years) with a maximum inspiratory pressure of < 50 cm H_2O. This is on the higher side and we must watch out for barotrauma.

Analgesics in Asthma

Non-steroidal anti-inflammatory drugs increase leukotriene production by inhibiting cyclooxygenase. They can, therefore, cause bronchospasm, laryngospasm, rhinorrhoea and periorbital oedema. Acetaminophen (paracetamol) has also been implicated in causing asthma but this is not common. Aspirin should be avoided as it causes Reyes syndrome (aspirin-induced asthma syndrome)

Post-Operative Care

Any child who is a known severe asthmatic or has had an episode of asthma under anaesthesia should be treated and monitored in the intensive care unit post-operatively. Nebulised drugs should be prescribed if the child is unable to use a metered inhaler. High-flow humidified oxygen may be used to improve oxygenation and decrease the work of breathing.

If his asthma is generally well controlled, he may be sent home on his regular medication regime.

Conclusion

- A 'tight bag' with inadequate ventilation is a nightmare.
- Form a protocol and approach the problem in a systematic manner – above all DON'T PANIC!
- There is no alternative than to stick to the basics which include a thorough machine and circuit check before anaesthetising ALL cases.
- Keep self-inflating bags like the AMBU (artificial manual breathing unit) and alternative breathing systems available.
- Optimise medical conditions before all elective cases, thus making it easier for yourself to handle these cases.

SUGGESTED READINGS

1. Goldschneider KR, Davidson AJ, Wittkugel EP, Skinner AV (eds). Clinical Pediatric Anesthesia – a Case-based Handbook. Oxford University Press, New York, 2012.
2. Wheeler M, Cote CJ, Todres ID. The Pediatric Airway. In: A Practice of Anesthesia for Infants and Children, 4th edition. Cote CJ, Lerman J, Todres ID (eds). Saunders Elsevier, Philadelphia 2009; pp. 237–278.
3. Alami AA, Ayoub CN, Baraka AS. Laryngospasm: Review of different prevention and treatment modalities. *Paediatr Anesth* 2008; 18(4):281–288.
4. Flick RP, Wilder RT, Pieper SF, et al. Risk factors for laryngospasm in children during general anesthesia. *Paediatr Anesth* 2008; 18(4):289–296.
5. Burgoyne LL, Anghelescu DL. Intervention steps for treating laryngospasm in pediatric patients. *Paediatr Anesth* 2008; 18(4):297–302.
6. Hampson-Evans D, Morgan P, Farrar M. Pediatric laryngospasm. *Paediatr Anesth* 2008; 18(4): 303–307.
7. Cass L. Intraoperative Wheezing. In: Clinical Pediatric Anesthesia – a Case-based Handbook. Goldschneider KR, Davidson AJ, Wittkugel EP, Skinner AV (eds). Oxford University Press, New York, 2012; pp. 191–201.
8. Woods BD, Sladen RN. Perioperative considerations for the patient with asthma and bronchospasm. *Br J Anaesth* 2009; 103(Suppl 1):157–165.
9. Collins S, Schedler P, Veasey B, et al. Prevention and treatment of laryngospasm in the pediatric patient: A literature review. *AANA J* 2019; 87:2.
10. Anderson N, Clarke s, von Ungern-Sternberg BS. Aerosolized drug delivery in awake and anaesthetised children to treat bronchospasm. *Pediatr Anesth* 2022: 32:156–166. doi: 10.1111/pan.14354.
11. Regli A, Sommerfield A, von Ungern-Sternberg. Anesthetic considerations in children with asthma. *Pediatr Anesth* 2022:32:146–155. doi: 10.1111/pan.14373.
12. Tait AR, Malviya S. Anesthesia for the child with an upper respiratory tract infection: still a dilemma? *Anesth Analg* 2005; 100(1):59–65. doi: 10.1213/01.ANE.0000139653.53618.91. PMID: 15616052.
13. Bernardo-Ocampo MC. Upper respiratory tract infection and paediatric anaesthesia. ATOTW 246 – 16/01/2012.

19 Recognition and Management of the Difficult Paediatric Airway

Rebecca Jacob • Aparna Williams

One of the greatest challenges in the practice of anaesthesia is the management of a child with a difficult airway (DA). A DA in anaesthesia is defined as a clinical situation in which a conventionally trained anaesthetist experiences difficulty with face mask ventilation, tracheal intubation, supraglottic airway device (SAD) insertion, invasive airway access or all of these. To handle these cases successfully, it is important to understand the normal airway anatomy and function in children of different ages, be familiar with common airway problems seen in childhood, be able to recognise the signs and symptoms of significant airway compromise and know the radiological features associated with various lesions. In addition, one should be familiar with the use of various equipment and techniques devised to deal with airway problems and be familiar with protocols to manage such patients, always having an alternative contingency plan in case of failure of the first protocol, such as a plan B and C when plan A fails or when there is a sudden complete loss of a patent airway.

Anatomy of Relevance

The child differs from the adult in many ways – in size, shape and position of the airways.

Upper Airway

The upper airway of the newborn infant is smaller than that of the adult. The tongue is relatively large and occupies the oral cavity and oropharynx fully. Most neonates are obligate nose-breathers as the epiglottis, which is highly placed, almost meets the soft palate making oral ventilation difficult. This lasts for the first 2–6 months of age. The neonate, unlike the older child, has very little lymphoid tissue in the upper airway. The tonsils and adenoids appear in the second year of life and generally reach their largest size by 4–7 years of age, after which they gradually diminish in size unless infected. In the 4–7 year old, enlarged lymphoid tissue is a common cause of airway obstruction, snoring and sleep apnoea.

The larynx is positioned higher, with the body of the hyoid bone between C3 and C4 vertebrae. As the baby grows, the glottis moves caudally to reach the C5-C6 vertebral level by maturity. The high position of the epiglottis and larynx allows the infant to breathe and swallow simultaneously. The larynx also differs in many ways. The epiglottis is more U-shaped and protrudes over the larynx at a 45° angle. It is funnel shaped in children below 8 years of age with the narrowest portion being at the level of the cricoid ring. The vocal cords of the neonate are slanted such that the anterior commissure is more caudad than the posterior commissure.

The tracheal direction in the infant is downwards and posteriorly, whereas in the adult it is directly downwards. Consequently, the application of cricoid pressure is more effective in an infant. The distance between the vocal cords and the bifurcation of the trachea is 4–5 cm. The endotracheal tube (ETT) must be carefully positioned and fixed as the tip of the tube can move about 2 cm with the flexion and extension of the head. In most cases, the right main bronchus is less angled than the left and is the one into which an ETT slips in most often, as does an aspirated foreign body. Neonates and infants have relatively large heads which tend to flex their small 'weak' necks.

Physiologically, children are more prone to hypoxaemia and bradycardia. Oxygen consumption is approximately 7 ml/kg in the neonate compared to 3 ml/kg in the adult. This implies that airway obstruction will produce hypoxia more rapidly. Airflow in the upper airway is turbulent during quiet respiration. Laminar flow begins only at the level of the 4th or 5th bronchial divisions where the rapid increase in the cross-sectional area increases airflow velocity. The resistance to turbulent gas flow is inversely proportional to the fourth power of the radius of the airway. Hence, 1 mm of oedema in the trachea of the newborn, which reduces the radius from 2 to 1 mm, increases the resistance to airflow approximately 16-fold.

Neonates and infants have a highly compliant chest wall and horizontally placed ribs which place them at a mechanical disadvantage and increase their work of breathing. The diaphragm is the major muscle of respiration in the neonate, but its muscle fibres are such that they are less efficient than in the adult.

Causes of a Difficult Airway

The causes of a DA are commonly classified as follows (**Table 19.1**):

- Congenital
- Structural
- Inflammatory
- Neoplastic

These are enumerated in the following text. However, this classification does not explain or describe the degree of difficulty the anaesthetist will encounter during mask ventilation or intubation. This is amply illustrated in **Figures 19.1–19.3**.

Assessment of the Airway

Assessment begins with a comprehensive history.

History

The history of respiratory problems such as snoring, noisy breathing, stridor, change of voice, sleep apnoea/apnoeic spells or recurrent croup is significant. Does the child prefer to lie on one side or prone? Is the breathing easier when he sits up? Does he have feeding problems with regurgitation and aspiration? Has he had prior head, neck or oral surgery such as cleft palate surgery? Is there any documentation of previous anaesthetics with a record of a difficult intubation? Is there a record of any congenital lesions such as a laryngeal web, neck mass, haemangioma, subglottic stenosis or laryngomalacia? Does he have any associated syndromes? Does he open his mouth wide when he cries? If the child has had prior surgery, try to see the anaesthetists' notes from the previous surgery for details of perioperative airway problems.

Examination

Physical examination should be both frontal and lateral (**Fig. 19.4**). Take into account the general appearance of the child including agitation, dyspnoea, stridor, cyanosis, chest retractions, weak or absent cry, drooling of saliva and the dysmorphic facies of the child with a craniofacial anomaly.

Assess what could the anatomic location of the problem be? Crowing on inspiration is indicative of extrathoracic airway obstruction whereas noise on exhalation is usually due to an intrathoracic lesion.

TABLE 19.1 Causes of Difficult Airway in Children

Causes of Difficult Airway	Clinical Examples
Congenital	Craniofacial anomaly: associated with micrognathia (Pierre Robin sequence, Treacher Collins), hemifacial microsomia (Goldenhar's), midfacial hypoplasia or facial clefts, Apert's, Crouzon's, Pfeiffer's and Saethre–Chotzen syndromes; macroglossia, Hurler's/Hunter's syndrome (mucopolysaccharidosis), Beckwith–Wiedemann syndrome, Down syndrome Cervical spine: Down, Klippel–Feil syndrome Laryngotracheal: Laryngeal web, tracheomalacia
Structural	Aspirated foreign body, trauma, tracheal stenosis, post intubation oedema, temporomandibular joint ankylosis, post burn contracture neck or circumoral contracture
Inflammatory	Croup, epiglottitis, laryngeal papillomatosis, diphtheria, retropharyngeal abscess
Neoplastic	Cystic hygroma, tumours, meningomyelocele

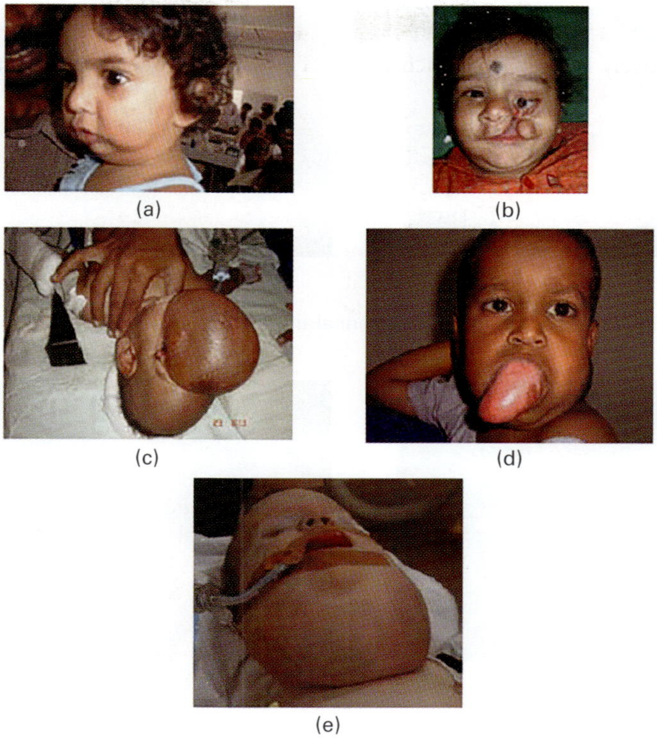

Figure 19.1 (a–e) Difficult mask ventilation. (a) Pierre Robin sequence. (b) Mid-facial deformity with a facial cleft. (c) Encephalocele. (d) Macroglossia due to a neurofibroma tongue. (e) Cystic hygroma and macroglossia.

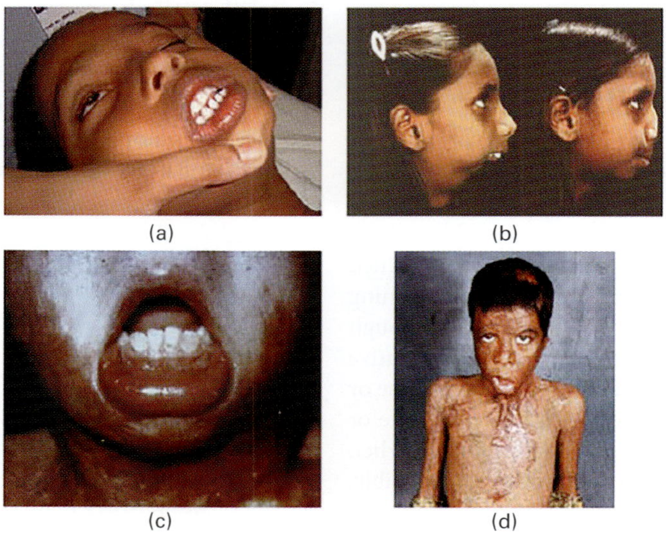

Figure 19.2 (a–d) Difficult intubation. (a) Temporomandibular joint ankylosis. (b) Long-standing temporomandibular joint ankylosis and after correction. (c) Limited mouth opening due to burn contracture. Note fibrosis in the mandibular space limits the 'give' for tongue displacement during intubation. (d) Limited neck extension due to burn contracture of the neck.

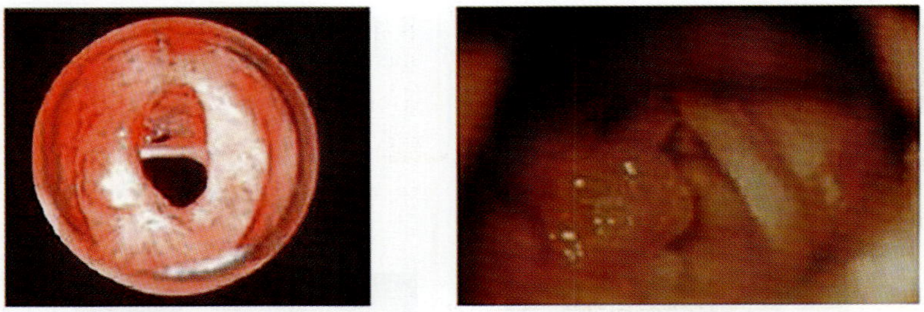

(a) (b)

Figure 19.3 (a and b) Structural abnormalities – congenital and acquired. (a) Laryngeal web. (b) Laryngeal papilloma.

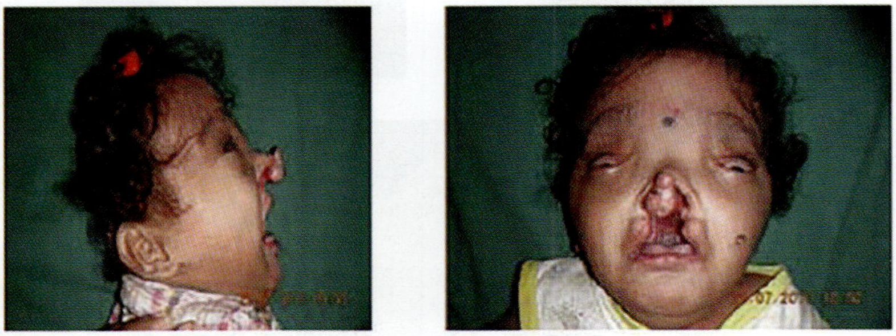

(a) (b)

Figure 19.4 (a and b) Clinical examination. (a) Bilateral cleft lip and palate. (b) Note the abnormal shape of the head.

Distress and noise during both inspiration and expiration could be due to a lesion at or just above the thoracic inlet.

Clinical Examination with the View to Predict a 'Difficult Airway'

Examination should start with the size of the head, the nares and proceed down the airway.

In the neonate, infant and young child, first rule out choanal atresia or in the older child, blocked nasal passages as with hypertrophied adenoids or tonsils. Then check mouth-opening and temporomandibular joint mobility though they may be difficult to assess in the uncooperative child. Check for a protruding pre-maxilla, loose or protruding teeth, evidence of cleft lip or palate or evidence of cleft surgery having been done earlier. Assess the tongue size in relation to the mandible, the mandibular size (mentohyoid distance – should at least allow the insertion of a fingertip) and symmetry. Look for the presence of soft-tissue masses such as cystic hygroma or haemangioma. Assess neck mobility and the child's ability to co-operate. Look for signs of airway obstruction as seen in **Figure 19.5**.

In the older child, in addition to the above, assess mouth-opening and visibility of the uvula in relation to the tongue (Mallampatti). Look for enlarged tonsils, loose or protuberant teeth, the compliance of the mandibular space and the mobility and thickness of the neck.

The commonly used assessment criteria for ease of intubation such as the Mallampatti classification and thyromental distance have not been validated for the smaller paediatric patient. What is more commonly used now is the more comprehensive COPUR Scale first described by Lane (**Fig. 19.6**).

Pre-Operative Investigations

Measurement of oxygen saturation with a pulse oximeter is essential; other investigations may be useful. Imaging with a plain X-ray, CT scan or MRI may be useful in selected cases to diagnose the cause or site of airway obstruction, or bony or soft-tissue abnormalities.

Most special investigations will require cooperation from the child, which is not always possible and therefore limits their use.

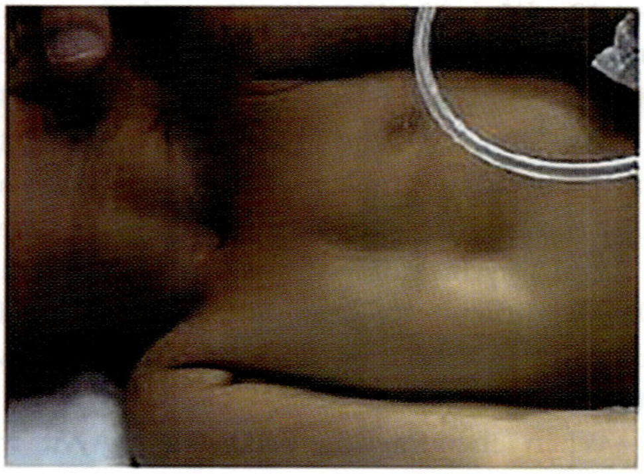

Figure 19.5 Signs of obstruction and respiratory distress. Note the suprasternal indrawing as well as indrawing at xiphisternum with inspiration.

- Arterial blood gases may be useful to assess the severity and progress of respiratory distress.
- Respiratory function tests may help to differentiate extrathoracic from intrathoracic obstruction.
- A sleep study may be useful to assess the severity of sleep apnoea, but is not routine.
  - Overnight pulse oximetry may be more practical.
- It may be possible to visualise the larynx using nasoendoscopy if the child is co-operative.

Clinical Classification of a Difficult Airway

After the history and examination have been completed and results of investigations obtained, a simple classification would be a useful guide to the management of the paediatric DA. The DA can be classified as follows:

- A known/anticipated DA: It includes children with a documented DA or with anatomical or clinical features suggestive of severe airway obstruction or deformity that prevents routine airway management. Successful management of the anticipated DA relies on meticulous planning. Airway experts should be involved at an early stage. The flowchart shown in Figure 19.6 on the management of the anticipated difficult paediatric airway is easy to follow.
- Unanticipated DA: It includes children whose history and clinical examination are not suggestive of a DA but who pose problems to the

COPUR Scale (Lane)			
C-Chin		**U-Uvula**	
Normal	1	*Mouth open tongue out*	
Small, moderately hypoplastic	2	Tip of uvula visible	1
Markedly recessive	3	Uvula partially visible	2
Extremely hypoplastic	4	Uvula concealed, soft palate visible	3
		Soft palate not visible	4
O-Opening			
Interdental space between front teeth		**R-Range**	
>40 mm	1	*Observe line from eye to orbit, estimate range of motion looking up and down*	
20–40 mm	2		
10–20 mm	3	>120°	1
<10	4	60°–120°	2
		30°–60°	3
P-Previous intubation or OSA		<30°	4
Previous attempt easy	1		
No previous attempt, no hx OSA	2		
OSA, previous hx difficult intubation	3		
Extremely difficult previous intubation, trach, or patient unable to lie supine	4		

Prediction Points	
5–7	Easy normal intubation
8–10	Laryngeal pressure may help
12	More difficult, fiberoptic may be less traumatic
14	Difficult intubation, fiberoptic orother advanced technique
16	Dangerous airway, consider awake intubation, potential tracheostomy

Figure 19.6 COPUR Scale (Lane) to predict difficult airway in children. COPUR, for **c**hin, **o**pening, **p**revious intubation, **u**vula and **r**ange; hx, history of; OSA, obstructive sleep apnoea; trach, tracheostomy.

of severe disease. Different sleep labs using different AHI or RDI cut-offs for mild, moderate and severe OSAS further confound interpretations of severity; the range of AHI cut-offs for a diagnosis of OSAS is 1–5 and the range for severe OSAS is between 10 and 30. Despite difficulties in interpretation, the PSG remains an important diagnostic test with important clinical implications.

Medical Conditions Associated with OSAS

While the majority of paediatric OSAS patients are not obese, OSAS is more common in obese children, which is a population that has grown substantially worldwide. Enlarged tonsillar tissue is associated with OSAS. A particularly high index of suspicion should exist for OSAS when there is tonsillar hypertrophy in association with history noted in Box 21.1. In addition, though removal of hypertrophied tonsils and adenoids does typically lead to significant improvement in severity of apnoea and quality of life, T&A does not guarantee that a child's OSAS has been cured, especially in children with severe OSAS. The majority of children with severe OSAS still have OSAS on post-recovery PSG, with a small percentage still having severe OSAS. Obese children are at a higher risk of persistent OSA after T&A. The American Academy of Otolaryngology-Head and Neck Surgery (AAO-HNS) clinical guidelines currently recommend a preoperative PSG for obese patients before T&A.

Numerous other medical conditions, including certain syndromes, are associated with OSAS (Table 21.1), and these same conditions may increase the need for numerous surgical interventions including T&A. The presence of these conditions, or others that reduce airway dimensions or increase airway collapse, should alert anaesthesia providers to the possibility of OSAS. The presence of a condition from Table 21.1, or a history of having had T&A to treat OSAS, should prompt thorough questioning of parents, which would include questions from Box 21.1.

Syndromes and sequences associated with OSAS are taken from Baum and O'Flaherty.[3] Other diagnoses associated with OSAS are collected from multiple sources.

Table 21.1 Syndromes and Other Diagnoses Associated with Paediatric OSAS

Syndromes and Sequences	Other Diagnoses
Beckwith–Wiedemann syndrome	Achondroplasia
Craniofacial syndromes Apert syndrome Crouzon syndrome Pfeiffer syndrome	Arnold–Chiari malformation Carney complex Cerebral palsy Choanal stenosis
Down syndrome	Cleft palate following repair
Goldenhar syndrome	Craniometaphyseal dysplasia
Hallermann–Streiff syndrome	Cystic hygroma
Klippel–Feil sequence	Hypothyroidism
Marfan syndrome	Myelomeningocele
Mucolipidosis (Sialidosis)	Obesity
Mucopolysaccharidoses Hunter syndrome Hurler syndrome Morquio syndrome Scheie syndrome	 Osteopetrosis Papillomatosis Pharyngeal flap surgery Sickle cell disease
Pierre Robin sequence	
Prader–Willi syndrome	
Rubinstein–Taybi syndrome	
Schwartz–Jampel syndrome	
Treacher Collins syndrome	

OSAS, obstructive sleep apnoea syndrome.

Paediatric OSAS–Associated Comorbid Conditions

Chronic untreated OSAS leads to pulmonary hypertension, resulting from pulmonary arterial vasoconstriction in response to chronic nocturnal hypercarbia, acidosis and hypoxaemia. Right ventricular dysfunction, cor pulmonale, hepatic congestion and peripheral oedema can develop if elevated pulmonary pressures are left unchecked. Biventricular hypertrophy can occur with paediatric OSAS, and though it occurs uncommonly, it is most likely to occur with severe OSAS. Fortunately, all these entities may be reversible if OSAS can be surgically reversed.

Paediatric OSAS is also associated with autonomic dysfunction, enhanced sympathetic activity, endothelial dysfunction and systemic hypertension. Anaesthetists performing pre-operative evaluation of children with OSAS should be on the lookout for manifestations of these OSAS-related comorbid conditions and request an echocardiogram when required, especially when OSAS is known to be severe.

Ambulatory Anaesthesia and the Child with OSAS

Ambulatory surgery is believed to be safe for patients with OSAS only when certain precautions are taken and when support services are good. The Society for Ambulatory Anesthesia published adult guidelines in 2012 stating that ambulatory surgery is safe for adults with OSAS as long as they use previously prescribed continuous positive airway pressure (CPAP), have optimised comorbidities, can have their post-operative pain managed predominately by non-opioid modalities and are otherwise good candidates for ambulatory surgery. Guidelines for ambulatory surgery for children with OSAS do not exist, but elements of the adult guidelines could be applied to paediatrics. For example, although children rarely present for surgery on CPAP, those who do should be required to use their CPAP post-operatively.

Children with OSAS may receive ambulatory T&A, with some exceptions; it is generally believed that those under 3 years of age, those with severe OSAS, and any patient with an underlying syndrome or medical conditions such as those in **Table 21.1** should be admitted for overnight observation. PSG is the only way to determine OSAS severity. When PSG is not available for patients with severe symptoms or high-risk features, a conservative approach that includes post-operative overnight observation is preferable. Children with OSAS who require overnight admission, whether due to OSAS severity, comorbid conditions or type of surgery, should have monitoring that allows rapid recognition of respiratory depression and airway obstruction.

Anaesthetic Management of Children with OSAS

Proper perioperative care for children with OSAS depends on identification of the condition. As noted above, the pre-operative history should include enquiry into whether a child snores, and further questions can be asked to parents of snoring children to improve the predictive value for OSAS (see **Box 21.1**). Micrognathia, retrognathia, midfacial hypoplasia as well as large tonsils should alert one to the possibility of OSAS. Specific paediatric medical conditions (see **Table 21.1**) should prompt suspicion of OSAS. Primary therapy for paediatric OSAS is T&A, and children coming for that procedure are likely to have OSAS or a milder form of SDB. Children requiring general anaesthesia for other surgeries, or for imaging studies, who have a high likelihood of having OSAS but have never been tested with PSG may need to have their procedure delayed until they can receive testing (and possibly T&A) or may need to proceed with an urgent procedure without testing, in which case it is prudent to assume that they have OSAS.

Pre-anaesthetic medication with midazolam appears to be safe for patients with SDB, though almost no data exists on this topic. A series by Francis et al. of 70 children between 1 and 12 years of age, receiving T&A, were administered 0.5 mg/kg of oral midazolam pre-operatively and monitored with pulse oximetry.[4] Only one 16 month old with severe OSAS (RDI of 39 and O_2 saturation nadir to 74% on PSG) experienced a brief self-limited oxygen desaturation pre-operatively while asleep. That data and personal experience indicate that oral pre-anaesthetic midazolam is safe in OSAS patients; however, caution should be exercised in those with severe OSAS, especially for younger patients, and patients should be under close observation once the premedication is given. Intranasal route may also be used for premedication. Recent studies indicate that intranasal dexmedetomidine (2 μg/kg) may be safer than intranasal midazolam (0.1 mg/kg) as premedication.

Both general anaesthesia and opioids worsen OSAS, giving rise to concern for post-operative exacerbation of apnoea. Anaesthetic induction for paediatric patients with OSAS may be safely performed with either volatile anaesthetics or intravenous agents. Anaesthetic induction is normally accompanied by narrowing of upper airway calibre and tendency for airway obstruction, which may be more pronounced in patients with OSAS. Partial or complete airway obstruction that occurs during inhalation induction of paediatric OSAS patients may be ameliorated or overcome by use of face mask CPAP, chin-lift or jaw thrust; by lateral position or by placing an oral airway. Complete airway obstruction should be addressed immediately with corrective measures because post-obstructive pulmonary oedema can develop rapidly when profound negative pressure is generated by strong inspiratory efforts against a closed airway. Intravenous induction may be a better choice for patients with very severe OSAS. OSAS is a known risk factor for difficult tracheal intubation in adults. Likewise, many of the entities associated with paediatric OSAS (such as those listed in **Table 21.1**) are also associated with difficult tracheal intubation, although tonsillar hypertrophy alone rarely causes difficulty with intubation. Tracheal intubation with deep anaesthesia, rather than with neuromuscular blockade, may be advantageous for patients undergoing T&A because the duration of the procedure is short and rapid return to spontaneous ventilation is desirable both for titration of narcotics (see the following text) and for emergence. Short-acting anaesthetics, such as desflurane or propofol, may be beneficial for the maintenance of anaesthesia in patients with OSAS. However, T&A is not easily managed using propofol as the sole anaesthetic unless combined with neuromuscular blockade. Desflurane is rarely available in low-resource nations. Alternative choices for children with OSAS include halothane or sevoflurane for anaesthetic induction, and halothane, isoflurane or sevoflurane for maintenance of anaesthesia.

Paediatric OSAS patients should be expected to have exaggerated responses to opioid analgesics; they are more susceptible to respiratory depressant effects and appear to be more sensitive to analgesic effects. Those exaggerated responses may be most pronounced in patients with severe OSAS. However, children undergoing T&A usually receive opioid medication due to the painful nature of the procedure, and those with OSAS should have small aliquots titrated to analgesic and respiratory responses. The American Society of Anesthesiologists, in 2014, updated and recommended reducing the opioid dose during surgery by half in these patients. Short-acting opioids tend to be most forgiving. Non-opioid alternatives for pain management, such as acetaminophen, NSAIDs, alpha-2 adrenergic agonists and regional anaesthesia, should be considered. Thus, in patients with severe OSAS undergoing T&A, an opioid-free intraoperative technique may be employed; analgesia can be supplied with acetaminophen, dexamethasone, dexmedetomidine and local anaesthesia injected into the tonsillar bed by the surgical team, with small amounts of opioid analgesics reserved for administration as needed in the recovery room.

However, intra-operative ketorolac should be avoided during T&A because it is associated with nearly a four-fold increase in the odds of requiring reoperation for post T&A haemorrhage.

Dexamethasone decreases pain post T&A, albeit a marginal effect, and is a worthwhile analgesic adjunct. Dexamethasone has the additional benefit of providing a strong antiemetic effect, and after T&A it speeds return to a normal diet.

Extubation in paediatric OSAS patients should be performed awake unless there is a compelling reason to do otherwise, such as severe reactive airways. After T&A, awake extubation is especially desirable due to elevated risk for aspiration and airway obstruction. Even after awake tracheal extubation, children with OSAS may require assistance to maintain airway patency, including lateral positioning, chin-lift or jaw thrust, placement of a nasal airway, or application of face mask CPAP.

Post-operative disposition depends on many factors. These children may need longer stay in the post-anaesthesia care unit (PACU) to ensure airway patency and maintenance of saturation. They may also require overnight SpO_2 monitoring or until they can maintain their oxygen saturation on room air. AAO-HNS guidelines recommend inpatient admission for paediatric patients with severe OSA, age <3 and/or SpO_2 nadir <80%.

Conclusion

Obstructive sleep apnoea syndrome is a common paediatric condition with important implications for the perioperative period. Perioperative management of children should include screening for OSA, understanding PSG results when available and understanding the potential for important comorbid conditions resulting from OSAS. Ambulatory anaesthesia may be appropriate for paediatric patients with OSAS, but patient factors and OSAS severity dictate suitability.

Paediatric OSAS patients require special considerations both intra- and post-operatively in order to provide safe and efficient care.

REFERENCES

1. Li AM, Cheung A, Chan D, et al. Validation of a questionnaire instrument for prediction of obstructive sleep apnea in Hong Kong Chinese children. *Ped Pulmonol* 2006; 41:1153–1160.
2. Schwengel DA, Sterni LM, Tunkel DE, Heitmiller ES. Perioperative management of children with obstructive sleep apnea. *Anesth Anal* 2009; 109:60–75.
3. Baum V. Anesthesia for Genetic, *Metabolic, and Dysmorphic Syndromes of Childhood*, 2nd edition. Lippincott Williams & Wilkins, Philadelphia, PA; 2007.
4. Francis A, Eltaki K, Bash T, Cortes S, Mojdehi K, Goldstein NA. The safety of preoperative sedation in children with sleep-disordered breathing. *Int J Ped Otorhinolaryngol* 2006; 70:1517–1521.

SUGGESTED READINGS

1. Scalzitti NJ, Sarber KM. Diagnosis and perioperative management in pediatric sleep-disordered breathing. *Paediatr Anaesth* 2018; 28(11):940–946. doi: 10.1111/pan.13506. Epub 2018 Oct 3. PMID: 30281185.
2. Mitchell RB, Archer SM, Ishman SL, et al. Clinical Practice Guideline: Tonsillectomy in Children (Update). *Otolaryngology–Head and Neck Surgery*. 2019;160(1_suppl):S1-S42. doi:10.1177/0194599818801757
3. Lee TC, Wulfovich S, Kettler E, et al. Predictors of overnight postoperative respiratory complications in obese children undergoing adenotonsillectomy for obstructive sleep apnea. *Int J Pediatr Otorhinolaryngol* 2022; 162:111334. doi: 10.1016/j.ijporl.2022.111334. Epub 2022 Oct 4. PMID: 36209625.
4. Pehora C, Faraoni D, Obara S, et al. Predicting perioperative respiratory adverse events in children with sleep-disordered breathing. *Anesth Analg* 2021; 132(4):1084–1091. doi: 10.1213/ANE.0000000000005195. PMID: 33002926.
5. Burns DW, Chan VWS, Trivedi A, et al. Ready to scan? A systematic review of point of care ultrasound (PoCUS) for screening of obstructive sleep apnea (OSA) in the pediatric population. *J Clin Anesth* 2022; 83:110973. doi: 10.1016/j.jclinane.2022.110973. Epub 2022 Sep 21. PMID: 36152603.
6. Shen F, Zhang Q, Xu Y, et al. Effect of intranasal dexmedetomidine or midazolam for premedication on the occurrence of respiratory adverse events in children undergoing tonsillectomy and adenoidectomy: A randomized clinical trial. *JAMA Netw Open* 2022; 5(8):e2225473. doi: 10.1001/jamanetworkopen.2022.25473. PMID: 35943745; PMCID: PMC9364121.
7. Adler AC, Daszkowski A, Tan JC, et al. The association of dexmedetomidine on perioperative opioid consumption in children undergoing adenotonsillectomy with and without obstructive sleep apnea. *Anesth Analg* 2021; 133(5):1260–1268. doi: 10.1213/ANE.0000000000005410. PMID: 33591119.
8. Friedman NR, Meier M, Tholen K, et al. Tonsillectomy for obstructive sleep-disordered breathing: should they stay, or could they go? Laryngoscope 2022; 132(8):1675–1681. doi: 10.1002/lary.29909. Epub 2021 Oct 21. PMID: 34672364.
9. Roberts C, Al Sayegh R, Ellison PR, et al. How pediatric anesthesiologists manage children with osa undergoing tonsillectomy. *Ann Otol Rhinol Laryngol* 2020; 129(1):55–62. doi: 10.1177/0003489419874371. Epub 2019 Sep 5. PMID: 31801377; PMCID: PMC7885167.
10. Scalzitti NJ, Sarber KM. Diagnosis and perioperative management in pediatric sleep-disordered breathing. *Paediatr Anaesth* 2018; 28(11):940–946. doi: 10.1111/pan.13506. Epub 2018 Oct 3. PMID: 30281185.
11. Arambula AM, Xie DX, Whigham AS. Respiratory events after adenotonsillectomy requiring escalated admission status in children with obstructive sleep apnea. *Int J Pediatr Otorhinolaryngol* 2018;107:31–36. doi: 10.1016/j.ijporl.2018.01.009. Epub 2018 Jan 31. PMID: 29501307.
12. Murto KT, Chen W, Katz SL, et al. research needs assessment for children with obstructive sleep apnea undergoing diagnostic or surgical procedures. *Anesth Analg* 2018; 127(1):198–201. doi: 10.1213/ANE.0000000000003309. PMID: 29481438.
13. Schnoor J, Busch T, Turemuratov N, et al. Pre-anesthetic assessment with three core questions for the detection of obstructive sleep apnea in childhood: An observational study. *BMC Anesthesiol* 2018; 18(1):25. doi: 10.1186/s12871-018-0483-y. PMID: 29458333; PMCID: PMC5819204.
14. Kako H, Tripi J, Walia H, et al. Utility of screening questionnaire and polysomnography to predict postoperative outcomes in children. *Int J Pediatr Otorhinolaryngol* 2017; 102:71–75. doi: 10.1016/j.ijporl.2017.09.006. Epub 2017 Sep 14. PMID: 29106880.

22 Anaesthesia for Diagnostic Airway Interventions

Gayatri Sasikumar

Children with congenital or acquired anomalies of the airway present with multiple challenges to the anaesthesiologist. These include sharing of the airway with the surgeon, the unique nature of the paediatric airway and possible association with other congenital anomalies. The diagnosis of airway anomalies requires varying depths of anaesthesia at different stages of assessment, so it is important for the anaesthesiologist to have some familiarity with the surgical steps. These children often present with acute respiratory distress and may require stabilisation in the intensive care unit before any elective procedure. A multi-disciplinary team is often involved in the management of such children, which includes a paediatrician, paediatric ENT surgeon, intensivist, pulmonologist, neurologist and anaesthesiologist. It is very important for the team to have a good understanding and communication with one another. The surgical plan and possible outcomes should be explained to the parents since most of these children may require multiple visits to the operating room.

Indications for Diagnostic Airway Procedures

The indication for these procedures includes a child who presents with one or more of the following symptoms: inspiratory stridor, cyanosis, worsening croup, feeding difficulties, noisy breathing, abnormal crying, and acute respiratory distress requiring supplemental oxygen and ventilation. Diagnostic endoscopy is also an important first step to delineate pathology prior to definitive surgery, for example, to identify the position and number of tracheo-oesophageal fistulae prior to tracheo-oesophageal fistula (TEF) repair, to identify the extent of the stenotic segment and vocal cord movement prior to tracheal resection and anastomosis, etc. The age of presentation ranges from newborn babies to older children.

The fundamentals of diagnosis are to conduct a systematic examination of the airway starting from the nares to the trachea and bronchi to rule out common anomalies.

Common anomalies of the airway and their presentation in the paediatric age group:

1. **Laryngomalacia:** It is one of the most common congenital anomalies of the larynx. In this condition, the supraglottic structures cave in during inspiration closing the laryngeal inlet. A defect in the neuromuscular support to the laryngopharynx is thought to be the aetiology. Children with this condition typically present at 2–4 weeks, with inspiratory stridor that worsens during crying, feeding and in the supine position. There may be associated feeding difficulty and gastroesophageal reflux.

   There are 3 main types of laryngomalacia:

   - *Type 1:* Inward migration of aryepiglottic (AE) folds during inspiration.
   - *Type 2:* Short AE folds with a curved tubular epiglottis that collapses on inspiration.
   - *Type 3:* Overhanging epiglottis that collapses into the laryngeal inlet, obstructing it.

   Surgical treatment is indicated if the child has feeding difficulties, failure to thrive and severe respiratory distress.

2. **Vocal cord palsies:** It is the second most common congenital anomaly of the larynx. A child with unilateral palsy presents with mild stridor, hoarse cry and aspiration. Bilateral palsy on the other hand presents with high-pitched inspiratory stridor, with normal voice, apnoeic spells and cyanosis.
3. **Congenital subglottic stenosis:** This is the third most common laryngeal anomaly and the commonest cause of tracheostomy in children under the age of one year. It is characterised by the narrowing of the airway below the glottis (Fig. 22.1). Most children may require emergency intubation which could lead to mixed (acquired on congenital) subglottic stenosis. Symptoms include biphasic stridor and recurrent croup with a 'barking' cough.
4. **Laryngeal web:** This is a relatively uncommon condition. Failed recanalisation of the primitive larynx during the 8–10th week of embryological development results in an anterior laryngeal web (Fig. 22.2). The child presents with varying degrees of dysphonia ranging from mild hoarseness to aphonia. Severe cases may need a tracheostomy.
5. **Laryngeal cleft:** It accounts for about 0.5–1.5% of all congenital anomalies of the larynx. It is characterised by a longitudinal slit-like defect between the laryngotracheal tract and the upper digestive tract (Fig. 22.3). There is a high prevalence of associated systemic (cardiac, urogenital and craniofacial) anomalies in these children. They often present with feeding and respiratory difficulties. The severity of symptoms depends on the extent of the cleft.
6. **Congenital tracheal anomalies:** These include, tracheomalacia, tracheal stenosis and tracheal webs (Fig. 22.4). Symptoms are non-specific and depend on the severity of the defect. These include biphasic stridor with expiratory wheezing, respiratory distress with chest retractions, cyanosis, apnoeic spells and barking cough.
7. **Recurrent respiratory papillomatosis, subglottic cysts and subglottic haemangiomas** (Fig. 22.5): These lesions of the airway may cause varying degrees of obstruction of the laryngeal inlet. The symptoms depend on the extent of the obstruction. Some conditions such as papillomatosis are recurrent and the child may need repeated operating room visits and anaesthesia. A good rapport with the child and the caregivers comes in handy.

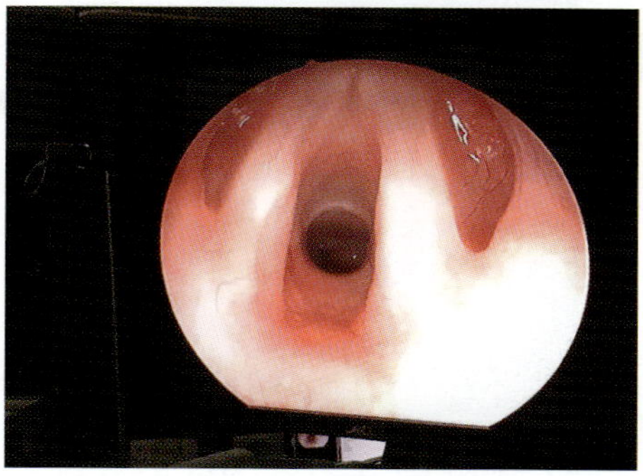

Figure 22.1 Subglottic stenosis: Narrowing of the airway below the level of the vocal cord. (*Courtesy*: Children's Airway and Swallowing Centre, Manipal Hospital, Old Airport Road, Bangalore.)

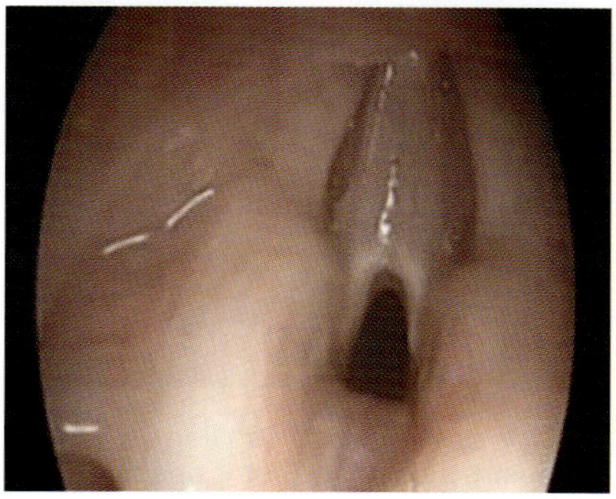

Figure 22.2 Anterior laryngeal web. (*Courtesy*: Children's Airway and Swallowing Centre, Manipal Hospital, Old Airport Road, Bangalore.)

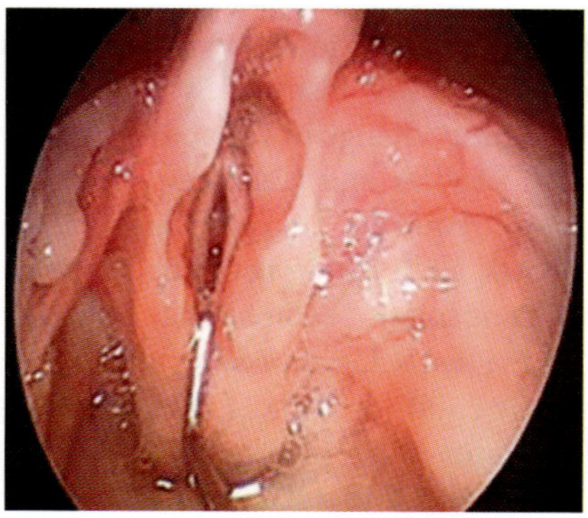

Figure 22.3 Laryngeal cleft: The cleft is identified by palpation of the posterior glottis using an L-Probe. (*Courtesy*: Children's Airway and Swallowing Centre, Manipal Hospital, Old Airport Road, Bangalore.)

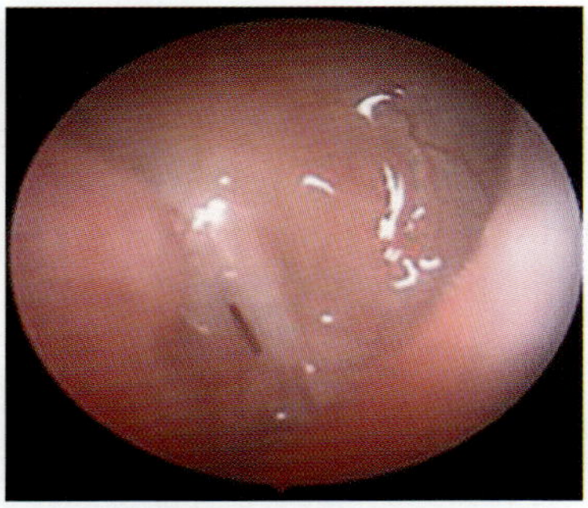

Figure 22.4 Tracheal stenosis. (*Courtesy*: Children's Airway and Swallowing Centre, Manipal Hospital, Old Airport Road, Bangalore.)

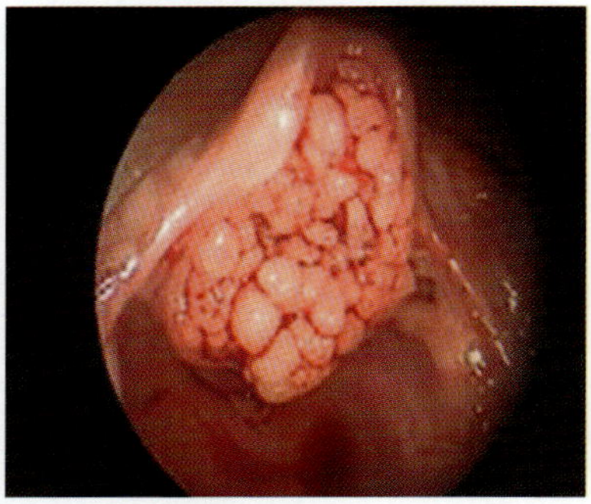

Figure 22.5 Laryngeal papillomatosis causes complete obstruction of the glottic opening. (*Courtesy*: Children's Airway and Swallowing Centre, Manipal Hospital, Old Airport Road, Bangalore.)

Pre-Operative Evaluation

The first step in clinical assessment involves taking a thorough history. Symptoms include noisy breathing, change in voice, abnormal crying, feeding difficulties and acute respiratory distress sometimes requiring oxygen and ventilatory support. Ask for a history of concurrent medical illness, congenital anomalies, developmental delays, previous ICU admissions and intubation. Observe the child for signs of respiratory distress, audible sounds during respiration and obvious indicators of the difficult airway such as retrognathia, micrognathia, cleft lip/palate, etc. Some of these children may be tracheostomised, which ensures a secure airway. Anaesthetic management in them is therefore easier than in the non-tracheostomised child. Make a note of the size of the tracheostomy tube and keep a similar sized polyvinylchloride (PVC) or reinforced tube stand-by for an emergency. Follow routine nil per oral (NPO) guidelines. If the surgical plan is to only diagnose the defect in the airway, the child will be comfortable in the post-op and can be shifted to the ward. However, if definitive corrective surgery is done, the respiratory distress of the child may worsen due to airway oedema, requiring post-operative ICU admission and monitoring. Close communication and planning with the intensive care team help prevent unnecessary delays in the transport of the child post-procedure.

In the operating room, a difficult airway cart (including video laryngoscopes, flexible and rigid bronchoscopes, and tracheostomy equipment) should be kept ready. In cases where a tracheostomy is thought to be inevitable (e.g., a laryngeal papilloma causing complete obstruction of the glottic opening), prior marking of the surgical landmarks before induction of anaesthesia can save precious time in an emergency. Airway ultrasound is a useful guide to identify landmarks especially in tiny babies. Appropriately sized tracheostomy tubes must be kept ready in such cases. Premedication with anticholinergic agents such as atropine or glycopyrrolate will decrease the oral secretions, steroids such as dexamethasone or hydrocortisone will decrease airway oedema, and bronchodilators either intravenous or nebulised will help open-up proximal and distal airways. Local anaesthetic applied to the tongue, glottis and subglottis will decrease the number of anaesthetic drugs needed and prevent laryngospasm. As with any other procedure, meticulous care must be taken to keep the baby warm and adequately hydrated.

Anaesthetic Management

An airway diagnostic procedure is a fact-finding mission by the surgeon to look for the cause of the child's symptoms. The surgical step begins with transnasal flexible endoscopy to assess the dynamic cause of laryngeal obstruction (diagnosis of laryngomalacia). During this phase, keep the child 'light' and spontaneously breathing so that the movement of the laryngeal structures will closely mimic the awake state. The next step is to look for any obvious lesions or defects in the supraglottic region. This is followed by the assessment of vocal cord movement. Stimulating the baby by stroking the face or feet leads to reflex glottic closure and makes the assessment of cord movement easy. Since at different stages of the assessment, the plane of anaesthesia required is different, choose an anaesthetic agent that can preserve spontaneous ventilation and reflex laryngeal closure, and allow the anaesthesiologist to switch from lighter to deeper planes of anaesthesia rapidly. Inhalational anaesthesia with sevoflurane is a good choice here compared to propofol because it maintains spontaneous respiration at deeper planes and has minimal effect on the pharyngeal muscle tone. Lignocaine spray should be avoided during dynamic airway assessment as it can cause muscle relaxation and exaggerated collapse of supraglottic structures, leading to a false diagnosis of laryngomalacia. Once dynamic assessment is done, the plane of anaesthesia is deepened to facilitate subsequent inspection of the glottic and infra glottic region. Additional boluses or infusion of propofol, dexmedetomidine, ketamine or remifentanil (if available) with good local anaesthetic spray to the glottic and subglottic region gives an adequate depth of anaesthesia.

A direct laryngoscope or suspension laryngoscope is used as a final step of airway examination, to get a good visualisation of the laryngeal structures. Diagnosis of laryngeal cleft and confirmation of earlier findings is done during this phase. A rigid bronchoscope is used to look for any defect in the infra glottic region like subglottic stenosis, haemangiomas, cysts, tracheomalacia, etc. Oesophagoscopy is done for completion to rule out signs of reflux oesophagitis.

Different anaesthetic techniques can be used during this time. These include spontaneous ventilation, apnoeic oxygenation with intermittent ventilation, jet ventilation and positive pressure ventilation via endotracheal tube.

- **Spontaneous ventilation:** In the majority of the diagnostic airway procedures, assessment of vocal cord mobility and neuromuscular structures is an essential first step. Therefore, in these cases, spontaneous ventilation is a requirement. This technique is called tubeless anaesthesia and there are different methods of providing oxygenation during airway assessment using this technique. These include delivering oxygen through, nasal prongs, a nasal endotracheal tube with the tip in the oropharynx (nasal insufflation technique), oral south pole Ring–Adair–Elwyn (RAE) tube placed in the oropharynx, etc. The advantage of using a nasal or oral tube fixed in the oropharynx is that it provides an unobstructed view of the laryngeal structures to the surgeon, allowing easy instrumentation of the airway and acts as a conduit for continuous oxygen and anaesthetic delivery (Fig. 22.6). In case of emergency if the child desaturates, the tube can be slipped into the glottis by the surgeon under vision. The challenge in these cases is to maintain spontaneous ventilation and at the same time allow laryngeal suspension, which is highly stimulating. As mentioned earlier, local anaesthetic to the oral cavity and vocal cords helps to decrease anaesthetic requirements. Anaesthesia can be maintained with either total intravenous anaesthesia (TIVA) (propofol with short-acting opioid, dexmedetomidine and ketamine, or a combination of these drugs) or volatile agents with intermittent intravenous propofol. As mentioned earlier, inhalational anaesthetics allow the anaesthesiologist to rapidly change the depth of anaesthesia during a dynamic assessment.
- **Jet ventilation:** This is another technique that can be used to provide oxygenation during airway procedures. Air/oxygen mixture is delivered at high pressure through a small-bore catheter placed within the airway. Jet ventilation can be classified as either low or high frequency depending on the frequency of pulsed gas; and supraglottic, trans-glottic or transtracheal based on the position of the oxygen delivery system. In low-frequency jet ventilation, the respiratory rate is manually controlled to 8–10 breaths min^{-1} to allow adequate time for exhalation. In high-frequency jet ventilation, special equipment is used to deliver heated and humidified jets at rates up to 10 Hz. In the paediatric population, jet ventilation in the supraglottic position can be used safely with a lower risk of airway fires. Caution must be taken to ensure that the jet is directed at the glottic opening to avoid gastric insufflation. This technique is not recommended in laryngotracheal stenosis, as there is the risk of air trapping and barotrauma due to inadequate gas exhalation. It is also contraindicated in papillomatosis since viral particles may get disseminated into the lungs. The transtracheal jet

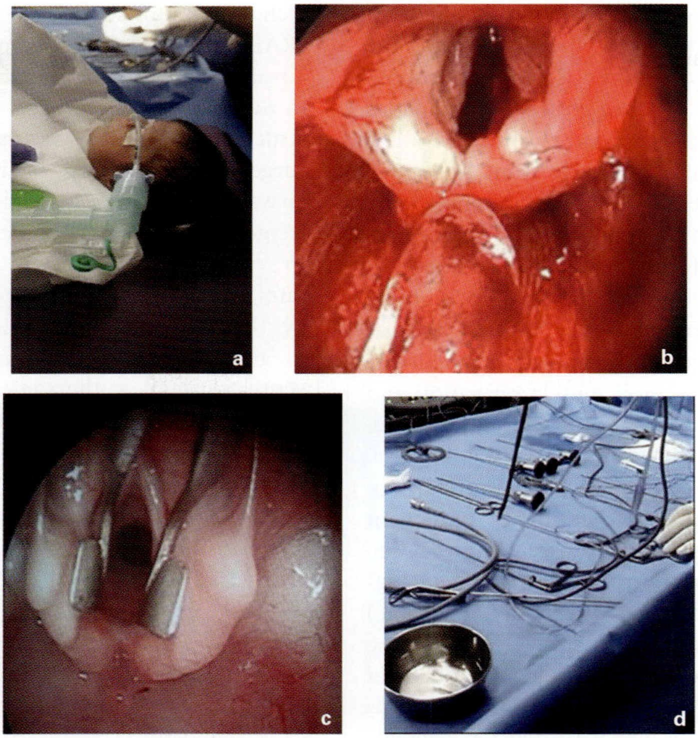

Figure 22.6 (a) Nasal insufflation. (b) Endotracheal tube tip in the oropharynx. (c) Lindholm vocal cord retractor. (d) Instruments for airway diagnostic procedures. (*Courtesy*: Children's Airway and Swallowing Centre, Manipal Hospital, Old Airport Road, Bangalore.)

ventilation technique is not commonly done in the paediatric population due to difficulty in placing the transtracheal cannula in the awake child. It is used only in specific cases where the airway is very narrow and there is no alternate way to ventilate the child other than tracheostomy or in older children. TIVA is required during jet ventilation since it is not possible to administer inhalational anaesthetic.

Jet ventilation in children requires close monitoring and a well-trained team familiar with this technique.

- **Apnoeic oxygenation with intermittent ventilation:** This technique requires optimal cooperation from the surgeon. Here, the child is first intubated and once the surgeon is ready the endotracheal tube is removed to allow the surgeon an unobstructed view. When saturation levels drop to 90%, the child is reintubated and this process is repeated. If the upper airway is patent, a nasal high-flow oxygen delivery systems like THRIVE can be used to provide apnoeic oxygenation. Anaesthesia in such cases should be maintained with TIVA. Remember that the pulse oximeter reading lags behind the actual drop in oxygen saturation. So, vigilant monitoring of saturation is required during this technique.
- **Positive pressure ventilation via endotracheal tube:** Intubation can be done orally, nasally or through the tracheostomy if the surgeon is not assessing the dynamic movement of the glottic and supraglottic structures. This technique ensures complete control of the airway and continuous ventilation. Smaller-size tubes should be used to provide a working room for the surgeon. If available, laser-safe tubes can be used to prevent airway fires. Laryngeal mask airways with special catheter mounts that allow flexible bronchoscope to be inserted without disconnecting the circuit can also be used. Anaesthesia can be maintained with either TIVA or volatile agents. When using smaller-sized tubes, the air leak present leads to an inadequate depth of anaesthesia with volatile anaesthetics whereas this is not a problem with TIVA.

Intraoperative Monitoring

As for all cases, basic American Society of Anaesthesiologists (ASA) monitoring standards are mandatory. When using the tubeless technique, specialised monitors like transcutaneous carbon dioxide monitor and respiratory impedance monitor (**Fig. 22.7**) are useful in monitoring respiration. It is important to keep in mind that, during these procedures, the whole team should be vigilant irrespective of the anaesthetic technique used.

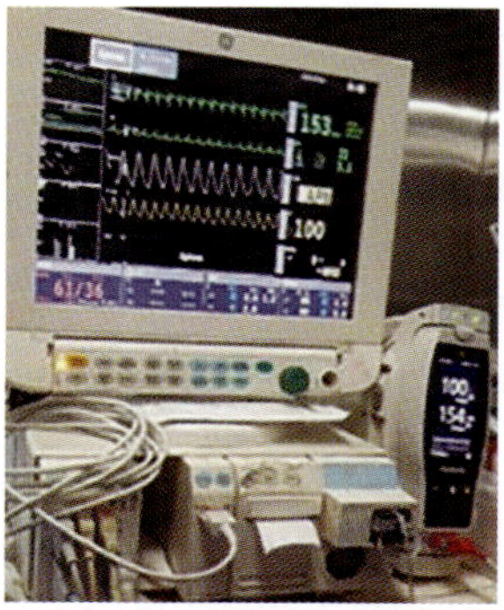

Figure 22.7 The respiratory impedance monitor shows continuous breathing patterns even in the absence of EtCO2 tracing. (*Courtesy*: Children's Airway and Swallowing Centre, Manipal Hospital, Old Airport Road, Bangalore.)

Complications and Troubleshooting

Complications include apnoea, laryngospasm, desaturation, pneumothorax, failed ventilation and loss of airway. The team must be on guard to deal with all complications and when needed, be prepared for an emergency tracheostomy. Liberal use of topical local anaesthetic and intravenous steroid help reduce the incidence of the above complications. One must be careful though to avoid exceeding the toxic dose of local anaesthetic. Effective communication within the team is pertinent to curb complications (**Fig. 22.8**).

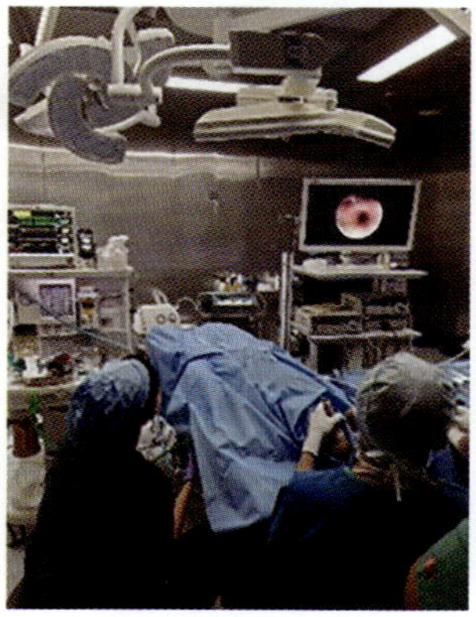

Figure 22.8 A vigilant team that communicates well is important. (*Courtesy*: Children's Airway and Swallowing Centre, Manipal Hospital, Old Airport Road, Bangalore.)

Conclusion

The anaesthetic technique chosen for diagnosis of airway anomalies depends on the surgical procedure, the type of laryngeal pathology, the age of the child and associated comorbidities, the duration of the procedure and most importantly, the experience of the surgeon and anaesthetist. It usually involves multiple steps requiring instrumentation and probing of the airway. A thorough discussion with the surgical team helps customise anaesthesia care for individual patients. Complications can occur even with the most experienced hands and it is therefore important for the whole team to be vigilant at all times. Good communication and understanding among the team members save the day in the majority of cases. Finally, it is prudent for the team to discuss with the parents the details of the procedure and expected outcomes.

SUGGESTED READINGS

1. Philippe Monnier, ed. Paediatric airway surgery: Management of laryngotracheal Stenosis in Infants and Children. Springer-Verlag Berlin Heidelberg; 2011.
2. Bradley J, Lee GS, Peyton J. Anesthesia for shared airway surgery in children. *Pediatr Anesth* 2020; 30:288–295. DOI:https://doi.org/10.1111/pan.13815.
3. Oshan V, Walker RWM. Anaesthesia for complex airway surgery in children. *Cont Educ Anaesth Crit Care Pain* 2013; 13(2):47–51. DOI:https://doi.org/10.1093/bjaceaccp/mks058.

23 FOREIGN BODY ASPIRATION

Rebecca Jacob • Swapna Thampi
• Gayatri Sasikumar

Foreign body (FB) aspiration is a leading cause of death in children aged between 1 and 3 years. Though older children are also known to aspirate foreign bodies, toddlers are more prone to do so. They are often busy exploring their environment, putting things in their mouths with inadequate dentition and immature swallowing co-ordination. They are often under the supervision of an older sibling who is busy 'doing his own thing'. Ninety-six percent of foreign bodies in this age group are organic in nature (peanuts, custard apple and tamarind seeds heading the list in southern India) whereas in older children it is usually non-organic products (pins, coins, pen caps, etc.). Anatomically, children have symmetrical bronchial angles till about 15 years of age when the aortic knuckle develops fully. The FB may thus pass to either mainstem bronchus. The location of the FB depends on its size and shape, the majority being found in the proximal airways. Organic matter such as tamarind seeds and peanuts swell over time worsening the obstruction. Small sharp objects tend to lodge in the subglottic area. Foreign bodies that obstruct the glottis cause acute respiratory distress and stridor. If aspirated foreign bodies are not removed in time, it puts the child at risk of chronic pneumonia, granulation tissue formation, atelectasis and even bronchiectasis.

Signs and Symptoms

FB aspiration may present in one of three clinical phases or may progress from one to the other:

1. Immediate phase
2. Asymptomatic phase
3. Clinical phase

Immediate Phase

The *immediate phase* occurs immediately after aspiration and the child may present with choking, gagging, coughing, wheezing, stridor and/or temporary cyanosis especially if the FB is lodged at or near the glottic opening or in the trachea. Mortality is high in this phase and there is an increased risk of hypoxic encephalopathy in those who survive. This phase requires emergency measures to relieve the obstruction. Smaller objects partially obstructing the glottis or those that pass into a distal bronchus may go unnoticed for weeks until the child presents with unexplained recurrent respiratory symptoms, pneumonia and focal or diffuse wheezing.

Asymptomatic Phase

The *second* or *asymptomatic stage* may last from a few minutes to months after the immediate phase. This varied duration depends upon the location of the FB, the degree of airway obstruction, the type of material aspirated and the ease with which the FB can change its location.

Clinical Phase

The *third clinical phase* is *the renewed symptomatic period* characterised by airway inflammation or infection. This is more probable if the FB is organic in nature. Symptoms include repeated bouts of cough with sputum production, fever, wheezing and occasionally haemoptysis. Because a considerable period has passed, a definitive history of FB aspiration is difficult to obtain. A high index of suspicion along with careful clinical examination helps clinch the diagnosis in such cases.

Diagnosis

Diagnosis of FB aspiration is based on history, clinical presentation and imaging.

History and Clinical Presentation

History of FB aspiration or potential aspiration or sudden onset of coughing, choking, stridor or cyanosis particularly while feeding is often obtained. If there is stridor, aphonia or hoarseness, the FB is most likely in the larynx or trachea. Voice changes or barking cough may also be the result of laryngeal oedema. Chest retraction is seen with upper airway obstruction (Fig. 23.1).

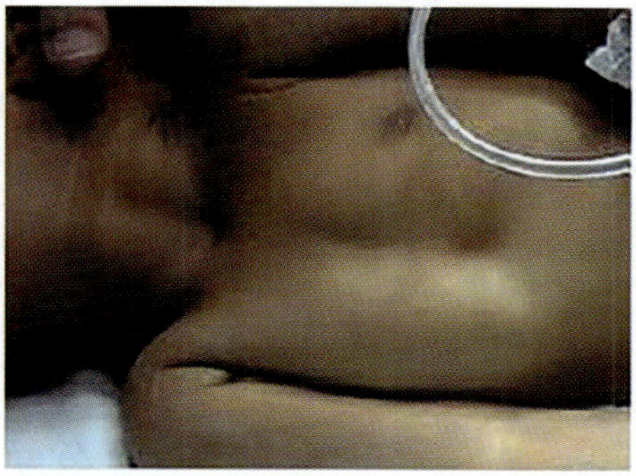

Figure 23.1 Retraction of the chest and suprasternal area due to upper airway obstruction.

The severity of the symptoms depends on the size and location of the FB, the complications related to the type of FB and the duration. Most often, there are unilateral diminished breath sounds and rhonchi. Bilateral decreased breath sounds help diagnose a tracheal FB. Alternating loss of breath sounds could mean that the FB is shifting. Sometimes, the physical examination may be normal but that should not exclude the suspicion of a FB aspiration.

Imaging

The workup of a stable patient should include a chest radiograph to identify the FB or look for its possible location based on its effects. Imaging gives a more definitive diagnosis if the FB is opaque. Lateral and anterior views help to locate the site of obstruction. Tracheal foreign bodies can be differentiated from oesophageal foreign bodies based on their alignment in the sagittal plane as opposed to the anterior plane. Most FBs are, however, not radio-opaque and will not be seen on chest X-ray or cause any radiographic abnormalities especially in the first 24 hours. One may have to rely on indirect findings such as mediastinal shift, atelectasis, hyperinflation or lobar collapse/consolidation that set in later (Figs 23.2 and 23.3). A comparison of inspiratory and expiratory films may reveal an area of unilateral hyperinflation and mediastinal shift. If both inspiratory and expiratory films look equally hyperinflated, it implies bilateral air trapping, due to the FB being lodged in the trachea involving both mainstem bronchi. However, young children cannot be instructed to hold their breath in one phase of respiration and a lateral decubitus film may be more helpful. Here, normally, the mediastinum should shift towards the dependent side. If, however, the mediastinal shift does not occur it implies that there is a hyperinflation of the lower, that is, dependent lung. There will also be a similarity in the decubitus and the upright film due to the air trapping in the dependent lung. Thoracic computed tomography and virtual bronchoscopy that can generate intraluminal views of the airway up to the sixth and seventh generation can be used to identify difficult-to-locate foreign bodies. However, remember that their use leads to significant radiation exposure to the child.

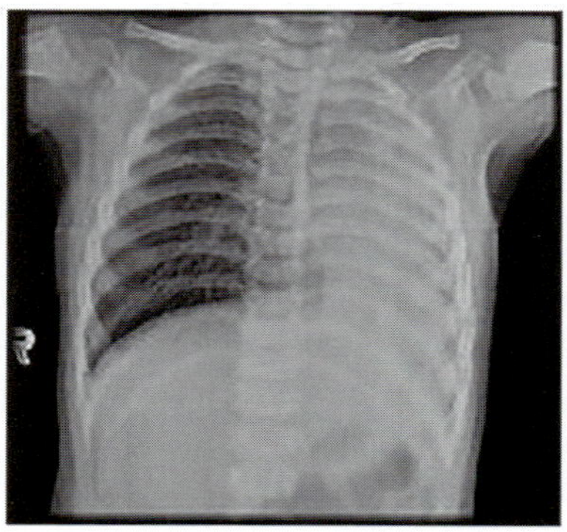

Figure 23.2 Aspiration of a custard apple seed leading to collapse of the left lung and hyperinflation of the right lung.

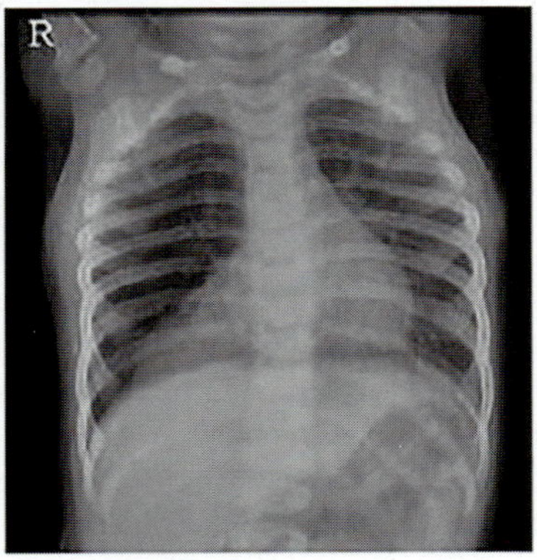

Figure 23.3 Effect of a peanut in the right lower lobe.

Differential Diagnosis

Differential diagnoses would include asthma, croup, pneumonia, bronchitis, tracheomalacia, bronchomalacia, vocal cord dysfunction or psychogenic cough.

Complications

Complications of FB aspiration depend on the location and type of FB aspirated (organic or non-organic, sharp versus blunt). If the FB is removed within 24 hours of aspiration, the complication rate is very low. Delayed removal leads to inflammation with the possibility of tracheal or bronchial stenosis, bronchiectasis, lung abscess, tissue erosion or perforation, pneumomediastinum or pneumothorax.

Management

Emergency treatment in the first clinical phase: The American Heart Association included the management of FB aspiration in its paediatric basic life support guidelines in 1995. When the airway obstruction is mild and spontaneous respiration is possible, the child should be encouraged to cough and transferred to the hospital as soon as possible. When the airway obstruction is severe, a Heimlich manoeuvre should be performed which involves giving subdiaphragmatic abdominal thrusts. In infants due to the risk of injury to the relatively large liver, this manoeuvre is not recommended. Instead, they should be given five back blows followed by five chest thrusts repeatedly till the airway is cleared. Blind finger sweeps should never be undertaken as this may push the FB further downwards into the airway. If the child becomes unresponsive then airway, breathing and circulation should be assessed, and management should proceed according to the basic life support guidelines.

Bronchoscopy

The gold standard for the removal of a FB is via a rigid bronchoscope. The patient may present for *bronchoscopy* in the first (acute) or third (clinical) phase or in case of recurrent pneumonia or atelectasis.

The instrument most used is a ventilating bronchoscope as marketed by Storz (**Fig. 23.4**). This provides both a means of visualising the airway and a means of ventilation. It is available in sizes 2.5–6.0 mm ID (internal diameter). The external diameter is 2 mm larger. With the glass eyepiece in place, it becomes a steel endotracheal tube (ETT). This bronchoscope is used preferably after 'deepening the child' with mask ventilation and topical spray with lignocaine 10% (each aliquot being 10 mg) (**Fig. 23.5**). The whole airway including the

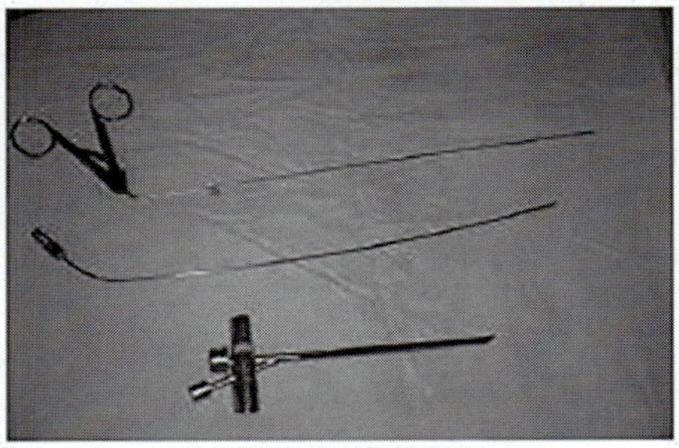

Figure 23.4 Rigid ventilating bronchoscope.

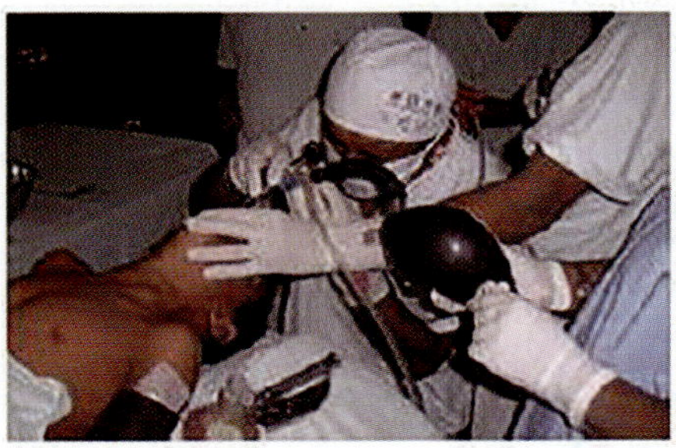

Figure 23.5 Rigid bronchoscopy depth of anaesthesia maintained through the side port of the bronchoscope.

subglottic area is visualised as it is instrumented, thus reducing the chance of dislodging a highly placed FB.

Whenever possible, rigid bronchoscopy should be done by an experienced operator or by a trainee being guided by an experienced endoscopist in a procedure room fully equipped to handle paediatric airway emergencies. Often, the lack of experience of the anaesthetist and bronchoscopist is a contributing factor to a poor outcome in the management of FB aspiration. Equally important is the communication and the teamwork between them for planning as well as the conduct of the procedure.

Rigid bronchoscopy is performed under general anaesthesia (GA) although anaesthesia may not be necessary if the patient is moribund. A flexible fibre optic bronchoscope (FOB) may be used as a diagnostic tool (refer to Chapters 2 and 19). Some centres have successfully used FOB for the removal of foreign bodies using ureteral stone baskets and forceps. The advantage is that the procedure can be done under mild sedation with topical lignocaine spray, but technically it is very difficult to remove foreign bodies using the FOB. Hence, rigid bronchoscopy remains the technique of choice in these situations. Peripherally located FB will have to be managed medically with bronchodilators, antibiotics and steroids. Physiotherapy with chest percussions has been advocated but beware that chest percussion can dislodge the FB into a proximal airway and cause complete obstruction.

Protocol for Bronchoscopy Under General Anaesthesia

- *Fasting:* When an aspirated FB causes minimal or no airway obstruction, time should be taken to fast the patient and complete preparation for bronchoscopy. Fasting is important, as the risk of aspiration is great because the airway cannot be protected during the procedure, especially if local anaesthetics are used to obtund the airway responses. Six hours are allowed for solids and 2 hours for clear fluids. In acute cases in a non-fasted child, a large bore gastric tube should be used to suction the stomach after induction and before inserting the bronchoscope so as to reduce the risk of aspiration. An alternative would be to use ultrasonography to assess the volume and contents of the stomach prior to bronchoscopy and aspirate stomach contents, if needed.
- Specific pre-operative laboratory investigations are usually not warranted.
- A minimum of two anaesthetists, with at least one being a specialist paediatric anaesthetist if the patient is less than 1 year of age, are desirable for a successful outcome. A trained anaesthesia technician or nurse should also be present.
- The anaesthetic machine, monitoring equipment and routine emergency drugs are checked.
- The use of anticholinergics pre-procedure may be beneficial in reducing airway secretions, preventing vagal-induced bradycardia and reflex cholinergic-induced bronchoconstriction. But their use is optional. However, it is worth having atropine drawn up and diluted for use in case of severe bradycardia. Also have propofol drawn up to supplement anaesthesia/sedation, if required.
- Monitoring is the same as that for any other procedure under GA, that is, pulse oximetry, ECG and non-invasive blood pressure monitoring. Note that oximetry has a lag period before showing a desaturation. However, it does show a desaturation before there is any marked change in skin colour. Thus, though it is worth having pulse oximetry one must also have a high index of suspicion for early detection of trouble. $EtCO_2$ is not reliable as most expired gases escape via or around the scope rather than through the side arm.

Anaesthesia

Before we begin, it is important to know the location of the FB in the airway and the surgical plan for its removal. The three questions to be asked is: 'What is the plan for induction?' 'How is the patient going to be ventilated during the procedure?' and 'What is going to be the technique used for maintenance of anaesthesia?' The induction of anaesthesia can be either inhalational or intravenous. Inhalational induction followed by IV access is acceptable in most situations. However, with a moribund child or if the FB is in the trachea IV access should be established as soon as possible as inhalation would take time and hypoxaemia is a possibility. Most anaesthetists prefer an inhalational mask induction using either sevoflurane or halothane. If an IV is already in place, propofol or thiopentone may be used. Propofol is preferred for its stability with a reactive airway. IV induction should, however, proceed cautiously maintaining spontaneous ventilation especially if the FB is proximally placed because of the theoretical risk of dislodging it with positive pressure ventilation. A topical lignocaine spray both to the vocal cords and into the trachea makes for a smoother anaesthetic as it prevents coughing on the scope. Doses of up to 4 mg/kg can be used. Reduce the dose in children below 2 years and those with dry mucosa.

Spontaneous ventilation must be maintained until it is certain that the child can be ventilated under anaesthesia. Rapid sequence IV induction is more likely to risk the loss of airway. Cricoid pressure is not advocated in these children as, if applied too early, it can cause laryngospasm and coughing or, if too enthusiastically, it can compress the trachea and cause airway obstruction.

The FB may be dislodged if an ETT is first used to secure the airway (occasionally, an ETT is used to dislodge a highly placed FB into a main bronchus so as to establish some means of ventilation – at least to one lung). In case of total airway obstruction due to a tracheal FB, which is difficult to remove, pushing it deeper into one main bronchus helps to ventilate and oxygenate through the other bronchus to provide temporary relief while a plan for removal is formulated. In the case of a large FB or a vegetable FB like a tamarind seed that has swollen with time, a tracheostomy may be required as it may be impossible to negotiate the foreign body through the cricoid area.

After induction of anaesthesia, the surgeon inserts the rigid bronchoscope through the glottic opening and the anaesthesia circuit is connected to the side port of the ventilating bronchoscope. Maintain deep planes of anaesthesia throughout the procedure using inhalational or IV agents as well as topical lignocaine through the bronchoscope to avoid coughing, bucking or spasm. Maintenance of anaesthesia is most often done with inhalational anaesthetics. However, more recently total intravenous anaesthesia (TIVA) with propofol and remifentanil or dexmedetomidine along with topicalisation of the airway is becoming a popular choice for these procedures. Hypoventilation and leak of gases around the bronchoscope lead to an inadequate depth of anaesthesia when using inhalational anaesthetics. With TIVA, a constant level of anaesthesia is maintained throughout the procedure and there is less operation theatre pollution.

A question often asked is 'Should we use controlled or spontaneous ventilation during the procedure?' Both techniques have been used successfully and have their proponents.

Spontaneous Ventilation

Advantages

- Lower risk of moving the FB distally which would cause a ball-valve obstruction of the airway or lead to greater difficulty in removing the FB.
- Ventilation continues during the manipulation of the FB and its removal. Though the removal of the eyepiece can lead to air dilution, the depth of anaesthesia may be maintained by increasing the concentration of the inhalational agents or supplementing with intravenous agents such as propofol or by using TIVA.
- Ventilation also continues if the bronchoscope is only partially inserted into the trachea and the side holes of the bronchoscope are outside the trachea.
- Once the FB is removed, the airway may be rapidly assessed.

Disadvantages

- An adequate depth of anaesthesia is required to insert and maintain the scope in the airway.
- The depth of anaesthesia required might cause hypoventilation, decrease cardiac output and cause arrhythmias. This may be avoided by supplementing the inhalational agent with topical local anaesthetic and intravenous agents such as propofol. Resistance to ventilation increases with the insertion of suction or forceps into the bronchoscope.
- Be prepared to assist with ventilation and treat arrhythmias.

Controlled Ventilation

Advantages

- The airway is immobilised and provides good working conditions for the surgeon.
- Less anaesthetic vapour is required as a balanced anaesthetic technique is used. This decreases

the incidence of cardiac depression and arrhythmias.
- Intermittent positive pressure ventilation (IPPV) may decrease atelectasis, improve oxygenation and overcome the increased airway resistance that occurs when using a small bronchoscope.

Disadvantages

- A proximal partially obstructing FB may rarely turn into total obstruction with paralysis.
- Ventilation may be difficult if the side holes of the bronchoscope are not completely in the trachea.
- Ventilation will be impossible during instrumentation either with the forceps or with the suction.
- If intravenous anaesthetic agents and drugs such as succinylcholine are used, their doses will have to be carefully calculated especially in difficult cases which take a long time.
- Movement of the FB distally is another possibility with IPPV.

Jet ventilation has been tried but it is more likely to cause dislodgement of the FB or cause barotrauma.

When using a fiberoptic bronchoscope (FOB), the use of laryngeal mask airway (LMA) has been described. LMA allows the maintenance of airway and ventilation during the procedure and also acts as a conduit to pass the FOB. A connector with a self-sealing valve can be used with LMA through which the FOB can pass. Often the removal of an FB may need the removal of the entire unit including LMA to avoid displacing the FB.

After the FB is removed or even if it is expectorated before the scopy, direct visualisation is recommended to ensure that there are no additional foreign bodies present and to determine whether there is any compromise to the airways by inflammation. In case of atelectasis, it may be worth intubating the patient and ventilating with positive pressure to help open up the airways. An oxygen air mixture is also useful, as the nitrogen in the air, which is not absorbed as rapidly as oxygen or nitrous oxide, will keep the alveoli distended. In the case of repeated scopies and in the presence of inflammation, a short course of corticosteroids (0.08–0.1 mg/kg BW), nebulised adrenaline (racemic if available but plain adrenaline works just as well) and humidified oxygen is recommended. Antibiotics need only be used in case of infection. Try and wake up the patient as soon as possible – a 'coughing' child will clear his own airway of fragmented FB particles and sputum!

Complications

Intraoperative complications that may occur include hypoxia, hypercarbia, haemodynamic instability and the need for continued post-operative oxygen supplementation or ventilation.

Complications associated with instrumentation for FB removal include the following:

- Trauma to the airway and teeth
- Dislodgement of the FB and complete obstruction of the airway
- Creation of a traumatic tracheo-oesophageal fistula
- Barotrauma

Conclusion

Providing safe anaesthesia to a child who has aspirated a FB could be one of the most challenging cases an anaesthetist will have to face in his career. When presented with such a case it is important to recognise the type, site, duration and pathology caused by the airway obstruction preoperatively, discuss the plan for the procedure with the surgeon or pulmonologist and other team members and always have a plan B available. Ensure that all equipment and monitors are checked and available.

During the procedure, obtund the deep airway reflexes to prevent coughing and bronchospasm using lignocaine and propofol as required. If there is total airway obstruction, push the FB into one main bronchus to be able to ventilate and oxygenate the other temporarily until another attempt or plan is formulated. Above all, DO NOT PANIC – THINK!

Post-operative intubation and ventilation with admission to the ICU may be necessary. Steroids and nebulised adrenaline can help reduce airway oedema. Repeat chest X-ray post-operatively.

SUGGESTED READINGS

1. Fong EW. FB aspiration. Case based pediatrics for medical students and residents. Department of Pediatrics, University of Hawaii (Manual) 2004; 311–314.
2. Campo S, Denman WT, Todres LD. Pediatric Emergencies. In: A Practice of Anaesthesia for Infants

and Children, 3rd edition. Cote CJ, Todres LD, Goudsouzian N (eds). WB Saunders, Philadelphia 2001; pp. 321–322.

3. Brett CM, Zwass MS. Eyes Ears Nose Throat and Dental Surgery. In: Paediatric Anaesthesia, 4th edition. Gregory GA (ed). Churchill Livingstone, New York 2002; pp. 675–679.
4. Farrell PT. Rigid bronchoscopy for foreign body removal: Anaesthesia and ventilation. *Pediatr Anaesth* 2004; 14:84–89.
5. Zur KB, Litman RS. Pediatric airway foreign body retrieval: Surgical and anesthetic perspectives. *Paediatr Anaesth* 2009; 19(1):109–117.
6. Fidkowski CW, Zheng H, Firth PG. The anesthetic considerations of tracheobronchial foreign bodies in children: A literature review of 12,979 cases. *Anesth Analg* 2010; 111(4):1016–1025.
7. Chidambaram V, Sadhasivam S. Foreign Body in the Airway. In: Clinical Pediatric Anesthesia – A Case-Based Handbook. Goldschneider KR, Davidson AJ, Wittkugel EP (eds). Oxford University Press, New York, 2012; pp. 122–130.
8. Kendigelen P. The anaesthetic consideration of tracheobronchial foreign body aspiration in children. *J Thorac Dis* 2016; 8(12):3803–3807.

24 Anaesthetic Considerations in Paediatric Laparoscopic and Thoracoscopic Surgery

Ekta Rai • Sarathkumar MS

The widespread adoption of minimally invasive surgery (MIS) in adults over the past two decades has led both to rapid developments in this field and to the progressive adoption of paediatric surgery. At the outset, it should be noted that MIS does not equate to minimally invasive anaesthesia.

The two main challenges for MIS in the paediatric population are the small size of the child leading to restrictive access to the surgical field and the need for appropriate-sized surgical equipment. The use of multiple small incisions and specialised equipment has many obvious benefits to the patient (**Fig. 24.1**): less pain, early mobilisation and feeding, shorter recovery time and hospital stay, etc. When compared with conventional surgery, there may also be an overall decrease in complication rates, which often comes with an increase in initial cost, equipment, skill and expertise.

The anaesthetic considerations for paediatric laparoscopic and thoracoscopic procedures require an understanding of the surgical technique, its physiological effects and other special anaesthetic requirements.

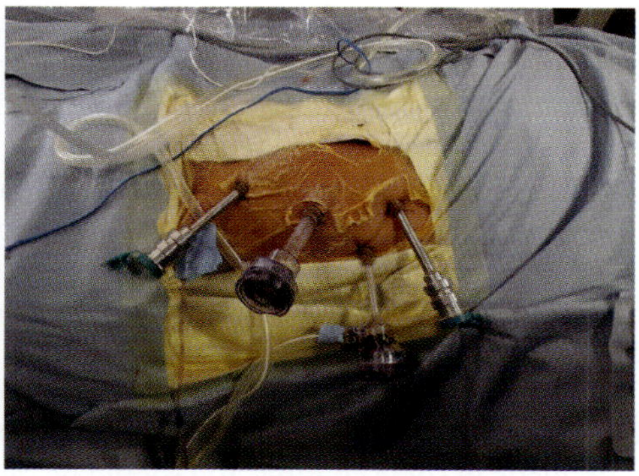

Figure 24.1 Laparoscopic ports. Please note the port size.

Laparoscopic Procedures

The basic tenet in laparoscopic surgery is the insufflation of the peritoneal cavity with a gas to aid the visualisation and dissection of surgical tissues. The various insufflating gas options are oxygen, air, carbon dioxide, helium and nitrous oxide. Carbon dioxide (CO_2) is the most preferred gas for insufflation as it is non-combustible, highly soluble in blood, easily excreted by the lungs and cost-effective.

The challenges faced during laparoscopy are mainly due to the mechanical effect of raised intra-abdominal pressure (IAP), extreme positions (Trendelenburg and reverse Trendelenburg), absorption of the gas and the volume/flow rate of insufflating gas. There is also an increase in the level of stress hormones which, in many cases, will parallel the rise seen in conventional surgery.

The gas insufflation has a two-fold impact on the patient's physiology: increased IAP and absorption into the circulation.

Acceptable IAP is far lower in children than adults, 6 mmHg in infants, 12 mmHg in children and up to 20 mmHg in adults.

The rise in IAP impacts the venous return (VR), systemic vascular resistance and contractility differently at different phases of increased IAP. Initiation of increasing IAP results in the mobilisation of pooled splanchnic blood, which in turn results in increased VR and cardiac output (CO). Further increase in abdominal pressure leads to direct pressure on the inferior vena cava and thus a reduction in VR and CO. The volume of insufflating gas required for creating pneumoperitoneum is approximately 0.9 L for a 10 kg child in comparison to 2.5–5 L for an adult. Gas flow rates, in infants, start as low as 0.5–3 L/min titrated to gas leaks so as to maintain abdominal distension. The flow of gas should be guided carefully as children have a high vagal tone and high gas flow may result in a sudden peritoneal stretch, leading to significant bradycardia and asystole. Management of this situation would include stopping the insufflation or desufflating the abdomen and pharmacologic treatment with intravenous atropine.

Respiratory effects of the pneumoperitoneum include cephalad displacement of the diaphragm which in turn results in a decrease in both functional residual capacity and overall lung compliance. There may be an increase in airway pressure and, though more commonly associated with the steep Trendelenburg (head-down) position, the tracheal tube which is just above the carina may become endobronchial. This should be ruled out by auscultation. Other less common respiratory effects include bronchospasm and atelectasis, due to cephalad displacement of the mediastinum and collapse of poorly ventilated infero-basal segments of the lung.

The absorption of CO_2 from the insufflation occurs gradually and progresses with the duration of the case. Neonates and infants have a higher CO_2 absorption risk because of the thin peritoneal layer compared to older children and adults. It is not abnormal to see an increase in the end-tidal CO_2 by 5–10 mmHg and this may require increased minute ventilation to maintain normocapnia.

This is achieved by increasing both the respiratory rate (RR) and the tidal volume (TV) keeping in mind that increasing only one parameter may not only be ineffective (dead space ventilation if only RR is increased) but also be harmful (volutrauma if only TV is increased). Controlled ventilation is always preferred, and novel ventilatory modes such as volume-guaranteed, pressure-regulated ventilation may maintain better TVs during periods of dynamic change in respiratory resistance and compliance thereby maintaining minute ventilation more effectively than pressure- or volume-controlled ventilation (VCV). Positive end-expiratory pressure (PEEP) of 4–5 cm H_2O is mandatory to prevent basal atelectasis.

A diminishing TV with pressure-controlled ventilation (PCV) is often an early sign of returning diaphragmatic function (i.e., waning neuromuscular blockade), kinked or blocked ET tube or the more ominous peritoneal-pleural disruption (i.e., pneumothorax). The surgeons sometimes rely on the anaesthetist to tell them that there is a slow increase in TV indicating abdominal parietal plane dissections (i.e., surgical emphysema) or a sudden increase in TV indicating an undetected leaking laparoscopic port site. While using PCV during laparoscopic procedures, it is essential to revert to VCV as soon as the abdominal insufflation has been discontinued to avoid the equally hazardous volutrauma.

In patients with severe congenital cardiac or pulmonary disease, even low IAPs may not be tolerated and conversion to an open technique may be the safest action. Safe levels of hypercarbia and duration of hypercapnia during paediatric laparoscopic and thoracoscopic surgery have not been defined and should be considered on an individual basis.

In upper abdominal surgery, especially in and around the diaphragm, there is a possibility that the insufflated gas will enter the pleural space. This may occur through the congenital pleuroperitoneal recesses or via the diaphragmatic hiatus. If there is an inadvertent injury to the pleura, the insufflated CO_2 can cause a pneumothorax. Unlike other gas in the pleural space, the CO_2 is almost always absorbed rapidly, and unless the patient demonstrates ventilatory insufficiency, it does not require intervention. It is almost always unnecessary to insert a chest tube or to decompress the CO_2 pneumothorax unless there is a cardiorespiratory compromise as the spontaneous absorption of the CO_2 is the rule rather than the exception. A tension pneumothorax after laparoscopic surgery is usually unrelated to the CO_2 and should be treated according to standard protocols.

The cardiorespiratory and CO_2 absorption effects of the pneumo-peritoneum can be rapid and dramatic in some children and should be carefully watched for. If any of these results is a serious compromise to the overall physiology, the pneumoperitoneum should be evacuated immediately and re-instituted gradually but only after adequate and appropriate resuscitation.

Two of the major complications from laparoscopic procedures are major gas embolism and bleeding. Both are fortunately very unusual. Gas embolism is attributed to the entrainment of insufflated gas via large open veins into the systemic circulation from where it reaches the pulmonary circulation, resulting in the presentation of acute right heart failure. The clinical signs are, however, rather non-specific with dilated neck veins, sudden drop in $EtCO_2$ followed by an increase in arterial CO_2, hypotension and bradycardia and increasing airway pressures. Prompt resuscitation should follow standard protocols and nitrous oxide, if used, should be discontinued. A precordial or oesophageal stethoscope may be useful to hear the eponymous millwheel murmur. This can be confirmed by transoesophageal or transthoracic echocardiography. In the presence of cardiovascular compromise secondary to suspected gas embolism, Durant's manoeuvre may be useful. Durant's manoeuvre involves the left lateral decubitus with the Trendelenburg position. Theoretically, by placing the right ventricular outflow tract inferior to the right ventricular cavity and permitting the emboli to migrate superiorly to a non-obstructing position, this manoeuvre will facilitate moving the entrained CO_2 from the ventricular outflow tract and improve cardiac output. Durant's manoeuvre may also allow for the removal of the gas embolism by aspiration from the right atrium via a central venous line (if available). Venous gas embolism will have more profound systemic effects if there is an intra-cardiac shunt (atrial septal defect [ASD], ventricular septal defect [VSD], etc.) or even a patent foramen ovale. The presentation can be dramatic with cardiovascular collapse and should be treated with immediate cessation of surgery and prompt resuscitation.

Major haemorrhage is also now rare with advances in surgical expertise and technique. This was previously reported as due to direct injury to the great vessels or more commonly the iliac vessels by the Veress needle or even by the trocar. Hypotension at this stage of surgery should prompt careful vigilance and it is expected that the anaesthetist will 'watch the surgical field' during the placement of the trocar. Unusual bleeding at this stage is obvious as it fills the operative field and should prompt the surgeon to abandon the laparoscopic approach in favour of conventional open surgery with the aim of establishing rapid control of the bleeding. Rapid fluid resuscitation and preparation to transfuse large volumes of blood should be initiated without delay.

Inadvertent injury to other normal tissue is still possible in laparoscopic surgery but may present days or weeks after surgery. Vigilance by the anaesthesia team cannot be understated in these procedures, while careful cooperative teamwork is essential to ensure the safety of the patient and the success of the surgery.

The post-operative care of the child who has undergone laparoscopic surgery is determined by pre-operative comorbidities including age and overall health, surgery performed and outcome. Patient care and monitoring in the early recovery period should be continued as per the standard practice. Adequate analgesia may be ensured by non-opioid techniques (acetaminophen and non-steroidal anti-inflammatory drugs [NSAIDs]) with rescue analgesia using short-acting opioids (fentanyl). Early mobilisation and feeding may be encouraged with the aim of having a short hospital stay and early discharge.

Thoracoscopic Procedures

Like laparoscopic procedures, thoracoscopic surgery requires the insufflation of the thoracic cavity (pleural space) with CO_2 such that visualisation of the surgical field is optimised. Recent advances in video-assisted thoracoscopic surgery (VATS) mean that it is increasingly utilised in children. Most of the benefits associated with VATS in the adult population, that is, less post-operative pain and shorter length of stay, are presumed true in the paediatric population as well. Thoracoscopic procedures have been successfully used on all children from newborns to teenagers. These include lung biopsy and resection, mediastinal mass examination and excision, sequestration, and congenital cystic adenoma malformation (CCAM).

Single-lung ventilation in children does not always require lung isolation. Infants can be managed without lung isolation if the induced capnothorax provides sufficient collapse of the lung undergoing surgery. However, the older the patient, the less likely this technique will work and therefore most patients will need to have the surgical lung isolated and one-lung ventilation initiated.

mediastinum into the dependent lung as discussed earlier. Gas embolism into the venous circulation is also possible, resulting in rapid haemodynamic instability. Maintaining the minimum capnothorax pressure that allows for good surgical vision is recommended.

End of surgery: When surgical resection is complete, ventilation to the isolated lung can resume. If possible (depending on the isolation technique), suctioning of the lung prior to this is recommended. Sterile saline instilled into the surgical field is often used to look for bubbling, indicative of air leak from the surgical lung as re-expansion of the lung commences. Re-expansion can be achieved by giving ever-increasing TV breaths until the lung re-inflates completely. Alternatively, continuous pressure holds of 20–30 cm H_2O will work. Re-expansion injury has been noted in several animal models if high pressures and/or high oxygen tensions are used. No single best method for lung re-expansion in the human population is known.

Children undergoing routine laparoscopic and thoracoscopic procedures are usually extubated at the end of the procedure. The need for post-operative mechanical ventilation depends on the pre-operative comorbid condition (e.g., congenital diaphragmatic hernia where lung compliance is already poor), intraoperative surgical course (major lung resections) and post-operative oxygen requirements.

Post-operatively, the patient will require a monitored setting with personnel familiar with this type of procedure. A chest tube may be present depending on the surgery performed. At a minimum, cardiorespiratory monitoring is required as well as providing supplementary oxygen. As mentioned earlier, most of these patients will be extubated and can be safely monitored on a high-dependency ward with 2:1 nursing care.

Pain can be secondary to gas insufflation and rapid distension of the peritoneum, tissue dissection, excessive stretching of the diaphragm and the phrenic nerve, or residual carbon dioxide gas in the abdomen. It is important to remove as much of the gas as possible from the abdominal cavity at the end of the procedure. A 'single shot' injection of long-acting local anaesthetics (ropivacaine 0.2%) along with adjuvants (dexmedetomidine, clonidine and morphine) either at the trocar sites or in peripheral nerves like intercostal nerve blocks, rectus sheath block, transversus abdominis plane block, erector spinae and paravertebral block may provide analgesia for as long as 10–16 hours.

Epidural morphine or other opiates may be used under close supervision. Paracetamol and parental opioids are used to manage post-operative pain. Thoracic epidurals are not usually required for VATS but can be used if the clinical scenario is appropriate. Neonates and infants accumulate local anaesthetics due to reduced clearance and protein binding. There is thus a potential for central nervous system and cardiovascular toxicities. This must be considered if they are started on continuous epidural infusions of local anaesthetics.

Recent Updates

Robotic surgery is on the horizon and being explored in the paediatric population as well. This confers many technical benefits such as improved ergonomics, motion scaling, 3D-HD vision and increased dexterity with 7 degrees of freedom that allows precise movements even to less accessible areas of the body. But the large size of robotic equipment and small working space limits its role in younger children. Currently, most of the surgeries in children are being performed as thoracoscopic or laparoscopic MIS.

There has been an emphasis on *early recovery after surgery (ERAS)*, which is a multidisciplinary approach towards early recovery. ERAS guidelines include the administration of carbohydrate drinks up to 2 hours before surgery, MIS, cautious intraoperative fluid management, minimal and only essential drains and tubes for the minimal possible duration in the post-operative period, early ambulation and the initiation of oral intake on the day of the procedure.

Newer modes of ventilation and the ability to deliver smaller TVs (as small as 20 ml) in new modern workstations have allowed feasibility and increased safety in sicker children and neonates.

Conclusion

For the overall success of MIS such as laparoscopic and thoracoscopic surgery, it is essential for each centre to develop a multidisciplinary approach to the perioperative protocols, with input from the surgeons, recovery room nurses and other healthcare providers involved, with the anaesthetist taking the lead.

SUGGESTED READINGS

1. Tobias JD. Anaesthesia for minimally invasive surgery in children. *Best Pract Res Clin Anaesthesiol* 2002; 16:115–130.
2. Tobias JD. Thoracic surgery in children. *Curr Opin Anaesthesiol* 2001; 14:77–85.
3. Slinger P. Principles and Practice of Anesthesia for Thoracic Surgery. Springer Media, New York 2011.
4. Mishra P, Gupta B, Nath A. Anesthetic considerations and goals in robotic pediatric surgery: a narrative review. *J Anesth* 2020; 34(2):286–293.
5. Templeton TW, Piccioni F, Chatterjee D. An update on one-lung ventilation in children. *Anesth Analg* 2021; 132(5):1389.
6. Jaichenco AL, Crivelli EL, Castellani GG, et al. Laparoscopic surgery in pediatrics. *Curr Anesthesiol Rep* 2019; 9(3):326–332.
7. Meng-Meng T, Xue-Jun X, Xiao-Hong B. Clinical effects of warmed humidified carbon dioxide insufflation in infants undergoing major laparoscopic surgery. *Medicine* 2019; 98(27):e16151.
8. Gupta R, Singh S. Challenges in paediatric laparoscopic surgeries. *Indian J Anaesth* 2009; 53(5): 560–566.
9. Anaesthesia for Paediatric Laparoscopic Surgery. WFSA Resource Library. Available from: https://resources.wfsahq.org/atotw/anaesthesia-for-paediatric-laparoscopic-surgery/. (accessed 01 Mar 2023).

25 Challenges of Thoracic Surgery in the Paediatric Patient

Rebecca Jacob • Rakhee Goyal

Neonates, infants and young children are very different from adults in that their systems are immature, with anatomical and physiological differences, with size constraints and differing pathology making dealing with their problems highly specialised. Anaesthetising children for thoracic surgery requires a clear understanding of the above. The anaesthetist must provide physiologic stability, adequate oxygenation and good perioperative analgesia.

An overview of the physiology in different patient positions, the approach to one-lung ventilation and the concept of per-operative analgesia are described in the following text.

Physiology of Ventilation and Perfusion in the Upright and Lateral Decubitus Positions

Upright Position

As we know, efficient gas exchange is dependent on the matching of ventilation and perfusion. Both ventilation and perfusion increase from apex to base in the upright position, ventilation being assisted by the excursions of the diaphragm and perfusion by gravity. The change in perfusion, however, is more extreme ranging from zero flows to high flows (**Fig. 25.1**). Compliance to ventilation is best at the bases as seen in **Figures 25.1** and **25.2**.

Lateral Decubitus Position

As in adults, the dependent lung in the older child is better ventilated due to increased excursions of the dependent diaphragm in the lateral position (see **Fig. 25.3**).

However, the infant has limited diaphragmatic excursion, thereby limiting the functional advantage seen in the adult/older child. The infant's small size also limits the hydrostatic pressure gradient between the non-dependent and the dependent lungs, and there is no remarkable increase in blood flow to the lower lung (as in an adult). In fact, in the spontaneously breathing neonate and infant V/Q distribution is similar to that seen in the adult during IPPV. In infants with unilateral lung disease, there is an improvement in oxygenation with the healthy lung up (awake state), as opposite to that in the older child or adult.

Closed Chest, Changes in the Ventilation/Compliance Curve in the Awake Versus Anaesthetised Patient in the Lateral Decubitus Position (Fig. 25.3)

Inspiratory and diaphragmatic muscle tone drops with induction of anaesthesia. There is a 15–20% drop in functional residual capacity (FRC) in both lungs. Anaesthesia also obtunds hypoxic pulmonary vasoconstriction (HPV).

The dependent lung now drops from the steep compliant portion of the compliance curve to the flatter non-compliant portion and the upper, non-dependent lung now takes the position on the steeper portion signifying a better ventilation. The distribution of ventilation is not affected by anaesthesia and the dependent lung (which is now poorly ventilated) receives the bulk of the perfusion. This results in a ventilation/perfusion (V/Q) mismatch. With the use of muscle relaxants and paralysis

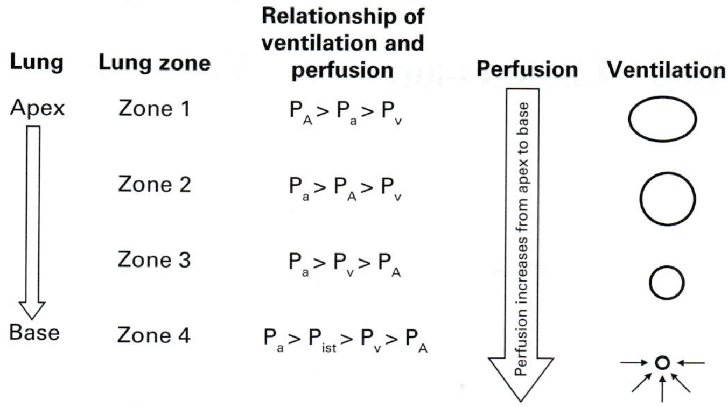

Figure 25.1 Ventilation and perfusion in the upright position through the different zones from the apex to base of the lung. P_A, alveolar pressure; P_a, pulmonary arterial pressure; P_v, pulmonary venous pressure; P_{ist}, pulmonary interstitial pressure.

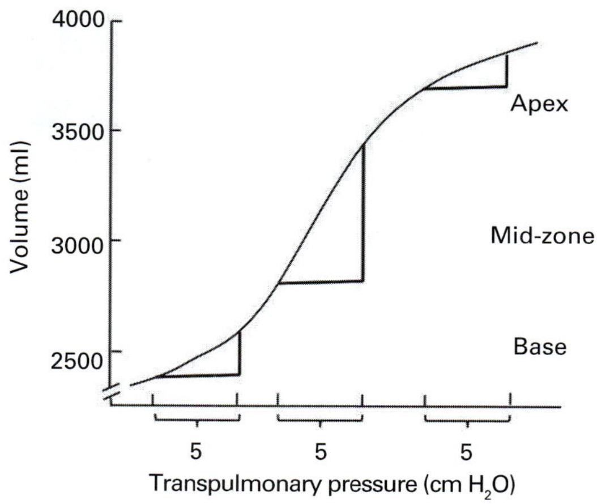

Figure 25.2 Compliance curve with regional variations in the upright position (in the older child). Note that the bases are most compliant with maximum respiratory excursions.

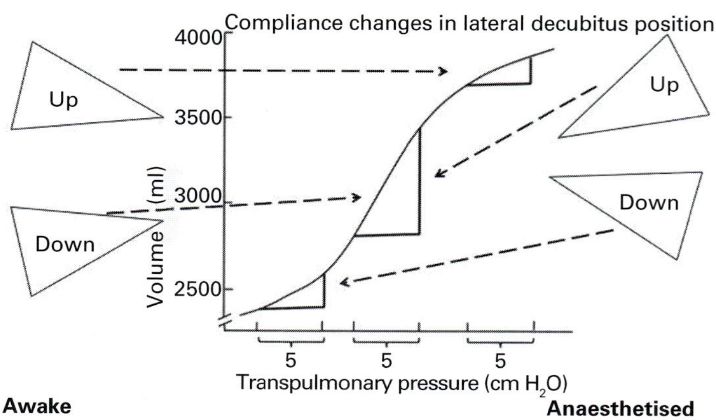

Figure 25.3 Ventilation/compliance changes in the lateral decubitus position in the awake and anaesthetised state in the older child. 'Up' and 'Down' signify the upper non-dependent lung and the lower dependent lung, respectively.

of the diaphragm, there is a static displacement 'headward' of the diaphragm by the abdominal contents further decreasing the compliance of the dependent lung. This is made worse by improper positioning (**Figs 25.4** and **25.5**).

The non-dependent lung is well ventilated but poorly perfused while the dependent lung is poorly ventilated but well perfused. Though perfusion increases, it is less so in the small child than in the adult due to less vertical height and therefore less gravitational influence on perfusion. In addition, the weight of the mediastinum and abdominal contents impedes the movement of a non-active lung, causing a circumferential compression of this lung. Rolls placed under the dependent thorax further compress the lung, especially in the infant/neonate who has a very compliant thoracic cage. The atelectatic shunt compartment increases because of compression (see **Figs 25.3** and **25.4**).

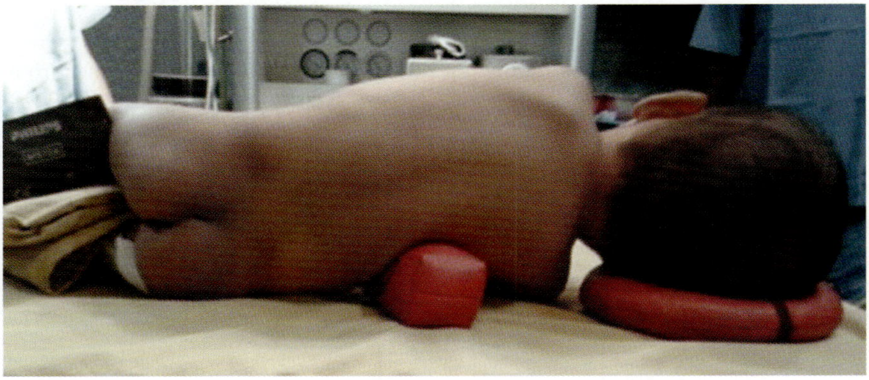

(a)

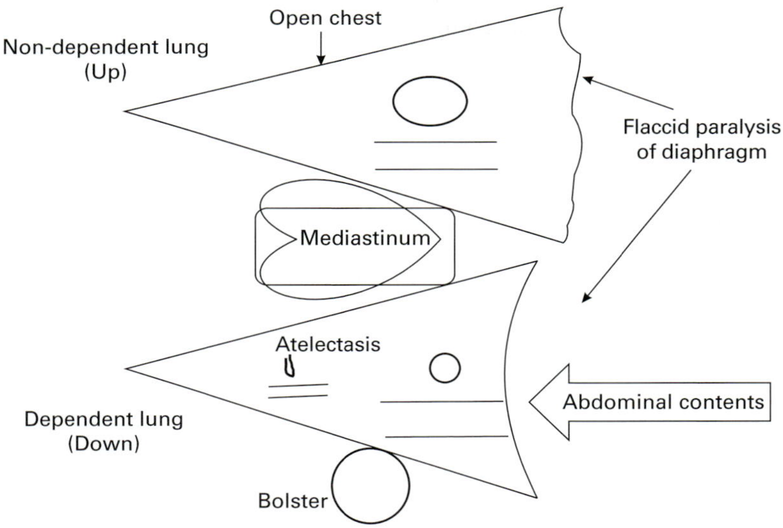

(b)

Figure 25.4 (a) Lateral decubitus position for left thoracotomy. (b) Anaesthetised, lateral decubitus, open chest, paralysed, sub-optimally positioned for right thoracotomy. The non-dependent lung is well ventilated but poorly perfused while the dependent lung is poorly ventilated but well perfused in the adult. Not much difference in perfusion in the infant due to less difference in vertical height between the two sides. The weight of the mediastinum and abdominal contents impedes the movement of a non-actively contracting diaphragm causing a circumferential compression of the dependent lung. Atelectatic shunt compartment increases in the dependent lung.

Open Chest Anaesthetised Patient – Lateral Decubitus Position (Fig. 25.4 a,b)

The opening of the chest causes a loss of pleural pressure and releases the weight of the mediastinum onto the dependent lung. The non-dependent lung either herniates out of the chest with a dramatic increase in Zone 1, that is, increase in ventilation with poor perfusion, or collapses due to application of one lung ventilation (OLV) when all ventilation is diverted to the well-perfused dependent lung resulting in an improvement in V/Q. However, the non-dependent collapsed lung could increase the atelectatic shunt fraction.

Factors which help to decrease blood flow to the non-dependent (upper) lung in the lateral decubitus position under anaesthesia are as follows:

1. **Passive mechanical factors**
   - Gravity
   - Surgical manipulation ligating/clamping large vessels
   - Severity of the existing disease
2. **Active vasoconstrictor mechanisms**
   - Hypoxic pulmonary vasoconstriction

Factors that decrease oxygenation in the lateral decubitus position under anaesthesia are as follows:

- Lung disease and HPV in ventilated lung
- General anaesthesia
- Circumferential compression
- Absorption atelectasis
- Difficult removal of secretions
- Transudation of fluids

Oxygenation can be improved by

- Ventilation methods
- Airway pressures – CPAP
- Increasing FiO_2
- Oxygen insufflation to the non-dependent lung

Open Chest – Spontaneous Ventilation

Mediastinal shift and paradoxical ventilation tend to complicate matters.

Indications for Thoracic Surgery

The indications for thoracic surgery in different age groups in children are as follows:

1. **Neonates and infants**
   (a) Tracheal stenosis
   - Acquired – subglottic
   - Congenital – segmental

   (b) Pulmonary sequestration
   - Intralobar
   - Extralobar

   (c) Pulmonary hypoplasia
   - Unilateral
   - Bilateral

   (d) Congenital cystic lesions
   - Bronchogenic
   - Dermoid
   - Cystic adenomatoid malformation

   (e) Congenital lobar emphysema

   (f) Tracheo-oesophageal fistula

   (g) Vascular
   - Patent ductus arteriosus
   - Coarctation of aorta
   - Vascular rings

   (h) Cardiac
   - Palliative procedures
2. **Infants and children**
   (a) Tumours (primary or metastatic)
   - Lung
   - Pleura
   - Mediastinum

   (b) Infection (wet lung)
   - Bronchiectasis
   - Lung abscess
   - Hydatid cyst
   - Empyema
   - Bronchopleural fistula

   (c) Congenital
   - Pulmonary arteriovenous malformation

   (d) Skeletal (in adolescents)
   - Pectus excavatum
   - Kyphoscoliosis

Video-assisted thoracic surgery (VATS) has been used safely in small children, including neonates, in recent years. The morbidity is less and outcomes are better with minimally invasive procedures. It can be useful for several thoracic surgeries in children including uncomplicated tracheoesophageal fistula, congenital diaphragmatic hernia, bronchogenic cysts, etc. One-lung ventilation is desirable for VATS usually with some carbon dioxide insufflation at low gas flows and low pressures of 4–8 mbar.

marketed BB. However, when they are not available, the Fogarty vascular embolectomy catheter has been used as a blocker.

Fogarty Catheter (Fig. 25.6)

The most commonly used blocker has been the *Fogarty* vascular embolectomy catheter, but it is far from ideal as it is not designed as a BB. It may be placed through an ETT pushed into the side to be blocked, the ETT withdrawn into the trachea, the cuff inflated and its position confirmed by a fibre-optic bronchoscope. It may also be placed through a rigid bronchoscope, the scope withdrawn and an ETT placed alongside it. It is close-ended and has a high-pressure, low-volume cuff. It is difficult to place and is often dislodged causing a catastrophic obstruction. The cuff can cause mucosal ischaemia and bronchial rupture. *Atrioseptostomy* and *pulmonary artery catheters* have the advantage of a central lumen that would permit suctioning or the application of oxygen and continuous positive airway pressure (CPAP) to the affected lung. An arterioseptostomy catheter is also advantageous because of its angled tip. *Swan–Ganz catheters* have been used similarly.

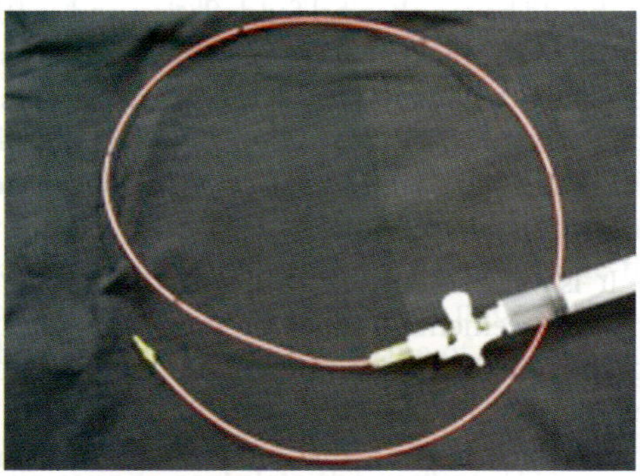

Figure 25.6 Fogarty vascular embolectomy catheter.

Arndt Endobronchial Blocker

They are available in sizes 5F, 7F and 9F. It can be placed through a multiport adapter with three connections: one connected to an ETT, the other to the bronchoscope and the side one to the BB (**Fig. 25.7**). The fibreoptic bronchoscope port has a sealing cap and the BB port has a connector that locks and secures the catheter in place and maintains an airtight seal.

There are two narrow lumens: one contains an adjustable wire loop and the other inflates a spherical low-pressure, high-volume balloon. The blocker is passed through its port and placed at the end of the ETT. The bronchoscope is then passed through its port through the wire loop at the end of the PWEB device. The bronchoscope and blocker are then passed under vision as a single unit into the diseased side. The bronchoscope is withdrawn slightly, the cuff inflated, again under vision and the bronchoscope removed. The blocker is fixed in place all the while, maintaining ventilation. The balloon is inflated so as to collapse the lung and deflated when ventilation of the lung is required. The central channel allows suction, though not very efficiently, and oxygen insufflation or CPAP if required. The balloon, which is coloured blue for ease of identification, is 1 cm in length in the 5F and corresponds with the length of the short right mainstem bronchus of a 2 year old.

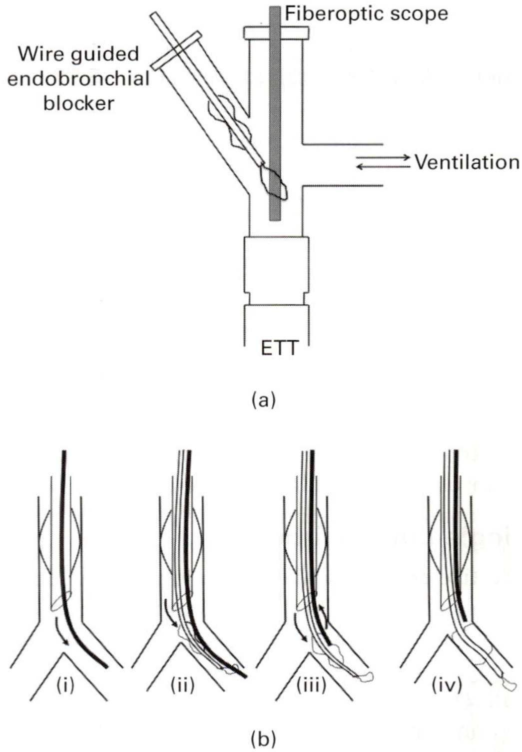

Figure 25.7 (a) Arndt blocker – machine end. (b) Placement of Arndt blocker – patient end during insertion. (i) ETT in place with fibreoptic bronchoscope passed into left main bronchus. (ii) Arndt blocker being inserted over the bronchoscope. (iii) Blocker deployed and bronchoscope being withdrawn. (iv) Blocker inflated in left main bronchus. ETT, endotracheal tube.

Univent Tube

The Univent Tube (Fig. 25.8) (Fuji Systems Corporation Tokyo, Japan) is a conventional ETT with a second lumen containing a small tube with a balloon located at its distal end, which may be advanced into the main bronchus or even provide lobar blockade. Because the blocker tube is firmly attached to the parent ETT, displacement of the blocker during surgery is uncommon. The blocker tube may be used to provide oxygen or CPAP.

The smallest sizes available are 3.5 and 4.5 mm ID. However, a large amount of the cross-sectional area is occupied by the blocker channel, so that the working channel is quite small. Also, the wall thickness of the tube adds to the external diameter so that the smallest tube has an external diameter of 8 mm and may only be used in a 6 year old. The balloon is high pressure, small volume and can cause mucosal damage. Placement requires a fibreoptic scope. The great limitation in the use of the Univent tube is that the ventilating channel, which is small, is shared by the fibreoptic scope during placement or later with a suction catheter. Also, Univent tubes below 6.5 mm ID do not have a central lumen in the bronchial blocker (as do the larger sizes). Therefore, oxygen and CPAP cannot be applied to the smaller Univent tubes.

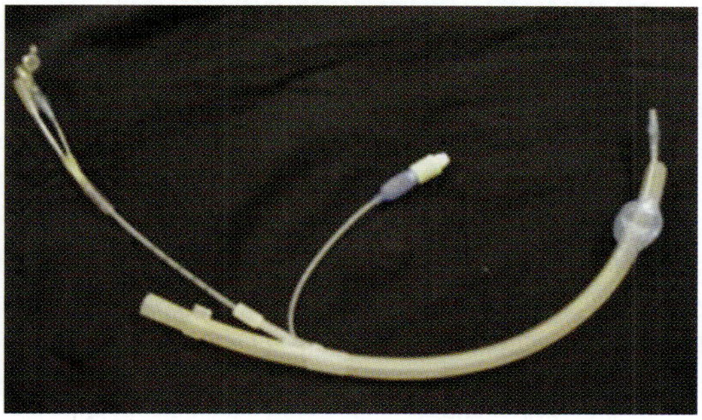

(a)

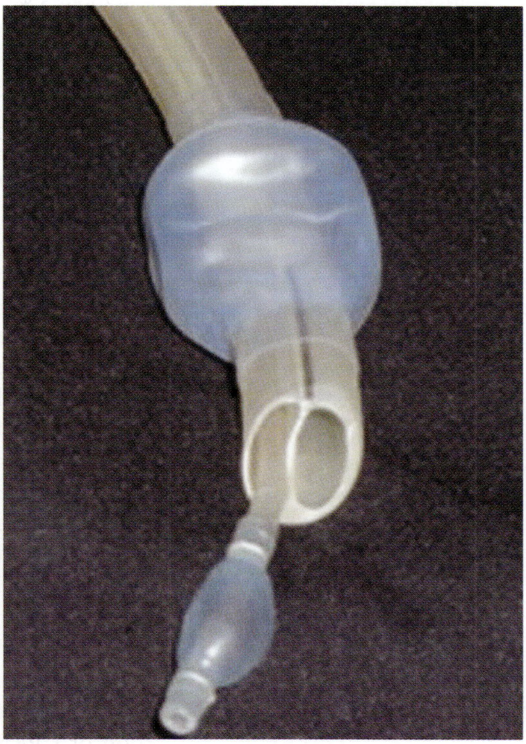

(b)

Figure 25.8 (a) Univent tube. (b) Univent tube – patient end.

Double-Lumen Tubes

All double-lumen tubes (DLTs) are essentially two tubes of unequal length moulded together: the shorter tube lies in the trachea and the longer tube in a bronchus. The smallest tubes designed are the Marraro tubes which may even be used in neonates. However, they do not provide airtight lung isolation and have very small lumens. They are not available in most countries (Fig. 25.9).

DLTs are available for older children (Fig. 25.10) in sizes 26F, 28F and 32F. These tubes have cuffs located on the tracheal and bronchial tubes. The tracheal cuff, when inflated, provides

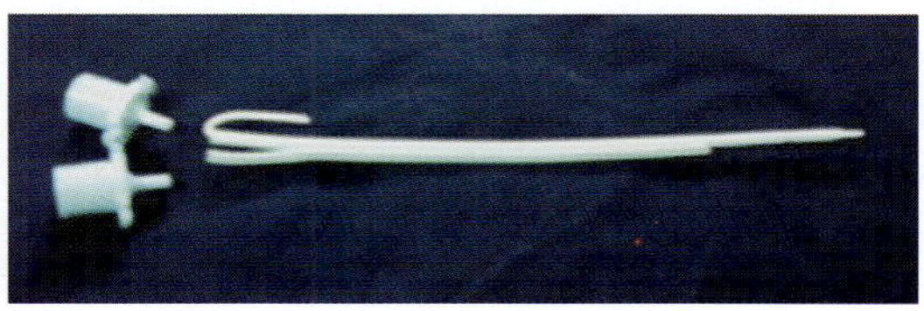

Figure 25.9 Marraro tube.

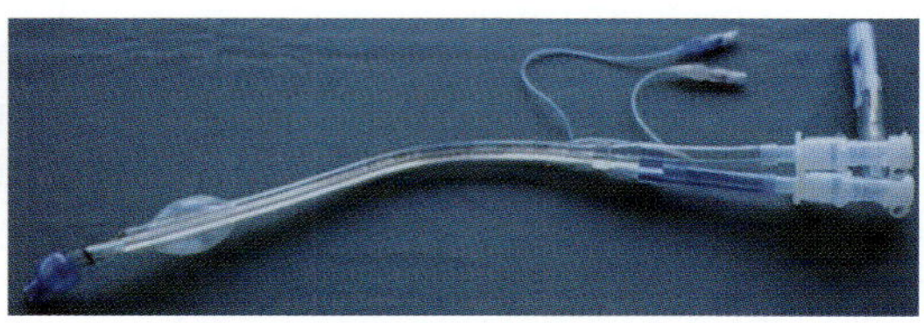

Figure 25.10 Left-sided double-lumen tube.

an airtight fit in the trachea permitting positive pressure ventilation. The bronchial cuff, usually coloured blue, when inflated allows ventilation to be diverted to either or both lungs and protects each lung from contamination from the contralateral side.

DLTs are safe and easy to use with very little airway damage reported. The cuffs are high volume, low pressure and cause little damage to the mucosa. Each lung may be ventilated and sucked separately and CPAP applied to the non-dependent lung when required.

Left-sided DLTs are safer and should be used in all cases, except perhaps in a left pneumonectomy where the left mainstem bronchus is to be divided. The bronchial tube of the right DLT has an additional opening to accommodate the right upper lobe bronchus. Accurate positioning of the right endobronchial tube is more difficult, considering the shorter length of the right main bronchus and the possibility of right upper lobe obstruction.

Anaesthesia

The combination of general anaesthesia with regional analgesia is particularly useful in thoracic surgery. Due to the factors mentioned in the preceding text, hypoxia and hypercapnia may prove to be a problem during surgery (see **Fig. 25.4**). Ventilation needs to be individualised for the particular patient and the underlying pathology. Too much ventilation or little or no ventilation has both been implicated in acute lung injury (ALI). Protective lung ventilation may be undertaken using small tidal volumes, low peak and plateau pressures, routine positive end-expiratory pressure (PEEP) and permissive hypercapnia. Pressure-controlled ventilation is typically used so as to minimise barotrauma and maximise the function of the dependent lung. The respiratory rate may be increased once one-lung ventilation (OLV) is established. Permissive hypercapnia is tolerated as long as haemodynamic function is preserved.

If hypoxia and hypercapnia persist, the usual manoeuvres in the adult population can be applied to children. Initially, 100% oxygen should be used and then titrated downwards, using air rather than nitrous oxide, as tolerated by the patient. Hypoxia rarely occurs but could be due to underventilation causing atelectasis. Its management should be aimed at recruitment of collapsed alveoli and decreasing the shunt fraction by the use of CPAP to the non-ventilated lung or two-lung ventilation (TLV). PEEP can be used on the dependent lung, but if it is increased (>10 mmHg) it may compromise PVR and divert blood away from that lung. In smaller patients, the use of CPAP to the surgical lung may compromise the exposure.

Positioning (Figs 25.4a and 25.11)

Ensure that the patient is placed in full lateral position with the scapula of the upper limb pulled forward. Rolls placed under the lower axilla should relieve the pressure on the lower arm but not distort the chest or compress the dependent chest too much. A soft pillow should be placed between the legs and the patient strapped in place. Protect all pressure points. Check that all monitors, intravenous and arterial lines are well fixed and accessible. The ETT or DLT should be accessible at all times for suctioning. A separate suction apparatus and catheters should be available for the surgeon and the anaesthetist.

Desaturation can be expected in infants because of their high oxygen consumption and the problems of anaesthesia and open chest in the lateral decubitus position as described in the preceding text. Try to minimise blood flow to the upper non-ventilated lung. 100% oxygen may be used when on OLV. At the end of surgery, while re-inflating collapsed lung an air oxygen mixture is good to retain the inflation and alveolar configuration. (Nitrogen which is present in air is

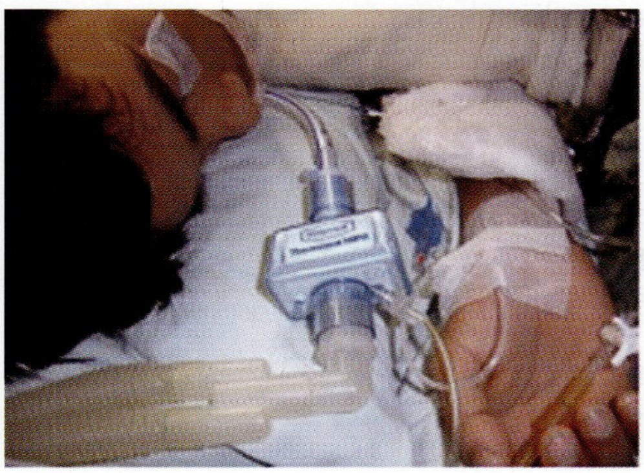

Figure 25.11 Patient in the lateral decubitus position. Ensure that the ETT is accessible for suction, the arterial line in view and the three-way tap of the IV are easily accessible. ETT, endotracheal tube.

not as easily absorbed as oxygen. It helps to keep the alveoli distended and a slightly inflated alveolus is easier to keep open than an atelectatic one.)

Monitoring

All patients should have a pulse oximeter, NIBP monitoring and a good peripheral intravenous line. For the very young child and those undergoing major surgery, an intra-arterial line is useful, both for continuous monitoring of blood pressure and for taking arterial samples for blood gas estimations. A central venous catheter is not always called for. Beware that a heat-moisture exchanger will not only add to the dead space but can also become blocked with secretions and blood.

Pleural Drainage

Air, blood and fluid collection in the pleural space prevents expansion of the lung and, if significant, may cause mediastinal shift. A pleural drain helps to drain the collection, facilitates expansion of the lung and helps to re-establish the ability to generate negative pleural pressure in the spontaneously breathing patient.

The pleural drainage system consists of three parts: first, a chest tube with low resistance, 1 metre in length, which drains the fluid or air; second, a one-way valve (usually an underwater seal), which allows expulsion of air during spontaneous expiration and positive pressure inspiration and prevents re-entry of air during spontaneous inspiration; and third, a collection chamber. Suction applied to the pleural drainage systems increases the pressure gradient between the pleural space and the collecting chamber, preventing reverse flow of air in the spontaneously breathing patient.

Important note: The depth to which the tube dips under the water or fluid is important, as the greater the depth, the more the resistance that is applied to respiration. This will occur especially if there is a lot of drainage.

The tube connecting the chest tube to the bottle should not be too long as looping of the tube also adds to resistance.

If suction is used, bilateral pleural drains should not be connected to the same suction as differential resistance to drainage may cause mediastinal shift. If suction is not being applied, the drainage bottle should be disconnected from the suction source as otherwise gas and fluid will be unable to escape.

Post-Operative Pain Relief

Multi-modal analgesia is commonly used in all thoracic surgeries, and this helps in reducing the opioid use in the post-operative period and facilitates on-table or early extubation (better spontaneous breathing with good analgesia). This may include a regional analgesia technique along with paracetamol (intravenous/oral/rectal) or diclofenac (in older children). All the regional techniques in children are performed under anaesthesia because of which there is a growing concern about the safety of central neuraxial blockade. There has been a shift from central to peripheral nerve blocks, and the increasing use of ultrasound guidance has helped it further. Thoracic paravertebral block and erector spinae plane block are gaining attention in the paediatric age group also. There are many reports on continuous catheter techniques especially in older children. These are used both for thoracotomy and thoracoscopy.

The availability of safer local anaesthetics such as ropivacaine and levobupivacaine has encouraged clinicians to use them in smaller children for longer periods. Additives such as clonidine, dexmedetomidine, fentanyl, etc., can also be used along with the local anaesthetic drug for better analgesia (see Chapters 13, 14 and 47).

Conclusion

For successfully anaesthetising a child for a thoracic procedure, a thorough understanding of the anatomy, physiology and pathology of the respiratory system is essential. In addition, a good outcome is dependent on good monitoring and equipment along with a good working relationship and understanding between the anaesthetist, surgeon, intensivist, blood bank, radiologist, physiotherapist and nursing staff.

SUGGESTED READINGS

1. Lecamwasam HS, Benumof JL, Triantafillou AN. Physiology of the lateral decubitus position, the open chest and one lung ventilation. In: Thoracic Anaesthesia, 3rd edition. Kaplan JA, Slinger PD (eds). Churchill Livingstone 2003; pp. 71–92.
2. Haynes SR, Bonner S. Anaesthesia for thoracic surgery in children – a review. *Paed Anaesth* 2000; 10:237–251.
3. Hammer GB. Pediatric thoracic anesthesia – a review. *Anesth Analg* 2001; 92:1449–1464.
4. Hammer GB. Single lung ventilation in infants and children. *Paed Anaesth* 2004; 14:98–102.
5. Yun ES, Saulys A, Popic PM, Arndt GA. Single lung ventilation in a pediatric patient using a pediatric fiberoptically directed wire-guided endobronchial blocker. *Can J Anesth* 2002; 49:256–261.
6. Hammer GB, Brodsky JB, Redpath JH, Cannon WB. The Univent tube for single lung ventilation in pediatric patients. *Paed Anaesth* 1998; 8:55–57.
7. Lohser J, Ishikawa S. Physiology of the Lateral Decubitus Position, Open Chest and One Lung Ventilation. In: Principles and Practice of Thoracic Anesthesia. Slinger P (ed). Springer, New York, 2011; pp. 71–82.
8. Lohser J, Ishikawa S. Clinical Management of One Lung Ventilation. In: Principles and Practice of Thoracic Anesthesia. Slinger P (ed). Springer 2011; pp. 83–101.
9. Schwartz R, Karsli C. Anesthesia for Pediatric Thoracic Surgery. In: Principles and practice of Thoracic Anesthesia. Slinger P (ed). Springer 2011; pp. 551–577.
10. Fabila TS, Menghraj SJ. One lung ventilation strategies for infants and children undergoing video assisted thoracoscopic surgery. *Indian J Anaesth* 2013; 57:339–344.
11. Letal M, Theam M. Paediatric lung isolation. *BJA Educ* 2017; 17(2):57–62.
12. Semmelmann A, Kaltofen H, Loop T. Anesthesia of thoracic surgery in children. *Pediatr Anesth* 2018; 28(4):326–331.
13. Ponde V. Recent trends in paediatric regional anaesthesia. *Indian J Anaesth* 2019; 63:746–753.
14. Yentis SM, Hirsch NP, Smith GP. Chest Drainage. In: Anaesthesia A-Z. Butterworth Heinemann, Oxford, 1993; p. 97.
15. Kam AC, O'Brien M, Kam PCA. Pleural drainage systems – a review. *Anaesthesia* 1993; 48:154–161.

26 Anaesthetic Management of Children with Common Congenital Heart Diseases for Non-Cardiac Surgery

Raj Sahajanandan • Rebecca Jacob

Congenital cardiac abnormalities occur in 4–9/1000 live births with a wide spectrum of disability ranging from trivial to lethal. Eighty percent of these lesions are represented by atrial septal defect (ASD), ventricular septal defect (VSD), tetralogy of Fallot (TOF), coarctation of aorta, patent ductus arteriosus (PDA), transposition of great arteries (TGA), aortic stenosis and pulmonary stenosis. About a third of these children also have extra-cardiac anomalies, such as tracheo-oesophageal fistula, anorectal abnormalities, and cleft lip and palate as syndromic associations, which may require surgery within the first year of life. The recent advances in medical and surgical techniques have significantly improved survival and have resulted in a significant number of these children presenting for noncardiac surgery.

Presentations for Non-Cardiac Surgery

Patients with congenital cardiac lesions may present for non-cardiac surgery in one of the following ways:

Before the lesion is diagnosed: The patients may present with an unexpected complication during anaesthesia like cyanosis, arrhythmias or ventricular dysfunction. Treatment consists of resuscitation and termination of surgery as soon as possible.

After diagnosis, before surgical intervention: These patients have the advantage of a previous cardiac work-up and are under the care of a cardiologist. If the non-cardiac surgery is elective and cardiac repair is due to be performed, then consider performing cardiac surgery first. Anaesthetic management in asymptomatic patients with small VSDs, atrial septal defects or minimal aortic coarctation may pose very few problems.

After surgical palliation: Review all records of the previous procedure and the current status of the patient. The timing of the corrective surgery, if planned, should be coordinated with the non-cardiac surgery. Monitoring and post-operative management depend on the degree of symptoms, exercise tolerance, presence of pulmonary hypertension and extent of the planned surgical procedure.

After surgical correction: There may be varying degrees of surgical repair. An otherwise healthy child who has had patch closure of a small atrial septal defect may be treated as completely normal, but a patient presenting for the same non-cardiac procedure with a history of pulmonary hypertension after repair of a large VSD will need special attention. Problems that could occur after repair of the congenital heart lesion are ventricular dysfunction, dysrhythmias, residual shunts and persistent obstruction.

Inoperable cardiac lesion: An example of an inoperable cardiac lesion is 'hypoplastic left heart syndrome with hypoplastic aorta'. These patients are at high risk for mortality and morbidity. Even a minimally invasive elective procedure demands full invasive monitoring and post-operative care.

Classification of Congenital Heart Disease

Congenital heart disease (CHD) has been variously classified.

One such classification simply divides CHD as follows:

- **Left-to-right shunts:** Septal defects (ASD and VSD) and shunt at the great arteries (PDA)
- **Right-to-left shunts:** Cyanotic (TOF)
- **Obstructive:** Aortic and pulmonary valvar stenosis and coarctation of the aorta
- **Miscellaneous:** Includes hypoplastic defects, mitral valve prolapse and coronary arterial anomalies

Another classification based on the haemodynamics of the lesion is as follows:

1. **Acyanotic heart disease**
   - *Left-right shunt:* ASD, VSD, PDA
   - *Left heart obstruction:* Coarctation of the aorta, aortic stenosis, mitral stenosis
2. **Cyanotic heart disease**
   - *Reduced pulmonary blood flow:* TOF, pulmonary stenosis, Ebstein's anomaly
   - *Increased pulmonary blood flow:* TGA, double outlet right ventricle (DORV), total anomalous pulmonary vein connection (TAPVC), truncus arteriosus (TA)
   - *Single ventricle:* Hypoplastic left heart syndrome (HLHS)

Whatever the classification, it is important to realise that many defects have more than one *pathophysiological consequence and it is important to understand this before anaesthetising a child with CHD* (**Table 26.1**).

Table 26.1 Pathophysiological Consequences of Common CHDs

Physiological Derangement	Haemodynamic Consequences	Clinical Consequences	Examples
Increased pulmonary blood flow	Inefficient systemic circulation, pulmonary congestion, pulmonary hypertension. Volume and pressure overload of pulmonary circulation	Failure to thrive, heart failure symptoms, tachypnoea, frequent respiratory symptoms	All post-tricuspid shunts, some large pre-tricuspid shunts (ASD, VSD and PDA)
Reduced pulmonary blood flow	Hypoxia in presence of atrial or ventricular septal defect; reduced cardiac output if both septa are intact. Reduced ability to oxygenate blood	Cyanosis and fatigue	All congenital defects that are associated with pulmonary stenosis
Mixing of systemic and pulmonary venous return (single ventricle physiology)	Some hypoxia will result but the exact oxygen saturation will be dictated by pulmonary blood flow. If pulmonary blood flow is increased (shunt ratio 2:1 or more) saturations are above 85%	Cyanosis of varying severity depending on pulmonary blood flow	All forms of univentricular hearts; double outlet LV or RV, tricuspid atresia
Elevated pulmonary vascular resistance	Inability to increase cardiac output during exercise or stress, increased left to right shunting across associated defects	Fatigue on effort, patients with defects in the atrial or ventricular septum will have increasing cyanosis	All conditions associated with increased pulmonary blood flow increase the risk for development of increased pulmonary vascular resistance
Left-sided atrioventricular valve regurgitation	Left ventricular volume overload, elevation in left atrial pressures, pulmonary venous congestion	Tachypnoea, fatigue on effort	Atrioventricular septal defects, corrected transposition, atrial septal defects with mitral valve prolapse and mitral regurgitation (MR), congenital MR, anomalous coronary artery from pulmonary artery

(*Contd.*)

Table 26.1 (*Contd.*)

Physiological Derangement	Haemodynamic Consequences	Clinical Consequences	Examples
Right-sided atrioventricular valve regurgitation	Right ventricular overload, elevated right atrial pressures, systemic venous congestion	Fatigue, right heart failure	Ebstein's anomaly, congenital anomalies of tricuspid valve
Left ventricular hypertrophy	Elevated filling pressures with resulting left heart failure	Tachypnoea from pulmonary venous congestion	All forms of left ventricular outflow tract obstruction, hypertrophic cardiomyopathy
Right ventricular hypertrophy	Elevated right-sided filling pressures with systemic venous congestion	Right heart failure, liver enlargement, fluid accumulation (oedema and ascites)	Advanced forms of RV outflow obstruction: critical pulmonary stenosis, advanced pulmonary hypertension
Reduced coronary perfusion	Left ventricular dysfunction	Tachypnoea, fatigue	Anomalous left coronary artery from pulmonary artery
Pulmonary valve regurgitation	Dilation of branch pulmonary arteries with airway compression, right ventricular dilation	Respiratory symptoms in infants with TOF and absent pulmonary valve, fatigue on effort in patients with long standing pulmonary valve incompetence	TOF with absent pulmonary valve
Aortic valve regurgitation	Left ventricular dilatation	Fatigue and palpitation	Bicommisural aortic valve associated with subpulmonic and some perimembranous defects
Obstructive lesions	Increased ventricular workload to overcome the obstruction, as well as a relatively reduced circulation distal to the obstruction	Failure and fatigue	Coarctation of aorta

ASD, atrial septal defect; LV, left ventricle; MR, mitral regurgitation; PDA, patent ductus arteriosus; RV, right ventricle; TOF, tetralogy of Fallot; VSD, ventricular septal defect.

It is also important to understand that cardiac lesions behave differently in children of different ages due to age-related haemodynamic considerations. Neonates have a higher cardiac index, smaller functional residual capacity, increased alveolar ventilation and a higher metabolic rate. Older children may develop irreversible pulmonary hypertension and cardiac asthma resulting from significant left-to-right shunts. This excessive pulmonary blood flow (PBF) may prevent normal regression of medial smooth muscle tissue in the pulmonary vascular tree.

Approach to a Child with CHD

A practical approach to a child with CHD is to have a checklist of assessment protocols and understand why each is being asked for or done. See **Table 26.2** for the suggested pre-operative checklist.

Also check the following:

- Birth history, history of prematurity and neonatal ICU admission/ventilation
- History of cyanotic spells, squatting, failure to thrive, poor feeding and sweating
- Current medications, for example digoxin levels and electrolytes, and beta-blockers. Generally, all medications should be continued. Anticoagulation management should be done after discussion with the surgical team and the cardiologist.
- Medications required in the past
- Known useful or ineffective medication used in the past, especially antiarrhythmics
- Allergies
- Whether prophylactic antibiotics have been given

Table 26.2 Pre-Operative Checklist

Pre-Operative Checklist	Purpose
Assessment and analysis of patient records History & Examination	• What is the complete clinical diagnosis? • Has the CHD been corrected, is it uncorrected or palliated? • Details of the operation or catheterisation performed • Is there an active URI? • Extracardiac effects of CHD/complications from previous surgery • Evidence of cardiac failure • Drug history (anti-hypertensive, anti-failure, antiarrythmic and anti-coagulant)
Consultation with paediatric cardiologist with the following investigations, if required • ECG • Chest X-ray • Oxygen saturation on room air • Arterial blood gases • Echocardiography • Exercise testing • Cardiac MRI • Serum electrolytes and blood sugar • Haematocrit	The investigations will reveal the following: • What is the current status of the CHD – pathophysiology and adequacy of cardiac output in particular? • Is there severe polycythaemia? • Is there a shunt? Intracardiac or extracardiac • Restrictive or non-restrictive and impact of PVR–SVR balance on the shunt • Is there an obstruction? Is it supravalvular, valvular or subvalvular? Severity of the lesion? Fixed (AS) or Dynamic (TOF) • What are the pulmonary arterial pressures? • Is there an increased PBF? Look for Qp/Qs in the cath study • Pulmonary hypertension: >30 mm Hg • Impact of ventilation and anaesthetic drugs on PVR/SVR for the lesion • Will PVR or SVR require manipulation to optimise systemic or pulmonary blood flow? • What haemodynamic changes can be expected with the stress of surgery and anaesthesia? • Is there a risk of worsening hypoxia? • Is there a need for endocarditis prophylaxis? • Is there a possibility of dysrhythmia? • Is there a risk of paradoxical embolisation because of R-L shunt? • Are there specific concerns during post-op recovery?

AS, aortic stenosis; CHD, congenital heart disease; ECG, electrocardiogram; PBF, pulmonary blood flow; PVR, pulmonary vascular resistance; Qp/Qs, pulmonary blood flow/systemic blood flow; SVR, systemic vascular resistance; TOF, tetralogy of Fallot; URI, upper respiratory infection.

- History of previous difficult intravenous access/ look for venous access now
- History of previous prolonged ventilation/ stridor during URI – may indicate tracheal stenosis
- History of 'difficult airway' access, re-examine thoroughly and discuss with colleague or senior
- Measure the blood pressure and saturation in all four limbs
- Look for non-cardiac anomalies which can increase the perioperative risk – Trisomy 21, Goldenhar, VACTERL, CHARGE and Di George

Look for URI – consider deferring the surgery in case of active URI

Risk Stratification

As there are many consequences of CHD (**Table 26.3**), it is important to stratify the risk in these patients to take appropriate informed consent and decide on the preoperative work up and tests, level of monitoring, anaesthesia technique, the level of postoperative care and suitability to do these procedures at a district general hospital or refer to a tertiary care with backup of cardiology/ ICU support. Age, especially less than 2 years, surgical complexity, functional status and severity of CHD are all associated with increased morbidity and mortality.

Thus, it is crucial to elucidate the following:

1. The complexity of the congenital heart disease
2. To look for long-term sequelae and factors associated with poor outcomes
3. To assess surgical risks
4. To assess whether the patient is physiologically compensated or compromised

Table 26.3 Consequences of CHD and its Implications

Consequences	Pathophysiology	Implications
Cyanosis	Response to chronic hypoxia because of decreased PBF and/or mixing. Compensatory polycythaemia	Cerebral and sinus vein thrombosis Myocardial depression due to chronic hypoxia
Congestive heart failure (tachypnoea, failure to thrive, poor feeding, cold extremity and poor weight gain)	Due to increased PBF resulting from shunt lesions, obstructive lesions and impaired ventricular contractility	Results in decreased systemic perfusion, increased pulmonary congestion and increased systemic venous congestion; 10% risk of cardiac arrest
Pulmonary hypertension	(L to R) shunts due to increased PBF. TAPVC – prolonged pulmonary venous obstruction HLHS – high left atrial pressure Truncus arteriosus – mixing lesions with increased PBF	Not usually a feature of R to L shunt. But can occur in associated non-cardiac pathologies like OSA Is dynamic – can be worsened by hypoxia, hypercarbia, acidosis and hypothermia Can become irreversible at any age
Arrhythmia	May be due to complications of CHD or a complication of surgery	Optimise the function of ICD or pacemaker before non-cardiac surgery Risk of cardiac arrest
Lungs Decreased compliance Recurrent laryngeal nerve injury Phrenic nerve injury Blunted response to hypoxia Airway compression by vascular structures	 Due to increased PBF Surgery Surgery	 Chronic aspiration and lung impairment Diaphragmatic palsy Resolves with full correction but, with palliative surgery, may remain life-long
Haematologic Polycythaemia and hyperviscosity syndrome Coagulation abnormality	 Response to chronic hypoxia Qualitative and quantitative abnormality of platelets Hypofibrinogenemia Fibrinolysis	 Thrombosis, embolism and brain abscess Consider venesection if PCV > 60 Avoid pre-operative dehydration
Neurological Hyperviscosity Paradoxical emboli to CNS Brain abscesses Cerebral thrombosis		Fatigue, tiredness, muscle weakness, myalgia, and paraesthesia of fingers, toes and lips, headache, depressed mentation, TIA and stroke

CHD, congenital heart disease; CNS, central nervous system; HLHS, hypoplastic left heart syndrome; ICD, intra-cardiac device; OSA, obstructive sleep apnoea; PBF, pulmonary blood flow; PCV, packed cell volume; TAPVC, total anomalous pulmonary venous connection; TIA, transient ischaemic attack.

Complexity of Congenital Heart Disease

Based on the functional status and residual disease burden, the American College of Surgeons National Surgical Quality Improvement Program (NSQIP) has classified CHD in children as minor, major or severe (Table 26.4).

The risk adjustment for congenital heart surgery (RACHS) can also be helpful. The RACHS was developed to compare outcome data for paediatric patients undergoing cardiac surgery. It stratifies anatomic diversity into six categories based on age, type of surgery performed and similar in-hospital mortality—RACHS 1 and 2: Minimal risk; 3–4: Moderate risk; >4: High risk.

Factors associated with poor outcomes of surgery are as follows:

1. Age < 2 years
2. Poor functional status (ASA 3 & 4)
3. Complex lesions (single ventricle physiology, uncorrected complex lesions)
4. Severe pulmonary hypertension (MPAP> 25 mmHg, PVRI> 3 Wood unit·m^2) with NYHA 3 or 4 status, PAP ≥ SBP and decreased cardiac index
5. Systemic to pulmonary artery shunts
6. Cardiomyopathy
7. Aortic stenosis
8. Preop hospital stay > 10 days
9. Inotropic support

Table 26.4 Classification of CHD According to 'Risk'

Classification	Criteria
Minor	• Unrepaired acyanotic heart disease with no medication (e.g., ASD, small-to-moderate VSD without symptoms) • Repair of CHD with normal cardiovascular function and no medication
Major	• Unrepaired symptomatic acyanotic heart disease • Repair of CHD with residual haemodynamic abnormality with or without medications (e.g., TOF with free pulmonary regurgitation, HLHS)
Severe	• Uncorrected cyanotic CHD • Patients with documented pulmonary hypertension • Patients with ventricular dysfunction requiring medication • Listed for heart transplant

ASD, atrial septal defect; CHD, congenital heart disease; HLHS, hypoplastic left heart syndrome; VSD, ventricular septal defect; TOF, tetralogy of Fallot.

10. Preoperative CPR
11. Acute kidney injury
12. Mechanical ventilatory support

Caveat: *Pulmonary hypertension after a cavopulmonary anastomosis is defined as a transpulmonary gradient >6 mmHg (mPAP minus mean left atrial pressure) even if mPAP < 25 mm Hg.*

High Surgical Risk

High-risk surgical procedures are those with anticipated haemodynamic instability, large fluid shifts, or high blood loss.

1. Emergency surgery
2. Intrathoracic/intraperitoneal surgery
3. Vascular reconstructive surgery
4. Surgical procedures with anticipated fluid shifts and blood loss

   Mortality rates can be as high as 16%.

Physiological Assessment

Cardiac failure: Look for tachypnoea, tachycardia, sweating on feed, frequent suck/pause/suck cycles during feeds, failure to thrive, hepatomegaly and rales. It carries 10% risk of cardiac arrest and >90% requirement of inotropes.

Pulmonary artery hypertension: (PAP >25 mmHg at rest, >30 mmHg on exercise). Chest infection is poorly tolerated by these children.

Arrhythmia: Right bundle branch block (RBBB) is very common, but ventricular ectopics are ominous.

Cyanosis: It is often found in patients with co-existent heart failure, pulmonary hypertension or arrhythmias. It is complicated by polycythaemia, coagulation abnormalities as well as thrombosis.

Who and Where Should These Patients Be Cared for?

The anaesthetists caring for these patients should have a good understanding of the anatomy and physiology, the proposed procedure and its haemodynamic implications as well as the potential complications.

These are suggested guidelines. However, if the children have associated non-cardiac anomalies, it would be better to refer them to a higher centre.

Communication and Informed Consent

All available information and reports should be collected from parents, cardiologists, surgeons and from old records. Ask specifically about previous anaesthesia and surgical experience and assess the need for premedication. Risk stratification which includes CHD risks, risks of proposed surgery and anaesthetic risks should be communicated to the family with the proposed anaesthetic plan and referred to specialists appropriately unless it is a life-threatening emergency (Fig. 26.1).

Anaesthetic Management – General Principles

A good understanding of the pathophysiology is the key to peri-operative management of these children.

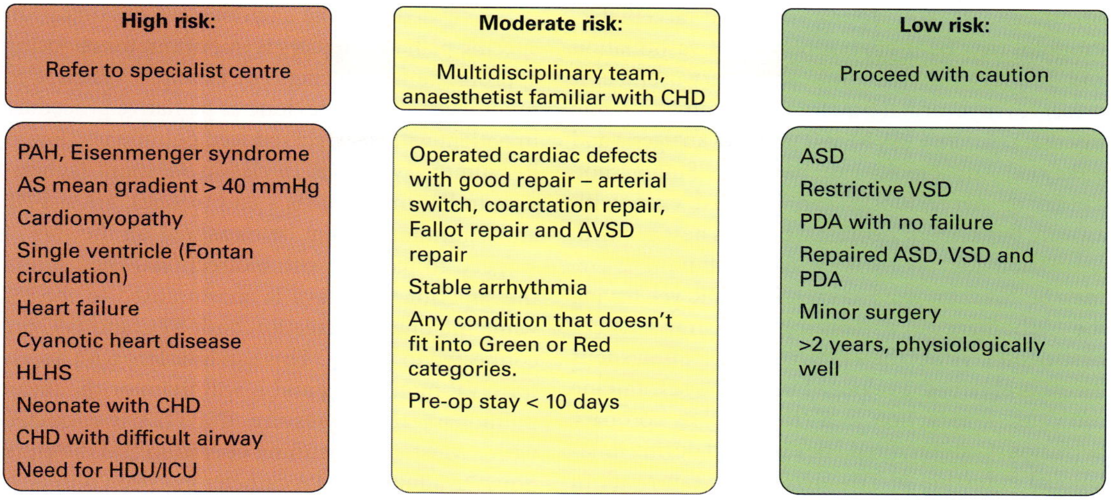

Figure 26.1 Risk stratification and communication. AS, aortic stenosis; ASD, atrial septal defect; AVSD, atrioventricular septal defect; CHD, congenital heart disease; HDU, high-dependency unit; ICU, intensive care unit; PAH, pulmonary artery hypertension; PDA, patent ductus arteriosus; VSD, ventricular septal defect.

Setting: Patients with simple lesions or well-compensated moderately complex lesions can have non-cardiac procedures in well-equipped and staffed community hospitals. However, if the patients are not well compensated or have complex lesions or a single ventricle, it is advisable that they undergo any procedure in a tertiary care hospital with necessary cardiology back-up. Avoid outpatient surgery, as there is increased incidence of post-operative cardiac dysfunction in patients with significant lesions.

Pre-operative sedation: With very few exceptions such as those with pulmonary hypertension (PHT), children with a congenital cardiac defect should be brought to the OT sedated so as to avoid the fear and stress associated with the procedure. Parental presence may be considered provided they are prepared with appropriate counselling/educative videos/ prior experience. Midazolam 0.5 $mg.kg^{-1}$, 20 to 30 minutes prior to induction is a good option.

The *anaesthetic management of children with CHD for cardiac catheterisation* follows the same principles except that fraction of inspired oxygen (FiO_2) need to be adjusted to know the response of pulmonary vascular resistance (PVR) to increased levels of oxygen.

Airway management: It can range from spontaneous respiration with sedation to general anaesthesia with a mask or a laryngeal mask airway or endotracheal tube with care to maintain normocarbia. Effects of positive pressure ventilation on the pathophysiology of the cardiac lesions should be minimised.

The ***Anaesthetic technique*** should be chosen in patients with CHD after careful assessment of the particular pathophysiology and the required haemodynamic goals. The haemodynamic effects of the different anaesthetic agents are discussed in Table 26.5. Inhalational induction with

Table 26.5 The Haemodynamic Effects of Induction Agents

Agent	Haemodynamic Effects		Caution
Propofol	SVR and MAP fall	HR, PVR and PAP unchanged	Children with AVSDs
Ketamine	MAP rises	No effect on PVR and PAP	
Etomidate	Minimal effect on haemodynamics		Adrenal suppression

AVSDs, atrioventricular septal defects; HR, heart rate; MAP, mean arterial pressure; PAP, pulmonary artery pressure; PVR, pulmonary vascular resistance; SVR, systemic vascular resistance.

sevoflurane is still appropriate and acceptable. Propofol may be used, but beware of vasodilation and drop in SVR. Ketamine can be very useful as it preserves myocardial function, maintains systemic vascular resistance (SVR) and provides analgesia and sedation. Any opioid can be used. 'Single shot' caudal or nerve blocks can be used even with aspirin, but a major neuraxial block is best avoided.

Halothane up to 0.5% or sevoflurane 2–3% may be used to avoid decreasing SVR yet having the advantage of reducing dynamic RVOT obstruction. After the child is asleep, intravenous access is obtained. Prolonged use of 8% sevoflurane can cause a reduction in SVR as well as coronary perfusion. Caution should be exercised during inhalational induction in Trisomy 21 as it can result in bradyarrhythmias. Ketamine may be used to supplement induction at this time as it maintains SVR and PBF. If there is a concern about the increase in pulmonary outflow obstruction, small doses of β-blocker (esmolol 0.5 mg/kg) may be used.

When considering anaesthetic agents in shunt lesions, remember

- Left-to-right shunt: Inhalational induction faster
- Right-to-left shunt: Intravenous induction faster while volatile is slower
- Balance between SVR and PVR affects the shunt pattern (see the following text)

If a surgical systemic to pulmonary shunt has been placed, the PBF increases and the speed of induction is increased. Intravenous induction can be more rapid because the induction agent would reach the brain quicker after bypassing the lungs. Systemic hypotension can result in a decrease in pulmonary blood flow, with subsequent arterial desaturation, in a patient with a systemic to pulmonary artery shunt (Blalock-Taussig shunt or central shunt).

Monitoring

Ensure that there is adequate ***monitoring***: What is *essential* are an electrocardiogram, pulse oximetry, non-invasive blood pressure, end-tidal carbon dioxide, temperature and a precordial stethoscope. *Optional* monitoring would include invasive arterial blood pressure and central venous pressure. Remember that the $EtCO_2$ will underestimate the true arterial CO_2, especially in R-to-L shunts.

Knowledge of the anatomy and physiology of specific palliative repairs is important for choosing appropriate monitoring. For example, systemic to pulmonary shunts are done as palliative procedure in patient with severely reduced pulmonary flow as in pulmonary atresia. In classic BT shunt (subclavian to PA anastomosis – end to side), arterial BP and saturation cannot be measured on the side of surgery. In patients with bidirectional Glen shunt, the superior vena cava is anastomosed to the PA while in Fontan circulation both SVC and IVC are connected to the PA. This can interfere with access for CVP monitoring and it will monitor the mean pulmonary artery pressure. If a TGA is corrected with a Mustard or Senning operation and the child grows to adulthood, PA catheter insertion is impossible with the atrial baffles.

It is important to have arterial blood pressure monitoring for major surgery as well as complex lesions.

Anaesthetists should be familiar with transthoracic echocardiography (ECHO) as it will help in fine-tuning peri-operative management.

Systemic air emboli are a constant threat in children with CHD regardless of their shunting pattern, because of the dynamic nature of shunts during anaesthesia and surgery. Air traps are advisable for all intravenous lines but are not a substitute for meticulous attention and constant vigilance and purging of air bubbles.

Consider ***regional anaesthesia*** when feasible but the same extent of monitoring should be used for general anaesthesia as decreased SVR may not be tolerated by some patients with mixed lesions and decreased coronary perfusion.

Caudal epidural and USG-guided blocks are very good options. Caution needs to be exercised in children with coagulation abnormalities.

Pacemakers or implanted defibrillators should be checked by the cardiologist and his advice sought. In general, pacemakers should be converted to an asynchronous mode just before the surgery, to avoid electrocautery interference. The defibrillator function in the patients on ICDs must also be turned off and there should be immediate access to an external defibrillator. The type of pacemaker device and reason for insertion must be known. Patients with pacemakers are better monitored with arterial waveforms to ensure that the electrical impulse is actually producing an ejection/stroke volume. The settings of these devices should be restored as soon as possible after the completion of the procedure.

Positioning

Trendelenburg position can increase central venous (superior vena cava) pressure and cause cerebral hypoperfusion in a patient with a Glenn shunt or Fontan circulation.

Post-Operative Care

Adequate pain relief and maintenance of normothermia are essential for a good recovery. Patients with Glenn or Fontan circulation (low-pressure shunt) benefit from spontaneous ventilation, head up and feet up position and a good preload to facilitate pulmonary perfusion and good oxygenation. So, facilitate early extubation without excessive sedation. Hypovolaemia, especially with cyanotic congenital heart disease, should be corrected immediately. Features associated with a high risk of peri-operative cardiac arrest are cardiomyopathy, cardiac failure, balanced circulation or single ventricle circulation and arrhythmias.

Infective Endocarditis Prophylaxis

Patients with structural congenital heart disease, including surgically corrected or palliated structural conditions are at increased risk of infective endocarditis. However, the National Institute for Health and Care Excellence (NICE) no longer recommends prophylactic antibiotics for gastrointestinal, genitourinary and dental procedures. Instead, the emphasis is on education regarding good oral hygiene and recognition of the symptoms of infective endocarditis. Infective endocarditis (IE) prophylaxis is described as per the American Heart Association guidelines. According to these guidelines, the patient must have both cardiac condition and surgical/procedural indication to receive infective endocarditis prophylaxis.

Cardiac Indications

1. Prosthetic cardiac valve or material
2. Previous infective endocarditis
3. Congenital heart disease*
    - Unrepaired cyanotic CHD including palliative shunts and conduits
    - Completely repaired CHD with prosthetic material or device during the first 6 months after the procedure
    - Repaired CHD with residual defects at or near the site of a prosthetic patch or device
    - Cardiac transplant recipients who develop valvulopathy

(**Antibiotic prophylaxis is no longer recommended for any other form of CHD.*)

Surgical/Procedural Indications

1. All dental procedures that involve manipulation of the gingival tissue or perforation of the oral mucosa
2. Invasive procedures of the respiratory tract such as tonsillectomy and adenoidectomy (not bronchoscopy) and drainage of abscess or empyema or procedures on infected skin or musculoskeletal tissue
3. Gastrointestinal (GI) or genitourinary (GU) tract procedures: Not routinely recommended except in those who have established GI or GU infections.

Drugs: Single-dose ampicillin IV/amoxicillin 'O' in a dose of 50 mg/kg 30–60 minutes before the procedure or as soon as IV access is secured is the recommended regimen, with clindamycin IM or IV (20 mg/kg), cefazolin/ceftriaxone (50 mg/kg), cephalexin 'O' 50 mg/kg 30–60 minutes before recommended for penicillin-sensitive individuals.

Pathophysiology of Common CHD

'Shunting': Communication between the systemic and pulmonary circulations is a common feature of CHD. The shunt may be a component of the heart lesion or have been created to palliate the lesion.

Simple shunt lesions (Fig. 26.2): The magnitude and direction of the flow of blood across the shunt are determined primarily by the size of the communication and the relative resistances of the pulmonary and systemic circulations. In case of a large cardiac defect (ASD or VSD), a pressure differential across the shunt is primarily dependent on the PVR and SVR. This is termed a ***non-restrictive shunt***. If the defect is small, the shunt is influenced primarily by the size of the defect and it is termed a ***restrictive shunt***. A non-restrictive defect is more difficult to manage as anaesthesia

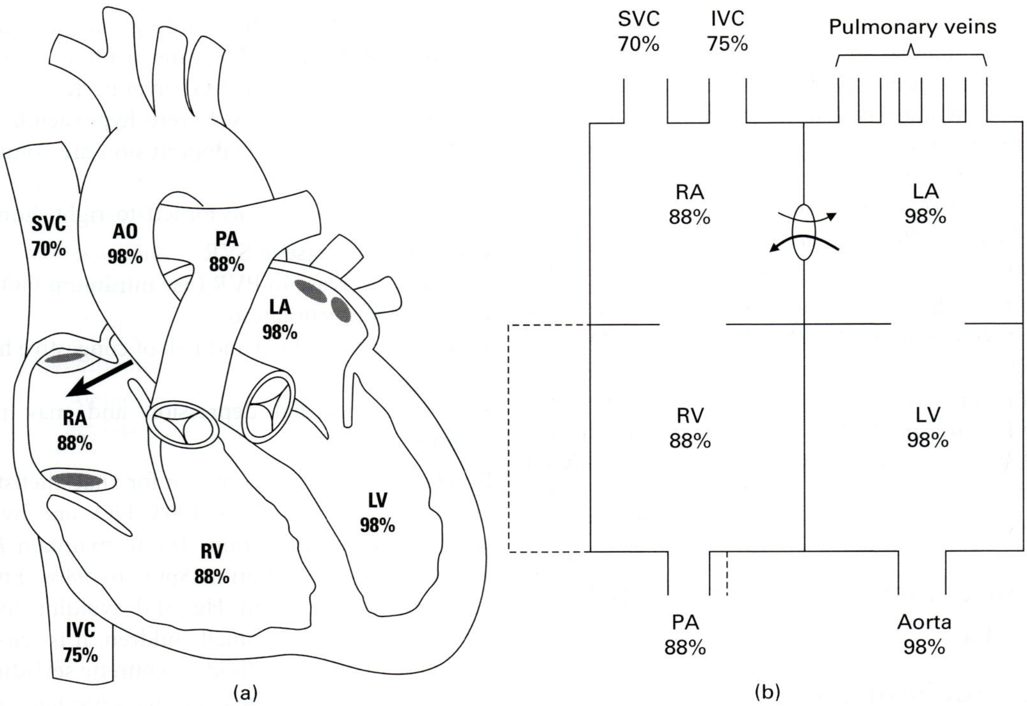

Figure 26.3 (a and b) Atrial septal defect with oxygen saturations in different chambers. AO, aorta; IVC, inferior vena cava; LA, left atrium; LV, left ventricle; PA, pulmonary artery; RA, right atrium; RV, right ventricle; SVC, superior vena cava.

General Haemodynamics

There is a left-to-right shunt at the atrial level with right ventricular volume overload. The RV versus LV compliance, rather than the size of the ASD, determines the amount of shunting. High PA pressures may occur with advancement in age.

Anaesthetic Considerations

Small-to-moderate size defects are well tolerated. Large defects lead to arrhythmias, exercise intolerance and rarely PHT. Pre-medication may be given as usual as they are minimally symptomatic.

The shunt is predominantly left to right so ***care should be taken to avoid venous air embolism as paradoxical arterial embolism*** may occur.

Interventions which increase right atrial pressures more than left atrial pressure such as positive airway pressure and Valsalva manoeuvre may reverse the direction of shunt flow.

Atrial dysrhythmias and heart block (varying degrees) may occur after ASD repair.

Ventricular Septal Defect

Location

Perimembranous VSD (**Fig. 26.4a,b**) is most common. Other types of VSDs are muscular, septal or infundibular. VSD may be associated with extra-cardiac congenital anomalies. Unrepaired defects, especially large ones, are at risk of PHT (50% by age 2). Small-to-moderate size defects are at risk for endocarditis (turbulent flow), sub-pulmonic obstruction, subaortic obstruction, aortic regurgitation (venturi effect), and right ventricular failure (volume overload). Repaired VSDs can develop complete heart block or arrythmias and rarely persistent PHT.

Haemodynamics

Left-to-right shunting causes increased PBF, increased left ventricular volume and increased left ventricular work.

In a large VSD (non-restrictive), the amount of shunting depends on the ratio of systemic to pulmonary vascular resistance.

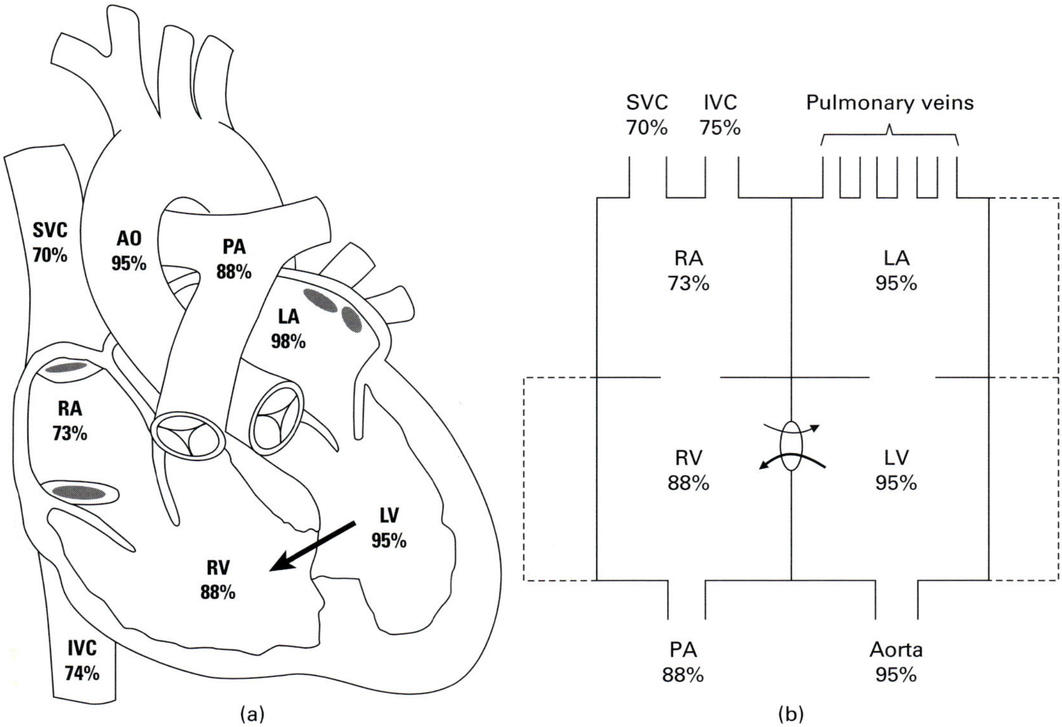

Figure 26.4 (a and b) VSD with oxygen saturations in different chambers. LV, left ventricle; RV, right ventricle; VSD, ventricular septal defect.

On the other hand, in a small VSD (restrictive) a pressure gradient exists between the two ventricles and the quantum of shunt depends on the size of the septal orifice.

Pressure-related problems are more common with VSD than with ASD considering that the defect lies between high-pressure cardiac chambers.

Anaesthetic Implications

Pre-medication depends on the amount of ventricular dysfunction.

Pulmonary vascular tone should be taken into consideration. As with an ASD, an acute and persistent increase in SVR or a decrease in PVR is undesirable as it increases the magnitude of the left-to-right shunt. Increasing the child's FiO_2 and lowering the pCO_2 will decrease PVR and consequently increase PBF at the expense of systemic flow. In large VSDs, ventilation needs to be adjusted to maintain normocapnia and limit FiO_2 to prevent reduction of PVR and further increases PBF (pulmonary steal). Fluid overload must be avoided. These children are at increased risk of postoperative pulmonary infection.

Induction also depends on the ventricular function. An inhalational induction may be used if the left ventricular function is good. With a poor LV function, an opioid/ketamine induction may be an option.

Patent Ductus Arteriosus (Fig. 26.5 a,b)

In this condition, there is failure of the ductus arteriosus to close.

Haemodynamics

Before birth there is bi-directional shunting of blood between the main pulmonary artery and the descending aorta while PVR is high. As PVR decreases, soon after birth the shunt becomes predominantly left to right. Subsequently increased PBF leads to pulmonary hypertension, increased lung water and increased work of breathing.

Anaesthetic Considerations

The ductus arteriosus is a vascular structure connecting the main pulmonary artery with the proximal descending aorta that is an essential part of the foetal circulation. Persistent patent ductus arteriosus may occur in isolation or as part of a

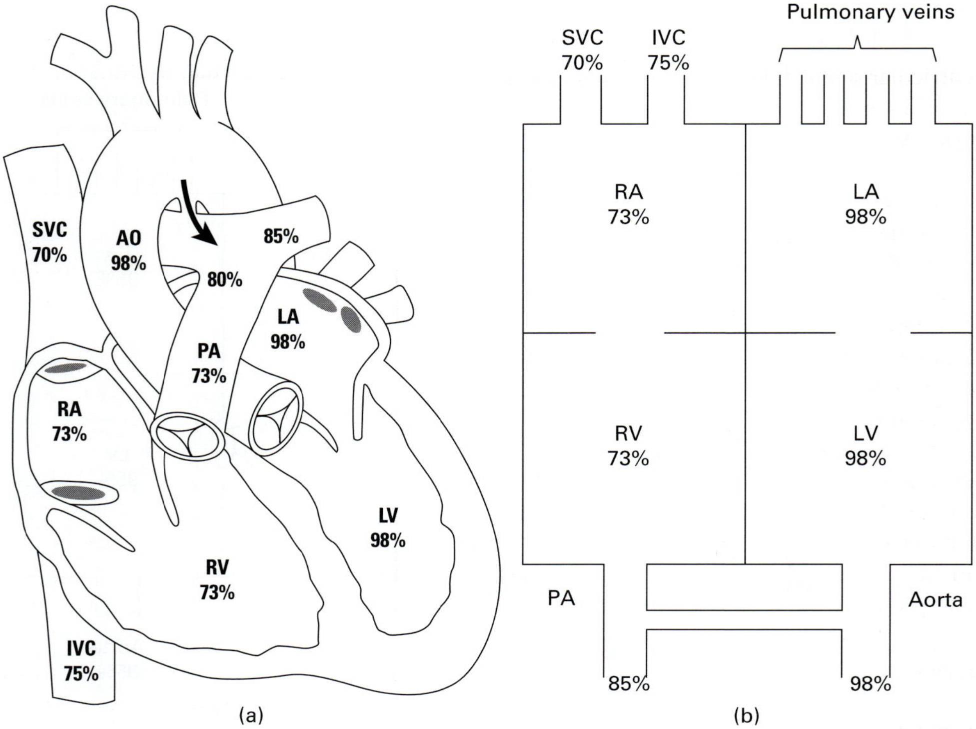

Figure 26.5 (a and b) Patent ductus arteriosus and oxygen saturations in different chambers. LV, left ventricle; RV, right ventricle.

complex heart disease. It is commonly seen in premature babies. Hypoxaemia retards ductus closure as do prostaglandins. The magnitude and direction of the shunting are dependent on the size of the communication and the PVR.

In neonates, corrective measures include fluid restriction, supplemental oxygen and indomethacin (unless the baby is 'ductus dependent' when prostaglandins need to be given to maintain ductus patency). Maintain SaO_2 at not more than 85–90% to minimise the risk of retrolental fibroplasia.

Older patients are usually asymptomatic if the ductus is small. With a large shunt left-to-right shunting results in left ventricular volume overload and increased PBF, which if left untreated may cause irreversible pulmonary vascular occlusive disease and Eisenmenger syndrome. It may also predispose to lower respiratory tract infection, atelectasis and congestive heart failure.

Definitive Treatment

PDA is a risk for endocarditis, paradoxical emboli and congestive heart failure. Therefore, the existence of PDA is an indication for closure. However, the presence of severe pulmonary vascular obstructive disease (PVOD) is a contraindication for PDA interruption.

Transcatheter device closure of PDA by a cardiologist is less invasive than open surgery and is often done in older children. Video-assisted thoracoscopic surgery (VATS) is another option. In neonates, the PDA may be ligated or divided via a left thoracotomy. After ligation/division, BP should be measured in the lower extremities to verify that the descending aorta has not been inadvertently ligated. As the afterload increases after PDA interruption, the LV may need support.

Critically ill neonates may require a high-dose narcotic technique to minimise the stress response to surgery. Fentanyl 20 µg/kg, midazolam 0.1 mg/kg and pancuronium 0.2 mg/kg may be used as anaesthetics for premature infants. Post-op ventilation is mandatory.

Atrioventricular Septal Defect

Atrioventricular septal defect (AVSD) is associated with an atrial septal defect usually ('primum ASD'), ±a ventricular septal defect. This results in a high-volume shunt which results in pulmonary plethora and presents with signs of severe cardiac failure in infancy leading to early pulmonary hypertension. It is usually associated with an abnormal atrioventricular valve. If left untreated the reactive pulmonary hypertension will change to an irreversible state. Children with AVSD develop Eisenmenger syndrome usually by the age of 1–2 years, with 4% survival beyond 5 years.

In babies with unrepaired AVSDs, it is better to target a saturation of 94% and avoid 100% O_2. Oxygen is a potent pulmonary vasodilator and the reduction in PVR with O_2 can increase PBF significantly in unrestricted shunts and worsen cardiac failure and present as breathlessness.

Eisenmenger Syndrome

The development of pulmonary hypertension secondary to long-standing left-to-right shunting is referred to as Eisenmenger syndrome. The PVR is more than the SVR at this stage and the flow through the shunt reverses. This may transiently improve the signs of cardiac failure with a reduction of PBF but with worsening cyanosis. Surgical closure of the shunt is not possible at this stage as the PVR is too high and the RV will fail without the shunting.

Non-cardiac surgery should only be performed if absolutely essential in patients with Eisenmenger physiology. Eisenmenger patients tend to be cyanotic with a saturation of about 85%. This results in polycythaemia and an increased risk of thrombosis. These patients are at risk of platelet number and function abnormality as well as coagulation abnormalities.

Predictors of mortality in Eisenmenger syndrome include the following:

1. Syncope
2. Age at presentation or development of symptoms
3. Poor functional class
4. Supraventricular dysrhythmias
5. Elevated right atrial pressures
6. Low oxygen saturation (less than 85%)
7. Renal insufficiency
8. Severe right ventricular dysfunction
9. Trisomy 21

Pulmonary Hypertension

The primary haemodynamic goal is ***to maintain the SVR and prevent increases in the PVR***. An acute increase in the PVR will cause right ventricular failure with decreased cardiac output whether there is an intracardiac shunt or not. In these cases, bradycardia precedes cardiac arrest. Prevention of pulmonary hypertensive crisis includes hyperventilating with higher FiO_2, correction of acidosis, maintenance of normothermia, inotropic support, suppression of surgical sympathetic stimulation and avoidance of high intrathoracic pressure. General anaesthesia with optimal control of ventilation with regional anaesthesia is a good anaesthetic choice. Spinal and epidural anaesthesia are relatively contraindicated due to a significant decrease in the SVR, especially in patients with unrestrictive shunts. Inhaled nitric oxide is highly desirable when managing these patients, but it requires special equipment for administration.

Avoid prolonged fasting and ensure intravenous hydration. Euvolemic phlebotomy is not a routine practise, but may be considered, in consultation with the cardiologist, when the haematocrit is >65%.

Management of Pulmonary Hypertensive Crisis

The PHT crisis is evident by a fall in oxygen saturation and blood pressure. The goal of treatment is to reduce the PVR and increase cardiac output by giving 100% O_2, optimising analgesia, treatment of metabolic acidosis, adrenaline infusion and pulmonary vasodilators (NO, Sildenafil via NG tube).

Shunt Lesions: Right-to-Left Shunt

Right-to-left (R→L) shunt results in deoxygenated blood entering the systemic circulation, which results in cyanosis. Haemodynamic consequences of right-to-left (R→L) shunts include *decreased PBF, hypoxaemia*, LV volume load and LV dysfunction.

A child with chronic hypoxaemia compensates by maintaining a high haematocrit. However, *haematocrit in excess of 60%* is known to increase the tendency to renal and cerebral thromboembolic phenomena, increased blood viscosity and vascular resistance, increased incidence of coagulopathies and decreased cardiopulmonary reserve.

Haemodynamic goals for right-to-left shunts include the following:

- Avoid increase in the PVR and oxygenate well but avoid hyperoxia
- Maintain high SVR. Avoid hypovolemia. Fluid administration to maintain good intravascular volume. Phenylephrine for treatment of hypotension (5 mcg/kg). Ketamine may be considered for induction.
- Maintain good BP (avoid hypotension).
- Minimise intrathoracic pressure: use pressure-controlled ventilation with low inspiratory pressures, low PEEP and ensure complete neuromuscular blockade. These should be adjusted to get a good balance between good ventilation and an increase in PVR. Also, if the increased peak airway pressure (PAW) is resulting in desaturations it may be due to the effect on preload.

In children with a (R→L) shunt, inhalational induction is slower than normal. In the presence of R→L shunts, the physiological dead space is more and results in end-tidal carbon dioxide ($EtCO_2$) consistently underestimating the $PaCO_2$. The lower the patient's arterial oxygen saturation (SaO_2), the greater the difference between arterial CO_2 and $EtCO_2$.

The onset of action of drugs administered intravenously (IV) may be more rapid in the presence of a R→L shunt since the dilutional effect in the lungs is not present. For this reason, it may be prudent to reduce the rate of IV injection of depressant drugs in these patients.

Great care needs to be taken to *avoid systemic hypotension* because this will increase the magnitude of the right-to-left shunt and worsen cyanosis. Pharmacological-induced responses that decrease SVR (volatile anaesthetics, histamine release, alpha adrenergic block, direct peripheral vasodilation) will increase the magnitude of the R→L shunt and accentuate arterial hypoxaemia. Spinal anaesthesia, which causes peripheral vasodilation and reduces venous return, similarly has deleterious haemodynamic effects in patients with R→L shunts. Acute hypovolaemia will also tend to increase the magnitude of the R→L shunt.

Positive end expiratory pressure (PEEP) can increase the magnitude of the R→L shunt and must be carefully titrated.

Meticulous avoidance of air in the venous line prevents the occurrence of paradoxical emboli. Nitrous oxide should be avoided, as this will cause air emboli, if they occur, to increase in size.

Practical Caveats

It is important to have a sleeping/sedated child for induction. Premedication should be considered to ensure this, but supplemental oxygen should be administered. Hypercyanotic spells can happen during an induction or during the perioperative period. Knee chest position/abdominal compression or bilateral femoral compression are effective manoeuvres to improve the SVR.

While it is important to maintain oxygenation remember that 100% oxygen will not correct desaturation as the reason for hypoxia is usually the worsening of the right-to-left shunt. Desaturation is best corrected by increasing the SVR and decreasing the PVR.

It is important to note the baseline saturations of the patient and titrate to that level.

Meticulous avoidance of air bubbles is crucial.

Tetralogy of Fallot (Fig. 26.6 a,b)

Pathology

Non-restrictive VSD (cyanosis), pulmonary outflow obstruction (valvular, supravalvular and infravalvular), overriding of the aorta and right ventricular hypertrophy (compensation for right ventricular outflow tract obstruction [RVOTO]).

The child may present with cyanosis at birth and may develop cyanotic 'spells' in infancy, due to spasms of muscle bundles in the right ventricular outflow tract in response to a stimulus like crying (adrenergic stimulation). An older child may 'squat', when tired, as a response to a 'spell' in order to increase pulmonary blood flow (by compression on the abdominal aorta increasing the SVR). Chronic hypoxia is associated with clubbing.

Haemodynamics

The aorta receives blood from the right ventricle as well as from the left ventricle. The amount of

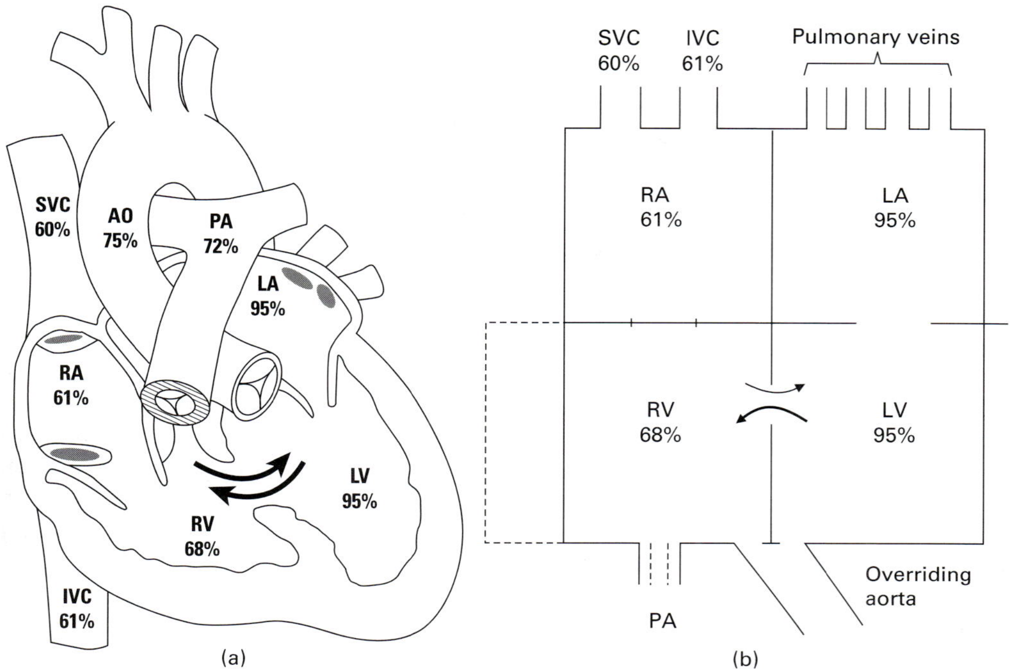

Figure 26.6 (a and b) (a)Tetralogy of Fallot. (b)Tetralogy of Fallot with oxygen saturations in different chambers. LV, left ventricle; RV, right ventricle.

shunt depends on the degree of pulmonary outflow obstruction, the relative SVR and the PVR (least important).

The degree of **cyanosis** depends on the magnitude and direction of the shunt. The resistance to flow across the right ventricular outflow tract (RVOT) is relatively fixed in patients with TOF; thus, *changes in SVR affect the magnitude of right-to-left shunting*. A decrease in SVR worsens right-to-left shunting, whereas an increase in SVR decreases right-to-left shunting. Therefore, ketamine, which increases the SVR, is often considered an ideal agent for induction of anaesthesia.

Modified Blalock–Taussig (innominate or subclavian artery-to-PA) shunts are sometimes used to palliate children, by increasing pulmonary blood flow, prior to definitive repair. The shunt is usually restrictive so as to ensure just enough PBF to maintain saturations of about 85%. Cyanosis persists if the shunt is too small. If there is increased PBF, pulmonary hypertension may result. If the shunt is too big, the increase in PBF can cause cardiac failure with systemic to pulmonary runoff resulting in low systemic blood pressure. BT shunt results in chronic left ventricular volume overload. In patients who have previously undergone a Blalock-Taussig (BT) shunt, preservation of SVR continues to be important for maintaining shunt flow. It is crucial to maintain blood pressure as a fall in blood pressure will reduce PBF, which results in desaturation. In these patients, BP and SpO_2 monitoring should not be attempted on the arm of the shunted side. Auscultation reveals a continuous murmur in the second right intercostal space in the midclavicular line.

Complete correction involves closure of VSD with relief of obstruction of the RV outflow tract, often with a 'patch'. In patients who have had a complete correction, do an ECG to look for sinus and AV node dysfunction or atrial and ventricular dysrhythmia. Residual pulmonary regurgitation (PR) is common with RVOT patch repair. This can result in free pulmonary regurgitation causing arrhythmia and RV failure later in life. With patch-less repair and preservation of the pulmonary valve leaflet, the PR is minimised. Other complications of complete correction are ascending aortic aneurysm, residual VSD, left ventricular dysfunction, persistent pulmonary hypertension from previous

Initially, management is with prostaglandin E_1 therapy to maintain ductal patency and encourage intercirculatory mixing. Newborns with significant cyanosis need to undergo a balloon atrial septostomy to enlarge or artificially create an ASD with left-to-right shunting of blood so as to increase arterial saturation to 80–90%. Definitive surgical treatment includes an **arterial switch operation** along with translocation of coronary arteries, thus achieving a normal physiology. After correction, they generally behave as well-compensated corrected CHD patients. Occasionally, residual problems such as coronary artery ischaemia due to anatomic problems with reimplantation, stenosis or incompetence of the neoaortic root are seen. Myocardial ischemia due to narrowed, occluded coronary arteries, as well as endothelial dysfunction and ascending aortic aneurysm are seen in survivors.

Mustard or Senning's procedure were older surgical techniques to repair TGA. Both reroute blood flow at the atrial level. The surviving patients have significant ventricular dysfunction and atrial arrhythmias. Sinus node dysfunction is common and 40–50% need pacemakers. Residual atrial or ventricular level shunts should be looked for in the ECHO.

Anaesthetic Management

Anaesthetic goals include *maintaining pulmonary blood flow by reducing PVR and increasing contractility*. Decrease PVR while maintaining or increasing SVR and while maintaining heart rate at above normal levels to ensure maximum mixing. *Hypotension below 60/30 mmHg should be avoided because it would worsen coronary perfusion pressure.* These patients may have haematocrits in excess of 70%, which may contribute to the high incidence of cerebral venous thrombosis. *Dehydration must be avoided* during the perioperative period. Oral fluids should not be withheld for prolonged periods. Manage dysrhythmia.

Drugs administered intravenously are distributed to vital organs with minimal dilution; hence, the dose and the rates of administration of intravenous anaesthetics may have to be decreased. The onset of inhalational anaesthesia is delayed as only small amounts of inhaled drugs reach the systemic circulation. Ketamine is a useful drug for induction. Opioids, muscle relaxants and benzodiazapines may be used to supplement anaesthesia. Volatile anaesthetics should be used cautiously as there is a risk of myocardial depression. The ability of pancuronium to mildly increase the heart rate and blood pressure may be useful. Avoid drugs causing histamine release which can result in a drop in SVR.

Congenitally Corrected TGA (L-TGA)

In these cases, the LV is the subpulmonic ventricle and the RV is the systemic ventricle. The potential issues in these cases include complete heart block, arrhythmias (atrial and ventricular), anatomic right ventricular failure and systemic AV valve regurgitation, which can happen in both unrepaired and repaired cases. These patients are prone to arrhythmia and heart failure.

Obstructive Lesions

A number of defects limit left ventricular outflow. They include aortic stenosis, hypoplastic left heart syndrome, interrupted aortic arch and coarctation of the aorta. The haemodynamic consequences of these left-sided obstructive lesions include decreased systemic perfusion, low cardiac output, hypotension, left ventricular pressure overload, left ventricular hypertrophy, diastolic dysfunction followed by left ventricular failure, subendocardial ischaemia and decreased coronary perfusion.

Neonates with severe obstruction need immediate intervention. The reduced left ventricular chamber size, left ventricular hypertrophy and endocardial fibroelastosis result in such poor LV function that intractable LV failure often persists after intervention. Mortality is high in them.

Older children with moderate-to-severe obstruction present with decreased exercise tolerance, syncopal episodes, myocardial ischaemia or left ventricular failure.

The *goals of anaesthesia* in left-sided obstructive lesions are to provide adequate coronary perfusion, decrease myocardial oxygen demands and maintain cardiac output so as to prevent subendocardial ischaemia and ischaemia to vital organs. This can be achieved by avoiding tachycardia or severe bradycardia, maintaining preload, SVR and diastolic pressure. Hypotension can be precipitated by tachycardia, bradycardia, hypovolaemia or dysrhythmias. Tachycardia may prevent adequate ventricular filling during diastole. Dysrhythmias should be treated aggressively, as atrial function is critical to the maintenance of an adequate cardiac output. Should there be a precipitous decline in blood pressure secondary to an atrial rhythm disturbance, cardioversion is required as inadequate diastolic pressure results in myocardial ischaemia.

Fasting times should be minimised or intravenous fluids should be started as these children do not tolerate dehydration. Volume losses and hypotension must be promptly treated. Volume replacement should be pursued cautiously because pulmonary oedema may result depending on the functional status of the left ventricle.

Sedation may be used for older children to prevent anxiety. In aortic stenosis and idiopathic hypertrophic subaortic stenosis, phenylephrine can be used to increase SVR and mean arterial pressure (MAP).

In dynamic obstructive lesions as is seen in infundibular stenosis in TOF, hypovolaemia, light anaesthesia, direct-acting inotropic drugs and low SVR should be avoided as these conditions aggravate the obstruction.

Aortic Valve Stenosis

Aortic valve stenosis (AS) is one of the most common congenital heart lesions accounting for 5–10% of all congenital heart defects. The obstruction to the left ventricular outflow tract may be at the valvular level (70%), subvalvular level (14%), supravalvular level (8%) or multiple levels. Aortic stenosis is characterised by LV pressure overload and hypertrophy. Twenty percent of cases may be associated with VSD, PDA or coarctation.

The age of presentation is a significant risk factor. The majority of patients who present before 3 months of age require ventilator and inotropic support. Neonates with critical AS will have circulatory failure as the ventricle is unable to generate flow through the obstructed LV outflow tract (LVOT). The R→L shunt through a PDA in the presence of a VSD decompresses the LV and perfuses the lower body. Alternatively, the RV will perfuse the entire body via the ductus arteriosus. In older children, the LV becomes hypertrophied and hyperdynamic. These patients have an imbalance between myocardial supply and demand and are at risk of subendocardial ischaemia. If left unrepaired, it can cause pulmonary oedema (elevated LV filling pressure secondary to LVH), PHT, myocardial ischemia (increased demand with reduced subendocardial perfusion) syncope (fixed cardiac output) and post-stenotic dilatation. These factors place the patient at an increased risk for sudden death. Complications of repair are aortic regurgitation and LV diastolic dysfunction.

For anaesthetic management, goals are to avoid tachycardia, hypotension and factors that increase myocardial oxygen consumption.

Coarctation of Aorta (Fig. 26.8)

In coarctation of the aorta, there is aortal narrowing opposite the insertion of the ligamentum arteriosum near the left subclavian artery. The type of coarctation is described by its relationship to the ductus arteriosus as pre-ductal, juxtaductal and post-ductal. The lesions presenting in infancy are usually **pre-ductal** and are characterised by poor collateral flow. The babies are dependent on ductal patency and will require prostaglandins to maintain ductal patency till corrective surgery. The juxtaductal and post-ductal coarctation are characterised by significant collateral blood flow. Collaterals develop from the subclavian artery initially and intercostal arteries later in childhood. As many as 50–85% of patients with coarctation

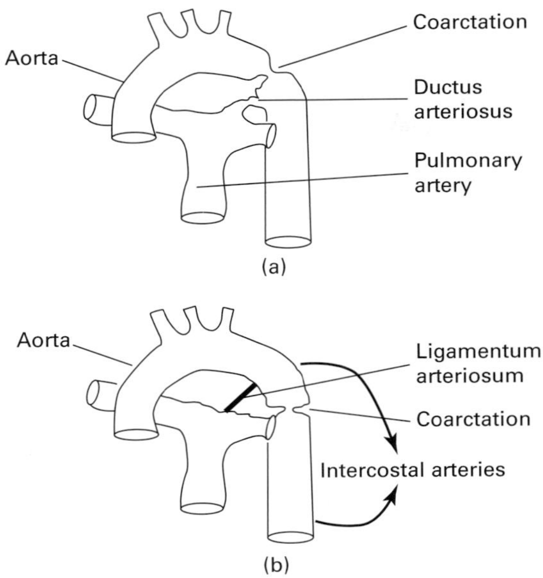

Figure 26.8 Coarctation of the aorta. (a) Pre-ductal coarctation and (b) post-ductal coarctation.

have a bicuspid aortic valve. These lesions are characterised by LV pressure overload hypertrophy. Endothelial dysfunction can cause diffuse aortopathy. Other pathologies to look for are aortic aneurysms, intracranial aneurysms (10%) and premature coronary artery disease.

The *diagnostic features* of coarctation of the aorta are systolic and mean blood pressure (BP) differences between the upper and lower extremities. The symptomatology varies depending on the severity of coarctation. Mild forms are nearly asymptomatic while in severe obstruction, the PDA may be the only source of systemic supply and LV dysfunction is common. Both LV systolic and diastolic dysfunction can occur. In the neonate, the aortic obstruction may precipitate congestive heart failure and cardiogenic shock. Such patients require inotropic support and diuretics. Metabolic acidosis should be corrected to improve left ventricular function.

Anaesthetic Management

The choice of the anaesthetic technique depends on the location of the coarctation, presence of good collaterals, severity of hypertension, coexisting cardiac anomalies, presence of congestive cardiac failure due to the marked increase in afterload and the presence of a left-to-right shunt. Preferred sites for blood pressure monitoring are from the preductal arteries (right arm) as inaccurate blood pressure (left arm) readings can be observed either in cases of residual/re-coarctation or if previous left subclavian angioplasty was performed. Aim to maintain the BP at or just below normal values but avoid dramatic reductions in the BP to prevent drastic falls in the cardiac output. Anaesthetic goals are to avoid tachycardia and hypotension. Post-operative hypertension is common and should be managed accordingly.

Blood pressure and pulse oximetry are best done on the right upper limb.

An overall view of the desirable haemodynamic changes in congenital heart disease is seen in **Table 26.8**.

Univentricular Hearts Undergone Stage 2 Palliation (Bidirectional Glenn Shunt)

In creating a bidirectional Glenn shunt (BDGS), the SVC is separated from the right atrium and anastomosed to the right pulmonary artery thus allowing the passive central venous pressure to be the driving force for pulmonary circulation. The inferior vena cava blood drainage mixes with pulmonary venous blood either at the atrial level or at the single ventricle and thus acts similarly to shunt physiology providing a reliable cardiac output. So, in this stage of palliation, the pulmonary circulation is

Table 26.8 Desired Haemodynamic Changes in Congenital Cardiac Disease

Congenital Heart Diseases	Pre-load	Pulmonary Vascular Resistance	Systemic Vascular Resistance	Heart Rate	Contractility
ASD	↑	↑	↓	N	N
VSD (R→L)	N	↓	↑	N	N
VSD (L→R)	↑	↑	↓	N	N
IHSS	↑	N	N → ↑	↓ *	↓ *
PDA	↑	↑	↓	N	N
Valvar PS	↑	↓	N	↓	↑
Infundibular PS	↑	↓	N	↓	↓ *
AS	↑	N	↑ *	↓ *	N → ↑
MS	↑	N → ↓	N	↓ *	N → ↑
AR	↑	N	↓	N → ↑	N → ↑
MR	↑	N → ↓	↓	N → ↑	N → ↑

AR, aortic regurgitation; AS, aortic stenosis; ASD, atrial septal defect; IHSS, idoppathic hypertrophic subaortic stenosis; MR, mitral regurgitation; MS, mitral stenosis; PDA, patent ductus arteriosus; PS, pulmonary stenosis; VSD, ventricular septal defect.

*Primary consideration.

essentially separated from systemic circulation thereby unloading the single ventricle and reducing the workload significantly. Superior cavopulmonary anastomosis, in the absence of an additional source of PBF, provides oxygen saturations ranging from 75 to 80%.

These subsets of children are amenable for non-cardiac surgery as the creation of a bidirectional Glenn shunt, i.e., superior cavopulmonary anastomosis has eliminated the dependency of the pulmonary circulation on the systemic circulation and created upper body venous drainage into the pulmonary circulation to provide a reliable but limited pulmonary blood flow. This stage 2 palliation is performed when the pulmonary vascular resistance declines after 2–3 months of life.

Anaesthetic and peri-operative management of these patients must involve a thorough understanding of the circulatory physiology of BDG shunt. The most important concept in managing these patients is that the PBF is dependent upon venous return from cerebral blood flow and the relative resistance of the pulmonary vascular bed (PVR). Cerebral blood flow is dependent on cerebrovascular resistance which in turn is influenced by alterations of physiological variables like $PaCO_2$ and H+ concentration (acidosis/alkalosis). The response to the alterations in these physiological variables has diametrically opposite effects on PVR and cerebrovascular resistance. So, the ventilator management is tailored to maintain a $PaCO_2$ of 40–45 mmHg and pH 7.37–7.4 to augment cerebral blood flow without increasing PVR. This mild hypercarbia enhances PBF and arterial saturations as well as tissue oxygen delivery due to reduced SVR. The positive pressure ventilation may impede PBF but by minimising the mean airway pressure as well as by providing adequate expiratory time it is possible to optimise the PBF. Spontaneous ventilation has definite advantages in this type of circulation so early extubation is recommended.

Summary

Non-cardiac surgery in children with cardiac lesions are often accomplished without any problems. However, it is essential to have a thorough knowledge of the anatomy and physiology of the lesion, and problems associated with it. It is ideal to have a cardiologist's opinion and investigations prior to surgery and a well-equipped ICU with good protocols where these children may be monitored and managed post-operatively. Special attention should be paid to very small babies and children who present with a history of congestive cardiac failure, severe pulmonary hypertension or residual lesion or sequelae after correction. These children run a higher risk of perioperative morbidity and mortality.

SUGGESTED READINGS

1. Clifford M. Children with congenital heart disease for non-cardiac surgery. In: Clinical Pediatric Anesthesia – a Case-based Handbook. Goldschneider KR, Davidson AJ, Wittkugel EP, Skinner AV (eds). Oxford University Press, New York, 2012; pp. 293–300.
2. Franco SA, Hines RL. Congenital heart disease. In: Stoeltings Anesthesia and Coexisting Disease. Hines RL, Marschall K, eds. Elsevier Saunders, Philadelphia, 2012:48–72.
3. Nishimura RN, Carabello BA, Faxon DP, Freed MD, Lytle BW, O'Gara PT, O'Rourke RA, Shah PM. ACC/AHA 2008 Guideline Update on Valvular Heart Disease: Focused Update on Infective Endocarditis: A Report of the American College of Cardiology/American Heart Association Task Force on Practice Guidelines: Endorsed by the Society of Cardiovascular Anesthesiologists, Society for Cardiovascular Angiography and Interventions, and Society of Thoracic Surgeons. *Circulation* 2008; 118:887–896.
4. Thomas J. Anaesthesia for the child with congenital heart disease: Pointers and pitfalls Congenital heart disease Nov/Dec 2011 Vol.29 No.11 CME 463, www.cmej.org.za.
5. Brown ML. Anesthesia in pediatric patients with congenital heart disease undergoing noncardiac surgery: Defining the risk. *J Cardiothorac Vasc Anesth* 2019; 00:1–9.
6. Flannery KM, Raviraj D. Anaesthesia in Children With Congenital Heart Disease for Noncardiac Surgery. ATOTW 467, https://resources.wfsahq.org/anaesthesia-tutorial-of-the-week/.
7. Smith S, Walke A. Anaesthetic implications of congenital heart disease for children undergoing non-cardiac surgery. *Anesth Int Care Med* 2021; 22(9):563–569.
8. Faraoni D, Zurakowski D, Vo D, et al. A postoperative outcomes in children with and without

congenital heart disease undergoing noncardiac surgery. *JACC* 2016; 67(7):793–801.

9. Cannesson M, Earing MG, Collange V, et al. Anesthesia for noncardiac surgery in adults with congenital heart disease. *Anesthesiology* 2009; 111:432–440.
10. Walker I. Anaesthesia for non-cardiac surgery in children with congenital heart disease. Update in Anaesthesia, www.wfsahq.org/resources/update-in-anaesthesia (March 8, 2022).

27 Arrhythmias – Causes, Diagnosis and Treatment

Basanth Kumar Rayani • Aanchal Bharuka

Rhythm disturbances are less common in children as compared to adults. They could be benign or point towards a systemic pathology and rarely may be life-threatening. Identification of arrhythmia and its management is very important for safe perioperative care.

Electrocardiogram (ECG) is an essential component of ASA (American Society of Anaesthesiologists) monitoring standards. A baseline 12-lead ECG is not advocated in a healthy child pre-operatively. However, it may be done under the following conditions:

- History of palpitations, syncope and cyanotic episodes
- History of arrhythmia
- History of sudden deaths in the family
- Presence of congenital heart disease
- Syndromic children or those with undiagnosed myopathies

Reading and analysing ECG in children as compared to adults requires the knowledge of normal variations.

Recording 12-Lead ECG in Children

Standardisation is to be kept at 5 mm/mV as children require a higher voltage and this should be ensured during interpretation. Avoiding movement artefacts could be challenging in younger children, and this can be reduced by applying limb leads in a proximal location, distracting or sedating the child. Additional right-sided leads (V3R and V4R) may be required (Fig. 27.1).

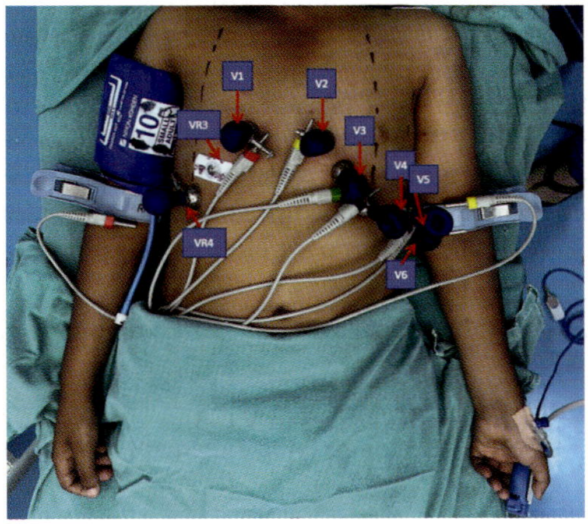

Figure 27.1 Electrocardiogram (ECG) leads placement in children.

V3R is placed in between V1 and V4R, and V4R is placed at the fifth intercostal space in the midclavicular line.

Differences in Paediatric ECG as Compared to Adult

A paediatric ECG is different from an adult ECG. Knowing these differences will prevent us from mislabelling them as abnormal. The basic mechanisms of depolarisation, repolarisation, electrical wave generation and re-entrant mechanisms are similar to that of adults. But the smaller size of the heart, lower thoracic impedance and a relative predominance of the right ventricle over the midazolam, etomidate, ketamine and bupivacaine may cause slight prolongation of QT interval. So, these medications should be avoided in cases of prolonged QTC interval and not be used in combination.

ECG features: Twisting QRS around the isoelectric baseline, prolonged QT interval.

Treatment: Magnesium – This is the cornerstone of treatment for torsades (Table 27.3).

Isoproterenol is indicated in cases where the heart rate is below 60 bpm to maintain the rate near 90 bpm.

Long QT Syndrome

Long QT syndrome is a disturbance with ventricular repolarisation of the heart predisposing the child to develop ventricular Torsades, ventricular tachycardia (VT), ventricular fibrillation (VF) or bradyarrhythmias. It can occur in congenital or acquired forms. In the *congenital form*, genetic defects exist in sodium and potassium channels. The *acquired form* may be caused by endocrine, neurologic or electrolyte abnormalities and due to certain medications like antipsychotics. The child is at increased risk of syncope, cardiac arrest and sudden death.

ECG features: Prolongation of corrected QT interval.

Treatment: Beta-blockers, magnesium, lidocaine and phenytoin (Table 27.3).

Avoidance of exacerbating factors like sympathetic stimulation, correction of electrolyte imbalance and treatment of the underlying cause.

Ventricular Fibrillation

Ventricular fibrillation is rare in children and is usually a result of the termination of ventricular tachycardia. Most of the time it does not occur as the first rhythm. It should be treated promptly, whenever present.

ECG features: Irregular chaotic rhythm; P-waves, QRS and T-waves cannot be identified on ECG

Treatment: Defibrillation

Cardioversion and Defibrillation

Defibrillation

Defibrillation is the asynchronous delivery of shock at any point of the cardiac cycle. It is indicated in ventricular fibrillation and pulseless ventricular tachycardia.

Defibrillator electrode/paddles in children: Infant paddles for children less than 10 kg and adult paddles for children weighing more than 10 kg (12 cm more superior than 8 cm)

Electrode/Paddle position

Anterior/Apex position: Right of sternum below the clavicle and the other one in left mid-axillary line at the level of nipples lateral to breast tissue.

Anterior/Posterior position: The centre of the anterior pad is placed slightly to the left of the sternum while the posterior is placed in the middle of the upper back.

For the conduction interface, jelly provided with a defibrillator should be used while saline or isopropyl alcohol is to be avoided. The minimum distance between the paddles should be 3 cm.

Energy for defibrillation – first attempt with 2 J/kg, second and subsequent doses are 4 J/kg to the maximum of 10 J/kg.

Figure 27.15 shows paediatric paddles, and Figures 27.16 and 27.17 show placement positions.

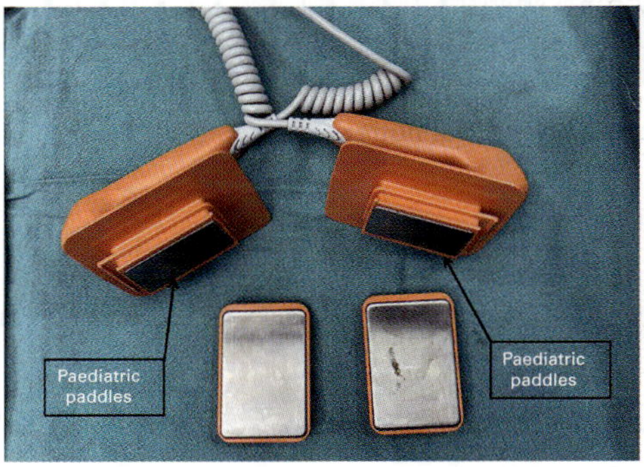

Figure 27.15 Paediatric paddles.

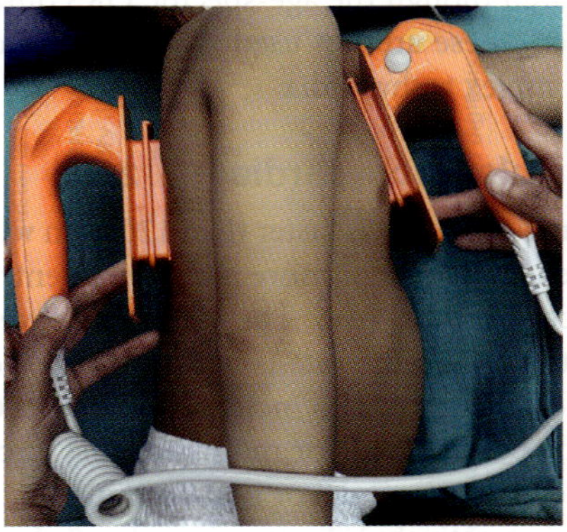

Figure 27.16 Anteroposterior paddle placement.

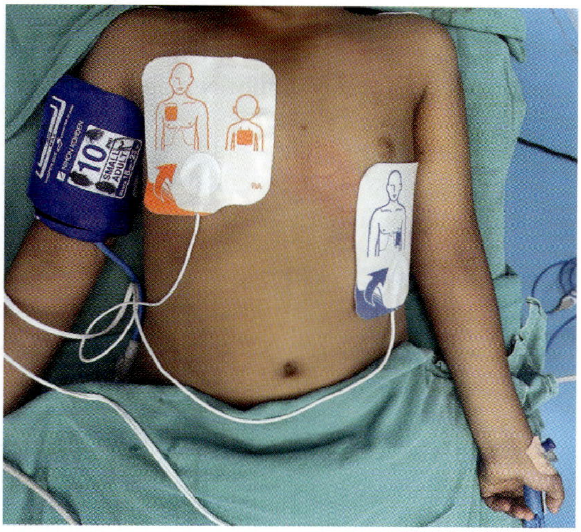

Figure 27.17 Anteroapical pad placement.

Cardioversion

Cardioversion is the delivery of shock synchronus with an R-wave during the cardiac cycle. It is indicated in unstable patients but with organised rhythms such as SVT, AF, atrial fibrillation and ventricular tachycardia with a pulse.

Energy for cardioversion is 0.5–1 J/kg for the first shock and 2 J/kg for subsequent shocks.

Automated External Defibrillator

These may be used in infants and children to deliver a shock in cases of out-of-hospital ventricular fibrillation or pulseless ventricular tachycardia. The devices used include the following:

1. Manual defibrillator for infants
2. Automated external defibrillator (AED) with dose attenuator for children <8 years and weight less than 25 kg
3. AED without dose attenuator for children of 9 years of age or older

Antiarrhythmic Medications

Table 27.3 depicts details on commonly used anti-arrhythmic medications as per Vaughan–Williams classification.

Bradyarrhythmias

Bradyarrhythmias are classified based on the site of the block as sinus bradycardia, AV block and bundle branch block, which are further subdivided as shown below. Figure 27.18 depicts the classification of bradyarrhythmias.

Sinus Bradycardia

Sinus bradycardia is a heart rate lower than the lowest normal for the age. It can be seen physiologically during sleep, rest or in athletic children. Pathologically, the commonest cause of bradycardia in children is hypoxia. It can also be seen during hypothermia, hyperkalemia, hypercalcemia, raised intracranial pressure, acute illness, hypothyroidism, beta-blockers, digitalis, etc. Intraoperatively, it can be seen when large doses of opioids like fentanyl are administered, with reversal agents like neostigmine and sugammadex, after phenylephrine administration, transiently and during tracheal suctioning. The child may have symptoms like syncope, fatigue, sleepiness, exercise intolerance

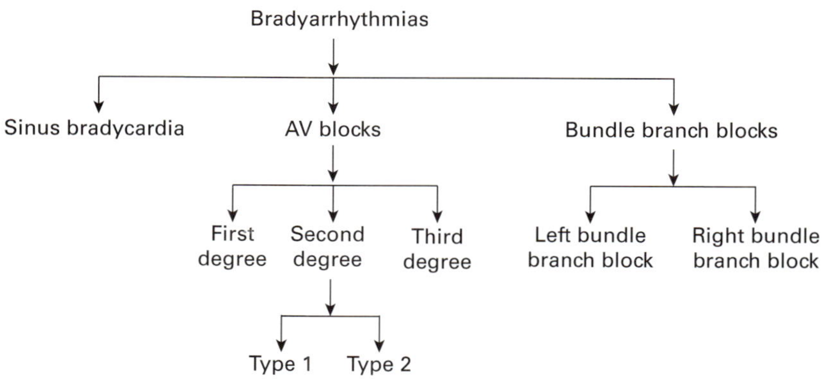

Figure 27.18 Classification of bradyarrhythmias. AV, atrioventricular.

and nightmares. Certain reflexes causing bradycardia, which are important for anaesthesiologists, include the following:

- Oculocardiac reflex: During ophthalmic surgery, activation of the ophthalmic branch of the trigeminal nerve due to traction of extraocular muscles causes significant bradycardia and may even cause asystole.
- Vagal reflex: In abdominal laparoscopic surgeries (due to rapid carbon dioxide insufflation for pneumoperitoneum), peritoneal stretching occurs during both laparoscopic and open procedures.
- Bezold-Jarisch reflex: Severe bradycardia, asystole associated with hypotension during spinal anaesthesia, though not very common in children.

ECG features: Sinus rhythm, decreased rate, P-wave followed by QRS complex

Treatment: If haemodynamically stable, no treatment is required.

Adrenaline: 0.01 mg/kg

Atropine: 0.02 mg/kg, if vagal mediated

Pacing in resistant cases

Heart Blocks/Conduction Abnormalities

This implies abnormal impulse conduction to ventricles from the atria through the AV node. Causes can range from enhanced vagal tone, structural heart disease, post-cardiac surgery for congenital heart disease, inflammation, infection, channelopathy, myocardial infarction and trauma. The various types of blocks have been described in Table 27.4.

Table 27.4 Heart Blocks

	First Degree	Mobitz Type 1	Mobitz Type 2	Third Degree
ECG	Prolonged PR interval	Progressive prolongation of the PR interval, progressive shortening of RR interval and failure to conduct a beat from atria to ventricle	Constant PP interval and normal PR interval before the dropped beat	Complete AV dissociation, an atrial rate more than ventricle, independent atrial and ventricular rates
Site of block	Delay in atrium or AV node or Bundle of His	Normal QRS: AV node or proximal to the bundle of His Wide QRS: AV node, at or below the bundle of His	Mostly below the bundle of His	AV node
Causes	High vagal tone, Rheumatic fever, ASD, Epstein's anomaly, AV canal defect, medications like digitalis, amiodarone and electrolyte imbalance (calcium, potassium and hypomagnesemia)	The high vagal tone in the majority of cases	Myocarditis, post-surgical complication, CAD post-transplant and rejection post-transplant	Congenital, structural cardiac disease, maternal connective tissue disorder, post-cardiac surgeries, following EP procedures and percutaneous catheter interventions
Treatment	In the majority of children, it can be normal, and no treatment is needed. If the PR interval is more than 300 ms, then evaluation for cause is required	If during sleep: No treatment During exercise: Look for conduction abnormality	If irreversible cause: Permanent pacemaker implantation	Pacemaker

ASD, atrial septal defect; AV, atrioventricular; CAD, coronary artery disease; ECG, Electrocardiogram; EP, electrophysiological; PR, pulse rate.

Table 27.5 ECG Changes Occurring in Common Conditions

Hypokalaemia	Increased P-wave amplitude, prolonged PR interval, ST depression, T-wave flattening or inversion, prominent U-wave, apparent long QT, ectopics, SVT, AF, atrial fibrillation, VT, VF and Torsade de pointes
Hyperkalaemia (mEq/L)	5.5–6.5 – Peaked P-wave 6.5–7.0 – P-wave widening PR prolongation P-wave disappearance 7.0–9.0 – Bradyarrhythmias >9.0 – Asystole, VF and PEA
Hypocalcaemia	Prolonged QTc due to prolonged ST segment
Hypercalcaemia	Short QT, Osborn J-wave and ventricular fibrillation
Hyponatraemia	No significant change
Hypernatraemia	No significant change
Hypomagnesemia	Prolong PR, QT, ectopics, VT and Torsade de pointes
Hypothermia	Bradycardia, prolonged PR, QRS, QT intervals, Osborn wave, AF, PVC and ventricular fibrillation
Digitalis toxicity	SVT with slow ventricular rate, PVC, sinus bradycardia, AV blocks, atrial fibrillation

AV, atrioventricular; PEA, pulseless electrical activity; PVC, premature ventricular complex.

Bundle Branch Blocks

- Right bundle branch block (RBBB) can be seen as a congenital form or can be caused due to arrhythmogenic right ventricular cardiomyopathy (ARVC), heart transplantation, myocarditis and Brugada syndrome.
- It is important to differentiate RSR's pattern of ventricular strain seen commonly in children from RBBB where a wide QRS will also be seen.
- Left bundle branch block (LBBB) can be caused due to Kearns–Sayre syndrome, myotonic dystrophy, etc.

ECG features: RBBB – RSR in V1, LBBB – RSR in V6

Treatment: If RBBB is asymptomatic, then no treatment is needed. If symptomatic a pacemaker is indicated; while in LBBB, an early pacemaker is the treatment.

ECG Changes Occurring in Common Conditions

Apart from arrhythmias, certain metabolic conditions have pathognomonic ECG features that could be life-threatening. These are depicted in Table 27.5.

Summary

Anaesthesiologists should be well versed in the knowledge of arrhythmias in children – the causes, the ECG features and management. In the perioperative period, they should be able to recognise, provide emergency treatment and seek expert advice from the paediatric cardiologist as appropriate.

SUGGESTED READINGS

1. Drago F, Battipaglia I, Di Mambro C. Neonatal and pediatric arrhythmias: Clinical and electrocardiographic aspects. *Card Electrophysiol Clin* 2018; 10(2):397–412.
2. Kafalı HC, Ergül Y. Common supraventricular and ventricular arrhythmias in children. *Turk Arch Pediatr* 2022; 57(5):476–488.
3. Cannon BC, Snyder CS. Disorders of Cardiac Rhythm and Conduction. In: Moss & Adams' Heart Disease in Infants, Children and Adolescents: Including the Fetus and Young Adult, 9th edition. Allen HD, Shaddy RE, Penny DJ, Feltes TF, Cetta F (eds). Wolters Kluwer, Netherlands 2016.
4. Valdes SO, Kim JJ, Miller-Hance WC. Arrhythmias: Diagnosis and Management. In: Anesthesia for Congenital Heart Disease, 3rd edition. Andropoulus DB, Stayer SA, Russell IA, Mossad EB, Miller-Hance WC (eds)., Wiley Blackwell, New Jersey 2015.
5. Sasikumar N, Kumar RK, Balaji S. Diagnosis, and management of junctional ectopic tachycardia in children. *Ann Pediatr Card* 2021; 14:372–381.

6. Lambrechts L, Fourie B. How to interpret an electrocardiogram in children. *BJA Educ* 2020; 20(8):266–277.
7. Park MK, Guntheroth WG. How to read pediatric ECGs, 3rd edition. Mosby, St Louis:;1992.
8. Davignon A, Rautaharju P, Boisselle E, et al. Normal ECG standards for infants and children. *Pediatr Cardiol* 1980; 1:123–213.
9. Saarel EV, Granger S, Kaltman JR, et al. Electrocardiograms in healthy North American children in the digital age. *Circulation: Arrhyth Electrophysiol* 2018; 11(7):e005808.
10. Adwan R, Thatcher S, Russo S, et al. Arrhythmias in children: Too fast or too slow. *Prog Pediatric Cardiol* 2022; 65:101520.

28 Cardiopulmonary Resuscitation

Smruthi S

Cessation of the heart and respiration leads to deprivation of oxygen to the brain and vital organs. This would lead to profound morbidity or even death unless it is dealt with promptly and effectively. Early identification and timely intervention are vital for improving survival particularly in paediatric patients, who may deteriorate rapidly. Each hospital should set up an emergency response team or code blue team so that sick kids receive expert care and resuscitation from the trained resuscitation team. As anaesthetists, we can take the lead in forming such teams and train team members in vital resuscitation skills.

The *paediatric chain of survival* given by AHA (American Heart Association 2020) is summarised by the following sequence:

- **IHCA** (in-hospital cardiac arrest) (**Fig. 28.1a**).
- **OHCA** (out-of-hospital cardiac arrest) (**Fig. 28.1b**).

Cardiac arrest alone rarely occurs due to cardiac problems, but usually follows a period of hypoxia and acidosis. Paediatric cardiopulmonary arrest occurs most commonly at either end of the age spectrum (<1 year and adolescence).

Cardiopulmonary Resuscitation

Cardiopulmonary resuscitation is discussed under the following headings: assessment and primary resuscitation, that is, basic life support, where no equipment or drugs are used, followed by continued resuscitation and advanced life support.

The 2020 AHA guidelines have combined the recommendations for both basic and advanced life supports, in infants, children and adolescents in a single document.

Assessment

To recognise the sick child, one must know the normal baseline values in children. **Table 28.1** shows the normal baseline haemodynamic values for different age groups.

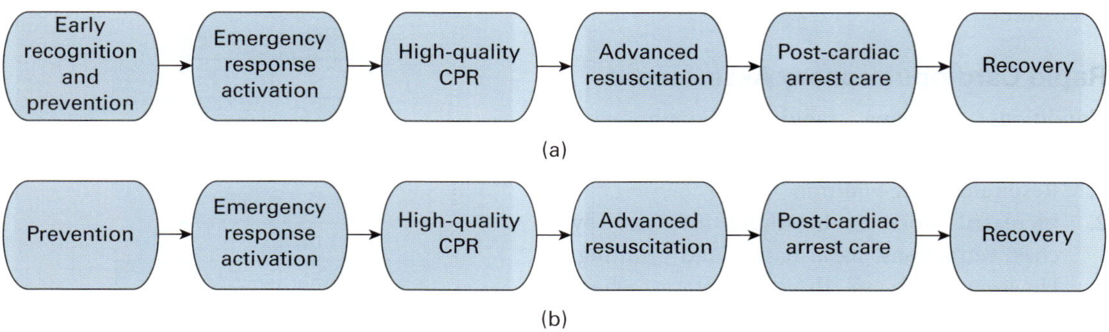

Figure 28.1 (a) IHCA (In-hospital cardiac arrest) paediatric chain of survival. (b) OHCA (Out-of-hospital cardiac arrest) paediatric chain of survival. CPR, cardiopulmonary resuscitation.

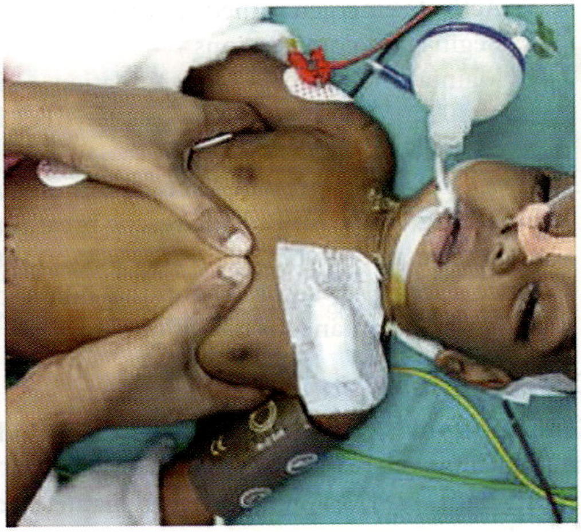

Figure 28.5 Chest compressions using encircling thumb technique in infants.

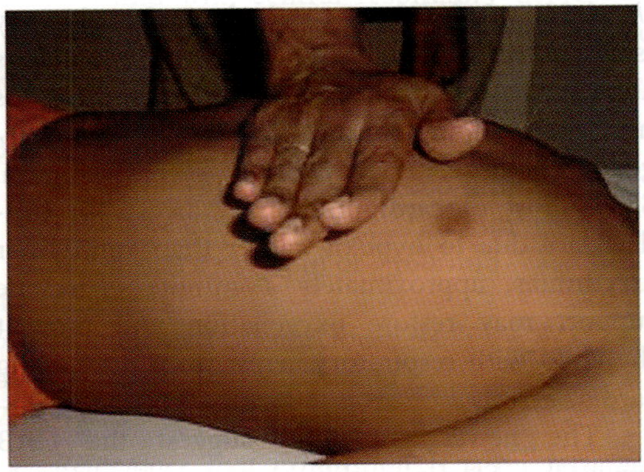

Figure 28.6 Cardiac massage in a child. Note the heel of rescuer's hand on lower sternum and fingers and not on the ribs.

side by side on the lower half of the sternum and encircle the lower part of rib cage with the rest of the hand. Press down the sternum at least 1/3rd the depth of the chest while the stretched fingers support the infants back.

2. **Chest compressions, for cardiac massage, in a child:** Steady the child's head. Place the heel of the rescuer's hand over the lower half of the sternum avoiding the xiphoid process and compress it with the elbows straight to approximately one-third to one-half the anteroposterior diameter of the chest (**Fig. 28.6**). Two-hand compression with fingers interlocked, similar to adults, may be used in bigger children if adequate depth cannot be achieved by one hand.

   Children over 8 years: Use adult technique with both hands in the centre of the chest between the nipples for chest compressions with a ratio of 15 compressions to 2 ventilations.

A – Airway

Relaxation of muscles and passive posterior displacement of tongue may lead to airway obstruction in an unconscious child. Open the airway by **head tilt and chin lift manoeuvre**. If neck injury is present, avoid head tilt and open the airway by **jaw thrust** alone.

Head Tilt – Chin Lift

Place one hand on the child's forehead and tilt the head gently back into a neutral position with the neck slightly extended (**Fig. 28.7**). Place the fingers of the other hand under the bony part of the lower jaw at the chin and lift the mandible upwards and outwards. Do not close the mouth or push soft tissue under the chin. This can worsen obstruction. If a foreign body or vomitus is present, remove it while being careful not to push it in further.

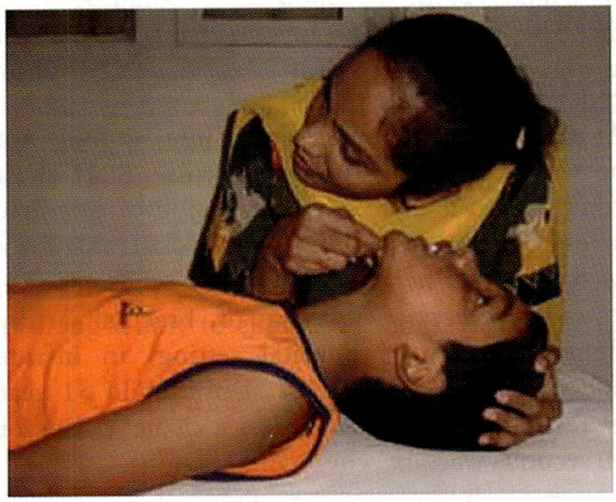

Figure 28.7 Head tilt and chin lift: Look, listen and feel.

Jaw Thrust

Place two to three fingers under each side of the lower jaw and lift the jaw upwards and outwards (**Fig. 28.8**).

If the child is conscious and demonstrates spontaneous respiratory efforts, time should not be wasted on attempts to open the airway further.

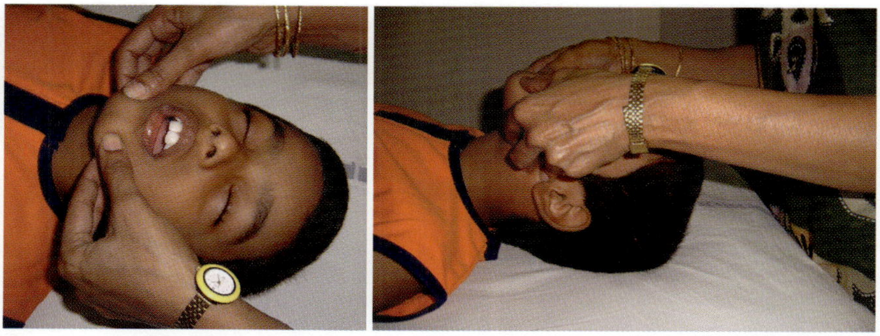

(a) (b)

Figure 28.8 Jaw thrust. (a) From the front and (b) side.

B – Breathing

- Look – for a rise and fall of chest or abdomen
- Listen –for exhaled air sounds
- Feel – for flow of exhaled air over the mouth

The classic 'Look – Listen – Feel' has been discouraged in newer guidelines due to inaccuracy and wastage of precious resuscitation time. Nevertheless, a quick assessment by a trained person like an anaesthetist need not be discouraged.

If the child is breathing effectively and there is no evidence of trauma, place him/her in the **recovery position** by turning him/her onto the side and holding the head, shoulders and torso simultaneously with the upper leg bent and knee moved forward so as to stabilise the child (**Fig. 28.9**).

If there is no spontaneous breathing, provide **rescue breathing** while maintaining a patent airway by chin lift or jaw thrust manoeuvre (**Fig. 28.10**).

The most effective way of providing rescue breathing (**Fig. 28.10**) is by bag and mask ventilation while maintaining the airway open. Assess the efficacy of rescue breaths by looking at the chest rise and fall with each rescue breath. The respiratory rate and compression:ventilation ratio is to be maintained at a ratio of 30:2 in case of a single rescuer, and 15:2 when a second rescuer arrives (AHA 2020 guidelines). To avoid confusion, European Resuscitation Council 2021 guidelines recommend the ratio of 15:2 to be followed irrespective of the number of rescuers. If the chest does not rise during rescue breathing, ventilation is not effective. Deliver rescue breaths slowly to avoid gastric distension giving enough time for expiration. Since improper opening of the airway is the most common cause of airway obstruction, a patent airway should be maintained during rescue breathing. High concentration-inspired oxygen needs to be provided during ventilation till the return of spontaneous circulation. If skills are available, use of a supraglottic airway or endotracheal intubation is preferred without much interruption of chest compressions.

Try to access an automated external defibrillator (AED)/defibrillator, check for the rhythm and proceed as per the advanced life support (ALS) protocol based on whether it is a shockable/ non-shockable rhythm.

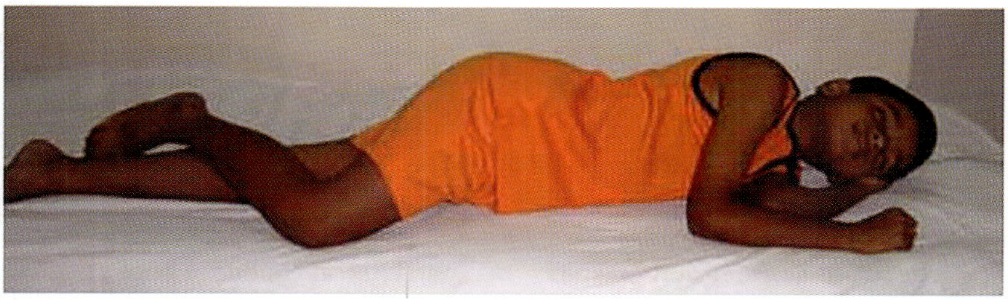

Figure 28.9 Recovery position.

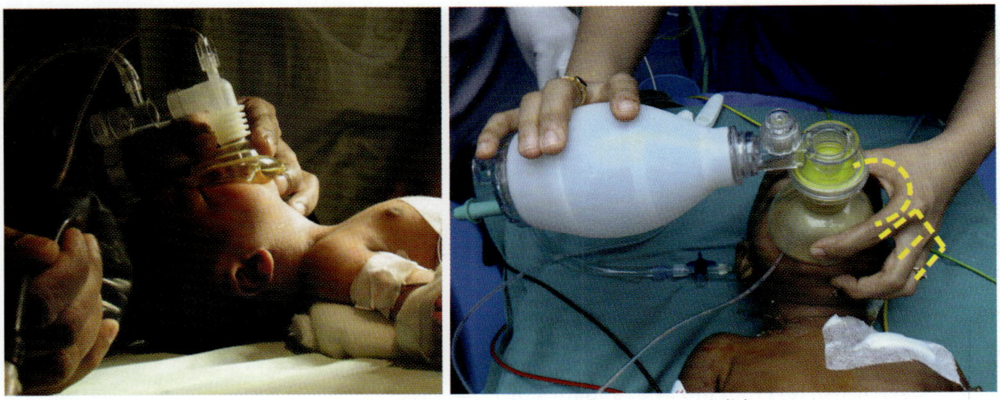

(a) (b)

Figure 28.10 (a) Rescue breathing using the anaesthesia circuit. (b) Rescue breathing using bag and mask. Note Reverse E-C clamp made by fingers over the jaw and mask to achieve a seal.

Basic life support in children may be summarised as shown in **Table 28.2**.

Table 28.2 Summary of Basic Life Support in Infants and Children

	Infant	1–8 Years
Pulse check	Brachial/femoral	Carotid
Compression area	Lower one-third of sternum	Lower one-third of sternum
Compression with	2 fingers/encircle technique	Heel of one hand
Depth	At least one-third depth	At least one-third depth
Rate	100–120/min	100–120/min
Ratio	30:2 (one rescuer) 15:2 (two rescuers)	30:2 (one rescuer) 15:2 (two rescuers)

Advanced Life Support in Infants and Children

If the above measures elicit no response, the following must be instituted rapidly. This would occur most commonly in cases of drowning, poisoning, trauma, hypovolaemic shock, burns or cardiac dysrhythmias. Rule out the 5Hs and 5Ts as the possible cause of arrest. 5Hs are Hypoxia, Hypovolaemia, Hydrogen ion excess (acidosis), Hypo/hyperkalaemia and Hypoglycaemia. 5Ts are Toxins, Tamponade (cardiac), Tension pneumothorax, Thrombosis (coronary or pulmonary) and Trauma.

In all cases, the same CAB should be followed with 'C' chest compression continuing. We describe the further management of the 'C' circulation with hypovolaemia and arrhythmias after reconsidering 'A' and 'B'. This is followed by 'D' for defibrillation and drugs.

- **A** – **A**irway should be maintained with a mask and oropharyngeal or nasopharyngeal airways of an appropriate size. An oropharyngeal airway can be used in an unconscious child while nasopharyngeal airway is used in the semiconscious. (Do not use a nasopharyngeal airway in case of head trauma.) Choose the correct size of oropharyngeal airway by measuring from the corner of the mouth to the angle of the jaw whereas for nasopharyngeal airway measure from the tip of the nose to the tragus of the ear (see Chapter 2). Laryngeal mask airways (LMAs) have also been used in resuscitation. Endotracheal intubation is of course the technique of choice to rapidly improve oxygenation, control the airway and prevent aspiration.
- **B** – **B**reathing may be accomplished by bag and mask ventilation or positive pressure ventilation through an LMA or endotracheal tube. (Remember that with LMA, the airway is not protected from regurgitation and aspiration.) The 2020 AHA Guidelines for resuscitation suggest one breath every 2–3 seconds (20–30 breaths/minute), accounting for the child's age and clinical condition once an advanced airway is in place. Capnography, when available, is strongly encouraged not only to confirm the

Table 28.3 Signs of Hypovolaemic Shock

	Compensated	Uncompensated	Pre-terminal
Blood volume loss	<25%	25–40%	>40%
Heart rate	+	++	+++ or decreased
Systolic blood pressure	N	Decreased	Unrecordable
Capillary refill	>2 sec	>2 sec	>5 sec
Skin	Cool	Cold/mottled	Cold/grey/dusky
Respiratory rate	+	++	Sighing
Mental state	Mild agitation	Uncooperative	Unresponsive
Urine output	+	Nil	Nil

placement of airway devices but also to aid decision making in CPR. $EtCO_2$ values of less than 15 mmHg suggest a need to improve the quality of chest compressions.

- **C – Circulation**: The signs of hypovolaemic shock are described in Table 28.3.

Treating hypovolaemia is an important component of resuscitation. In children with septic shock, it is recommended to administer isotonic crystalloids at 10–20 mL/kg in aliquots based on frequent assessment. The superiority of colloids has not been clearly documented and the use of hypotonic and glucose-containing solutions for volume resuscitation is to be avoided. In children who are not responsive to fluids, it is recommended to use either norepinephrine (noradrenaline) or epinephrine (adrenaline) as the initial vasopressor agent of choice. Stress doses of corticosteroids may also be considered in these children. The use of vasopressors and corticosteroids in children with refractory septic shock is mainly recommended in order to prevent morbidity associated with fluid overload. Blood and blood products should be used in clinical scenarios of cardiac arrest related to haemorrhage, rather than using crystalloids for volume resuscitation (see Chapter 8). Balanced resuscitation using packed red blood cells, fresh frozen plasma and platelets is recommended.

Vascular access may be difficult in these patients and unusual approaches for administration of drugs may sometimes be necessary. These are described in Table 28.4 (see Chapter 10).

Advanced life support in infants and children can be summarised in the following cardiac arrest algorithm (Fig. 28.11).

Table 28.4 Vascular Access (Refer to Chapter 10)

Route of Access	Remarks
Peripheral venous access	Route of choice
Intraosseous route	Easy in children less than 6 years. All drugs and fluids can be given through this route
Endotracheal route	Only if no intravenous/intraosseous routes. Only lignocaine, atropine, naloxone and adrenaline can be given
Cut down – peripheral or central line	As advanced vascular access

The following is a brief look at arrhythmias in children that may cause cardiovascular compromise. A detailed account of arrhythmias, their causes, recognition and treatment is given in Chapter 27.

Paediatric Bradyarrhythmias

Bradycardia in a child is defined as a heart rate of <60/min. The possible causes are hypothermia, hypoxia or medications. According to the AHA 2020 recommendations, when we come across a child with bradycardia with a pulse, the following steps have to be followed:

1. Check for signs of cardiopulmonary compromise, i.e.,
   - Acutely altered mentation
   - Signs of shock
   - Hypotension

- If there are *no signs of cardiopulmonary compromise*, the child's ABCs have to be supported. Consider administering oxygen and observing the child, a 12-lead ECG is done and eventually the underlying cause is identified and treated
- If there are *signs of cardiopulmonary compromise*
  - Maintain a patent airway
  - Breathing is assisted with positive pressure ventilation
  - Attach a cardiac monitor to identify the rhythm; simultaneously monitor pulse, BP and oximetry

2. If heart rate remains <60/min despite oxygenation and ventilation, start high-quality CPR
3. Check for a pulse:

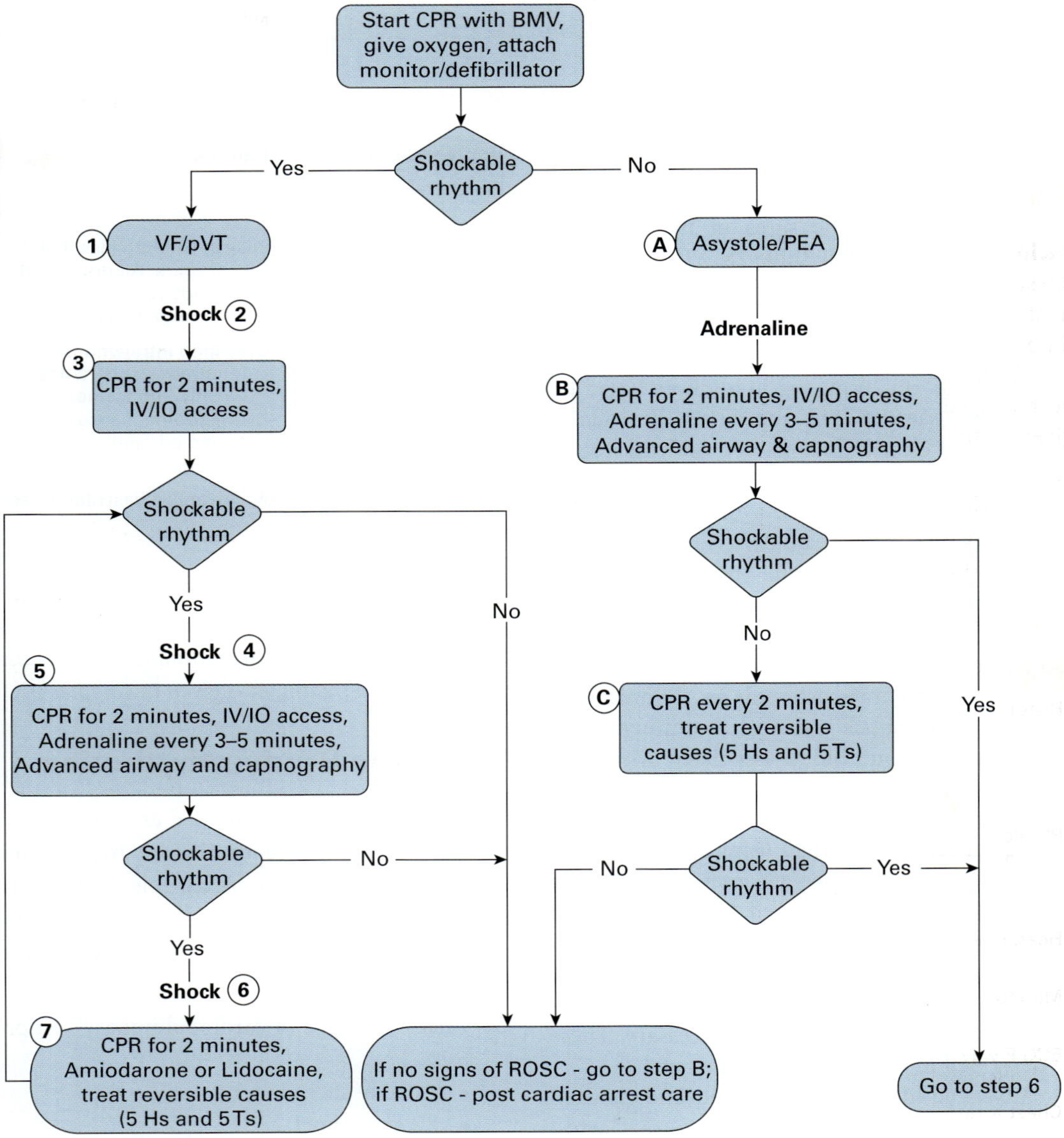

Figure 28.11 Paediatric cardiac arrest algorithm. BMV, bag mask ventilation; CPR, cardiopulmonary resuscitation; IV/IO, intravenous/intraoral; PEA, pulseless electrical activity; pVT, pulseless ventricular tachycardia; ROSC, return of spontaneous circulation; VF, ventricular fibrillation.

If bradycardia is still persistent
- Continue CPR
- Secure an IV/IO access
- Administer epinephrine or atropine (atropine only in increased vagal tone or primary AV block)
- Consider transthoracic/transvenous pacing
- The underlying cause has to be identified and treated

4. Pulse is checked every 2 minutes, if bradycardia is persistent, continue resuscitation for the same
5. If the pulse is absent, resuscitation is followed as per the paediatric cardiac arrest algorithm

Paediatric Tachyarrhythmias

Tachyarrhythmias can be confusing as some are physiological and others are pathological requiring treatment. Tables 28.5 and 28.6 could help in differentiating them.

A child with tachycardia with a pulse should be managed by the following stepwise approach given by the AHA 2020 guidelines:

1. Initial assessment and support:
   - Maintain a patent airway, and assist breathing
   - Administer oxygen
   - Attach a cardiac monitor to identify rhythm, also monitor pulse, blood pressure and oximetry
   - Secure an IV/IO access
   - Get a 12-lead ECG
2. If it is a sinus tachycardia, i.e., P-waves are normal, variable RR interval, HR <220/min in infants, <180/min in children; look for the probable cause and treat accordingly
3. If it is not a sinus rhythm, look for signs of cardiopulmonary compromise:
   - Acutely altered mentation
   - Signs of shock
   - Hypotension
4. Also, evaluate the QRS duration on ECG to differentiate between narrow complex tachycardia (≤0.09 seconds) and wide complex tachycardia (>0.09 seconds).

Table 28.5 Causes of Narrow Complex and Wide Complex Tachycardia

Narrow Complex Tachycardia	Wide Complex Tachycardia
Sinus tachycardia SVT Atrial flutter	Ventricular tachycardia SVT with aberrant intraventricular conduction (this is rare in children)

SVT, supraventricular tachycardia.

Table 28.6 Comparison between ST and SVT

Characteristics	ST	SVT
History	Gradual onset compatible with clinical conditions such as fever/ pain/dehydration/ hypovolaemia	Abrupt onset or termination with symptoms of CCF in infants and palpitations in older children
Physical examination	Signs of the underlying clinical conditions such as fever/hypovolaemia, anaemia/dehydration	Signs of CCF rales/hepatomegaly/oedema
Heart rate	Infant: Usually <220/min Child: Usually <180/min	Infant: Usually >220/min Child: Usually >180/min
Monitor	Heart rate varies with level of activity and rest	Minimal heart rate variability with changes in activity or stimulation
ECG P waves may be difficult to identify with very fast rates	P waves present/normal/ upright in leads I/aVF	P waves absent/ abnormal/inverted in leads II/III/aVF
Chest X-ray	Small heart and clear lungs unless the cause of ST is cardiac or pneumonia	Signs of CCF such as pulmonary oedema and cardiomegaly

CCF, congestive cardiac failure; ST, sinus tachycardia; SVT, supraventricular tachycardia.

Hepatic Arterial Buffer Response or Arteriovenous Reciprocity

- This response is the phenomenon by which hepatic arterial blood flow increases in response to a decrease in portal venous blood flow. This results in the maintenance of hepatic oxygen supply, which is essential for hepatocyte function and maintenance of total hepatic blood flow for clearance of endogenous waste products. However, this response is limited to a 50% decrease in portal venous flow, which results in a twofold increase in hepatic artery flow. Also, this response is limited in its ability to compensate during conditions of hypoperfusion, inflammation and shock.
- Washout of adenosine and other neural, myogenic and metabolic factors such as oxygen content or pH of portal venous blood may significantly influence the buffer response.

Extrinsic Regulation

Changes in the Composition of Systemic and Portal Venous Blood

They affect liver blood flow, for example,

- Arterial hypoxaemia, systemic hypercarbia, hypocapnia and alkalosis
- Hepatic arterial blood flow is increased by decreased portal oxygen content and pH
- Post-prandial hyperosmolarity increases both portal and hepatic arterial blood flow

Neural Control

The sympathetic and parasympathetic nerves supplying the liver run along the blood vessels and bile ducts. These form an intercommunication plexus which terminates on the arterioles and venules.

Stimulation of the sympathetic system due to hypercarbia, pain or hypoxia reduces liver blood flow and blood volume and about 500 ml of hepatic blood can be expelled within a few seconds. This indicates that the liver is a large reservoir of whole blood, which can be redistributed in response to autonomic activity.

Humoral Factors

- Both α- and β-receptors exist in the hepatic arterial bed. Only α-receptors are present in the portal vessels.
- Experimentally, adrenaline injected into the hepatic artery causes vasoconstriction via the α-receptors, followed by vasodilation by action on the β-receptors.
- Adrenaline injected into the portal circulation only produces vasoconstriction.

Regeneration of Hepatocytes

Normally, only 0.005% of hepatocytes are in the cell cycle (G1 phase) while the remaining are in the dormant phase. After a partial hepatectomy when there is a loss of hepatocytes, the dormant cells are mobilised from G0 to G1 phase until the original liver volume is achieved. This along with the ability of hepatocytes to regenerate by mitosis allows restoration of the original liver volume in liver donors and after hepatectomy.

Relevant Pharmacology

All volatile agents decrease hepatic blood flow. But sevoflurane and desflurane have the least effect on total hepatic blood flow and hepatic oxygen delivery while halothane decreases hepatic blood flow the most.

Patients with advanced liver disease such as cirrhosis and end-stage liver disease may have problems dealing with and eliminating certain drugs, thus potentiating their clinical effects.

Drugs used in anaesthesia and most commonly affected are narcotics such as morphine and pethidine, muscle relaxants such as vecuronium and rocuronium, and sedatives such as benzodiazepines and dexmedetomidine.

The action of suxamethonium can be prolonged due to a decrease in the levels of psuedocholinesterase in liver disease that affects hepatic function.

However, patients with asymptomatic elevation of transaminases can undergo surgery with minimal impact on the outcome.

For more on pharmacology and the liver, refer to Chapter 3.

SUGGESTED READINGS

1. Butterworth JF, Mackey DC, Wasnick JD. Hepatic Physiology and Anaesthesia. In: Morgan and Mikhail's Clinical Anaesthesiology, 5th edition. Edward Morgan G, Larson CP (eds). McGraw-Hill Medical Publishing, New York, 2013; pp. 708–709.
2. Rothenberg DM, O'Connor CJ, Tuman KJ. Anesthesia and the Hepatobiliary System. In: Millers Anesthesia, 7th edition. Eriksson LI, Fleisher LA, Wiener-Kronish JP, Young WL (eds). Churchill-Livingstone, Philadelphia, 2010; pp. 2135–2153.
3. Kaufman BS, Roccaforte JD. Hepatic Anatomy, Function and Physiology. In: Clinical Anesthesia. Barash PG, Cullen BF, Stoelting RK, Cahalan MK, Stock MC (eds). Wolters Kluwer, Philadelphia, 2009; pp. 1246–1250.
4. Furchtgott LA, Chow CC, Periwal V. A model of liver regeneration. *Biophys J* 2009; 96:3926–3935. doi:10.1016/j.bpj.2009.01.061

to the biliary anastomosis, enteral feeds may be delayed for 3–4 days. A 5 Fr triple lumen or 4 Fr double lumen catheter may be placed in the internal jugular vein guided by ultrasound. This helps in fluid administration and sampling for the next few days. The inhalational agent may then be changed to isoflurane/air and oxygen as hepatic blood flow and oxygen supply are better maintained. Nitrous oxide is avoided at this stage to avoid troublesome bowel distension. A nasogastric tube also helps to decompress the stomach.

Maintenance crystalloid solutions must contain dextrose so as to avoid hypoglycaemia. Maintenance fluids should contain at least 1% dextrose in Ringer's lactate increasing to 5% as required. Blood sugar estimations should be done at least after induction and at the end of surgery. Replacement of losses should be with Ringer's lactate without added dextrose. Unlike in adults with obstructive jaundice, the use of diuretics or volume loading is not required for the prevention of renal failure because this virtually does not occur in this age group. Blood loss is assessed by swab weight and suction loss. Generally, there is very little blood loss and blood replacement is not necessary. However, blood that is warmed to body temperature should be replaced as soon as the loss exceeds 10% of the estimated blood volume. Ascites are not usual but if present, 4.5% albumin in 0.9% sodium chloride should be used to replace losses. Urine output is not usually easy to assess in this age group.

Monitoring is with an ECG, pulse oximeter, non-invasive blood pressure and temperature (both core and peripheral). Ventilation should be controlled and end-tidal gases monitored for oxygen, carbon dioxide and volatile anaesthetic agents.

In general, haemodynamic stability is maintained without the need for vasoactive substances. There is usually no need for invasive arterial or venous monitoring unless the baby has associated sepsis, pneumonia, cholangitis or severe cirrhosis. However, one must watch out for decreasing venous return, and therefore decreased cardiac output, if there is compression or kinking of the inferior vena cava.

Analgesia can be provided with calculated doses of short-acting opioids such as fentanyl 2 mcg/kg. Caudal catheters can be placed after ruling out coagulopathy and infusions of 0.1% bupivacaine or ropivacaine with 1 mcg/ml fentanyl can be used as an infusion during surgery and post-operatively.

Ultrasound-guided abdominal wall blocks such as rectus sheath block and right subcostal transversus abdominis plane blocks can have an opioid-sparing effect (see Chapter 14). Paracetamol can be used in a smaller dose 10–15 mg/kg IV 8th hourly while monitoring the liver functions.

Hypothermia is a very real problem as in addition to the large surface-to-volume ratio in infants and their lack of insulation, a large surface of the liver is often exposed to the cold operating room. OT temperatures should be kept higher than normal, IV fluids warmed, all cleaning solutions warmed and hot air blowers used to maintain surface warmth. Wrapping the limbs of the baby with plastic cling film is an effective way to preserve core temperature.

Most babies can be successfully extubated at the end of surgery. Elective post-op ventilation is considered in children with other organ system failures (specifically sepsis, cholangitis and pneumonia), hypothermia or those who have needed large-volume transfusions.

Intravenous antibiotics are given for 5 days post-op to prevent ascending cholangitis which can lead to significant morbidity. In uncomplicated cases, inj. ofloxacin 7.5 mg/kg twice daily and inj. metronidazole 7.5 mg/kg thrice daily are given for the first five days after surgery. Meropenem has been suggested as an effective first-line empirical antibiotic.

Post-Operative Management

Balancing adequate pain control, respiratory depression and return of bowel function can be a challenge. Large amounts of opioids may cause respiratory depression, prolonged intubation, delayed return of bowel function and lengthen the hospital stay.

Children with caudal catheters can be managed with post-operative infusions of local anaesthetic 0.1% with 1mcg/kg fentanyl for 2–3 days. In centres where experience with caudal catheters is limited then paracetamol intravenously and opioids such as fentanyl in doses of 0.5 mcg/kg can be given as needed or as continuous infusions. ERPs may be considered with the use of IV dexmedetomidine or ketamine and ultrasound-guided abdominal regional blocks as part of pain management.

SUGGESTED READINGS

1. Kasai M, Mochizuki I, Ohkohchin N, et al. Surgical limitation for biliary atresia. Indications for liver transplant. *J Paediatr Surg* 1989; 24:851.
2. Kelly DA, Davenport M. Current management of biliary atresia. *Arch Dis Child* 2007; 92:1132–1135.
3. Schwarz SM. Pediatric Biliary Atresia Treatment and Management. Medscape. Updated on 2 February 2021. Accessed on 17 May 2015. Available from at: https://emedicine.medscape.com/article/927029-treatment accessed on 29th May 2023
4. Rivera MR, Squires RH, Davies PJ. Essentials of Hepatology. In: A Practice of Anesthesia for Infants and Children, 4th edition. Cote CJ, Lerman J, Todres ID (eds). Saunders Elsevier, Philadelphia, 2009; p. 595.
5. Green DW, Howard ER, Davenport M. Anesthesia, perioperative management and outcome of correction of extrahepatic biliary atresia in the infant: A review of 50 cases in the King's College Hospital series. *Paediatr Anaesth* 2000; 10:581–589.
6. Hartley JL, Davenport M, Kelly DA. Biliary atresia. *Lancet* 2009; 374:1704–1713.
7. Hammer G, Hall S, Davis PJ. Anaesthesia for General Abdominal, Thoracic, Urologic and Bariatric Surgery. In: Smith's Anesthesia for Infants and Children, 7th edition. Motoyama EK, Davis J (eds). Elsevier, Philadelphia, 2006; pp. 695–697.
8. Khalil BA, Perera MTPR, Mirza DF. Clinical practice: Management of biliary atresia. *Eur J Pediatr* 2010; 169:395–402 (Review).
9. Jacob R. Anaesthesia for biliary atresia and hepatectomy in paediatrics. *Ind J Anaesth* 2012; 56:479–484.
10. Sundaram SS, Mack CL, Feldman AG, et al. Biliary atresia: Indications and timing of liver transplantation and optimization of pretransplant care. *Liver Transpl* 2017; 23(1):96–109.
11. Vogt P, Tolly R, Clifton M, et al. The development of an enhanced recovery protocol for Kasai portoenterostomy. *Children (Basel)* 2022; 9(11):1675.

In the event of metabolic acidosis, sodium bicarbonate should be intravenously administered according to the base deficit. However, it is important to avoid hyperventilation, which can lead to respiratory alkalosis, resulting in the release of lactate from muscle tissue, which, if not efficiently metabolised, can aggravate metabolic acidosis. Cannulation of a peripheral artery during major surgeries facilitates monitoring arterial blood acid–base status as well as blood glucose concentrations.

The presence of hepatomegaly can lead to perioperative respiratory compromise. A reverse Trendelenburg position during airway manipulation may lessen the effect of hepatomegaly on respiratory function. Another result of hepatomegaly and subsequent displacement of the abdominal contents is gastro-oesophageal reflux and the risk of aspiration. In patients with hepatic dysfunction, additional recommendations include maintenance of the hepatic oxygen supply–demand ratio, provision of adequate cardiorespiratory function and avoidance of medications that could accelerate hepatocellular damage.

Another issue in patients with GSD is the possibility of the occurrence of malignant hyperpyrexia (MH). Although no clinical association with MH has been established, many of these patients have a positive in vitro contracture test, and simple prophylactic measures, such as avoiding 'MH-trigger agents', may be recommended, if otherwise not contraindicated. It is important to be aware of the clinical signs of MH (increased oxygen consumption, rise in blood pressure, tachycardia, rise in $EtCO_2$ and tachypnoea during spontaneous ventilation; rise of temperature >2°C) and institute treatment in the event of suspicion of an MH crisis.

Postoperative Care

It may be worthwhile to consider a 24-hour supervision of the patient in an intensive care or high dependency unit (ICU or HDU) to monitor for post-operative respiratory failure, acidosis or muscle fatigue, rhabdomyolysis, myoglobinuria and renal failure.

Conclusion

In conclusion, of primary importance to the anaesthesiologist are issues related to the associated cardiomyopathy, myopathy and alterations in the regulation of serum glucose concentrations. Airway concerns include the potential for airway problems related to macroglossia and the associated myopathy. Associated with myopathy are the usual concerns related to non-depolarising neuromuscular blocking agents and the potential for adverse effects with succinylcholine.

To summarise, it is important to have a clear picture of the pre-operative condition of the patient, as well as an understanding of the implications of anaesthesia to be able to anticipate perioperative problems that may arise during the conduct of anaesthesia in these patients. Although potentially dangerous, it is possible to have a smooth, uneventful course of anaesthesia with meticulous attention to the metabolic and homeostatic details.

SUGGESTED READINGS

1. Rivera M, Squires RM Jr, Davis PJ. Essentials of Hepatology. In: A Practice of Anaesthesia for Infants and Children, 5th edition. Cote CJ, Lerman J, Anderson B (eds). Elsevier Saunders, Philadelphia 2013; pp. 595–604.
2. Tautawy H, Myslajek T. Inborn Errors of Metabolism. In: Stoelting's Anesthesia and Co-Existing Disease, 6th edition. Hines RL, Marschall KE (eds). Elsevier Saunders, Philadelphia 2012; pp. 311–313.
3. Baum VC, O'Flaherty JE. Anaesthesia for Genetic, Metabolic and Dysmorphic Syndromes of Childhood, 2nd edition. Lippincott's Williams & Wilkins, Philadelphia 2007; pp. 156–158.
4. Ciarallo CL, Galinkin JL. Metabolic Diseases and Inborn Errors of Metabolism. In: A Practical Approach to Pediatric Anaesthesia. Holzman RS, Mancuso TJ, Polaner DM (eds). Lippincott's Williams & Wilkins, Philadelphia 2008; pp. 556–558.
5. Gurrieri C, Sprung J, Weingarten TN, et al. Patients with glycogen storage diseases undergoing anesthesia: a case series. *BMC Anesthesiol* 2017; 17(1):134.

32 HEPATITIS IN CHILDREN

Lakshmi Kumar

Hepatitis is an inflammation of the liver and can result in liver cell damage and destruction. It may be acute or chronic.

Acute Hepatitis

Acute hepatitis is most often due to a virus but can also be caused by drugs and toxins.

Viral Hepatitis

Viral hepatitis is a major worldwide public health issue and continues to be an important cause of liver disease in children. Acute viral hepatitis is typically caused by one of six viruses: hepatitis A virus (HAV), hepatitis B virus (HBV), hepatitis C virus (HCV), hepatitis D virus (HDV), hepatitis E virus (HEV) and hepatitis G virus (HGV). Cytomegalovirus (CMV), Epstein–Barr virus (EBV), Herpes simplex virus (HSV), Varicella zoster virus (VZV), Enteroviruses, Rubella, Adenovirus and Parvovirus are other viruses that cause hepatitis.

Drug-Induced Hepatitis

Drug-induced hepatitis can result from the direct dose-dependent toxicity of a drug (or a metabolite), from an idiosyncratic drug reaction or from a combination of the two.

The most common drugs affecting the paediatric population are acetaminophen, inhalational agents (halothane), phenytoin, aspirin, isoniazid and diclofenac.

Fulminant or acute liver failure can occur in children either due to viral hepatitis or as an idiosyncratic drug reaction. This may be an emergent situation that requires liver transplantation. Encephalopathy and cerebral oedema are the feared complications. Utmost care must be taken to prevent a rise in intracranial pressures during the surgery.

Halothane Hepatitis

This is rarely encountered today with decreasing use of this agent in clinical practice. Halothane damages the liver in two ways:

1. **Halothane hepatotoxicity** is a mild self-limited post-operative toxicity due to changes in hepatic blood flow that affect hepatic oxygenation. It is a non-immune phenomenon and recovery is the rule.
2. **Halothane hepatitis** is an extremely rare life-threatening immune-mediated response after repeat exposure to halothane due to the tri-fluoroacetyl metabolite initiated by oxidative metabolism. The occurrence of halothane-associated hepatitis in children is between 1 in 82,000 and 1 in 200,000. It can potentially lead to hepatic necrosis, hepatic encephalopathy and acute liver failure. Symptoms generally develop about 2 days to 3 weeks after exposure and present as fever, anorexia, nausea, myalgias, arthralgias and rash. All inhalational anaesthetics are capable of producing it.

The treatment of both halothane hepatotoxicity and halothane hepatitis is supportive. Corticosteroids are of no proven value. The most effective preventive tool is to avoid the use of halothane, especially if repeated anaesthetics are required.

Signs and Symptoms

Low-grade fever, fatigue, anorexia, nausea, emesis, pruritis, light-coloured stools and dark urine.

Treatment

Treatment of hepatitis varies and depends on the underlying cause of the disease. The goal of treatment is to stop damage to the liver and alleviate symptoms. Treatment may include one or more of the following:

- Supportive care (healthy diet and rest)
- Significant nausea and vomiting may require intravenous fluids and electrolyte replacement
- Medications to help control itching
- Avoidance of alcohol and drugs
- Preventing the spread of the disease if the cause is viral hepatitis
- Interferon drug therapy
- Antivirals for acute viral hepatitis

Chronic Hepatitis

Chronic hepatitis is an inflammatory disease of the liver lasting for more than 6 months as evidenced by elevated serum aminotransferases. The most common causes of chronic hepatitis are autoimmune hepatitis, chronic viral hepatitis (HBV with or without HDV co-infection, and infection with HCV), drug-induced and steatohepatitis (in diabetic and obese children). Patients can usually be classified as having one of three distinct entities based on a liver biopsy: chronic persistent hepatitis, chronic lobular hepatitis or chronic active hepatitis.

Signs and Symptoms

The most common symptoms of chronic hepatitis are fatigue, malaise, abdominal pain and jaundice. Portal hypertension, ascites and encephalopathy manifest as the disease progresses.

Treatment

The current standard of care for patients with chronic HBV hepatitis is the combined regimen of interferon and nucleotide analogues. IFN-α is approved for use in children as young as 12 months of age. No antiviral drugs are approved for the treatment of children under the age of 1 year. For chronic HCV hepatitis, newer oral direct-acting antivirals have demonstrated higher efficacy in viral suppression and hence are preferred, They are approved for use in children >3 years of age. Corticosteroids and immuno-suppressant drugs are administered for autoimmune hepatitis.

Anaesthetic Management

Anaesthetic management for acute and chronic hepatitis is dealt with separately in the following text.

Anaesthetic Management of Acute Hepatitis

Pre-Operative Assessment

Children with acute hepatitis should have any elective surgery postponed until acute hepatitis has resolved, as indicated by the normalisation of liver tests. Only truly emergent surgery should be considered in patients with acute hepatitis as patients with acute hepatitis are at risk for deterioration of hepatic function and the development of complications from hepatic failures, such as encephalopathy, coagulopathy or hepatorenal syndrome.

- Laboratory tests that need to be done include liver function tests, coagulation profile, blood urea nitrogen, serum electrolytes, creatinine, glucose, platelet count and viral serology.
  - If transaminase levels are >3 times normal, non-essential, non-emergent procedures requiring a general or regional anaesthetic should be postponed.
  - The prothrombin time (PT) is the best indicator of hepatic synthetic function. Persistent prolongation >3 seconds (international normalised ratio [INR] >1.5), following administration of vitamin K, is indicative of severe hepatic dysfunction. Appropriate blood products should be available for surgery.
  - Jaundice is apparent when bilirubin levels exceed 3–4 mg/dl. Severely jaundiced patients (>8 mg/dl) are more likely to develop post-operative renal failure and sepsis.

- Blood glucose may be low with severe liver injury and should be corrected.
- Hypokalaemia and metabolic alkalosis might occur due to vomiting.
- Evaluate side effects resulting from specific drug therapy.
- In patients with acute hepatitis who need emergent surgery:
  - Determine the cause and the degree of hepatic impairment
  - Vitamin K or fresh frozen plasma to correct coagulopathy
  - Pre-medication is generally not given in patients with advanced liver disease, in an effort to minimise drug exposure and not confound hepatic encephalopathy

Pre-operative fasting should follow normal guidelines. Intravenous fluids may need to be started for those children with vomiting.

Pre-Medication

Pre-medication should be avoided in children with encephalopathy. In others, midazolam, oral – 0.5–1 mg/kg, IV – 0.05–0.1 mg/kg, rectal – 1 mg/kg, intranasal – 0.1–0.2 mg/kg is an option.

Lorazepam or oxazepam is better because of phase II metabolism. The newer benzodiazepine and remimazolam now available in some Asian countries undergo dose-dependent ester hydrolysis and can be safely used in liver dysfunction.

Chloral hydrate (trichloryl) is not recommended in neonates and patients with liver disease because of impaired metabolism and the potential accumulation of toxic metabolites.

Intraoperative Monitoring

Routine monitoring includes ECG, pulse oximetry, non-invasive blood pressure, end-tidal CO_2 and temperature. Invasive arterial pressure monitoring and central venous monitoring should be used in major cases where there may be large fluid shifts and blood loss.

Anaesthetic Considerations

- The goal of intraoperative management is to preserve the existing hepatic function and avoid factors that may be detrimental to the liver. Focus is needed on optimising liver perfusion and preventing secondary ischaemic injury.
- Factors known to reduce hepatic blood flow, such as hypotension, excessive sympathetic activation and high mean airway pressures during controlled ventilation, should be avoided. Hypoxia is to be avoided and normocarbia maintained.
- Some patients with viral hepatitis may exhibit increased central nervous system sensitivity to anaesthetics.
- Most anaesthetics are central nervous system depressants; hence, the fewest number of agents should be used.
- Inhalation anaesthetics are generally preferable to intravenous agents because most of the latter are dependent on the liver for metabolism or elimination. Isoflurane is the volatile agent of choice because it has the least effect on hepatic blood flow. Sevoflurane may be used as an induction agent in children.
- Standard induction doses of intravenous induction agents can generally be used because their action is terminated by redistribution rather than metabolism or excretion. Repeat doses need to be titrated. Propofol is the induction agent of choice.
- Atracurium and cis-atracurium are cleared independent of liver function and are the muscle relaxants of choice. Pseudo-cholinesterase deficiency is rare so that succinylcholine and mivacurium action should not be prolonged.
- In the case of opioids, fentanyl may be the best option since it is short-acting and is excreted by the kidney. Fentanyl has unaffected pharmacokinetics in the presence of significant hepatic dysfunction. Metabolism of morphine is dependent on the liver and its elimination can get delayed. Accumulation of its active metabolite can occur if there is renal impairment. Morphine administration should be carefully titrated.
- Blood glucose, acid–base status and urine output should be monitored.
- Regional anaesthesia may be employed in the absence of coagulopathy, provided hypotension is avoided.
- Prevent nosocomial transmission of the virus.

Post-Operative Concerns

The perioperative physician should be vigilant to monitor liver functions after surgical stress. The transaminases may be elevated following perioperative hypotension, blood loss or after partial clamp of the inflow to the liver.

Anaesthetic Management of Chronic Hepatitis

Pre-Anaesthetic Assessment

- Look for the presence of hepatic dysfunction.
- Hepatocellular insufficiency can be assessed by measurements of serum bilirubin, serum albumin and PT (INR).
- Look for any features of cirrhosis and complications of chronic liver disease such as portal hypertension, hepatorenal and hepatopulmonary syndrome.
- Look for any extrahepatic manifestations such as arthritis, serositis glomerulonephritis, skin rashes and thrombocytopenia.

Paediatric end-stage liver disease and Child and Pugh scores are often used to evaluate the prognosis of liver disease in cirrhotic patients awaiting transplantation and are further discussed in Chapter 33.

Intraoperative Management

Patients with chronic persistent or chronic lobular hepatitis should be treated similar to those with acute hepatitis (see the preceding text). In contrast, those with chronic active hepatitis should be assumed to already have cirrhosis and should be treated accordingly.

Pre-existing liver function impairment causes various degrees of drug metabolism reduction due to

- alteration of liver perfusion due to increased portal pressure;
- hepatocellular insufficiency;
- reduced serum proteins altering the availability of protein-bound systemic drugs;
- unpredictable drug redistribution due to ascites, hypervolaemia and high cardiac output;
- enzyme induction-associated drug therapy;
- pre-existing organ dysfunction, mainly encephalopathy and kidney impairment.

Anaesthetic implications are similar to those of acute hepatitis. In addition,

- Hepatocellular insufficiency is associated with a hyperkinetic state which when combined with general anaesthesia often results in an intraoperative low systemic arterial pressure. This may require vasopressor therapy like norepinephrine in order to maintain adequate blood pressure and urinary output.
- Judicious use of paracetamol in patients with any pre-existing liver impairment. Supplementation of n-acetylcysteine may help in the elimination of the products of paracetamol metabolism.
- Non-steroidal anti-inflammatory drugs are avoided as they are likely to worsen pre-existing renal dysfunction.
- Adequate circulatory volume should be maintained, and 5% albumin can be used. The use of splanchnic vasopressors such as noradrenaline and terlipressin can have a beneficial impact in reducing acute kidney injury associated with chronic liver disease.

In conclusion, knowledge of physiology and pathophysiology is critical when dealing with patients with liver damage or failure. Elective surgery is avoided in acute hepatitis and is to be undertaken with caution in chronic liver diseases. The anaesthesiologist should be alert to rapid changes in the patient's condition caused by anaesthetic drugs, haemodynamic instability or the insult of surgery. An affiliation with a centre performing hepatobiliary surgery with the support of multidisciplinary units can improve outcomes in this patient group.

SUGGESTED READINGS

1. Rivera MR, Squires RH Jr, Davis PJ. Essentials of Hepatology. In: A Practice of Anesthesia for Infants and Children, 5th edition. Cote CJ, Lerman J, Anderson B (eds). Elsevier Saunders, Philadelphia, 2013; pp. 595–604.
2. Lentschener C, Ozier Y. What anaesthetists need to know about viral hepatitis. *Acta Anaesthesiol Scand* 2003; 47:794–803.
3. Malde AD. Viral hepatitis and the anaesthesiologist. *Ind J Anaesth* 2004; 48:264–275.
4. Marschall KE. Diseases of the Liver and Biliary Tract. In: Stoelting's Anesthesia and Co-Existing Disease, 5th edition. Hines RL,

Marschall KE (eds). Churchill Livingstone, Philadelphia, 2008; pp. 259–279.

5. D'Agata ID, Balistreri W. Evaluation of liver disease in the pediatric patient. *Pediatr Rev* 1999; 20:376–389.
6. Davis PJ, Bosenberg A, Davidson A, et al. Pharmacology of Pediatric Anesthesia. In: Smith's Anaesthesia for Infants and Children, 8th edition. Davis PJ, Cladis FP, Motoyama EK (eds). Elsevier Mosby, Philadelphia, 2011; pp. 179–261.
7. Ramsy M. Anesthesia for Patients with Liver Disease. In: Morgan and Mikhail's Clinical Anesthesiology, 5th edition. Belval B, Lebowitz H (eds). McGraw-Hill Medical, USA, 2013; pp. 707–726.
8. Jonas MM, Block JM. Treatment of children with chronic hepatitis B virus infection in the United States: Patient selection and therapeutic options. *Hepatology* 2010; 000:1–14.
9. Hepatitis in Children. University of Rochester Medical Centre. Available at https://www.urmc.rochester.edu/encyclopedia/content.aspx?contenttypeid=90&contentid=P02517. Accessed on May 29 2023.
10. Vaja R. Anaesthesia for patients with liver disease. *Contin Educ Anaesth Crit Care Pain* 2010; 10:15–19.
11. The ABCs of Hepatitis. Centers for Disease Control and Prevention. Updated 2020. Accessed on May 29 2023. Available from https://www.cdc.gov/hepatitis/resources/professionals/pdfs/abctable.pdf.
12. Martin JL. Toxicity of Inhaled Anesthetics. In: Miller's Anesthesia, 7th edition. Miller RD, Eriksson LI, Fleisher LA, Wiener-Kronish JP, Young WL, (eds). Elsevier, Philadelphia, 2010; pp. 644–650.
13. Shneider BL, Neimark E, Frankenberg T, et al. Critical analysis of the pediatric end-stage liver disease scoring system: A single center experience. *Liver Transpl* 2005; 11:788–795.

33 Cirrhosis of the Liver in Children

Lakshmi Kumar

The destruction of normal liver tissue by fibrosis, with the formation of regenerative nodules caused by any of the following conditions, is defined as cirrhosis of the liver.

Aetiology

Aetiology of liver cirrhosis in children can be considered under the following main headings – metabolic, biliary tract-related and other causes.

Biliary atresia and Wilson's disease are the commonest indications for liver transplants amongst children.

1. **Metabolic/inherited disorders**
   (a) Wilson's disease
   (b) Primary hyperoxaluria
   (c) Glycogen storage diseases
   (d) Hemosiderosis
   (e) Congenital hypofibrinogenemia
   (f) Urea cycle disorders
   (g) Maple syrup urine disorder
2. **Bile duct diseases**
   (a) Biliary atresia
   (b) Progressive fibrosing intrahepatic cholestasis
   (c) Congenital hepatic fibrosis
   (d) Choledochal cysts (Caroli's disease)
3. **Other causes**
   (a) Drug-induced liver injury
   (b) Viral aetiology

Hepatotoxic groups of drugs range from paracetamol, antibiotics, antifungals and some herbal supplements. While paracetamol and anti-tubercular medications are known to cause acute or fulminant failure, insidious progression to liver disease may also occur with hepatocyte injury.

Pathophysiology

Cirrhosis can impact multiple systems.

Cardiovascular System

This is characteristically hyperdynamic with a high cardiac output (CO) and low systemic vascular resistance. In general, the systemic arterial pressure is decreased, the heart rate is slightly increased and central filling pressure is normal. The mixed venous oxygen saturation is high. In advanced disease, there are widespread arteriovenous (AV) communications through collateral vessels within the splanchnic organs, lungs, muscles and skin, which may be caused by increased cirrhosis-induced endogenous vasodilators such as glucagon, nitric oxide, vasoactive intestinal polypeptide and ferritin. The presence of these endogenous vasodilators may also explain the poor cardiovascular response to physiologic and pharmacologic vasoconstrictors. Alcoholic liver disease and haemosiderosis may also be associated with cardiomyopathy. They are commonly seen in adolescents or young adults.

Respiratory System

Cirrhosis is often associated with pulmonary dysfunction and hypoxaemia. The causes of hypoxaemia are multiple. They are as follows:

- Diaphragmatic splinting from ascites or the presence of pleural effusion restricts alveolar ventilation, reduces functional residual capacity and predisposes to atelectasis and hypoxia.

- Intrapulmonary AV shunting may occur, worsening hypoxia.
- The presence of endogenous vasodilators impairs the development of hypoxic pulmonary vasoconstriction.
- The erythrocyte 2,3-diphosphoglycerate levels increase and shift the oxyhaemoglobin dissociation curve to the right.

As the AV channels are more dilated at the bases rather than the apex of the lung, the sitting position worsens hypoxemia while the lying down position allows redistribution of blood to the apices and improves oxygenation.

Haematology

Anaemia may be present secondary to hypersplenism-induced haemolysis, bleeding varices, chronic illness, bone marrow suppression due to drugs and malnutrition. Reduced capacity to synthesise clotting factors results in coagulopathy. Prothrombin time (PT) and activated partial thromboplastin time are elevated. Thrombocytopaenia and platelet dysfunction are common.

Renal Dysfunction

The extreme splanchnic vasodilatation predisposes to the development of hepatorenal syndrome resulting from renal vasoconstriction and activation of the renin–angiotensin aldosterone axis. In addition, hypovolemia from any cause can affect renal function in a manner akin to the injury/risk of acute kidney injury.

Hypovolaemia can occur because of the formation of ascites, overzealous diuretic therapy, gastrointestinal haemorrhage or sequestration of blood in the splanchnic vasculature.

Vasodilatation associated with general anaesthesia may result in renal hypoperfusion and the development of prerenal kidney failure.

Endocrinopathies

Plasma levels of glucagon and growth hormone increase and insulin resistance can occur. Adolescent girls may experience oligomenorrhoea and amenorrhoea. Depletion of hepatic and muscle glycogen storage may result in perioperative hypoglycaemia. Muscle wasting is common due to impaired protein synthesis and malnutrition.

A decrease in cortisol levels has been observed in chronic liver disease and may be significant enough to warrant supplementation.

Gastric Emptying

An increase in gastric volume and a delay in emptying time have been documented in chronic liver disease. Practically, however, the need for a rapid sequence intubation can be reserved for those patients with tense ascites, active variceal bleeding and encephalopathy. The evidence for an increased aspirate after adherence to the standard fasting requirements is very low.

Portal Hypertension

Ascites in chronic liver disease is a result of resistance to blood flow through the portal system. The stasis of blood in the splanchnic circulation, associated hypoalbuminemia due to defects in the liver's synthetic function, favours an egress of fluid in the abdominal cavity. As liver disease progresses the stellate cells in the perisinusoidal space of Disse are replaced by collagen and lymphatic reabsorption is compromised.

Hepatic encephalopathy in patients with chronic liver disease can be precipitated by infection, gastrointestinal haemorrhage, electrolyte or acid–base disturbance, sedative drugs, hypoglycaemia, hypoxia, hypotension or excessive dietary intake of proteins.

In acute and fulminant liver failure, the onset of encephalopathy is sudden and intracranial pressures may be very high. All measures to reduce intracranial pressures must be undertaken, as death from coning is a feared complication in this group.

Symptoms and Signs

The symptoms and signs can be insidious in onset. It may often be undetected in the absence of jaundice, ascites or encephalopathy. The earliest manifestation could be jaundice and a darkening of the skin. Ascites, if present, suggests increased portal venous pressure and worsening liver function.

Measurement of liver span, the distance between the edge of the liver and the upper margin of dullness obtained by percussion along the right midclavicular line, is a useful adjunct to palpation at initial presentation and at follow-up. The mean span changes from 4.5 to 5 cm at 1 week of age to 6 to 7 cm in early adolescence. In cirrhosis, the lower margin may not be palpable.

Signs of advanced liver disease include muscle wasting, spider naevi, pleural effusions, ascites, splenomegaly and encephalopathy. Auscultation of the liver may reveal vascular bruits. These can be due to anatomic malformations of the intrahepatic vessels or increased flow to the liver.

Children who have end-stage liver disease can have significant morbidity and mortality after anaesthesia and surgery. Any interventions can worsen liver function and can result in fatal hepatic failure. Therefore, end-stage liver disease is usually a relative contraindication to surgical intervention except in life-threatening situations.

Investigations

- A full blood count will detect anaemia, thrombocytopaenia or raised white cell count if the infection is present.
- Prothrombin time (PT)/international normalised ratio (INR) is a useful indicator of hepatocellular synthetic function and is used as a prognostic indicator in acute liver failure and after surgery in patients with chronic liver disease. If low, vitamin K should be administered for at least 3–5 days before the operation, whenever possible.
- Measurement of albumin levels is also useful in the evaluation of liver synthetic function.
- Baseline renal function, electrolytes and acid–base status.
- Hyponatraemia or potassium abnormalities before surgery.
- Check blood glucose levels to rule out hypoglycaemia.
- Cardiac investigations should include ECG, and echocardiography for associated cardiac defects, LV function and volume status and pulmonary artery pressures based on the RV pressures.
- Chest X-ray or ultrasound may be useful for demonstrating pleural effusion and ascites in need of drainage before surgery.
- Lung function tests should be considered before major surgery. However, room air saturations and baseline arterial blood gases should be done in all cases.

Predictors of Outcome

The Child–Turcotte–Pugh classification (Table 33.1) is commonly used to estimate the risk of mortality in patients with liver disease undergoing surgical intervention. Points are given for each of the five entities with a possible maximum score of 15. Child–Turcotte–Pugh's total score of 5–6 is class A and is associated with a low operative mortality risk (<5%); a total score of 7–9 (Child's class B) has moderate mortality risk (25%) and total score of 10–15 (Child's class C) carries high-risk mortality (>50%). Other predictors which affect the outcome poorly include emergency surgery, malnutrition, blood loss and sepsis.

Paediatric end-stage liver disease (PELD) is a system of scoring the severity of disease for children with liver disease under 12 years of age.

Table 33.1 Child –Turcott–Pugh Classification

Parameter	Points Assigned		
	1	2	3
Ascites	Absent	Slight	Moderate
Hepatic encephalopathy	None	Grade 1–2	Grade 3–4
Serum bilirubin micromol/L (mg/dL)	<34.2 (<2)	34.2–51.3 (2–3)	>51.3 (>3)
Serum albumin g/L (g/dL)	>35 (>3.5)	28–35 (2.8–3.5)	<28 (<2.8)
Prothrombin time (Seconds over control) INR	<4 <1.7	4–6 1.7–2.3	>6 >2.3

Child A: Score 5–6 (well compensated); Child B: Score 7–9 (significant functional compromise); Child C: Score 10–15 (decompensated).

It is calculated using the child's albumin, bilirubin, INR for PT, child's age and degree of growth failure. It is calculated according to the following formula:

PELD score

$\{(0.436 \times \text{age}^{a}) - (0.687 \times \log(\text{albumin})) + (0.480 \times \log(\text{bilirubin})) + 1.857 \times \log(\text{INR})) + (0.667 \times \text{growth failure}^{b})\} \times 10$

[a]*Age <1 year is assigned a value of 1. Age >1 year is assigned a value of 0.*

[b]*Growth failure is assigned a value of 1 and no growth failure is assigned 0.*

The PELD score calculated for any given patient is correlated with their prognosis and how likely they are to die within a certain time period. A higher score correlates with a more critical condition. This score is also for prioritising the allocation of liver transplants.

Anaesthesia and Surgery

High PELD scores are not considered for elective surgery as the risks are very high.

General anaesthesia can worsen hepatic and neurologic function due to the associated alterations in hepatic blood flow and perfusion.

Emergency surgery requires rapid optimisation of existing problems in the limited time available. In these cases, morbidity and mortality can be very high.

The optimisation includes improving the intravascular volume status, preferably with albumin, correcting coagulopathy with vitamin K1, fresh frozen plasma if PT is greater than 1.5 times the control, platelets if the platelet count is less than 50,000/mm^3 and cryoprecipitate if fibrinogen levels are low (<100 mg/dL).

Packed red blood cells may be required if anaemia is severe, <8.0g/dL. Drainage of ascites may be considered to improve respiratory parameters but this should not be done rapidly to avoid haemodynamic decompensation. Each litre of ascites drained should be replaced with 7–8 g albumin to prevent paracentesis-induced circulatory dysfunction and drainage slowed to over 2–4 hours when possible.

Premedication: It is better to avoid a sedative premedication (see the following text) but an H2 receptor antagonist such as ranitidine may be given. Note that the patients may be on β-blockers as part of the medical therapy for portal hypertension.

Induction of anaesthesia: In compensated patients, careful attention to fasting and low pressure assisted ventilation can be used. In patients with tense ascites, a rapid sequence protocol should be followed due to slow gastric emptying and raised intra-abdominal pressure.

During surgery aim to maintain adequate hepatic arterial blood flow and thus hepatic oxygenation. Portal circulation has a much smaller role to play due to its involvement in the disease process. Factors decreasing hepatic blood flow and thus potentially harmful to the patient include all forms of anaesthesia and sedation, surgical traction on the liver, intermittent positive pressure ventilation, hyperventilation and hypocapnia, α-adrenoreceptor agonists and laparoscopic surgery. Care to minimise the intra-abdominal pressures during laparoscopy, minimise the use of PEEP and a dual ventilatory mode that allows the least peak airway pressures during dynamic changes in intra-abdominal pressure are strategies that help in the preservation of liver blood flow.

Administration of Anaesthesia: Relevant Pharmacology

In general, the effect of various drugs is influenced by hepatic blood flow, protein binding (considering that protein synthesis is markedly affected in liver failure) and their usage of various intrahepatic metabolic pathways on their way to elimination.

Sedatives

Sedative drugs such as midazolam are dependent on hepatic blood flow. Their clearance is halved while their half-life is doubled. Also 95–97% is bound to albumin and decrease in albumin levels means an increase in the free fraction of the drug with a greater pharmacodynamic effect.

Ketamine is highly lipophilic and is metabolised in the liver, but it does so by methylation so its clearance is minimally affected in cirrhosis.

Induction Agents

Etomidate is considered the safest agent for liver disease. Propofol has a short half-life but may cause hypotension due to vasodilation. A combination of ketamine with propofol may overcome the circulatory side effects of propofol. It is eliminated in the urine so liver failure does not affect its pharmacokinetics.

Thiopentone may be unsuitable due to an increase in the unbound fraction, redistribution and hypotension on induction.

Neuromuscular Blocking Drugs

Depolarising muscle relaxants: Pseudocholinesterase is required in the breakdown of succinylcholine. Low levels of pseudocholinesterase, an enzyme produced by active hepatocytes, result in a prolongation of the action of succinylcholine.

Non-depolarising muscle relaxants: Increase in volume of distribution and altered protein binding results in resistance to non-depolarisers. Steroid-based neuromuscular blocking drugs such as vecuronium and rocuronium have an elimination phase in the liver, and their action is prolonged in liver disease and should be avoided. On the other hand, atracurium and cis-atracurium are metabolised independently of the liver and are therefore considered ideal for use in patients with liver failure.

Opioids

The effect of opioids is produced by their direct binding to specific receptors. The total effect depends on the concentration of the opioids at the receptors and this may be altered by changes in hepatic blood flow and protein binding. The major metabolic pathway for opioids in the liver is oxidation. However, both morphine and buprenorphine undergo glucuronidation, whereas remifentanil undergoes ester hydrolysis. Most opioids have a decreased first-pass metabolism with a decreased drug clearance and an increased bioavailability (pethidine). Morphine, in spite of glucuronidation, has a poor clearance in the presence of cirrhosis.

Remifentanil is considered the ideal opioid in liver failure as it is metabolised by tissue and RBC esterases and is not dependent on the liver for metabolism.

Fentanyl, in low doses, may be used intraoperatively as it is renally excreted and does not have an active metabolite. However, it does accumulate with repeated dosing.

Morphine elimination is delayed due to poor hepatic blood flow and extraction ratio. It may, therefore, precipitate hepatic encephalopathy.

Volatile Anaesthetic Agents

Desflurane is considered the ideal anaesthetic in liver disease as it is the least metabolised in the liver. It also provides a quick emergence from anaesthesia. Isoflurane and sevoflurane are also considered relatively safe as they undergo minimum hepatic metabolism. Halothane is metabolised to a greater degree. It also produces cardiac depression and hypotension and is considered unsuitable for liver disease. Halothane can affect the hepatic arterial buffer response in liver disease.

Monitoring

All patients should be monitored with pulse oximetry, electrocardiography (ECG), non-invasive blood pressure (NIBP) and end-tidal capnography. In addition, invasive monitoring of both arterial and central venous pressure (CVP) is recommended for major surgery. Monitoring of core body temperature, neuromuscular blockade and urine output is also recommended.

As these patients have portal hypertension and often have oesophageal varices, insertion of nasogastric tubes and oesophageal temperature probes should be avoided. If considered necessary, they can be placed either by the endoscopist or the senior anaesthesiologist with utmost caution.

IV Fluids

Most of these patients are vasodilated with low systemic vascular resistance and high cardiac output (CO).

Large-bore intravenous (IV) access is mandatory. Lactate-containing fluids are best avoided and acetate-containing fluids are the preferred choice. All fluids should be administered via a fluid-warming device and access to a rapid infusion device is important for all major surgeries.

Fluid replacement should be guided by cardiovascular variables, blood loss and urine output. Maintenance of intravascular fluid volume and appropriate cardiovascular management are critical to achieve an adequate urine output of 0.5–1 mL/kg/hr. However, loop diuretics or mannitol may be needed occasionally. Only when preload is optimised vasopressors such as noradrenaline/phenylephrine should be used to treat hypotension. Glucose must be monitored closely and a background infusion of 5% dextrose started if necessary.

Ventilation is controlled to maintain arterial PCO_2 between 4.5 and 5.3 kPa (34–40 mmHg).

Post-Operative Pain Management

IV patient-controlled analgesia using fentanyl is often the treatment of choice.

If bleeding parameters and platelets are normal, a regional anaesthetic technique may be considered.

As a rule, central neuraxial blocks (CNB) are contraindicated in Child class C and need to be used to weigh risks versus benefits in Child class B patients.

Transversus abdominis plane blocks and erector spinae blocks with catheters are superficial blocks and are considered safe even in the presence of coagulopathy and offer a reasonable alternative to central neuraxial blocks (CNB) (see Chapter 14).

Non-steroidal anti-inflammatory drugs (NSAIDs) are not recommended owing to the risk of gastrointestinal haemorrhage due to platelet dysfunction and nephrotoxicity. Acetaminophen is not contraindicated but should be used with care and liver function should be monitored carefully.

Post-Operative Care

Post-operative ICU admission should be anticipated for patients with advanced liver disease. Sedative drugs should be discontinued early and patients should be allowed to recover from anaesthesia so that neurological assessment can be performed. Worsening encephalopathy, jaundice and ascites are very important clinical markers of decompensation of liver function. Careful fluid management is continued to avoid the development of post-operative renal failure.

Intravascular catheters should be removed as soon as they are no longer required because of the increased risk of catheter-related sepsis.

SUGGESTED READINGS

1. Ziser A, Plevak DJ, Wiesner RH, et al. Morbidity and mortality in cirrhotic patients undergoing anesthesia and surgery. *Anesthesiology* 1999; 90:42–53.
2. Maze M, Bass NM. Anaesthesia and the Hepatobiliary System. In: Anesthesia, 5th edition. Miller RD (ed). Churchill Livingstone, Philadelphia 2000; pp. 1960–1972.
3. Strunin L, Eagle CJ. Hepatic Diseases. In: Anesthesia and Uncommon Diseases, 4th edition. Benumof JL (ed). WB Saunders Company, Philadelphia 1998; pp. 147–174.
4. Wiklund RA. Preoperative preparation of patients with advanced liver disease. *Crit Care Med* 2004; 32:S106–15.
5. Haberer JP, Schoeffler P, Couderc E, et al. Fentanyl pharmacokinetics in anaesthetized patients with cirrhosis. *Br J Anaesth* 1982; 54:1267–1270.
6. Zaleski L, Abello D, Gold MI. Desflurane versus isoflurane in patients with chronic hepatic and renal disease. *Anesth Analg* 1993; 76:353–356.
7. Vaja R, McNicol L, Sisley I. Anaesthesia for patients with liver disease. *Contin Educ Anaesth Crit Care Pain* 2010; 10(1):15–19.
8. Fischer SP, Bader AM, Sweiter B. Hepatic Disorders Under Preoperative Evaluation. In: Millers, 7th edition. Miller RD, Eriksson LI, Fleisher LA, et al. (eds). Churchill Livingstone/Elsevier, Philadelphia 2010; pp. 1026–1028.
9. Mushlin PS, Gelman S. Cirrhosis and Portal Hypertension. In: Millers, 7th edition. Miller RD, Eriksson LI, Fleisher LA, et al. (eds). Churchill Livingstone/Elsevier, Philadelphia 2010; pp. 431–438.
10. Bromley P, Bennett J, Anaesthesia for children with liver disease. *Cont Educ Anaesth Crit Care Pain* 2014;14: 207–212.
11. Steadman RH. Anaesthesia for the Patient with Liver Disease. Available from: www.uptodate.com. (accessed 16 March 2023).
12. Dalal A, Lang JD. Anesthetic Considerations for Patients with Liver Disease. In: Hepatic Surgery. InTech, London 2013.

34 Liver Tumours and Hepatic Resection

Lakshmi Kumar • Rebecca Jacob

Liver tumours are uncommon in children, but 72% of those that occur are malignant. Of these, the most common are hepatoblastomas and hepatocellular carcinomas. Unlike in adults, metastatic tumours only account for 10% of cases. Neuroendocrine tumours, though rare, are notorious for their intraluminal venous extension and may have to be removed on cardiopulmonary bypass.

Hepatoblastomas usually occur in low-birth-weight babies below the age of 2 years. The presenting symptom is an abdominal mass that is not usually associated with ascites, anaemia or jaundice. Liver functions are often normal. Hepatoblastomas are often associated with isosexual precocity, as a result of the liver's production of ectopic gonadotrophic hormone, Beckwith–Wiedemann's syndrome, polyposis coli, Wilm's tumour and foetal alcohol syndrome. Survival rates are up to 90% if the histology type is foetal and about 50% if the histology type is embryonal. Other types with poorer survival rates are macrotubular and anaplastic.

Hepatocellular carcinoma occurs in two age peaks of below 4 years and between 12 and 15 years, respectively. The survival rates in both groups are poor at 5–10%. Patients present with weight loss, jaundice, fever and lethargy. Only about 5% have cirrhosis. Other associated diseases include Von Gierke's disease, type I glycogenesis, cystinosis, extrahepatic biliary atresia, hypoplasia of intra-hepatic bile ducts, Wilson's disease and giant cell hepatitis. Many of these children would have been subjected to chemotherapy, and the chemotherapy protocol should be reviewed prior to surgery. Adriamycin and anthracycline are often used and are associated with dose-dependent irreversible cardiomyopathy. These patients will require special tests to assess cardiotoxicity and cardiac reserve, such as history, physical examination, ECG, chest X-ray and echocardiogram.

Anatomic hepatic resection is dependent on the segmental infrastructure of the liver (refer to Chapter 29) and saves a considerable amount of normal liver tissue. *Non-anatomic resection* is independent of structural planes and excessive bleeding is a common problem.

Anaesthesia for Hepatic Resection

Pre-Operative Check

Pre-operative investigations should include complete blood count, coagulation profile, renal and liver function tests, chest X-ray and blood grouping with reserve. CT or MR abdomen with volumetric analysis is done to assess the liver tumour size and involvement of hepatic veins. If the future liver remnant (FLR) is more than 25% of healthy liver then it is considered acceptable. In selected children with FLR less than 25%, pre-operative portal vein embolisation/ligation can be considered to allow for compensatory hypertrophy of the remnant liver. In children, the residual liver is often normal unlike in adults whose liver is often cirrhotic. However, patients with pre-existing liver disease often present with coagulation defects, acidosis, electrolyte disturbances and hypoglycaemia. Pulmonary function may be impaired due to the presence of shunts (that are also a part of hepatopulmonary syndrome) or diaphragmatic splinting due to ascites and hepatomegaly. They should be specifically assessed for gas exchange impairment, nutrition-associated cardiomyopathy, infection, cirrhosis, decompensation and kidney impairment. The response of hypoxaemia to 100% oxygen should be measured to assess the degree of shunt.

The influence of *anaesthetic techniques and drugs* on liver function after liver resection has not been studied. However, the pharmacokinetics of fentanyl and sufentanil are not altered nor is the liver function responsible for the elimination of remifentanil. Theoretically, muscle relaxants used should be those not metabolised or eliminated by the liver such as atracurium and cisatracurium, and these should be the agents of choice in liver resection.

Sevoflurane is the inhalational agent of choice for induction and isoflurane or desflurane is 'marginally preferred' for maintenance. Nitrous oxide has an additive effect on depressing cardiac function when used with other volatile agents. Halothane, given the risk of hepatotoxicity and its implications on hepatic blood flow, has been completely replaced by newer safe agents.

Monitoring

There is a potential for massive blood loss in these children, and invasive monitoring with intra-arterial blood pressure (IABP) and central venous pressure (CVP) with Foley's catheter for measuring urine output is considered mandatory. Minimally invasive cardiac output (CO) monitoring lacks accuracy in children. In centres equipped with multidisciplinary units, transoesophageal echocardiography (TOE) may be used to assess cardiac function and volume status if a multifactorial problem arises.

Intraoperative blood loss has been correlated with high CVP and venous congestion. Therefore, intravenous fluid replacement should be restricted as far as the haemodynamics allow until parenchymal resection is completed. Maintaining a CVP of less than 5 cm of H_2O has been shown to reduce bleeding, thus decreasing the need for blood transfusion, prolonged dissection, prolonged portal occlusion time and increase in the hepatic ischaemic reperfusion injury. However, any intraoperative decrease in systemic arterial blood pressure (SAP) should be treated aggressively to preserve liver blood flow and avoid post-operative impairment of liver function.

The recording of CVP may, however, prove fallacious as it is much less reliable during liver resection. CVP may increase during surgery when the pressure of surgical retractors on the diaphragm raises the intrathoracic pressure or compression on the liver releases a significant amount of blood into the circulation. Clamping of liver vessels decreases venous return to the heart and thus the CVP. This may also occur when the liver is mobilised and the vena cava and the portal vein get compressed or twisted. The potential for air embolism, while maintaining a low CVP, during liver dissection is significant. A negative CVP can rapidly allow large volumes of air to be entrained through small, unrecognised lacerations of the hepatic veins. The presence of an air embolus may be diagnosed by a sudden fall in $EtCO_2$, hypoxaemia, hypercarbia, fall in SAP and rise in pulmonary artery pressure. This problem has been minimised by newer techniques of surgery and the maintenance of CVP between 3 and 5 cm of H_2O.

Blood and Fluid Replacement

Hepatic resections carry an inherent risk of bleeding due to the highly vascularised liver parenchyma. Surgical techniques such as clamp and crush, bipolar cautery and ultrasonic surgical aspirator help reduce blood loss. Should massive bleeding occur, the major criteria for blood volume expansion include the adequacy of systemic arterial pressure, expired carbon dioxide levels and the waveform of the peripheral pulse oximetry curve.

Massive blood volume replacement with volume expanders, blood and blood products may create physiological derangements requiring close monitoring and correction of arterial blood gases, acid–base balance, electrolytes, coagulation profiles and tissue oxygenation. Haemodynamic instability can be accentuated during surgical manipulation. Lower haemoglobin values are well tolerated, and restricting intraoperative fluids to decrease haemodilution may contribute to a reduction in the need for blood transfusion.

Liver vessel occlusion may be resorted to decrease blood inflow to the liver. This may be done by clamping of the vascular triad and more rarely with total vascular occlusion. In these cases, inotropes, vasopressors and vasodilators must be used appropriately. Intermittent clamping of the portal vascular triad is better tolerated than prolonged continuous periods of ischaemia.

Antibiotics

Antibiotics are given pre- and intraoperatively because of long operating times, large post-surgery dead spaces and inevitable areas of dead tissue. Translocation of intestinal enterobacteria to the systemic circulation and peritoneal inoculation is seen after major liver resection. The drug recommended is cefazoline. Biliary obstruction is a potential source of sepsis, and piperacillin with tazobactam (or sulbactam) combined with an aminoglycoside or a fluoroquinolone is recommended.

Postoperative Considerations

Hypothermia is commonly associated with this surgery, and adequate warming during and after surgery is important.

Post-Operative Ventilation

Post-operative ventilation should be considered in children who are cold, have had massive transfusions, still have some acid–base or coagulation abnormalities and have other associated anomalies.

Post-Operative Ascites

Post-operative ascites always develops at the expense of circulating fluid and occurs whether the liver is healthy or diseased. Intra- and post-operative fluid limitation does not prevent this ascites and volume expansion with diuretics and vasopressor therapy should be initiated early to prevent kidney failure.

Post-Operative Pain Relief

Liver surgery may cause post-operative liver disturbances even in patients with normal pre-operative coagulation functions undergoing uncomplicated hepatectomy. The extent of liver resection appears to affect the magnitude and duration of the coagulation defect with the prothrombin time (PT) and platelets showing an inverse relationship to the amount of hepatic tissue resected. Matot et al. found that PT returned to normal within a day in minor resections but took 5–7 days in uncomplicated major resections necessitating the use of fresh frozen plasma prior to removal of epidural catheters. The availability of point-of-care tests of coagulation has given insights into the coagulation which may not be as deranged as suggested by the PT. In fact, the viscoelastic tests may reveal a near-normal coagulation due to compensatory hyperfibrinogenaemia explaining why epidurals have been safe despite an apparent coagulopathy.

With the widespread availability of ultrasound and expertise in blocks, the need for central neuraxial blockade is diminishing. Equivalent analgesia can be obtained by a combination of abdominal plane blocks or right thoracic paravertebral block with multimodal analgesia which includes paracetamol at 10–15 mg/kg 8 hourly (see also Chapters 14 and 47).

Morphine is a very effective analgesic either as a bolus or as an infusion. However, its half-life will be dependent upon the residual liver function. Shorter-acting opioids such as fentanyl infusions may be safer in children. Paracetamol can be used safely even after liver resections with a slightly lower dose. Co-administration of N-acetylcysteine commonly used in liver resections can prevent the accumulation of paracetamol metabolites by providing glutathione. Nonsteroidal anti-inflammatory drugs (NSAIDs) are better avoided as they worsen the pre-existing poor renal function, especially in the presence of cirrhosis.

Right thoracic paravertebral blocks have been used in managing post-hepatectomy pain in adults, but there are no reports of their use in paediatrics (see also Chapters 14 and 47).

REFERENCE

1. Matot I, Scheinen O, Eid A, Jurim O. Epidural anesthesia and analgesia in liver resection. *Anesth Analg* 2002; 95:1179–1181.

SUGGESTED READINGS

1. Rivera MR, Squires RH, Davies PJ. Essentials of Hepatology. In: A Practice of Anesthesia for Infants and Children, 4th edition. Cote CJ, Lerman J, Todres ID (eds). Saunders Elsevier, Philadelphia 2009; p. 595.
2. Hammer G, Hall S, Davis PJ. Anaesthesia for General Abdominal, Thoracic, Urologic and Bariatric Surgery. In: Smith's Anesthesia for Infants and Children, 7th edition. Motoyama EK, Davis J (eds). Elsevier, Philadelphia 2006; pp. 695–697.
3. Green DW, Ashley EMC. The choice of inhalation anaesthetic for major abdominal surgery in children with liver disease. *Paediatr Anaesth* 2002; 12:665–673.
4. Lentschener C, Ozier Y. Anaesthesia for major liver resection – some points should be revisited. *Eur J Anaesthesiol* 2002; 19:780–788.
5. Jones RM, Moulton CE, Hardy KJ. Central venous pressure and its effect on blood loss during liver resection. *Br J Surg* 1998; 85:1058–1060.
6. Kwan AL. Epidural analgesia for patients undergoing hepatectomy. *Anesth Intens Care* 2003; 31:236–237.
7. Ng A, Hall F, Atkinson A, et al. Bridging the analgesic gap. *Acute Pain* 2000; 3:194–199.
8. Jacob R. Anesthesia for biliary atresia and hepatectomy in pediatrics. *Ind J Anaesth* 2012; 56:479–484.
9. Howard R, Carter B, Curry J, et al. Good practice in postoperative and procedural pain management. *Pediatr Anaesth* 2008; 18:1–81.
10. Li K, Jiang F, Aizpuru M, et al. Successful management and technical aspects of major liver resection in children: A retrospective cohort study. Medicine (Baltimore) 2021; 100(6):e24420.

35 Pyloric Stenosis

Rebecca Jacob

Pyloric stenosis, also called an olive tumour, occurs due to the hypertrophy of the gastric outlet musculature. It is one of the most commonest gastrointestinal tract (GIT) abnormalities in the first 3 months of life. It is important to realise that pyloric stenosis is an acute medical emergency and not a surgical emergency. Pre-operative correction of severe fluid and electrolyte deficits may require several days, but careful pre-operative preparation is essential for a positive outcome.

Incidence

It is variably quoted as 3:1,000 to 1:500 live births.

It is more common in first-born males than in females (4:1) and is more common in the offspring of affected parents.

Aetiology

The definitive aetiology remains unknown.

Various theories proposed are as follows:

- Polygenic mode of inheritance
- Hypoganglionosis
- Deficient production of nitric oxide synthase causing impaired relaxation of pyloric smooth muscle
- *Helicobacter pylori* infection
- Hypergastrinaemia with duodenal hyperacidity pylorospasm and hypertrophy of the pyloric muscle
- Macrolide antibiotics such as erythromycin used by pregnant and breastfeeding mothers or given to babies in the first 2 weeks of life

Associated congenital abnormalities are rare.

Clinical Features

Symptoms: Present between the third and fifth weeks of life with a history of progressive non-bilious vomiting which may become projectile. This occurs immediately after a feed and the baby is hungry soon after vomiting. Concurrent constipation is common. Loss of weight and failure to gain weight are common. Jaundice occurs as a result of glucuronyl transferase deficiency due to starvation (17%). Pre-renal failure may also occur due to severe dehydration.

Signs: The child is dehydrated with visible gastric peristalsis and a palpable olive-shaped firm tumour (felt best soon after vomiting) in the epigastrium or right hypochondrium (**Fig. 35.1**). Ultrasound examination helps in early diagnosis (see investigations below.)

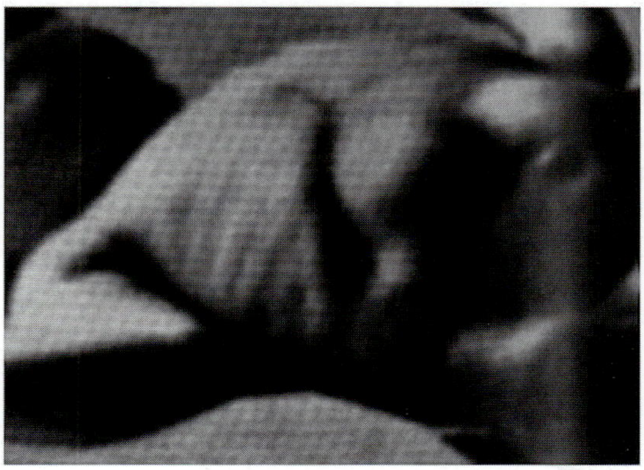

Figure 35.1 Note the presence of an 'olive tumour' in the right hypochondrium in the case of severe dehydration.

Pathophysiology

The basic pathology involves hypertrophy of the pyloric musculature with narrowing of the gastric outlet (Fig. 35.2).

The child with pyloric stenosis may show a wide range of metabolic disturbances, the most common being a chloride (or saline) responsive hypochloraemic, hypokalaemic, hypovolaemic and hyponatraemic metabolic alkalosis. Hypocalcaemia may be associated with hyponatraemia. Normally, each mEq of gastric acid secreted causes a mEq of HCO_3^- to be generated. This gastric acid passes into the duodenum and is neutralised by the pancreatic HCO_3^-. In this case, the gastric acid that is produced is lost to the body in the vomitus or gastric aspirate while the generated HCO_3 continues to rise in the plasma. This increased HCO_3 load cannot be handled by the proximal tubule of the kidney, and increasing amounts of $NaHCO_3$ are delivered to the distal tubule, which cannot reabsorb it. So, the kidney passes alkaline urine with a pH > 7.0 along with Na. As there is also an extracellular fluid volume (ECFV) depletion, the kidney attempts to conserve Na^+ by stimulating aldosterone secretion. Hypokalaemia occurs as K^+ is lost in the vomitus, lost in the urine in exchange for H^+ (in an effort to conserve Na^+) and also shifts intracellularly as the pH becomes more alkalotic. With the depletion of Na^+ and K^+, the kidneys secrete more acidic urine (paradoxic acidosis) thus further increasing metabolic alkalosis. Hypochloraemia occurs due to loss of Cl^- from the gastric secretion and in an effort to conserve Cl^- the urinary Cl^- drops to <20 mEq/l. Usually, urinary Cl^- and Na^+ concentrations are similar and both are low in hypovolaemic states as both are reabsorbed together. However, in pyloric stenosis some Na^+ loss is obligatory with the excess HCO_3^- presented to the distal tubule so that the Na^+ found in the urine is inappropriate for ECFV depletion. In contrast, all the Cl^- is reabsorbed in exchange for HCO_3^- and the urinary Cl^- levels are a more accurate predictor of the patient's volume status.

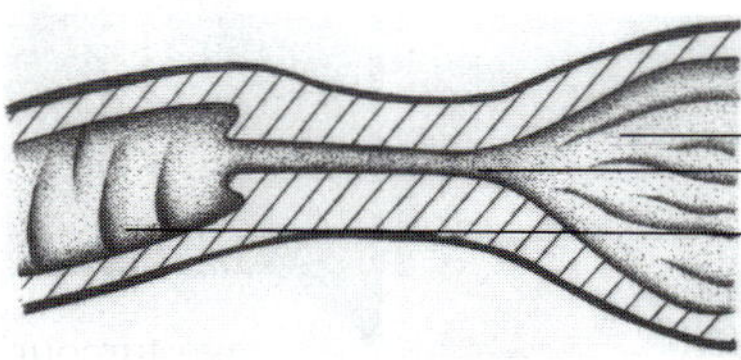

Figure 35.2 Pathology showing hypertrophy of the pylorus and narrowing of the gastric outlet.

Clinically, the baby shows varying signs of dehydration as shown in Table 35.1. It is important to accurately assess the baby's condition as further management is based on the clinical findings.

Table 35.1 Clinical Signs of Dehydration in Infants

Severity	Mild	Moderate	Severe
Fluid loss (%BW)	5%	10%	15%
Anterior fontanelle	Normal	Sunken	Markedly depressed
Skin turgor	Normal	Decreased	Greatly decreased
Mucous membrane	Moist	Dry	Very dry
Eyes	Normal	Sunken	Markedly sunken
Pulse	Normal	Increased	Greatly increased and feeble
Respiration	Normal	Tachypnoea	Rapid and deep
Urine output (ml/kg/hr)	<2	<1	<0.5

BW, body weight.

Investigations

1. **Blood**
   (a) Haemoglobin (haemoconcentration may result in polycythaemia)
   (b) Electrolytes (hypokalaemia, hypochloraemia, hyponatraemia and hypocalcaemia)
   (c) Arterial blood gas (metabolic alkalosis and metabolic acidosis)
2. **Urine**
   Cl - low, Na - normal to high, pH - initially alkaline but may become acidic paradoxically.
3. **Radiological**
   Ultrasound abdomen: The size of the pylorus is measured and compared to a standard value. The pylorus muscle thickness >4 mm, length >14–20 mm and pyloric diameter >10–14 mm is diagnostic in term infants. This investigation is less accurate in premature infants. It must be noted that accuracy is operator dependent.

A barium meal is no longer done as it exposes the baby to radiation and it is difficult to remove/aspirate all the barium after the investigation (**Fig. 35.3**).

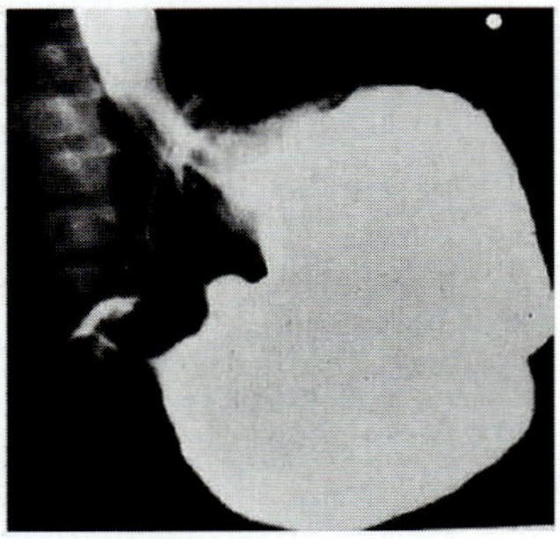

Figure 35.3 Radiological appearance after a barium swallow. Note the distended stomach.

Differential Diagnosis

The differential diagnosis of pyloric stenosis includes *gastro-oesophageal reflux disease and sepsis.*

Management

The management is primarily medical:

- Start an intravenous line and take samples of haemoglobin and electrolytes
- Pass a nasogastric (NG) tube – 8 Fr
- Gastric washout 4 hourly with saline till it clears. Then aspirate every 2 hours (this is especially important if a barium swallow has been done).
- Fluid management is according to the degree of dehydration – mild, moderate and severe (see **Table 38.1** for grading severity of dehydration).

Severe Dehydration

Greater than 15% fluid loss, severe alkalosis and impending cardiovascular failure

- Give bolus 20 ml/kg of normal saline (NS) or 5% dextrose normal saline or colloid.
- Then continue as for moderate dehydration with half the estimated deficit being given as NS over 6–8 hours.

Mild-to-Moderate Dehydration

- Glucose saline (5% glucose in 0.45% NS and 10 mmol potassium chloride [KCl] in a 500 ml bag) at 6–8 ml/hr
- The KCl is to be added only after the child starts passing urine. More KCl may be required if the serum K^+ is low (refer to Chapter 7)
- NG tube washout to be replaced with an equal amount of NS
- Once the target is reached, glucose saline, at the rate of 4 ml/kg/hr, should be administered as maintenance
- Conservative management with nasoduodenal feeding may be considered for those in whom surgery is contraindicated.

Targets for Resuscitation

- Serum chloride ≥ 106 mmol/l
- Serum $Na^+ > 135$ mmol/l
- Serum $HCO_3^- \leq 26$ mmol/l
- Urine $Cl^- > 20$ mmol/l
- Urine output > 1 ml/kg

Surgical Management

Surgery is the definitive treatment where a pyloromyotomy, Ramsted's procedure, is done and the pyloric muscle is widely split down to the submucosa. It is a simple operation, and morbidity and mortality are very low (**Figs 35.4 and 35.5**).

Laproscopic pyloromyotomy is an option.

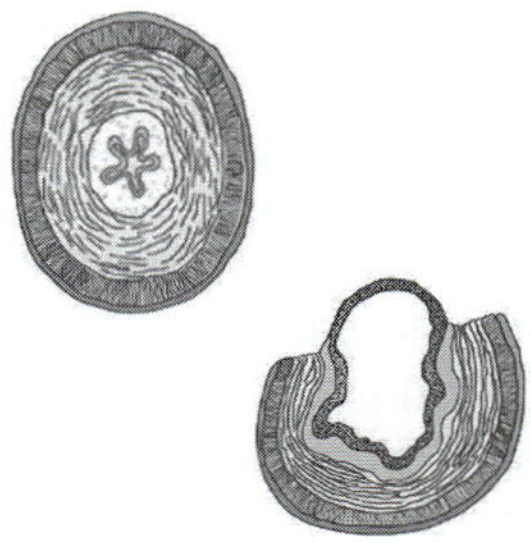

Figure 35.4 Pyloric stenosis before and after pyloromyotomy.

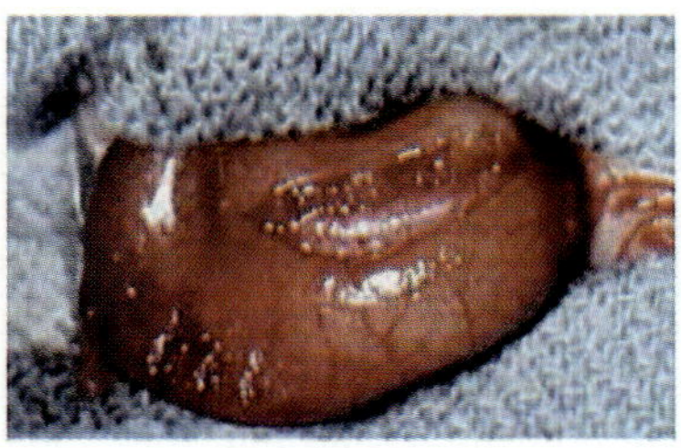

Figure 35.5 Pylorus after pyloromyotomy. Note that muscle has been cut down to the submucosa.

Anaesthetic Management

Acid–base abnormalities and dehydration are to be corrected prior to surgery because

- hypokalaemia leads to perioperative arrhythmias,
- metabolic alkalosis leads to post-operative apnoea and
- dehydration predisposes to hypotension and subsequent acidosis.

Monitoring

ECG, pulse oximetry, non-invasive blood pressure monitoring, $EtCO_2$, temperature and a precordial stethoscope.

Glucose and electrolyte levels should be monitored pre- and post-op and glucose may be monitored intraop if glucose-containing fluids have been stopped.

Preparation

If the patient is not awake and vigorous, the resuscitation is not adequate and the patient is not ready for anaesthesia and surgery.

The gastric outlet obstruction prevents gastric emptying and there is a risk of pulmonary aspiration of gastric acid secretions. It is therefore important to remove these secretions before anaesthesia suppresses the protective airway reflexes. An NG tube should be passed and aspirated prior to induction with the baby in the left and right positions as well as supine and prone so as to access the residual volume from the stomach. This has been quoted to be as high as 30–100 ml. Leave the NG tube open after aspiration. Ultrasound assessment of the gastric volume and contents can be helpful (see Chapter 15).

Induction

Pre-oxygenation and an intravenous induction are preferred as the child already has an IV line placed for resuscitation. Follow this with a rapid sequence induction with pre-oxygenation, a sleep dose of thiopentone sodium or propofol and suxamethonium 2 mg/kg. The use of cricoid pressure is controversial because of the difficulty in applying appropriate pressure in the right place in a child with a small pliable trachea.

An awake intubation may be considered if the intubation is anticipated to be difficult. However, some mucosal damage can be expected in a vigorous crying child.

The risk of vomiting or regurgitation is greatest during airway stimulation by laryngoscopy. So, ensure that after oxygenation an adequate depth of anaesthesia with neuromuscular blockade is achieved.

If any trouble is anticipated, *get help – the safety of the patient is of paramount importance and it should never be compromised because of inexperience or an inappropriate environment – the surgery can wait and the patient maintained on IV fluid!*

Maintenance

Sevoflurane or halothane and oxygen and nitrous oxide or air, muscle relaxation with atracurium, fentanyl (1–2 mcg/kg) for analgesia, intermittent positive pressure ventilation (IPPV), appropriate fluid management at 4 ml/hr and maintenance of body temperature.

At the end of the procedure, air may be injected through the NG tube to test the integrity of the pyloric mucosa. Intraoperative replacement fluid should be with isotonic NS or Ringer's lactate. Maintenance fluid should have at least 1% dextrose (refer to Chapter 7).

Post-Operative Analgesia

- **Non-opioids:** Rectal paracetamol given intraoperatively as a loading dose of 30–40 mg/kg, at the beginning of surgery, followed by 15–20 mg/kg post-operatively
- **Local anaesthesia:** 0.25% bupivacaine (2 mg/kg) or ropivacaine 0.2% as wound infiltration
- Avoid opioids to prevent post-operative apnoea.
- Ultrasound-guided rectus sheath blocks, TAP blocks and local infiltration by the surgeon are good alternatives (see Chapter 14).

Extubation

After the reversal of neuromuscular blockade, the child should be extubated fully awake, vigorous, with some purposeful movements, spontaneous respiration and an active gag reflex.

Post-Operative Period

Supplemental oxygen if pulse oximetry is <95%. Keep the child in the left lateral position.

Premature or ex-premature infants and those with significant alkalosis should be monitored for apnoea for at least 12 hours post-op. If there is an episode of apnoea, monitoring should be continued for a further 12 hours.

Feeding can be started 12–24 hours post-operatively. The first feed should be water followed by gradually increasing volumes of milk

Watch out for post-operative hypoglycaemia, which is a common complication.

SUGGESTED READINGS

1. Craig R, Deeley A. Anaesthesia for pyloromyotomy. *BJA Educ* 2018; 18(6):173–177.
2. Roberts JD, Romanelli TM, Todres ID. A Practice of Anaesthesia for Infants and Children. In: Neonatal Emergencies, 4th edition. Cote CJ, Lerman J, Todres ID (eds). WB Saunders Company, Philadelphia 2009; pp. 761–762.
3. Bissonnette B, Sullivan PJ. Pyloric stenosis. *Can J Anaesth* 1991; 38:668–70.
4. Fell D, Chelliah S. Infantile pyloric stenosis. *Br J Anaesth CEPD Rev*2001; 1:85–88.
5. Hammer G, Hall S, Davis PJ. Surgery for Pyloric Stenosis. In: Smiths Anesthesia for Infants and Children, 8th edition. Davis PJ, Cladis FP, Motoyama EK (eds). Elsevier Mosby, Philadelphia 2011; pp. 750–751.
6. Davies I. Infantile Hypertrophic Pyloric Stenosis. WFSA Resource Library 2012. Available at: https://resources.wfsahq.org/atotw/infantile-hypertrophic-pyloric-stenosis-anaesthesia-tutorial-of-the-week-276/. Accessed on Jan 2015.

36 Intestinal Obstruction in Children

Rebecca Jacob

Intestinal obstruction in children is an emergency and should be quickly diagnosed and treated. Excellent outcomes can be achieved with appropriate early treatment and a team approach to these acute problems.

Causes of Acute Intestinal Obstruction

Neonatal

- Stomach: Hypertrophic pyloric obstruction and atresia
- Duodenal: Atresia, stenosis and web
- Jejunal: Atresia and stenosis
- Ileal: Atresia
- Colonic: Meconium plug (Fig. 36.1), small left colon and atresia
- Anorectal: Imperforate anus and atresia

Infancy

- Intussusception (Figs 36.2 and 36.3)
- Hirschsprung disease
- Incarcerated hernia

Older children

- Meckel's diverticulum
- Adhesive obstruction
- Hernia

Causes of chronic partial obstruction include caecal volvulus and duplication cysts and occasionally faecal impaction leading to chronic strictures.

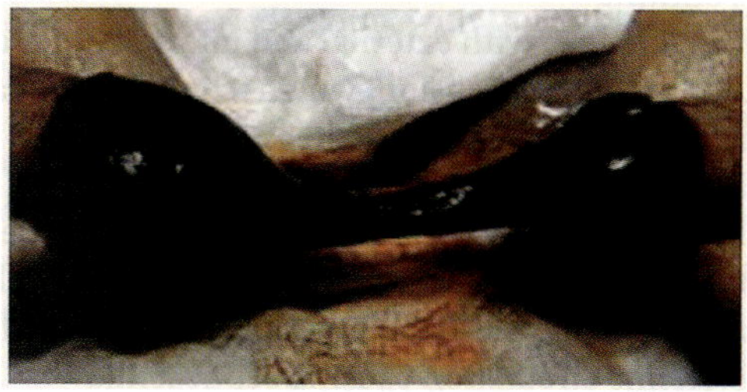

Figure 36.1 Inspissated meconium.

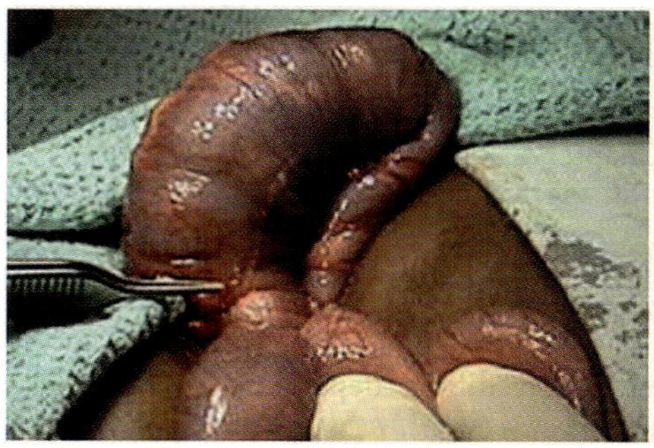

Figure 36.2 Intussusception.

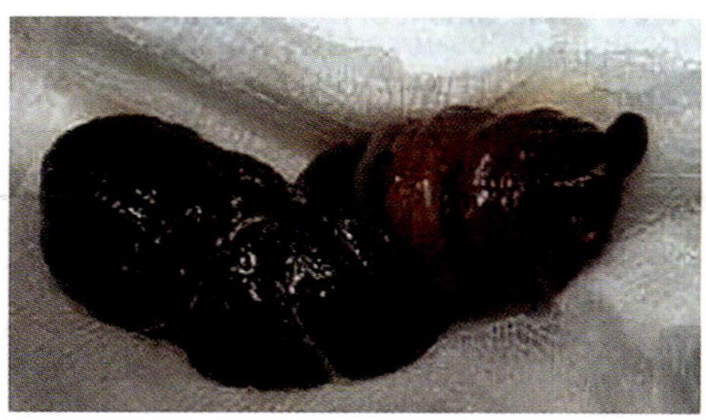

Figure 36.3 Appendix intussuscepted.

diagnosis as well as show the site of and often the aetiology of obstruction. Care must be taken to ensure that renal functions are normal before giving contrast. In children with borderline renal function, N-acetylcysteine can be administered along with adequate hydration to prevent contrast-induced acute renal failure.

Anaesthetic Management

Aggressive fluid resuscitation should be done before general anaesthesia except in acute haemorrhage, compromised enteric circulation or dead bowel where the emergent situation dictates resuscitation should be done along with the surgery.

Full stomach rules are to be followed.

Intravenous Induction

Intravenous induction can be used in children who already have IV access.

***Rapid sequence induction* of anaesthesia**: Apply suction to the nasogastric tube if already present and leave the nasogastric tube open

Pre-oxygenate by mask: Administer IV atropine/glycopyrrolate if tachycardia is not severe

Induce with IV induction agents. However, thiopentone 4–6 mg/kg can cause hypotension in the inadequately resuscitated child as does propofol 2–3 mg/kg. Ketamine 1–2 mg/kg is very often chosen in the hypovolaemic child as it helps maintain systemic blood pressure.

Cricoid pressure: It is difficult to apply cricoid pressure properly in the younger child as (a) it is difficult to identify the cricoid, (b) it is difficult to apply pressure without compressing the pliable trachea, and (c) it is ineffective with a nasogastric tube in place. It may be considered in the older child during rapid sequence intubation.

Succinylcholine: 1 mg/kg

Of *paramount importance* is that adequate time must be allowed for the drugs to achieve their full effect. The tendency to intubate immediately must be avoided to avoid unnecessary complications such as laryngospasm and regurgitation. Gastric regurgitation is stimulated in patients who are only partially anaesthetised and partially paralysed at the time of laryngoscopy.

Inhalational Induction

Inhalational induction may be used in well-hydrated children in whom there is neither ileus nor gastric distension and no functional IV line. This technique requires a smooth, rapid and closely monitored induction of anaesthesia, and excessive depth of anaesthesia should be avoided. The anaesthetist should be aided by an experienced assistant who can start an IV line when the patient is anaesthetised and apply cricoid pressure properly (if choosing to do so) during intubation of the trachea.

Choice of the Inhalational Agent

Sevoflurane and halothane are well-tolerated as induction agents. Isoflurane is an irritant and is unpleasant. Cardiac arrhythmias and myocardial depression are uncommon with isoflurane and sevoflurane.

Avoid nitrous oxide in patients with bowel obstruction as it will make bowel distension worse.

Supplement with narcotics such as fentanyl and morphine. Avoid excessive doses in pre-terms (who are prone to apnoea) and in haemodynamically unstable children.

Abdominal surgery is often associated with increased intra-abdominal pressure due to distended bowel loops and resultant oedema. Compartment syndrome must be considered in this setting. Ventilation should be controlled and end-tidal carbon dioxide closely monitored. Inspired oxygen saturation should be adjusted to a level slightly higher than what is necessary for full oxygen saturation. The oxygen saturation of preterm infants should be maintained between 87 and 92% to decrease the possibility of retinopathy of prematurity.

Intermediate-acting muscle relaxants such as atracurium are preferred for maintenance since they are well-tolerated and easily reversed. The effect of muscle relaxants should be closely monitored by electrical neurostimulation to prevent overdosing with muscle relaxants. Concurrent administration of IV or intraperitoneal aminoglycoside antibiotics may potentiate non-depolarising muscle relaxants.

Careful fluid balance is of utmost importance in major abdominal surgery. The rate of IV fluid administration depends on the sum of maintenance requirements, pre-existing deficits and ongoing losses including that in the third space. If the child is febrile, additional fluid should be administered. Many anaesthetists administer only plain lactated Ringer's solution for reasons of simplicity, especially when working without skilled assistants and to avoid hyperglycaemia. In neonates and infants, it is necessary to provide dextrose along with maintenance fluid. This may be given as a 1% solution (refer to Chapter 7).

In patients in whom significant blood loss is anticipated, the maximum allowable blood loss must be calculated before surgery to prevent blood loss below a target haematocrit. Actual blood loss should be carefully replaced. Coagulation studies are indicated when actual blood loss exceeds the estimated total blood volume. Blood given to premature infants should be irradiated to prevent graft versus host reaction (refer to Chapter 8).

After surgery, the endotracheal tube is left in place until the patient is wide awake, adequate spontaneous ventilation is demonstrated, core temperature is near normal, muscle relaxants are fully reversed, and the concentration of narcotic and inhalational agents is sufficiently diminished so that they will not impair ventilation. Analgesia may also be provided by caudal injection. Patients with large incisions, overwhelming sepsis, unstable cardiovascular systems and CNS depression may require prolonged ventilatory support. The decision to ventilate should be made early – well before the end of surgery so as to make appropriate arrangements for transfer. These patients are best managed post-operatively in a unit where intensive ventilatory and circulatory support can be provided.

SUGGESTED READINGS

1. Steward DJ. Manual of Paediatric Anaesthesia, 3rd edn. Churchill Livingstone, Philadelphia, 1992; 235–237.
2. Hall SC. Anaesthesia for abdominal surgery. In: Paediatric Anaesthesia, 4th edn. Gregory GA (ed). Churchill Livingstone, Philadelphia, 2002; pp. 567–584.
3. Fraser B. Acute fluid resuscitation for intussusception In: Clinical Pediatric Anesthesia. Goldschneider KR, Davidson AJ, Wittkugel EP, Skinner AV (eds). Oxford University Press, 2012; pp. 32–40.

37 Anaesthesia for Cleft Lip and Palate Repair*

Sarah Hodges • Rebecca Jacob

Cleft lip and palate (CLP), along with neural tube defects and congenital heart defects, is one of the most common congenital abnormalities worldwide, although there is considerable racial variability. It is highest amongst Asians with an incidence of 1:500 live births, 1:750 in Caucasians and approximately 1:1,000 in Blacks, although there are too few incidence studies from Africa to be definite about that figure.

Due to the rapid and striking improvement in appearance after surgery, it is popular for surgical camps especially in developing countries where there is often a backlog of patients requiring surgery. These surgical camps do not address the issue that the facial deformity from a cleft and palate requires multiple operations extending into early adulthood. The surgery is not confined to the primary CLP repair but may also include palatal lengthening, pharyngeal flaps, alveolar bone grafting, orthognathic surgery and rhinoplasty. The holistic management of a patient with CLP also entails involvement of a multidisciplinary team.

For successful CLP surgery, it is essential that the anaesthetist and surgeon communicate closely not just intraoperatively as they are sharing the airway but also for the pre-operative preparation, the decision for surgery and the post-operative care.

Embryology

By the fourth week of conception, the facial prominences begin to appear. During the fifth week, the nasal pits form from the frontonasal prominence, which is the mesenchyme ventral to the brain vesicles. These nasal pits become the nostrils with the medial and lateral nasal prominences on the either side. During the next 2 weeks of development, the maxillary prominences (Fig. 37.1) increase in

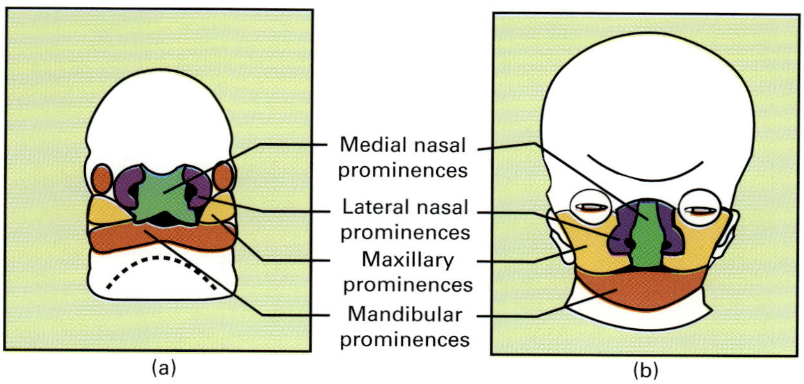

Figure 37.1 Stages of development of the face.

* Photographs in this chapter are also contributed by Andrew Hodges (FRCS Plast).

size and grow medially pushing the medial nasal prominences to the midline. The cleft between these prominences fuses, resulting in the formation of the upper lip. The lateral nasal prominences form the nasal alae. The lower lip and jaw are formed as the mandibular prominences merge across the midline.

The two medial nasal prominences merge not just on the surface of the face but deeper as well. On the surface, they form the philtrum (central portion) of the upper lip, the upper jaw with four incisor teeth and deeper they form the triangular primary palate. The secondary palate is formed from two shelf-like outgrowths of the maxillary prominences. These appear at 6 weeks and grow obliquely downwards on either side of the tongue. In the seventh week, these shelves move up as the tongue moves down and they fuse to form the secondary palate. They also fuse with the primary palate. At the same time, the nasal septum grows down to join the cephalic part of the newly formed palate. By 10–12 weeks, the development of the face is complete.

Cleft lip results from partial or complete lack of fusion of the maxillary prominence with the medial nasal prominence on one or both sides. Cleft palate results from failure of the fusion of the palatine shelves.

The clefts can vary in severity from a small defect in the vermilion of the upper lip to a complete cleft of the face extending beyond the nose and up to the eye (**Figs 37.2–37.5**).

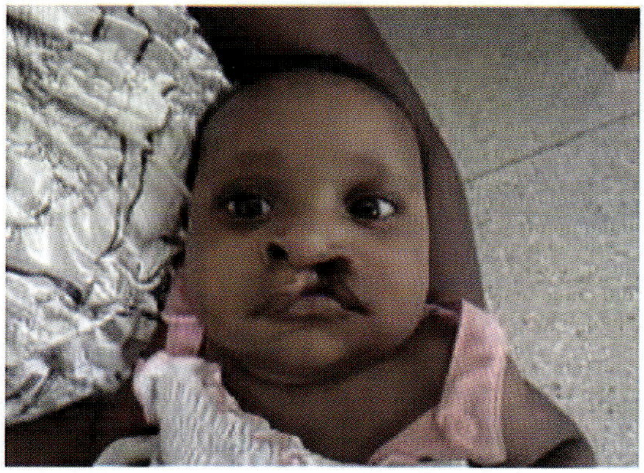

Figure 37.3 Unilateral complete cleft lip.

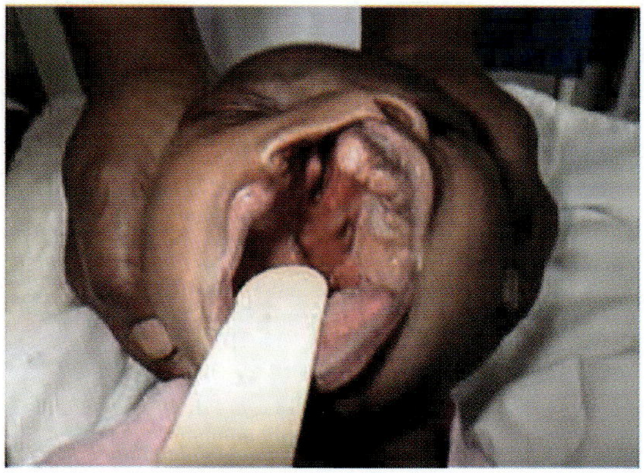

Figure 37.4 Unilateral cleft palate and palate.

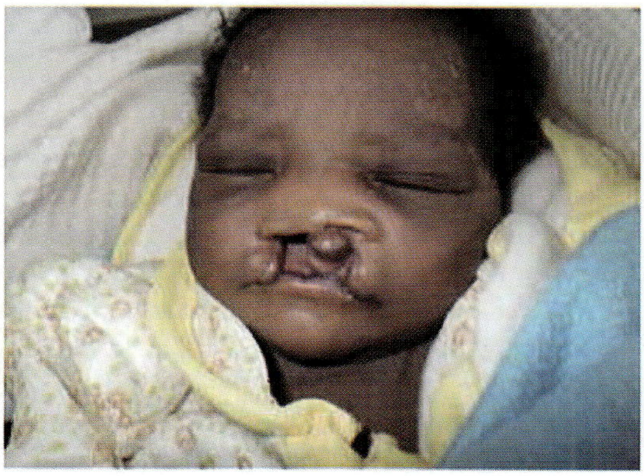

Figure 37.2 Bilateral cleft lip.

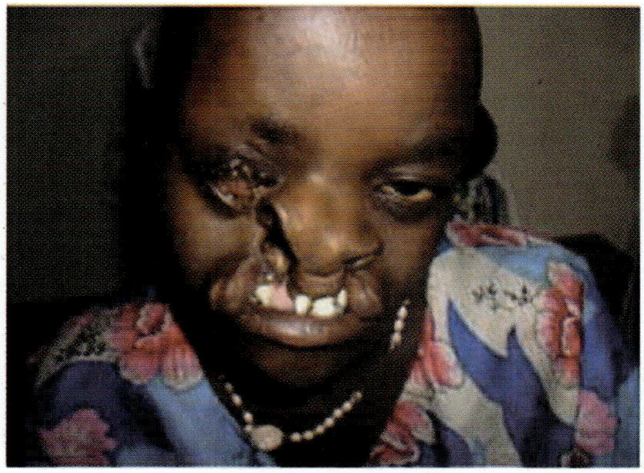

Figure 37.5 Extensive craniofacial cleft.

Associated Anomalies

Most cases of CLP are isolated, but they can be part of several syndromes, notably Pierre Robin sequence, Treacher Collins syndrome, Goldenhar syndrome, Patau syndrome (trisomy 13), Holoprosencephaly sequence and many others (Figs 37.6–37.8). The other associated anomalies are other defects of branchial arch development, especially middle ear and upper airway development. Clefts are also frequently associated with cardiac, renal or skeletal defects. They seem to occur more frequently in males compared to females, and cleft lips are usually left sided. The aetiology is often unknown though it is likely to result from both environmental and genetic causes. Notably there seems to be a small association with maternal ingestion of alcohol and anticonvulsant medication. The incidence is greater than expected amongst first-degree relatives of patients with CLP. The palatal shelves fuse 1 week later in females compared to males, which may explain why isolated cleft palate occurs more commonly in females compared to males.

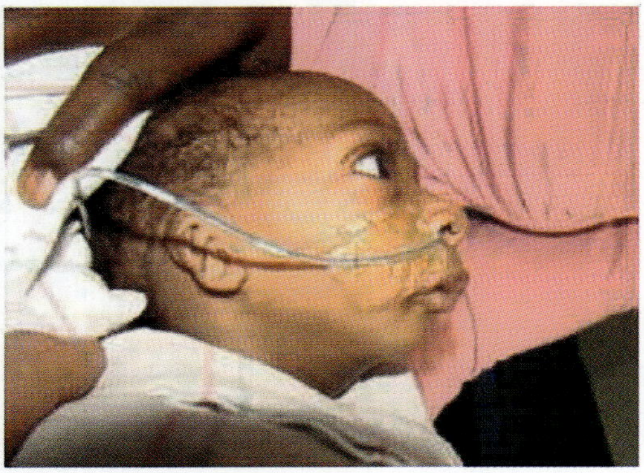

Figure 37.6 Pierre Robin sequence.

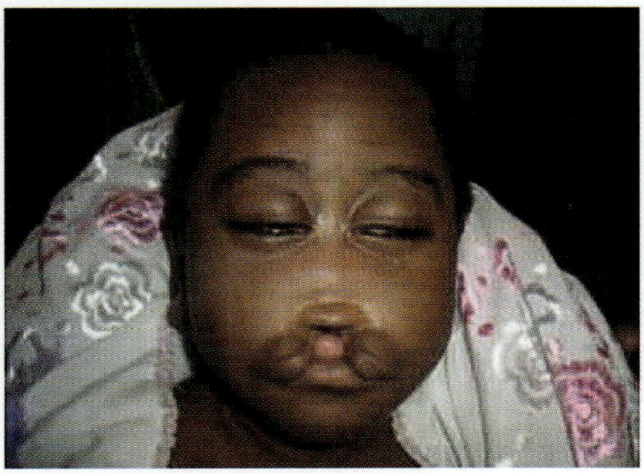

Figure 37.7 Infant with holoprosencephaly.

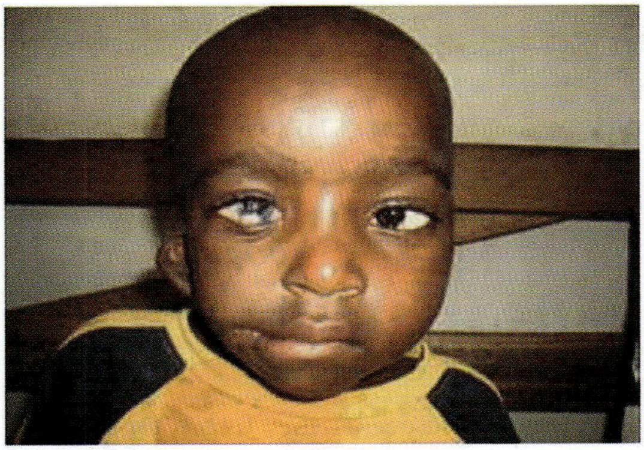

Figure 37.8 Child with Goldenhar syndrome.

Associated Problems

- **Feeding:** An isolated cleft lip rarely causes problems with feeding, but a baby with a cleft palate is unable to suckle as it cannot produce the necessary suction and the lack of palate reduces the let-down reflex in the mother's breast as the nipple is not being stimulated by touching the baby's palate. The babies become exhausted trying to suckle and often take in large amounts of air. Babies with a cleft palate have higher caloric requirements and it can be a challenge to keep up with this extra demand so they often have some degree of 'failure to thrive'. These babies will need specialised feeding advice possibly using dedicated feeding devices or the insertion of a nasogastric tube in the most severe cases. In low-income countries, these babies often present with severe malnutrition, anaemia and a history of recurrent chest infections due to repeated episodes of aspiration. With teaching and excellent support some mothers can breast feed a baby with a unilateral cleft palate.
- **Swallowing:** Many babies with a cleft palate are unable to coordinate the 'breathe, suck, swallow' reflex, which results in frequent nasal regurgitation of feeds or intermittent choking spells. This is for the most part a temporary problem as the actual swallowing mechanism is usually

normal, but upright positioning during feeding will reduce the nasal regurgitation.

- **Hearing:** Cleft palate is frequently associated with Eustachian tube dysfunction, which results in middle ear effusions and conductive hearing loss. Many centres insert grommets (pressure equalising tubes) at the time of cleft palate repair to relieve the middle ear fluid and equalise the pressure.
- **Speech:** A chid with an unrepaired cleft palate will never speak normally due to excessive nasal escape of air. Even after successful surgery, he/she will need speech and language therapy to ensure normal articulation and pronunciation. The child may also require further speech surgery to lengthen the palate and treat the velopharyngeal dysfunction (VPD).
- **Dental:** A child with a cleft of the alveolus will require alveolar bone grafting and orthodontics at around the age of mixed dentition.
- **Psychological:** Cleft patients may have several psychological problems due to the abnormal looking face, incomprehensible speech or just repeated visits to hospital and many surgeries. They may develop a phobia of doctors and hospitals or become excessively demanding. All this needs to be taken into consideration at the pre-operative assessment.

Timing of Surgery

Although the timing of surgery varies across the world, the primary surgery is best done in early infancy. This will reduce parental anxiety and improve bonding, ensure a better cosmetic and functional result, and increase the chances of better feeding. Although historically the 'rule of tens' was used: 10 weeks of age, 10 lbs in weight and 10 g/dl haemoglobin, many centres are repairing both the lip and the palate at a much earlier age in fact even in the neonatal period if there are no anticipated airway problems, although waiting until 3 months of age gives time to detect most congenital abnormalities and allows for anatomical and physiological maturation. It has been suggested that in low-income countries where the prevalence of malaria and worm infestations is high, a haemoglobin of 8 g/dl for a cleft lip repair in an otherwise healthy child is acceptable and 3 kg (6.6 lbs) is an adequate weight to guarantee a smooth recovery. However, this should only be attempted by an experienced anaesthetist with good support services and post-op care. It is always better to play safe and wait till the child is bigger with a haemoglobin of at least 10 g/dl in case of palate surgery.

Pre-Operative Assessment

When managing any patient with CLP, a high index of suspicion for other underlying problems should be maintained. Clinical history must include gestational age, feeding habits, recurrent respiratory tract infections and/or otitis media and possible obstructive sleep apnoea. Pre-medication is rarely required and is not advisable in any infant with a potential airway problem.

Airway

Clefts of the lip or palate per se do not lead to upper airway obstruction. But airway obstruction is usually a result of other associated problems which may be mechanical or neuromuscular. It is essential at the pre-operative visit to find out about noises when sleeping, for example, snoring and episodes of choking, and whether certain positions can alleviate these problems, for example, prone. This will enable the anaesthetist to anticipate some of the possible post-operative airway problems that can be avoided with the insertion of a nasopharyngeal airway prophylactically at the end of surgery. The usual airway assessment should be done to look for micrognathia and glossoptosis in particular. As clefts are associated with defects of branchial arch development, it is essential to note the position of the ears as low-set ears may well alert the anaesthetist to a difficult intubation.

Respiratory

Upper respiratory tract infections are particularly common at that young age and especially in cleft babies and they carry an increased risk of airway complications and impaired wound healing. Routine or targeted treatment of low-grade nasal infections with antibiotics will reduce the incidence of a post-operative pyrexial illness. It can be a difficult decision as many of these infants, especially the cleft palate patients, have a persistent nasal discharge without overt infection. Any signs of a more extensive respiratory tract infection (pyrexia, chest signs and raised white cell count) warrant treatment with antibiotics and postponement of surgery. Pre-operative treatment with nebulised bronchodilators may smooth the induction process.

Cardiac

In the history, the mother might report exhaustion and sweating during feeding, cyanotic spells and repeated chest infections. These are possible indicators of congenital heart disease but all babies with a cleft should have a full examination, pulse oximetry in air and an echocardiogram and ECG if a murmur is heard or a cardiac lesion suspected.

Nutritional Status

An infant with even just a submucous cleft palate has increased caloric requirements and it is essential to check that the energy that a child expends during feeding does not exceed the nutritional and caloric intake from the feeding. This problem may occur if feeding takes more than 30 minutes. In low-income countries, it might be worth considering routine deworming medication and iron supplementation for chronic anaemia.

Pre-Operative Investigations

- Haemoglobin and differential white cell count
- Full cardiac assessment (echocardiogram [ECHO], ECG and chest x-ray [CXR]), if a congenital cardiac lesion is suspected
- Blood group and possibly cross-match, if required for cleft palate patients
- Blood smear in zones prevalent with malaria

Fasting Pre-Operative Orders

Fasting pre-operative orders are identical to other types of surgery: 6 hours for solid food and formula feeds, 4 hours for breast milk and 2 hours for clear fluids.

Intraoperative Management

As the airway is shared with the surgeon, it is essential that there is excellent communication between the anaesthetist and the surgeon. The airway must be secured with an endotracheal tube, the trachea protected from blood and the infant accessible to the anaesthetist. Most of the morbidity from cleft surgery is associated with airway problems either intraoperatively or post-operatively.

Pulse oximetry, capnography, ECG, NIBP and a precordial stethoscope are the ideal monitors but in low resource settings, only the pulse oximeter and stethoscope may be available.

Induction

Basic monitoring is established and induction can be intravenous, intramuscular or inhalational. Sevoflurane in 100% oxygen is commonly used for inhalational induction, although halothane is equally effective and will give a longer time for intubation if muscle relaxation is not used. However, it is essential to be aware of the cardio-depressant effect of halothane and reduce the amount delivered as soon as possible. Intravenous access is secured as soon as possible. IV access may be placed prior to surgery if there is no skilled assistant, or an airway problem is expected. Intravenous induction is possible with propofol, thiopentone or ketamine. In poor resource settings without all the monitoring and skilled assistance, it is possible to use intramuscular ketamine for induction, secure IV access and establish monitoring in theatre when the infant is settled. It is important to confirm face mask ventilation before achieving paralysis with either a depolarising or a longer acting neuromuscular blocking agent. Lignocaine can be squirted directly on the vocal cords to facilitate intubation if neuromuscular blockers are not used or available. If the ability to inflate the lungs is in doubt, do not paralyse the infant. Always maintain spontaneous ventilation in a potentially difficult paediatric airway. The incidence of difficult laryngoscopy in cleft children under 3 years of age is only about 4.77% and difficult intubation 0.91%, but this increases markedly with associated micrognathia (50% difficult laryngoscopy). A large alveolar defect can make laryngoscopy difficult as the blade falls into the cleft. This can be managed with either a rolled piece of gauze, a Guedel airway upside down placed in the cleft or a paraglossal approach to intubation. Occasionally, a second pair of hands is of use (**Figs 37.9 and 37.10**). Videolaryngoscopy has improved visualisation and intubation success of the larynx especially in patients with difficult airways.

Difficult face mask ventilation is rare, but in cases where the airway becomes obstructed after the loss of consciousness, rescue manoeuvres include positioning the individual in a lateral or semi-prone position, using a nasal or an oral pharyngeal airway, or utilising a laryngeal mask airway (LMA). Cleft repair is an elective procedure, and it may be more prudent to defer surgery until the child is older and the airway is easier to manage. Some severe cases of Pierre Robin sequence may require tracheostomy to maintain a patent airway with or without surgery. Check air entry bilaterally after intubation. The Ring–Adair–Elwyn (RAE) tube being a pre-configured tube may slip endobronchially during intubation or after placement of the gag leading to one lung ventilation and hypoxia. Always auscultate for equal air entry after placement of the mouth gag. Shorten the tube if necessary, by withdrawing it and refixing. Ensure that all monitors and IVs are well fixed, and extensions are in place prior to draping the patient to always ensure access to the patient.

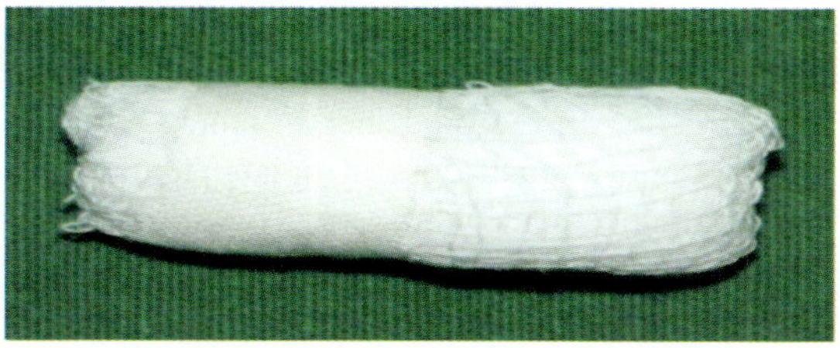

(a)

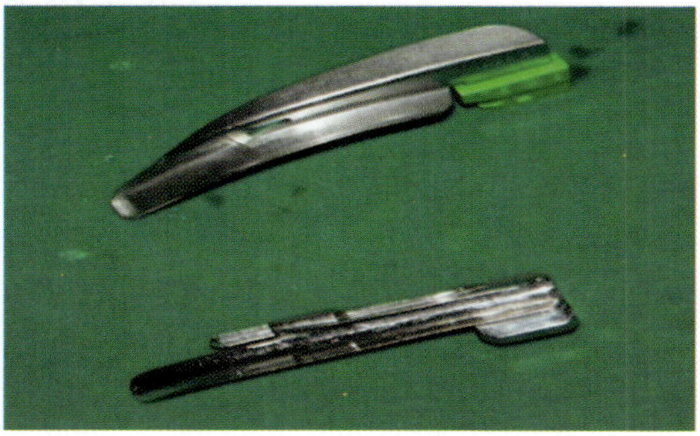

(b)

Figure 37.9 (a) Obliterate the cleft with a roll of gauze or (b) use a laryngoscope with a wider flange.

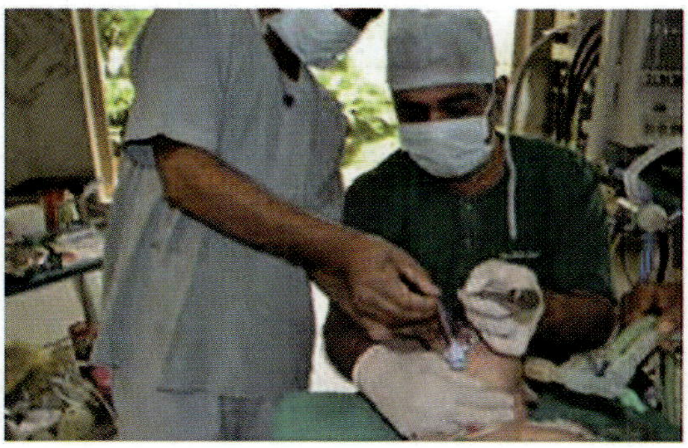

Figure 37.10 Two-person technique for difficult intubation.

Maintenance

The ideal endotracheal tube is the south-facing RAE tube (see Chapter 2), which is fixed centrally over the lower lip giving optimum surgical access. Some mouth gags have a groove for insertion of the tube to avoid occlusion as the gag is opened. A throat pack is inserted and must be well compacted down around the endotracheal tube so as not to abolish surgical view and access. The presence of the pack should be documented and the time of it's removal should also be documented (**Fig. 37.11**).

A head ring and roll under the shoulders are used to extend the neck. The extension is much more in case of a cleft palate repair. This makes the larynx very anterior and if there is an accidental extubation, reintubation is very difficult unless the neck is flexed (**Figs 37.12 and 37.13**). The eyes must also be protected.

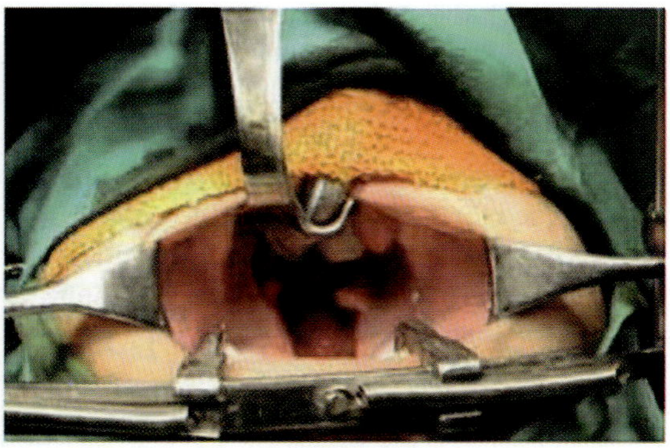

Figure 37.11 Gag with tube in groove. Note throat pack in situ.

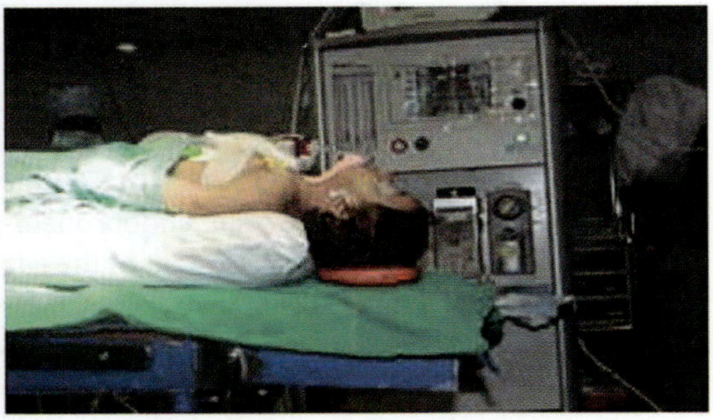

Figure 37.12 Position for cleft palate surgery.

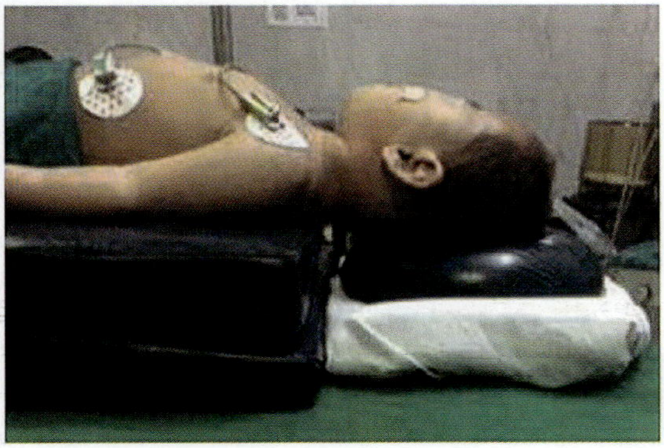

Figure 37.13 Sheets under the head to elevate head and reposition the baby for intubation in case of accidental extubation.

Sharing the airway with the surgeons does have some problems. Kinking of the tube when the gag is introduced is one such problem (see **Fig. 37.11**). It is diagnosed by rising airway pressures, difficulty in ventilation, a 'tight bag', limited chest movements and later rising $EtCO_2$ and falling SpO_2. Ask the surgeon to loosen the gag and reposition again. If the endotracheal tube is persistently occluded when the gag is opened, then the barrel of an empty 2 ml syringe can be inserted alongside the tube to prevent this. Accidental extubation is another problem and can occur when the patient is positioned for surgery or when the gag or throat pack is removed. Often the surgeon notices the dislodgement first, the $EtCO_2$ trace disappears, there is an inability to ventilate the patient and hypoxia soon follows. If a precordial stethoscope is used, a change or lack of breath sounds will be audible immediately. Shout for help, suction the throat and place a pillow or rolled sheets under the patient's head to get him back to the intubation position (see **Fig. 37.13**). Always have another RAE and standard ET tube of the same size or one size smaller available in the operating room. Also have a mask and LMA available as rescue devices in case of a failed intubation at the first try and a need to oxygenate.

Anaesthesia is maintained with controlled or assisted ventilation with volatile agents (halothane, isoflurane or sevoflurane) noting that mean alveolar concentration (MAC) values in infants are higher than in adults. Total intravenous anaesthesia (TIVA) may also be used as an alternative. Intraoperative analgesia is provided with a combination of acetaminophen rectally or intravenously, local infiltration of the operation site by the surgeon, infraorbital nerve blocks (for lip surgery) and a small dose of opiate (fentanyl) at the commencement of surgery. The utilisation of bilateral suprazygomatic maxillary nerve block for palate repairs and palatal lengthening surgery has been shown to accelerate post-operative recovery and decrease the requirement for post-operative opiates. This can be performed either by landmark technique or by using ultrasound guidance. Tramadol has also been used in centres where other narcotics are not available. Non-steroidal drugs can also be used in children over 6 months of age with no other contraindications. Surgery usually lasts 1–3 hours depending on the type of cleft and whether a combination operation is being performed, but there is rarely any need to repeat the dose of opiate. Most centres give at least one dose of a broad-spectrum antibiotic as soon as the intravenous line is secured. Dexamethasone (0.25 mg/kg) is a useful adjunct, which appears to reduce the incidence of respiratory complications in recovery and has a combined antiemetic and analgesic effect. It takes time to act and should be given at least half an hour before the end of surgery.

The surgeon will usually want to infiltrate the lip or palate with epinephrine (adrenaline) to reduce bleeding. A local anaesthetic agent, such as lignocaine or bupivacaine, when added to this infiltrate decreases the requirement of analgesics intraoperatively and post-operatively. The risk of arrhythmias is high, especially with the concomitant use of halothane, and keeping the $EtCO_2$ in the low to normal range will minimise this risk, reduce vasodilation and prevent excessive bleeding. Although infants do not tolerate hypothermia well, maintaining normothermia is usually not a problem in cleft surgery.

Fluid losses (pre-operative starvation, maintenance and ongoing losses) are typically replaced with a balanced salt solution with a small amount of added glucose (making it 1–2% dextrose in Ringers lactate or normal saline) especially in smaller babies. Blood transfusion is occasionally needed for palate repairs.

Extubation and Recovery

At the completion of the surgery, visualise the oropharynx directly, remove the pack, suction any clots and assess haemostasis. Prior to extubation, it is important to allow for the elimination of anaesthetic agents to ensure that the infant is fully awake and all muscle relaxants have been reversed. It is advisable to give supplementary oxygen at this stage and look for any signs of airway obstruction, which are more common in infants with pre-existing problems such as obstructive sleep apnoea or rhinorrhoea. Airway obstruction may be due to laryngospasm, retained pack, blood clot, upper airway narrowing, tongue swelling due to prolonged retraction or inadequate mouth breathing. If pre-operatively or intraoperatively any concerns are noticed, such as severe micrognathia, glossoptosis or a very long palate, it is advisable to insert a nasopharyngeal airway or endotracheal tube nasally just prior to extubation with the tip just above the epiglottis, to overcome the obstruction (Fig. 37.14). This can be done in theatre by the surgeon to avoid any damage to the palate repair. It is normally only required for 24 or 48 hours. Some surgeons use a tongue stitch placed

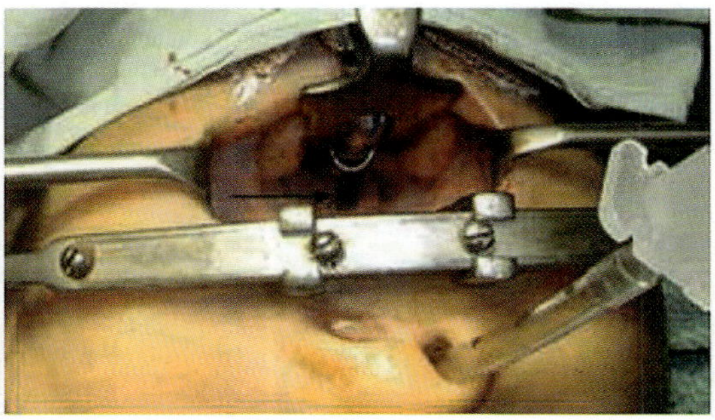

Figure 37.14 Nasopharyngeal airway in situ. Note the position of tip.

posteriorly and fixed onto the chin. Positioning the infant in the lateral or prone position might also assist respiration and relieve any obstruction. Very occasionally, it is necessary to re-intubate and perform a tracheostomy to overcome the pharyngeal incoordination. Laryngospasm is more common post cleft surgery, but its incidence can be reduced with judicious use of a small dose of dexmedetomidine or clonidine 15–20 minutes prior to extubation. This might also diminish the occurrence of emergence delirium.

Close observation should continue in the recovery period for bleeding and respiratory problems. It is critical not to try and rush the recovery period; the post-anaesthesia care unit (PACU) is a much safer area than the ward. Parental presence in the recovery might assist in keeping the child calm and content.

Oral acetaminophen and non-steroidal analgesics are usually sufficient for post-operative analgesia and have the added benefit of not sedating the child. Post-operative analgesia can be supplemented with small doses of opiates given intravenously cautiously (morphine 0.05 mg/kg or fentanyl 1–2 μg/kg) if extra analgesia is deemed necessary. Again, this should only be used if you have dependable nursing care and monitoring post-op. In most cases, it is not necessary to splint the arms to prevent the baby from touching the lip or palate and this often only serves to increase the baby's frustration and induce crying.

Post-Operative Feeding

The timing of post-operative feeding is a contentious issue and varies with different centres. With cleft lip repairs, babies can return to breastfeeding within 2–4 hours after surgery; the only limitation may be discomfort or the lack of sensation due to an infraorbital nerve block. In most cases, these babies rarely require post-operative intravenous fluids, but they must be observed closely for any signs of dehydration in case of inadequate oral intake. Older children may prefer to use a straw to drink. Cleft palate infants are a different problem as their oropharynx has been disrupted by surgery, they may have a narrowed airway due to oedema and they must learn to breathe through their mouth. They are also often the hungriest patients, and the parents are anxious to feed them as soon

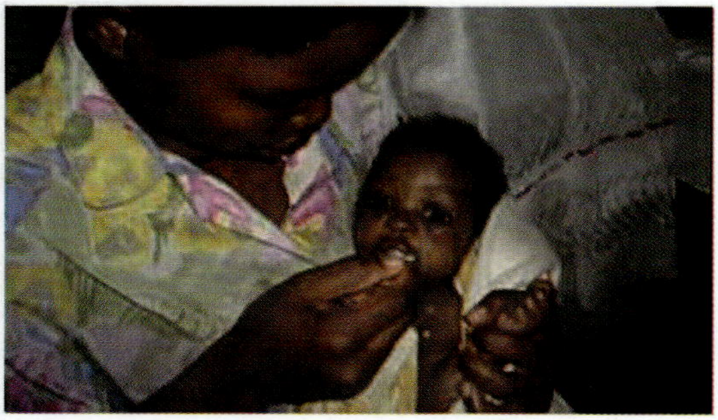

Figure 37.15 Feeding a baby post cleft lip and palate repair.

as possible. All feeding should be done under close nurse supervision for the first 48 hours with only small amounts to avoid any possibility of aspiration (**Fig. 37.15**).

Conclusion

Anaesthesia for CLP surgery requires constant communication with the surgeon and vigilance to ensure excellent outcomes. The anaesthetist needs to have a high index of suspicion for conditions associated with CLP and be prepared for a potential difficult airway. Extubation when wide awake is mandatory and close observation for signs of airway obstruction must continue throughout the recovery period.

SUGGESTED READINGS

1. Dunnet J. Anesthesia for repair of cleft palate. In: Paediatric Anaesthesia (Problems in Anaesthesia). Lauder GR, Stoddart PA (eds). Informa Health Care, London, 2004: 35–37.
2. Sommerville N, Fenlon S. Anaesthesia for cleft lip and palate surgery. *Contin Educ Anaesth Crit Care Pain* 2005; 5(3):76–79.
3. Xue FS, Zhang GH, Li P, et al. The clinical observation of difficult laryngoscopy and difficult intubation in infants with cleft and palate. *Paediatr Anaesth* 2006; 16(3):283–289.
4. American Cleft Palate Craniofacial Association. Core curriculum for cleft lip/palate and other craniofacial anomalies. Available from: http://www.Cleft palate-cranio facial.org.
5. Ahmed, M, Xue Yand Ayub A. Strategies to Optimize Global Cleft Care. Available from: http://dx.doi.org/10.5772/67186
6. Cawthorn TR, Todd AR, Hardcastle N, et al. Optimizing outcomes after cleft palate repair: Design and implementation of a perioperative clinical care pathway. *Cleft Palate Craniofac J* 2021; 59(5): 561–567.
7. Bateman MC, Conejero JA, Mooney EK, et al. Short-stay cleft palate surgery with intraoperative dexamethasone and marcaine. Ann Plastic Sur 2006; 57:245–247.
8. Mesnil M, Dadure C, Captier G, et al. A new approach for peri-operative analgesia of cleft palate repair in infants: The bilateral suprazygomatic maxillary nerve block. *Pediatr Anesth* 2010; 20: 343–349.
9. Chiono J, Raux O, Bringuier S, et al. Bilateral suprazygomatic maxillary nerve block for cleft palate repair in children. A prospective, randomized, double-blind study versus placebo. *Anesthesiology* 2014; 120:1362–1369.
10. Mireault D,. Cawthorn TR, Todd AR, et al. Suprazygomatic maxillary nerve block: an ultrasound and cadaveric study to identify correct sonoanatomical landmarks. *J Anesth* 2021; 35:150–153.
11. Elyazed MMA, Mostafa SF. Bilateral suprazygomatic maxillary nerve block versus palatal block for cleft palate repair in children: A randomized controlled trial. Egypt J Anaesth 2018; 34(3): 83–88.

38 Hydrocephalus and Meningomyelocele

Ramamani Mariappan

Hydrocephalus

The word hydrocephalus (HCP) is derived from the Greek word (Hydro – water, Cephalus – brain). It is an abnormal accumulation of cerebrospinal fluid (CSF) within the ventricle of the brain. This common paediatric neurosurgical condition is due to the mismatch between CSF production and absorption, resulting in increased intracranial CSF volume. The estimated prevalence of HCP is about 1–1.5%. The incidence of congenital HCP is about 0.9–1.8/1000 births (range: 0.2–3.5/1000).

Classification (Fig. 38.1)

Based on Mechanism

HCP may be due to ***subnormal CSF reabsorption*** (common) or ***overproduction*** (rare). Overproduction of CSF is due to choroid plexus papilloma or carcinoma. Subnormal CSF reabsorption may be of two types – (1) Non-obstructive or communicating HCP and (2) Obstructing or non-communicating HCP.

- **Non-obstructive or communicating type:** There is a defect in the CSF absorption at the level of arachnoid granulation. All the ventricles are dilated.
- **Obstructive or non-communicating type:** Here, there is an obstruction proximal to arachnoid granulation along the CSF pathway. Hence, there is a ventricular enlargement proximal to the level of obstruction.

Based on Aetiology

- **Congenital:** Aqueductal stenosis, agenesis of the foramen of Monro and vein of Galen malformation are some of the causes of congenital HCP. Dandy–Walker malformation, Arnold Chiari malformation (ACM) Type I and II, and Bickers-Adams syndrome are the common syndromes in newborns with HCP. X-lined inheritance has been reported as the cause of congenital HCP (gene location Xq28).
- **Acquired:** Post-infectious (most common), post-haemorrhagic (subarachnoid and intraventricular haemorrhage) or neoplastic (posterior fossa tumours, choroid plexus papilloma and suprasellar tumours causing obstruction to the CSF pathway)

Clinical Features

Untreated HCP almost always results in reduced intracranial compliance and intracranial hypertension. Delay in treatment can result in brain herniation and death, especially in acute HCP. In children with HCP, the reported mortality rate is about 0–3%.

The symptoms and the signs of HCP depend on the intracranial compliance and how acutely HCP develops; that is, in an infant or in younger children, if the HCP develops slowly, the cranial vault expands (Fig. 38.2). In older children, the cranial bones are fused; hence, the cranium cannot expand, and the signs of herniation develop rapidly.

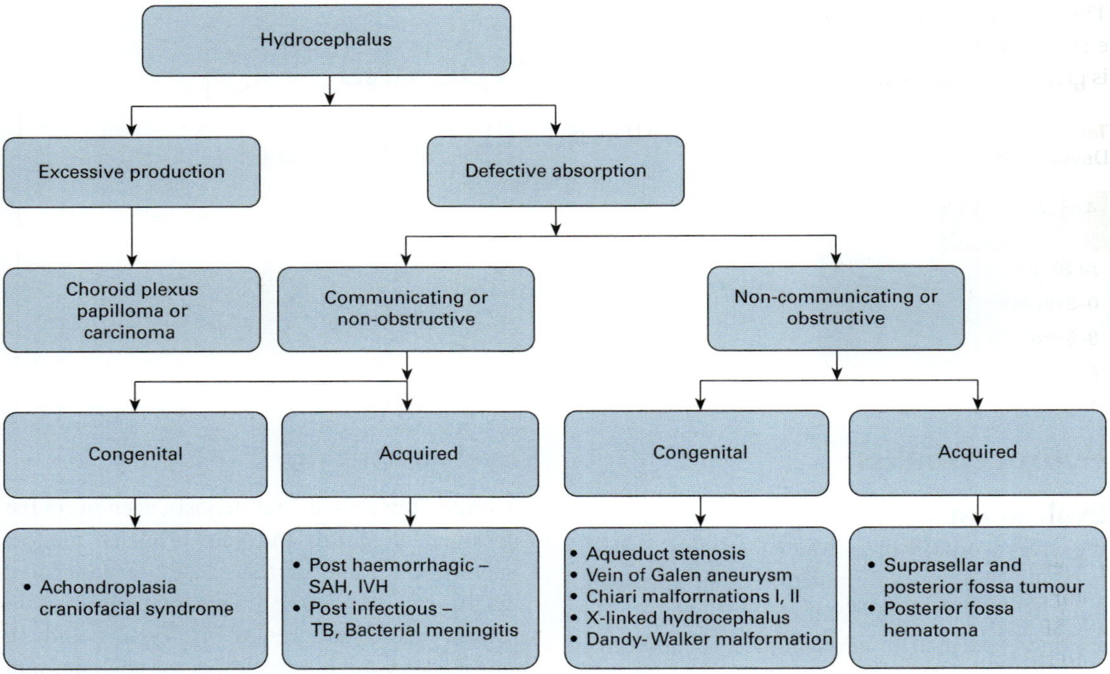

Figure 38.1 Classification of hydrocephalus. IVH, intraventricular haemorrhage; SAH, subarachnoid haemorrhage; TB, tuberculosis.

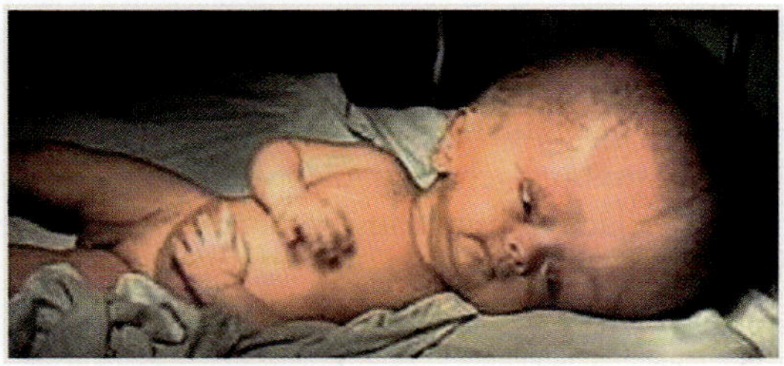

Figure 38.2 An infant with large HCP.

Symptoms

Increased irritability, weak cry, poor feeding, dysphagia, nausea and vomiting, lethargy, headache on awakening, gait and visual disturbances, delayed milestones, and weakness of lower limbs are the symptoms of HCP.

Signs

Large head (head circumference > 2 SD of normal for the age and sex), frontal bossing, bulging anterior fontanelle, dilated scalp veins, sutural diastasis (more in infants), 'sunset sign'(upward gaze palsy due to pressure on the region of suprapineal recess), ptosis (third nerve palsy), strabismus (sixth nerve palsy), lower limb weakness (enlarging anterior horn of lateral ventricle stretches the fronto-ponto-cerebellar fibres), papilloedema and absent pulsation of retinal vessels, irregular respiration, apnoeic spells and Macewen's sign (cracked pot sound on percussion of the skull near the frontal temporal and parietal bones) are some of the signs of HCP. Children can develop visual field defects or blindness (rare) due to posterior cerebral artery occlusion due to the downward transtentorial herniation, injury to the optic nerve at the optic disc due to chronic papilloedema or compression of the optic chiasma due to the dilatation of the third ventricle.

Measurement of the Head Circumference (Occipital-Frontal Circumference)

The occipital-frontal circumference (OFC) of a normal infant is approximately equal to the distance from the crown to the rump. It is about 33–35 cm at birth. At the age of one year, the infant's head circumference reaches 90% of the adult's head circumference. It reaches adult size by 6 years of age.

The expected increase in normal head circumference at different stages of development in children is given in Table 38.1.

Table 38.1 The Expected Head Circumference During Development

Age (Months/Year)	Expected Head Circumference (cm)
At Birth	33–35
0–3 months	2 cm/month
3–6 months	1 cm/month
6–12 months	0.5 cm/month
1–3 years	0.25 cm/month
4–6 years	1 cm/year

Evaluation

- Genetic testing and counselling should be done for congenital HCP with syndromic associations.
- CSF analysis (counts, protein, sugar and culture) to rule out infective aetiology.
- X-ray skull lateral view – 'Beaten Copper appearance' and erosion of sella turcica – but it is seldom performed now.
- Cranial ultrasound (USG) through the anterior fontanelle – to evaluate the ventricular size and to assess the progression.
- Neurological imaging – CT-brain and magnetic resonance imaging (MRI)-brain. The findings are discussed in detail below.

CT/MRI Criteria for Hydrocephalus (Fig. 38.3)

- Mickey Mouse Sign (ballooning of frontal horns [FHs] of the lateral ventricle and the third ventricle)
- The axial width of the temporal horn (TH) > 2 mm (TH is not visible in a patient without HCP)
- The ratio of FH/internal diameter (ID) is >0.5 (FH – largest width of FH; ID – internal diameter from inner-to-inner table at the same level of FH)
- Evans ratio – FH/biparietal diameter (BPD) > 0.3 (FH – largest width of FH; BPD – ID from inner-to-inner table at the maximum parietal diameter)

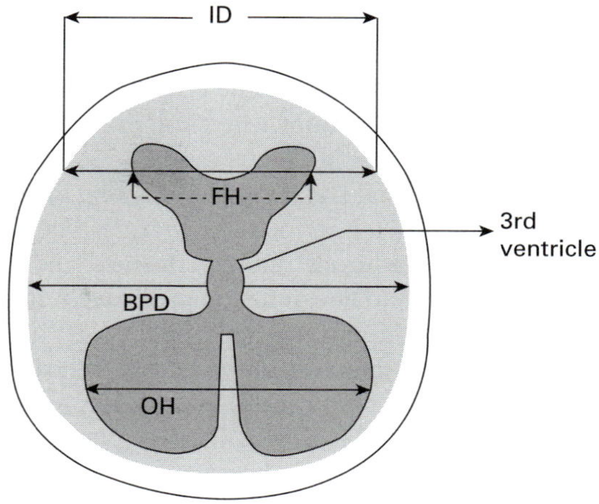

Figure 38.3 Radiological (CT/MRI) features of hydrocephalus. BPD, biparietal diameter; FH, frontal horn; ID, internal diameter; OH, occipital horn.

- Periventricular hypodensity on CT, or periventricular high-density signal on T2W sequence of MRI, indicates high intraventricular pressure causing periventricular seepage of fluid
- Thinning of the corpus callosum or upward bowing of corpus callosum seen in a sagittal section of MRI (common in chronic HCP)

Approach to Patients with Symptomatic Hydrocephalus

Surgical management: Surgical management is the mainstay of treatment for HCP. The aim of surgery is to control the intracranial pressure (ICP) and rapidly relieve the obstruction by diverting the CSF from the lateral ventricle to the peritoneal cavity, which is termed as ***ventriculoperitoneal (VP)*** shunt. It is a commonly performed surgery with a good success rate compared to other methods of diversion procedures (described below).

If the aetiology of the HCP is due to a posterior fossa tumour, tumour excision helps to relieve the HCP. Some children need placement of a VP shunt after surgery despite the removal of the tumour.

When there is an abnormality in the peritoneal cavity (infection and previous abdominal surgery), then the distal tip of the shunt is placed in the right atrium via the internal jugular vein and superior vena cava, and it is termed a ***ventriculo-atrial (VA) shunt***. It needs repeated revision because as the child grows the distal end of the catheter shortens compared to the VP shunt where a longer length may be placed in the abdominal cavity.

Rarely, the distal end of the shunt is kept in the pleural cavity, and it is termed a ***ventriculo-pleural shunt***. This procedure is rarely performed and is considered a second line of treatment for HCP. It is performed for children >7 years of age.

Ventriculo-subgaleal shunt (lateral ventricle to subgaleal space of the scalp) is done in premature children with SAH, where there is a possibility of normalisation of CSF reabsorption over a short period of time.

Lumboperitoneal shunt is performed for children with communicating HCP who are >2 years of age.

An alternative to a shunt is an ***endoscopic third ventriculostomy (ETV)*** using a neuro endoscope. The ventriculostomy (communication) can be made through the floor of the third ventricle to the adjacent basal CSF cisterns. The success of ETV can be assessed using the ETV score (based on age, aetiology and previous shunt history), which ranges from 0 to 100%. The score of >80% is associated with a high success rate and a score of <40% is associated with low success following ETV. *Coagulation of the choroid plexus* is a treatment option for choroid plexus papilloma where there is increased CSF production.

Medical management: Medical therapy using acetazolamide and diuretic can be tried as a temporary measure in premature infants with intraventricular haemorrhage without HCP and the features of raised ICP. Studies have shown that HCP is controlled in >50% of infants without signs of raised ICP and normal renal function. The following drugs are used to control HCP:

- Acetazolamide (a carbonic anhydrase inhibitor) 25 mg/kg/day divided TID (thrice daily) per oral (PO); the dose can be increased slowly daily to 25 mg/kg/day to a maximum of 100 mg/kg/day
- Along with acetazolamide, furosemide 1 mg/kg/day may be given orally in divided dosesTID
- To counteract the acidosis caused by acetazolamide, tricitrate (Polycitra) can be used in a dose of 4 ml/kg/day QID (four times per day) dose (each ml contains 2 mEq of bicarbonate, 1mEq K^+ and 1 mEq Na^+)
- Electrolytes must be measured frequently to maintain the serum HCO_3^- to > 18 mEq/L. Also, watch for the symptoms of acetazolamide side effects (lethargy, tachypnoea, diarrhoea and paraesthesia over the fingertips)

Anaesthetic Management

- **Assessment:** Level of consciousness (GCS – Glasgow Coma Scale), ability to protect the airway, fasting status, coexisting pathology or organ system compromise such as poor lung compliance or immature renal function, drug history, especially of steroids and anticonvulsants and its associated anaesthetic interactions. When dealing with children who have congenital HCP and syndromic associations, it is important to consider the involvement of other organ systems.
- **Investigations:** Haemoglobin, total and differential WBC count, USG-abdomen to look for any other congenital anomalies/CT/MRI-brain to study the pathology and the ventricle size.
- **Pre-medication:** Avoid sedation in the presence of signs and symptoms of raised ICP or altered sensorium.
- **Monitoring:** Pulse oximetry, ECG, non-invasive blood pressure monitoring, capnography, temperature, TEE (trans-oesophageal echocardiography) and precordial doppler (for VA shunt).
- **Induction:** High ICP and vomiting increase the risk of pulmonary aspiration. So, rapid sequence induction with thiopentone or propofol followed by succinylcholine or rocuronium is indicated. In the absence of intravenous access, inhalational induction with sevoflurane can be considered. The trunk can be elevated over a flat pillow and head stabilised using a large head ring/jelly ring (**Figs 38.4 and 38.5**). *Avoid* moving the child's head over the edge of the table as it is difficult to maintain stability of a large head.
- **Maintenance:** Communication with the operating surgeon about positioning is important. Patients are placed with a 30° head-up position and minimal neck flexion or rotation to improve venous drainage and prevent any rise in ICP.

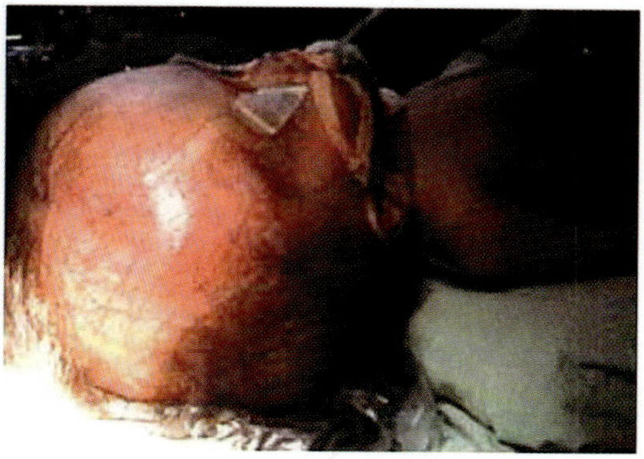

Figure 38.4 Positioning of a child for intubation and surgery.

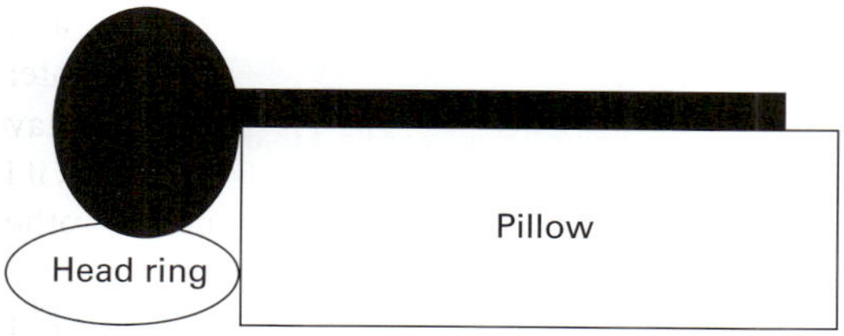

Figure 38.5 Position for intubation and surgery.

Placement of an axillary roll may be required to avoid pressure on the dependent arm (especially in the lateral position). Maintain normocarbia by keeping the CO_2 to a lower normal range ($PaCO_2$ 35–40 mmHg). Avoid both hyper and hypocapnia. *Avoid* spontaneous ventilation in ventriculo-pleural (to prevent pneumothorax) and in VA (to prevent air embolism) shunts. A combination of air, oxygen, isoflurane or sevoflurane, fentanyl (avoid morphine as it interferes with the assessment of the conscious level in the immediate post-operative period), paracetamol and intermediate-acting non-depolarising muscle relaxants is used. N_2O must be used with caution. Replace the loss of intravascular volume due to emesis or diuresis with saline or balance salt solution. The procedure itself is not associated with blood or third space loss. Maintain normothermia during the procedure as these children are prone to hypothermia due to their large heads which increase the surface area exposed to cold cleaning solutions and air conditioning. Glucose needs to be checked especially for infants and small children as these children are prone for hypoglycaemia, also to compare the serum sugar with the CSF sugar value (CSF sugar should be two-thirds of the serum value)

- **Emergence and extubation:** Allow adequate time to eliminate anaesthetics and ensure adequate reversal of neuromuscular blockade is achieved. Ensure normothermia is achieved at the time of reversal of neuromuscular blockade. Extubate when the child is fully awake. Post-operatively, monitor the mental status as re-obstruction and deterioration can occur.

Each shunting procedure is associated with its own complications (immediate and delayed). They are depicted in **Table 38.2**.

Special Concerns

- **EVD care:** Those with shunt infection must have their shunt removed, and an external ventricular drain (EVD) placed. Care should be taken to *avoid* displacing the EVD. Clamp the drain while transferring to the operating table so that there is no sudden change in ICP. Lowering the drain will cause siphoning of CSF, collapse of the ventricle and rupture of cortical veins leading to intraventricular haemorrhage.
- **Slit ventricle syndrome:** In 5–10% of patients following a shunt procedure, there is over drainage of CSF and a slit-like ventricle results. They do not have adequate CSF to compensate for brain or blood volume alterations. Therefore ***avoid*** excess or hypotonic intravenous solutions to minimise brain swelling, as these patients can develop cerebral herniation after an uneventful surgery.

Spina Bifida (Spinal Dysraphism)

It is a congenital neural tube defect in which the caudal part of the neural tube fails to close during the early part of embryogenesis (fourth week). Depending on the extent of involvement, it is classified as spina bifida occulta (failure of fusion of vertebral arch without the protrusion of spinal canal content) and spina bifida aperta or spina bifida cystica (herniation of content of spinal canal

Table 38.2 Complications of the Shunting Procedures

Procedure	Cranial End Complications	Caudal End Complications
Ventriculo-peritoneal shunt	Seizure, intracranial haematoma, shunt tip malposition, disconnection, leakage, obstruction, infection, slit ventricle syndrome and subdural hygroma due to over drainage	Inguinal hernia, hydrocele, ascites, pseudocyst, peritonitis, intestinal obstruction, perforation, volvulus, malposition of distal tip to stomach, bladder and intestine
VA shunt	Same as above	Bleeding, injury to major vessels of the neck, air embolism while insertion, heart failure (over drainage), septicaemia, vessel wall perforation, pulmonary microembolism and nephritis
Ventriculo-pleural shunt	Same as above. Over drainage is common in this shunt because of negative pressure in the intrapleural space	Hydrothorax and pyothorax
Endoscopic third ventriculostomy	Seizure and intracranial haematoma	Basilar artery and perforator vessel injury, midbrain, hypothalamus injury, bradycardia, life-threatening arrhythmia, asystole and delayed awakening

through the defective vertebral arch). The word (Latin) Aperta means 'open'. The incidence of spina bifida is about 0.5 of 1000 births worldwide and in the United States is estimated to be >3 per 10000 births.

Types of Spina Bifida

- **Spina bifida occulta:** Congenital absence of spinous process and various amount of lamina. There is no protrusion or exposure of meninges/neural tissue. A tuft of hair, skin dimple or capillary angioma may be seen at the site of the defect. It is often asymptomatic till adulthood. Sometimes it may be associated with a lipomeningomyelocele, lipoma of the cord, tethered cord, or dermoid tumour. These children can present with various neurological symptoms with bowel and bladder involvement.
- **Spina bifida aperta or cystica:** Congenital absence of spinous process and various amount of lamina along with herniation of the contents of the spinal canal such as meninges or neural tissue.
  - Meningocele: Cystic distention of meninges without the neural tissue.
  - Meningomyelocele (MMC): Cystic distention of meninges with neural tissue. Children often present with various neurological deficits with cauda equina symptoms.

Meningomyelocele

The incidence of meningomyelocele is 1–2/1000 (0.1–0.2%) live births, and its incidence increases to 2–3% if there is a previous child with MMC, and the incidence increases to 6–8% after two previous children with MMC. The most common site of occurrence is in the lumbosacral region, but this can occur at any level in the neuraxis (**Fig. 38.6**). The MMC at the cervical or thoracic level constitutes <5% of MMCs.

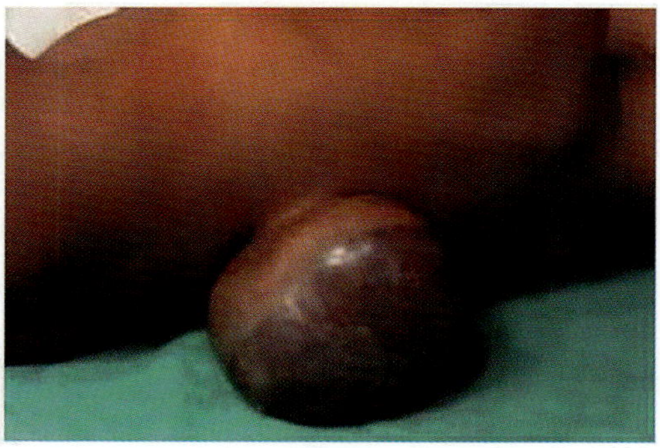

Figure 38.6 Lower thoracic meningomyelocele.

Risk Factors for the Development of MMC

- Folic acid deficiency or hypervitaminosis A during the prenatal period
- Exposure to the TORCH infection during early pregnancy. TORCH is an acronym for a group of diseases that cause congenital (present at birth) conditions if a foetus is exposed to them in the uterus. TORCH stands for **t**oxoplasmosis, **o**ther (such as syphilis, hepatitis B), **r**ubella, **c**ytomegalovirus (CMV) and **h**erpes simplex.
- Methylenetetrahydrofolate reductase deficiency
- Use of carbamazepine/sodium valproate/ovulation-inducing drug use during early pregnancy
- Maternal cocaine abuse, smoking and alcohol consumption
- Obesity and insulin-dependent diabetes mellitus
- Lower socioeconomic status
- Maternal heat exposure during the first trimester
- Exposure to environmental pollutants, pesticides and radiation
- Genetic factors – Chromosomal anomalies of Trisomy 18 and 13

Antenatal Diagnosis

Laboratory Studies

- Elevated maternal serum alpha-fetoprotein level (more than two multiples of median for the appropriate week of gestation) between 15 and 20 weeks of gestation.
- If the foetal USG did not show any abnormality, amniotic fluid alpha-fetoprotein assay at 13–15 weeks of pregnancy can be done.
- The presence of acetylcholinesterase (nerve-specific enzyme) in amniotic fluid also aids in diagnosis.

Imaging Studies

- *Foetal Ultrasonography (USG):* Foetal spine USG (sagittal plane) at 18–22 weeks' gestational age will show **the osseous defect** in the thoracolumbar spine with a **sac containing neural elements.** This confirms the neural tube defect. Additionally, a biparietal diameter of >5th percentile is seen in 50% of patients with spina bifida. The absence of neural tube defect with elevated alpha-fetoprotein indicates the possibility of an omphalocele.

Ventriculomegaly and hindbrain herniation with crowding of the posterior fossa, and tectal beaking indicate the presence of Arnold Chiari malformation (ACM) Type II. Dilated renal system and talipes also can be seen.

- *Foetal cranial USG signs:*
  - Lemon sign: Indentation and scalloping of frontal bones are predictive of spina bifida. This sign is seen in 80% of cases of MMC.
  - Banana sign: Convex-shaped cerebellum wrapping the brainstem tightly appears like a banana along with the obliteration of cisterna magna due to the spinal cord tethering and the downward migration of the cerebellum. This sign is positive in 90% of cases of MMC.
- *MRI of the foetus*: Better visualisation of the spinal cord and its contents if foetal surgery is planned.
- *Foetal Karyotyping*

Presenting Symptoms

Depending on the location of the lesion, sensory and motor, bowel, bladder and sexual functions are affected. The higher the lesion, more the deficits and hence the prognosis is worse. Children with cervical MMC present with quadriparesis/plegia and those with thoracic lesion present with paraparesis/plegia. MMC is one of the most common causes of neurogenic bladder in the paediatric population. As the children grow, the functional disability worsens. MMC can be associated with multiple congenital anomalies involving the brain, musculoskeletal, renal, gastrointestinal and vertebral system. Associated congenital anomalies are shown in **Table 38.3**.

Pre-Anaesthetic Assessment

- These infants and children can have a variety of neurologic deficits with bladder and bowel dysfunction depending on the level of the lesion. Pre-operative neurological status must be documented in the anaesthesia record.
- Children with MMC often have Arnold Chiari malformation (ACM) Type II. The symptoms of Chiari II malformation include difficulty in swallowing, inspiratory stridor, apnoea, impaired cough or gag reflex (cranial nerves IX and X involvement), weakness or spasticity of the upper limbs and difficulty with balance or coordination. Other signs and symptoms may

Table 38.3 Congenital Anomalies Associated with MMC

Organ System Involved	Associated Anomalies
Central nervous system	Aqueductal stenosis, corpus callosal agenesis, ventriculomegaly, ACM Type II with lower cranial nerves involvement and quadriparesis
Cardiovascular system	CHD: Atrial septal defect, ventricular septal defect, anomalous pulmonary venous return, tetralogy of Fallot, bicuspid aortic valve, coarctation and hypoplastic left heart syndrome
Vertebral	Sacral agenesis, hemivertebra, fused vertebrae and ribs, scoliosis and kyphosis
Musculoskeletal	CTEV, congenital dislocation of hip, arthrogryposis congenita, absent fibula and syndactyly
Renal	Single kidney, horseshoe kidney, hydroureteronephrosis, posterior urethral valve, hypospadias, congenital megaureter, duplex system and neurogenic bladder
Gastrointestinal system	Imperforate anus and tracheoesophageal fistula
Others	Cleft lip and palate

ACM, Arnold Chiari malformation; CHD, congenital heart disease. CTEV, congenital talipes equino varus.

include hypotonus, opisthotonos, nystagmus or weak cry. These children are more prone to neurological worsening during airway manipulation and prone to aspiration pneumonia and stridor during the perioperative period. Hence, these should be noted during the pre-anaesthetic evaluation and necessary precautions taken.

- Look for other organ system involvement, such as congenital heart disease (CHD) and renal anomalies and their associated anaesthetic problems. As well as age-related pathophysiology, especially in the presence of prematurity.
- HCP develops in 65–85% of children with MMC, and 5–10% of patients have clinically overt HCP at birth. About 80% of children develop HCP by the age of 6 months. Hence, measures need to be taken to prevent a further rise in ICP by facilitating smooth induction and intubation.

Special note should be made of the following remembering that

- An infant with a large head can have an associated difficult airway.
- Their hydration status should be assessed and optimised before surgery, especially in children with the features of raised ICP with vomiting.
- Adequate amount of blood to be arranged for infants with very large MMCs.

Pre-Operative Investigations

- **Laboratory investigations:** Complete blood count, creatinine, electrolytes, blood sugar, cross-match for surgery, urine routine and microscopic examination
- **Imaging:**
  - *Ultrasound:* Abdomen – renal anomalies; cranial USG – HCP
  - *Trans-thoracic ECHO*: CHD.
- **X-ray:**
  - *X-ray spine*: Anteroposterior and lateral view - scoliosis and kyphosis - spine consultation
  - *X-ray chest:* If the child is symptomatic (cardiomegaly and aspiration 'patch')
  - *X-ray hip and knee:* Hip and knee deformity – orthopaedic consultation

Surgical Management

Intrauterine closure of MMC defect: Foetal surgery is done when the foetal USG shows HCP and ACM Type II. The procedure is still controversial. The MOMS trial (management of meningomyelocele) is a randomised trial, which compared the prenatal (<26 weeks) versus postnatal surgery for MMC, its effect on the foetal outcome and the need for a shunt at 12 months of age. The mental and motor function at 30 months of age were also assessed. The study results showed that prenatal surgery reduced the need for shunting and improved motor outcomes at 30 months but was associated with maternal and foetal risks.

Postnatal MMC repair: MMCs with intact skin cover can wait for proper assessment and 'work up' before elective surgery. Ruptured MMC or MMC without the skin cover should be operated on within 24 to 36 hours in a 'latex-free' environment.

After 36 hours of birth, colonisation starts to occur, and then the chance of post-operative infection increases. Some surgeons prefer to do the MMC repair and the VP shunt surgery at the same sitting. Some prefer to do the MMC repair in the first stage and closely watch the babies post-operatively by measuring the head circumference, doing cranial USG and observing them for clinical deterioration, and then subject them to VP shunt surgery if deemed necessary. Children with ruptured MMC should be started on antibiotics (Gram-positive and negative cover), to be discontinued 6 hours after surgery. If the VP shunt is planned after the MMC repair, antibiotics should be continued for 5 days.

Anaesthetic Management

Monitoring

- **Standard monitors:** Pulse oximetry, ECG, non-invasive blood pressure monitoring, temperature, capnometry and urine output monitoring.
- **Specific monitors:** Especially if the MMC is big and major blood loss and fluid shift are anticipated – invasive arterial blood pressure (BP), central venous pressure (CVP) monitoring, pulse pressure variation (PPV) or stroke volume variation (SVV) guided fluid therapy.
- **Optional:** Precordial stethoscope, coagulation monitoring (standard vs point-of-care) and depth of anaesthesia monitoring.

Induction and Intubation

- **Position for intubation** is a major concern. In most cases, induction and tracheal intubation can be performed with the infant in the supine position, and the uninvolved portion of the patient's back supported with towel, cushions or a 'doughnut' ring so that there is no direct pressure on the MMC. For very large defects, it is occasionally necessary to place the infant in the lateral position. One in three patients with MMC will be symptomatic from their Arnold Chiari II malformation. So, one must handle airway management and neck positioning with care. Video laryngoscope-assisted intubation will help to reduce neck movements.
- **Anaesthetic agents:** Intravenous induction with thiopentone or propofol and preferably a non-depolarising muscle relaxant (preferably atracurium) must be used, especially in the presence of a neurological deficit. Alternatively, an inhalational induction with sevoflurane may be done.
- **Airway management:** Mask ventilation and intubation may be difficult in neonates with massive HCP or an infant with large cervical MMC. In such cases, inhalational induction or even awake intubation may be indicated. Video laryngoscope-assisted fiberoptic intubation may reduce the apnoea time during asleep intubation. High flow apnoeic oxygenation should be considered to avoid hypoxia during intubation.

Maintenance of Anaesthesia

- **Positioning:** For surgery, the patient is turned to a 'prone' position after intubation. Maintenance of anaesthesia either by using inhalational anaesthetics (isoflurane or sevoflurane) with air and oxygen or total intravenous anaesthesia (TIVA) with propofol and fentanyl or remifentanil. If the motor evoked potential monitoring is planned, avoid using muscle relaxants during the maintenance phase of anaesthesia. Appropriate size bite blocks should be placed to prevent tongue injury.
  - The airway should be secured properly to avoid accidental extubation. Extremities should lie in a relaxed position and should be well-padded to prevent hypothermia.
  - Excessive flexion or rotation of the neck should be avoided as some of these children may have an associated ACM Type II.
  - Lungs should be mechanically ventilated. Barotrauma to the immature lung must be prevented. Premature infants (especially <32 weeks) are at increased risk for retinopathy of prematurity and lung injury from prolonged exposure to high oxygen concentration. Hence, high FiO_2 should be avoided in premature neonates.
  - Ensure that the abdomen is free by placing chest and hip rolls to facilitate ventilation and decrease intra-abdominal pressure, which in turn decreases the bleeding from the epidural plexus.
- Prevent injury to and drying of exposed neural tissue by covering it with Ringer's lactate (RL)

or saline-soaked sterile gauze. Avoid the scrub solution or the anti-microbial solution from touching the exposed neural tissue so as to avoid neuronal damage.

- The CSF should be sent for cell counts and protein, sugar and culture at the time of surgery so that appropriate antibiotic therapy can be started, if indicated.
- Intraoperatively sugars must be checked intermittently to prevent hypoglycaemia. A 'cocktail' containing 10% dextrose should be continued for neonates.
- These children are prone to excessive third space loss from the exposed MMC. Hence, fluid and blood loss should be replaced appropriately using an isotonic balanced salt solution. Blood loss may be considerable during the repair of the MMC when large amounts of skin are to be undermined to cover the defect or a local rotation flap is needed to cover a large defect. Hence, blood should be readily available.
  - Age-appropriate systolic blood pressure must be maintained (70 + 2 [age in years]) to maintain spinal cord perfusion.
  - The large area of exposed tissue and the liberal use of cold surgical preparation solutions increase the risk of hypothermia. Care must be taken to prevent drying or thermal injury to the exposed neural tissue by radiant heat lamps.

Special Considerations – Latex Allergy

Seventy-three percent of these children are allergic to the protein present in latex because of repeated exposure to latex products since birth such as repeated bladder catheterisation and surgery. Hence, latex-free products should be used to avoid life-threatening allergic reactions during the perioperative period. They may also have an increased incidence of allergies to other substances, so anticipate and be ready to treat anaphylaxis.

Post-Operative Care

- Nurse the children in the prone position and keep them flat or in a slight Trendelenburg position with a urinary catheter in place.
- Watch for signs of raised ICP or brainstem herniation – children should be monitored in intensive care unit (ICU) during the post-operative period.
- Daily measurement of head circumference and bi-weekly or weekly assessment using cranial USG for ventriculomegaly to rule out HCP if the shunt is not done simultaneously along with MMC repair and to assess the shunt function if it was done simultaneously with MMC repair.
- Avoid narcotics as the babies are very sensitive to their respiratory depressant effect.

Late Complications of MMC Repair

- HCP
- Tethered cord syndrome (10–20%)
- Scoliosis
- Syringomyelia/Syringobulbia
- Dermoid tumour at the surgical site (16%)
- ACM Type II

Anaesthesia for the In-Utero Repair of MMC

Anaesthesia for the in-utero repair of MMC poses multiple challenges to the anaesthesiologist, which include inducing profound uterine relaxation, monitoring foetal and maternal well-being, extreme vigilance on maternal and foetal blood loss, providing adequate analgesia to both mother and foetus, providing tocolysis during the post-operative period. The detailed discussion on this topic is beyond the scope of this chapter. Students should refer the article by Ferschl M et al. (2013) for further details on this topic.

Conclusion

In all cases, it is important to properly assess the baby pre-operatively for signs and symptoms of raised ICP, neurological deficits and for associated congenital anomalies. During surgery, ensure proper positioning, fluid and electrolyte balance and warmth. Reverse and extubate when fully awake and monitor closely post-operatively.

SUGGESTED READINGS

1. Vavilala MS, Soriano SG. Hydrocephalus in anaesthesia for neurosurgery. In: Smiths Anesthesia for Infants and Children, 8th edn. Davis PJ, Cladis FP, Motoyama EK (eds). Elsevier Mosby, Philadelphia, 2011; pp. 725–726.
2. Crean P, Hicks E. Hydrocephalus in essentials of neurology and neuromuscular disease.

In: A Practice of Anaesthesia for Infants and Children, 4th edn. Cote CJ, Lerman J, Todres ID (eds). WB Saunders Company, Philadelphia, 2009; pp. 495.
3. Boat AC, Sadhasivam S. Meningomyelocele repair. In: Clinical Pediatric Anesthesia. Goldschneider KR, Davidson AJ, Wittkugel EP, Skinner AV (eds). Oxford University Press, New York, 2012; pp. 561–572.
4. Keyes M. Anesthetic considerations in the child with myelomeningocele. Sem Anesth Periop Med Pain 2003; 22(2):125–133.
5. Koleya M, De Jesus O. Hydrocephalus. In. Stat Pearls. Treasure Island (FL): Stat Pearls Publishing; 2022. Available from https ://www.ncbi.nih.gov/books/NBK60875/ (accessed on 25 July 2022).
6. Primary Spinal anomalies. In: Handbook of Neurosurgery, 9th edn, Greenberg MS (ed). Thieme, New York 2020; pp. 280–291.
7. Primary Craniospinal anomalies. In: Handbook of Neurosurgery, 9th edn, Greenberg MS (ed). Thieme, New York 2020; pp. 29–310.
8. Alruwaili AA, M Das J. Myelomeningocele. In: StatPearls. Treasure Island (FL): StatPearls Publishing. Available from: https://www.ncbi.nlm.nih.gov/books/NBK546696/ (accessed on 27 June 2022)
9. Krovvidi H, Flint G, Williams AV. Perioperative management of hydrocephalus. *BJA Educ* 2018; 18(5):140–146.
10. Ferschl M, Ball R, Lee H, et al. Anesthesia for in utero repair of myelomeningocele. *Anesthesiology* 2013; 118(5):1211–1123.

39

Bleeding Tonsil

Rebecca Jacob

Bleeding in the post-operative period following tonsillectomy and/or adenoidectomies may be as high as 1–2% of all tonsillectomies. A basic understanding of the pathology of the bleeding tonsils and familiarising oneself with the most effective methods by which this potentially hazardous and fatal complication can be prevented is considered in the following text.

Types of Haemorrhage

- **Primary haemorrhage:** Occurs at the time of operation due to injury to the vessels.
- **Reactionary haemorrhage:** Occurs within the first 24 hours. Approximately 75% of post-tonsillar bleeds occur in the first 6 hours after surgery and the remaining 25% occur within the first 24 hours. Ligature slippage and/or dislodging of clots are the main causes of reactionary haemorrhages. Return to normal blood pressure during the recovery period opens up collapsed blood vessels which also contribute to bleeding.
- **Secondary haemorrhage:** Secondary to infection of the tonsillar fossa with sloughing of tissue and the fibrin clot separates from the tonsillar bed; it occurs after 24 hours and within 10–14 days.

Anaesthetic Problems

Bleeding tonsil is an emergency situation and instead of panicking. It is good to consider problems under the following headings. The options for action are as follows:

- **Hypovolaemia:** Post-tonsillectomy bleeding is often a slow ooze rather than brisk bleeding. The patient's swallowing reflex conceals the large volumes of blood lost. The hypovolaemic patient presents clinically with tachycardia and hypotension. Orthostatic hypotension indicates loss of at least 20% of the circulating blood volume. Hypotension at rest could mean a much larger volume loss. Caution! Anaesthetic induction with its attendant vasodilatation can lead to cardiovascular collapse. Therefore, the need for urgent fluid resuscitation before surgery.
- **Full stomach:** Due to food and swallowed blood.
- **Bleeding in the upper airway:** Blood in the upper airway makes it difficult to intubate. A large bore suction (two are preferable), a 'tilting table', several laryngoscope blades (in case the light fails on one) and different sizes of endotracheal tubes (ETTs) should be checked and kept ready.
- **Sharing the airway:** Both the anaesthetist and the surgeon have to work in the mouth and oropharynx.
- **Previous recent anaesthesia:** Residual effects of narcotics may be a problem. A mild subglottic oedema may necessitate a smaller-sized ETT.

Assessment of the Patient

- **History:** From the notes, patients, parents and nurses
- **Previous anaesthesia record:** Any difficult intubation, and anaesthetic agent used

- **Observation:** Level of consciousness, signs of restlessness and signs of dehydration or pallor
- **Examination:** Tachycardia and hypotension

Any other medical problems (obesity, sleep apnoea and asthma are the most common associated problems)

Resuscitation and Transfer to the Operating Room

- **IV access:** Before re-anaesthetising the patient, a good intravenous access should be obtained and intravascular volume restored. Prompt IV access is crucial to the outcome but may be difficult in a severely hypovolaemic patient. Intraosseous access or IV access using ultrasound guidance should be considered (see Chapter 10)
- **Blood for haematocrit, cross-match and coagulation:** Serial haematocrits should be checked and patients should be transfused if necessary. Deaths have occurred due to ill-timed anaesthetic inductions in patients who were rushed to the operating room while still hypovolaemic.
- **Coagulation:** The status must be carefully evaluated and appropriate correction made.
- **Resuscitate with crystalloid, plasma or blood:** Blood loss is replaced with crystalloids, colloids or whole blood depending on the amount of blood loss. Frequent observations of peripheral temperature and capillary filling, blood pressure, pulse and respiratory rate should be made.
  - The volume and contents of the stomach may be assessed by ultrasonography (see Chapter 15). This will help in assessing the danger of aspiration but do not waste time organising this if there is the danger of a massive bleed. Accept that the child may have a 'full stomach'.
- **Transfer:** The patient should be stabilised before transfer. The patient must be transferred in the lateral position to prevent aspiration, and accompanied by a nurse and doctor. The vitals must be frequently monitored. IV fluids should be on flow during transfer.
- **Sedation:** It is preferable not to sedate these patients heavily for fear of loss of protective airway reflexes.

Prepare Staff, Theatre and Equipment

The anaesthetic machine should be checked before the patient is brought into the operating room. The operating room should be warmed. The anaesthetic assistant should be instructed properly regarding the things needed and how to apply cricoid pressure properly. Different sizes of ETTs, laryngoscopes and a mask with a self-inflating bag should be available. The suction apparatus should be checked and a spare one kept available in case one gets occluded with blood clots. Blood in the airway may impair the visualisation of the vocal cords and cause plugging of the ETT or suction apparatus. Secondary intubation equipment such as video laryngoscopes should be available as well as nasal prongs connected to an oxygen supply to provide apnoeic oxygenation during laryngoscopy.

Induction

Resuscitate adequately prior to induction.

- **Supine position:** Once the patient is stabilised and the theatre ready, the patient is placed supine and the monitors connected.
- **Pre-oxygenate:** Hypoxia is a very common complication in children with a difficult airway. Pre-oxygenation is a safe, simple and effective technique to increase safe apnoea time by increasing the oxygen content of the functional residual capacity technique. Ideally, this should be done for at least 3 minutes or eight vital capacity breaths (the latter is avoided in patients who have blood or secretions in the mouth).
- **Rapid-sequence induction and intubation (RSII)** in a supine position with cricoid pressure is advocated but may be difficult in a small child. A controlled rapid sequence RSII that incorporates low pressure (<12 cm H_2O) mask ventilation before laryngoscopy under a deep plane of anaesthesia may be used in case of slow venous bleeding. Supplemental oxygen delivery via a nasal cannula during laryngoscopy can help provide apnoeic oxygenation.
- **Ketamine** is the induction agent of choice in hypovolaemia and hypotension and *suxamethonium (or rocuronium)* is the muscle relaxant of choice in 'full stomach'.

- **Secure the airway with an ETT:** A cuffed ETT may be chosen, which is 0.5–1.0 mm smaller in diameter than the appropriate-sized uncuffed tube (check the record of previous anaesthetic, for tube size, if available). A cuffed tube decreases the risk of pulmonary aspiration in these high-risk patients. It is better to use a standard ETT to rapidly secure the difficult airway rather than a preformed tube such as the oral Ring–Adair–Elwyn tube, which may be difficult to insert rapidly in this situation.

The passage of a *nasogastric tube (NG)* pre-operatively is controversial. Passing an NG tube to an awake child can be distressing both to the child and his parents, raising the blood pressure and traumatising both the adenoid and the tonsillar bed thus causing further bleeding. Also, the clotted blood will not be easy to aspirate via an NG tube. However, the removal of swallowed blood will help in decreasing post-operative nausea and emesis. This may be achieved by passing a large-bore orogastric tube under vision after the surgeon has controlled the bleeding. However, this does NOT guarantee that the stomach is empty.

- **Steroids:** Dexamethasone at a dose of 0.1 mg/kg can be given intravenously to reduce airway oedema. It is also a good anti-emetic.
- **Ondansetron** is also a useful anti-emetic.
- **Tranexamic** *acid* has been used effectively for coagulation abnormalities.

Maintenance

Maintenance is with

- positive pressure intermittent ventilation,
- volatile anaesthetic and adequate opioid analgesia and
- non-depolarising muscle relaxant

Emergence

The muscle relaxant must be antagonised with neostigmine and atropine.

Extubation may be performed in a lateral, head-down position with the child fully awake. Some authorities prefer the supine head-down position as they feel more comfortable securing the airway in this position.

Adequate analgesia during the post-operative period is necessary.

Post-Operative Position

The *tonsil position* can aid in maintaining a clear airway during the recovery period. The body is placed semi-lateral, inclined at 45° forward, stabilised by the upper arm under the head, and the lower leg straight with the upper leg bent. The absence of a pillow under the head permits the width of the shoulder to incline the pharynx downwards, facilitating drainage away from the larynx (**Fig. 39.1**).

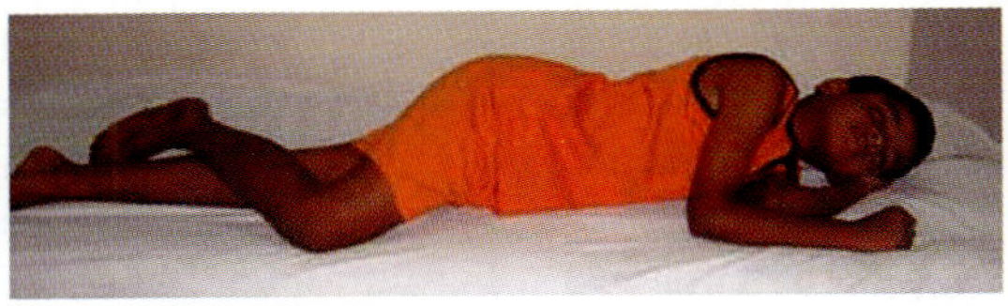

Figure 39.1 Recovery position.

Recovery

- Oxygen therapy till fully awake
- Maintain body temperature
- Maintain intravenous fluids
- Continue monitoring the patient
- Provide adequate analgesia

SUGGESTED READINGS

1. Lee AC, Hache M. Pediatric anesthesia management for post-tonsillectomy bleed:: Current status and future directions. *Int J Gen Med* 2022; 15:63–69.
2. Snijdelaar DG, Doyle DJ. Anesthesia for ENT Procedures and Laser Surgery. In: Wylie and Churchill-Davidson's A Practice of Anesthesia, 7th edition. Healy TEJ, Knight PR (eds). Arnold Press, London, 2003; p.840.
3. Hannallah RS, Brown KA, Verghese ST. Post Tonsillar Bleeding. In: A Practice of Anaesthesia for Infants and Children, 4th edition. Cote CJ, Lerman J, Todres ID (eds). WB Saunders Company, Philadelphia, 2009; pp. 670–671.
4. Landsman IS, Werkhaven JA, Motoyama EK. Bleeding After Tonsillectomy. In: Smiths Anesthesia for Infants and Children, 8th edition. Davis PJ, Cladis FP, Motoyama EK (eds). Elsevier Mosby, Philadelphia, 2011; pp. 799–800.

40 Major Paediatric Trauma

Georgene Singh • Riya Sarah Abraham

Trauma is a major cause of morbidity and mortality in children between 1 and 19 years of age. Each year, more than 10 million children – nearly 1 of every 6 children – in the United States require emergency care for the treatment of injuries, with more than 10,000 dying from serious injuries. No such numbers are available in India, but they could be a lot more considering the size of the population and the dearth of immediate medical care. Failure to secure a compromised airway, assist breathing, and recognise and respond to intra-abdominal and intracranial haemorrhage are the leading causes of unsuccessful resuscitation in paediatric patients with severe trauma.

Injuries associated with motor vehicles are the most common cause of death in children of all ages. Deaths due to drowning, house fires, homicides and falls follow in descending order. Other important causes for childhood injuries, which are commonly overlooked, are physical and sexual abuse. Child maltreatment accounts for the great majority of homicides in infants (i.e., children younger than 12 months of age). Falls account for the majority of all paediatric injuries but infrequently result in death.

Paediatric trauma deaths have a trimodal distribution, with 50% being immediate mortalities due to either severe head injury or major haemorrhage. A further 30% of the deaths occur within the first few hours from the head injury, haemorrhage or airway emergencies. Late deaths due to organ failure and sepsis are often due to inadequate initial resuscitation. Morbidity associated with trauma is time sensitive. Early goal-directed therapy and prompt referral and transport of injured children to an appropriate level of care are critical to survival.

Anaesthetists, who are often involved in the initial evaluation and management of a child with trauma, should have a clear understanding of the anatomical and physiological differences between paediatric and adult patients (**Table 40.1**).

In addition to the anatomical and physiological differences listed in **Table 40.1**, one must also be aware of the normal values of vital parameters across all age groups in infants and children (**Table 40.2**).

Nature and Pattern of Injury

The nature of injury relates to the mechanism and severity of injury and is assessed during the secondary survey (see below). Mechanisms of injury vary with age.

- **Accidental**
  - Blunt trauma – mostly by falls and motor vehicle collisions
  - Penetrating – as in gunshot injuries and stab wounds
- **Non-accidental:** Those sustained as a result of deliberate action by another person.
  - Bruises, abrasions and lacerations

The severity of trauma may be obvious such as degloving injuries and fractures or concealed as in systemic injuries. Often, an injury which may seem trivial such as a scalp injury may cause bleeding significant enough to cause a hypovolaemic shock.

Table 40.1 Paediatric Anatomy and Physiology Which Make a Significant Difference in Trauma

S.No.	Relevant Changes in Paediatric Anatomy and Physiology		Significance in Trauma
1.	Airway	Small oral cavity Large tongue/tonsillar enlargement	Predispose to airway obstruction
		Relatively large occiput, causing a passive cervical flexion in the supine position	Adds to airway obstruction, necessitating a roll under the shoulder which may exacerbate unstable cervical spine injury
		Anterior and Cephalad larynx U-shaped, floppy epiglottis Short trachea	Difficult direct laryngoscopic visualisation May project into the airway and obscure the glottic aperture Risk of endobronchial intubation and accidental tube dislodgement
		Smaller airway diameter Narrowest at cricoid ring	Increased resistance with obstruction due to oedema/secretions Use of uncuffed ET tubes (by convention)
		Narrow trachea, shorter distance between tracheal rings	Difficult to perform needle cricothyroidotomy
		Preferential nasal breathers	If the nose is obstructed by secretions/ oedema, there is a significant increase in the work of breathing, since the nares account for half the total airway resistance
2.	Head	Relatively large head (infants and children <8 years of age)	A particular risk of head trauma and cervical spine injury, scalp/face burns account for up to 19% of body surface area in infants (as against 9% in adults)
3.	Brain	Open fontanelles, increased subarachnoid and extracellular space	Better tolerance to an expanding intracranial hematoma
		Less myelinated brain and thinner cranium	Mild forces resulting in skull fractures and parenchymal injury
4.	Spinal cord	Flexible cervical spine	SCIWORA
		Weak musculature of the neck	Predisposed to pseudo-subluxation of the cervical spine
5.	Chest	Compliant chest wall	Prone to pulmonary contusions without bony/rib fractures
		Mobile mediastinal structures	More likely to develop a tension pneumothorax
		Limited functional residual capacity, increased oxygen utilisation relative to adults Smaller tidal volumes	Early development of hypoxia with inadequate ventilation (shorter safe apnoea time) Aggressive mechanical ventilation may result in iatrogenic barotrauma
		Lower percentage of slow twitch (type 1) skeletal muscle fibres in their intercostal muscles in infants	The use of accessory muscles to facilitate airflow during respiratory distress makes them prone to early fatigue and respiratory failure.
6.	Abdomen	Poor protection of abdominal organs by the ribcage	Prone to direct injury of the liver and spleen
7.	Musculoskeletal system	Immature skeletal framework	Predisposes to physeal and greenstick fractures

(*Contd.*)

Table 40.1 (*Contd.*)

S.No.	Relevant Changes in Paediatric Anatomy and Physiology		Significance in Trauma
8.	Vascular access	More difficult to achieve than for adults	Delay in fluid resuscitation A low threshold to obtain intraosseous access
9.	Circulation	Increased physiologic reserve allows maintenance of blood pressure despite 30–45% loss of total blood volume	Shock manifests initially as tachycardia with poor skin perfusion, followed by hypotension and finally bradycardia, if blood loss continues unchecked
10.	Autonomic system	Higher vagal tone	Infants may have a pronounced vagal response to airway manipulation. Hypoxia potentiates the risk for bradycardia.
11.	Metabolism	Large body surface area to weight ratio, and higher metabolic rate	Prone to insensible fluid losses and hypothermia which may worsen metabolic acidosis, exerting a negative cardiac inotropic effect

ET, endotracheal; SCIWORA, Spinal cord injury with or without radiological abnormality.

Table 40.2 Normal Values for Children

Age	0–6 Months	6–12 Months	1–3 Years	3–6 Years	6–12 Years	>12 Years
Respiratory rate (/min)	30–55	25–40	20–40	20–25	14–22	12–18
Heart rate (/min)	90–150	80–120	70–110	65–110	60–95	55–85
Blood pressure (SBP/DBP) mmHg	65–90/45–65	80–100/55–65	90–105/55–70	95–110/60–75	100–120/60–75	110–135/65–85
Body weight	3–7.5 kg	8–10 kg	10–14 kg	14.5–20 kg	20–40 kg	>35 kg
Blood volume	90–100 ml/kg	80–90 ml/kg	70–80 ml/kg	70–80 ml/kg	70–80 ml/kg	70 ml/kg

DBP, diastolic blood pressure; SBP, systolic blood pressure.

A thorough examination of the injuries in each anatomic region can help assess the severity of the injury and dictate further management.

The pattern of injuries sustained by a child depends on the nature of the trauma. Blunt injuries often result in multisystem trauma. Children, specifically, are more susceptible to multiple organ injuries due to their relatively smaller body size, are at particular risk for head and cervical spine injury due to the relatively large size of the head with respect to their body and are more prone to hypothermia and dehydration due to their larger surface area to mass ratio. The pliant skeleton can cause injury to internal organs without evidence of fractured bones and other tell-tale external signs, leading to disastrous consequences if these are missed during the initial assessment. It is, therefore, imperative that the injuries to all systems are carefully sought for in the initial evaluation of the injured child.

Although the incidence of penetrating trauma in children is less, the approach is similar to that in blunt trauma, with a higher likelihood of significant injury and the need for operative intervention. Those to the head, neck, torso and extremities proximal to the elbow or knees have the highest potential for abrupt decompensation. A low threshold for obtaining surgical consultation and early transfer to a higher trauma facility may improve outcomes.

Classification of Trauma

Classification of trauma is essential to predict morbidity, mortality and for prioritisation of treatment modalities. There are different classification systems that are aimed at the following:

1. Triage scoring systems
2. Scoring systems for assessment of the severity of the injury
3. Outcome analysis systems (combination of the above)

Triage Scoring Systems

Triage scoring systems are typically used in the field to determine physiologic risk and referral patterns for pre-hospital personnel. The ideal triage score should be simple, easy to calculate and based upon rapidly obtainable clinical findings. It should also be sensitive enough to include all patients who require a higher level of trauma services. The most validated among the paediatric triage scoring systems are the paediatric trauma score (PTS) and the Paediatric Glasgow Coma Scale. Others include the trauma score (TS), revised trauma score (RTS) and the age-specific paediatric trauma score (ASPTS).

Paediatric Trauma Score

The PTS was developed to reflect the vulnerability of children to traumatic injury. It is a sum of six measures incorporating size as a surrogate for age, along with vital signs and markers of organ-specific injury. It is used as a predictor of mortality and correlates with the severity of the injury. It can also guide resource utilisation and the decision for transport to a paediatric trauma centre. The minimal score is −6 and the maximum score is +12. There is a linear relationship between the decrease in PTS and the mortality risk (i.e., the lower the PTS, the higher the mortality risk). Mortality is estimated at 9% with a PTS > 8 and at 100% with a PTS ≤ 0. In most cases, the severity of a paediatric trauma injury is determined by the PTS (Table 40.3).

Paediatric Glasgow Coma Scale

Modification of the Glasgow Coma Scale (GCS) to the paediatric population, in both verbal and pre-verbal children, has been an important advancement. The use of the motor component of the GCS instead of the entire scale (tGCS) had been proposed to simplify field triage for trauma patients. A retrospective systematic review of 14 studies showed the tGCS to have significantly better utility. The modified GCS is shown in Table 40.4.

Scoring Systems for Assessment of Severity of Injury

Injury scoring systems, as opposed to triage scoring systems, are based upon anatomic injury and are only accurate after all injuries have been diagnosed. Once all injuries have been identified, the score remains constant. This scoring system is primarily used for the comparison of injury severity among trauma populations and to accurately predict risk for adverse outcomes.

The Abbreviated Injury Scale (AIS) is the most commonly used scoring system and was designed to categorise the injuries of victims of motor vehicle collisions. It ranges from 1 (least severe) to 5 (survival uncertain) within six body regions: head/neck, face, chest, abdomen/pelvis, extremities

Table 40.3 Paediatric Trauma Score

Score	+2	+1	−1
Weight	>20 kg	10–20 kg	<10 kg
Airway	Normal with oral or nasal airway positioning	Maintainable without advanced airway intervention	Unmaintainable
Blood pressure	>90 mmHg	50–90 mmHg	<50 mmHg
Level of consciousness	Awake, alert	Obtunded and loss of consciousness	Comatose
Open wound	None	Minor	Major or penetrating
Fractures	None	Single and simple	Open or multiple

Table 40.4 Modified (Paediatric) Glasgow Coma Scale

Infants	Score	Children
	Eye Opening	
Spontaneous	4	Spontaneous
To speech or sound	3	To speech
To painful stimulus	2	To pain
None	1	None
	Best Verbal Response	
Coos, babbles and smiles	5	Cries appropriately, oriented
Irritable cry, but consolable	4	Confused
Cries/screams in pain	3	Inappropriate crying/ words
Grunts/groans to pain	2	Grunts incomprehensible words
None	1	None
	Best Motor Response	
Spontaneous movement	6	Obeys commands
Localises pain	5	Localises pain
Withdrawal from pain	4	Withdrawal from pain
Flexion to pain (decorticate)	3	Flexion to pain (decorticate)
Extension to pain (decerebrate)	2	Extension to pain (decerebrate)
None	1	None

and skin/general. Non-survivable conditions are assigned an AIS of 6. However, it does not accurately measure the effect of multiple injuries.

The Injury Severity Score (ISS) and the anatomic profile (AP) are scores derived from the AIS. The ISS is a valid predictor of mortality, length of stay in the hospital or intensive care unit and cost of trauma care. It is calculated from the highest AIS for the three most severely injured regions. The AP uses the AIS descriptors of severity but takes into account only four body regions: head/brain/spinal cord, thorax/neck, all other serious injuries and all non-serious injuries.

Outcome Analysis Systems

Outcome prediction systems use both physiologic and anatomic data to estimate morbidity and mortality for an individual patient or for trauma populations. Examples include:

- Trauma Injury Severity Score (TRISS)
- Paediatric age-adjusted trauma injury severity score (PAAT)
- A Severity Characterisation of Trauma (ASCOT)
- Paediatric Risk of Mortality (PRISM III)
- Paediatric trauma BIG score
- International Classification injury severity score

The TRISS combines TS or the RTS (physiologic) and ISS (anatomic) data and age to estimate the probability of patient survival. The PAAT combines the age-specific PTS with the ISS and was shown to better predict survival than the TRISS and ASCOT. The PRISM III is used in paediatric ICUs and is the only validated predictor of critical care outcomes in paediatrics as it incorporates cardiovascular and neurologic parameters, as well as acid–base, electrolyte and haematologic values. The BIG score is calculated from the admission base deficit, international normalised ratio (INR) and the GCS as follows:

BIG score = Base deficit + [2.5 × INR] + [15 − GCS]

The BIG score was more accurate in predicting mortality than the RTS, ISS, ASPTS or PAAT.

Validation studies have shown that a BIG score < 16 was associated with a high likelihood of survival.

Approach to Major Trauma

The goals of initial trauma management in children, as in adults, are to rapidly assess injuries, determine management priorities and provide critical interventions. Achieving these goals requires a systematic and logical approach according to the tenets of Advanced Trauma Life Support (ATLS). Prompt recognition and treatment of life-threatening airway obstruction, inadequate breathing, and intra-abdominal and intracranial haemorrhage significantly increase the survival rate after major trauma. The first hour or 'the golden hour' is critical.

Early management of trauma may be divided into the following four phases:

- **The Primary survey or initial assessment:** It is a quick, 2-minute assessment and treatment of basic life functions. This is done with a simple systematic ABCDE guide (see below) to evaluate and re-evaluate the most important functions that are at risk in the traumatised child. The primary survey is kept simple so that it is easy to teach, learn and execute in an orderly manner, even in a stressful situation, so as to ensure that no essential component is missed.
- **Resuscitation phase:** It may be done along with the initial assessment, while also utilising the adjuncts to the primary survey. The goals of essential therapy include providing adequate oxygen delivery and ventilation, controlling haemorrhage and replacement of volume and preventing secondary damage to target organs.
- **Secondary survey:** It follows the resuscitation phase and consists of a complete physical examination, radiological assessment (X-rays, computed tomography [CT] scan and ultrasound), laboratory investigations, essential interventions and appropriate antibiotic administration.
- **Definitive care:** During this period, definitive management of life- and limb-threatening injuries are planned and executed as per priority.

Primary Survey

The primary survey is a quick assessment to identify and treat critical events. It follows a sequential order of assessment and treatment. It may often involve basic or advanced life support depending on the situation. The paediatric BLS algorithm is dealt with in Chapter 28. Relevant modifications to standard paediatric life support with respect to trauma in children will be dealt with under the respective sections given below.

Primary Survey – A-B-C-D-E

A – Airway Maintenance with Cervical Spine Protection

Maintenance of Airway

Give OXYGEN!

Establishing a patent airway to provide adequate oxygenation is a priority since airway obstruction with hypoxia is the most common cause of paediatric cardiopulmonary arrest following trauma. If the child is crying, then one can assume that the airway is patent, at least for the time being. Hypoxaemia should be suspected in a child who is agitated or extremely quiet. Signs to suggest airway compromise are in-drawing of the suprasternal area, paradoxical chest movements, inspiratory stridor and cyanosis, especially in a child with facial injuries or who is vomiting.

In children, there is a disproportion between the size of the head and the face and this is more pronounced in the smaller child. The large occiput flexes the cervical spine causing obstruction of the pharynx. Placing a layer of padding under the torso of the child, especially the shoulders, helps to align the cervical spine in a neutral position and keep the plane of the mid-face parallel to the spine board. Other factors that make a paediatric airway a challenge have been detailed in **Table 40.1**. Chin lift, jaw thrust, insertion of nasal or oral airways, bag and mask ventilation and maintaining a continuous positive airway pressure are all manoeuvres which can relieve airway obstruction. Do not use a nasopharyngeal airway in case of a head injury.

Cervical Spine Protection

Children are prone to spinal cord injury with or without radiological abnormality because of the flexible cervical spine and weak musculature of the neck. Hence, cervical spine immobilisation should be undertaken prior to securing the airway.

Indications for cervical spine motion restriction:

- Mechanism precluding potential C-spine injury (motor vehicle collisions, fall from height and diving)
- Anatomic predisposition to the neck injury (e.g., Down's syndrome, prior neck injury and history of cervical spine surgery)
- Altered mental status or intoxication
- Neck pain, torticollis and/or guarding of the neck
- Neurologic deficit

Cervical spine motion restriction is usually addressed by the application of a rigid cervical collar. One-person, manual in-line techniques to restrict motion must be used if immobilisation devices need to be removed for access to the airway or for performing airway manoeuvres. The use of a spine-board is ideal during patient transfer.

Endotracheal Intubation in an Injured Child

Indications:

- An unresponsive, apnoeic and hypoxic child
- Inadequate ventilation with a self-inflating bag or an obstructed airway
- Severe head injury requiring controlled hyper-ventilation
- Penetrating chest or neck injuries, facial injuries and burns
- Flail chest or an open chest wound
- Shock unresponsive to fluid resuscitation

Emergency endotracheal (ET) intubation performed by a non-anaesthetist causes complications as high as 44% in paediatric patients. Rapid sequence induction (RSI) is ideal to secure the airway as patients are presumed to have a full stomach due to traumatic gastroparesis, placing them at risk for pulmonary aspiration. They may also have varying levels of consciousness. It entails a coordinated, sequential process of preparation, sedation and paralysis in rapid succession to facilitate safe, emergency tracheal intubation. The suggested sequence for RSI in children is detailed in **Figure 40.1**.

Performing an RSI requires assistance with manual in-line immobilisation, intubation, application of cricoid pressure, administration of drugs and monitoring. It is important not to persist with repeated intubation attempts without ventilating the patient. When all other methods of providing oxygenation fail, needle cricothyroidotomy with an intravenous (IV) cannula should be considered. Surgical cricothyroidotomy is not recommended due to the high incidence of laryngeal mobility and difficulty in laryngeal reconstruction when attempted later. Laryngeal mask airway and video laryngoscopes are useful alternatives for children with facial and head and neck trauma. Maintaining spontaneous ventilation is important for children with tracheal injuries.

Pearls

- The size of the ET tube approximates the size of the child's external nares or the tip of the child's index finger.
- Fix the tube well for transport.
- The latest AHA 2020 Paediatric advanced life support (PALS) guideline has endorsed the use of a cuffed endotracheal tube (ETT) in children less than 8 years old but beyond the newborn period. However, the cuff pressure needs to be kept below 20 mmHg.
- It also recommends the discontinuation of cricoid pressure while securing the airway if it interferes with ventilation or ease of intubation.

B – Breathing and Ventilation

The respiratory rate in children varies with age, ranging from nearly 40/min in an infant to around 20/min in a 12 years old. To ensure adequate ventilation, it is important to look, feel and listen to detect abnormality in breathing.

Inspection (Look)

- Respiratory rate and depth – children normally have a higher respiratory rate than adults
- Penetrating injury to the chest and sucking chest wounds
- Presence of flail chest
- Use of accessory muscles and ala nasi flaring

Palpation (Feel)

- Tracheal shift
- Broken ribs and subcutaneous emphysema

1. Preparation

- Identify specific concerns (increased intracranial pressure, septic shock and bronchospasm)
- Look for predictors of difficult intubation or bag-mask ventilation
- Check monitors, equipment and oxygen source
- Oxygen saturation, heart rate, respiratory rate, blood pressure and end-tidal CO_2 detection
- Atleast one, and preferably two functional intravenous lines
- Tested and functioning suction (Yankauer and flexible catheter) and airway equipment (appropriate sizes for age)
- Call for additional, trained help when required

2. Pre-oxygenation

- Spontaneously breathing: 100% FiO_2(>7 L/min oxygen flow) by non-rebreather mask for 3 minutes
- Apneic or inadequate breathing: Bag-mask ventilation with small tidal breaths using 100% FiO_2

3. Anti-cholinergics and induction agents

Atropine (0.02 mg/kg i.v/i.m) may be given as pretreatment for:

- Children <1 year of age
- Children <5 years of age, receiving succinylcholine

Choice of induction agent

- If haemodynamically unstable, etomidate (0.2–0.4 mg/kg) or ketamine (1–2 mg/kg) may be preferred
- For their neuroprotective effects, propofol (2–3 mg/kg) may be used in haemodynamically stable patients with head injury and etomidate in those who are haemodynamically unstable.

4. Neuromuscular blockade

Succinylcholine (1–1.5 mg/kg): Absolutely contraindicated in the following scenarios:

- Chronic myopathy/denervating neuromuscular disease
- > 48–72 hours after burns, multiple trauma
- Extensive crush injury
- H/o malignant hyperthermia
- Pre-existing hyperkalemia

Rocuronium (1.2 mg/kg): used in children with contraindications for succinylcholine or as primary paralytic if sugammadex is available.

5. Placement of ET

Choice of tube: Cuffed endotracheal tubes are equally safe as uncuffed tubes, as long as the cuff pressures are limited to <20–25 cm H_2O to avoid tracheal mucosal ischaemia.

- Uncuffed tube: 4+ (age in years/4)
- Cuffed tube: 3.5+ (age in years/4)

Choice of laryngoscopy blades: Miller straight blade in infants and preschool toddlers, curved Macintosh in older children

Cricoid pressure: AHA 2020 guidelines do not recommend routine use of cricoid pressure.

6. Post-intubation Management

- Confirmation of tube position: Auscultation of bilateral equal air entry and $EtCO_2$ monitoring
- Ventilator settings and maintenance of anaesthesia

Figure 40.1 Suggested sequence for RSI in children. ET, endotracheal, RSI, rapid sequence intubation.

Percussion

- Dullness (for haemothorax or hydrothorax)
- Hyper resonance (for pneumothorax)

Auscultation (Listen)

- Pneumothorax/haemothorax – decreased air entry
- Abnormal sounds – bowel sounds in the chest with a ruptured diaphragm
- After intubation, check the correct placement of the tube with bilateral equal expansion, breath sounds, exhaled moisture in the tube and absence of breath sounds over the stomach
- Adequacy of ventilation should be assessed by auscultation over each side of the chest and the use of a pulse oximeter and a capnogram

Desaturation with absent breath sounds and hyper-resonance on percussion over one side could indicate a tension pneumothorax. A definitive diagnosis may be made by the use of ultrasound. Management includes administration of high oxygen concentration, bag-valve-mask ventilation if respiratory efforts are inadequate and needle decompression in case of a tension pneumothorax (by inserting an 18-14G over-the-needle catheter just above the third rib in the mid-clavicular line a smaller catheter should be used in infants and smaller children).

An open pneumothorax should be sealed and a chest tube inserted. Monitoring the end-tidal CO_2 and obtaining an arterial or venous blood gas measurement may be considered. It is crucial to have adequate intravenous access before inserting a chest tube for haemothorax, since the decompression may lead to hypotension, requiring a rapid infusion of fluid and blood.

In patients with traumatic brain injury, hyperventilation ($PaCO_2$ < 35 mmHg) may worsen cerebral perfusion by decreasing cerebral blood flow. Ventilation should be aimed at maintaining a $PaCO_2$ between 35 and 40 mmHg unless there is evidence of impending herniation.

In paediatric cardiopulmonary arrest, the updated AHA 2020 guideline for Basic Life Support (PBLS) recommends a ventilation rate of 1 breath every 2–3 seconds (20–30 breaths/min) as data has shown improved rates of return of spontaneous circulation and survival with paediatric in-hospital cardiac arrests. For children in respiratory arrest due to suspected opioid overdose, in addition to providing standard PALS, intramuscular or intranasal naloxone (dose: <20 kg or <5 year old – 0.1 mg/kg IV/IO/IM/IN up to a maximum of 2 mg; >20 kg or >5 years old – 2 mg IV/IO/IM/IN) may be administered.

Pearls

- Children have high oxygen consumption, lower functional residual capacity and respond to hypoxia by rapid bradycardia.

C – Circulation with Haemorrhage Control

The clinical assessment of blood loss in an injured child is difficult since his/her increased physiological reserve can maintain systolic pressure in the normal range even up to 30% loss of blood volume.

The blood loss may be obvious as from a lacerated scalp or concealed in the thoracic, retroperitoneal or pelvic spaces. Usual sources of bleeding or causes of haemodynamic compromise are as follows:

- External bleeding (e.g., large vessel injury and limb amputation)
- Significant chest trauma with possible tension pneumothorax, haemothorax, cardiac tamponade or blunt cardiac injury
- Abdominal tenderness suggesting internal haemorrhage (e.g., liver/splenic laceration)
- Pelvic pain/instability, indicating a fracture
- Open fractures of the long bones
- Spinal cord injury with shock

Compensated shock occurs when there has been significant blood loss, but the blood pressure is maintained by tachycardia and vasoconstriction. Tachycardia, poor skin perfusion and a cold, anxious child may be the only manifestations of hypovolaemic shock. Other signs of shock include delayed capillary refill, narrowing of the pulse pressure to less than 20 mmHg, mottling of the skin, decreased level of consciousness and an absence of a brisk response to pain. The best site to palpate for a pulse in a child is either the antecubital fossa for the brachial artery or the groin for the femoral artery.

Table 40.5 Classification of Haemorrhagic Shock Classes I, II, III and IV in Children and Their Clinical Presentation

System	Clinical Signs	Class I Up to 15%	Class II 15–30%	Class III 30–40%	Class IV ≥40%
Cardiovascular	Pulse rate	Normal	Mild tachycardia	Moderate tachycardia	Severe tachycardia
	Blood pressure	Normal/ increased	Normal/ decreased	Decreased	Decreased
Skin	Capillary blanch test	Normal	Positive	Positive	Positive
Respiratory	Respiratory rate	Normal	Mild tachypnoea	Moderate tachypnoea	Severe tachypnoea
Renal	Urine output	1–2 ml/kg/hr	0.5–1 ml/kg/hr	0.25–0.5 ml/kg/hr	Negligible
Central nervous system	Mental status	Slightly anxious	Mildly anxious	Anxious/confused	Confused/lethargic
	Fluid replacement (3:1 rule)	Crystalloid	Crystalloid	Crystalloid/blood	Crystalloid/blood

Table 40.5 describes the classification of haemorrhagic shock in children and their clinical presentation.

Haemorrhage control with intravenous access for administration of crystalloids or blood and management of persistent haemodynamic compromise constitutes the mainstay for the circulation phase of the primary survey.

Haemorrhage Control

Extremity bleeding can be controlled using subfascial gauze packs, with minimal compression on the proximal artery, and careful application of a compressive dressing to the entire injured limb. Reduction and splinting of long bone fractures and stabilisation using external fixation devices (e.g., suspected pelvic fracture) may also provide haemostasis. Anti-fibrinolytics, specifically, tranexamic acid (loading dose – 15 mg/kg over 10 minutes, followed by an infusion of 2 mg/kg/hour for at least 8 hours or until the bleeding stops), has been associated with a significant reduction in mortality when given within 3 hours of blunt or penetrating trauma in adults.

Establishing Venous Access (see Chapter 10)

Peripheral venous access is essential for administering fluid, medication and drawing blood samples. Establish IV access preferably with two large bore (appropriate to age) cannulas with at least one in the upper extremity (in case of inferior vena cava tear). Since this could be a challenge in a small infant, intra-osseous (IO) access is a recommended alternative. IO is a rapid, safe and effective route for the administration of medications, fluid and blood. The usual site is the upper end of the tibia of an uninjured leg.

Percutaneous central access or venous cutdown is for establishing more permanent vascular access for ongoing care. Ultrasound guidance facilitates central venous catheterisation in challenging situations.

Resuscitation

An initial bolus of 10 or 20 ml/kg of warm isotonic crystalloid is given in aliquots, with frequent reassessment. If a third bolus seems essential, 10 ml/kg of packed red blood cells (PRBCs; type-specific or O negative) should be considered. There is very little evidence to support the use of colloids in children with a traumatic injury. The choice between using normal saline or Ringer's lactate has little significance when crystalloid resuscitation is limited to 60 ml/kg. The new AHA 2020 PALS guideline for the management of hypotensive haemorrhagic shock advocates the administration of blood products when available, instead of crystalloids, for ongoing volume resuscitation. Early, balanced resuscitation using PRBCs, fresh frozen plasma (FFP) and platelets in a ratio of 1:1:1 is supported by recommendations from several international trauma societies. A massive transfusion protocol may be appropriate for patients who have profound haemorrhage or ongoing internal bleeding with an anticipated need to replace total blood volume over 24 hours. The presence of coagulopathy in children with severe trauma undergoing blood transfusion is significantly associated with mortality. Patients with documented coagulopathy, especially those with head trauma, warrant FFP even in the absence of transfusion. There is no evidence-based consensus on an optimal volume trigger for initiating massive transfusion protocol in children; however, some experts use the following weight-based approach:

- <5 kg (neonate) – 55 ml/kg
- 5–25 kg (infant) – 50 ml/kg
- 25–50 kg – 45 ml/kg
- >50 kg (adolescent) – 40 ml/kg or 6 units packed red cells

Urine output is a good measure of volume resuscitation. It is essential to catheterise the child to obtain an accurate estimate of the same (check the nappies/diapers in small babies).

Vasopressors

If the response is still inadequate, vasopressors such as epinephrine (adrenaline) may initially be given as a bolus (2–10 mcg/kg), followed by an infusion of either epinephrine (0.02–1 mcg/kg/min) or norepinephrine (0.02–0.2 mcg/kg/min). Controlled hypotension may be detrimental to blunt trauma patients with brain injury, as it reduces cerebral perfusion and increases mortality. Hence, controlled hypotension is not recommended in paediatric blunt trauma victims. The AHA PALS 2020 recommends the administration of epinephrine (10 mcg/kg) early into paediatric cardiopulmonary resuscitation (CPR), with better survival rates observed when administered within 5 minutes of initiation of chest compressions.

Refractory Shock

Recalcitrant hypotension despite appropriate fluid therapy may be suggestive of massive haemorrhage or mechanical disruption of cardiac contractility. The latter, in trauma, is most commonly due to cardiac tamponade, manifesting as Beck's triad (see **Table 40.8**). These features may be absent in a hypovolemic child. When available, bedside ultrasound can reliably diagnose or exclude significant cardiac tamponade and should be used appropriately, if time permits.

Pearls

- Tachycardia is the first response to hypovolaemia.
- Hypotension is a late sign (25–35% blood volume loss).
- Establishing early adequate venous access is paramount to resuscitation to facilitate prompt administration of epinephrine during CPR and for the sampling of blood for laboratory investigation and cross-matching.

D – Disability and Neurological Assessment

The modified Paediatric GCS (**Table 40.4**) can provide an overview of consciousness and indicates a need for intervention. It should also be included in the secondary survey, thereby allowing serial assessment of the neurological status of the patient and prognostication. A rapid neurological assessment can be done by noting the pupillary size and its reaction to light and the 'AVPU' assessment, which stands for

- A – *Awake*
- V – Responds to *verbal* commands
- P – Responds to *painful* stimuli
- U – *Unresponsive*

Trauma patients with a GCS ≤ 8 or who are unresponsive or respond only to pain require rapid resuscitative efforts. One must look out for signs of raised intracranial pressure (ICP), predisposing to impending herniation, which includes the following:

- Hypertension with bradycardia or tachycardia (using age-based standards for heart rate and blood pressure) and slow irregular respirations – Cushing's triad
- Unequal or fixed and dilated pupils
- Any abnormal breathing pattern (Cheyne-Stokes respiration)
- Hemiparesis
- Decorticate, decerebrate or absent motor responses to pain

Patients with concerns for significant intracranial injury or raised ICP must be managed appropriately to reduce secondary insult from hypoxia, ischaemia and cerebral oedema. Maintaining an oxygen saturation >95%, initiating controlled ventilation through ET intubation in patients with GCS < 8 and fluid resuscitation to maintain cerebral perfusion are critical for management. For most paediatric patients with evidence of cerebral herniation, hyperosmolar therapy with mannitol 0.5–1 g/kg i.v. or IV hypertonic saline (3% NaCl) 2–6 ml/kg is initially effective at reducing ICP.

E – Exposure and Environment

It is important to undress the child and look for other injuries. It is vital to ensure enough help to 'log roll' and stabilise the neck while examining the back and spine. The tone of the anal sphincter should be assessed. Hypothermia is an important problem in the traumatised child, even in the tropics. Children, owing to their relatively large surface area, are prone to hypothermia due to heat exchange with the environment. It is, therefore, critical to keep the injured child warm using blankets, increasing ambient room temperature, radiant warmers, warmed IV fluids/blood, warm and humidified inspired oxygen.

Pain relief is an important part of the treatment of an injured child. Also, the presence of a parent or guardian in the resuscitation room may help the trauma team by minimising the injured child's fear and anxiety. Nearly 25% of children suffer from post-traumatic stress disorder after a motor vehicle collision.

Table 40.6 summarises the immediate life-threatening injuries and appropriate interventional procedures in trauma.

Adjuncts to Primary Survey

The primary survey relies largely on clinical examination. Haematological and imaging studies, serum chemistries and urinalysis have low sensitivity for identifying serious injuries in children with trauma. However, they serve as adjuncts to diagnosis and treatment modalities are not to be considered substitutes for clinical assessment. Table 40.7 lists the commonly used adjuncts to the primary survey. These may be chosen based on clinical suspicion.

Table 40.6 Immediate Life-Threatening Injuries and Life-Saving Procedures in Trauma

Clinical Markers	Immediate Life-Threatening Injuries	Life-Saving Procedures
Airway	Laryngeal/tracheal trauma Faciomaxillary trauma	Oxygen; simple airway Positioning manoeuvres Oropharyngeal airway ET intubation Cricothyroidotomy Tracheostomy
Breathing	Tension pneumothorax Flail chest haemothorax Sucking chest wound (open pneumothorax) Central depression of respiration	Intercostal cannula Intercostal tube ET intubation Cover-sucking chest wound
Circulation	Haemorrhage Internal External Cardiac tamponade/rupture	Pressure over bleeding sites Two large-bore IV cannulae IO infusion Pericardiocentesis Emergency thoracotomy
Disability	Neurological dysfunction	Avoid secondary brain insult By optimising ABC
Exposure	Hypoglycaemia Hypothermia	Substrate as 10% glucose Warming of patient Warming of all fluids

ET, endotracheal tube; IO, intraosseous; IV, intravenous.

Table 40.7 Commonly Used Adjuncts to Primary Survey

S. no.	Commonly Used Adjuncts	Findings of Significance
1.	Blood investigations	Type and cross-match Complete blood count with haematocrit Coagulation studies (Pt, aPTT, INR), including point-of-care tests (TEG, ROTEM) Serum electrolytes, blood urea and creatinine Liver enzymes, serum amylase Blood glucose Blood gas analysis Continuous non-invasive Hb monitoring (pulse co-oximetry)
2.	Urinalysis	≥50 RBCs per high-powered field suggests intra-abdominal injury after blunt trauma
3.	Screening radiographs	Lateral cervical spine Antero-posterior chest Antero-posterior pelvis
4.	eFAST (Extended focussed assessment of sonography in trauma)	Five views: right upper quadrant (perihepatic), left upper quadrant (perisplenic), suprapubic, subxiphoid (pericardial) and thoracic
5.	Procedural adjuncts	EVD Central venous catheter Nasogastric tube insertion Urinary catheterisation

eFAST, extended focussed assessment of sonography in trauma; EVD, external ventricular drain.

Role of e-FAST

Extended focussed assessment of sonography in trauma (eFAST) is a rapid ultrasound examination of the five aforementioned views to identify an underlying aetiology and to focus on further management in haemodynamically unstable patients, and also in stable patients if the performance of ultrasound does not cause any delays. It can be done in 3 minutes, is non-invasive, portable and can be performed during resuscitation. The primary goal of e-FAST is to detect free fluid in Morrison's pouch, the pelvis, the perisplenic region and the pericardium and air/fluid in the pleural cavity.

Positive abdominal findings on e-FAST (low frequency 2–5 MHz, curvilinear/phased array probe) may warrant operative intervention in lieu of an abdominal CT (Computed Tomography) scan. It may also permit prompt detection of pneumothorax, haemothorax or cardiac tamponade with greater sensitivity but lower specificity than a supine chest radiograph. To maximise the sensitivity of the chest examination, scanning may be done along various parts of the anterior and lateral chest walls. The linear, high-frequency (5–10 MHz) probe may be kept perpendicularly over the second to third spaces anteriorly. The absence of a pleural slide and the barcode sign when viewed in motion mode is suggestive of a pneumothorax.

Secondary Survey and Definitive Care

The secondary survey includes a detailed head-to-toe examination to rule out other injuries.

- Insertion of chest tubes, if needed
- X-rays of the chest, cervical spine and pelvis and of any other area of interest
- Consider antibiotics and anti-tetanus
- Follow-up on the laboratory results

Chest Trauma

The majority of chest injuries in children are due to blunt trauma, such as in road traffic accidents. Children have thin, compliant, flexible chest and abdominal walls which do not offer much protection to the viscera. Since the ribs and chest wall are pliable, the forces are transmitted to the underlying structures causing pulmonary and cardiac contusions without signs of rib fractures. Rib fractures in a child indicate severe impact. Children are more prone to tension pneumothorax, as the mediastinal structures are mobile. Advanced cardiac monitoring to measure cardiac output, pulmonary arterial occlusion pressure, mixed venous oxygen saturation and stroke volume variation may be used when indicated to improve outcomes.

ABCDEs is crucial. Restoration of the circulating volume and avoiding hypoxia are mandatory. A seizure following the impact of trauma is common in children but is usually self-limiting. Since children are at a high risk of post-traumatic seizure, prophylactic anticonvulsant therapy should be given for the first 7 days post-trauma. All children with seizures require a CT scan. A neurosurgical consultation is required if the GCS is ≤8 or has motor scores of 1 or 2, or the CT scan shows brain haemorrhage, cerebral swelling or intracranial herniation.

The Brain Trauma Foundation 2019 guidelines for the management of severe traumatic brain injury (TBI) in paediatrics provide recommendations on baseline care, first- and second-tier therapies including monitoring as well as threshold recommendations to guide management. These guidelines were formed from observations of the Approaches and Decisions in Acute Paediatric TBI Trials.

Figure 40.2 outlines the basic algorithm and treatment in the management of severe TBI in children.

The timing of instituting first-tier therapies depends on various factors such as the ICP and rate of progression of the disease process. Accordingly, interventions may need to be bypassed, repeated or initiated concurrently. Second-tier therapies represent the treatment options for refractory intracranial hypertension when Tier 1 approaches have been inadequate. They may be used singly, serially or in combination with the use of advanced monitoring. **Figure 40.3** represents the evidence- and consensus-based algorithm of second-tier therapies for the management of severe TBI.

Brain Trauma Foundation Recommendations for Paediatric TBI

Threshold recommendations (for better outcomes)

- ICP threshold of <20 mm Hg
- CPP threshold between 40 and 50 mmHg
- $PbrO_2$ of >10 mmHg

Hyperosmolar Therapy

The 2019 update of this guideline confers a level 2 recommendation on the use of hyperosmolar therapy for ICP control. A bolus of hypertonic saline (3%) is recommended in patients with intracranial hypertension. Recommended effective doses for acute use range between 2 and 5 ml/kg over 10–20 min. Dose of continuous infusion of 3% saline range from 0.1 to 1.0 ml/kg of body weight per hour, administered on a sliding scale. The bolus of 23.4% hypertonic saline is suggested for refractory ICP. The suggested dose is 0.5 ml/kg with a maximum of 30 ml. Avoiding sustained (>72 hours) serum sodium >170 mEq/L is suggested to avoid complications of thrombocytopenia and anaemia, whereas avoiding sustained serum sodium >160 mEq/L is suggested to avoid the complication of deep vein thrombosis.

Temperature and Nutrition

Instituting normothermia over prophylactic moderate (32–33°C) hypothermia is suggested to improve overall outcomes. The use of an immune-modulating diet is no longer recommended. If hypothermia is used and rewarming initiated, it should be carried out at a rate of 0.5–1°C every 12–24 hours to avoid complications. Initiation of early enteral nutritional support (within 72 hours of injury) is suggested to decrease mortality and improve outcomes.

Recommendations on Other Pharmacotherapy

- With the use of multiple ICP-related therapies, as well as appropriate use of analgesia and sedation in routine ICU care, avoiding bolus administration of midazolam and/or fentanyl during ICP crises is suggested as a level 3 recommendation due to risks of cerebral hypoperfusion.
- Prophylactic treatment is suggested to reduce the incidence of early (within 7 days) post-traumatic seizures (PTS). (*Note: PTS is also used for paediatric trauma score and for post-trauma stress disorder.*) At present, there is insufficient evidence to recommend levetiracetam over phenytoin based on either efficacy in preventing early PTS or toxicity.
- High-dose barbiturate therapy, with continuous arterial blood pressure monitoring, is suggested in haemodynamically stable patients with refractory intracranial hypertension despite maximal medical and surgical management.
- Routine use of corticosteroids is not suggested to improve outcomes or reduce ICP.
- The use of antiplatelets following trauma as a measure to control bleeding has been debated.

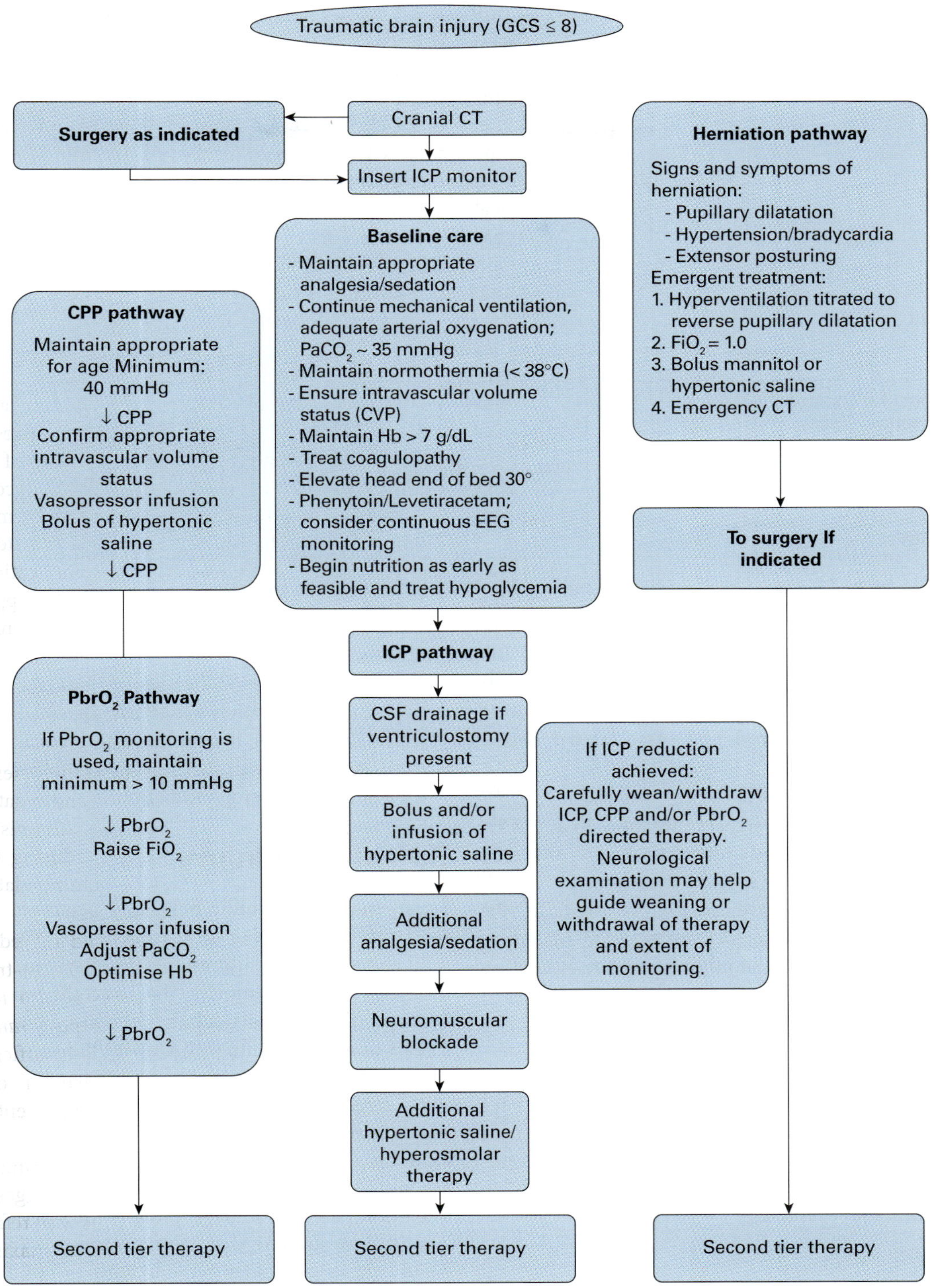

Figure 40.2 Evidence- and consensus- based algorithm of **first tier therapies** for the management of severe TBI in infants, children and adolescents. Adapted from Brain Trauma Foundation guidelines 2019. CPP, cerebral perfusion pressure; CVP, central venous pressure; EEG, electroencephalogram; FiO_2, fraction of inspired O_2; ICP, intracranial pressure; $PaCO_2$, Partial pressure of CO_2; $PbrO_2$, regional brain tissue oxygen.

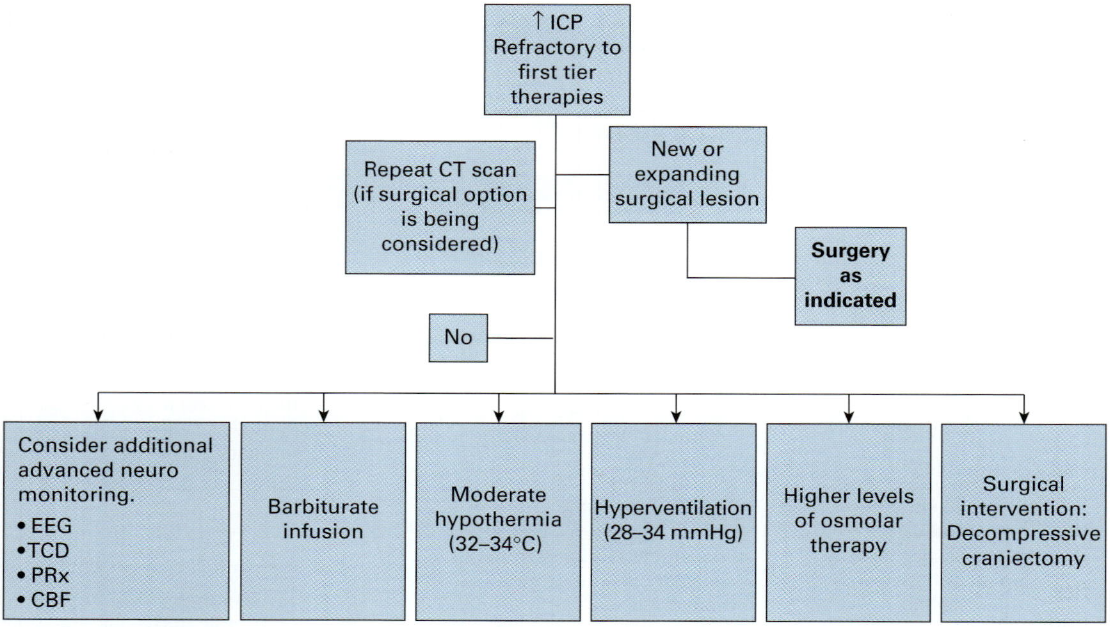

Figure 40.3 Evidence- and consensus-based algorithm of **second-tier therapies** for the management of severe TBI in infants, children and adolescents. CBF, cerebral blood flow; CT, computed tomography; EEG, electroencephalography; ICP, intracranial pressure; PRx, pressure reactivity index; TCD, transcranial Doppler.

The CRASH-3 trial concluded that tranexamic acid is safe in TBI and that administration within 3 hours reduces head injury associated deaths.

Ventilation Strategies

Prophylactic severe hyperventilation to a $PaCO_2$ < 30 mmHg in the initial 48 hours after the injury has not been suggested to improve overall outcomes. If hyperventilation is used in the management of refractory intracranial hypertension, advanced neuromonitoring for the evaluation of cerebral ischaemia is suggested.

Operative Recommendations

Cerebrospinal fluid drainage through an external ventricular drain (EVD) is suggested to manage increased ICP. Decompressive craniectomy is suggested to treat neurologic deterioration, herniation or intracranial hypertension refractory to medical management.

Pearls

The management of a child with the head injury includes the following:

- Early management of ABCDE.
- Early involvement of neurosurgical expertise.
- Early ET intubation to avoid hypoxia and hypercarbia. It is advisable to use pharmacological sedation and neuromuscular blockade to intubate a child with the head injury to prevent the rise in ICP during intubation.

Spinal Cord Injury

Spinal injuries in children usually occur during road traffic accidents or sporting activities. Though only about 10% of children with multiple injuries have cervical spine injuries, the possibility should be kept in mind particularly in children below 2 years of age and those with Down syndrome who are especially susceptible. The child's head is relatively larger compared to the neck and therefore the momentum forces tend to move it more than in an adult. The ligaments connecting the vertebrae are more flexible allowing movement of the vertebral bodies without actual rupture of the ligaments.

Studies showed that cervical injury can be ruled out in the older patient with no midline cervical tenderness, no focal neurologic deficit, normal alertness, no intoxication and no painful, distracting injury. But nearly 30–40% of children with traumatic myelopathy have spinal cord injury without radiological abnormality (SCIWORA). So, a thorough neurological examination is imperative to rule out cervical spine injury in children. Non-verbal children, those who are comatose or those who have neck pain should have a lateral X-ray of the neck which exposes the spine from C1 to C7 and flexion and extension cervical X-ray under the supervision of the neurosurgeon before the injury is ruled out. Till these criteria are met, consider the C spine injured and maintain immobility using a rigid cervical collar and spine board.

Radiological Considerations

- Pseudo-subluxation – anterior displacement of C2 over C3 is seen in about 40% of children less than 7 years of age. This is more evident when the child is lying supine on the spinal board as it flexes the cervical spine. Placing a 1 inch thick pad under the torso of the child will place the head in a neutral position and reduce this subluxation.
- Skeletal growth centres may be mistaken for fractures.
- SCIWORA is common in children. Therefore, if there is a high index of suspicion for spinal cord injury, based on the mechanism of injury, it may be prudent to maintain immobilisation of the head and neck till expert advice is available.

Following are the National Emergency X-Radiography Utilization Study (NEXUS) criteria, which identify patients at risk of significant cervical spine injury who will benefit from spinal cord immobilisation techniques before a definitive diagnosis is made:

1. Midline cervical tenderness
2. Evidence of intoxication
3. Altered level of alertness
4. Focal neurological deficit
5. Distracting painful injury

Note that if none of these is present, the patient is at very low risk for clinically significant cervical spine injury.

Battered, Abused Child

Any child with intentional injury caused by the parent, guardian or acquaintances is considered a battered, abused child. If such a situation is suspected by the primary care provider, it is vital to take a detailed history and do a careful examination and document them. History should be obtained not only from the parent but also from the patient, if appropriate. In many countries, physicians are bound by law to report such incidents to the authorities in order to manage the physical and psychological consequences of maltreatment and to promote the safety and well-being of children.

Abuse is suspected if:

- There is a discrepancy between the history and the degree of physical injury, for example, loss of consciousness after a fall from a sofa or bed and lower extremity fracture in a child too young to walk
- A discrepancy between the caregivers about the sequence of the event
- A delay in seeking medical attention after the injury
- History of repeated trauma and treatment in the emergency department
- Inappropriate behaviour by the parent or caregiver
- Evidence of bruises in different stages of healing
- Evidence of previous injuries such as scars and healed fractures
- Perioral or perineal injuries
- Multiple subdural haematomas
- Retinal haemorrhages
- Unusual injuries such as sharply demarcated burns, cigarette burns, rope marks, bites, etc.

In-Hospital and Inter-Hospital Transport

Each institution should have written protocols pertaining to this including which patients should be transported and who should do the transporting, the number of escorts, minimum monitoring and resuscitative equipment and which elevator may be used. Most adverse events during transfer occur due to ineffective communication, inappropriate escort personnel, inadequate equipment or equipment failure and inappropriate monitoring. There should always be a portable source of oxygen, self-inflating resuscitation bag, an emergency medication box, equipment for emergency airway management (laryngoscope, tubes and stylet),

Step	Actions
1. Assessment	• Assess patient condition (stable/unstable) • Document need for transfer • Involve multidisciplinary team
2. Risk Evaluation	• Identify risks and benefits of transfer • Proceed with transfer if benefit outweighs risk
3. Communication	• Communicate with receiving personnel regarding condition of the patient • Inform the parent/primary caregiver regarding the need for transfer and may allow one parent to accompany the patient • Obtain all necessary permissions required for transfer
4. Preparation	• Assign accompanying personnel • Arrange equipment–monitors, airway devices, sedative and emergency drugs, infusion pumps, etc. • Adequate battery back-up for necessary equipment
5. Handover	• Relay necessary information regarding patient condition, ongoing treatment, need for transfer, any adverse events during transport and required monitoring • Ensure closed-loop communication • Document patient condition at the end of transfer

Figure 40.4 Algorithm for in-hospital and inter-hospital transport of the paediatric patient.

battery-powered multichannel monitor, infusion pumps and portable suction. One team member should assume the role of team leader. The ability to communicate and call for help is very important. Before transport, reassess the patient and ensure haemodynamic stability, adequate oxygenation and functionality of the monitors. All handovers should be documented with a record of vital signs, personnel involved, etc.

Figure 40.4 describes the suggested algorithm for in-hospital and inter-hospital transport.

Anaesthesia for an Injured Child

An anaesthesia provider may have to take care of an injured child in the following circumstances: initial stabilisation in the emergency department, provide sedation and monitoring for imaging, emergent surgery such as laparotomy or craniotomy, semi-elective surgeries such as stabilisation of long bone fractures, management in the intensive care unit and control of pain including regional analgesia.

An important fact to consider is that the 'child' ranges from a less than 3 kg neonate to a 100 kg teenager and everyone in between! It is therefore crucial to remind oneself of the changes, in the growth of the child, with respect to vital signs, weight, height, blood volume, ETT size and the dosage of drugs to be administered.

Preparation for Surgery

Operation Room Set-Up

In addition to the basic requirements of the operating room (refer to Chapters 1 and 2), preparation should include the availability of age-appropriate equipment, dilution and labelling of medications in age-appropriate doses, raising the ambient temperature in the room to 26°C, checking the availability of rapid infusion devices, fluid warmers, access to imaging (X-ray chest, fluoroscopy) and laboratory tests (haematocrit, blood gases and coagulation tests).

Pre-Operative Evaluation

Although a detailed history and examination are preferred, it may not be possible in an urgent situation. A brief history as outlined by the mnemonic AMPLE (A – allergies, M – medications, P – past medical history, L – last oral intake and tetanus immunisation, E – events related to the injury) may be feasible. History and consent for anaesthesia must be obtained from the parent or primary caregiver.

Initial priorities in the operating room are to reassess vitals and volume replacement, continue resuscitation (if needed), establish monitoring and then proceed with induction. Most cases present as emergencies; hence, pre-oxygenation followed by a rapid sequence intubation is required. If a child arrives already intubated, it is prudent to check the tube for size, length at the lips, bilateral air entry, capnogram and radiological confirmation, if needed.

Intraoperative Management

Apart from ECG, pulse oximeter, blood pressure and end-tidal CO_2, temperature monitoring is crucial in children.

It must be remembered that the post-trauma child is often hypovolaemic and haemodynamically unstable. Induction of anaesthesia causing vasodilatation and suppression of sympathetic response will lead to precipitous hypotension. Institution of intermittent positive pressure ventilation will further reduce venous return and thus cardiac output. Major procedures may warrant invasive arterial access to facilitate beat-to-beat monitoring of blood pressure, monitoring of fluid responsiveness, pulse pressure variation (PPV) and allow frequent arterial blood sampling. Although central lines are not routinely indicated, they may enable reliable administration of vasopressors/inotropes in haemodynamically unstable patients.

Intravenous Agents

The requirements for intravenous anaesthetics are decreased after trauma and haemorrhage because

- the volume of distribution is decreased and
- dilution of serum proteins occurs so that less drug is bound and more free active drug is available.

As described in **Figure 40.1**, haemodynamically stable patients may receive propofol (neuroprotective) during induction. If haemodynamically unstable, ketamine or etomidate may be used.

Maintenance of Anaesthesia

Inhalational or intravenous routes may be used for the maintenance of anaesthesia. Depth of anaesthesia may be monitored using minimum alveolar concentration (in case of inhaled anaesthetics), along with the use of neuromonitoring such as BIS (bispectral index) and entropy.

Neuromuscular Blocking Agents

Succinylcholine (1–1.5 mg/kg) is the muscle relaxant of choice for RSI. Hyperkalaemia, secondary to the administration of succinylcholine, is not of concern in the early burn (<48 hours) and trauma situation. Although it causes a transient increase in ICP, this effect has not been shown to adversely affect the outcome in a head-injured patient. However, in the case of a child with an open eye injury, its use is to be avoided. Atracurium and mivacurium have histamine-releasing properties that may result in hypotension. So, rocuronium (1.2 mg/kg) is considered the relaxant of choice due to its cardiovascular stability and relatively better safety profile. Neuromuscular monitoring may be instituted intraoperatively to guide the dosage of neuromuscular blocking administration.

Intraoperative Fluid Management

A delay in fluid resuscitation may lead to significant hypovolaemia due to smaller blood volume in children. Dextrose-containing fluids are usually avoided because hypotonic solutions are not retained in the circulation for a long and may contribute to the development of cerebral oedema. Balanced, isotonic fluids such as normal saline or Plasma-lyte may be used for resuscitation.

The concept of damage control resuscitation (DCR) has been associated with improved survival and shorter hospital stay in adults. The core principles of DCR include rapid surgical control of bleeding, permissive modest hypotension that helps preserving the freshly formed thrombus, minimal use of isotonic colloids with prevention of haemodilution-related complications, and early administration of PRBCs in combination with plasma and platelets in 1:1:1 unit ratio. Massive transfusion may be required in cases of severe trauma.

Temperature Maintenance

In a child post-severe trauma, there are several factors contributing to ongoing heat loss, including exposure to a cold environment at the scene of the accident, large open wounds, rapid infusion of fluids and blood, exposure of body cavities during operative procedures, which are often overlooked in the face of resuscitation. Hypothermia has a severe deleterious effects that may hinder resuscitative efforts. They include myocardial dysfunction, cardiac irritability and dysrhythmias. Other effects of hypothermia include acid–base disturbances, a leftward shift of the oxyhaemoglobin curve and coagulopathies that can exacerbate ongoing haemorrhage. Continuous temperature monitoring and measures to prevent heat loss is therefore essential in all paediatric trauma patients.

Extubation

The decision to extubate depends on the extent of the injury, type of injury, course of surgery, anticipated problems, the need for airway protection or continued ventilation and the plan for post-operative pain management. A child with facial and airway trauma requires a reassessment of the airway with a laryngoscope or fibreoptic scope. The absence of an air leak around the tube prior to extubation is probably due to oedema and is a strong factor in predicting post-extubation stridor. Children who cannot be extubated immediately will require special care during transport to the intensive care unit and possibly to the imaging facilities.

Analgesia

Acetaminophen is a commonly used drug, either in the oral, per rectal or intravenous route, and is associated with a good safety profile. Ibuprofen is more effective than acetaminophen in treating pain from musculoskeletal trauma. In major trauma, careful titration to the effect of morphine or other opioids can be used. For children over 6 months of age, the analgesic effects of morphine or fentanyl are similar to those in an adult and hence opioids need not be withheld. Although regional anaesthetic techniques such as epidural and plexus block can provide better pain relief, especially in limb revascularisation surgeries, it should be carefully analysed on a case-to-case basis, since it can mask the symptoms and signs of compartment syndrome.

Post-Operative Management

Most children with severe trauma would need monitoring and further stabilisation after the surgery to correct fluid shifts, acidosis and tissue swelling. Hence, monitoring in a high-dependency unit until they are stable is ideal. They should be nursed in a pain-free setting with adequate psychological and emotional support which would provide for a better and faster recovery. A multidisciplinary dedicated team should take care of the injured child. Early diagnosis and quick intervention are required to limit the morbidity and mortality associated with trauma in children.

SUGGESTED READINGS

1. Management of Pediatric Trauma. A policy statement of the American Academy of Pediatrics. *Pediatrics* 2008; 121:849–852.
2. McFadyen JG, Ramaiah R, Bhananker SM. Initial assessment and management of pediatric trauma patients. *Int J Crit Illness Inj Sci* 2012; 2(3):121–127.
3. Ivashkov Y, Bhananker SM. Perioperative management of pediatric trauma patients. *Int J Crit Illness Inj Sci* 2012; 2:143–148.
4. Bhalla T, Dewhirst E, Sawardekar A, et al. Perioperative management of the pediatric patient with traumatic brain injury. *Paediatr Anaesth* 2012; 22(7):627–640.
5. https://lapedsready.org/wp-content/uploads/2017/03/PediatricTraumaCareGuidelines2011.pdf. Accessed on May 30 2023.

6. Reynolds P. Pediatric Trauma. In: Smith's Anesthesia for Infants and Children, 8th edition. Davis PJ, Cladis FP, Motoyama EK (eds). Elsevier Mosby, Philadelphia 2011.
7. Barker SJ, Shander A, Ramsay MA. Continuous noninvasive hemoglobin monitoring: A measured response to a critical review. *Anaesth Analg* 2016; 22(2):565–572.
8. Brain Trauma Foundation 2019 guidelines for Paediatric Traumatic Brain Injury. Available at: https://braintrauma.org/coma/guidelines/pediatric. Accessed on 30th May 2023.
9. Kliegman R, St Geme J, Blum NJ, et al. Nelson Textbook of Pediatrics, 21st edition. Philadelphia, PA, Elsevier 2019.
10. American College of Surgeons, 2018. Advanced Trauma and Life Support course manual, 10th edition. Chicago, IL.
11. Marcin JP, Pollack MM. Triage scoring systems, severity of illness measures, and mortality prediction models in pediatric trauma. *Crit Care Med* 2002; 30(11):S457.
12. Kochanek PM, Tasker RC, Carney N, et al. Guidelines for the management of pediatric severe traumatic brain injury, third edition: Update of the brain trauma foundation guidelines. *Pediatr Crit Care Med* 2019; 20(1):S1–S82.
13. Kochanek, Patrick M, Tasker, Robert C, Bell, Michael J, et al. Management of pediatric severe traumatic brain injury: 2019 Consensus and Guidelines-Based Algorithm for first and second tier therapies. *Pediatric Crit Care Med* 2019; 20(3): 269–279.
14. Principi T, Schonfeld D, Weingarten L, et al. Update in pediatric emergency medicine: Pediatric resuscitation, pediatric sepsis, interfacility transport of the pediatric patient, pain and sedation in the emergency department, pediatric trauma. *Update Pediatr* 2018; 17:223.
15. Neff LP, Cannon JW, Morrison JJ, et al. Clearly defining pediatric massive transfusion: Cutting through fog and fiction with combat data. *J Trauma Acute Care Surg* 2015; 78(1):22–28; discussion 28-9.

41 Burns: Acute, Subacute and Delayed with Contracture Neck

Rebecca Jacob • Amitha Varmma Aredath

Burns are the leading cause of fatal injury in children. The outcome and the mortality rates depend upon the total body surface area (TBSA) involved, depth of burns, age of the patient and the level of care and expertise available locally.

Globally, there were 8,991,468 new fire, heat and hot substance injuries in 2017 with 120,632 deaths.

The death rate in low-income and middle-income countries is seven times higher than that in high-income countries.

Burns

Burns may be caused due to the following reasons:

- **Dry:** Fire, firecrackers/hot metal objects, motorcycle exhausts, household heaters
- **Smoke:** Trapped in a burning building
- **Moist:** Boiler/geyser/kitchen/tea, coffee and tar
- **Electrical:** Live wire
- **Chemical:** Acid/alkali – household-cleaning solutions
- **Ballistic:** Bullets/mines/bombs
- **Cold:** Frostbite or chilblains
- **Radiation**

Assessment of Burns (Table 41.1; Figs 41.1 and 41.2)

- Degree: The severity of the burn depends on the temperature (amount of heat) and duration of contact with the heat. Damage is done by intradermal heat
- Percentage of total body surface area (TBSA) burned
- Depth of burn
- Anatomical site of burns
- Severity and prognosis
  - Other injury
  - Other medical conditions
  - Age of patient <3 or >45 years
  - Physiological status of the patient

Assessment of the body surface area (BSA) involved in the burn. This should include the areas that are red, inflamed and have blisters. Wherever possible, Lund and Browder charts should be used to accurately assess the area. In the casualty situation, the area covered by the patient's palm and fingers represents roughly 1% of BSA. A straightforward way of calculating the BSA involves taking into account the changing proportion of head to trunk and limbs. This is shown in **Figure 41.2**. Smartphone technology, with for example, the Mersey Burns App may be used to assess the burn severity and fluid resuscitation.

Definition of Major Burns in Children

- Third-degree burns involving >5% of the TBSA
- Second-degree burns involving >10% of the TBSA
- Large burns involving the face, hands, feet and perineum (and major joints)
- Electrical, chemical and inhalational burn injuries
- Burns in a child with a serious pre-existing medical disease
- Circumferential burns, especially on the chest

Table 41.1 Classification of Burn Injuries

Degree of Burns	Depth of Injury	Outcome and Treatment
First-degree (minimal tissue damage)	Epidermis (superficial)	Sharp, uniform pain; erythematous Heals without scar Heals in about 7 days
Second-degree (partial thickness)	Epidermis and varying proportion of dermis	Blistering, excruciating pain Heals with minimal scarring May need grafting Demarcates and heals over 14–21 d
Third-degree (full-thickness)	Destruction of epidermis and dermis – all skin elements	Dry, leathery appearance with firm pearly white discoloration May not be very painful
Fourth-degree (underlying structures)	Prolonged exposure to extreme heat	Charred and skeletonised requires extensive debridement

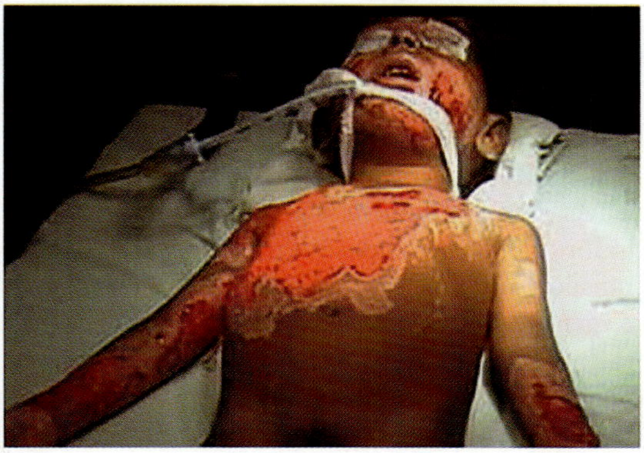

Figure 41.1 Many burn injuries have a mix of different burn depths.

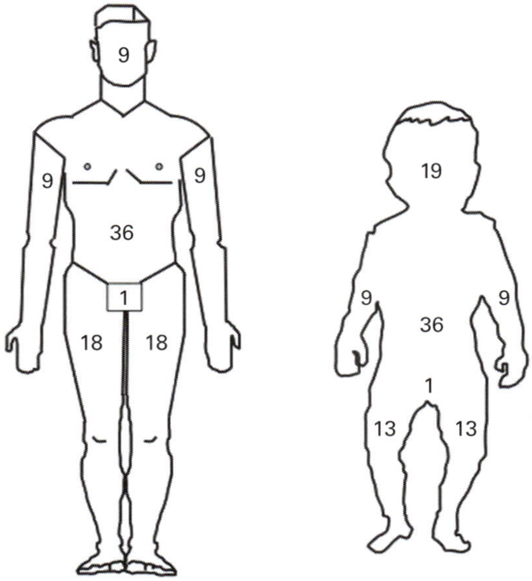

Figure 41.2 Body surface area showing the percentage distribution of burns. Note that 10% is added to the head and 5% is subtracted from each leg when the count is done on children.

Pathophysiology

Pathophysiological responses to burns may be divided into three phases:

Ebb phase or low cardiac output phase or resuscitative phase. In the first 24–48 hours after a major burn, cardiac output may be reduced up to 60% from baseline due to hypovolemia from increased capillary permeability-induced plasma loss, reduced myocardial response to catecholamines, reduced contractility and increased systemic vascular resistance due to high vasopressin levels.

Flow phase or high cardiac output phase. During the recovery phase, 72- to 96-hour post-burn, hyperdynamic and hypermetabolic responses result in increased cardiac output (CO), tachycardia, increased myocardial oxygen consumption and decreased systemic vascular resistance. In major burns, the circulating mediators, especially cytokines, result in systemic responses characterised by a systemic inflammatory response syndrome. It is at this stage that nutrition and prevention of sepsis are important.

Recovery phase. The recovery phase, which follows, could last up to a year during which catabolism requiring good nutritional support continues.

Circumferential burns can impair blood supply and compromise venous drainage. They will need immediate escharotomies.

Cardiovascular Changes

The cardiac output drops dramatically in the initial 24 hours of the post-burn period. This is attributed to circulating myocardial depressants and the loss of intravascular fluid volume due to widespread capillary leakage caused by inflammatory mediators and hypoproteinaemia. From the second post-burn day, the circulatory system enters a hyperdynamic state and capillary integrity is restored.

About 30% of children with major burns develop systemic hypertension, which persists for several weeks and may require anti-hypertensives. This is probably due to increased serum catecholamines and/or activation of the renin–angiotensin system.

Airway and Respiratory System

It could have one of three distinct components – upper airway injury, lower airway and pulmonary parenchymal injury and systemic intoxication byproducts of burning material such as carbon monoxide and hydrocarbons.

A history of 'closed space injury' with any of the following symptoms and signs is suggestive of inhalational injuries:

- Burns of the face/inside the mouth
- Singeing of eyebrows and nasal hairs
- Soot in the oro-pharynx, carbonaceous sputum
- Dysphonia, wheezing, dyspnoea, cough, tachypnoea, rales and rhonchi
- Hypoxia and hypercapnia

Direct thermal injury above the vocal cords is common. There can be serious upper airway compromise secondary to oedema in cases of burns involving the head and neck with steam, extremely hot air or chemicals. If there is any suggestion of it occurring, it is better to intubate the child and secure the airway early – before oedema sets in and intubation becomes impossible.

Direct thermal injury below the level of vocal cords is rare, except in cases of steam inhalation. However, direct injury of the tracheobronchial mucosa and lung parenchyma can occur with inhalation of toxic chemicals and particulate matter.

Chemical pneumonitis may occur due to inhalation of smoke particles and products of incomplete combustion such as chlorine, cyanide, sulphur and nitrogen dioxide.

Pulmonary oedema results from an increase in vascular permeability and it may progress over the first 48 hours as the systemic inflammatory response progresses. It may be exacerbated by overly aggressive fluid resuscitation. The surfactant is deactivated, thus decreasing lung compliance, increasing work of breathing and increasing metabolic demands. Severe injury results in the desquamation of airways with inflammation leading to atelectasis and areas of compensatory emphysema.

Hypoxia and carbon monoxide toxicity are the commonest cause of death in children who have been burned in an enclosed space. Carbon monoxide has 230–270 times the affinity for haemoglobin as oxygen and it shifts the oxygen dissociation curve to the left decreasing oxygen delivery to the tissues. It also inhibits mitochondrial cytochrome oxidase activity blocking oxygen transport and binds to myoglobin, thereby reducing oxygen delivery to the muscle. It affects the heart (tachycardia, hypertension, angina and arrhythmias) and brain (headache, nausea, vomiting, confusion, dizziness, syncope, seizures and coma). Long-term neurological and psychological sequelae can occur. The cherry red colour of the child misleads the clinician into thinking that oxygenation is adequate. Even pulse oximetry is undependable as carboxyhaemoglobin is measured as haemoglobin. It is better, therefore, to consider the possibility of carbon monoxide poisoning and administer 100% oxygen early.

Cyanide inhalation can occur with incomplete combustion of nitrogenous material during fires. Severe cyanide poisoning is fatal. Mild cyanide poisoning can occur along with carbon monoxide poisoning and should be identified. Metabolic acidosis with high lactate points towards cyanide poisoning and should be treated with amyl nitrate and sodium thiosulphate.

Metabolism and Endocrine Responses

For a short time after the burn, metabolism decreases but soon rises with an outpouring of catabolic hormones – catecholamines, glucocorticoids and glucagon with the maximum rise of noradrenaline on day 4 post-burn. These lead to the following adverse effects: a rise in the metabolic rate with a rise in temperature (hyperthermia), heart rate, stroke volume and increase in oxygen consumption, massive proteolysis, oxidation of active muscle and lipolysis leading to hypoalbuminaemia, body wasting, vasoconstriction, gastric ulceration, disseminated intravascular coagulation, and cardiac dysfunction. Levels of adrenocorticotrophic hormone, antidiuretic hormone (ADH), renin, angiotensin and aldosterone are raised. Insulin may be high or low but plasma glucose is usually high. Hyperosmolar ketosis and coma may be seen, especially in those on total parenteral nutrition (TPN).

Daily evaporative loss is almost 4,000 ml/m^2 of burn surface in children. Assuming 0.58 calories for each ml of water loss, daily energy loss is about 2,400 calories. The increase in metabolic rate leads to an increase in core temperature, which must be differentiated from sepsis. In such burns, the only way to return the metabolic rate to normal is to excise the burn and cover the resultant defect.

Gastrointestinal System

Gastric stasis and ileus are common in major burns. Acute stress ulceration of the duodenal mucosa, called Curling's ulcer, is the most frequent life-threatening gastrointestinal complication.

Stress hormones including catecholamine levels being high lead to mesenteric vasoconstriction decreasing gut immune function and mucosal integrity. Small bowel ischaemia with stasis causing bacterial translocation and areas of necrosis are also seen.

Acalculous cholecystitis and superior mesenteric artery syndrome are other complications that may occur.

Renal System and Electrolyte Abnormalities

Initially, there is a decrease in renal blood flow (RBF) and glomerular filtration rate (GFR) secondary to hypovolaemia and increased catecholamine levels. This leads to activation of the renin–angiotensin system and anti-diuretic hormone (ADH) release. The net effect is sodium and water retention and exaggerated losses of K^+, Mg^{2+} and Ca^{2+}.

Serum potassium concentrations may increase in the first 2 days due to tissue necrosis and haemolysis. Beware of the use of suxamethonium, which causes a surge of potassium release from the multiple extrajunctional neuromuscular receptors which form post-burn. With the resumption of kidney function, gastric aspiration and diarrhoea, there can be marked hypokalaemia in the next few days. Beware of the use of drugs that encourage the intracellular movement of potassium such as calcium, insulin and glucose.

Ionised calcium decreases during the post-burn period. Supplement with calcium gluconate if administering large volumes of blood and blood products.

The post-burn systemic inflammatory response in combination with overly aggressive fluid resuscitation may lead to intra-abdominal compartment syndrome, decreased renal blood flow (RBF) and ultimately renal injury from hypoperfusion.

Rheology

The immediate post-burn period is a prothrombotic state due to an acute increase in blood viscosity (secondary to hypovolaemia) and the concentrations of fibrinogen, factors V and VIII.

Immune System and Sepsis

Burn patients are more prone to sepsis because of the disruption in skin integrity, the presence of dead tissue, impaired blood supply to and from the burn area and impaired immune systems. Leukocyte function and IgG and IgM levels are low, with altered phagocytic and lymphocytic functions. Initially, infection is from exogenous sources and is mainly due to gram-positive bacteria. Endogenous infections are usually gram-negative due to translocation from the gut. Vascular access lines are an ongoing source of infection so care should be taken with their placement and maintenance.

Liver

Minor abnormalities in liver functions are common but overt liver failure is rare in the post-burn period. Increased acute-phase protein synthesis in the liver includes C-reactive protein, fibrinogen, alpha-2-macroglobulin and complement. Fatty infiltration of the liver may occur in major burns. Serum cholinesterase is decreased.

Prior to surgery, check glucose and International Normalised Ratio (INR).

Management of Burns

Immediate Care on Site

Stop the burning process. 'Cool the burn' with tepid or cool clean running water for 20 minutes. This reduces tissue damage and is an effective analgesic. Do not use ice. Even if cool water has not been applied at once, it is effective up to 4 hours post-burn and may be used before then. Remove clothing and anything that is constrictive like jewellery. Silver sulphadiazine ointment may be applied to the burn area. Avoid tight dressings and elevate the limbs. Once cooled, cling film is useful to prevent evaporation. If this is not available, use layers of clean dressings (even cloth will do in an emergency setting). This will reduce the loss of temperature and fluids. Cover the patient with blankets – keep him warm.

Chemical burns – Wash copiously with water until the burning sensation settles.

All major burns are traumatic injuries and should be treated as per advanced trauma life support (ATLS) protocol. The initial primary and secondary survey is applicable in these patients.

Airway

Primary Survey

- Stabilise cervical spine
- Check airway patency
- Observe for signs of inhalation injury

Burns to the head and neck and inhalational burn injuries may cause airway obstruction due to massive oedema. If there are signs of airway compromise, the best course of action is to intubate and ventilate early. Complete obstruction can occur within 6–24 hours of injury. Steroids have no place in the treatment of burns.

Breathing

Administer 100% oxygen – humidified, if possible. This is done in an unintubated children using a face mask with a reservoir bag and with oxygen flow at 15 l/min.

Ventilation is required in the following patients:

- Unconscious or coexisting trauma
- Carbon monoxide poisoning
- Developing acute respiratory failure, in need of extensive resuscitation, sedation and analgesia

Circulation and Fluid Therapy

Primary Survey

- Check pulses and blood pressure (BP). Check distal pulses and capillary return
- Consider good IV access - two if possible.
- Circumferential deep dermal to full-thickness burns may cause a tourniquet effect which may require release by escharotomy

Insert two large bore cannulae through the intact skin wherever possible. Any paediatric burns > 10% BSA require IV fluid replacement. A delay in fluid replacement can increase the risk of multiorgan failure and acute renal injury. Hypovolaemic shock is unusual in burn patients without coexisting injury but, if present, treat with a fluid bolus of 20 ml/kg of isotonic crystalloid. There are a number of recommendations as to how the fluid loss should be replaced. The most widely accepted and followed guideline is to replace 4 ml/kg per percent of the BSA involved (Parkland's formula) with a balanced salt solution (Hartmann's Ringer lactate [RL]) in the first 24 hours. Half of the total calculated volume is given over the first 8 hours and the remaining over the next 16 hours.

There have been concerns about under and over-estimation of fluid loss with this formula, so some centres suggest goal-directed fluid therapy and escalate or de-escalate the fluid therapy accordingly. Most common and easiest is targeting 0.5–1 ml/kg/hr of urine output. But other causes of reduced urine output like rhabdomyolysis, renal tubular necrosis, increased ADH due to injury, abdominal compartment syndrome should also be considered. Peripheral perfusion, acid–base balance and haematocrit may be used as a guide. Concerns of fluid extravasation, worsening of oedema and compartment syndrome with excessive crystalloid use have led to the use of colloids, especially 5% albumin. Colloid or hypertonic saline in the initial resuscitation is controversial.

The clinical end-point of fluid resuscitation:

- Intact sensorium
- Normothermia
- Age-appropriate haemodynamics

- Sustained urine output
- Minimal systemic acidosis, with base deficit <2

Once resuscitation is complete, fluids may be given at a maintenance rate which considers the burn size and extra evaporative losses.

It is important to maintain an adequate circulating blood volume at all times without overloading the patient (fluid overload worsens airway oedema and abdominal compartment syndrome). Therefore, all these formulae are only guidelines for fluid management, which must be dictated by the patients' response to fluid therapy.

Victims of burns require high caloric intake. This may be done as intravenous alimentation if the patient has paralytic ileus or requires to be NPO prior to surgery. Check blood glucose levels to assess hypo or hyperglycaemia. If they are allowed oral fluids, porridge or soup with high calories is encouraged.

Disability – Assess Conscious State

A rapid neurological assessment can be done by noting the pupillary size and its reaction to light and the 'AVPU' assessment, which stands for

A – Awake
V – Responds to Verbal commands
P – Responds to Painful stimuli
U – Unresponsive

Secondary Survey

Brief History

- Allergies, past medical history, tetanus status, medications and last meal
- Ensure that tetanus prophylaxis is given
- Burn history
  - Time of injury
  - Mechanism of injury – scalds contact, flame, electrical
  - Location of event – confined space with risk of inhalation
  - Any associated injuries

A head-to-toe assessment for other injuries. Assess for corneal injury. Electric burns are at risk of rhabdomyolysis.

Analgesia

A significant burn is one of the most painful conditions known. Morphine IV titrated to effect is an excellent analgesic. Ensure that respiration, pulse oximetry and sedation are monitored during the administration of morphine or fentanyl. Paracetamol and non-steroidal anti-inflammatory drugs are useful adjuncts. Midazolam is an incredibly good sedative in this setting. Ketamine has also been used for post-burn analgesia in children, both for initial wound care and for subsequent dressing changes. The dose of ketamine varies from 0.2 to 2 mg/kg depending on the procedure.

Children with major burn injuries become rapidly tolerant to both analgesics and sedatives. Do not worry about the high doses as long as the airway is secured, and adequate ventilation assured. Opioid withdrawal will require slow tapering of doses when the child recovers. The development of multiorgan failure with major burns will affect the clearance of morphine and its metabolites. Dexmedetomidine has been used for sedation and analgesia or as an adjunct.

Apart from being painful, burns induce severe stress and *psychological* trauma. The patient should never be left alone – they require encouragement and comfort.

Monitoring and Investigations

Continuous pulse oximetry, ECG and frequent non-invasive BP recording should be done routinely.

In cases of severe burns with rapid fluid shifts, invasive BP monitoring is recommended. A urinary catheter should be inserted, and urine output measured on an hourly basis. Core temperature should be monitored. A nasogastric tube should be inserted for large burns to prevent gastric distension and assist with caloric supplementation.

Full blood count including haematocrit, urea, creatinine, electrolytes, blood sugar, carboxyhaemoglobin levels and arterial blood gases are necessary in all cases of major burns in a child requiring admission. Serial evaluation of these investigations is needed in major burns. Watch out for anaemia, which may be caused by frequent blood testing in the smaller child.

Management of Anaesthesia

In the early phase, patients may present for anaesthesia for debridement and collagen placement or skin grafting, tracheostomy in case of airway burns, and escharotomy and fasciotomy for relief of compartment syndrome. Repair of fractures and exploratory procedures related to blunt trauma may also require surgery.

Pre-Operative Evaluation

The focus is on assessing the extent and location of burns, physiologic derangements, current drug therapy and expecting the need for blood transfusion remembering that there is a potential for major blood loss. Intravascular volume, acid–base status, current metabolic state, oxygenation, electrolytes and coagulation parameters should all be normalised. Adequate analgesia should be provided pre-operatively. The patient should be kept warm during transport and in the operating room. Gastric emptying is delayed, and the patient should be considered a full stomach. IV access is often difficult, and the application of monitors is also difficult. Safe transport to and from the OT with oxygen, monitoring and warmth should be ensured.

The most profound pharmacologic change involves muscle relaxants. Burnt patients have an increased sensitivity to the effects of succinylcholine and are less sensitive to non-depolarising muscle relaxants. This is because of the proliferation of extrajunctional acetylcholine receptors on the damaged or denervated muscle membrane. This may lead to lethal hyperkalaemia following succinylcholine. Succinylcholine may be safely used in the first few hours following a burn but after that it is contraindicated until the burn has healed and the patient has resumed normal activity.

Resistance to non-depolarising muscle relaxants develops soon after injury and is related to the magnitude of the burn. The dosage of non-depolarising muscle relaxants may need to be increased by two to five times the normal dose, in patients with >20% TBSA burns. Ketamine and halothane have been extensively used in burnt patients, and repeated administration of halothane has been shown to be safe in children. Children need analgesia for repeated burn dressings. Opioids, ketamine and dexmedetomidine are some of the commonly used drugs. Patients can develop tolerance and higher doses may be required for subsequent dressings.

Intraoperative Management

- The greatest challenges in anaesthetising burn victims are heat conservation, providing adequate analgesia and management of blood loss.
- Monitoring includes pulse oximetry, ECG and non-invasive BP. In cases where large losses of blood or fluid shifts are expected, an arterial line for BP monitoring (and blood sampling) and a central venous line for central venous pressure monitoring are essential.
- The pharmacological alterations given in **Table 41.2** are to be borne in mind while deciding on the anaesthetic. Succinylcholine is avoided.
- Maintenance fluid requirements are higher than normal. If the child is on TPN, it is discontinued, and glucose-containing solutions are used intraoperatively to avoid hypoglycaemia.
- These patients need higher-than-normal doses of opioids for intraoperative and post-operative analgesia as burn surgery involving grafting is very painful and burned patients develop opioid tolerance rapidly.
- Temperature control: When tissues denuded of skin are exposed, the patient rapidly becomes hypothermic. General anaesthesia blocks thermoregulation and aggravates the problem. Burnt patients have a higher-than-normal core temperature, due to their hypermetabolic state, and are most comfortable in a higher-than-normal ambient temperature. Fluid warmers, hot air blowers (Bair Hugger) and plastic covers to wrap up the patient to prevent evaporative water loss are very useful in preventing hypothermia. Remember that the higher core temperature in burned patients means that the post-operative patient may shiver at relatively 'normal' core temperatures.
- Blood loss during excision and grafting is difficult to assess and manage. Measures to limit blood loss include the use of tourniquets

Table 41.2 Pathophysiology and Its Effects on Anaesthesia

System	Pathology	Effects
Plasma proteins	↓ Albumin	↑ Free fraction (e.g. benzodiazepines, phenytoin, salicylic acid)
	↑ α_1-acid glycoprotein	↓ Free fraction (e.g. lignocaine, pethidine, imipramine)
Cardiovascular system	Early low output state	Poor redistribution of IM/oral drugs
	Late hyper dynamic circulation	↑ Organ blood flow and drug clearance
Kidney	Increased RBF and GFR	• Increased excretion of some drugs (e.g. amino glycosides) • Sodium and water retention with loss of potassium, magnesium and calcium.
Liver	Enzyme induction	• Minor abnormalities • Accelerated metabolism of some drugs.
Neuromuscular junction	Increased acetylcholine receptor sites	• Hyperkalaemia after scoline
		• Decreased effect of non-depolarising relaxants

over extremities, adrenaline (1:10,000) soaked sponges applied to the bleeding surface, and thrombin and collagen pads applied locally. Injection of high volumes of dilute adrenaline solutions (1:100,000 to 1:500,000) into the burnt tissue prior to excision has also been shown to reduce blood loss and decrease transfusion requirements. High total doses (80–100 mcg/kg) may be given safely as long as the anaesthetist is alert to intravascular injection.

- Post-operatively, these patients need oxygen for longer than usual. Analgesia is provided with opioids. The requirements change from patient to patient and from time to time in the same patient.

Escharotomy

Burned tissue becomes inelastic. This inelastic non-expansile tissue is called an eschar. If the burn is circumferential this stiff, inelastic tissue can cause serious problems. In the limbs, it is seen as compartment syndrome; on the chest wall, a restrictive ventilation failure is likely; and on the abdomen, an intra-abdominal compartment syndrome raises intra-abdominal pressure with restriction of ventilation, decreased venous return and hypotension. On the neck, it can cause airway problems and difficulty in swallowing. Management consists of urgent escharotomy which can be done even at the bedside under ketamine. Injecting adrenaline under the eschar can reduce blood loss. (Monitor carefully for signs of systemic absorption of adrenaline such as tachycardia and hypertension.)

Anaesthesia for Secondary Burn Reconstruction

Late complications of burn injuries include hypertrophic scars and contractures. Hypertrophic scars are treated surgically by excision or shaving followed by primary closure or skin grafting.

Contractures may involve any joint, but airway management may be particularly hazardous when neck contractures are present. Neck contractures impair neck extension and thus make glottis visualisation difficult as shown in **Figures 41.3–41.6**.

In an anticipated difficult airway in the older child, the primary management strategy would be an awake or an awake but sedated approach. However, in the younger age group, this is often difficult due to the lack of patient co-operation.

Assisted spontaneous ventilation under general anaesthesia is then the preferred technique until the contracture is released by the surgeon under local anaesthetic infiltration (**Fig. 41.7**). Maintaining spontaneous gas exchange benefits in two ways. It protects against total airway obstruction due to loss of upper

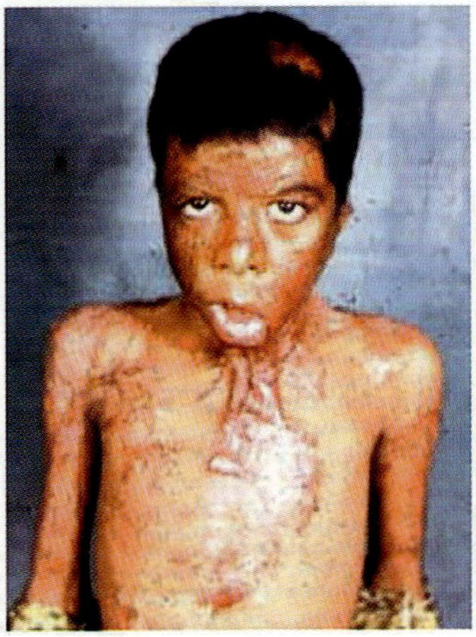

Figure 41.3 Burn contracture – neck.

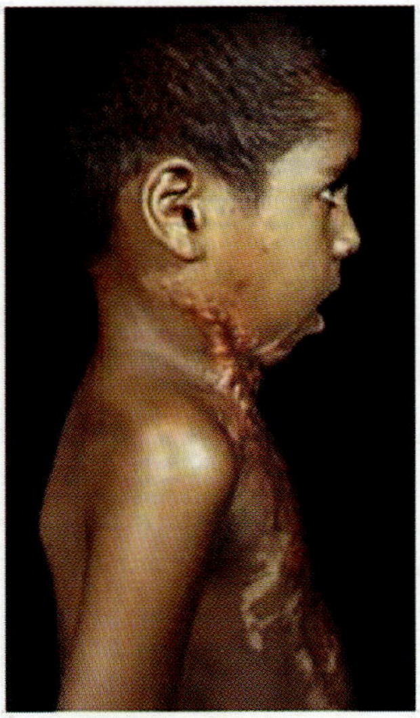

Figure 41.4 Burn contracture – neck and face.

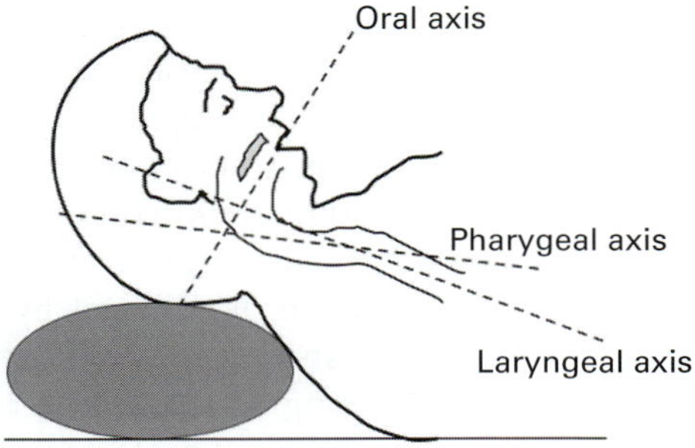

Figure 41.5 Demonstration of limitation of neck extension, making visualisation of the glottis difficult.

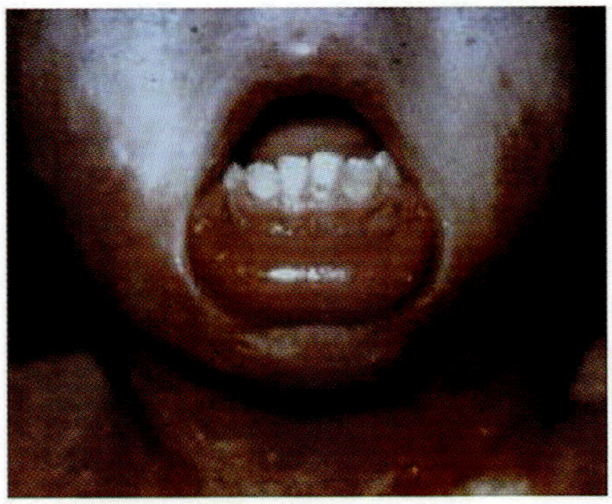

Figure 41.6 Contractures of mouth limiting mouth opening.

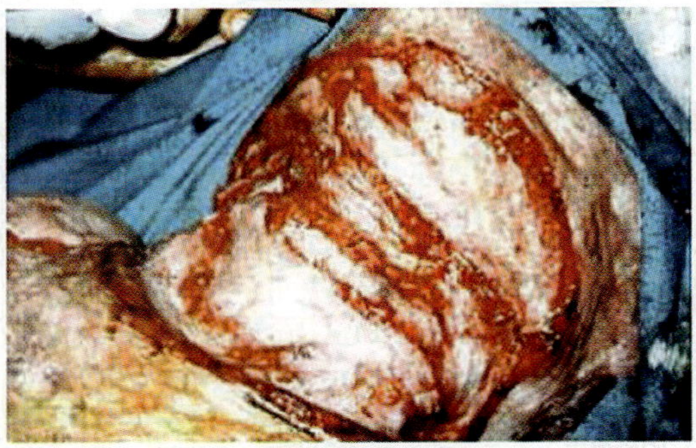

Figure 41.7 Contracture neck released.

airway muscle tone, and spontaneous breath sounds may function as a valuable guide to locate the glottis. A laryngeal mask airway (LMA; especially the LMA supreme) is particularly useful in this situation.

Anaesthetic Agents

- A combination of opioids and benzodiazepines like fentanyl and midazolam, where the opioids blunt airway reactivity and benzodiazepine provides anxiolysis and amnesia, can be used.
- Dexmedetomidine is an alternative. It is an alpha-2 adrenergic agonist, acts at the locus coeruleus of the pons, and provides good analgesia and sedation.
- Inhalational anaesthetics: In the frightened young child, sedation with an opioid technique may not be sufficient. Here intubation can be carried out under deep inhaled anaesthesia with

spontaneous ventilation. Halothane and sevoflurane are the commonly used agents as they are the least irritant to the airway.

Halothane offers smooth induction, and its pharmacokinetic profile allows inhalational induction and intubation possible without rapid offset of its effects. Watch out for arrhythmias. There is no data to show hepatotoxicity with repeated use of halothane in burned children.

Sevoflurane is being increasingly used for inhalational induction in a burned child with a possible difficult airway, but its rapid offset of effect must be borne in mind. Supplemental doses of intravenous propofol may be needed to maintain adequate depth of anaesthesia if sevoflurane is used for intubation purposes without muscle relaxants. All anaesthetics cause concentration-dependent depression of cardiac output.

- Propofol: Propofol in titrated doses may be a useful agent, but it may be difficult to achieve profound sedation yet maintain spontaneous ventilation in the paediatric age group.
- Ketamine: It provides both hypnosis and analgesia. It can be used in conjunction with midazolam and usually preserves adequate spontaneous ventilation while providing anaesthesia to prevent laryngeal reactions to airway manipulation. Ketamine may cause increased secretions and the administration of an antisialagogue, and pre-endoscopy suctioning is recommended following the administration of ketamine.
- Topical anaesthesia can be used in conjunction with sedation or general anaesthesia. Regional blocks of the upper airway and larynx may be technically difficult due to the anatomical distortion by burn contractures.

Techniques for securing the airway in children with a difficult airway would depend on individual experience and the availability of equipment. The child may be maintained under general anaesthesia using a nasopharyngeal airway in one nostril, while the other nostril is used for intubation attempts (refer to Chapter 19 on the difficult paediatric airway).

- Fibreoptic endoscopy and intubation may be considered the techniques of choice in experienced hands. Nebulised lignocaine, topical application of local anaesthetic sprays/jellies, 'spray as you go' through the channel of the fibreoptic scope may be used.
- A blind nasal technique may be used. Nasal packs soaked in a vasoconstrictor such as ephedrine should be used to minimise bleeding during the passage of the tube through the nose.
- Lighted wands or stylets have been used. However, a thick scar on the anterior aspect of the neck may make visualising the light in the trachea difficult.
- LMA may be a useful adjunct to airway management in such cases. It may be used to maintain oxygenation in an emergency in a 'cannot ventilate cannot intubate' situation. It can also be used as a guide to fibreoptic intubation or as an access for blind passage of the ET tube or an intubating stylet and thus enhance the success rate.
- Release of the contracture under local anaesthesia aided by ketamine or inhalational anaesthesia may be needed in some cases to facilitate intubation.

SUGGESTED READINGS

1. James SL, Lucchesi LR, Bisignano C, et al. Epidemiology of injuries from fire, heat and hot substances: global, regional and national morbidity and mortality estimates from the Global Burden of Disease 2017 study. *Inj Prev* 2020; 26: i36–45
2. Thomas J, Heinz R. Practical Guide to Paediatric Burns. SAMA Health and Medical Publishing Group, Cape Town 2006.
3. Shank ES, Sheridan RI, Cote CJ, et al. Burn Injuries. In: A Practice of Anesthesia for Infants and Children, 4th edition. Cote CJ, Lerman J, Todres ID (eds). Saunders Elsevier, Philadelphia 2009; pp. 715–734.
4. Palmisano BW, Rusy LM. Anesthesia for plastic surgery. In: Pediatric Anesthesia, 4th edition. Gregory GA (ed). Churchill Livingstone, London 2002; pp. 732–741.
5. Suman A, Owen J. Update on the management of burns in paediatrics. *BJA Educ* 2020; 20(3):103–110.
6. McCann C, Watson A, Barnes D. Major burns: Part 1. Epidemiology, pathophysiology and initial management. *BJA Educ* 2022; 22(3):94–103.
7. McGovern C, Puxty K, Paton L. Major burns: Part 2. Anaesthesia, intensive care and pain management. BJA Educ 2022; 22(4):138–145.

42 ANAPHYLAXIS

Rebecca Jacob • Amitha Varmma Aredath

Definition

The Australasian Society of Clinical Immunology and Allergy (ASCIA) defines anaphylaxis as a rapidly evolving generalised multisystem hypersensitivity reaction characterised by one or more symptoms or signs of respiratory and/or cardiovascular involvement and involvement of other systems such as the skin and/or the gastrointestinal tract.

Diagnosis

World allergy criteria, Amended in 2020

Highly likely when one of the following two is fulfilled:

1. Acute onset of skin and or mucosal involvement with at least one of the systemic involvement, i.e. Gastrointestinal tract (GIT), cardiovascular or respiratory system
2. In the case of a patient with a known allergy either hypotension, bronchospasm or laryngeal involvement

Pathophysiology

Anaphylaxis is classified as immunological and non-immunological.

Immunological anaphylaxis *can be IgE mediated or non-IgE mediated.*

- IgE mediated includes type 1 hypersensitivity reactions and accounts for 60% of perioperative anaphylaxis. These reactions are not dose related and can occur even with a minute dose of drug administered or food ingested. They tend to become more severe on re-exposure.
- Non-IgE-mediated anaphylaxis includes complement system or IgG-mediated anaphylaxis.

Non-immunological anaphylaxis also formerly known as anaphylactoid reaction is caused by agents that induce sudden, massive mast cell or basophil degranulation in the absence of immunoglobulins. It has been described for ethanol, exercise or some drugs; where the mast cells may be activated through Mas-related G-protein-coupled receptors. Also, mast cell independent mechanism through COX-1 inhibition for NSAIDs has been described.

In all cases, there is a sudden release of mediators into the plasma of vasoactive and bronchospastic substances including histamine, leukotrienes, serotonin and tryptase. H1-receptor stimulation stimulates the synthesis of nitric oxide, which causes massive vasodilatation. In general, anaphylactic mediators cause vasodilation, fluid extravasation, smooth muscle contraction and increased mucosal secretions. The systems that are commonly affected are the respiratory, cardiovascular, gastrointestinal, skin and mucous membranes.

Biphasic anaphylaxis: Recurrence of symptoms after an apparent resolution of the initial attack even without an additional trigger. It occurs in about one-fifth of the cases. The mechanism of recurrence is still unclear.

Protracted anaphylaxis: Anaphylactic reactions may last for hours, days or even weeks in extreme cases.

Common Trigger Agents

Neuromuscular Blocking Agents

Neuromuscular blocking agents (NMBA) are responsible for 60–70% of anaphylactic reactions under anaesthesia. Primary sensitisation may have occurred through a tertiary or a quaternary ammonium compound (antigen) found in other drugs, food, cosmetics and hair products. Therefore, a reaction can occur without previous exposure to the NMBA. Suxamethonium is more likely to produce anaphylaxis than non-depolarising muscle relaxants.

Antibiotics

Pre-dominantly, beta-lactam antibiotics like penicillin and cephalosporins cause IgE response. Vancomycin causes direct histamine release from mast cells. NAP 6 audit has implicated teicoplanin in a third of antibiotic-induced anaphylaxis cases.

Latex Allergy

Latex allergy is more commonly seen in patients with meningomyelocele, in those with urogenital problems, in those requiring frequent catheterisation and in children with atopic conditions – eczema, asthma and food allergies.

Anaesthetic Agents

Anaphylaxis with thiopentone and propofol is rare. Ketamine and etomidate are considered safe. Sugammadex hypersensitivity has been reported but the mechanism is unclear and appears to be dose related. Opioids may cause urticaria and flushing when given intravenously due to direct histamine release, but they do not cause anaphylaxis.

Others

Chlorhexidine, dyes such as methylene blue, radiocontrast media, NSAIDS, insulin, protamine, local anaesthetics, plasma expanders such as dextrans, starches and gelatins.

Risk Factors

Risk factors include female sex, multiple past procedures or surgeries, history of previous drug reactions or anaphylaxis and allergic conditions like asthma, eczema or hay fever.

Clinical Features of Anaphylaxis Under General Anaesthesia

Over 90% of anaphylaxis will occur at or shortly after induction, but reactions can occur at any time during the anaesthetic. The 6th UK National Audit Project (NAP 6) reported an incidence of perioperative anaphylaxis as 1;11,000. Clinical manifestations are not consistent and therefore diagnosis can be difficult. Skin features (erythema, urticaria and rash) are almost universal if reactions are closely observed, but erythema (and even angio-oedema) may be subtle and missed if not carefully looked for. Respiratory symptoms (bronchospasm and upper airway oedema) are more common in children. Death may occur from *hypoxaemia* (due to upper airway angio-oedema and acute upper airway obstruction, bronchospasm and mucus plugging).

Shock in anaphylaxis may be *distributive* due to severe reduction in venous tone or *hypovolaemic* due to massive fluid shifts out of circulation due to increased permeability of the vascular bed. In severe anaphylaxis, up to 35% of intravascular volume can shift to the extravascular space within 10 minutes. In addition, there is a depression of myocardial function affecting the cardiac output. This can manifest as pulseless electrical activity.

While compensatory tachycardia in response to hypotension is considered a characteristic feature, sudden bradycardia with cardiovascular collapse and cardiac arrest may occur before any skin features become apparent.

Gastrointestinal smooth muscle constriction can cause GI disturbances.

Ring and Messmer have described a *clinical severity scale*.

Grade I: Mild cutaneous and mucous signs

Grade II: Moderate involvement of the respiratory and cardiovascular systems

Grade III: Severe involvement

Grade IV: Where there is a cardiac arrest

In addition to this scale, there are three factors that can predict *severe anaphylaxis*: (a) rapid onset, (b) absent cutaneous signs and (c) paradoxical bradycardia. Bradycardia in this situation is considered an adaptive mechanism that allows maximal ventricular filling in the presence of massive hypovolaemia. *Atropine is therefore contraindicated.*

Differential Diagnosis of Anaphylaxis Under General Anaesthesia

- Other causes of *respiratory symptoms*: Asthma, post-extubation stridor, pulmonary oedema, pulmonary embolus, tension pneumothorax and tube malposition
- Other causes of *hypotension*: Arrhythmias, cardiogenic shock, haemorrhage, hypoglycaemia, overdosage of vasodilator, pericardial tamponade, vasovagal reaction, sepsis, venous air embolism, bone cement implantation syndrome and partial sympathectomy after spinal or epidural anaesthesia
- Other causes of *angio-oedema*: Hereditary or acquired angio-oedema, treatment with angiotensin converting enzyme (ACE) inhibitors

Management

The range and severity of presentation and response to treatment are extremely variable, and management will vary accordingly. The diversity of presentation requires a high index of suspicion by the treating anaesthesiologist.

Immediate Management

1. Stop injection or infusion in progress
2. Call for help/inform the surgeon
3. 100% oxygen and reduce volatile anaesthetics. Intubate if not already intubated. Delaying intubation will make intubation difficult with the progression of airway oedema
4. Adrenaline
   - Adrenaline 0.5–1 ml of 1:10,000 intravenously and titrate to response (consider an intra-arterial line for monitoring BP and blood gases). Adrenaline is the drug of choice in the treatment of anaphylaxis because its alpha-1 effects help to support the blood pressure while its beta-2 effects provide bronchial smooth muscle relaxation.
   - If intravenous access is not available, immediate intramuscular adrenaline 0.01 mg/kg should be administered and intravenous access secured
   - Paradoxical bradycardia may occur in some cases. Adrenaline is preferred over atropine in these scenarios
   - Resistant hypotension may require noradrenaline or arginine vasopressin
   - In patients on beta-blockers or sub-optimal response to adrenaline, glucagon may be considered
5. Rapid intravenous volume expansion with crystalloids – Ringer lactate or Normal saline
6. Elevate legs
7. In case of cardiac arrest, resuscitate as per ACLS guidelines

Follow-Up With

1. Antihistamines – chlorpheniramine maleate – IV slowly as it can worsen vasodilatation and hypotension
2. Hydrocortisone – may help to prevent the biphasic or protracted reactions that can occur in up to 20% of patients. Useful in angio-oedema.

Persistent Bronchospasm

1. Salbutamol (beta-2 agonist) – nebulise via the breathing circuit or give IV bolus followed by infusion
2. Aminophylline – check whether the child is already on a theophylline to avoid theophylline toxicity

Check arterial blood gases (ABG) – if acidosis is severe, give sodium bicarbonate

If CVS instability persists, consider infusion of adrenaline and noradrenaline.

The appearance of erythema or urticaria, when initially absent, most likely indicates restored cutaneous perfusion.

The decision to proceed with surgery or reschedule will depend on the type of surgery (emergency or elective), severity of anaphylaxis and the clinical condition of the patient. The parents should be informed of the incident and involved in the decision making.

Consider ICU admission if:

- ***Airway***
  - Oedema – check for laryngeal oedema by checking for a leak around ETT
- ***Breathing***
  - Persistent bronchospasm
  - Hypoxia

  - Pulmonary oedema
  - ARDS
- *Circulation*
  - Ongoing CVS instability and dependence on inotropes to maintain BP
  - Severe metabolic acidosis

Investigations

- Check the coagulation profile
- ABG

Diagnostic Tests for Anaphylaxis

Plasma concentrations of histamine and tryptase and skin testing based on the likely antigen (a gold standard for IgE-mediated reactions)

Immediate-Serum Tryptase Levels

Mast cell tryptase is the main protein of mast cell granules. Ninety-nine percent of this enzyme is found in mast cells, and it is not found in red or white blood cells. So plasma levels are not affected by haemolysis. The half-life is 2.5 hours with peak levels occurring rapidly and within 1 hour. In countries with the facility to measure serum tryptase, it is recommended to take four blood samples:

- Immediately after initial treatment
- 1-hour post-exposure (for the peak)
- 6 hours post-exposure
- 24 hours after the resolution of symptoms and signs to capture the true baseline values

All samples should be carefully labelled with timings. Samples should be stored at –20°C. Even post-mortem serum tryptase may give meaningful results to aid diagnosis. Raised serum tryptase merely indicates that there has been mast cell degranulation which occurs in both anaphylactic and anaphylactoid reactions. The basal level is 0.8–1.5 ng/ml.

Prevention of Anaphylaxis

After an episode of anaphylaxis, the history, events, symptoms and management should be documented. Patient/family must be informed about the incident and details of probable allergen should be included in the patient card. They should be educated to never fail to inform the treating doctors of the probable allergen whenever undergoing any medical treatment anywhere. To prevent further episodes skin testing may be done after 4 weeks of an episode.

SUGGESTED READINGS

1. Hosu LG, Aronson LA. Anaphylaxis. In: Clinical Pediatric Anesthesia. Goldschneider KR, Davidson AJ, Wittkugel EP, Skinner AV (eds). Oxford University Press, New York, 2012; 84–92.
2. Rees S. Anaphylaxis. Anaesthesia Tutorial of the Week 38. 2006;1–5.
3. Brown SGA, Mullins RJ, Gold MS. Anaphylaxis: Diagnosis and management. *Med J Aust* 2006; 185(5): 283–289.
4. Lieberman PL. Recognition and first-line treatment of anaphylaxis. *Am J Med* 2014; 127:S6–S11.
5. Lieberman PL, Nicklas RA, Oppenheimer J, et al. The diagnosis and management of anaphylaxis practice parameter: 2010 update. *J Allergy Clin Immunol* 2010; 126:477–480.
6. Schwartz LB. Systemic anaphylaxis, food allergy, and insect sting allergy. In: Goldman's Cecil Medicine, 24th edn. Goldman L, Schafer AI, eds. Elsevier Saunders, Philadelphia, 2011; chap 261:1633–1638.
7. Harper NJN, Cook TM, Garcez T, et al. Anaesthesia, surgery, and life-threatening allergic reactions: Epidemiology and clinical features of perioperative anaphylaxis in the 6th National Audit Project (NAP6). *Br J Anaesth* 2018; 121(1):159–171.
8. Dewachter P, Savic L. Perioperative anaphylaxis: pathophysiology, clinical presentation and management. BJA Educ 2019; 19(10):313–320.
9. Cardona V, Ansotegui IJ, Ebisawa M, et al. World Allergy Organization Anaphylaxis Guidance 2020 - Position paper. *World Allergy Organ J* 2020; 13:100472.
10. Gouel-Cheron A, Neukirch C, Kantor E, et al. Clinical reasoning in anaphylactic shock: addressing the challenges faced by anaesthesiologists in real time: A clinical review and management algorithms. Eur J Anaesthesiol 2021; 38(11):1158–1167.

43 Malignant Hyperthermia

Amitha Varmma Aredath • Rebecca Jacob

Malignant hyperthermia or malignant hyperpyrexia (MH) is a pharmacogenetic disease or syndrome characterised by a potentially life-threatening hypermetabolic state in susceptible individuals. This disease entity was first described in 1962 by Denborough et al.[1] The incidence of MH episodes during anaesthesia is between 1:10,000 and 1:25,000.

Pathophysiology, Genetics and Disease Mechanism

MH is an autosomal dominant defect and is typically located on the long arm of chromosome 19 involving the ryanodine receptor (RYR1) located on the sarcoplasmic reticulum within skeletal muscles. More than 15 different mutations in this gene are linked to MH. The other genetic defects associated with MH are CACNA1S and STAC3. When exposed to certain anaesthetic triggers such as volatile anaesthetic agents and suxamethonium (scoline), the receptor opens and releases calcium into the cell resulting in a marked increase in intramyoplasmic calcium. The calcium released may be from the sarcoplasmic reticulum stores or from the extracellular environment. This increase in calcium causes a sustained skeletal muscle contraction and stimulation of the enzyme calcium ATPase which produces a hypermetabolic state involving both the aerobic (O_2 consumption) and the anaerobic (glycogen breakdown) metabolic pathways. Heat is generated, hyperthermia and muscle rigidity set in and worsen, O_2 demand increases and the body is unable to eliminate the CO_2 produced. This rapidly progresses to circulatory collapse and death, if not treated quickly.

Conditions identified to be associated with MH are King Denborough syndrome, central core disease, multi-minicore disease, hypokalaemic periodic paralysis and central nuclear myopathy.

Presentation

The presentation of MH may be insidious or dramatic. The early symptoms usually develop within an hour of exposure to the triggering agent. However, MH may even occur after an hour or early post-operative period.

Early symptoms and signs are primarily due to the hypercatabolic state.

- Hyperthermia – rapid increase in core body temperature at a rate of 1–2°C every 5 minutes and sweating
- Muscular rigidity, masseter spasm and spasm of the lateral pterygoids. Difficulty in ventilation and rising airway pressures
- Tachycardia arrhythmias and unstable BP
- Respiratory acidosis with increasing $EtCO_2$ and $PaCO_2$
- Hypoxia and cyanosis
- Metabolic acidosis with increasing lactate production

Late symptoms and signs are due to rhabdomyolysis.

1. Hyperkalaemia seen on the ECG as peaked T waves and ventricular ectopics. Severe cardiac arrhythmias and hyperkalaemic cardiac arrest.
2. Rhabdomyolysis and myoglobinuria (dark coloured urine) leading to

- Grossly elevated blood creatinine phosphokinase
- Grossly elevated myoglobin levels
- Renal failure
- Acute cerebral oedema. Hyperthermia, acidosis and fluid shifts can lead to neurological collapse, coma and fixed dilated pupils
- Disseminated intravascular coagulation (DIC) and thromboembolism and release of tissue thromboplastin
- Compartment syndrome

Management

If unrecognised and untreated, MH has a mortality rate of >90%. Early management is the key to success and MH management protocol posters should be available in all OTs to recognise and treat this uncommon but potentially fatal disease.

Immediate Action

- Stop all trigger agents – remove the vaporiser
- Call for help
- Inform the surgeon and stop surgery or finish as soon as possible
- Replace the breathing circuit including the heat and moisture exchange (HME) filters and soda lime
- Activated charcoal filter, if available
- 100% oxygen with high fresh gas flows (FGF)
- Hyperventilate up to three times the minute ventilation
- Change to non-trigger anaesthesia – TIVA
- Dantrolene – IV with a bolus of 2.5 mg/kg followed by 1 mg/kg every 5–10 minutes until reversal of signs of MH (temperature and $EtCO_2$). Sometimes, a higher dose of up to 10 mg/kg may be required

  Continue at 1 mg/kg every 4–6 hours or run an infusion of 0.25 mg/kg/hr for 24–48 hours.

Symptomatic Treatment

- **Hyperthermia:** Cool the patient. Switch off warming devices, expose the patient, ice packs to vascular plexuses (axillae, groin and neck), cold lavage of stomach and bladder. Cold IV fluids must be administered with care as they may cause arrhythmias. Stop cooling at 38.5°C.
- **Hyperkalaemia:** Insulin 10 U in 50 ml of 50% dextrose, calcium (with care) 10 ml of 10% calcium carbonate, dialysis (refer to Chapter 7).
- **Acidosis:** Typically, mixed respiratory and metabolic. Sodium bicarbonate 1–2 mEq/kg IV only if base deficit >8 mEq/L, and the patient is ventilated (refer to Chapter 7).
- **Arrhythmias:** Avoid calcium channel blockers. Use beta-blockers or amiodarone. If life-threatening, treat arrhythmia as per ACLS guidelines.
- **Maintain urine output:** Place a urinary catheter. Give furosemide 1 mg/kg or mannitol 0.5–1 g/kg so as to maintain a urine output of at least 1 mL/kg/hr.
- Give inotropes, if necessary.

Monitor

- Along with standard monitoring of pulse oximetry, $EtCO_2$, BP and ECG.
- Monitor urine colour and output.
- Insert an arterial line and use it to monitor blood pressure, arterial blood gases (especially CO_2 and acidosis), electrolytes (especially K^+ and Ca^{++}), creatinine kinase, complete blood picture ([CBC] to rule out infection as a cause of hyperthermia) and coagulation studies.
- Insert a central venous line for measuring CVP and to give inotropes and other medications.
- Measure core and peripheral temperature.

Dantrolene

Dantrolene sodium is the specific treatment for MH. It is a hydantoin derivative that acts as a muscle relaxant but is not a paralysing agent. It appears to work directly on the RYR1 to prevent the release of calcium from the sarcoplasmic reticulum. Dantrium (Norgine Limited, UK) ampoule contains 20 mg of dantrolene presented as a lyophilised powder which is very difficult to dissolve. Each vial requires 60 ml of sterile water to dissolve the powder. Shake the vial till the solution is clear.

Ryanodex (Eagle Pharmaceuticals, USA) is available as 250 mg/vial and requires 5 mL of sterile water as a solvent. This solution with a pH of 9.5 should be used within 6 hours of mixing, kept at 20–25°C, away from light. Capsules of 25, 50 and 100 mg are also available. Complications of dantrolene include muscle weakness, thrombophlebitis, GI disturbances, hepatotoxicity and pulmonary oedema. Hyperkalaemia, increasing lactate production and myoglobin abnormalities can occur for a number of hours or days after the insult. Further dantrolene may be needed hours later if symptoms and signs of increased metabolic activity recur. The patient has to be monitored 24–48 hours after dantrolene administration.

Anaesthesia for Patients Suspected or Susceptible for MH

Consensus guidelines from the European Malignant Hyperpyrexia Group (EMHG)

- Trigger-free anaesthesia
  - Regional or local anaesthesia, if possible
  - If GA use TIVA and avoid succinylcholine and inhalational agents
- Preparation of an anaesthesia machine
  - Clean the machine, if available
  - Remove the vaporiser, change the soda lime, filters and breathing circuit
  - Flush the circuit with oxygen or air with a maximum flow rate for 90 seconds or >10 L/min for 20 minutes
  - Use activated charcoal filters, if available
- Monitoring. Standard anaesthesia monitoring including ECG, pulse oximetry, $EtCO_2$, non-invasive blood pressure (NIBP) and core temperature
- Patients receive standard care in post-anaesthesia care unit (PACU) after surgery
- Ambulatory surgery can be considered if trigger-free anaesthesia can be administered.

Differential Diagnosis

Any clinical condition that causes hyperthermia, rising $EtCO_2$ and intractable tachycardia arrhythmias must be considered. They include the following:

- Inadequate depth of anaesthesia
- Inadequate ventilation due to a defective or inappropriate breathing circuit, too low a fresh gas flow (FGF), low minute volumes, mechanical ventilator fault, exhausted or ineffective soda lime, blocked ETT or airway obstruction
- Anaphylaxis and transfusion reaction
- Endocrine causes: Thyroid storm or phaeochromocytoma
- Neurolept malignant syndrome and serotonin syndrome
- Drugs (glycopyrrolate, hyoscine, ecstasy)
- Cerebral ischaemia or hypothalamic injury
- Other muscular diseases such as isolated masseter spasm and Duchenne's muscular dystrophy
- Tourniquet ischaemia, especially after release of the tourniquet
- Overzealous warming of the patient

Definitive Diagnosis and Susceptibility Testing

- Re-review the history: with information of previous anaesthetics, triggering agents, family members having incidents during anaesthesia
- Creatine kinase levels may be raised in the patient or immediate family (done at rest or fasting). Though normal levels are not predictive, raised levels may have some correlation with susceptibility to MH
- Quadriceps muscle biopsy with contracture studies. Usually, it requires a large piece of vastus lateralis muscle (about 3–5 cm long and up to 1 cm wide). This cannot therefore be done in very small children. Australian centres suggest a minimum age of 12 years and North American centres a lean body weight of 20 kg. In case the child is smaller, the parents may be tested for susceptibility to MH.
- DNA testing for mutation of the *ryanodine* gene. Family members who have 1 of 15 known RYR1 mutations are considered sensitive.

The patient and family members should be informed as to the results of the testing and if susceptible be given documentary proof of the same and advised to wear a Medic – Alert bracelet.

REFERENCE

1. Denborough MA, Forster JF, Lovell RR, Maplestone PA, Villiers JD. Anaesthetic deaths in a family. *Br J Anaesth* 1962; 34:395–396.

SUGGESTED READINGS

1. Davis PJ, Brandon BW. The association of malignant hyperthermia and unusual disease: when you're hot or maybe not. *Anaesth Analg* 2009; 109(4): 1001–1003.
2. Hopkins PM. Malignant hyperthermia: Advances in clinical management and diagnosis. *Br J Anaesth* 2000; 85(1):118–128.
3. Zhou J, Allen PD, Pessah IN, Naguib M. Neuromuscular disorders and malignant hyperthermia. In: Millers Anesthesia, 7th edn. Miller RD, Eriksson LI, Fleisher LA, Wiener Kronish JP, Young WL, eds. Elsevier, Philadelphia, 2010; pp. 1181–1195.
4. Parness J, Lerman J, Stough RC. Malignant hyperthermia. In: A Practice of Anaesthesia for Infants and Children, 4th edn. Cote CJ, Lerman J, Todres ID, eds. Elsevier Saunders, Philadelphia, 2009; pp. 847–866.
5. Hopkins PM, Rüffert H, Snoeck MM, et al. European Malignant Hyperthermia Group guidelines for investigation of malignant hyperthermia susceptibility. *Br J Anaesth* 2015; 115(4):531–539.
6. Ruffert H, Bastian B, Bendixen D, et al. Consensus guidelines on perioperative management of malignant hyperthermia suspected or susceptible patients from the European Malignant Hyperthermia Group. *Br J Anaesth* 2021; 126(1):120–130.

44 Anaesthesia for Patients with Haematological Diseases

Verghese T Cherian • Vibhavari Naik

Haematological Diseases in Children

The common haematological diseases in children are as follows:

1. Inherited coagulation disorders
   - Haemophilia
   - Von Willebrand disease
2. Haemoglobinopathies
   - Sickle cell disease
   - Thalassaemia
3. Malignancies
   - Leukaemia
   - Lymphoma
4. Others
   - Aplastic anaemia
   - Thrombocytopaenia
   - IgA deficiency

The common reasons for anaesthetising children with haematological diseases are for therapeutic and diagnostic procedures as well as for incidental surgery.

Therapeutic Procedures

Therapeutic procedures include the following:

- Insertion of the central line for chemotherapy (mediport/Hickman)
- Lumbar puncture for cerebrospinal fluid (CSF) analysis and chemotherapy injection
- Splenectomy
- Bone marrow transplantation
- Radiation for malignancy
- Procedures that would also be performed in other children, for example, appendectomy

Diagnostic Procedures

Diagnostic procedures include the following:

- Bone marrow biopsy
- Biopsy – Liver, renal and lymph nodes
- Mediastinoscopy and lymph node biopsy
- CT scans and MRI scans

Haemophilia

Haemophilia is an X-linked inherited disorder that leads to insufficient production of Factor VIII (Haemophilia A), Factor IX (Haemophilia B) or Factor XI (Haemophilia C). Since the platelet function is normal, the formation of the primary platelet plug is normal, but the stabilisation is defective as the production of thrombin is impaired. Haemophilia severity is categorised based on the factor levels in the blood – mild (>5%), moderate (1–5%) and severe (<1%).

Diagnosis

- Family history
- Prolonged partial thromboplastin time
  - Normal prothrombin time and platelet count
- Low levels of Factor VIII or IX

Management

Preanesthetic evaluation should include factor assays, inhibitor (antibody) levels, haematology consult and administration of recombinant factor. NSAIDs should be avoided for analgesia and suitable alternatives should be chosen. Airway instrumentation should be avoided when possible and, if indicated, should be done gently to avoid mucosal injury.

Administration of Recombinant Factor

In those with severe deficiency, prophylactic factor administration at regular intervals is used to prevent spontaneous bleeds. The aim is to raise the factor level to 40% of the normal. Major surgery and trauma would need the levels to be raised to 80–100% of normal, just prior to surgery and maintained post-operatively. Recently, the minimum factor activity of more than 50% is considered adequate if planning for the neuraxial block.

Cryoprecipitates may be used only if the clotting factors are not available. Emicizumab is a monoclonal antibody that mimics activated Factor VIIIa and promotes haemostasis. Desmopressin (DDAVP) is a synthetic vasopressin, which can release Factor VIII from endothelial cells and can be used for mild Haemophilia A. A single dose per day for not more than 3 days is recommended. Tranexamic acid may be used as an adjunct to improve clot stability and reduce fibrinolysis.

von Willebrand Disease

This is one of the most common hereditary bleeding disorders (1%) and is due to the deficiency of von Willebrand factor (vWF), a glycoprotein produced by the endothelial cells and megakaryocytes. vWF is essential for the adhesive linkage between the platelets and the damaged endothelium for the 'initiation' of primary haemostasis. It is also required as a template for the functioning of Factor VIII. vWD is classified into three types: Type 1 (quantitative defect), type 2 (qualitative defect) and type 3 (absence of vWF).

Diagnosis

- Prolonged bleeding time, prolonged PTT
- Low levels of vWF

Management

- Factor VIII concentrate
- DDAVP (0.3 μg/kg) induces the release of vWF from the endothelial cells

Sickle Cell Disease

Sickle cell is an inherited haemoglobinopathy characterised by haemolysis, painful vaso-occlusion and end-organ damage. It is most common among people of African and Mediterranean descent.

Pathophysiology

A single point mutation in the sixth codon leads to the substitution of valine for glutamic acid on the α-chain in haemoglobin A making it haemoglobin S. The deoxygenated HbS polymerises to form long fibres causing the normally pliable biconcave red cell to assume a rigid sickle shape ('sickling' of the red cells), which is irreversible.

This causes cell membrane damage, haemolysis, clogging of the microcirculation and ischaemia of the tissues.

Risk Factors for 'Sickling'

- Hypoxaemia: Hypoventilation
- Decreased perfusion: Hypotension, hypovolaemia
- Venous stasis: Tourniquets, prolonged immobility, improper positioning
- Metabolic: Hypothermia, acidosis, infection
- Lifestyle: Alcohol binges, high altitude, long flights

Anaesthetic Implications

These patients usually present for splenectomy, cholecystectomy, skin grafting for skin ulcers, recurrent osteomyelitis and acute abdomen.

The aim is to prevent 'sickling' by avoiding acidosis, hypoxaemia, dehydration, venous stasis and hypothermia as well as to provide adequate pain control.

- Shorter fasting times, especially for clear fluids
- Neuraxial blocks cause vasodilatation, but need adequate fluid preloading, to prevent hypotension
- Adequate oxygenation
- Measures to maintain normothermia

Thalassaemia

Thalassaemia is a group of diseases with reduced or no synthesis of one or more globin chains of haemoglobin. It is named after the chain that is affected: α-thalassaemia, β-thalassaemia. The production of defective haemoglobin leads to early red cell destruction and anaemia.

Diagnosis

- Microcytic, microchromic, haemolytic anaemia
- Abnormal haemoglobin
- The clinical presentation depends on the severity of the defect (major, intermediate, trait or silent carrier)

Management

- Repeated transfusions of leukodepleted red blood cells
- Bone marrow transplantation

Anaesthetic Implications

- Often have hepatosplenomegaly
- Pulmonary hypertension, conduction defects, pericarditis and cardiac failure may be present secondary to hemosiderosis
- A child with beta-thalassaemia with repeated transfusions may have difficult airway due to frontal bossing and maxillary prominence

Leukaemias and Lymphomas

Haematological malignancies, i.e., leukaemia and lymphomas are the commonest, forming more than 60% of childhood cancers. Amongst them, acute lymphoblastic leukaemia (ALL) is commonest in children less than 5 years and lymphomas are commoner in adolescents.

Anaesthetic Implications

These children need multiple diagnostic and therapeutic procedures over their treatment period that runs over months and years. Hence developing a good rapport with patients and families can go a long way in reducing their anxiety and improving their cooperation. They can be scheduled for lumbar puncture, bone marrow aspiration, long-term vascular access placement, radiation therapy, CT or MRI scans. The following could be the concerns in these children:

- Initial presentation of acute leukaemia could have hyperleukocytosis with WBC counts higher than 50×10^9/L. It could be associated with anaemia, which should not be treated as transfusion increases the blood viscosity further causing capillary obstruction, micro-infarction and organ damage. These patients are also at a high risk of developing tumour lysis syndrome, which can be fatal if not recognised in time and treated.
- Lymphomas present with lymph nodal masses for biopsy or excision. Anterior mediastinal mass, depending on the size and location can cause airway and cardiovascular compromise and need meticulous planning of treatment.
- **Immunosuppression:** It can frequently occur due to their treatment regimens which include high-dose steroids, chemotherapy, radiotherapy and haemopoietic stem cell transplantation. They can develop neutropenic sepsis. Care should be taken when handling these children. Absolute neutrophil count should preferably be more than 1500 for major procedures. Granulocyte colony-stimulating factor is administered to improve neutropenia.
- **Thrombocytopenia:** Platelet transfusions should be judiciously used in these children as they often develop alloantibodies to platelets. For platelet refractoriness, single donor platelets or human leukocyte antigens (HLA)-matched platelets are preferred and timed as close to the procedure as possible.
- **Cardiotoxicity:** Anthracyclines are commonly used in these children and cause dose-dependent cardiotoxicity. Echocardiography should be done before taking them up for major surgery.
- **Thrombosis:** Children receiving L-asparaginase are at a high risk of deep vein thrombosis. They may have upper extremity thrombosis secondary to repeated central intravenous access lines.
- **Hepatotoxicity:** Many chemotherapeutic drugs like methotrexate, cytarabine and asparaginase may cause hepatotoxicity and liver function tests (LFTs) should be checked before major surgery.
- **Mucositis:** It is common in these children (Fig. 44.1) and may cause difficulty in intubation as the gums bleed on touch.
- **Long-term vascular access:** Anaesthesiologists should be well-versed in accessing indwelling catheters and maintain strict aseptic precautions to avoid bloodstream infections. Flushing these

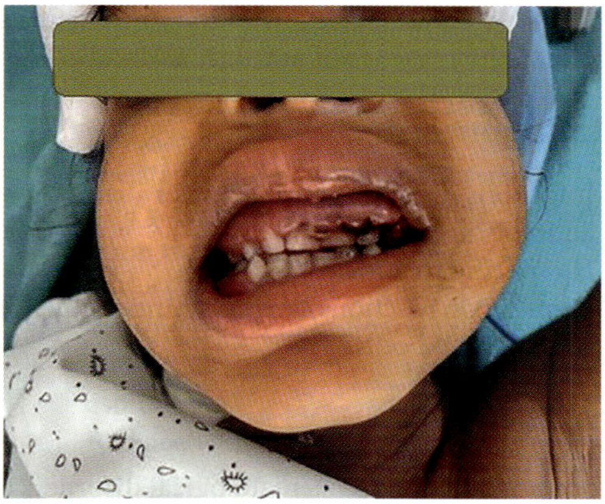

Figure 44.1 Child with mucositis and gum hypertrophy.

devices with normal saline using the turbulent flush technique and locking them with heparin after use helps maintain their patency. Many centres now practice saline locking instead of heparin locking to avoid heparin-induced thrombocytopenia.

- **PONV:** Children receiving chemotherapy are at high risk of PONV and multimodal prophylaxis is recommended.
- **Wound healing:** children receiving immunosuppressive chemotherapies are at higher risk of wound infection and delayed wound healing. Certain drugs like bevacizumab (vascular endothelial growth factor antibody) inhibit angiogenesis and may require deferring elective surgery for 4 to 6 weeks.

Aplastic Anaemia

Aplastic anaemia is a syndrome of haematopoietic failure causing pancytopenia – anaemia, neutropenia and thrombocytopenia. It may be congenital (Fanconi anaemia) or acquired – after exposure to drugs, viruses, radiation and toxins.

Diagnosis

The diagnostic criteria include bone marrow hypocellularity and two or more cytopenias of the following:

1. Reticulocytes < 1%
2. Neutrophils < 550/microliter
3. Platelets < 50,000/cu.mm

It is considered severe when bone marrow cellularity is <25% of normal. Treatment includes stopping the offending drug or thymectomy if associated with thymoma. For irreversible cases, systemic immunosuppression or allogenic hematopoietic stem cell transplantation is considered.

Anaesthetic Implications

Bleeding and infections are the dreaded complications perioperatively. Pre-operative optimisation should be done in coordination with a haematologist depending on the type and severity of surgery. These children tolerate anaemia well and often do not require transfusion if Hb > 6 g/dL unless major blood loss is anticipated. A platelet count > 50,000/cu.mm is recommended for surgery. Platelet transfusions should be timed immediately before surgery or HLA-matched platelets should be used to avoid being destroyed by antibodies which these children frequently develop. A good antibiotic cover is required to avoid infections. Regional anaesthesia is often contraindicated due to low platelets. Details of the anaesthetic technique for the specific procedures are mentioned in the procedure section below.

Thrombocytopaenia

When the platelet count falls below 50,000/cu.mm as compared to the normal of above 150,000/cu.mm

Diagnosis

- History of easy bruising, petechiae, purpura, bleeding from nose or gums
- Asymptomatic and detected on routine blood tests
- Prolonged bleeding time with normal prothrombin time and partial thromboplastin time

Causes

- Decreased production – sepsis, dengue fever, myelodysplastic syndrome and hereditary syndromes

be avoided in children receiving methotrexate as it potentiates neurotoxicity.

While positioning, the airway must always be well controlled and basic monitoring, especially oximetry, instituted.

The possibility of coning must be considered if there is unexplained CNS deterioration.

Bone Marrow Aspiration

This is mainly diagnostic or to monitor the progress of disease or treatment.

The anaesthesia considerations are as for LP (above). Most often both lumbar puncture and bone marrow aspiration are done at the same time.

The only thing to note is that the need for post-operative analgesia in the bone marrow aspiration category is much higher. Subcutaneous and periosteal infiltration of local anaesthetic can help reduce the pain post-operatively along with oral or IV paracetamol.

Radiation Therapy

Radiotherapy is given to children with haematological malignancies to prevent CNS spread. The procedure is not painful but requires immobilisation to strategically deliver radiation at the intended site. Radiation masks are applied after the child is sedated and can interfere in the airway management (**Fig. 44.2**). The radiation suite limits access to the patient and a good distant monitoring system should be used (**Fig. 44.3**). Since these children require repeated exposure to anaesthetics for a month, gradually increasing doses of propofol

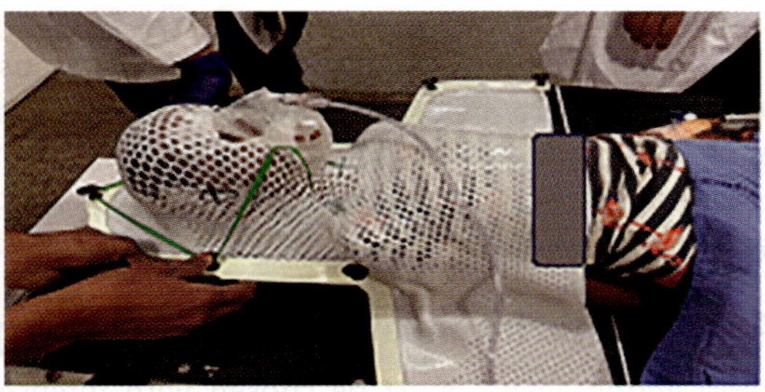

Figure 44.2 Radiation mask applied to the child's upper body.

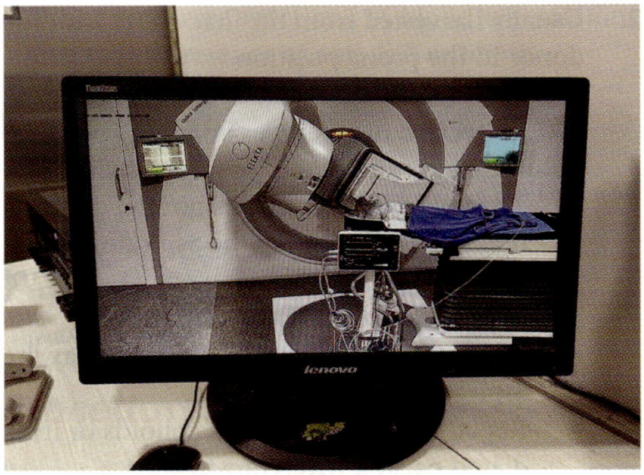

Figure 44.3 Showing the distant monitoring system in the radiation suite.

are needed. Antiemetics should be used as they are prone to nausea and vomiting.

SUGGESTED READINGS

1. Culshaw V, Yule M, Lawson R. Considerations for anaesthesia in children with haematological malignancy undergoing short procedures. *Paediatr Anaesth* 2003; 13:375–383.
2. Roizen MF, Fleisher LA. Hematologic Disorders and Oncologic Disease. In Millers, 7th edn. Miller RD, Eriksson LI, Fleisher LA, Wiener-Kronish JP, Young WL (eds). Churcill Livingstone, New York, 2010; pp. 1126–1132.
3. Haberkern CM, Webel NE, Eisses MJ, et al. Essentials of Hematology. In: A Practice of Anaesthesia for Infants and Children, 5th edn. Charles J Cote, Jerrold Lerman, Todres ID (eds). Elsevier Saunders publ., Philadelphia, 2009; pp. 177–194.
4. Adjepong KO, Otegbeye F, Adjepong YA. Perioperative management of sickle cell disease. *Mediterr J Hematol Infect Dis* 2018; 10(1):e2018032.
5. Srivastava A, Santagostino E, Dougall A, et al WFH Guidelines for the Management of Hemophilia, 3rd edition. *Haemophilia* 2020; 26(6):1–158.
6. Nagrebetsky A, Al-Samkari H, Davis NM, et al. Perioperative thrombocytopenia: evidence, evaluation, and emerging therapies. *Br J Anaesth* 2019; 122(1):19–31.
7. Forster VJ, Bell G, Halsey C. Should nitrous oxide ever be used in oncology patients receiving methotrexate therapy? *Paediatr Anaesth* 2020; 30(1):9–16.

45

Infection, Sepsis and the Anaesthetist

Kristy Xinghan Fu • Swapna Thampi

Infection is still the leading cause of death in children worldwide, despite the substantial progress made in prevention, early recognition and treatment of infectious diseases in recent decades. The World Health Organization (WHO) Global Health Observatory estimates that about 17,000 children die every day worldwide, with about half of these deaths due to infectious causes.

Although the vast majority of childhood infections are acquired in the community and not in hospital, hospital-acquired or 'nosocomial' infections such as ventilator-associated pneumonia (VAP) and catheter-related bloodstream infection (CRBSI) are associated with worse outcomes in children cared for in hospital. This population is often already disadvantaged by primary or secondary immunodeficiency, malnutrition and comorbidities such as chronic lung disease, congenital heart disease and neuromuscular disorders, which confer a higher risk of acquiring infection and developing sepsis.

The anaesthetist is often called upon to manage children suffering from infection and sepsis. Children may present for elective surgery and be found to have evidence of infection, children may present for management of a condition requiring anaesthesia to diagnose or treat a problem causing sepsis and the anaesthetist may be called upon to assist in the resuscitation or management of patients with severe infections or septic shock in the emergency room, intensive care unit or paediatric ward. An understanding of the common approaches to the diagnosis and management of infection and sepsis are therefore fundamental to safe and effective anaesthetic practice.

Prevention is the most important step in the fight against infection and sepsis. In the fight against child deaths due to sepsis, the WHO promotes 'Interventions that work' which include exclusive breastfeeding for 6 months, the use of vaccines against the most common bacteria causing pneumonia (*Streptococcus pneumoniae* and *Haemophilus influenzae* type B, Hib), measles and pertussis vaccination, the use of standardised guidelines in assessing sick children, the use of modern oral rehydration solutions, and ensuring a supply of clean water and clean air. Malnutrition, an avoidable cause, is associated with secondary immunosuppression and a reduced ability to survive severe sepsis.

Sadly, despite taking preventative measures infections will occur. All expert guidelines stress the importance of early recognition and treatment of infection, the early administration of appropriate antimicrobials and early resuscitative measures, which aim to prevent the escalation of infection to systemic sepsis, multi-organ failure and septic shock. Significant progress has been made in understanding sepsis epidemiology, the role of hyperlactatemia and risk stratification in septic shock, the use of extracorporeal therapy and the advantage of infection bundle approach such as antibiotic administration within an optimal time and choice of vasoactive medication.

Sepsis Epidemiology

Several large studies (SPROUT[1], ANZPIC registry[2], and PHIS database[3]) conducted between 2002 and 2014 report a significant prevalence of septic shock (6–23%) among children in the paediatric intensive care units (PICUs) with a mortality of 14–24%.

Clinical Presentation of Inflammation, Sepsis and Septic Shock

Terminology in the field of infection and sepsis is often used loosely, for instance, 'infection' is used as a synonym for 'sepsis', which is inaccurate and misleading.

Infection is defined as the presence of clinically suspected or proven infection. Infection may be localised with no systemic effects or through spread of the microbe or the effects of toxins. It may provoke a systemic inflammatory response (the so-called systemic inflammatory response syndrome, SIRS). It is likely that genetic factors influence the evolution of sepsis to some extent, as not all children with similar causal infections develop severe sepsis and/or septic shock. It is important to understand that inflammation is a non-specific response to an insult of which infection is but one trigger. For instance, inflammation occurs commonly in direct trauma, burns, pancreatitis and following major surgical interventions.

When infection is the cause of SIRS, the clinical picture is termed 'sepsis'. Sepsis is characterised above all by abnormal temperature and/or abnormal white blood cell count usually accompanied by tachycardia and/or tachypnoea (see **Tables 45.1** and **45.2**). Characteristic presentation of specific diseases can vary and will be noted later in this chapter.

Unrecognised or untreated sepsis has the potential to progress to cause multi-organ dysfunction – *severe sepsis*. In the context of severe sepsis, hypotension which is unresponsive to volume infusion during resuscitation (40 mL/kg in 1 hour), the patient is categorised as having *septic shock*.

Progression from Infection to Sepsis and Septic Shock

- Fever (or hypothermia) + leukocytosis (or leukopaenia) = SIRS

Table 45.1 Definitions of Infection, Systemic Inflammatory Response Syndrome, Sepsis, Severe Sepsis and Septic Shock in Children

Infection Suspected or proven infection caused by any pathogen or Clinical syndrome with high probability of infection noted on examination, laboratory test or imaging
SIRS At least two of the following criteria, with either *a* or *b* are obligatory: a. core temperature (rectal, oral, bladder or central catheter probe) >38.5°C or <36.0°C b. leukopaenia or leucocytosis for age or more than 10% immature neutrophils (excluding drug-induced findings) c. tachycardia (mean heart rate (HR) > 2 SD above normal for age) not related to external or painful stimuli or drugs, or unexplained persistently elevated HR over 0.5–4.0 hours or bradycardia in children <1 year old (mean HR < 10th percentile for age) not related to external vagal stimuli, drugs or congenital heart disease; or unexplained persistently depressed HR over 0.5 hour d. tachypnoea (mean RR > 2 SD above normal for age) or need for mechanical ventilation due to an acute process not related to neuromuscular disease or general anaesthesia
Sepsis SIRS plus suspected or proven infection
Severe sepsis Sepsis *and* one of the following: cardiovascular dysfunction with hypoperfusion, raised lactate, oliguria, prolonged capillary refill time or acute respiratory distress syndrome or two or more organ dysfunctions (e.g. disseminated intravascular coagulation, acute kidney injury, hepatic dysfunction or neurologic dysfunction)
Septic shock Sepsis and cardiovascular dysfunction – fluid refractory hypotension, signs of hypoperfusion or need for vasoactive drug to maintain normal blood pressure for age

HR, heart rate; SD, standard deviation; RR, respiratory rate; SIRS, systemic inflammatory response syndrome.

Modified from Goldstein B, Giroir B, Randolph A, Sepsis ICCoP. International pediatric sepsis consensus conference: definitions for sepsis and organ dysfunction in pediatrics. *Pediatr Crit Care Med* 2005; 6(1):2–8.[4]

Table 45.2 Age-Specific Guidelines of Abnormal Vital Signs and Leukocyte Counts

Age	Tachycardia[a] (beats/min)	Bradycardia[a] (beats/min)	Tachypnoea (breaths/min)	Hypotension[b] (SBP, mmHg)	Leukocytes[a] ($\times 10^3/mm^3$)
0 days–1 week	>180	<100	>60	<60	>34
1 week–1 month	>180	<100	>60	<60	>19.5 or <5
1 month–11 months	>180	<90	>50	<70	>17.5 or <5
1 year	>160	<90	>40	<70	>17.5 or <5
2–5 years	>140	–	>30	<74	>15.5 or <6
6–12 years	>130	–	>25	<82	>13.5 or <4.5
13–<18 years	>110	–	>20	<90	>11 or <4.5

SBP, systolic blood pressure.

[a]5th percentile for lower values and 95th percentile for upper values.

[b]Estimated values, varies according to patient's gender, height and age in years. The abnormal vital sign triggers in this table must be considered only as potential indications of physiological abnormality, requiring further careful assessment of the sick child.

Modified from Goldstein B, Giroir B, Randolph A, Sepsis ICCoP. International pediatric sepsis consensus conference: definitions for sepsis and organ dysfunction in pediatrics. *Pediatr Crit Care Med* 2005; 6(1):2–8.[4]

- SIRS + infection = sepsis
- Sepsis + multiorgan dysfunction = severe sepsis
- Severe sepsis + refractory hypotension = septic shock

Hypotension is not necessarily a prominent feature in children with septic shock as children often maintain normal blood pressures due to compensatory mechanisms including tachycardia and vasoconstriction. The presence of hypotension in children is an indication of advanced septic shock and must be managed aggressively.

Multi-organ dysfunction is prominent in severe sepsis and septic shock. Even in the absence of lung infection, presence of a rapid respiratory rate and a requirement for supplemental oxygen often heralds the onset of acute inflammatory lung injury, characterised by non-cardiogenic pulmonary oedema and ultimately paediatric acute respiratory distress syndrome. Oliguria or biochemical evidence of renal impairment due to impaired renal perfusion, deteriorating mental status due to decreased cerebral perfusion, hepatic impairment, thrombocytopenia and impaired liver synthetic function are also prominent features of established septic shock. Other common features in some sepsis syndromes include cutaneous rashes, vomiting, diarrhoea, abdominal distension, neck stiffness and meningeal signs.

The early recognition of sepsis is crucial for good outcomes and is essentially arrived at through taking an accurate clinical history, along with careful observation and clinical examination of the child. Healthcare workers must have a high index of suspicion when assessing the sick child and 'think sepsis'. The presence of clinical signs of sepsis on examination is sufficient to start initial management. One need not await laboratory confirmation to initiate treatment.

Investigation of Sepsis

An important aspect of managing sepsis is to determine the microbiological cause. Although sophisticated investigations such as viral PCR and immunofluorescence are widely available in resource-rich healthcare environments, they often do not radically alter treatment as few effective agents exist for viral infections. Conversely, the readily available, inexpensive techniques of microscopy and bacterial culture (blood, site-specific cultures) usually determine which bacteria are responsible for an episode of sepsis and therefore underpin effective management by confirming the appropriate antimicrobial to be administered. **Table 45.3** shows the core investigations in sepsis.

Table 45.3 Core Investigations in Sepsis

Core Investigations in Sepsis	Commentary
Source identification (guided by clinical presentation)	
Culture and microscopy	
Blood	
Sputum or tracheal aspirate	Try to take cultures before the first antimicrobial dose
Urine	
Cerebrospinal fluid (if meningitis suspected)	
Stool	
Any exudates (e.g. wound, skin lesions)	
Blood microscopy	
If malaria suspected: thick and thin blood smears	
PCR/ELISA	
If dengue suspected: PCR/ELISA (<5 days) or IgM/IgG	
Viral immunofluorescence/PCR	If viral infection suspected ± rapid antigen tests if available
Respiratory viruses: respiratory syncytial virus, adenovirus, influenza, parainfluenza, etc.	Nasal secretions if respiratory viral infection suspected
Markers of inflammation	
ESR or C-reactive protein or procalcitonin	Relatively non-specific markers raised in acute inflammatory states including sepsis
Differential white blood cell count	Absolute leukopaenia or leukocytosis for age with >10% immature neutrophils
Markers of organ/system dysfunction	Identifies failing organ/systems needing support and tracks clinical trends
Plasma urea	Raised in dehydration and in renal failure
Plasma creatinine	Raised in renal impairment/failure
Plasma electrolytes	High sodium in dehydration Low sodium due to water retention in sepsis-associated SIADH
Liver function tests	
Coagulation (prothrombin time, activated partial thromboplastin)	
Lactate	> 4 mmol/L has higher risk of developing organ dysfunction
Central venous oxygen saturation	< 65% in child with normal SaO_2

Trends in lactate levels are emerging as an important prognostic indicator in paediatric sepsis. Children with SIRS and elevated venous lactate ≥ 4 mmol/L have a relative risk of 5.5 for developing organ dysfunction within 24 hours of presentation and a longer duration of organ dysfunction.[5] Lactate normalisation within 4 hours of septic shock is associated with decreased incidence of persistent organ dysfunction at 48 hours.

Management of Sepsis

Bundled approaches to recognition of shock and management in paediatric patients can improve outcomes as there is better adherence to guidelines and decreased time to therapy.

Whenever the diagnosis of sepsis or septic shock is made, treatment should be rapidly commenced to minimise morbidity and mortality of the patient. Early aggressive resuscitation including fluids and antimicrobial administration within the first hour for septic shock, and within the first 3 hours for suspected sepsis, has been shown to significantly improve sepsis outcomes. The Surviving Sepsis Campaign's (SSC) International Guidelines for Management of Severe Sepsis and Septic Shock is recognised as an authoritative guideline to management and its highlights are described below.

Initial Resuscitation

As in any emergency scenario, the management of a child with severe sepsis starts with systematic assessment of the child's airway, breathing and circulation.

Airway

If the airway is not clear, use an airway opening manoeuvre and consider use of a Guedel airway or similar adjunct to maintain airway patency.

Breathing

All children with proven or suspected severe sepsis or septic shock should receive supplemental oxygen therapy, ideally via a high-flow face mask. If there is increased work of breathing, a trial of non-invasive ventilation may be useful. Respiratory distress or increased work of breathing often results in a further mismatch in the delivery of oxygen and consumption of oxygen, which is already present in severe sepsis or septic shock states. If the child's respiratory effort is inadequate, breathing should be supported with bag-valve-mask, prior to tracheal intubation and ventilation.

In the severely shocked child, cardiovascular status may worsen during anaesthesia for tracheal intubation. Adequate volume loading prior to intubation is recommended, and the choice of anaesthetic agents should aim to minimise the possibility of inducing myocardial depression or vasodilatation. Ketamine is frequently the induction agent of choice in the unstable septic child. High-dose opioids, benzodiazepines and thiopentone are relatively contraindicated because of the risk of more profound circulatory depression; and if used should be titrated slowly.

Tracheal intubation and mechanical ventilation is usually considered necessary if there is obvious hypoventilation, severe respiratory distress or when resuscitation requires more than 40 mL/kg fluids to be administered. Mechanical ventilation reduces the work of breathing and improves oxygenation, thereby improving oxygen delivery. It also helps to facilitate placement of venous and arterial cannulae necessary for advanced resuscitation.

Circulation

Crucial steps while assessing and managing shock related to sepsis are as follows (Fig. 45.1):

- **Access:** Two wide bore peripheral intravenous cannulae or, if peripheral venous access is difficult, an intraosseous access should be inserted. Experienced personnel may choose to access the femoral, internal jugular or subclavian veins but these attempts should not delay initial resuscitation, which whenever possible should use rapidly sited peripheral or intraosseous devices.
- **Blood samples:** Take blood samples for blood gas, glucose, full blood count, biochemistry, C-reactive protein or procalcitonin, blood culture, cross match and clotting studies.
- **Fluids:** An initial fluid bolus of 10–20 mL/kg should be given over 15–20 minutes to all patients with severe sepsis and septic shock, followed by reassessment to review response, which should include measurement of capillary refill time, HR, blood pressure, central venous pressure and liver size. Normal saline (0.9% sodium chloride) is widely recommended for initial fluid resuscitation and has the advantage of being relatively cheap and widely available. If available, balanced crystalloids may have conferred benefits over normal saline as emerging evidence show reduced morbidity and mortality in patients given balanced crystalloids versus normal saline. Further cycles of 10–20 mL/kg of fluid boluses should follow unless there is evidence of normalising haemodynamic status. If hepatomegaly or rales develop during fluid resuscitation, further fluid administration may be harmful. If shock persists after 40–60 mL/kg, inotropic support should be started to augment cardiac output (see below). Children with severe septic shock may require 100–200 mL/kg fluids in the first 24 hours of their illness. The 2011 FEAST trial[7] results encourage early vasopressor use in septic shock while avoiding excessive fluid bolus resuscitation, especially so in healthcare settings without intensive care support.
- **Inotropic support:** Shock that persists after 40–60 mL/kg should be further managed with inotropic support. Ideally, inotropic infusion should be given via a central venous cannula; however, therapy must not be delayed if central venous access is not available. Inotropes can and should be administered through an intraosseous needle or a peripheral cannula until a central access is obtained. In shock states with abnormal perfusion without hypotension, consider starting an epinephrine (adrenaline) infusion (0.05–2 μg/kg/minute) and titrating the dose according to clinical response. In shock states with

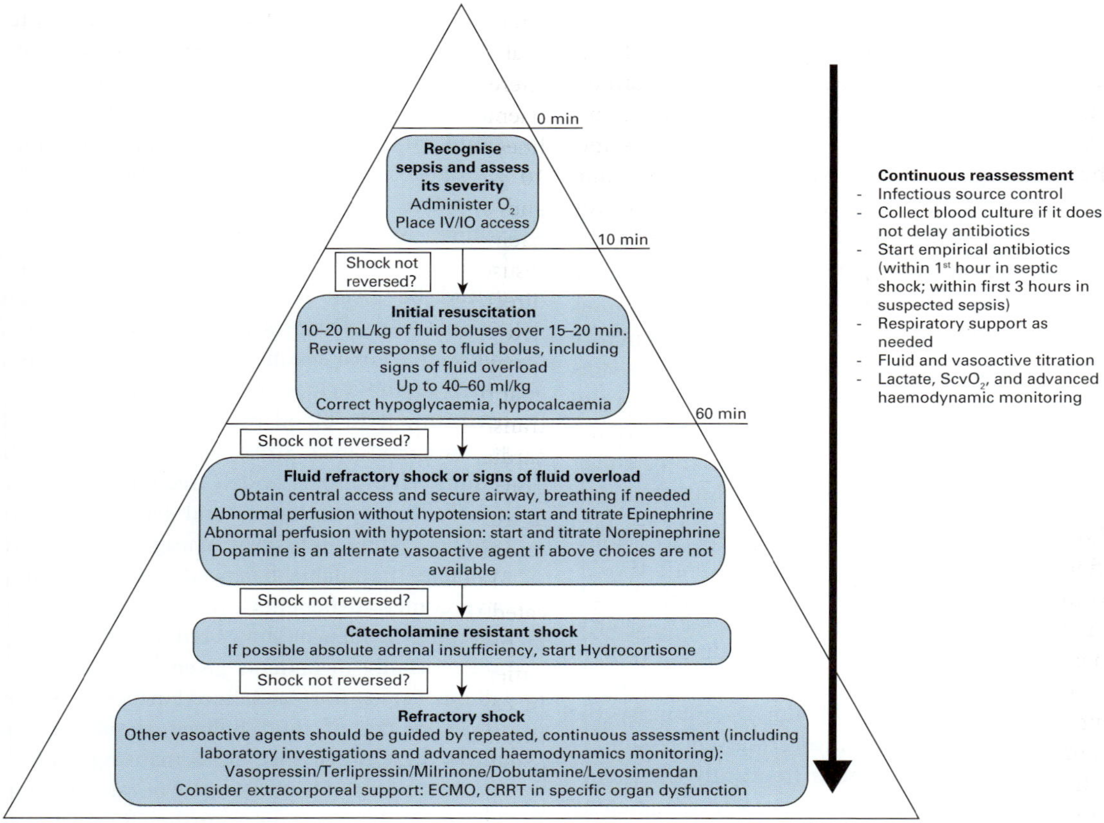

Figure 45.1 Important steps in the haemodynamic stabilisation of infants and children with sepsis. IV, intravenous; IO, intraosseous; $ScvO_2$, central venous oxygen saturation; ECMO, extracorporeal membrane oxygenation; CRRT, continuous renal replacement therapy. Modified from Davis AL, Carcillo JA, Aneja RK, et al. American college of critical care medicine clinical practice parameters for hemodynamic support of pediatric and neonatal septic shock. *Crit Care Med* 2017; 45(6):1061–1093. doi: 10.1097/CCM.0000000000002425.[6]

abnormal perfusion with hypotension, consider starting norepinephrine (noradrenaline, 0.05–2 μg/kg/minute) and titrating the dose according to clinical response. Dopamine infusion is an alternative if epinephrine or norepinephrine is unavailable; consider starting at 5–10 μg/kg/minute in shock states without hypotension, and at a higher dose of 10–20 μg/kg/minute if hypotension is present. There are some emerging data suggesting higher mortality risk in patients who are supported on dopamine versus norepinephrine. Finally, in children with persisting low systemic vascular resistance and hypotension already receiving norepinephrine, the use of intravenous vasopressin or terlipressin infusions can be considered although there is little evidence to support their impact on outcome of paediatric severe septic shock.

The main goals of resuscitation for children with septic shock are capillary refill equal to or less than 2 seconds, normal blood pressure for age, normal pulses (central and peripheral equally palpable), warm extremities, urine output greater than 1 mL/kg/hour and normal mental status. When invasive advanced monitoring is available, central venous oxygen saturation ($ScvO_2$) should be maintained above 70% and cardiac index between 3.3 and 6.0 L/minute/m^2.

Care should be taken if a child presents in a shocked state of possible cardiac aetiology such as myocarditis, or with signs of raised intracranial pressure, as excessive fluid resuscitation will worsen cardiac failure and cerebral oedema, respectively. In such circumstances, a cautiously administered bolus of 10 mL/kg is recommended with rapid reassessment thereafter.

Ongoing cardiovascular management of the child with severe sepsis is beyond the scope of this chapter, but is likely to include continuing cardiovascular assessment and reassessment with whatever monitoring modalities are available to guide the bedside clinician. Serial measurements and observation of trends, for example, blood pressure, HR, plasma lactate and $ScvO_2$ can be extremely valuable to the decision-making clinician.

Antimicrobial Therapy and Source Control

Antimicrobial treatment is central to the successful management of sepsis and should be ideally administered within 3 hours after establishing a probable diagnosis of sepsis. Antimicrobial therapy should be administered even earlier, within 1 hour after recognition of severe sepsis or septic shock. Newer literature is emerging supporting better outcomes with earlier initiation of antimicrobial therapy. Whenever possible blood cultures should be taken prior to antimicrobial administration, but administration must not be delayed if blood samples cannot be obtained easily. The choice of antimicrobial drug should follow local guidelines based on the knowledge of local common diseases and pathogens and their likely sensitivities to antimicrobials. Faced with probable bacterial sepsis, cefotaxime or ceftriaxone 80 mg/kg are widely recommended. Specific situations are discussed in 'Infective syndromes associated with sepsis' section in this chapter.

In addition to antimicrobial therapy, cases where the source of sepsis can be identified, it is imperative to take action to control it where possible. Procedures such as drainage of infected fluid (abscesses, effusions), debridement of infected wounds, laparotomy or removal of infected devices should be undertaken as rapidly as possible and are as important as antimicrobial therapy.

Further Management

A range of other interventions is frequently required in the management of early severe sepsis and septic shock, as described below.

Blood and Blood Products

The use of blood transfusion and the optimisation of haemoglobin levels in sepsis and septic shock are controversial. The WHO recommends that red blood cells transfusion should be administered in cases of severe anaemia, defined as a haemoglobin level less than 5 g/dL. The SSC guidelines suggest aiming haemoglobin levels of at least 10 g/dL for haemodynamically unstable patients and a minimum of 7 g/dL for those in whom haemodynamic stability is achieved after initial resuscitation. The SSC supports the use of goal-directed therapy in sepsis to maximise tissue oxygen delivery, recommending a target for $ScvO_2$ of 70%. Oxygen delivery can be improved to achieve this goal by raising Hb concentration through red cell transfusion and/or taking measures to improve cardiac output. The evidence to support the additional benefit of therapy based on $ScvO_2$ goals is weak, and it may be difficult to implement in resource-constrained settings.

Prophylactic platelets transfusion is indicated when platelet counts are below 20,000/mm^3 in patients with high risk of bleeding and in all patients with platelet counts below 10,000/mm^3. In cases where there is active bleeding or when surgical or invasive procedures are required, platelet counts should be kept above 50,000/mm^3.

Fresh frozen plasma or factor concentrates may be required to correct coagulopathies in sepsis. Administration should be ideally guided by laboratory measurement of clotting profiles including prothrombin time, activated partial thromboplastin, fibrinogen and a measure of fibrin degradation, in addition to a full blood count.

Mechanical Ventilation

Most patients with severe sepsis and septic shock will require intubation and mechanical ventilation at some point. It may be due to impaired mental status, inability to maintain airway patency, respiratory distress due to the onset of acute lung injury or paediatric acute respiratory distress syndrome.

A lung protective ventilatory strategy should be adopted, aiming to avoid supplementary damage due to excessive ventilatory volumes or pressure while aiming to maintain lung recruitment. Authorities recommend aiming for tidal volumes of no more than 6–8 mL/kg and peak pressures less than 30 cm H_2O. High positive end-expiratory pressure (10–20 cm H_2O) may be required to maintain lung recruitment. To facilitate achievement of these goals, accept higher than normal $PaCO_2$ levels (aim for pH 7.2–7.25) and lower SpO_2 (~90%). When it is not possible to maintain reasonable oxygenation and CO_2 removal with these settings, high-frequency oscillatory ventilation or extracorporeal oxygenation should be considered if these advanced therapies are available.

Corticosteroids

Corticosteroids supplementation may be considered when shock is not reversed after initial fluid boluses and inotropic support (epinephrine, norepinephrine and dopamine) where there is evidence of, or a strong likelihood of, absolute adrenal insufficiency. Hydrocortisone at stress doses of 25–50 $mg/m^2/day$ should be given as initial treatment. There is no evidence from clinical trials to support the routine use of supplementary steroids in sepsis in the absence of adrenal insufficiency.

Nutrition

Severe sepsis leads to a catabolic state which can seriously compromise children, especially those with pre-existing malnutrition. Early feeding should be established preferably by enteral routes. If enteral feeding is not tolerated or when there is concern about intestinal perfusion, parenteral nutrition should be established, if available.

Glycaemic Control

Evidence is emerging from paediatric trials that the use of insulin to treat stress-induced hyperglycaemia leads to reduced inflammation and shorter hospital stay in critically ill children.[8] Hypoglycaemia is also a prominent feature of sepsis in many children. Newborns and children should be closely monitored for the onset of either hyperglycaemia or hypoglycaemia. A continuous glucose infusion must be established in all critically ill children to deliver 6–8 mg/kg/minute in newborns and 4–6 mg/kg/minute in children. If hyperglycaemia occurs, consideration should be given to use a continuous infusion of insulin titrated to blood glucose level to a 'high normal' range (5–7 mmol/L), and certainly to maintain a blood glucose < 10 mmol/L. (Note for conversion of mmol/L to mg/dL use the following formula: mg/dL = mmol/L × 18.)

Diuretics and Renal Replacement

Fluid overload has been found to be associated with worst outcomes and higher mortality in patients with acute lung injury and acute respiratory distress syndrome, after cardiac surgery and sepsis. The American College of Critical Care Medicine 2014 update recommends excess fluid removal using diuretics, peritoneal dialysis or renal replacement therapy if fluid is overloaded. There is no evidence to support the prophylactic use of dopamine or other agents in the prevention of acute kidney injury. However, known nephrotoxic agents should be avoided in children at risk of acute kidney injury, and all drug doses must be adjusted to 'renal doses' in children with impaired renal function.

Mechanical Circulatory Support

Extracorporeal membrane oxygenation is recommended in children who present with refractory septic shock, especially if cardiac performance is disproportionately impaired, or if severe paediatric acute respiratory failure is a prominent feature.

Anaesthesia Management

Initial resuscitation and stabilisation of these patients prior to anaesthesia should be based on the previously discussed (as above) management of sepsis and in-shock patients. They are vulnerable to the haemodynamic effects of sedatives and analgesics and require appropriate fluid resuscitation and inotrope infusion (peripheral or central) prior to securing the airway in spontaneously breathing patients. Anaesthetic induction prior to adequate volume resuscitation can lead to severe hypotension and arrest. Severe cardiac dysfunction may predispose these children to pulmonary oedema and rapid desaturation during intubation. Most experienced anaesthetists should perform the intubation and manage mechanical ventilation to reduce the work of breathing, improve oxygenation and organ perfusion.

Atropine may be useful particularly in babies against bradycardia. Ketamine is the agent of choice in septic shock as it maintains or augments systemic vascular resistance. Etomidate is discouraged due to its adrenal suppression effect. The role of hydrocortisone supplementation is unclear.

Fentanyl and remifentanil may be preferred over morphine as they are more cardio stable. Small doses of benzodiazepines may be titrated to effect. Barbiturates are not preferred due to their direct myocardial depression and reduction of systemic vascular resistance causing hypotension. Propofol should be avoided as it causes hypotension.

Neuromuscular blocking agents such as suxamethonium or rocuronium may be used to intubate these patients. Hypotension may occur during intubation despite adequate fluid resuscitation. Additional vascular access should be obtained as soon as possible. Appropriately titrated analgesia and sedation (e.g., fentanyl and midazolam) may be used for the transportation of these patients to the intensive care unit in an intubated state postoperatively. Arterial pressure and central venous pressure monitoring may be needed with point-of-care echocardiography being a useful non-invasive tool to rule out pericardial effusion and evaluate myocardial contractility and intravascular volume.

Infective Syndromes Associated with Sepsis

All types of infection can result in sepsis and septic shock. The patterns of infectious syndromes commonly presenting in children are outlined briefly below. Further reading is highly recommended for detailed information on each disease (please refer to References and Suggested Readings given at the end of the chapter).

Community-Acquired Pneumonia

Pneumonia kills more children per year than any other illness: more than malaria, AIDS and measles combined, killing two million children worldwide each year. The WHO estimates that less than 20% of children with pneumonia receive antibiotics.

Children with pneumonia may have a range of symptoms depending on their age and the cause of the infection. Bacterial pneumonia usually causes children to become severely ill with high fever and rapid breathing. Viral infections, however, often come on gradually and may worsen over time. Some common symptoms of pneumonia in children and infants include rapid or difficult breathing, cough, fever, chills, headaches, loss of appetite and wheezing. Children under five with severe cases of pneumonia may struggle to breathe, with intercostal recession and 'increased work of breathing'.

The leading causes of pneumonia are *S. pneumoniae* and *H. influenzae*. Other less common causes worldwide include important viruses such as respiratory syncytial virus and influenza, other bacteria such as *Staphylococcus aureus* and *Klebsiella pneumoniae*, and the fungus *Pneumocystis jiroveci* (PCP), which is particularly an important cause in young children with AIDS.

While adjuncts to diagnosis include chest X-ray and laboratory test, in resource-limited settings children should be assumed to have pneumonia if they have cough and rapid breathing (respiratory rate >50 breaths/minute for infants and >40 breaths/minute for children over 1 year of age). The presence of recessions in addition to rapid breathing suggests the pneumonia is severe.

Early antibiotic treatment of pneumonia underpins the successful management of pneumonia in all settings. Cotrimoxazole and amoxicillin are effective drugs against bacterial pathogens and are often used to treat children with pneumonia in developing countries, with the choice determined by known local patterns of resistance. Amoxicillin, co-amoxiclav and azithromycin are recommended as first-line treatments in developed health economies. Intravenous penicillin or ampicillin with gentamicin or a third generation cephalosporin are recommended in severe pneumonia. Treatment strategies need to be developed to reflect local resources and local epidemiology, for example, incidence of HIV/AIDS. If the child develops empyema in association with pneumonia, percutaneous drainage of the effusion, with or without anti-thrombolysis instilled or surgical intervention, is usually required.

General management of the child with pneumonia includes oxygen therapy and maintenance of sufficient enteral or intravenous fluid intake to maintain hydration. Hospitalisation and intravenous antibiotic therapy are recommended for those children presenting with severe sepsis, severe respiratory distress and those presenting with empyema. If fever persists or there is no improvement after 48 hours of antimicrobial therapy, the child should be rigorously reassessed.

Meningitis and Meningococcemia

Meningitis is inflammation of the meninges, most often caused by infection (bacterial, viral, or fungal) but can also be produced by chemical irritation, subarachnoid haemorrhage, cancer and other conditions.

Bacterial meningitis can occur at any age but is particularly prevalent in neonates, infants, and young adults. In developed countries, *Neisseria meningitidis* and *S. pneumoniae* are the common causes of acute bacterial meningitis. Previously, haemophilus influenzae bacteria (Hib) accounted for up to 50% of cases, but Hib vaccination programmes have since been highly effective and have dramatically reduced the prevalence of Hib infections in vaccinated populations. *Neisseria meningitidis* is a significant problem in many countries and is the only bacteria which can cause epidemics of meningitis; a particular problem with *N. meningitidis* group A in the sub-Saharan 'meningitis belt'. In neonates and infants, group B *Streptococcus*, *Escherichia coli*, other Gram-negatives and *Listeria monocytogenes* are seen. *Mycobacterium tuberculosis* should be considered in at-risk populations. Other causes of meningitis with sepsis include fungi, especially *Cryptococcus neoformans* in children with HIV, who have primary immunodeficiency or are immunosuppressed due to underlying conditions; protozoae including *Toxoplasma gondii*, *Acanthamoeba*, *Naegleria*; viruses including cytomegalovirus, herpes simplex, varicella, arboviruses (e.g. Japanese B encephalitis) and flaviviruses (dengue, see below). For management of the rarer forms of meningitis, one should follow local guidelines.

The clinical presentation of bacterial meningitis is usually non-specific in children under 18 months of age: fever, tachycardia, poor feeding, lethargy, irritability and vomiting. Signs of fulminant sepsis can occur in all types of bacterial meningitis, but are most common in meningococcal infections where purpuric rash and disseminated intravascular coagulation and shock may progress rapidly. Classical signs of meningitis such as neck stiffness and photophobia are found to be more common in older children and adults. Seizures are seen in 20–30% children with bacterial meningitis.

A lumbar puncture (LP) should be performed when a diagnosis of meningitis is suspected clinically. Contraindications to LP include raised intracranial pressure (altered level of consciousness, papilloedema, focal neurological signs, prolonged seizures), known structural CNS diseases, immunocompromised states, coagulopathy, haemodynamic instability and local skin infection.

The diagnosis of meningococcemia is primarily clinical, as LP may not be possible due to clinical instability on arrival. Isolation of *N. meningitidis* on blood or cerebrospinal fluid (CSF) Gram stain or culture confirms the diagnosis. When available, PCR may confirm infection even when blood or CSF samples are taken after the first dose of antimicrobials. **Table 45.4** shows characteristics of CSF in bacterial and viral meningitis.

Treatment options for bacterial meningitis in immunocompetent children according to age are as follows:

- Neonates (<28 days) up to 90 days old: Ampicillin + Gentamicin or Cefotaxime
- Children and adolescents (immunocompetent): third-generation cephalosporins: Ceftriaxone ±Vancomycin for community MRSA or known Methicillin-resistant *Staphylococcus aureus* (MRSA) carrier ± Metronidazole if suspected intra-abdominal source.

Table 45.4 CSF Characteristics in Bacterial and Viral Meningitis

Characteristics	Normal	Viral	Bacterial
White cell count (per mm^3)	<5	<1000	>1000
Polymorphs	0	20–40%	>85%
Protein (mg/dL)	<40	Normal or <100	>100
Glucose (mmol/L)	>2.5	Normal	<2.2
Blood to glucose ratio	>0.6	Normal	<0.4
Gram stain	No organisms	No organisms	75–90% positive
Culture	No growth	No growth	70–85% positive

CSF, cerebrospinal fluid.

Antibiotic choice should be modified to reflect known prevalence and resistance patterns. Likewise, antibiotic therapy in immunocompromised patients should follow local guidelines.

Adjunctive treatment of meningitis with corticosteroid must follow specific indications, and meningococcemia should not be treated with high-dose corticosteroids. The presence of adrenal insufficiency must be considered in the case of fluid refractory, catecholamine resistant shock. Septic shock is managed as outlined above.

Acute Epiglottitis

Epiglottitis presents with acute onset of high fever, sore throat, dysphagia and airway obstruction, varying from mild stridor to life-threatening obstruction. The diagnosis is usually based on clinical signs and symptoms, and confirmed by visualisation of an inflamed epiglottis during intubation. Various bacteria may cause acute epiglottitis, with Hib being historically the most common causative agent. Hib vaccination has lowered the incidence of Hib epiglottitis in countries that has adopted it as a routine.

The common sense of acute epiglottitis management is not to cause additional respiratory distress, thus not upsetting the child is highly encouraged. Keeping parents around and performing procedures only under analgesia and/or anaesthesia is fundamental. Maintaining the child with the head upwards is reasonable, as lying down may increase the airway obstruction. Children with significant airway obstruction will require anaesthesia for tracheal intubation. Inhalational anaesthesia is usually recommended, as it is safer than an intravenous-relaxant technique. Empiric combination antibiotic therapy with a third-generation cephalosporin and an anti-staphylococcal agent is usually recommended. Vancomycin is the anti-staphylococcal agent of choice in patients with epiglottitis complicated by sepsis. Patients with a penicillin allergy should be treated with vancomycin and a quinolone antibiotic agent. Antibiotics should be altered as culture sensitivities are identified by the laboratory and adjusted to ensure the completion of a 10-day course.

Dengue Fever

Dengue fever is one of the most common viral diseases in tropical and sub-tropical areas. Both *Aedes aegypti* and *Aedes albopictus* mosquitoes are vectors of dengue virus, which present four serotypes. The disease presents in three subsequent phases: febrile, critical and recovery.

During the critical phase, which commences around day 3 to day 7 of illness when fever subsides and capillary leakage increases, patients with severe dengue will present substantial plasma losses and massive haemorrhage – dengue shock syndrome and dengue haemorrhagic fever. Leukopaenia and rapid decrease in platelets count along with increasing haematocrit are early signs of this phase. The clinical picture will be of severe shock with single or, more commonly, multi-organ dysfunction and disseminated intravascular coagulation with severe bleeding.

Viral isolation in cell culture and viral RNA or antigens detection by PCR or ELISA techniques may confirm dengue diagnosis. However, these tests must be done before day 5 of the disease and are often not available. After day 5 of disease, the diagnosis relies on serological tests with IgM and IgG antibodies detection.

Dengue treatment is mainly supportive and patients will be managed according to clinical presentation (**Table 45.5**). Those presenting dengue with warning signs will require hospital admission with close haemodynamic monitoring. Intravenous fluid administration with isotonic crystalloid solution is usually required and given in continuous infusion so as to maintain perfusion and urine output.

Severe dengue demands urgent fluid resuscitation with isotonic crystalloid solutions in both continuous infusion and boluses administration as required. Clinical signs and haematocrit will guide the amount of fluid to be administered, avoiding fluid overload. Colloid solutions such as albumin may be used in persistent shock despite resuscitation with crystalloids. Blood transfusion with either whole blood or red blood cells may be required in severe bleeding. Haematocrit levels should not guide transfusion as it is usually elevated due to massive plasma leakage and, therefore, normal/elevated haematocrit levels could mislead the need of transfusion. Platelets and plasma transfusion may be required in specific cases. Fortunately, critical phase usually lasts 24–48 hours and patients who survive this period are likely to recover.

Table 45.5 Dengue Classification According to Severity[9]

Dengue without Warning Signs	Dengue with Warning Signs	Severe Dengue
Probable dengue: patient who live in/travel to endemic regions and present fever plus two of the following: • Nausea, vomiting • Rash • Aches and pains (myalgia, arthralgia, headache, retro-orbital pain) • Positive tourniquet test • Leukopaenia *Laboratory-confirmed dengue*: important if no signs of plasma leakage	Same as without warning signs plus any of the following: • Abdominal pain or tenderness • Persistent vomiting • Clinical fluid accumulation (ascites, pleural effusion) • Mucosal bleeding • Lethargy, restlessness • Liver enlargement >2 cm • Laboratory: increased haematocrit with rapid decrease in platelets count	Dengue with at least one of the following: • Severe plasma leakage leading to shock (DSS), fluid accumulation with respiratory distress • Severe bleeding as evaluated by clinician (DHF) • Severe organ involvement: AST or ALT ≥1000, impaired consciousness, cardiac or other organs dysfunction

ALT, alanine transaminase; AST, aspartate transaminase; DHF, dengue haemorrhagic fever; DSS, dengue shock syndrome. Modified from WHO Dengue Guidelines for Diagnosis, Treatment, Prevention and Control (2009).

Malaria

Malaria is a common parasitic disease in developing countries and a major health problem, which may present high morbidity and mortality, especially among the paediatric population. Resembling dengue fever, malaria also occurs in tropical and sub-tropical areas. *Anopheles* female mosquito inoculates sporozoites of *Plasmodium* into the human host, most commonly *Plasmodium falciparum* but also *P. vivax*, *P. ovale* and *P. malariae*.

Clinical manifestations of uncomplicated malaria comprise general symptoms of febrile illness. Paroxysmal fever may be present, but is not essential. Severe malaria may be the initial presentation in some cases, although it is usually a deterioration of uncomplicated cases. It presents with confusion and coma (cerebral malaria), metabolic/lactic acidosis, severe anaemia, bleeding, jaundice, hypoglycaemia, haemoglobinuria and acute renal failure, pulmonary oedema and acute respiratory failure. Shock with circulatory collapse and death may follow if untreated.

Microscopic diagnosis is the gold standard with analysis of both thick and thin blood smears to identify parasites presence and species, respectively. Negative smears do not rule out the infection and it should be repeated daily for 3 or more days if there is clinical suspicion of malaria. Rapid diagnostic test to detect *Plasmodium* antigens is an alternative, though not widely available. Antibodies detection with indirect immunofluorescence is unreliable to diagnose acute cases of malaria.

Treatment is based on both supportive management and antimalarial drugs. Supportive measures are addressed as required, with fluid resuscitation, electrolyte abnormalities and hypoglycaemia correction, fever treatment, blood transfusion, ventilatory support and renal replacement. Special attention must be given to glucose levels, as hypoglycaemia is frequent in young children. Fluid resuscitation should be carefully conducted in patients who present with neurological signs, as cerebral oedema is a common finding in cerebral malaria, the presentation and management of which is beyond the scope of this chapter.

Antimalarial drugs are the most important feature of treatment. However, prescription of antimalarial drugs must follow strict regional guidelines, as resistant malaria is of increasing concern worldwide. Administration should be based on recommendation of local public health policies, which are guided by drug resistance status and parasite species' incidence.

Toxic Shock Syndrome

Toxic shock syndrome (TSS) is a severe, acute, toxin-mediated disease, usually presenting rapid progression to multi-organ dysfunction with high morbidity and mortality. This is due to an exaggerated response of the immune system to bacterial toxins known as superantigens, which are found to be produced by certain strains of *S. aureus* and *S. pyogenes*. TSS may develop following a localised infection such as otitis, pharyngitis, primary skin infection or secondary to burns or varicella, necrotising fasciitis, pneumonia, tracheostomy or surgical site infection. Staphylococcal TSS can be associated with the use of tampons and, in this case, is classified as menstrual TSS.

The clinical presentation includes general symptoms of high fever, nausea, vomiting, diarrhoea, myalgia and malaise. An erythematous rash mainly on palms and soles followed by desquamation after a couple of weeks is characteristic of TSS, although it may not be present in all cases. Clinical deterioration usually develops rapidly with shock, hypotension and multi-organ dysfunction. Diagnosis is based on clinical presentation and laboratory findings of multi-organ involvement.

Treatment relies on early aggressive resuscitation and antimicrobial administration. Initial antimicrobial therapy is usually penicillin plus clindamycin, with the latter having the additional effect of reducing bacterial toxin production. Patients allergic to penicillin or with suspected or confirmed infection by methicillin-resistant *S. aureus* (MRSA) should receive vancomycin. Intravenous immunoglobulin, when available, is also recommended to help neutralise bacterial toxins. Septic shock management and multi-organ support must be carried out as required. Controlling the source of infection is extremely important, and many patients will require debridement of infected tissue.

Tetanus

Tetanus is another acute, toxin-mediated disease with potentially fatal outcome. It is caused by *Clostridium tetani*, which is inoculated through skin or mucosal injuries and produces the neurotoxin tetanospasmin, responsible for its clinical manifestations. Generalised tetanus is commonly characterised by trismus ('lockjaw'), risus sardonicus and opisthotonus.

Neuromuscular symptoms are related to hyperreflexia, generalised muscle rigidity and painful spasm, which may lead to dysphagia, laryngeal obstruction and acute respiratory failure following thoracic muscles spasms. Autonomic instability may be present, with labile HR and blood pressure, fever, sweat, salivation and increased respiratory secretions. Arrhythmias can also occur. The diagnosis is mainly clinical.

Tetanus management is based on several measures to avoid further spreading from inoculation site, neutralise circulating toxin and control clinical manifestations, especially muscle rigidity and autonomic instability. Intubation with rapid sequence technique and ventilatory support may be the first step required in the management of patients with tetanus due to muscles spasms, especially thoracic, laryngeal and pharyngeal. The port of entry wound, if obvious, should be explored and appropriately treated.

Metronidazole is the antibiotic of choice, although penicillin may still be used. Human tetanus immunoglobulin should be given as soon as possible and tetanus vaccination in acute tetanus must follow local guidelines. Benzodiazepines and magnesium sulphate are used to control muscle spasm. Magnesium is also useful to control autonomic instability along with morphine. Preventative measures to avoid pressure ulcers, muscle weakness and VAP are highly recommended as patients are likely to need high dose of sedation and muscle relaxants.

Urinary Tract Infection

Urinary tract infection (UTI) is common in children, especially those with vesicoureteric reflux, congenital anomalies in the kidney and urinary tract system (CAKUT), voiding dysfunction, constipation and spinal lesions such as spinal dysraphism. The use of urinary catheter is the main risk factor for hospital-acquired UTI, a common nosocomial infection in the intensive care unit. Sepsis secondary to UTI, the so-called urosepsis, is uncommon but may occur in young infants and in hospital-acquired UTI, especially if misdiagnosed or if treatment is delayed. In older children and adolescents, the diagnosis of a UTI should be accompanied by further social history investigation, including the HEADSS assessment (home, education and school, activities/employment, drugs, suicidality and sex).

UTI should be suspected in all infants younger than 3 months with fever and in children older than 3 months with fever and one or more symptoms among vomiting, poor feeding, lethargy, irritability, abdominal pain or tenderness, urinary frequency or dysuria. Definite diagnosis is made in the presence of positive urine culture obtained by aseptic method. *Escherichia coli* is the most frequent causative agent, followed by other Gram-negative bacteria and fungi.

Antibiotics are the mainstay of treatment. In urinary catheter-associated UTIs, the infected

46 INTRAOPERATIVE VENTILATION

Giuseppe A Marraro • Subramanyam Mahankali • Vibhavari Naik

The following will be discussed under intraoperative ventilation:

1. Ventilation modalities
    (a) Spontaneous breathing
        - Without a face mask
        - With a face mask or a laryngeal mask
    (b) Assisted ventilation
        - Manual positive pressure ventilation
        - Mechanical positive pressure ventilation
    (c) Ventilators type
        - Constant flow generators
        - Constant pressure generators
    (d) Ventilator characteristics
        - Compressible volume
        - Fraction of inspired oxygen
        - Tidal volume
        - Respiratory rate
        - Peak inspiratory pressure (PIP)
        - Flow waveform
    (e) Ventilatory modes
        - Assisted spontaneous breathing
            – Continuous positive airway pressure (CPAP)
        - Controlled mechanical ventilation
            – Volume-controlled ventilation (VCV)
            – Pressure-controlled ventilation (PCV)
            – Dual-control ventilation
        - Supported spontaneous breathing
            – Pressure support ventilation (PSV)
            – Volume support ventilation (VSV)
        - Use of positive-end expiratory pressure
2. Protective lung strategy during ventilation in anaesthesia
    (a) Toxicity of anaesthetic gases on the lung
    (b) Oxygen toxicity
    (c) Barotrauma and volutrauma
    (d) Atelectasis and atelectrauma during anaesthesia
        - Recruiting manoeuvres
            – Manual ventilation by the bag
            – Increase in end-inspiratory pause
            – 'Sigh'
    (e) Biotrauma
3. Ventilation of neonates during anaesthesia

General anaesthesia, using inhalation agents or intravenous drugs, can depress ventilation resulting in variations in pulmonary mechanics and alteration of gas exchange. This is due to depression of the central nervous system and due to reduced activity of the respiratory muscles, particularly the intercostal muscles which are responsible for the stability of the chest wall. Also, the central neuraxial blockade can affect ventilation if the level of the block is too high and the diaphragm and respiratory muscles are involved.

General anaesthetics depress the ventilatory response to hypercapnia and may predispose to prolonged apnoea. The use of volatile anaesthetic agents, such as halothane, isoflurane, desflurane and sevoflurane with spontaneous ventilation, produces a decrease in tidal volume and an increase in respiratory rate, causing a progressive increase of $PaCO_2$. Moreover, they blunt the response to hypoxaemia which continues into the postoperative period, further reducing the ability to regulate ventilation.

Sedative and analgesic drugs, depending on their strength and dose employed, may severely depress ventilation. When sedatives, analgesics, intravenous and inhalational anaesthetics are combined, they potentiate each other and may induce a respiratory depression more severe than that caused when they are used as sole agents.

The complications created by sedative and anaesthetic drugs are more evident in cases of pre-existing cardiorespiratory pathology.

Compliance decreases during general anaesthesia due to the reduction of functional residual capacity (FRC) and the formation of atelectatic areas. FRC reduction has several major effects on pulmonary function and in particular influences pulmonary mechanics, ventilation and perfusion distribution, and gas exchange. High chest-wall compliance, as seen in neonates, favours the occurrence of paradoxical 'pendeluft' movements, which generate a reduction in intrapleural pressure and poor increases in lung volumes.

Some differences exist between children and adults with regard to ventilation and perfusion distribution. In the spontaneously breathing adult, ventilation and perfusion are distributed preferentially to the dependent lung areas, whereas during intermittent positive pressure ventilation (IPPV) ventilation is mostly diverted to non-dependent areas. In contrast, in the spontaneously breathing neonate and infant, ventilation/perfusion distribution is similar to that of the adult during IPPV. The small airway diameter, lack of cartilage and FRC reduction all increase airway resistance.

Intraoperative Ventilation

Mechanical ventilation is a commonly used technique in the operating room.

Several concerns exist regarding the ventilation of infants and children during anaesthesia:

- How to ventilate neonates, infants and children according to their anatomical and physiological development?
- Is it only necessary to support gas exchange?
- How do we prevent side effects due to ventilation support that could influence post-operative care and surgical outcome?
- Can a short anaesthetic create lung damage?

The aims of intraoperative ventilation are as follows:

- To maintain gas exchange avoiding respiratory failure
- To facilitate surgery
- To avoid atelectasis, lung barotrauma and biotrauma
- To ameliorate pre-existing lung pathology
- To not cause surfactant inactivation or inhibition that can create terminal bronchioles and alveolar instability and collapse
- To not cause alteration of mucociliary activity that can be followed by difficulty in mucus elimination
- To not produce thick secretions that can lead to airway obstruction and consequent atelectasis and hypoxaemia

Ventilation Modalities

See classification given at the beginning of this chapter.

Spontaneous Breathing

Spontaneous breathing without a face mask is indicated during pain-free and short operations. Maintaining spontaneous breathing helps to avoid lung baro-volutrauma and haemodynamic complications.

This mode of ventilation is not recommended in infants and in long-duration surgery due to the difficulty in maintaining the patency of airways and avoiding hypoventilation caused by pharmacological depression and muscle fatigue. Its use is not suggested for newborns and infants less than 2 months, in children with difficult airways or in an emergency, except in cases of minor operations of brief duration.

Spontaneous breathing with a face mask or a laryngeal mask implies the use of special equipment (masks, breathing circuits, etc.) as well as the use of air and/or medical gases. It allows assissted ventilation and a means of monitoring assisted respiration. This method is indicated in children over 1 year, during short- and medium-duration surgeries. It is unsuitable in newborns, in emergency and shocked patients, in major cardiothoracic and abdominal surgery, and in head and neck surgery.

Assisted Ventilation

The most common *modes of assisted ventilation* during anaesthesia are manual or mechanical positive pressure ventilation.

Manual Positive Pressure Ventilation

Every breath is assisted or controlled. It is ideally used in intubated patients with a patent and protected airway and easily controlled ventilation. It is usually achieved by using ventilatory circuits such as the Ayres' T piece with the Jackson-Rees modification together with medical gases and volatile anaesthetics. This is the best method of evaluating the patency of the airway and the performance of correct pulmonary ventilation in patients at high risk. It can be helpful to evaluate the endotracheal tube patency (obstruction or malposition), control hypoventilation and hypoxaemia, and perform recruiting manoeuvres. The presence of the tube in the airway can allow tracheobronchial suctioning. However, respiratory rate and tidal volume are not uniform and can cause hypo- or hyperventilation. This mode of ventilation does not allow a stable level of positive-end expiratory pressure (PEEP) to be applied if it is necessary. The anaesthetist is exposed to pollution from expired gases, is at risk of fatigue and finds it impossible to use both hands, thus increasing the need for two anaesthetists during surgery.

Mechanical Ventilation

Mechanical ventilation represents a major advance in the administration of anaesthesia and allows difficult surgical operations, especially in very small and malformed neonates. It avoids irregularity in ventilation typical of manual ventilation. Mechanical ventilation has also given impetus to the development of ventilation assistance in post-operative intensive care.

Intraoperative-controlled ventilation is mandatory in newborns, infants and children of all ages during a surgical emergency, major surgery and surgery of long duration. It is also necessary for patients with a full stomach and specific clinical conditions, such as the need for hypocapnia in neurosurgery.

Advantages derived from mechanical ventilation are clearly recognised, but there are also some disadvantages which need to be recognised. They are as follows:

- Loss of physiologic humidification and heating of inspired gases
- Lung baro- or volutrauma, with consequent disruption of bronchioles and alveoli
- Hypo- or hyperventilated lung areas according to different compliances and resistances
- Need for deep general anaesthesia or muscle paralysis
- Hypoxaemia related to endotracheal tube obstruction or dislocation
- Technical problems related to ventilator malfunctioning

Ventilator Types

Positive pressure ventilators consist of a compressible air reservoir or turbine, air and oxygen supplies, a set of valves and tubes, and a disposable or reusable 'patient circuit'. The air reservoir is pneumatically compressed several times a minute to deliver room air or in most cases a mixture of air/oxygen and halogenated gases, to the patient. If a turbine is used, the turbine pushes air through the ventilator, with a flow valve adjusting pressure to meet patient-specific parameters. When positive pressure is released, the patient will exhale passively due to the lung's elasticity.

Most modern ventilators originate conceptually from Ayres' T-tube in which fresh gas flow is intermittently interrupted by electronically activated occlusion of the expiratory limb.

Constant Flow Generators

Volume pre-set (controlled) ventilators supply the same tidal volume for each breath, despite changing inflation pressure (PIP).

Constant Pressure Generators

Pressure-controlled ventilators supply constant pressure, which means that the tidal volume will vary according to pulmonary compliance and resistance.

Ventilator Characteristics

Compressible Volume

Compressible volume is represented by the circuit volume, which can be expanded and compressed during a respiratory cycle but is not involved in gas exchange. It is dependent on the type of ventilator, tightness of connections, humidification system volume and airway resistance. Current paediatric ventilators show a 50–75% volume loss, which is increased whenever a change in lung compliance occurs. In several paediatric ventilators, the compressible volume ranges between 1.0 and 1.5 ml/cm H_2O, which is too high for newborns and infants. The ideal compressible volume should be 0.3 ml/cm H_2O.

Fraction of Inspired Oxygen

A fraction of inspired oxygen (FiO_2) from 10 to 15% higher than that of air is used during intraoperative ventilation.

In children with pathologic lungs or those previously ventilated, it is necessary to increase FiO_2 to improve arterial tension and peripheral oxygen saturation (SpO_2). In children artificially ventilated before surgery, the same FiO_2 can be used or/modified as indicated by oxygenation monitoring.

The use of 100% oxygen must be avoided, except in children who are in a severe state of shock or cardiopulmonary disease, since this (oxygen) can promote atelectasis due to the rapid absorption of alveolar gas. The use of FiO_2 higher than 0.4 may expose patients to the risk of oxygen-free radical toxicity and, in premature newborns, to retinopathy of prematurity.

Tidal Volume

As a general rule, it is advisable to use a low tidal volume, at the same minute volume, in order to avoid lung overinflation (volutrauma), which can lead to lung fluid imbalance, increase in endothelial and epithelial permeability, and severe microstructural lung damage. An appropriate tidal volume must be chosen to compensate for the patient's and circuits' dead space in order to assure effective gas exchange and avoid hypoventilation. The recommended tidal volumes during intraoperative ventilation are described in **Table 46.1**.

Table 46.1 Recommended Tidal Volumes for Different Age Groups

Age Groups	Tidal Volume (ml)
Premature babies	5–10
Full-term newborns	20–30
Infants up to 6 mon	40–50
Infants up to 1 yr	70–90
Children up to 3 yrs	110–120
Children up to 6 yrs	250–300
Adult	500–800

Respiratory Rate

Respiratory rate together with tidal volume determines minute ventilation. As a general rule, it is useful to employ a respiratory frequency close to the one which the child would have during spontaneous breathing or the one used during ventilation support before anaesthesia.

Low respiratory rates improve pulmonary compliance but cause a larger excursion of the chest wall and diaphragm and overdistension of the alveoli and bronchioles. A high respiratory rate inactivates the Hering–Breuer reflex and improves gas diffusion by increasing mean intrapulmonary pressure.

Moderately high frequency (30–60 breaths/min) allows a reduction in PIP, smaller thoracic excursion and induces hypocapnia which in turn favours apnoea. High frequency (>60 breaths/min) can be useful in newborns with pulmonary hypertension and right-to-left shunt. It favours an increase in FRC and achieves a reduction in $PaCO_2$ and an increase in pH. If the tidal volume is inadequate in relation to dead space, it can lead to hypercarbia. Insufficient lung emptying in the expiratory phase results in air trapping.

Peak Inspiratory Pressure

For a long time, high PIP was considered to be mainly responsible for ventilation-induced lung trauma (barotrauma). Recent studies in intensive care demonstrate that the primary determinant for lung injury is alveolar overdistension rather than high peak airway pressures, that is, volutrauma instead of barotrauma. It is prudent to keep PIPs in neonates below 20 cm H_2O and below 30 cm H_2O in older children to avoid barotrauma. All ventilators must be provided with a pressure limit valve which gets activated at any time if the pre-set maximum limit is reached. PIP must be strictly monitored while ventilating the lungs of premature babies and those with pulmonary abnormalities such as cysts, interstitial emphysema, tracheo-oesophageal fistula and congenital diaphragmatic hernia, in order to avoid the risk of severe short-term (e.g. pneumothorax) or long-term (e.g. bronchopulmonary dysplasia [BPD] and chronic lung disease [CLD]) side effects.

Flow Waveform

Two waveforms are basically used – the sinusoidal and the square wave. The first is similar to that of physiologic spontaneous breathing, permits a gradual and smooth intrapulmonary pressure increase and generates lower mean airway pressure (MAP). The second one, with the same PIP, generates higher MAPs, thus favouring the re-opening of atelectatic areas and improving ventilation distribution.

Requirements for Paediatric Ventilators.

- Tidal volume from 5 ml and minute volume under 12 litres
- Respiratory rate up to three times that of adults (60 bpm)
- Low internal compressible volume
- Possibility to switch to manual ventilation
- High sensitivity and short triggering time

A suitable humidifying filter must be used during anaesthesia and the ventilator must have an appropriate device to humidify and warm ventilated gases if necessary. Safety valves to limit ventilation pressure and flow are recommended.

Ventilatory Modes Associated with Ventilators

Mechanical ventilation can be applied both invasively and non-invasively in the following ways:

- **Assisted spontaneous breathing:** Continuous positive airway pressure (CPAP)
- **Controlled mechanical ventilation:** Volume-controlled ventilation (VCV), pressure-controlled ventilation (PCV) and dual-control ventilation
- **Supported spontaneous breathing:** Pressure-supported ventilation (PSV) and volume-supported ventilation (VSV)

Mixed respiratory support such as intermittent mandatory ventilation and synchronised intermittent mandatory ventilation are not frequently used in anaesthesia.

Assisted Spontaneous Breathing

Continuous Positive Airway Pressure. CPAP is a mode of ventilation, which uses PEEP (positive end expiratory pressure) to increase total lung volume and FRC, thus favouring improved oxygenation. The optimum level of CPAP or PEEP is the lowest level of pressure that maintains a normal PaO_2 without increasing $PaCO_2$ excessively. If the pressure is too low, it will not increase the PaO_2 effectively and if too high it can overdistend the lungs and produce dead-space ventilation. CPAP application requires an intact respiratory drive. Its use reduces the occurrence of apnoea but cannot be used for treating apnoea, especially if apnoea is prolonged over 20 seconds or recurrent and complicated by bradycardia. The severe respiratory effort to maintain ventilation and hypercapnia ($PaCO_2 > 50$ mm Hg) are contraindications of its use.

CPAP can be applied using an endotracheal tube, head box, face chamber, face mask and nasal or pharyngeal prongs. Its use is suggested to improve airway patency, improve oxygenation without increasing FiO_2 and reduce the tendency to atelectasis. CPAP is also indicated in the post-operative care of neonates and infants who are at a high risk of respiratory failure. Newborns being obligatory nose breathers accept nasal CPAP, which can be effective even in prematures. Face mask CPAP should be used only for short periods as longer periods can predispose to pressure necrosis of the face and eyes. Gaseous distension of the abdomen occurs with nasal or mask CPAP, often requiring nasogastric or orogastric tubes to vent the stomach.

CPAP presents several advantages because of

- increased lung volume and FRC and improvement in the ventilation/perfusion ratio
- prevention and treatment of atelectasis
- reduced work of breathing, normalising respiratory frequency and preventing muscle fatigue
- reducing sternum and chest deformities

The increase in FRC is accomplished by increasing alveolar volume and through the recruitment of alveoli that would not otherwise contribute to gas exchange, thus increasing oxygenation and lung compliance.

Controlled Mechanical Ventilation

Intermittent Positive Pressure Ventilation and Continuous Positive Pressure Ventilation. IPPV is achieved by intermittently inflating the lungs with a positive pressure delivered by a ventilator or a bag and applied via an endotracheal tube, a tracheostomy or a facial or laryngeal mask. Continuous positive pressure ventilation (CPPV) is similar to IPPV, but the free flow of expired gases is arrested at a pressure level above zero (PEEP) and the whole respiratory cycle remains in a positive phase.

IPPV and CPPV can be applied using different modes of ventilation. The most common ones are as follows:

1. Volume-controlled ventilation
2. Pressure-controlled ventilation
3. Dual-controlled ventilation

1. **Volume-controlled ventilation:** It is delivered with a constant inspiratory flow, which delivers the pre-fixed tidal volume, resulting in increasing airway pressure through inspiration. Inspiration is active. The actual pre-set tidal volume remains constant as lung compliance and resistance change (**Fig. 46.1**).

Expiration is passive and thus requires more time to allow alveolar units to empty.

Ventilation is controlled by three factors: (1) tidal volume, (2) respiratory rate and (3) I:E ratio. The I:E is the ratio of time spent in inspiration to that spent in expiration. If the expiration is of insufficient duration, gas is trapped in the alveoli (at end-expiration), a process known as 'auto-PEEP'.

If the ventilator is time-cycled between inspiration and expiration, an inspiratory pause (no fresh gas flow during this pause) occurs and the pressure drops below the PIP (plateau pressure) due to alveolar re-distribution. High inspiratory flow during VCV has detrimental effects on lung ventilation. Therefore, low inspiratory flow rates should be used to keep the peak ventilatory pressure as low as possible. This ensures more homogeneous ventilation.

The main advantage of volume-controlled ventilators is guaranteed tidal volume and minute ventilation. This is particularly important in the operating room, where lung compliance may be influenced by the type of surgery involved (abdominal or chest surgery),

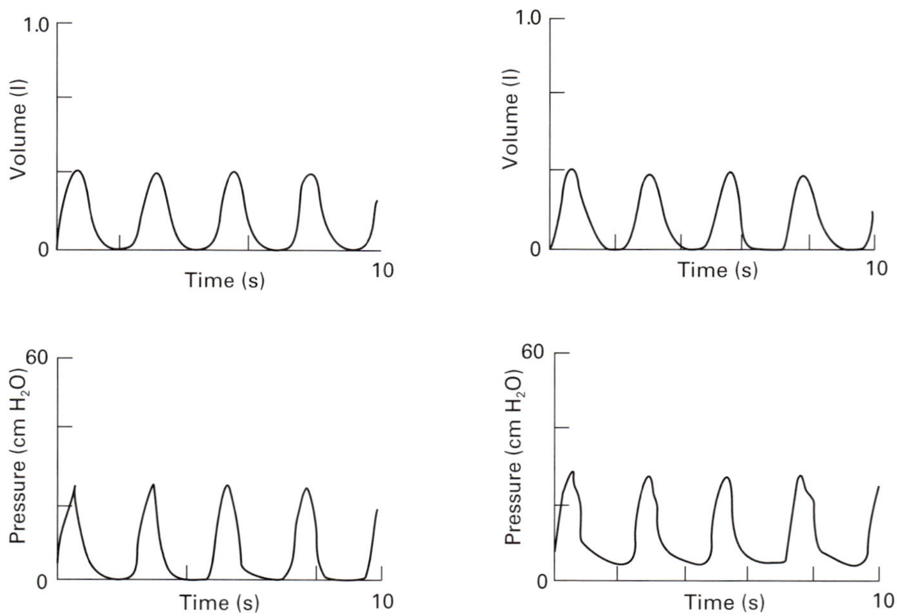

Figure 46.1 Volume-controlled ventilation (on the left) and volume-controlled ventilation with positive-end expiratory pressure (on the right).

Recently, ultrasound is being used to help diagnose lung collapse due to atelectasis as well as assess the effectiveness of recruitment manoeuvres.

Recruiting Manoeuvres

1. **Manual ventilation by a bag.** This manoeuvre is simple and can be applied when atelectasis can occur. At present, the safe peak pressure to reach during distension and how many seconds the lung must be maintained in distension are controversial. In adults, it is suggested to apply 40 cm H_2O maintained for 8–15 seconds. The same pressures could be applied to children and adolescents over 8 years of age. In infants and young children, this pressure could be harmful and 8–10 cm H_2O *over the pre-set inspiratory peak pressure* could be safer. In neonates, recruiting pressure must avoid increasing intrathoracic pressure over 25–30 cm H_2O. In children > 8 years, it has been recommended that a plateau pressure is maintained below 35 cm H_2O and recruiting manoeuvre should be affected in maintaining a PEEP level of 15 cm to avoid collapse of the recruited lung.
2. **Increase in end-inspiratory pause.** Alveolar recruitment can be increased by lengthening end-inspiratory pause during VCV using a square wave. At the end of inspiration, when the flow is interrupted, delaying the beginning of the expiratory phase favours the re-distribution of the gases in the alveoli, leading to progressive re-opening of the collapsed alveoli. The advantage of this method derives from alveolar recruitment at the end of PIP when the lung is distended (**Fig. 46.5**).

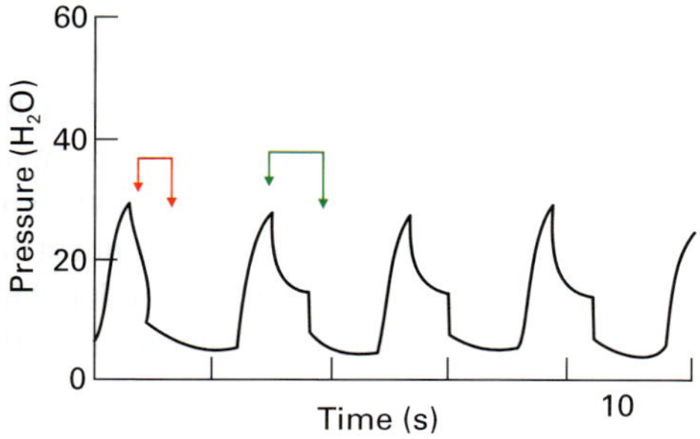

Figure 46.5 Increase of end-inspiratory pause from 10% (on the left) to 25% (on the right).

3. **'Sigh'.** The application of the 'sigh' during mechanical ventilation is an optional device in newer ventilators. A sigh was used until 1970 in anaesthesia to compensate for the tendency to atelectasis that appears during surgery. The ventilator doubles the pre-fixed tidal volume automatically for one or more breaths (**Fig. 46.6**). The increase in tidal volume can prevent the tendency to de-recruit and can expand atelectatic areas.

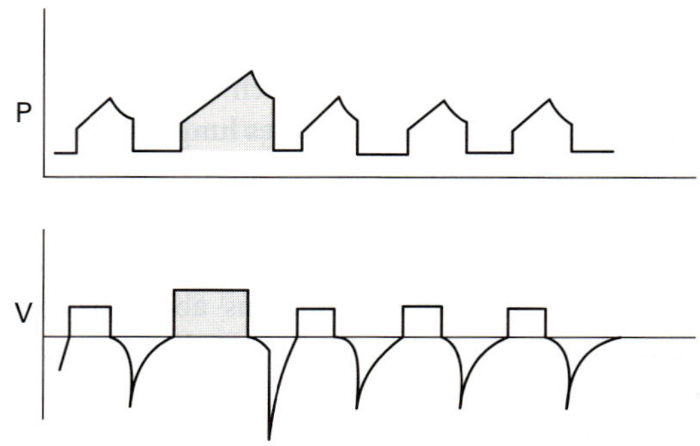

Figure 46.6 Sigh. Tidal volume is automatically doubled for one breath.

4. **Staircase step PEEP increments**

- PEEP is gradually increased from the baseline value by 1–2 cm H_2O every minute. With the increase in PEEP, the tidal volume and dynamic compliance increase till the critical opening pressure is reached. This is identified as a pressure at which there is a decline in tidal volume and dynamic compliance. At this point, the further increments in PEEP are stopped, and gradually the PEEP is reduced till the critical closing pressure is reached. This pressure is identified as the pressure at which a decline in tidal volume and dynamic compliance will occur if the set PEEP is below the closing pressure. This promotes the concept of open lung ventilation where the ventilation is maintained between the critical opening pressure and the critical closing pressure.
- Gradually increasing PEEP till a PIP of 30 cm H_2O is achieved during PCV and then gradually reduced.

Biotrauma

A large number of concomitant causes may favour the appearance of biotrauma during anaesthesia such as traumatic ventilation and oxygen supplementation.

Animal studies have demonstrated that overdistension of the lungs can cause elevations in inflammatory cytokines, increase endothelial and epithelial permeability, alter lung fluid balance and result in severe ultrastructural tissue damage. This hypothesis is attractive and has experimental support, but it is extremely difficult to prove in clinical practice.

Inflammatory mediators released by the lung owing to the increased pulmonary stresses entering the circulation could lead to distal organ dysfunction and multi-organ failure (MOF), which seriously limit the patient's recovery.

Reduction of lung stress, control of inflammation, reduction of FiO_2 and the use of protective lung strategies are fundamental in reducing biotrauma. The recommendation is made to limit end-inspiratory lung stretch to protect the lung from injury.

Ventilation of Neonates During Anaesthesia

Intraoperative ventilation of neonates requires knowledge and a thorough understanding of lung development according to gestational age. Bronchioles and alveoli develop progressively until 8 years of age.

Alveolus and terminal bronchioles of the neonate, and particularly of the premature baby, are unstable and collapse easily. Specifically, terminal bronchioles do not have a cartilaginous structure and for this reason, they have a great tendency to high-volume closure during the expiratory phase.

Airway resistance is increased due to the small diameter of bronchi and their instability. Chest and lung compliance are high.

The air–liquid interface requires a great quantity of surfactant to maintain the alveoli open. The quantity of surfactant to stabilise the alveolus and terminal bronchioles is strictly correlated with the development of the lung.

Closing volumes are greatly elevated in children up to 2 years of age and FRC is reduced during anaesthesia, leading to the formation of hypoventilated/atelectatic areas and hence hypoxaemia.

Central nervous centres controlling PaO_2 and $PaCO_2$ are not completely developed, and the chemoreceptors are less sensitive to changes in PaO_2 and $PaCO_2$. Irregularity in respiratory rhythm and apnoea are frequent patterns. In addition, ventilatory control is reduced during REM (rapid eye movement) sleep.

Persistence or appearance of pulmonary hypertension creates difficult oxygenation and favours hypoxaemia.

Persistence of ductus arteriosus and foramen ovale could produce cardiocirculatory instability and an easy return to foetal circulation.

The presence of foetal haemoglobin (Hb) could reduce peripheral oxygenation due to the ability of foetal Hb to capture oxygen and the difficulty in releasing it at the peripheral level.

A number of babies undergoing neonatal surgery have various degrees of pulmonary problems, and consequently, the need for more advanced means of mechanical ventilation might become necessary during surgery.

The most common severe pre-existing pulmonary diseases of neonates are as follows:

- RDS of premature infants
- Meconium aspiration syndrome
- Pneumonia and bronchopneumonia
- Chemical pneumonia from aspiration of gastric contents

Thus, two main lung conditions influence the ventilation of neonates during anaesthesia:

1. The neonate with healthy lungs. In this case, ventilation must guarantee gas exchange and avoid VILI.
2. The neonate with pathological lung. In this case, ventilation must guarantee gas exchange, avoid VILI and favour the resolution of lung pathology.

The mode of ventilation differs slightly depending on the age of the neonate and the type of surgery. Generally, PCV is preferred in premature infants, in newborns with respiratory distress or with any pre-existing pulmonary pathology, and during the first days of extra-uterine life. In the above-mentioned patients, VCV can also be used successfully, and it is especially useful when surgical manipulations are likely to interfere with intraoperative ventilation. If available, the neonatal anaesthesiologist must be prepared and equipped to perform anaesthesia and surgery during the administration of iNO and/or high-frequency oscillatory ventilation (HFOV).

High-Frequency Oscillatory Ventilation

HFOV is a lung-protective ventilatory modality for neonates with high airway resistance – respiratory distress syndrome, meconium aspiration, congenital diaphragmatic hernia, BPD, etc. It utilises a high ventilatory rate (10 Hz), and low tidal volumes (smaller than the anatomical dead space) to generate constant airway pressure in sinusoidal form, thereby providing oxygenation. It avoids the physical stress of opening and closing of alveoli, thus preventing lung injury.

High-Flow Nasal Oxygen

High-flow nasal oxygen (HFNO) provides warm and humid oxygen delivery at high FiO_2 (close to 100%) at high-flow rates (up to 60 litres/min). It helps in oxygenation, passive ventilation, providing positive airway pressure, reducing dead space, maintaining airway patency and reducing airway resistance. It can roughly generate 4–6 cm H_2O PEEP in the airway.

HFNO was extensively used during the COVID-19 pandemic as a step-up oxygenation strategy in early hypoxic respiratory failure. In many patients, it could avoid the need for intubation. Recently, there is increased interest in the utility of HFNO in the operating rooms.

HFNO is being considered in a difficult airway for pre-oxygenation and during the apnoea period till the definitive airway is secured.

HFNO-based oxygenation strategies are being used to prolong the duration of apnoea during airway endoscopy and tubeless airway procedures. Anaesthesia is usually maintained with propofol TIVA (total intravenous anaesthesia). THRIVE (Trans-nasal humidified rapid insufflation ventilatory exchange) and STRIVE-Hi (Spontaneous respiration using intravenous anaesthesia and hi-flow nasal oxygen) are similar in that both use HFNO devices, but the former is described in anesthetised and paralysed child while the latter in spontaneous respiration. The flows in children are set at 1–2 L/kg/min. THRIVE has been shown to nearly double the apnoea time. HFNO also delays the carbon dioxide rise by the following mechanisms:

- Passive insufflation of oxygen along the upper airway down to the alveoli causing a passive movement of carbon dioxide out of the system.
- Highly turbulent supraglottic flow vortices that produce movement of the gas.
- Cardiogenic oscillations may also partly contribute to gas movement.

SUGGESTED READINGS

1. Marraro GA. Protective lung strategies during artificial ventilation in children. *Paediatr Anaesth* 2005; 15(8):630–637.
2. Marraro GA, Sawant P, et al. eds. Mechanical ventilation in pediatric age. The National Book Depot. Mumbai, 2009
3. Plataki M, Hubmayr RD. The physical basis of ventilator-induced lung injury. *Expert Rev Respir Med* 2010; 4(3):373–385.
4. Sherman TI, Blackson T, Touch SM, et al. Physiologic effects of CPAP: Application and monitoring. *Neonatal Netw* 2003; 22(6):7–16.
5. D'Angio CT, Chess PR, Kovacs SJ, et al. Pressure-regulated volume control ventilation vs synchronized intermittent mandatory ventilation for very low-birth-weight infants: A randomized controlled trial. *Arch Pediatr Adolesc Med* 2005; 159(9):868–875.
6. Gruber PC, Gomersall CD, Leung P, et al. Randomized controlled trial comparing adaptive-support ventilation with pressure-regulated volume-controlled ventilation with automode in weaning patients after cardiac surgery. *Anesthesiology* 2008; 109(1):81–87.
7. Farias LL, Faffe DS, Xisto DG, et al. Positive end-expiratory pressure prevents lung mechanical stress caused by recruitmen/derecruitment. *Appl Physiol* 2005; 98(1):53–61.
8. Tusman G, Boehm SH, Tempra A, et al. Effects of recruitment maneuver on atelectasis in anesthetized children. *Anesthesiology* 2003; 98(1):14–22.
9. Sola A. Oxygen in neonatal anaesthesia: friend or foe? *Curr Opin Anaesthesiol* 2008; 21(3):332–339.
10. Edmark L, Kostova-Aherdan K, Enlund M, et al. Optimal oxygen concentration during induction of general anaesthesia. *Anesthesiology* 2003; 98(1):28–33.

11. Nakos G, Tsangaris H, Liokatis S, et al. Ventilator-associated pneumonia and atelectasis: evaluation through bronchoalveolar lavage fluid analysis. *Intensive Care Med* 2003; 29(4):555–563.
12. Jeong H, Tanatporn P, Ahn HJ, et al. Pressure support versus spontaneous ventilation during anesthetic emergence-effect on postoperative atelectasis: A randomized controlled trial. *Anesthesiology* 2021; 135(6):1004–1014.
13. Engelhardt T, Virag K, Veyckemans F, et al. Airway management in paediatric anaesthesia in Europe-insights from APRICOT (Anaesthesia Practice In Children Observational Trial): A prospective multicentre observational study in 261 hospitals in Europe. *Br J Anaesth* 2018; 121(1):66–75.
14. Moharana S, Jain D, Bhardwaj N, et al. Pressure support ventilation-pro decreases propofol consumption and improves postoperative oxygenation index compared with pressure-controlled ventilation in children undergoing ambulatory surgery: A randomized controlled trial. *Can J Anaesth* 2020; 67(4):445–451.

47

Paediatric Pain

Priya Nair • Ilamurugu Kaliaperumal

Pain, as described by the International Association for the Study of Pain, *is an unpleasant sensory and emotional experience associated with or resembling that associated with actual or potential tissue damage.*[1] Acute pain in children involves a combination of physiologic, psychologic, behavioural, developmental and situational factors. Persisting acute pain can result in a lower threshold for pain later in life, prime the patient for chronic pain and decrease his/her ability to cope with stress, ultimately resulting in an increased financial and social burden to society.

Mechanism of Pain

The paediatric population is a heterogeneous population. Understanding the differences in the physiology of pain within the group makes the management of pain easier. We now know that infants, regardless of age, feel pain. Even the premature infant has the anatomic and physiologic components to perceive pain and demonstrate a severe stress response to painful stimuli.

Complete myelination of nerve pathways is not required for pain transmission. Incomplete myelination results in slower conduction velocity, but it is offset by shorter conduction distances. Neural pathways required for nociception are present in the 26-week-old foetus, and though by birth almost all the pathways are developed, neonates are less able to discriminate between noxious and non-noxious stimuli. In the peripheral nervous system, C-fibres are mature but their cortical connections at the level of the dorsal horn are immature. A-β fibres, on the other hand, have well-developed connections within the spinal cord that can produce nociceptive signalling from lower-intensity stimuli. A-β fibres only recede once C-fibres have matured. Afferent transmission of nociceptive information occurs comparatively early. Descending pathways in the spinal cord involved in the modulation or inhibition of pain sensation develop comparatively later. This results in neonates having a lower threshold for pain.

Paediatric Pain: An Ignored Entity

Paediatric pain is often under-recognised and inadequately treated. Inadequate management of pain in early life leads to changes at the cortical and subcortical levels altering pain thresholds with subsequent stimuli, later in life. Management of pain differs in children when compared to adults. It is very important to remember that children are not small adults. The physiological differences between adults and children are a higher body water content, which can lead to a higher volume of distribution of water-soluble medications. They also have smaller fat and muscle stores and therefore less drug uptake by these pharmacologically inactive tissues, resulting in higher plasma concentrations of many medications. Other than the physiological differences, paediatric pain management involves a lot of patience on the clinician's part, interviews with caregivers, understanding their fears, distinguishing other issues like separation anxiety and also taking care of their goals like going to school, other activities and playing.

Acute Pain in Children

Physiological Signs of Pain in Children

The signs of pain in children are increased heart rate, respiratory rate, shallow respirations and consequently desaturation.

Decreased vagal tone (shrill cry), flushing, diaphoresis, palmar sweating and EEG changes are also some of the physical signs.

Behavioural Changes Associated with Pain

Vocalisation, changes in sleep–wake cycle, swiping or thrashing, rigidity, flaccidity, clenching of fists and facial expressions are the behavioural changes commonly associated with pain.

Stress Responses to Pain in the Neonate

Pain causes biochemical changes such as increased secretion of corticosterone, adrenaline, noradrenaline, glucagon, increased production of aldosterone and an increase in the blood level of metabolites such as glucose, lactate and pyruvate.

Assessment of Pain in Children

Pain assessment in a child is done by interviewing the child, parent(s), nursing staff and also doing a physical examination (**Box 47.1**).

Box 47.1 Factors Affecting Pain Assessment

Child factors
- Age
- Gender issues
- Cognition
- Development
- Past experiences
- Social, school and peer influences

Parent factors
- Education level and understanding of pain
- Over-solicitous parents
- Marriage/divorce

Pain factors
- Acute vs chronic pain
- Procedural, operative pain
- Simple vs complex pain

Contextual factors
- Levels of experience of nursing staff
- Beliefs and attitudes

Age-appropriate and context-appropriate assessment tools are recommended as there is no single ideal assessment tool (**Table 47.1**).

All objective rating systems rely on the physical signs of sympathetic activity coupled with behavioural assessment. There is always some difficulty in separating behaviour associated with pain from that caused by fear, need for parents and apprehension. The opinion of a parent is often valuable in making these assessments, keeping in mind that some parents lose objectivity in some situations.

Table 47.1 Commonly Used Tools in the Assessment of Pain

Scales	Age	Type	Details
VAS	7 yr onwards	Self-report	10 cm Horizontal line with 0 = no pain; 10 = max pain
Numeric	7 yr onwards	Self-report	0 = no pain; 10 = max pain
Wong-Baker Faces Pain Rating Scale	3–18 yr	Self-report faces	Six line-drawn faces range from no pain to worst pain in addition has description of faces (no hurt, hurts a little, hurts a lot, etc.)
FLACC	<3 yr and children who are unable to report	Observational (behavioural)	F – Facial expression L – Leg movement A – Activity C – Cry C – Consolability Each category scores 2; thus a possible total of 10
Children's Hospital of Eastern Ontario Pain Scale (CHEOPS)	1–12 yr	Observational (behavioural)	Cry, facial, child verbal, torso, touch and legs. Each behaviour scores 0–3

VAS, visual analogue scale.

48 ANAESTHESIA FOR CHILDREN WITH ENDOCRINE DISORDERS

Anita Shirley Joselyn • Smithamol P B •
Chris Maria Joseph • Ramamani Mariappan

Central Nervous System Causes for Paediatric Endocrinopathies

Paediatric brain tumours cause various endocrinopathies due to the tumour (size, location and invasion) or its treatment effect (surgery, chemotherapy and radiation). Endocrine deficits may be present at or even before the diagnosis of brain tumours in children. Even if they present with normal endocrine function at diagnosis, these deficits can occur during or immediately after surgery. Endocrine dysfunction is highly prevalent in brain tumour survivors who had surgery and chemotherapy/radiotherapy. Central nervous system (CNS) trauma and infection also can cause hypopituitarism. However, cranial surgeries for tumours other than the central location (diencephalon tumours) are not commonly associated with post-operative endocrine dysfunction.

Supratentorial tumours found in the diencephalon (central tumours) cause various endocrinopathies due to direct compression/invasion of the pituitary, hypothalamus and hypothalamic–pituitary–adrenal axis (HPA axis) or due to their treatment (surgery/radiation causing damage to HPA axis). Tumours arising from the third ventricle, tectum, pineal gland, pituitary gland, thalamus, hypothalamus, optic pathway and basal ganglia are considered central tumours. Craniopharyngiomas account for 80–90% of neoplasms in the pituitary and hypothalamic regions, which make up 5–13% of paediatric brain tumours. Tumours on the pituitary/hypothalamic region affect the growth hormone secretion initially, followed by gonadotropins, then adrenocorticotropic hormone (ACTH) and finally, thyroid-stimulating hormone (TSH) secretion. Posterior pituitary involvement can cause arginine vasopressin deficiency (AVP-D) (previously called diabetes insipidus) or a syndrome of inappropriate antidiuretic hormone secretion (SIADH). Alterations in sleep, appetite and temperature regulation, and weight gain show hypothalamic involvement. These children often present with pituitary gigantism/stunted growth (growth hormone alteration), precocious/delayed puberty (gonadotropic hormone alteration), central hypocortisolism (ACTH alteration), central hypothyroidism (TSH alteration) and panhypopituitarism.

Effect of Cranial Surgery (Diencephalon and Pituitary Surgery) on Endocrine Function and Its Management in Children

Alterations of water homeostasis with electrolyte disturbances such as hypernatraemia or hyponatraemia, central hypocortisolism with adrenal crisis and central hypothyroidism are the three perioperative endocrine complications in patients undergoing diencephalon or pituitary/hypothalamus surgery.

Perioperative endocrine dysfunction has many anaesthetic/perioperative implications, which can increase perioperative morbidity and mortality.

Alteration in water homeostasis: Arginine vasopressin deficiency (AVP-D), SIADH and cerebral salt wasting syndrome (CWS) are the three conditions associated with alteration in water homeostasis.

- *Arginine vasopressin deficiency (AVP-D):* previously called central diabetes insipidus (DI), is one of the most common complications during and after diencephalon and pituitary surgery and often presents with polyuria with or without polydipsia. Prompt identification and treatment are essential to prevent neurological morbidity. It can present in transient or permanent form after surgery. The reported incidence of post-operative transient and permanent AVP-D following craniopharyngioma resection surgery is 13% and 80%, respectively. Transient AVP-D can occur during surgery and lasts 5–7 days after surgery. The criteria for diagnosing intra-operative and post-operative AVP-D and its treatment are given in **Table 48.1**. Permanent AVP-D often presents as a triphasic response. During the initial phase (1–2 days), there is hypotonic polyuria causing hypernatraemia and dehydration followed by increased

Table 48.1 Criteria for Diagnosis and Management of Perioperative AVP-D Deficiency

Timeline	Criteria for Diagnosing Arginine Vasopressin Deficiency (AVP-D)	Management
Pre- and post-operative criteria	Excretion of a urinary volume >2 L/m²/day, >150 ml/kg/day in neonates, >100–110 ml/kg/day in children up to age 2, and >40–50 ml/kg/day in older children. Serum osmolality >300 mOsm/kg at the same time as inappropriately dilute urine (urine Osmol <300 mOsmol/kg)	• Patients with intact thirst mechanisms are allowed to drink water to compensate for the water deficit • In small children who cannot access free water or in older children who are adipsic and drowsy, maintenance fluid in the form of 5% D with 0.45% NS or 5% D is administered. Two-thirds of urine output can be replaced with 2.5% D + 0.2% NS • In the presence of fluid deficit with hypotension, Ringer's lactate solution (RL) or plasmalyte can be used along with the ADH analogue • Persistent polyuria with hypernatraemia should be treated with ADH analogue as it has prolonged antidiuretic with less vasopressor effect – *Oral desmopressin (DDAVP):* 25–500 μg/day in three divided doses – *Nasal spray*: 2.5–20 μg/day in one–three doses – *Sublingual*: 1–4 μg/kg/day. (Dose needs to be cautiously individualised and titrated with the lowest possible dose until stable euvolemic status and normal sodium levels throughout the day are achieved) *Overdosing of desmopressin will cause water intoxication with anuria and hyponatraemia and can cause cerebral oedema, and fluid overload.* In patients with severe fluctuation in sodium and serum osmolality, ***vasopressin infusion*** should be started with close titration
Intra-operative criteria	Urine output > 4 ml/kg/hr Serum sodium >145 mEq/L Serum osmolality > 300 mOsm/kg Urine osmolality < 300 mOsm/kg Urine specific gravity < 1.005 (Exclude other causes of increased urine output such as mannitol, furosemide, hyperglycaemia and osmotic contrast agents before diagnosing as AVP-D)	Vasopressin infusion at 1 mU/kg/hr and increase the infusion rate every 5–10 min max up to 10 mU/kg/hr to decrease the urine output to <2 ml/kg/hr. Replace the fluid deficit with RL or 0.45% NS during surgery if hypernatraemia persists IVF at two-thirds of maintenance + fluid for blood replacement and haemodynamic support Replace the blood loss with 0.9% NS/RL/5% albumin/blood product Check serum sodium every Q 4–6 hourly with or without serum osmolality
Caution: Overzealous treatment with vasopressin/DDAVP can cause dilutional hyponatraemia, cerebral oedema, seizures and fluid overload. Hence, frequent sodium monitoring is needed.		

secretion of antidiuretic hormone (ADH) from the degenerated hypothalamic and posterior pituitary cells causing SIADH (3–14 days), which manifests as hyponatraemia with fluid overload and hypertonic oliguria. Finally, during the third phase, permanent AVP-D occurs (after 14 days) due to irreversible damage to the hypothalamus or posterior pituitary and presents with hypotonic polyuria and hypernatraemia needing permanent replacement of AVP. Small children <4 years, radical excision and severe fluctuations in serum sodium during the immediate perioperative period are some of the risk factors for developing permanent AVP-D.

Craniopharyngioma is the common tumour (80–90%) involving the hypothalamic and the pituitary region in children; it peaks between 5 and 14 years of age and often presents with signs and symptoms of hypopituitarism and AVP-D. Paediatric anaesthesiologists may meet children with AVP-D when they come for craniopharyngioma resection, adjuvant radiation (post-surgery partial excision status), neuroimaging, various non-neurological surgeries or for repeat cranial surgery for tumour recurrence. Hence, paediatric anaesthesiologists should have a thorough knowledge of the perioperative management of children with hypothalamic and pituitary dysfunction.

- *Syndrome of inappropriate ADH secretion (SIADH):* This syndrome is associated with increased secretion of ADH causing dilutional hyponatraemia with fluid overload and hypertonic oliguria. It is treated with fluid restriction and sodium replacement for symptomatic hyponatraemia. There are no studies in children about the use of ADH antagonists (vaptans), which competitively interfere with the binding of ADH to the vasopressin 2 receptor in the kidney. Before treating patients with SIADH-induced hyponatraemia, one should rule out CSW and adrenal crisis. The treatment of SIADH and CSW are completely different as SIADH needs fluid restriction while CSW needs volume and sodium replacement with 0.9% NaCl.
- *CSW syndrome*: CSW syndrome is due to the inappropriate (increased) secretion of natriuretic peptides such as pro-brain natriuretic peptides and atrial natriuretic peptides leading to natriuresis and diuresis, resulting in salt and volume depletion. Volume replacement and sodium supplementation are necessary while treating this condition. Since cortisol deficiency is common after pituitary surgery, one should also rule out cortisol deficiency while treating CSW syndrome. The signs and symptoms of CSW and adrenal crisis are almost similar, except that hyperkalaemia and hypoglycaemia are seen in patients with an adrenal crisis. Adrenal crisis needs the administration of hydrocortisone along with volume and sodium replacement. **Table 48.2** depicts the

Table 48.2 Difference between SIADH and CSW Syndrome and Adrenal Crisis

Parameters	SIADH	CSW Syndrome	Adrenal Crisis
Extracellular volume status	Normo to hypervolemia	Hypovolemia	Hypovolemia
Vital signs	Heart rate and blood pressure - normal	High heart rate and low blood pressure	High heart rate and low blood pressure
Serum sodium	Low	Low	Low
Serum cortisol	Normal	Normal	Low
Urine sodium Net sodium loss	High Normal	High High	High High
Serum osmolality	Low	Low	Low
Urine osmolality	High	High	High
Urine output	Oliguria	Polyuria	Polyuria
Treatment	Fluid restriction symptomatic hyponatraemia: 3% NaCl	Volume replacement with 0.9% NaCl After volume replacement, symptomatic hyponatraemia can be treated with 3% NaCl	Volume replacement with 0.9% NaCl along with hydrocortisone After volume replacement, symptomatic hyponatraemia can be treated with 3% NaCl

difference between SIADH, CSW syndrome and adrenal crisis.

Central hypocortisolism with an adrenal crisis: Children with pre-operative cortisol deficiency due to dysfunction of the HPA axis should be started on oral hydrocortisone/prednisolone supplements. Based on the recent recommendation, 8–10 mg/m^2/day of hydrocortisone in three divided doses should be given in patients with adrenal insufficiency (AI). Children who are on pre-operative steroid replacement who are undergoing surgery should receive a stress dose of intravenous hydrocortisone (2 mg/kg or 50 mg/m^2) before the start of anaesthesia and should be continued for 24 hours as an intermittent bolus or as a continuous infusion based on the body weight or age (dose information in 'Adrenal Disorders' section).

Central hypothyroidism: Central hypothyroidism has many intra-operative anaesthetic implications, such as delayed drug metabolism and awakening, myocardial depression, bradyarrhythmia and hypothermia. Hence, children should be made euthyroid before surgery. Isolated central hypothyroidism is rare during the post-operative period and is always associated with central hypocortisolism. Starting the children on levothyroxine without starting the stress dose of hydrocortisone prior to levothyroxine can precipitate an adrenal crisis because of increased cortisol metabolism. The dose of levothyroxine is 3.0–5.0 μg/kg/day for small children and 2–4 μg/kg/day for adolescents.

Hypothalamic obesity: Children undergoing sellar or suprasellar surgeries are more prone to hypothalamic damage. Hypothalamic damage can cause hyperphagia (due to damage to the centres of appetite regulation), sleep disturbances, decreased energy expenditure, hyperinsulinism and hypopituitarism, all can lead to the hypothalamic syndrome. The hypothalamic syndrome is characterised by morbid obesity and its metabolic consequences in combination with neurocognitive symptoms. Some of the anaesthetic implications are a difficult airway, difficult intravenous cannulation, delayed awakening due to impaired metabolism of anaesthetic drugs and hypothermia, and obesity-related metabolic complications.

Effect of Radiotherapy on Endocrine Function and its Anaesthetic Implication in Brain Tumour Survivors

Studies have shown that the technique of radiotherapy (proton vs photon therapy) and the dose used for radiation (<20 Gy vs 20–40 Gy vs >40 Gy) have an influence on post-operative endocrine dysfunction in children undergoing radiotherapy. Photon therapy and high radiation dose are associated with an increased incidence of post-operative endocrine dysfunction. Growth hormone deficiency is commonly seen as both short- and long-term consequences of radiation in children with brain tumours. Gonadotropic dysfunction (precocious/delayed puberty), thyroid deficiencies (central and peripheral hypothyroidism) and ACTH deficiency (adrenal crisis) are also common after radiotherapy. Current guidelines recommend six-monthly evaluations of clinical (height/pubertal growth) and biochemical (thyroid function test, morning cortisol level and gonadotropic hormone levels) parameters for children of prepubertal and peripubertal age groups and yearly evaluation for children of the adolescent age group who underwent radiotherapy for a brain tumour. A prompt diagnosis and treatment with the right hormonal therapy are crucial for improving the quality of life and psychosocial well-being and best bone mineralisation for brain tumour survivors. Children who have undergone radiation and are scheduled for repeat neurosurgical (tumour recurrence) or non-neurosurgical surgeries should undergo thorough endocrine evaluation before surgery. Positioning for surgery should be done carefully as these children are at risk for vertebral and long bone fractures due to decreased bone mineral density.

Effect of Chemotherapy on Endocrine Function and its Anaesthetic Implications in Brain Tumour Survivors

Children who are treated with chemotherapeutic drugs can have associated endocrine dysfunction. Compared to radiotherapy, the incidence of endocrine dysfunction is less with chemotherapy. Alkylating agents used for chemotherapy can cause premature ovarian insufficiency in females and impaired secretion of testosterone and spermatogenesis in male.

Thyroid Disorders

The foetal thyroid gland begins to function at 10–12 weeks of gestation, and it is the primary source of thyroid hormone in the developing foetus. There are two biologically active hormones: thyroxine (T_4) and 3, 5, 3′-triiodothyronine (T_3). The production of normal quantities of thyroid hormones depends on the availability of exogenous iodine, with diet being the primary source. The thyroid hormone production is controlled by the hypothalamic–pituitary–thyroid axis. Regulation of thyroidal biosynthesis and secretion of T_4 and T_3 is by TSH, which is produced from the anterior pituitary. The thyroid hormones are critical determinants of brain and somatic development in infants and of metabolic activity in adults. These hormones affect the function of every organ system. The hormones influence growth and maturation of tissues, enhance tissue function, and stimulate protein synthesis and carbohydrate and lipid metabolism. Thyroid disorders account for a considerable proportion of paediatric endocrine disorders. The disorder can be due to the deficiency or excess of thyroid hormone.

Hypothyroidism

It is the most common thyroid disorder in children and occurs due to abnormally low production of thyroid hormone. Untreated hypothyroidism in childhood has permanent adverse effects on physical, intellectual and neurological development. The cause of hypothyroidism may be due to a pathology in the thyroid gland (primary hypothyroidism:congenital and acquired), pituitary gland (secondary hypothyroidism) or in the hypothalamus (tertiary hypothyroidism).

Thyroid function tests include serum TSH, total T_4 or free T_3. Serum TSH is the most sensitive test for diagnosing primary thyroid disorders and includes noticeable changes in total T_4 and T_3 values. Since thyroid hormone affects all metabolically active cells in our body, the deficiency causes a wide range of systemic features. Typical symptoms and signs in children include short stature, fatigue or exercise intolerance, hypothermia and cold intolerance, slow heart rate, narrow pulse pressure, weight gain, muscle pseudohypertrophy, slow relaxing deep tendon reflexes, hair loss or thinning of hair, dry, coarse skin, hoarse voice, constipation and coarse facial features. Severe hypothyroidism is rare but can be associated with coma, cardiovascular collapse, hyponatraemia, hypothermia and respiratory failure. Myxoedema coma can occur in profoundly hypothyroid individuals exposed to an external stress like infection, surgery, hypnotics or cold temperature. It is a medical emergency with a mortality rate higher than 50%. Testing of congenital hypothyroidism occurs with the neonatal screen. Early detection and starting of thyroid replacement are essential to avoid permanent neurologic sequelae.

Thyroid replacement with levothyroxine (LT_4) is to normalise T_4 and TSH. The dose in neonates is 10–15 μ/kg/day, in young children aged 1–3 years is 4–6 μ/kg/day, aged 3–10 years is 3–5 μ/kg/day, and aged 10 years to adolescents is 2–4 μ/kg/day. The treatment should start with one-fourth of the expected dose, with gradual titration every 4–6 weeks. After dose stabilisation, children and adolescent should undergo regular follow-up with clinical examination and serum TSH level and the dose adjusted accordingly.

Thyroid function should be assessed in the pre-operative period to ensure that the patient is clinically and biochemically euthyroid. If the patient is recently diagnosed with thyroid disease or hypothyroid even if on medication, elective surgery is deferred till a euthyroid state is achieved. Children with subclinical or mild hypothyroidism can undergo urgent surgery without delay. Thyroid replacement can be started and continued with the same regimen as outpatients. For children with moderate-to-severe hypothyroidism, surgery should be postponed, if possible. If urgent surgery is indicated, pre-operative treatment with IV LT_4 with or without glucocorticoids should be given to prevent myxoedema coma. An exception to this strategy applies to children who are scheduled for cardiovascular surgery or cardiac catheterisation in which hormone replacement could precipitate or worsen unstable coronary syndromes. Hormone replacement could be initiated post-operatively in children with cardiovascular disease undergoing cardiac surgery or cardiac evaluation. Assess for features of severe hypothyroidism like coma, pericardial effusion and heart failure. Due to the instances of sudden death in children with myxedematous heart diseases, they should receive one-fourth of the maintenance dose of thyroid hormone with gradual increments over 2–4 weeks till maintenance dose is achieved. Stress dose of steroids is needed if associated with adrenal insufficiency (AI). Proper airway assessment and plan if goitre is compromising the airway.

Anaesthesia Management

Mild or well-controlled hypothyroidism hardly affects anaesthesia. The anaesthetic management of the symptomatic patient with hypothyroidism can be problematic and requires caution when any depressant medications are given. Prolonged effects may result from decreased drug metabolism. The ASA standard monitors are enough in well-controlled patients. Invasive monitoring may be needed when significant fluid shift or blood loss is anticipated. Adequate precautions should be taken to minimise heat loss intraoperatively. If difficult intubation is anticipated due to goitre, decision on airway management to be based on thorough pre-operative evaluation of mass with imaging. Extubation should be performed after assessment for readiness as there is a tendency for delayed emergence from ventilatory support.

In the post-operative period, heart rate, oxygen saturation, blood pressure and respiratory rate should be monitored. Patients with delayed emergence from anaesthesia need post-operative ventilation. In case of a thyroid surgery, complications of airway (nerve injury, cervical hematoma and tracheomalacia) and hypocalcaemia need to be anticipated and dealt with.

Hyperthyroidism

Hyperthyroidism refers to hyperfunctioning of the thyroid gland, with excessive secretion of active thyroid hormones. Thyrotoxicosis refers to the clinical and biochemical manifestations of excess thyroid hormones. Hyperthyroidism occurs less frequently than hypothyroidism in children. The most common causes are congenital hyperthyroidism and Graves' disease (toxic goitre).

Congenital hyperthyroidism is a transient phenomenon seen in newborns due to the transplacental transfer of thyroid-stimulating antibody from mothers with Graves' disease. Most of these babies have a goitre and typically appear restless and anxious or irritable. Graves' disease is an autoimmune disorder, which is the most common cause of childhood hyperthyroidism. Its peak incidence occurs during adolescence, and it is most often seen in girls in the 10–15 years of age group.

Signs and symptoms of hyperthyroidism are those of a hypermetabolic state. Early features include emotional disturbances, motor hyperactivity and nervousness. Affected children are progressively more restless and irritable, and may have sweatiness, weight loss despite a normal or increased appetite, palpitations, brisk reflexes, heat intolerance, insomnia, diarrhoea, tremors and fidgetiness. Most children have obvious exophthalmos and a palpable diffuse goitre. The cardiopulmonary symptoms include tachycardia with a wide pulse pressure, systolic hypertension, palpitations, dyspnoea and cardiac enlargement, which may progress to frank cardiac failure. Rarely mitral regurgitation or atrial fibrillation may be present. Other medical conditions associated with long-term hyperthyroidism include irregular menstruation and osteoporosis.

Laboratory investigations: serum T_3 and T_4 levels are high in hyperthyroidism. As TSH secretion is suppressed, it may be unmeasurable. If needed neck X-rays, CT or MRI can be done to assess airway compromise.

Treatment is aimed at controlling the cardiovascular effects. Commonly used β-blocker drug is propranolol (1–2 mg/kg/day), and dose slowly titrated to effect. Methimazole is the antithyroid drug recommended in infants, children and adolescents. The FDA recently recommended that propylthiouracil cannot be used in paediatrics due to reports of liver failure. Saturated solution of potassium Iodide can be given orally, one drop 8 hourly. The clinical response to drugs is evident in 1–3 weeks and then may need up to

Adrenal disorders can be adrenal cortical disorders and adrenal medullary disorders.

Adrenocortical Disorders

Adrenocortical disorders result from insufficiency of one or more of adrenal steroids or from adrenal steroid excess. Cushing syndrome (hypercortisolism), primary hyperaldosteronism (Conn syndrome), hypoaldosteronism and adrenal insufficiency (AI) will be discussed here.

Cushing Syndrome (CS)

Cushing syndrome (CS) is a multisystem disorder due to the prolonged exposure to excess glucocorticoids. CS can be classified into ACTH-dependent (e.g. ACTH-secreting pituitary adenoma) and ACTH-independent types (exogenous steroid and adrenal tumours). In children, the most common cause of CS is exogenous administration of steroid. In childhood, the most common symptom is weight gain, with lack of height gain consistent with weight gain. Other features are muscle wasting, moon facies, hypertension, headaches, hirsutism, amenorrhea, delayed sexual development, hyperglycaemia, osteopenia, skin changes and growth deceleration. The appropriate treatment of CS depends on the accurate diagnosis and classification of the disease. Screening tests are overnight small dose dexamethasone suppression test, 24-hour urinary free cortisol and creatinine, and measurement of nocturnal salivary cortisol concentrations.

Anaesthesia Management

Anaesthesia management for a child presenting with CS for adrenal or extra-adrenal surgeries should take into consideration the secondary manifestations like obesity, airway concerns, hypertension, and skin and bone fragility. Stress dose of steroid should be administered during induction of anaesthesia.

Conn Syndrome

Primary aldosteronism is also known as Conn syndrome. It is the most common cause of mineralocorticoid excess. It is characterised by hypertension, polyuria and muscle weakness. Biochemical investigations show a hypokalaemic metabolic alkalosis with high aldosterone concentrations and low plasma renin activity. Surgical resection is the treatment for unilateral adrenal lesion. Bilateral adrenal hyperplasia is managed with spironolactone and eplerenone (competitive aldosterone antagonist). Treatment is surgical resection and adjuvant chemotherapy.

Anaesthetic Management

Anaesthesia management includes pre-operative restoration of intravascular volume, correction of electrolyte imbalance and renal dysfunction, and control of hypertension. No specific anaesthesia technique or medications are recommended. Invasive blood pressure monitoring is needed for children with uncontrolled pre-operative blood pressures. Bilateral manipulation of the adrenal glands to excise multiple functional tumours may need supplemental cortisol if transient hypocortisolism is a consideration.

Hypoaldosteronism

Hypoaldosteronism is a rare but potentially severe condition. It is due to either insufficient production of aldosterone or lack of responsiveness to aldosterone. It can be isolated or in the context of primary adrenal failure. Causes of hypoaldosteronism in children include salt wasting forms of congenital adrenal hyperplasia (CAH), adrenal hypoplasia congenita, aldosterone synthase deficiency and pseudo hypoaldosteronism. Biochemically, it is characterised by hyponatraemia, hyperkalaemia, prerenal azotaemia and hyperchloremic metabolic acidosis. Affected infants present with salt wasting, failure to thrive, fatal hyperkalaemia and shock. Investigations include essential serum hormonal levels, renal ultrasound and urine culture to find the underlying cause. Initial treatment includes restoration of intravascular volume and management of electrolyte imbalance. In case of salt wasting crisis, affected children are initially treated with both hydrocortisone and fludrocortisone while waiting for the hormonal investigations.

Anaesthesia management includes supportive measures for metabolic and electrolyte disorders.

Adrenal Insufficiency (AI)

Adrenal insufficiency is a potentially life-threatening and rare condition defined by glucocorticoid deficiency, with or without associated mineralocorticoid deficiency. AI can be primary, secondary and iatrogenic. Primary AI results from defects in the adrenal gland and is also known as Addison's disease. Approximately 75% of cases of primary AI in childhood are due to CAH, which is caused by 21-hydroxylase deficiency. In primary disease, the glands are unable to produce enough glucocorticoid, mineralocorticoid and androgen hormones.

Cortisol levels follow a proper circadian rhythm, with peak levels resulting from an ACTH surge in the early morning and trough levels later in the day. Morning serum cortisol level of less than 5 µg/dl is suggestive of AI. The classic definition of AI includes baseline plasma cortisol level of less than 20 µg/dl and a cortisol level of less than 20 µg/dl after ACTH stimulation. The short 250-µg ACTH stimulation test is a reliable test to assess the integrity of the HPA axis. All steroids except dexamethasone must be discontinued before the test. A normal ACTH stimulation test result is a plasma cortisol level more than 25 µg/dl. A positive test means a poor response to ACTH, which indicates an impairment of the adrenal cortex. Absolute AI is characterised as a low baseline cortisol level and a positive result on the ACTH stimulation test. Relative AI is indicated when the baseline cortisol level is higher, but the result of ACTH stimulation test is positive.

The signs and symptoms of AI depend on hormone that are deficient and the severity of the defects. Those presenting with the acute condition (Addisonian crisis) may have abdominal pain, nausea, vomiting, dehydration and postural hypotension. The chronic condition has an insidious onset with a wide range of symptoms like headache, dizziness, abdominal pain, weight loss, weakness and fatiguability, hypoglycaemia, dehydration and electrolyte disturbances (hyperkalaemia, hyponatraemia and acidosis).

Perioperative Steroid Management

Mineralocorticoid deficiency can be managed by using saline infusion and avoiding potassium in IV fluid. A single daily oral dose of 9-α-fluorocortisol acetate is sufficient if the patient can tolerate it. Neonates require high doses like 0.4 mg daily. If oral route is not feasible then 20 mg of IV hydrocortisone (equivalent to 9-α-fluorocortisol) can be given. Glucocorticoid deficiency is treated with cortisol (hydrocortisone) replacement. The normal replacement dose in unstressed children is 10–15 mg/m^2/day, which is twice the normal production. In conditions of physiological stress like trauma, fever, acute illness, and surgery, three to ten times of normal cortisol may need to be used.

Hypothalamic–Pituitary–Adrenal Axis Suppression Caused by Exogenous Steroid Therapy

HPA axis suppression can occur with exogenous steroid usage for treatment of conditions like inflammatory and autoimmune disease. HPA suppression places steroid-dependent children at increased risk for complications in the perioperative period because they are unable to respond to stress with an appropriate increase in the adrenal secretion of glucocorticoid. Dosage of cortisol or its equivalent that exceed 15 mg/m^2/day for more than 2–4 weeks produces HPA suppression. If treatment is less than two weeks, prompt recovery happens in 2 weeks. If it is more than 2 weeks, the HPA suppression may last for 1 week to 6 months.

Stress Dose for Children on Replacement Steroids

The latest practice is to use stress dose only for moderate and major surgeries not for minor ones.

- If the dose of glucocorticoid was less than the replacement dose (10–15 mg/m^2/day), independent of the duration there is no need of supplementary dose.
- If the dose of glucocorticoid was more than the replacement dose, HPA suppression will occur, and steroid will be required – see dose below.

Stress Dose Based on Type of Surgery

Children on long duration of high dose steroids should receive stress dose based on the type of surgery. The most common recommendation for perioperative steroid coverage is with IV hydrocortisone hemi succinate at the time of induction of anaesthesia. The stress dose for minor procedure is single dose of 25 mg/m^2 of hydrocortisone and for moderate one is 50 mg/m^2 with induction of anaesthesia. For major stress 100 mg/m^2 is can be given as continuous infusion or divided into four doses per day. This dose is usually continued for 1–3 days after more complex surgical procedures. Then, the dose is tapered post-operatively and replaced with the usual regimen once tolerating the oral route. The physiological stress of surgery and anaesthesia usually lasts for 48–72 hours.

Stress Dose Based on the Body Weight

The following dose is recommended. The child with

- <10 kg weight: 25 mg /24 hours
- 11–20 kg weight: 50 mg/24 hours
- >20 kg weight: 100 mg/24 hours

Based on age, the following dose is recommended. The child

- <1 year: 25 mg/24 hours
- 1–6 years: 50 mg/24 hours
- >6 years: 100 mg/24 hours

HPA suppression can also occur due to chronic use of oral, nasal, topical and inhaler steroids. Adrenal suppression is rarer in these modes, but some drugs like fluticasone propionate in high doses can cause HPA suppression. Anaesthesiologist should have a high index of suspicion of possible adrenal suppression in an asthmatic child on inhaler steroid who develop hypotension or hypoglycaemia in the perioperative period.

Acute AI or Adrenal Crisis

Acute AI should be considered in the differential diagnosis of haemodynamic instability, especially unresponsive to the usual measures. In patients with Al, an adrenal crisis is precipitated by absolute or relative glucocorticoid deficiency. Recognition and treatment of salt-losing adrenal crisis is especially important for survival. Clinical presentation is hyponatraemia, hyperkalaemia, dehydration, hypotension and shock in the severe stage. Treatment includes repletion of circulating glucocorticoids, and replacement of water and sodium deficits. IV dose of hydrocortisone sodium hemisuccinate is 50 mg/m^2 (maximum dose is 100 mg). Initial bolus dose is followed by the same dose divided over the next 24 hours, either as a constant IV infusion or as four divided doses. Bolus of D5 normal saline, 10 ml/kg IV to be given and repeat if needed. Haemodynamic support with vasopressors. Metabolic acidosis and electrolyte imbalance usually resolve with fluid and steroid administration. Throughout the treatment, electrolytes and water balance must be monitored to prevent water retention and its complications.

No specific anaesthesia technique or agents are recommended in managing patients with or at risk of AI. Etomidate is to be avoided in these group of patients as it inhibits the cortisol synthesis transiently. Patients with untreated AI for emergency procedures should be managed with invasive monitoring, corticosteroids, fluid and electrolyte resuscitation. Minimal doses of anaesthetic drugs are recommended as myocardial depression and muscle weakness are a part of the clinical presentation.

Adrenal Medullary Disorders

The adrenal medulla is composed of chromaffin (pheochromoblast) cells, which synthesise and store catecholamines (CCAs) norepinephrine, epinephrine and dopamine. CCAs are responsible for the body's 'fight-or-flight' response. Tumours that arise from the adrenal medulla are termed pheochromocytomas and they secrete CCAs. Pheochromocytomas and paragangliomas are rare neuroendocrine tumours (NETs) arising from neural crest-derived cells or organs known as paraganglia. In children these tumours are more frequently familial, extra-adrenal, bilateral and multi-focal compared to adults. Tumours with extra-adrenal origins are called paragangliomas and either secrete CCAs or are non-functional. Paragangliomas are seen anywhere along the abdominal sympathetic chain and in other sites like neck, mediastinum, walls of the bladder or ureters. Pheochromocytomas has less than 5% incidence and can be associated with hereditary syndromes like Von Hippel–Lindau (VHL) disease, familial paraganglioma and MEN type 2A or 2B (**Table 48.3**).

Among hypertensive children, the incidence of surgically confirmed pheochromocytoma or paraganglioma ranges from 0.8 to 1.7%. Children around 11–12 years of age are usually affected with a male predominance (2:1). Pheochromocytoma release substantial amounts of catecholamines (CCAs) like adrenaline, noradrenaline, dopamine,

Table 48.3 Multiple Endocrine Neoplasia Syndromes

MEN Syndrome	Affected Organs	Disorder
Werner syndrome Type I (Familial)	Parathyroid gland Pancreas Pituitary gland	Hypercalcaemia Hypoglycaemia Peptic ulcer
Sipple syndrome Type 2A (Autosomal dominant)	Thyroid gland Parathyroid Adrenal medulla	Medullary carcinoma Hypercalcaemia Pheochromocytoma
Wagenmann-Froboese syndrome Type 2B Autosomal dominant	Nervous system Thyroid gland Adrenal medulla	Multiple neuromas Medullary carcinoma Pheochromocytoma

somatostatin, calcitonin, oxytocin, vasopressin, insulin and ACTH. Adrenal pheochromocytoma secretes adrenaline and noradrenaline, while extra-adrenal tumours secrete only noradrenaline.

The most characteristic feature is hypertension. These tumours can produce paroxysms of hypertension and other symptoms. In between the paroxysms the patient can be asymptomatic, making the diagnosis challenging. Uncontrolled blood pressures can cause hypertensive encephalopathy and seizures. Wide fluctuations in blood pressure are characterised and may be followed by hypotension and syncope. In severe cases, patients can present with chest pain, pulmonary oedema and cardiac failure.

Other clinical symptoms include paroxysmal hypertension, headache, tachycardia, palpitation, pallor, sweating and vomiting. As well as weight loss despite excessive appetite, polyuria, polydipsia, hyperglycaemia and abdominal pain. Affected children are often emotionally labile and have an anxious expression. Hypercalcaemia can be seen in familial cases.

It is very important to diagnose pheochromocytoma in the pre-operative period. Life-threatening complications can happen in the perioperative period in undiagnosed cases. The most specific diagnostic test is demonstration of increased level of CCAs. Urine CCA concentrations are directly proportional to circulating levels. Twenty-four-hour urinary excretion of the primary CCAs and their metabolites 3-methoxy-4-hydroxy vanillyl mandelic acid and metanephrine is the primary means of establishing the diagnosis. The plasma-free metanephrine has 100% sensitivity and 94% specificity. Normal values change with age, so use age-specific norms while interpreting the results. Radiological investigations like CT, MRI and I^{131} meta-iodobenzylguanidine scan help to locate the tumour. Differential venous catheterisation may be required to obtain blood from various sites for CCA levels if multiple tumours are suspected.

Surgical resection is the only curative procedure. Surgical options are open adrenalectomy for large tumours, laparoscopic anterior transperitoneal or posterior retroperitoneal adrenalectomy, and cortical sparing resection for VHL, MEN etc. Anaesthesia care should be same for diagnostic tests and tumour resection.

Pre-operative investigations include serum electrolytes, renal function test, fasting blood sugar, ECG and ECHO. There may be hyperglycaemia, hypokalaemia and cardiomyopathy. The patient should be evaluated for MEN syndromes. Pre-operative medical preparation of the patient to block the effects of released CCAs is a prerequisite for definitive surgery. Commonly used antihypertensives are α-blockers like phenoxybenzamine and phentolamine. Symptomatic treatment includes starting oral phenoxybenzamine over a period of several days to weeks before surgery. Starting dose of phenoxybenzamine is 0.2 mg/kg once daily, maximum (adult) dose is 10 mg. Adjust the dose and frequency based on the clinical response, maximum three doses per day. The clinical effect is obtained once haematocrit is decreased and dose adjustment is needed if orthostatic changes occur with vital signs. Increased oral fluid intake is needed to avoid severe orthostatic changes with phenoxybenzamine. Phentolamine can be used for rapid α adrenergic blockade. Dose of phentolamine is 1–2 mg/kg/day in four divided doses, which can be increased until blood pressure returns to normal. If needed β-blocker drugs like propranolol to be added to control the heart rate. β-Blocker drug should never be used without prior or concurrent α-blocker therapy as unopposed α agonism can cause cardiac failure due to increased afterload. Proper pre-operative sedative premedication is needed to alleviate anxiety. Oral or IV midazolam with or without opioids can be used.

Anaesthetic management for pheochromocytoma excision can be divided into two stages. The first stage includes efforts to keep the blood pressure down while the tumour is isolated, and its blood vessels are ligated. The second stage involves efforts to keep the blood pressure elevated thereafter. The main goals of anaesthesia include normalisation of blood pressure, heart rate and functions of other organs, restoration of volume depletion and prevent surgery-induced CCA storms. Induction of anaesthesia is extremely critical as inadequate sedation may cause severe hypertension, whereas excessive α-blockade with inadequate blood volume re-expansion may cause severe hypotension. Intravenous induction can be done if IV access is present. Ketamine is contraindicated due to CCA release. Mask induction with sevoflurane is well tolerated if haemodynamic parameters are well-controlled. Then, IV cannula can be inserted slowly in proper plane of anaesthesia. Halothane is not safe due to its arrhythmogenic nature. Stress response of laryngoscopy to be prevented with IV lignocaine 1 mg/kg or IV fentanyl 1 μ/kg. Muscle relaxant with minimum cardiac effects like vecuronium is preferred. Pancuronium is to be avoided as it causes tachycardia. Meticulous monitoring and management of blood pressure should be done with automated blood pressure device before and during induction. After induction intra-arterial catheter should be inserted for beat-to-beat monitoring of blood pressure. Central venous line to be inserted for better fluid management and for infusion of emergency drugs. Anaesthesia is maintained with isoflurane/sevoflurane, air and oxygen. Desflurane should be avoided due to chance of tachycardia and hypertension. Addition of fentanyl 5–10 μ/kg or remifentanil 0.3–1 μg/kg/min will reduce the stress response and provide better haemodynamics. As remifentanil is shorter acting, a longer acting opioid should be given before the end of surgery to avoid hypertension due to pain while awakening. Epidural analgesia is an excellent method to reduce the stress response and CCA release due to surgical stimulation.

None of the anaesthesia techniques can block the CCA release due to direct surgical manipulation of tumour tissue. Hypertensive episodes during tumour manipulation can be managed by deepening the plane of anaesthesia, and infusions of sodium nitroprusside (0.5–5 μg/kg/min), nitroglycerine (0.5–1.5 μg/kg/min), phentolamine as an infusion or incremental doses of 1–2 mg, esmolol (bolus 500 μg/kg followed by an infusion of 50–200 μg/kg/min), dexmedetomidine (1 μg/kg over 10 minute followed by 0.5 μg/kg/hr), nicardipine 0.5–2.5 μ/kg/min and magnesium (loading dose 50 mg/kg followed by an infusion of 15–30 mg/kg/hr). A single drug or a combination regimen might be used depending on the severity, familiarity and availability of above medications. Infusions of only short-acting vasodilators are recommended for control of blood pressure before tumour resection because with removal of the tumour, vasodilatation due to persistent α-blockade and loss of excess CCAs may cause precipitous hypotension.

Hypotension is treated with discontinuation of vasodilator infusions, titration of anaesthetic agents, crystalloids, colloid, blood and blood products as per need. If all these measures fail, direct acting vasoconstrictors like noradrenaline, adrenaline or vasopressin infusion may be necessary. During surgery, temperature, blood glucose, arterial blood gases and urine output should be monitored. Hyperglycaemia occur with high CCA level and hypoglycaemia can occur after tumour resection. Vigilant monitoring with ECG is needed due to high chance of arrythmias. Decision for post-operative extubation or elective ventilation is based on the haemodynamic and other vital parameters. Postoperatively the patients should be monitored in ICU with ECG and arterial blood pressure monitoring. Hypertension usually settles in 24–72 hours. If hypertension persists rule out residual tumour. Good post-operative analgesia should be provided.

Diabetes Mellitus

Diabetes mellitus (DM) is a chronic metabolic condition characterised by hyperglycaemia. Type 1 diabetes is caused by autoimmune β-cell destruction and is commonly seen in children whereas Type 2 DM is commonly seen in middle aged adults with insulin resistance and relative insulin deficiency. Other causes of DM in children include mitochondrial disorders, disease of exocrine pancreas (cystic-fibrosis related diabetes), drug induced (steroids) and genetic syndromes (Prader Willi syndrome, Down syndrome, Turner's syndrome and Wolfram syndrome).

In a perioperative setting, it is important to maintain glycaemic levels under control as the perioperative fasting and surgical stress can push a patient into hypo/hyperglycaemia, respectively. Vigilant monitoring of blood glucose at the onset of the procedure and at regular intervals helps with prompt management of dysglycemia in children.

Management of Perioperative Hypoglycaemia

Blood sugars less than 70 mg/dl in children and less than 50 mg/dl in neonates in the peri-operative period must be considered as hypoglycaemia. The symptoms of hypoglycaemia can range from asymptomatic to those with irritability, confusion, slurred speech and seizures. In the neonatal period, it is physiologically normal to find low blood sugar levels and they require strict glycaemic monitoring as the symptoms can be masked.

Patients with diabetes and on insulin should be scheduled for their procedures early in the day. Prolonged fasting should be avoided, and the usual dose of insulin should be withheld or administered based on the pre-operative blood sugars in the ward. The management strategies for hypoglycaemia in a paediatric patient are given below in Table 48.4. Blood sugars should be checked within 15 minutes following correction of hypoglycaemia in the perioperative period.

Table 48.4 Treatment Regimen for Hypoglycaemia

Route of Administration	Dose
Per oral (glucose)	<2 years: 5 g 2–5 years: 10 g >5 years: 15 g
Intravenous	1–2 ml/kg 10% dextrose. Re-check blood sugars in 15 min
Intramuscular (glucagon)	<25 kg: 0.5 mg and >25 kg: 1 mg Only if Intravenous access not obtained

Known diabetics on regular oral hypoglycaemic agents (OHAs) or insulin often present for surgery. Their management is described in Figure 48.1.

Management of Perioperative Hyperglycaemia

Hyperglycaemia is associated with poor wound healing and high rate of post-op infections. A pre-operative consultation with the primary endocrinologist and evaluation of glycaemic control, serum electrolytes and ketones in patients with Type 1 DM are important to make a management plan in the intra-operative period. The type and duration of surgery are also important as the risk of hypo/hyperglycaemia is increased with emergency surgeries and those lasting for longer duration with major fluid shifts. On the day of surgery, the target blood glucose should be maintained between 90 and 180 mg/dl. Frequent blood glucose monitoring (1 hour) must be done in the intra-operative period and frequency increased to 30 minutes if there is a change in treatment plan. Insulin can be administered via subcutaneous injection with insulin pump or as intravenous injection. Regular insulin is used for intravenous infusion, and it is important to use a dextrose containing maintenance fluid at the same time. Maintenance fluid of choice is 0.45% saline with 5% dextrose. If sodium is low, 0.9% normal saline can be used along with 20 mmol/l of potassium added as maintenance fluid. After starting the insulin infusion, the dose must be titrated at the rate of 0.01–0.01 units/kg/hr to attain blood sugar target range (90–180 mg/dl). As the regular insulin has a short half-life, it is important to administer the subcutaneous insulin dose before discontinuing the insulin infusion. The intravenous insulin infusion starting rates are shown in Table 48.5.

Management of Diabetic Ketoacidosis (DKA)

Diabetic ketoacidosis (DKA) is a medical emergency, which requires prompt recognition and management. DKA must be ruled out for any child with diabetes, scheduled for an emergency surgery by doing urine ketones and serum electrolytes in the perioperative period. The diagnosis of DKA is made by symptoms such as abdominal pain, vomiting, polyuria, altered mental status and

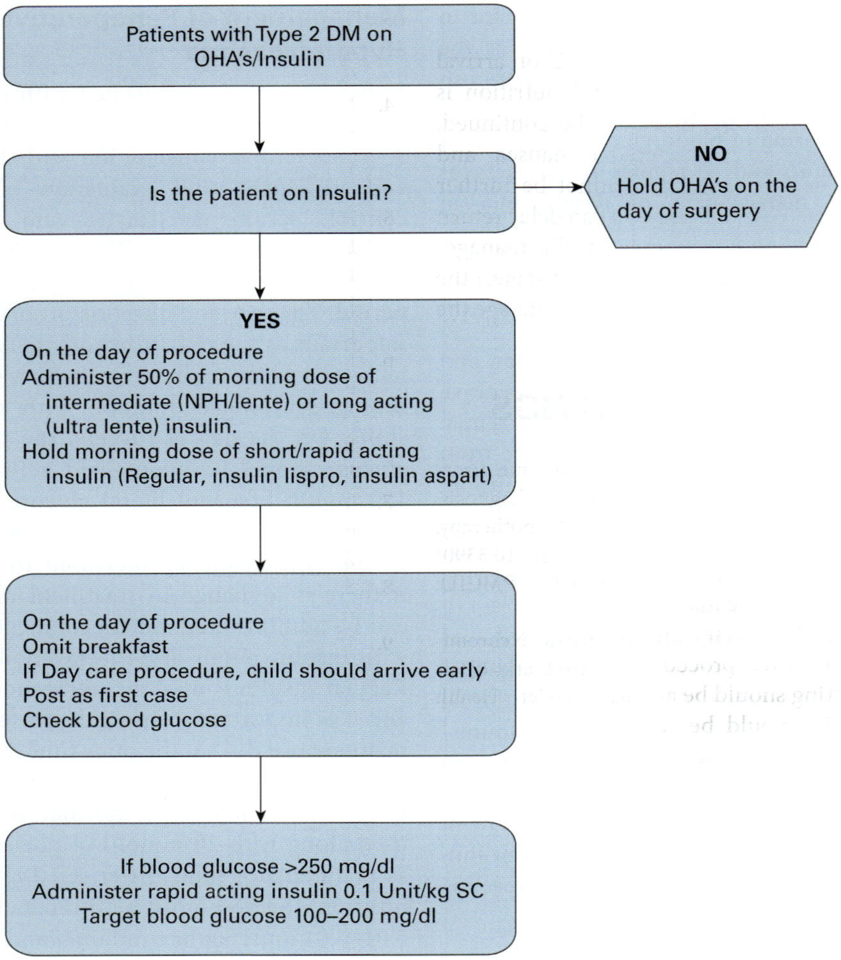

Figure 48.1 Perioperative management of patients on oral hypoglycaemic drugs/insulin. DM, diabetes mellitus; NPH, neutral protamine hagedorn; OHA, oral hypoglycaemic agent; SC, subcutaneous.

Table 48.5 Insulin Infusion Range for Hyperglycaemia

Blood Glucose (mg/dl)	Insulin Infusion (units/kg/hr)
110–140	0.025
140–200	0.05
220–270	0.075
>270	0.1

change in breathing pattern. Biochemical values of blood sugars >200 mg/dl, pH <7.3 with HCO_3 less than 15 mmol/l is suggestive of DKA. The treatment plan for DKA management must be done with the following goals:

- Initial resuscitation (airway, breathing and circulation)
- Insulin infusion (0.1 units/kg/hr)
- Addition of 10% dextrose if blood sugars <150 mg/dl
- IV fluids: initial bolus of 10 ml/kg of normal saline/Ringer's lactate (RL)
- Monitoring of serum electrolytes
- Hypokalaemia management
- Stop insulin infusion once patient takes orally, blood sugars <200 mg/dl, anion gap closed, pH > 7.3, HCO_3 > 15 meq/l

Note, ketones take longer to come back to baseline than do blood sugars

Post-Operative Management

Blood sugars must be checked in PACU on arrival and hourly till discharge. Once oral nutrition is started, home insulin regimen can be continued. The importance of postoperative nausea and vomiting (PONV) prophylaxis cannot be further stressed upon in these patients as it can delay return to normal food intake and home insulin management. Any signs of refractory PONV must alert the anaesthesiologist to consider DKA and manage the patient for same.

SUGGESTED READINGS

1. Claude F, Ubertini G, Szinnai G. Endocrine disorders in children with brain tumours: At diagnosis, after surgery, radiotherapy and chemotherapy. *Children (Basel)* 2022; 9(11):1617. doi: 10.3390/children9111617; PMID: 36360345; PMCID: PMC9688119.
2. Soriano SG, McManus ML. Paediatric Neuroanaesthesia and Critical Care. In: Cottrell and Patels Neuroanesthesia, 6th edition. Elsevier Health Sciences, Philadelphia pp. 337–350.
3. Khadilkar V, Karguppikar M. Endocrinological Management of Sellar and Supra-Sellar Tumors in Children. *Neurol India* 2022: 68(7);28–32.
4. Maxwell LG, Weintraub. Endocrine disorders. In: Smith's Anesthesia for Infants and Children, 9th edition. Davis PJ, Cladis FP (eds). Elsevier: Philadelphia 2017; pp. 1106–1114.
5. Krane EJ, Rhodes ET, Wolfsdrof JI. Essentials of Endocrinology. In: A Practice of Anesthesia for Infants and Children, 5th edition. Cote CJ, Lerman J, Anderson B (eds). Elsevier: Philadelphia 2013; pp. 547–553.
6. Martin LD, Hoagland MA, Rhodes ET, et al. Perioperative management of pediatric patients with Type 1 diabetes mellitus, updated recommendations for anesthesiologists. *Anesth Analg* 2020; 130(4): 821–827.
7. Tjen C, Wilkinson K. Perioperative care of children and young people with diabetes. *BJA Education* 2016; 16(4):124–129.
8. Steel S, Tibby S. Paediatric diabetic ketoacidosis. *Contin Edu Anaesth Crit Care Pain* 2009; 9:194–199.
9. Indian Academy of Paediatrics (IAP) growth charts. https://iapindia.org/iap-growth-charts/ accessed on 9th July 2023.

49 SIMULATION

Purva Makani • Dave Wright

Professor Gaba, widely known as the father of simulation-based education, defines simulation as *'a technique – not a technology – to replace or amplify real experiences with guided experiences that evoke or replicate substantial aspects of the real world in a fully interactive manner'*. Healthcare is a risky business and is ranked as a hazardous industry, even more unsafe than extreme sports such as bungee jumping and mountain climbing. Death from medical error has previously been estimated as the third most common cause of death in the United States, and the World Health Organisation attributes significant direct, financial, social and productivity harm from adverse healthcare events (**Fig. 49.1**).

There are several reasons for this poor safety record, but the most significant is our failure to train and learn from ultra-safe industries such as aviation. Aviation is long recognised as having widely embraced simulation as a tool to train and learn from errors. The practice and safety profile of anaesthesia has continued to improve. However, some inherent risk factors are unavoidable: working in relative isolation or isolated sites, especially out of hours; increasingly complicated and challenging patients with chronic disease; the background of rising public expectations, with the associated psychological pressure to perform safely. Paediatric anaesthesia has additional specific risks associated with accuracy of drug dosing, variations in equipment due to age and the associated training requirements. How well equipped are we to work under such conditions?

It appears we are not well trained (or at least not uniformly trained to perform reliably, especially in high-stake situations). If we specifically look at our technical skills, we do not seem to do that well. Our ability to perform a critical rescue intervention when most needed, such as the front of neck access in a 'cannot intubate cannot oxygenate' scenario is poor.

Adverse events occur in 1:10 hospital episodes in (high-income countries) and 1:4 episodes (low/middle-income countries).

Globally, this represents 134 million adverse events and 2.6 million deaths annually.

Unsafe care causes approximately US$ 1.5 trillion direct productivity losses annually.

Secondary social costs are valued at US$ 1–2 trillion.

Figure 49.1 The World Health Organisation Global Safety Action Plan 2021–2030.

The NAP4 study demonstrated a 75% failure rate in the emergency setting. Are our non-technical skills any better? Non-technical or human factors skills are a broad domain of individual and team competencies, which has traditionally been categorised as *social* (teamwork, leadership and communication), *cognitive* (situational awareness, decision-making, readiness and task management) and *personal* (management of stress and fatigue). More recently, these core non-technical principles are being considered in the wider context of human factors applied to systems and cultures. This is aligned with the transition of safety culture from the principles of safety 1 to safety 2, as first proposed by Hollnagel.[1]

Interestingly, non-technical skills contribute more to errors than technical skills. Atul Gawande in his pivotal work on surgical safety checklists highlights that 80% of errors are due to lack of good communication within teams. This is particularly pertinent in the complex and dynamic operating theatre setting. Poor communication has also been highlighted as a contributory factor to adverse outcomes for mothers and babies. In the UK, the triennially conducted Confidential Enquiries into maternal and child outcomes (MBRRACE-UK) has cited failures of communication in every report over a period of several decades. As anaesthetists, we work as part of the wider team in high-risk/high-consequence situations and should therefore ask 'on both an individual and team level, are we trained to be safe?'. The answer is a resounding no.

Simulation-based education (SBE) has long been cited as the educational tool for teaching these technical and non-technical skills. Evidence that SBE and training can improve our technical skills performance is well-established in areas such as cricothyroidotomy success rates, bronchoscopy skills, reduced central venous line complications and management of shoulder dystocia. Evidence translating improvements in non-technical skills performance from simulated environments into patient outcomes has proved a more challenging journey. Studies by Riley and Draycott were amongst the first to demonstrate this.[2,3]

In Riley's study, three hospital maternity units in the mid-west US participated in a unique programme over a 3-year period. Two control hospitals received lectures only or current best practice team safety training using the didactic TeamSTEPPS® model. An intervention hospital received TeamSTEPPS training plus in situ simulation (ISS). A sustained statistically significant 37% improvement in perinatal morbidity was seen in the hospital receiving ISS. There were no differences between control hospitals, despite perceptions of safety culture being high at all sites. This illustrated that it is not adequate to simply have learning content, which includes non-technical skills. it is the utilisation of ISS as the modality to deliver this learning, which is key to sustained change.

Draycott's study analysed neonatal outcomes in the period before and after simulation-based team training was introduced to a tertiary referral centre. A total of 19,460 cases were included: 8,430 pre-training and 11,030 post-training. The incidence of infants with low 5-minute APGAR scores (≤6) decreased from 88.6 to 44.6 per 10,000 births and hypoxic ischaemic encephalopathy from 27.3 to 13.6 per 10,000 births. One can see how the impact of simulation on the life outcomes of these infants can begin to contribute to reductions in the direct and consequential harms that the WHO has identified. Importantly, these improvements were sustained over time, an effect the authors attributed to the continued delivery of the simulation programme. This leads us onto the factors required for simulation to be effective. The five most influential factors driving the outcome of simulation are content, fidelity, dose/frequency, location and integration into improvement science.

- **Content:** Standardisation of SBE is important, but there is an optimal and variable point on the continuum of standardisation/local adaptation, which must be considered. For example, outcome improvements from Draycott's work on shoulder dystocia using the PROMPT (practical obstetric multi-professional training) approach were not always transferrable to other units. Training must be designed or modified to account for local environment, resources (including staff), procedures and patients. Content must also be quality assured and kept up to date.
- **Fidelity:** In its purest sense, fidelity is the accuracy with which simulation reproduces a clinical situation. It is often framed as the complexity of simulator technology used, with the term 'high-fidelity' representing technically advanced manikins. This is a false paradigm as technology

in isolation does not dictate fidelity. Instead, fidelity can be experienced through a number of themes including physical, environmental and psychological. It is more important to use what is most appropriate for your intended outcomes, i.e. the choice of simulation modalities, equipment or techniques aligns with the learning construct. For example, an experienced simulated patient may recreate seizures with greater fidelity than an expensive manikin (learning outcome: recognise the fitting child), but be of lower fidelity/unable to simulate teaching airway technical skills (learning outcome: perform rapid sequence intubation). The Helping Babies Breathe programme in Tanzania, which uses low technology simulation, showed a reduction in early neonatal mortality from 13.4 to 7.1 per 1000 births.

- **Dose and Frequency:** Decay of learning at individual, team and system levels is an important consideration when designing simulation programmes. Simulation has to be repeated at frequent intervals to maintain performance. A number of studies have shown that short refresher training for neonatal nurses, conducted at the bedside, consistently improves performance. This suggests that easily accessible, brief and targeted ISS may be as or more effective than traditional, simulation centre-based full-day courses. This may be due to a number of factors: skills are topped up and do not drop below an acceptable minimum; the total 'dose' may be higher due to consistent, repeated exposure; retention of key messages may be greater when not diluted with other content; and there is the opportunity for spiral learning.
- **Location:** ISS has advantages over training conducted in a stand-alone simulation centre. It is more realistic, affordable, involves real teams and local clinical faculty. Systematic reviews of ISS in improving patient outcomes suggested that by identifying latent errors, patient safety could be enhanced.
- **Integration into improvement science:** Framing simulation in its widest possible scope allows groups not traditionally directly associated with simulation to appreciate its role and, therefore, support its implementation and sustainable delivery. For example, non-clinical managers, administrators and those commissioning care may value the efficiency and productivity gains separately from patient outcomes. In this regard, ISS should be integrated into local care pathways, patient journeys and risk management systems.

Design and Planning of Simulation Activity

Planning Frameworks

Simulation is particularly relevant to paediatric anaesthesia as care often involves multiple clinicians, teams and specialties; specific requirements for drugs, equipment and environment; consideration of emotional well-being, psychosocial factors and parents or carers.

When planning simulation activity, simulation classification systems, such as that originally proposed by Gaba, are useful tools to explore the rational basis, methodology and intended outcomes. We would suggest adding current developments in simulation into this framework, including simulation for improvement science; use of extended reality technology (XR) such as virtual and augmented reality; hybrid (mixed modality) simulation and multi-site/remote simulation (**Fig. 49.2**).

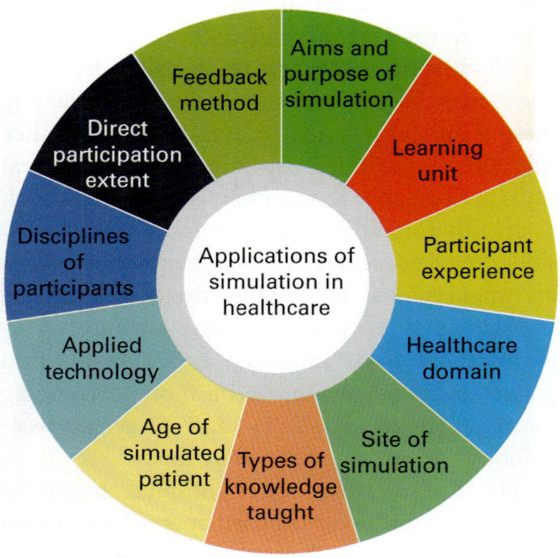

Figure 49.2 Domains of simulation.

Types of Simulators

A broad range of paediatric simulators are available (Fig. 49.3). These include part-task trainers for procedural skills, such as airway management, vascular access or lumbar puncture; simple manikins often used for resuscitation training; and manikins with advanced features such as automated movement, facial expression, skin colour and muscle tone. As it is the thoughtful design of simulation activity that creates high-fidelity learning environments, not the complexity of simulator technology, consideration should always be given to the most suitable simulator in the context of intended simulation output and available resources. Recent developments in 3D printing can facilitate deployment of low unit cost part-task trainers, often based on open-source designs, with the ability to make modifications to suit local requirements. This allows on-site and on-demand production of simulators, which may have practical and economic benefits in low resource or remote settings. A common application of 3D-printed simulators is emergency front of neck access, and various adaptations of this are produced by different centres to suit local requirements (Fig. 49.4).

The Simulation Experience

The typical model for conduct of simulation activity usually includes a number of elements:

- Familiarisation with equipment, simulator(s) and environment
- Defining boundaries, principles of psychological safety and principles of debriefing (pre-briefing)
- Scenario initiation (scripted introduction, phone call or incident alert)
- Conduct of scenario, including strategies for managing unanticipated events ('escape routes')
- Diffusing and/or capturing any psychological and physiological stressors
- Debriefing, learning and application to clinical practice

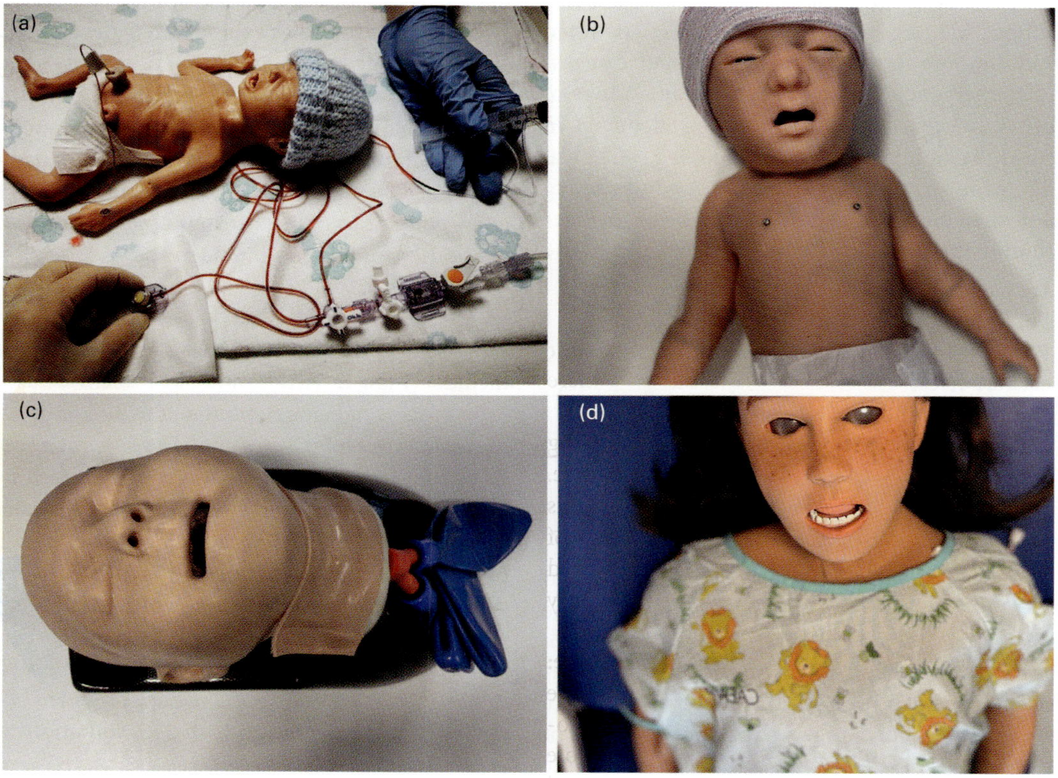

Figure 49.3 Paediatric simulators. (a) Umbilical artery cannulation task trainer. (b) SuperTory (Gaumard). (c) Pierre Robin airway trainer (TruCorp). (d) Paediatric airway simulators CAE Aria Healthcare.

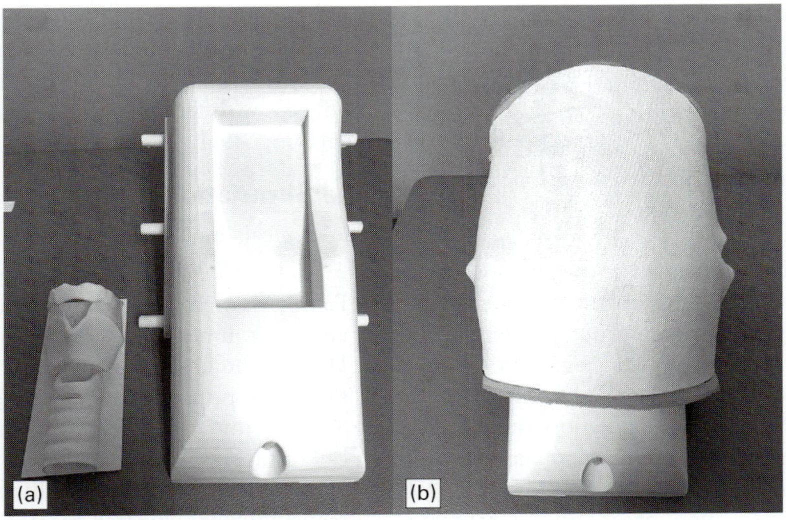

Figure 49.4 3D-printed front of access trainer. (a) Structure in polylactic acid (PLA). (b) Soft tissue overlay (Hull Institute of Learning and Simulation).

These elements can be incorporated into both activity in simulation centres and ISS. The logistics of centre-based simulation lends itself to formal, planned training events, whereas ISS is often deployed more flexibly. A typical paediatric anaesthesia emergencies course may include a range of acute scenarios, each incorporating elements of clinical reasoning and decision-making, technical skills, teamwork and human factors. A good starting point when planning a course would be to consider including the following example scenarios:

- Laryngospasm
- Foreign body inhalation
- Pre-operative hypovolaemia, resuscitation and cardiac arrest
- Equipment failure
- Bronchospasm
- Anaphylaxis
- Time critical transfer for definitive care exceeding local capacity

Whilst scenario selection should be based on a multifactorial assessment of the needs of the participating team, patients and wider system requirements, certain topics have particular relevance to paediatric practice: laryngospasm is more frequent than in adults; paediatric equipment varies widely based on age and requires specific training; drug calculations mandate attention to detail; and highly specialist tertiary care is often not available in all localities, increasing transfer requirements. We recommend the use of standardised scenario templates, which are available from a range of sources and often developed or adapted locally (**Appendix 49.1A and B**). These ensure that all aspects of the scenario are prepared and due consideration given to factors such as equipment requirements and dealing with unanticipated behaviours by scenario participants. It is also good practice to rehearse or pilot new scenarios to check they function as intended.

In Situ Simulation

Delivery models for ISS can vary widely and include: high-fidelity immersive team learning experiences; ad-hoc, spontaneous/unannounced or incident-responsive simulations, which capitalise on learning opportunities; focused technical or procedural skills; and simulation that includes a social component such as 'tea trolley training'. Tea trolley training involves a small faculty delivering very focused and brief ISS, whilst maintaining normal theatre clinical activity. Often a member of faculty will relieve an anaesthetist from their case to participate and refreshments are provided. This makes it easy to engage with ISS and motivates people to attend.

ISS should include the whole interdisciplinary team whenever possible, as whole team training in natural clinical environments facilitates high quality learning and improvements to patient safety. The use of in situ safety checklists (Appendix 49.2) is recommended to reduce the risks to the clinical environment, through loss of clinical equipment, contamination with simulation equipment and disruption to systems. Consideration should be given to 'no-go' conditions, under which the risk of ISS may outweigh the benefits. These can be broadly categorised into staffing needs, work flow patterns, clinical load/acuity, equipment needs, unanticipated events and threats to psychological safety. The latter is particularly relevant to simulation in paediatric environments. Children may be less able to understand the simulated nature of events, place it in the context of improving care and be more likely to have an emotional response to environmental cues. However, simulation in paediatric settings is well-established and these considerations can be mitigated through appropriate planning and sensitive engagement with children, families and the clinical team. The use of in situ planning tools may assist in identifying and managing these issues in advance.

A significant secondary benefit of ISS is the identification of latent errors also known as latent conditions or latent threats. These are inherent *system* weaknesses that have the potential to cause harm if certain precipitating factors are met and can be considered as a dormant pathology waiting to be triggered. The rate of error detection can be high – one study showed that for every ISS of only 10 minutes duration conducted in emergency departments, 1.2 latent errors were identified. Latent errors and actions required to remove or mitigate associated risks can be documented in standard templates, which facilitate categorisation and risk stratification (Appendix 49.3). These reporting templates facilitate integration of ISS into robust and reliable pathways for delivering necessary changes.

These benefits reminds us of the importance of applying Gaba's domains when planning simulation. Should we be planning ISS for learning, with the passive benefit of latent error detection or should we be planning ISS to probe and challenge systems, with the specific aim of identifying these threats? This led us on to the principles of how to utilise simulation in the context of improvement science.

Designing Simulation for Improvement Science

Simulation for improvement science has been described as 'translational simulation', building on Berwick's model of healthcare improvement. This recommends a close focus on improving health system performance through both 'simulation interventions' and 'diagnostic simulation'.

Simulation interventions may include the following:

- Improving relationships and culture
- Improving interfaces (handovers and systems)
- Authentic team training across patient journeys
- Embedding of guidelines and pathways
- Focused technical and non-technical skills training

Diagnostic simulation may include the following:

- System probing (identifying latent threats)
- Recreation of adverse events
- Trialling and iterating new equipment or processes
- Identifying culture or professionalism issues
- Exploring the patient experience
- Assessment of global system efficacy

Applying a conceptual model of ISS such as that proposed in the Genesis 1 and 2 reviews when planning ISS helps to deconstruct the broader system benefits and identify the widest range of stakeholders who may benefit. This incorporates concepts including science of complexity and systems thinking, systems engineering and resilience, adaptive complex systems and clinical competence/knowledge transfer. Highlighting these wider system gains can facilitate engagement with non-clinical staff, who may have a critical role in ensuring that delivery is sustainable.

Case Study: Opening a New Paediatric Day Surgery Complex

Our hospital is constructing a new theatre complex for paediatric day surgery, and we have been tasked with utilising simulation to aid in the preparation for its opening. How can we accomplish this, and what outcomes should we strive to achieve?

Use of simulation to prepare for operational readiness is well-established and offers risk reductions to patients. However, if we apply the principles of diagnostic simulation from the point of inception, the entire process of building design, through construction to the first patient use, can be informed and improved. Indeed, guidance issued by the Association of Anaesthetists and the Difficulty Airway Society in the UK, specifically, recommends utilising a human factor and simulation-based approach when designing and planning anaesthetic environments.

Architects are often able to generate 3D images of building plans. This allows the physical layout of the unit including patient waiting areas, corridors, operating theatre, and recovery and discharge areas to be recreated virtually. Experiencing these plans using virtual or augmented reality headsets such as Oculus® or Hololens® gives the ability to perform a virtual 'walk through' of the unit. This can identify problems at an early stage, improving layouts and reducing subsequent expensive alterations. In the later stages of construction, simulating whole patient journeys can identify ergonomic challenges and influence design and the location of equipment, for example, the location of anaesthetic machines and monitoring for optimal viewing, correct siting of medical gas outlets and suction, need for automatic doors and the line of sight visibility for nursing staff in recovery areas. Theatre productivity can be optimised by using these techniques to ensure effective flow of patients.

The experience of patients and families is especially relevant to paediatric anaesthesia. Conducting scenarios using simulated patients or staff acting in the role of patients and families can help us to understand how a child might experience care in our unit. This can influence the design of play rooms and family waiting areas as well as the support measures we provide for children, including distraction/anxiety management, assistive communication devices, play therapy and lighting.

ISS immediately prior to opening allows us to test systems for latent threats that could present an immediate or serious risk to patients. This can include location, visibility and awareness of resuscitation or airway rescue trolleys; availability of emergency drugs; access to blood product storage units and communication processes such as phone numbers or pager systems. Once the unit is fully commissioned, ISS can be used for ongoing trouble shooting and embedding of any new theatre pathways and processes required to work in the new physical infrastructure.

Conclusion

Simulation can have a major impact on the quality of care and clinical outcomes for children. Its use should be considered as a tool for improving and maintaining high standards in all aspects of patient care. Its place in the education and training of individual clinicians and whole teams is well-established, and there are many applications for both technical and non-technical skills. There is a well-established evidence base and guidance regarding the factors that influence successful learning from simulation. It is crucial to apply this knowledge when designing and delivering simulations. For the greatest impact, it is equally important to remember to tailor simulations to meet local needs, involving learners and other stakeholders in the process. Embracing simulation as a powerful tool when applied to improvement science has the potential to help create environments, systems and processes which encourage high quality care and minimise the latent conditions that predispose to risk. It is this integration of simulation with systems thinking that may unlock the true potential of simulation and reduce the global harms from error.

REFERENCES

1. Hollnagel E, Wears R, Braithwaite J. From Safety-I to Safety-II: A White Paper. 2015. Available from: https://www.researchgate.net/publication/282441875_From_Safety-I_to_Safety-II_A_White_Paper (accessed 01 Feb 2023)
2. Riley W, Davis S, Miller K, et al. Didactic and simulation nontechnical skills team training to improve perinatal patient outcomes in a community hospital. *Jt Comm J Qual Patient Saf* 2011; 37(8):357–64.
3. Draycott TJ, Collins KJ, Crofts JF, et al. Myths and realities of training in obstetric emergencies. *Best Pract Res Clin Obstet Gynaecol* 2015; 29(8): 1067–1076.

SUGGESTED READINGS

1. Gaba DM. The future vision of simulation in health care. *Qual Safety Health Care* 2004; 13(1):i2–10.

2. Makary MA, Daniel M. Medical error—The third leading cause of death in the US. *BMJ* 2016; 353:i2139.
3. Non-Technical Skills. Applied Psychology and Human Factors Group, University of Aberdeen. Available from: https://research.abdn.ac.uk/applied-psych-hf/non-technical-skills/ (accessed 01 Feb 2023)
4. Sankaranarayanan G, Odlozil CA, Hasan SS, et al. Training on a virtual reality cricothyroidotomy simulator improves skills and transfers to a simulated procedure. *Trauma Surg Acute Care Open* 2022; 7(1):e000826.
5. Versantvoort JMD, Kleinhout MY, Ockhuijsen HDL, et al. Helping babies breathe and its effects on intrapartum-related stillbirths and neonatal mortality in low-resource settings: A systematic review. *Arch Dis Child* 2020; 105(2):127–133.
6. Cheng A, Brown LL, Duff JP, et al. Improving cardiopulmonary resuscitation with a CPR feedback device and refresher simulations (CPR CARES Study): A randomized clinical trial. *JAMA Pediatr* 2015; 169(2):137–44.
7. Fent G, Blythe J, Farooq O, et al. In situ simulation as a tool for patient safety: A systematic review identifying how it is used and its effectiveness. *BMJ STEL* 2015; 1(3):103–110.
8. Parotto M, Jiansen JQ, AboTaiban A, et al. Evaluation of a low-cost, 3D-printed model for bronchoscopy training. *Anaesthesiol Intensive Ther* 2017; 49(3):189–197.
9. Association for Simulated Practice in Healthcare. Simulation-based eduction in healthcare: standards framework and guidance. 2016. Available from: http://aspih.org.uk/wp-content/uploads/2017/07/standards-framework.pdf (accessed 25 June 2023).
10. O'Farrell G, McDonald M, Kelly FE. 'Tea trolley' difficult airway training. *Anaesthesia* 2015; 70(1):104.
11. Patterson MD, Geis GL, Falcone RA, et al. In situ simulation: Detection of safety threats and teamwork training in a high risk emergency department. *BMJ Qual Saf* 2013; 22(6):468–477.
12. Raemer DB. Ignaz Semmelweis Redux? *Simul. Healthcare* 2014; 9(3):153–155.
13. Bajaj K, Minors A, Walker K, et al. "No-Go Considerations" for in situ simulation safety. *Sim Healthcare* 2018; 13(3):221–224.
14. Brazil V. Translational simulation: not 'where?' but 'why?' A functional view of in situ simulation. *Adv Simul* 2017; 2(1):20.
15. Evans K, Woodruff J, Cowley A, et al. GENESISS 2—Generating Standards for In-Situ Simulation project: A systematic mapping review. *BMC Med Educ* 2022; 22(1):537.
16. Ventre KM, Barry JS, Davis D, et al. Using in situ simulation to evaluate operational readiness of a children's hospital-based obstetrics unit. *Simul Healthc* 2014; 9(2):102–111.
17. Kelly FE, Frerk C, Bailey CR, et al. Implementing human factors in anaesthesia: Guidance for clinicians, departments and hospitals: Guidelines from the Difficult Airway Society and the Association of Anaesthetists. *Anaesthesia* 2023; 78(4):458–478.

Appendix 49.1A Scenario Template

HILS Hull Institute of Learning and Simulation

www.thehils.org.uk

NHS Hull University Teaching Hospitals NHS Trust

Scenario			
Scenario Name:		Time / Order:	
Target Audience:		Length:	

SITUATION :

EXPECTED PROGRESSION :

ESCAPE ROUTES :

CANDIDATE PRE-BRIEF :

KEY LEARNING OBJECTIVES:

KEY DISCUSSION POINTS:

Faculty	
Roles:	Name:
Facilitator:	
Debriefer:	

Role 1:

Role / Position:	Stooge? :	
	Y	N

Demeanour:

Actions / Verbal :

Role 2:

Role / Position:	Stooge? :	
	Y	N

Demeanour:

Actions / Verbal :

Role 3:

Role / Position:	Stooge? :	
	Y	N

Demeanour:

Actions / Verbal :

Appendix 49.1B

Baseline

HR	Rhythm	SPO2	BP	RR	⊙⊙	Obs

Demeanour:	
Verbal / Sounds:	

Trainee expected to:	Scenario Progression:

Stage 1

Trigger:						
HR	Rhythm	SPO2	BP	RR	⊙⊙	Obs

Demeanour:	
Verbal / Sounds:	

Trainee expected to:	Scenario Progression:

Stage 2

Trigger:						
HR	Rhythm	SPO2	BP	RR	⊙⊙	Obs

Demeanour:	
Verbal / Sounds:	

Trainee expected to:	Scenario Progression:

Stage 3

Trigger:						
HR	Rhythm	SPO2	BP	RR	⊙⊙	Obs

Demeanour:	
Verbal / Sounds:	

Trainee expected to:	Scenario Progression:

Stage 4

Trigger:						
HR	Rhythm	SPO2	BP	RR	⊙⊙	Obs

Demeanour:	
Verbal / Sounds:	

Trainee expected to:	Scenario Progression:

Patient Profile

Name:		Date of Birth:		
Age:		Gender?:	M	F
Manikin/ Actor:				
Patient History:				
Drug History/ Allergies:				

Manikin Set-Up

Model:		Monitoring ?	ON	OFF
Arrangement :				
Appearance :				
Moulage :				
Monitor Layout :				

SMOTS Set-Up

Live View?	YES	NO	Playback?	YES	NO
Phone Audio?	YES	NO	Vitals View?	YES	NO

Room Set-Up

Room(s):		Location:	
Representative Place:		Time:	
Layout:			

Environmental :

Equipment / Props / Consumables :

Considerations / Hazards :

Appendix 49.2 In Situ Simulation Checklist

HILS Hull Institute of Learning and Simulation

NHS Hull University Teaching Hospitals NHS Trust

In situ simulation checklist

Sim Hardware	Used?	Packed away?
Manikin		
SimPad		
AV equipment		
Trolley/cases		
Pre and Post Questionnaires		
Medical Equipment	**Used?**	**Disposal**
Airway Kit (adjuncts, tubes, laryngoscope blades, anaesthetic circuits)		
Oxygen systems (nasal, masks, neb)		
IV fluids and giving sets		
IV dummy drugs		
Blood sampling (ABG, sample bottles, Culture bottles)		
Suction		
Obs chart / Case notes		
Other		
Environment	**Used?**	**Cleaned?**
ECG machine		
Monitoring (cardiac monitor, DynaMAP)		
Bed space/ trolley		
Anaesthetic machine/ Resuscitaire		
Other		

Notes

All medical equipment used should be placed together in a "kit dump" so that the person responsible for re-stocking knows exactly what has been used.

The exception to this would be sharps and dummy drugs.

The person responsible for re-stocking should be agreed upon in advance of the in situ exercise.

Person responsible for re-stocking:

Final check of environment should take place at close of exercise

Appendix 49.3A In Situ Report

HILS Hull Institute of Learning and Simulation

NHS Hull University Teaching Hospitals NHS Trust

<Title>

<Date>

Aims of the session

- <Learning outcomes>
- <Learning outcomes>
- <Learning outcomes>

Overview:

<Brief outline of the case relating to the above outcomes>

Participants:

<List of all candidates, observers and faculty>

Themes from debriefing:

- <Bullet point list of the topics covered in the debrief, whether led by facilitator or the candidate's agenda>
- <Avoid specifics about how candidates performed>

Feedback from pre/post questionnaires

	Mean Response (1= Strongly disagree to 10=Strongly Agree)	
Question	Pre	Post
I feel confident to manage an unwell patient		
I feel confident working within a team managing an unwell patient		
I feel aware of my limitations and know when to call for help		
I feel I am able to communicate effectively in an emergency situation		
I enjoyed today's session		
The scenario was useful and relevant to my practice		
I received constructive feedback		
Regular simulation would be useful		
The session was disruptive to departmental running		
I learned something to change my practice		

Appendix 49.3B Latent Errors

Hull Institute of Learning and Simulation

NHS Hull University Teaching Hospitals NHS Trust

<Title> <Date>

Take home messages:

Latent errors

<This should detail any latent errors in the four categories below, with a score from the NPSA risk matrix (available on google images). Action plans should include any specific actions and named individuals who will carry them out>

	Risk Identified	Risk Score (NPSA matrix)	Action taken
Medication			
Equipment			
Environment			
Training			

Further reading

<This should contain suggested reading relevant to the case, such as NICE guidelines, BMJ clinical knowledge summaries or FOAMed resources>

50

Safety Concerns in Paediatric Anaesthesia

Erlinda Oracion • Rebecca Jacob

Anaesthesia is safe. This is what the anaesthetists will usually say to ASA 1 or 2 patient who is about to undergo a routine operation. The past half a century has seen a vast improvement in patient safety – a core principle of anaesthesia care worldwide. The increasing awareness of safety issues among anaesthetists, technological advances, the availability of newer and safer drugs, and updated guidelines and standards have seen the speciality evolve as a leader in patient safety. The implementation of standards of care, patient safety research and system-based improvements together with easy access to knowledge and training through computers and web-based learning have improved the quality of care and perioperative anaesthetic management of our patients. Critical incident monitoring has been used as a focus for improving the standard of care and formulating protocols and guidelines to help in providing the best care at all times.

Access to safe anaesthesia and surgery for patients of all ages should be considered a basic human right, but this is not available to a large segment of the world's population. Many developing and underdeveloped countries spend a very small portion of their GDP on health care, and this is the greatest barrier to providing good anaesthetic services and surgical care. However, there is much that can be done to make sure that the existing resources are used efficiently. The WHO, acknowledging the fact that the global volume of surgery is significant and adverse events resulting from surgeries constitute a significant public health concern, launched the Patient Safety Initiative in 2004 and the Safe Surgery Saves Lives Initiative in 2008. With these initiatives, they have set a core set of safety standards that can be applied to all countries in all settings.

The Surgical Safety Check List, together with the WHO-WFSA International Standards for a Safe Practice of Anesthesia (2010) enhanced patient safety cultures in most hospitals through the implementation of these guidelines. The checklist may initially sound simplistic and repetitive, but it has proven to improve and reiterate safety over time. It helps in various aspects, such as identifying the correct patient and surgery, ensuring administration of antibiotics, encouraging teamwork, maintaining equipment checks or providing status and identity to surgical nurses or anaesthetists.

Documentation

Routine charting is important. This should include the pre-anaesthetic check and checking of the anaesthesia machine. This should include pre-operative checklists and anaesthesia checklists. Safety minefields that provide the anaesthesiologist with important information are the targeted history, physical examination, informed consent and assent and a safe anaesthetic plan that are clearly documented and available for all healthcare personnel involved in the care of the patient. The use of drugs, monitors in use and documentation of vital parameters *sequentially* are also vitally important. Documentation of all interventions and drugs used, whether routinely or in case of a critical event including airway problems, anaphylaxis or cardiac arrest, in an accurate and 'time-related' (contemporaneous) manner, are essential. Remember that it is the manner of delivery, and not the drugs themselves, that results in anaesthetic morbidity and mortality.

Protocols

Standard protocols should be followed for fasting guidelines, for the delivery of anaesthesia and for difficult situations such as management of the difficult airway, dealing with children with a 'full stomach' and the management of cardiac arrest. There should also be protocols for checking the availability of equipment such as LMAs, gum elastic bougies or tracheostomy tubes, protocols for the maintenance of equipment such as defibrillators and resuscitation bags, and protocols for the availability and maintenance of drugs including checking of maintenance of the cold chain and expiry dates. Another important protocol to consider would be that of the safe performance of paediatric sedation. This requires proper selection and assessment of patients, adequate preparation, and the performance of sedation by providers with appropriate training and organisational support. Persons responsible for following these protocols should be identified and held responsible for carrying out these tasks, and guidelines designed and updated to maximise patient safety.

Monitoring

Maintaining minimum safety standards should follow the best practice guidelines enunciated by the national society of each country. Monitoring the implementation of this should be a matter for local bodies, hospitals and institutions. Anaesthetic outcomes improved dramatically with the introduction of the pulse oximeter in the 1980s. Fifty-eight countries in the world have made pulse oximetry part of their minimum monitoring standards, but data suggest that 78,000 operating rooms in low-income countries around the world have no access to pulse oximetry. The Life Box Project (Global Oximetry Project) – a collaborative partnership of the World Federation of Societies of Anaesthesiologists, the World Health Organisation, Harvard School of Public Health, the Association of Anaesthetists of Great Britain and Ireland and Smile Train – is hoping to correct this deficit over time with the provision of a small robust, easy-to-use pulse oximeter along with teaching material as to its use. Ideally, capnography ($EtCO_2$), temperature monitoring, electrocardiography and non-invasive blood pressure monitoring should also be considered as a standard of care for all children undergoing anaesthesia or deep sedation. The anaesthetist should make sure that backup equipment is available, and one should know the location of emergency supplies and equipment. But finding resources for these is still a problem.

Technology in paediatric anaesthesia is constantly evolving. We cannot accept all of it as good or necessary for our practice of safe paediatric anaesthesia. Ensuring the appropriate equipment, the right size of equipment like BP cuffs and pulse oximeter probes for all children being anaesthetised, is often very difficult in low-resource settings. The solution lies in integrating information regarding technology and gaining a clear understanding of its limitations, as well as the limitations of available resources.

The purpose of monitoring is to detect potential problems. It is not a substitute for close observation of the patient by the anaesthetist. Coupled with a good basic knowledge of physiology and pharmacology, appropriate training and continuous education, this is what is required to improve safety and reduce morbidity and mortality.

Medications

The objectives of medication administration are often summarised in the '5 rights': the right patient, the right medication, the right dose at the right time and by the right route of administration. Merry and Anderson suggest a sixth right – a right record of medications administered and medications wasted (notably any unused portions of ampoules of controlled drugs).

Anaesthesia is perhaps the only area where medications are typically prescribed, administered, recorded and outcomes measured by a single individual – the anaesthetist. Chances of error, violations of the norms, practices and protocols of the institution and misuse are high in this situation. In the interest of patient safety, both the system and the mindset of the individual practitioner should be addressed.

Measures that have been shown (evidence-based) to reduce medication errors include standards to improve the labelling of ampoules and syringes – labels to always be legible and colour coded to improve safety by decreasing between class errors (however, it does not eliminate within class errors; **Fig. 50.1**).

The organisation of workspaces and drug drawers should be uniform in similar work areas, for example, in all the operating rooms of a given institution.

It is worth advocating the retention of all ampoules and vials used in each case, beginning afresh for the next case. This will help track medications given in case of an adverse event.

Sedation drug regimens advocating the administration of three or more drugs increase morbidity and should be eliminated. The routine use of drugs with a long half-life should be reviewed. One should consider the fact that all drug combinations used to provide targeted sedation for painful procedures may still result in general anaesthesia depending on the initial dose and frequency of dosing.

Drug delivery systems should be mutually exclusive with special attention given to colour coding and labelling of lines. Errors in administering drugs ('wrong route errors') can prove fatal such as epidural bupivacaine being given into an intravenous line.

On an individual level, labels should always be read before drawing up the drug. Drugs such as narcotics and blood and blood products should be counter-checked by another individual, signed and documented prior to administration.

Many countries do not have paediatric formulations as in the case of intravenous fluids. Some strategies to develop institutionally are to standardise formulations and decrease the number of formulations available for use. We can consider providing pre-calculated doses for medication ordering and administration. This should be taken up with the pharmaceutical companies and pressure brought on them to manufacture and provide paediatric-specific formulations as has been done with intravenous fluids in some European countries.

Technological advances such as bar codes may be available in the future to ensure drug safety.

Sedation

Sedation/anaesthesia is performed outside the operating rooms for many procedures in children and helps to allay pain and anxiety. Each site and procedure will give rise to certain anaesthetic implications and challenges. A number of studies on sedation practices have reported that severe

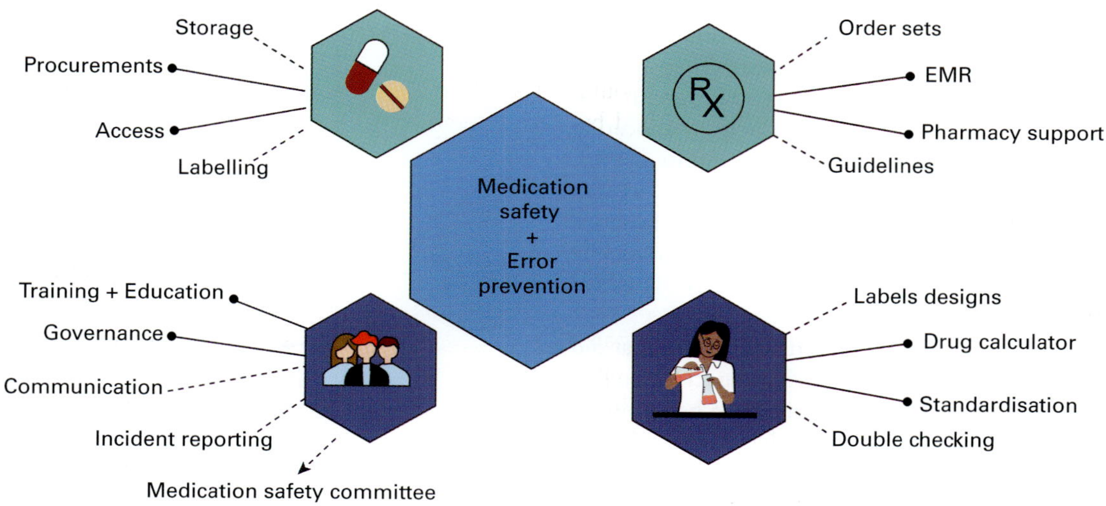

Figure 50.1 Medication safety and error prevention. EMR,

Source: Department of paediatric Anaesthesia, KK Women's and Children's Hospital, Singapore.

injury and death are rare, but problems such as stridor, laryngospasm and wheezing requiring respiratory interventions do occur. The authors of a 2006 review point out that the results should not simply reassure providers that sedation of children is of minimal risk but rather that they highlight the efficiency of core competencies and support services. Caregivers must be trained to manage the 'next level of sedation', be prepared to manage the airway, have access to emergency equipment and also have access to an anaesthetist at all times. In addition, one needs to be familiar with each off-site location because the anaesthetic environment and equipment demands may be unique in each area. Adverse events have been reported with all drugs even when given in prescribed 'safe doses'. Aside from having a predefined target, it is important for the analgesia and sedation to be regularly assessed and documented. So, the providers' competence and skills require rigorous evaluation and re-evaluation with a check on protocols and support systems available in each area where sedation is required.

Audits and Incident Reporting

Audits and incident reporting, whether done on a national scale (e.g. National Confidential Enquiry into Perioperative Deaths [NCEPOD] and Australian Incident Monitoring System [AIMS]) or in a particular institution or department, help to assess errors, violations, omissions and avoidable events, and place them in context. They help to identify areas of risk and put in place preventive or corrective measures. They also help in allocating resources where they may be best utilised. With increased incident reporting and analysis, we can investigate incidences, root causes, complications and adverse events. This has certainly proven to be an effective system to improve the safety of care for our paediatric patients.

What should be reported? Any event that did or had the potential to negatively impact the quality of care of the patient. What needs to be reported/documented should include what happened, how was it detected, contributing factors both active and latent, preventive ideas and outcomes.

The analysis of the event should be by the department safety officer (every department should have one), department incident reporting sessions, multidisciplinary medical reviews, thematic reviews – categories, patterns and context to plan interventions that will improve outcomes (**Figs 50.2–50.5**).

There are different frameworks for analysis, but the fishbone diagram or root cause analysis (**Fig 50.3**) is the most common. This process identifies the primary causal factor(s) underlying system failures (the root or source below the surface that may be obscured). The limitation of this method, however, is that sometimes it needs to reflect the multifactorial or multidimensional factors in the system.

Sometimes, it may be better to include another framework in the analysis, such as the Human Factors Analysis and Classification (**Fig. 50.4**). This may reveal systems and work process vulnerabilities, such as organisational influences, supervisory factors, and preconditions for unsafe and unsafe acts. This allows us to have a more complete and holistic system review to craft the necessary action plans.

The analysis aims to determine causes and develop ideas for intervention. The analysis enables one to determine appropriate strategies to address root causes and any additional strategies required to improve the overall quality of care (**Fig. 50.5**).

There are many challenges, however, to the reporting of incidents and their analysis. It is resource intensive. There may be a lack of expertise for analysis and improvement. Difficulties may

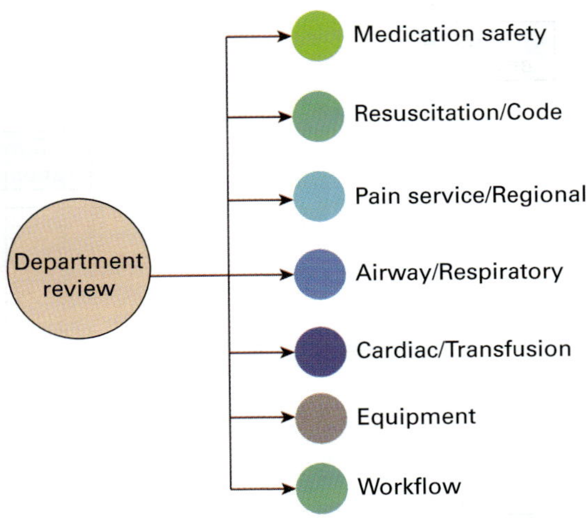

Figure 50.2 Departmental review.

Source: Department of Paediatric Anaesthesia, KK Women's andChildren's Hospital, Singapore.

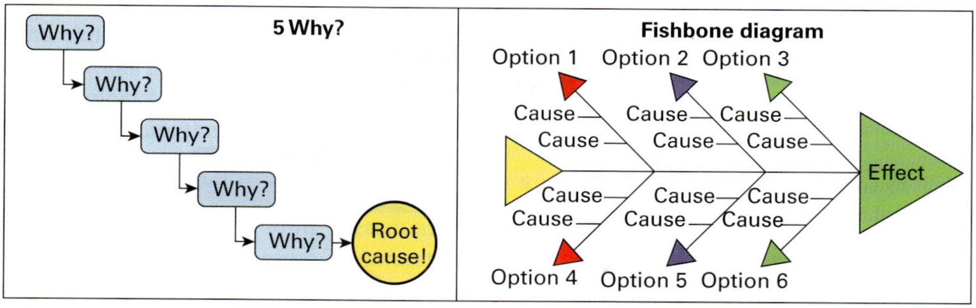

Figure 50.3 Analysis – determining the root cause of the problem – the 'WHY'.

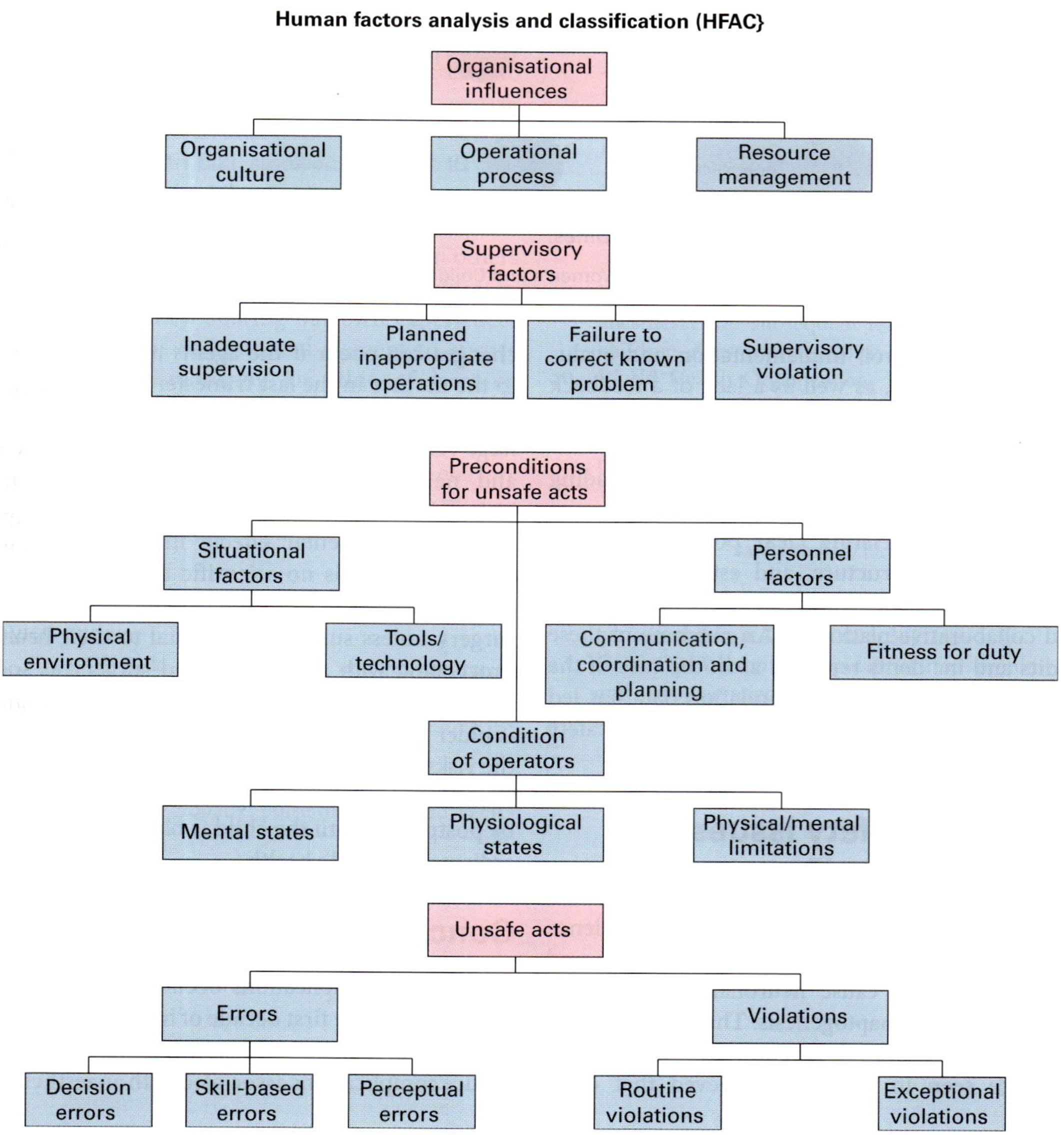

Figure 50.4 Human Factors Analysis and Classification.

Source: https://www.hfacs.com/hfacs-framework.html

Appendix 1

Drugs Commonly Used Perioperatively

Amar Nandhakumar

Reasonable care has been made to ensure correct dosage; however because of the wide range of age (0–17 years) and co-existing medical conditions, drug dosage may have to be modified upon user discretion.

Intravenous drugs contain various preservatives. Avoid benzyl alcohol-containing drugs in neonates and not more than 90 mg/kg/day in children <3 years, as they may cause the gasping syndrome.

Drug	Description and Perioperative Indications	Cautions and Contraindications	Side Effects	IV Dose (Paediatric)
Aceclofenac	Fever, pain, ankylosing spondylitis and arthritis	Contraindicated in patients with severe ulcers, gastrointestinal bleeding and hypersensitivity	• Diarrhoea, nausea, headache, indigestion, heartburn, abdominal pain, flatulence, feeling sick, dizziness and rash • Nephrotoxic, antiplatelet effect, can increase serum potassium and decrease serum sodium	• 2 mg/kg 12 hr oral • No IV preparation • Avoid in children < 6 years • Safety not established in paediatrics
Adenosine	Endogenous nucleoside with antiarrhythmic activity. Slows conduction through AV node. Treatment of acute paroxysmal SVT, duration 10 s	• Second- or third-degree heart block • Asthma • Caution in heart transplant recipients due to increased sensitivity • Theophylline and caffeine reduce the efficacy of adenosine	Flushing, dyspnoea and headache – all transient	• Up to 1 year: Initial 0.15 mg/kg, increasing by 0.05–0.1 mg/kg (max.) 0.3 mg/kg, IV • 1–11 years: Initial 0.1 mg/kg, increasing by 0.05–0.1 mg/kg (max.) 0.5 mg/kg (max. 12 mg), IV • 12–17 years: Initially 3 mg, followed by 6 mg and 12 mg if needed.

(*Contd.*)

Drug	Description and Perioperative Indications	Cautions and Contraindications	Side Effects	IV Dose (Paediatric)
Adrenaline	• Endogenous catecholamine with alpha and beta action: 1. Treatment of anaphylaxis 2. Bronchodilator 3. Positive inotrope 4. Given by nebuliser for croup 5. Prolongation of local anaesthetic action • 1:1000 contains 1 mg/ml • 1:10,000 contains 100 μg/mL	• Arrhythmias especially with halothane. • Via central catheter whenever possible • Incompatible with alkaline solutions	Hypertension, tachycardia, anxiety, hyperglycaemia and arrhythmias. Reduce uterine blood flow	• IV/IM 0.1 ml/kg of 1:10,000 (10 μg/kg) • Intraosseous/ET 0.1 ml/kg of 1:1000 (100 μg/kg) • Infusion 0.05–1 mcg/kg/min • Nebulisation 0.5 ml/kg (up to 5 ml) 1:1000 • Max dose for Infiltration 2 μg/kg
• Albumin 20% • Albumin 4%	Acute nephrosis, acute liver failure, ARDS, burns, cardiopulmonary bypass, hypoproteinaemia, renal dialysis, hypovolaemic, shock, haemolytic disease of newborn, hepatic surgery/transplantation	Hypersensitivity to commercially available albumin products, severe anaemia, cardiac failure, 25% solution in preemies (risk of IVH)	Anaphylaxis, CHF precipitation, oedema, hypertension/ hypotension, hypervolaemia, tachycardia, decreased myocardial contractility, bronchospasm, pulmonary oedema, salt and water retention, chills, fever, headache, nausea/ vomiting, pruritus, rash and urticaria	• 2–5 ml/kg IV of 20% solution • 10–20 mg/kg of 4% solution
Aminophylline	Methylxanthine bronchodilator is used in the prevention and treatment of asthma. Converted to theophylline, a phosphodiesterase inhibitor. Serum levels 10–20 mg/L (55–110 μmol/L)	• Caution in patients already receiving oral or IV theophyllines. Where serum level known as aminophylline 0.6 mg/kg should increase level by 1 mg/L • Avoid ephedrine along with Aminophylline	• Palpitations, tachycardia, tachypnoea, seizures, nausea • Severe hypokalaemia	• 5 mg/kg over 30 min, then 0.5–1 mg/kg/h IV • Not licensed for children less than 6 months
Amiodarone	Mixed class IC and III antiarrhythmic useful in the treatment of supraventricular and ventricular arrhythmias	• Via central catheter. Sino-atrial heart block, thyroid dysfunction • Avoid in cardiomyopathy, cardiac failure and circulatory collapse • Prolongs QT interval	• Commonly causes thyroid dysfunction and reversible corneal deposits • Can cause hypotension if administered rapidly	Loading dose 5 mg/kg then 25 μg/kg/min for 4 h, then 5–15 μg/kg/min, IV
Aprepitant	• Neurokinin 1 (NK-1) receptor antagonist • Nausea and vomiting – Chemotherapy induced • PONV	Acute porphyria	Asthenia, decreased appetite, headache, hiccups	• 6 months to 11 years: 3 mg/kg day 1(max. 125 mg) followed 2 mg/kg day 2 and 3 (max. 80 mg) • 12–17 years: 125 mg, 1 hour before chemotherapy, then 80 mg once daily for 2 days
Atracurium	Non-depolarising muscle relaxant, Hoffman elimination, plus non-specific enzymatic ester hydrolysis. Useful in severe renal or hepatic disease. Duration 20–35 min	• Store at 2–8°C • Dose based on ideal body weight in obese children	Histamine release and rash, hypotension, bronchospasm, administering over one minute reduces histamine-mediated side effects	• Intubation 0.3–0.6 mg/kg • Maintenance 0.1–0.2 mg/kg • An infusion 0.3–0.6 mg/kg/hr IV

(*Contd.*)

Drug	Description and Perioperative Indications	Cautions and Contraindications	Side Effects	IV Dose (Paediatric)
Atropine	• Muscarinic acetylcholine antagonist. Vagal blockade at AV and sinus node increases heart rate (transient decrease at low doses due to weak agonist effect). Crosses blood–brain barrier • Used to dry secretions prior to intubation in the past	• High fever • Angle-closure glaucoma	Decreases secretions, lowers oesophageal sphincter tone, relaxes bronchial smooth muscle	• IV: 10–20 μg/kg. Control of muscarinic effects of neostigmine: 10–20 μg/kg. • IM/SC: 10–30 μg/kg • PO: 40 μg/kg. • Organo-phosphorus compound poisoning 0.05–1 mg/kg, then 0.02–0.05 mg/kg every 15–60 min until atropinised
Alprostadil (prostaglandin E1, PGE1)	Maintain PDA	• Apnoea, hypotension, seizure and fever. • Avoid in hyaline membrane disease	Cardiac arrhythmias, respiratory distress, diarrhoea, bleeding disorders	5 nanograms /kg/ minute titrate by increasing 5 nanograms/kg/ minute to max 100 nanograms/kg/ minute
Amiodarone	Mixed class IC and III antiarrhythmic useful in the treatment of supraventricular and ventricular arrhythmias	• Via central catheter. Sino-atrial heart block, thyroid dysfunction • Avoid in cardiomyopathy, cardiac failure and circulatory collapse • Prolongs QT interval	Commonly causes thyroid dysfunction and reversible corneal deposits	25 μg/kg/min for 4 h, then 5–15 μg/kg/min, IV
Beclomethasone	• Asthma • Inhalational use	Steroid card for high-dose inhalational steroid	Throat Irritation	Aerosol/Powder: • 2–11 years: 100–200 micrograms twice daily • 12–17 years: 200–400 micrograms twice daily
Budesonide	• Asthma • Bronchopulmonary dysplasia • Inhalational Use	Steroid card for high-dose inhalational steroid	Nausea, headache, sore throat	• For BPD: 500 μg/kg twice daily • For Asthma: – 6 months–11 years: 125–500 micrograms twice daily, – 12–17 years: Initially 0.25–1 mg twice daily, maximum 2 mg per day

(*Contd.*)

Drug	Description and Perioperative Indications	Cautions and Contraindications	Side Effects	IV Dose (Paediatric)
Bupivacaine	Amide-type local anaesthetic used is for infiltration, epidural and spinal anaesthesia. Slower onset than lidocaine (lignocaine). Duration 200–400 min (slightly prolonged by adrenaline)	Greater cardiotoxicity than other local agents. Do not use for IVRA	Toxicity: tongue/circumoral numbness, restlessness, tinnitus, seizures, arrhythmias, cardiac arrest	• Infiltration/ regional blockade/ epidural/spinal: maximum dose dependent on injection site – 2 mg/kg for infiltration and nerve blocks recommended. • Epidural infusion 0.1–0.125% concentration at 0.1–0.4 mL/kg/hr. • Not recommended in neonates
Bicarbonate	• Alkaline salt used for the correction of acidosis. Dose (mmol) = weight (kg) × base deficit × 0.3 • To enhance the onset of action of local anaesthetics. 8.4% = 1000 mmol/L	• Precipitation with calcium-containing solutions, increased CO_2 production, necrosis on extravasation. • Via central catheter if possible	Alkalosis, hypokalaemia, hypernatraemia. Intraventricular bleed when given as rapid IV fast in neonates	1 mL/kg 8.4% solution (1 mmol/kg) IV
Buprenorphine	Opioid with both agonist and antagonist actions. Duration 6 h–12 hr	Only partially reversed by naloxone	Nausea, respiratory depression, constipation	>6 months. Slow IV/ IM: 3–6 μg/kg qds. SL: 3–6 μg/kg tds epidural – up to 3 μg/kg
Caffeine citrate	• CNS stimulant, structurally related to methyl-xanthines • It is recommended for short-term treatment of apnoea of prematurity	Hyper irritable baby, trauma, raised intracranial tension	Restlessness, irritability, tachycardia, necrotising enterocolitis	• 2 mg citrate = 1 mg base, 1–5 mg/kg of citrate 4–8 hr oral, PR, • neonate: 20 mg/ kg stat of citrate, then 5 mg/kg daily oral or IV over 15 min
Calcium chloride	Electrolyte replacement, positive inotrope, hyperkalaemia, hypermagnesaemia. 1 ml of Calcium chloride 10% contains 27 mgs or 0.68 mmol of elemental calcium	Necrosis on extravasation. Incompatible with bicarbonate	Arrhythmias, hypertension, hypercalcaemia	0.1–0.2 ml/kg 10% solution IV
Calcium gluconate	As calcium chloride 1 ml of calcium gluconate 10% contains 9 mg or 0.22 mmol of elemental calcium	Less phlebitis than calcium chloride	As calcium chloride	• 0.3–0.5 ml/kg • 10% solution (max. 20 mL) IV • 2–5 ml/kg/24 hr q6h
Cetirizine	Non-sedative antihistamine relief of allergy/urticaria	Urinary retention, glaucoma and porphyria	Dry mouth	PO: 0.2 mg/kg up to 10 mg
Chlorphenazine (chlorpheniramine)	Sedative antihistamine, relief of allergy, urticaria and anaphylaxis	Prostatic hypertrophy, urinary retention, glaucoma, porphyria and Epilepsy	• Drowsiness, dry mouth • Avoid in neonates: severe antimuscarinic effect	0.1–0.2 mg/kg/dose

(*Contd.*)

Drug	Description and Perioperative Indications	Cautions and Contraindications	Side Effects	IV Dose (Paediatric)
Cisatracurium	S-isomer of atracurium with greater potency, longer duration of action and less histamine release. Duration 55 min	Neuromuscular block potentiated by aminoglycosides, loop diuretics, magnesium, hypothermia, hypokalaemia, acidosis and volatile anaesthetic agents. Store at 2–8°C	Enhanced effect in myasthenia gravis, effect antagonised by anticholinesterases, e.g., neostigmine	• Intubation: 100 µg/kg IV. • Maintenance: 20 µg/kg every 0–30 min IV • Infusion: 0.06–0.1 mg/kg/hr
Clonazepam	Anticonvulsant activity	• Drowsiness • Porphyrias • Cerebellar/spinal ataxia	Hypersalivation	• 1 drop = 0.1 mg, 0.01 mg/kg (max. 0.5 mg) 12 hr oral, slow increment to 0.05 mg/kg (max. 2 mg) 6–12 hr oral. • Neonate 0.25 mg child 0.5 mg adult 1 mg (max.)
Clonidine	Selective α_2 agonist. Reduces the requirement for opioids and volatile anaesthetics. Enhances epidural analgesia	• Bradycardia and hypotension • Drowsiness • second- and third-degree heart block	Hypotension and sedation	3–5 µg/kg IV slowly. PO premed: 4 µg/kg Caudal: 1 µg/kg
Dantrolene	Direct-acting skeletal muscle relaxant used in the treatment of malignant hyperpyrexia and neuroleptic malignant syndrome. 20 mg/vial – reconstitute in 50 ml water	• Avoid combination with calcium channel blockers as may cause hyperkalaemia and cardiovascular collapse. • Extravasation causes tissue necrosis	Skeletal muscle weakness, hepatotoxicity	1–3 mg/kg IV repeated every 5 min till signs of MH disappear – to a maximum of 10 mg/kg. May have to repeat if signs of MH reappear
Desmopressin	A synthetic analogue of vasopressin (ADH) with longer duration of action and reduced pressor effect. Used for neurogenic diabetes insipidus and haemophilia (enhances factor VIII activity)	Caution in hypertension and CVS disease	Hypertension, abdominal pain, flushing and hyponatraemia	• IV/IM/SC: 0.4 µg/day. • Intranasal: 5–20 µg/day. • PO: 100–200 µg tds
Dexamethasone	Prednisolone derivative corticosteroid. Less sodium retention than hydrocortisone. Cerebral oedema, oedema prevention in airway manipulations	Interacts with anticholinesterase agents to increase weakness in myasthenia gravis	See prednisolone	• IV/IM/SC: 0.1–1 mg/kg • Cerebral oedema: 0.25–1 stat, then 0.6–1 mg/kg daily IV reducing over 3–5 days to 0.1 mg/kg • Croup: 0.6/kg IV/IM, then prednisolone 1 mg/kg 8–12 hr oral. • Anti-emetic: 0.5 mg/kg daily IV, IM, oral
Dexmedetomidine	Selective α_2 agonist. Reduces requirement for opioids and volatile anaesthetics	• Hypertension if given in boluses. • Caution in patients on digoxin and following congenital heart surgery – bradycardia • Inhibits non-shivering thermogenesis in neonates – hypothermia.	Hypotension, bradycardia, sedation	1 µ/kg IV over 15 min, then 0.2–0.7 µg/kg/hr for max 24 hr

(Contd.)

Drug	Description and Perioperative Indications	Cautions and Contraindications	Side Effects	IV Dose (Paediatric)
Diamorphine	Potent opioid analgesic	• Spinal/epidural use associated with respiratory depression • Causes withdrawal symptoms in neonates of dependent mothers	Histamine release, hypotension, bronchospasm, nausea, vomiting, pruritus and dysphoria	IV/SC: 50 μg/kg, then 15 μg/kg/h. Epidural 2–3 mg in 60 mL 0.125% bupivacaine at 0.1–0.4 mL/kg/hr
Diazepam	Long-acting benzodiazepine. Sedation or termination of status epilepticus	Thrombophlebitis Respiratory depression	Sedation and circulatory depression	• Premedication PO 0.1–0.2 mg/kg (max. 10 mg) • Sedation IV 0.05–0.3 mg/kg • Sedation IM 0.05–0.3 mg/kg
Diclofenac	Potent NSAID analgesic for mild to moderate pain	Hypersensitivity to aspirin, asthma, severe renal impairment, peptic ulceration	Gastrointestinal upset or bleeding, bronchospasm, tinnitus, fluid retention, platelet inhibition	PO/PR: 1 mg/kg tds. Maximum 3 mg/kg/day (>1 yr)
Digoxin	Cardiac glycoside. Weak inotrope and control of ventricular response in supraventricular arrhythmia therapeutic levels 0.5–2 μg/L	Enhanced effect/toxicity in hypokalaemia/ hypercalcaemia/ hypomagnesaemia/ hypoxia. Avoid cardioversion in toxicity	Anorexia, nausea fatigue, arrhythmias	• Rapid IV/PO • loading:15 μg/kg stat, then 5 μg/ kg qds, then 5 μg/ kg bd. • PO: 4 μg/kg bd
Dobutamine	β_1 adrenergic agonist, positive inotrope and chronotrope, cardiac failure	• Arrhythmias and hypertension, phlebitis but can be administered peripherally • Correct hypercapnia, hypoxia, acidosis during treatment	• Tachycardia. • Decreased peripheral and pulmonary vascular resistance • Tolerance develops after 72 hours	Infusion: 2–20 μg/ kg/min
Domperidone	• GERD • Nausea and vomiting	Mechanical GI obstruction, cardiac disease	Dry mouth, diarrhoea	250–400 micrograms/kg 3 times a day (max. per dose 10 mg)
Dopamine	• Naturally occurring catecholamine with α, β_1 and dopaminergic • Activity inotropic agent	Via central catheter Phaeochromocytoma (due to noradrenaline release)	Tachycardia, arrhythmias	Infusion: 2–20 μg/ kg/min
Enoxaparin	• Low molecular weight in the prophylaxis of deep vein thrombosis • May be used at the start of haemodialysis	• Blood dyscrasias • Hypersensitivity	The multidose vial contains benzyl alcohol, which is associated with gasping syndrome in premature infants	• <2 months- 1.5 mg/kg • 2 months–18 yr- 1 mg/kg 12 H • SC Prophylaxis- 0.75 mg/kg 12 hr (<2 months), 0.5 mg/kg SC (2 months–18 yr)
Esmolol	Short-acting cardio-selective beta-blocker, metabolised by red cell esterase. Treatment of supraventricular tachycardia or intra-operative hypertension	• Asthma, heart failure • AV block, verapamil treatment	Hypotension, bradycardia	SVT: 0.5 mg/kg over 1 min, then 50–200 μg/kg/min IV
Etomidate	• IV induction agent • Cardiostable in therapeutic doses	• Pain on injection • Reduce in liver cirrhosis	Nausea and vomiting. Myoclonic movements,? adrenal suppression	0.1–0.4 mg/kg IV
Fentanyl	• Synthetic phenyl piperidine derivative • Opioid analgesic • High lipid solubility and cardiostability • Duration 30–60 min	• IV: delayed respiratory depression • Epidural/spinal: pruritus	Circulatory and ventilatory depression. High doses may produce muscle rigidity	• 1–5 μg/kg, up to 25 μg/kg IV if post-op. Ventilation • Infusion: 2–4 μg/ kg/hr

(*Contd.*)

Drug	Description and Perioperative Indications	Cautions and Contraindications	Side Effects	IV Dose (Paediatric)
Flumazenil	• Benzodiazepine receptor antagonist • Duration 45–90 min	Benzodiazepine dependence (acute withdrawal), resedation if long-acting benzodiazepines	Arrhythmia, seizures Avoid in raised ICP and epilepsy	• 5 μg/kg, then repeat up to 40 μg/kg IV • Infusion: 2–10 μg/kg/hr
Fosphenytoin	• Status epilepticus • Neurosurgery associated seizures	Acute porphyrias, Heart block	Asthenia, dry mouth, dizziness, hypotension, bradycardia	Initially 20 mg/kg, at a rate of 2–3 mg/kg/minute, maximum 150 mg/minute, then 4–5 mg/kg daily in 1–4 divided doses
Furosemide (frusemide)	Loop diuretics are used in the treatment of hypertension, congestive cardiac failure, renal failure, fluid overload	• Prepare infusions in 0.9% saline and protect from light • Caution in hypoproteinaemia	Hypotension, tinnitus, ototoxicity hypokalaemia and hyperglycaemia	• 0.5–1.5 mg/kg bd • Oral/IM or IV once daily in prematures. 6–24 hourly in others
Gabapentin	Gamma-aminobutyric acid analogue, used as adjunctive therapy of partial seizures	Caution in patients with respiratory disease and on CNS depressant drugs	Dizziness, somnolence, peripheral oedema, asthenia, infection and diarrhoea	• Anticonvulsant: oral 10 mg/kg once day 1 oral, 12 hr day 2, 8 hr day, 3 then adjusted to 10–20 mg/kg 8 hr. Premed oral 25 mg/kg 1 hr preop • Analgesia: oral 2 mg/kg 8 hr, increased if reqd to 15 mg/kg or higher if tolerated
Glucose (Dextrose)	• Treatment of hypoglycaemia in an unconscious patient • Treatment of hyperkalaemia	50% solution irritant, therefore, flush after administration administer with insulin for the treatment of hyperkalaemia	• Not given alone without electrolytes – hyponatraemia. • Polyuria, localised pain	• Hypoglycaemia 0.05 ml/kg of 50% Dextrose • Solution or 2.5 ml/kg of 10% solution slow IV • Hyperkalaemia: 0.1 units/kg of insulin with 2 mL/kg 50% D
Glyceryl trinitrate	Organic nitrate vasodilator. Controlled hypotension, angina and congestive cardiac failure	Remove patches before defibrillation to avoid electrical arcing	Tachycardia, hypotension, headache, nausea, flushing, methhaemoglobinaemia	12–60 μg/kg/hr as infusion starting dose up to 300 μg/kg/hr
Glycopyrrolate	Anticholinergic	• High fever • Angle-closure glaucoma	Decreases secretions and lowers oesophageal sphincter tone, relaxes bronchial smooth muscle	10 mcg/kg
Haloperidol	• Antipsychotic, butyrophenones dopamine antagonist, not FDA approved below 3 yr. • It can be used in hyperactive behaviour, psychosis, schizophrenia	prolonged QT syndromes	Agranulocytosis, neuroleptic malignant syndrome, seizures, tardive dyskinesia,	0.01 mg/kg daily, increase up to 0.1 mg/kg 12 hr IV or oral

(*Contd.*)

Drug	Description and Perioperative Indications	Cautions and Contraindications	Side Effects	IV Dose (Paediatric)
Heparin	Endogenous mucopolysaccharide used for anticoagulation. Half-life 1–3 h. 100 units = 1 mg	• Monitor activated partial thromboplastin time. • Monitor platelets if used for more than 4 days • Reversed with protamine	• Haemorrhage • Heparin-induced thrombocytopenia • Prolonged usage-hyperkalaemia	• Low dose: 50–75 units/kg IV, then 10–15 units/kg/hr. • Full dose: 200 units/kg IV, then 15–30 units/kg/hr
Hydralazine	• Direct-acting arteriolar vasodilator used to control arterial pressure • Duration 2–4 hr	Higher doses required in rapid acetylators	Increased heart rate, cardiac output, stroke volume	0.1–0.2 mg/kg IV/IM q 4–6 hr PRN
Hydrocortisone	The endogenous steroid with anti-inflammatory and potent mineralocorticoid action (steroid of choice in replacement therapy). Treatment of allergy		Hyperglycaemia, hypertension psychic disturbance, muscle weakness, fluid retention	4 mg/kg, then 2–4 mg/kg qds IV
Hyoscine Hydrobromide (Scopolamine)	• Antimuscarinic sedative • Anti-emetic agent used as premedication reduces secretions and provides some amnesia	See atropine	See atropine	IV/IM/SC: 10 μg/kg
Ibuprofen	Closure of PDA Mild to moderate pain	Renal impairment, uncontrolled hypertension, heart disease	GI bleed and Hypersensitivity	• For PDA closure:10 mg/kg followed by 5 mg/kg every 24 hours for two doses. Maybe repeated after 48 hours if necessary. • For pain: 5 mg/kg 3–4 times daily • Maximum 30 mg/kg/day in divided doses
Indomethacin	NSAID analgesic for moderate pain. High incidence of side effects. Also used for neonatal ductus arteriosus closure	Hypersensitivity to aspirin, asthma, severe renal impairment, peptic ulceration	Gastrointestinal upset or bleeding, bronchospasm tinnitus, fluid retention, platelet inhibition	Ductus closure: 100–200 μg/kg IV over 30 min three doses
Insulin	Human soluble pancreatic hormone facilitates intracellular transport of glucose and anabolism. Diabetes mellitus, ketoacidosis and hyperkalaemia	• Monitor blood glucose and serum potassium • Store at 2–8°C	Hypoglycaemia, hypokalaemia	Ketoacidosis: 0.1–0.2 units/kg, then 0.1 units/kg/hr as an infusion
Isoprenaline	Synthetic catecholamine with potent beta-adrenergic agonist activity. Emergency treatment unresponsive to atropine and beta-blocker overdose		Tachycardia arrhythmias	Infusion: 0.1–2 μg/kg/min
Ketamine	Phencyclidine derivative producing dissociative anaesthesia. Induction maintenance of anaesthesia in high-risk or hypovolaemic patients	Emergence delirium reduced by benzodiazepines. Caution in hypertension. Control excess salivation with an antimuscarinic agent	• Bronchodilation, increased ICP, blood pressure, uterine tone, salivation. • Respiratory depression if given rapidly	• Induction: 1–3 mg/kg IV, 5–10 mg/kg IM • Infusion: 1–3 mg/kg/hr

(Contd.)

Drug	Description and Perioperative Indications	Cautions and Contraindications	Side Effects	IV Dose (Paediatric)
Ketorolac	NSAID analgesic for mild to moderate pain	Nephrotoxic, antiplatelet effect, hyperkalaemia, hyponatraemia	Gastrointestinal upset or bleeding, bronchospasm, tinnitus, fluid retention and platelet inhibition	Slow IV/IM: 0.5 mg/kg up to 30 mg
Labetalol	Combined α (mild) and β adrenergic receptor antagonist. Blood pressure control without reflex tachycardia. Duration 2–4 h	Asthma, heart failure, AV block and verapamil	Hypotension bradycardia, bronchospasm	• 0.2–1 mg/kg IV boluses until the response is seen, then 0.25–2 mg/kg/hr as an infusion. • Oral: 1–2 mg/kg/dose 12 hr (adult 50–100 mg) increased weekly up to max 10 mg/kg/dose 6 hr
Lacosamide	Focal seizures with or without generalisation	Heart block	Asthenia, confusion, depression, prolongation of the PR interval	• 50 kg and above: Loading dose 200 mg, followed by 100 mg twice daily, 12 hours after the initial dose. • <50 Kg: Consult product literature
Lansoprazole	• Proton pump inhibitor. • Reduction of gastric acid secretion	Reduce dosage in hepatic impairment	Headache, diarrhoea	PO: 0.3–0.6 mg/kg od
Levetiracetam	Focal/myoclonic/generalised seizures	Caution in liver and renal impairment	Confusion, Hallucination, muscle weakness	• 1–5 months: 7 mg/kg OD increased by 7 mg/kg bd max 21 mg/kg BD) • 6 months to 17 years: 10 mg/kg increase by 10 mg/kg bd max 30 mg/kg BD) increase the dose once in two weeks. • More than 50 kg: 250 mg bd increase to 500 mg bd max 1.5 g/dose
Levobupivacaine	The levorotatory enantiomer of bupivacaine with reduced cardiotoxicity	See bupivacaine	See bupivacaine	See bupivacaine
Lidocaine (lignocaine)	• Amide-type local anaesthetic: 1. Treatment of ventricular arrhythmias 2. Reduction of pressor response to intubation 3. Local anaesthetic – rapid onset, duration 30–90 min (prolonged by adrenaline)	Adrenaline-containing solutions contain preservative	Toxicity: Tongue circumoral numbness, restlessness, tinnitus, seizure, cardiac arrest	• Antiarrhythmic 1 mg/kg, then 10–50 μg/kg/min • Attenuation of pressor response: IV 1.5 mg/kg • Local anaesthesia: 0.5–2% solution. Maximum dose dependent on injection site – 3–4 mg/kg/4 hr (6 mg/kg with adrenaline)

(*Contd.*)

Drug	Description and Perioperative Indications	Cautions and Contraindications	Side Effects	IV Dose (Paediatric)
Lipid 20% (Intralipid)	• Local anaesthetic toxicity • Sodium channel blocker toxicity	• Severe liver damage • Hypersensitivity to soya or egg proteins	Fat overload syndrome	IV 1.5 ml/kg over 1 min, then 0.25 ml/kg/min over 20 min till haemodynamic stability is restored, can be repeated. Max dose of 10 mL/kg in 30 min
Lorazepam	• Benzodiazepine: 1. Sedation or premedication 2. Status epilepticus. Duration 6–10 hr	• Decreased requirement for anaesthetic agents • Can cause paradoxical effects of aggression.	Respiratory depression in combination with opioids. Amnesia	Sedation: 0.05 mg/kg/dose oral. Status epilepticus: 0.05–1 mg/kg IV over 2–5 min. May repeat 0.01–0.1 mg/kg/hr
Magnesium sulphate	• Essential mineral used to treat: 1. Hypomagnesaemia 2. Arrhythmias 3. Asthma 4. Persistent pulmonary hypertension of the newborn	Potentiates muscle relaxants. Monitoring of serum levels essential during treatment. Heart block	• CNS depression hypotension • Monitor Urine output, blood pressure and respiratory rate for signs of overdose	• Hypomagnesaemia: 0.2 ml/kg 50% solution over 20 min IV Magnesium sulphate 50% = 500 mg/mL = 2 mmol/ mL • Normal plasma level: 1.5–2.2 mEq/L
Mannitol	Osmotic diuretic used for renal protection and reduction of intracranial pressure, 20% solution = 20 g/100 mL	Anuria, intracranial bleeding except during craniotomy, cardiac failure, pulmonary oedema	• Extracellular volume expansion especially in severe renal or cardiovascular disease • Dehydration	0.25–2 g/kg IV
Melatonin	Insomnia, premedication	Autoimmune disorders	Arthralgia, abnormal behaviour	Initially, 2 mg once daily, increased to 5 mg once daily, dose to be taken 30–60 minutes before bedtime; maximum 10 mg per day
Methohexitone	• Short-acting barbiturate • Induction agent useful for ECT. Duration 5–10 min. 1% solution = 10 mg/mL	Porphyria. Premedication reduces excitation at induction	Hypotension, respiratory depression and hiccups	Induction. 1–2 mg/kg IV
Metoclopramide	Dopaminergic anti-emetic which increases gastric emptying and lowers oesophageal sphincter tone	Inhibits plasma cholinesterase	Extrapyramidal/dystonic reactions (treat with benztropine or procyclidine)	PO/IM/IV: 0.15 mg/kg up to 10 mg tds
Midazolam	• Short-acting benzodiazepine Sedative, amnesic, anticonvulsant • Duration 20–60 min. Oral administration of IV preparation effective though a larger dose required	Reduce dosage in debilitated patients, hypovolemia	Hypotension, respiratory depression and apnoea more common in neonates	• 0.1–0.2 mg/kg. • PO:0.5 mg/kg (use IV preparation in orange juice). • Intranasal: 0.2–0.3 mg/kg (use 5 mg/mL IV preparation)
Milrinone	Selective phosphodiesterase inhibitor used in cardiac failure with increased filling pressures, inodilator used after cardiac surgery	Stenotic valvular disease cardiomyopathy	Arrhythmias, hypotension, nausea	• IV 50 µg/kg over 10 min, then 0.375–0.75 µg/kg/min • Maximum 1.13 mg/kg/day

(*Contd.*)

Drug	Description and Perioperative Indications	Cautions and Contraindications	Side Effects	IV Dose (Paediatric)
Promethazine	• Phenothiazine, antihistamine, anticholinergic and anti-emetic sedative. • Paediatric sedation	• Children less than 2 years, respiratory depression • Epilepsy, angle-closure glaucoma	Extrapyramidal reactions	• >2 years sedation/premed • PO: 1–2 mg/kg • Anti-emetic: 0.2–0.5 mg/kg
Propofol	Di-isopropylphenol intravenous induction agent. Rapid recovery and little nausea. Agent of choice for daycare surgery, sedation or laryngeal mask insertion	• Reduce dose in haemodynamically unstable. • Allergy to eggs or soybean oil Caution in epilepsy	Apnoea, hypotension pain on injection. Myoclonic spasms, rarely convulsions	• Induction: IV 2–5 mg/kg. • Infusion: 4–15 mg/kg/hr. • NR induction <1 month. • NR maintenance <3 years
Propranolol	Non-selective β adrenergic antagonist, controlled hypotension	Asthma, heart failure and AV block verapamil treatment	Bradycardia, hypotension, AV block, bronchospasm	0.1 mg/kg IV over 5 min
Protamine	• Basic protein produced from salmon sperm • Heparin antagonist	Weakly anticoagulant and marked histamine release. Risk of allergy	Severe hypotension, pulmonary hypertension, bronchospasm and flushing	Slow IV: 1 mg per 1 mg heparin (100 units) to be reversed
Pyridostigmine	For treatment of myasthenia gravis			1 mg/kg 4–6 hr oral, 0.05–0.15 mg/kg/dose q4–6 hr, max dose 10 mg increase to max 2–3 mg/kg 4–6 H if required
Ranitidine	Histamine (H_2) receptor antagonist. Reduction in gastric acid secretion	Porphyria	Tachycardia	IV: 1 mg/kg slowly tds PO: 2–4 mg/kg bd
Remifentanil	• Ultra short-acting opioids are used to supplement general anaesthesia. Metabolised by non-specific esterases not plasma cholinesterase. • Duration 5–10 min and adjust dose as necessary	Be prepared to manage ventilation	Muscle rigidity, respiratory, depression, hypotension and bradycardia	0.1–0.4 μg/kg/min IV
Remimazolam	• Ultra-short acting benzodiazepine • Similar property to midazolam. • Safe for procedural sedation • Can be used for induction	• QT prolongation • Monitor respiration with concomitant usage of benzodiazepines, opioids and other respiratory depressant drugs	Hypotension, vomiting headache, somnolence	• Adults: – Sedation: 0.2 mg/kg/min, followed by 1–2 mg/kg/h – Anaesthesia induction: 6 or 12 mg/kg/h for induction, followed by 1 mg/kg/h (2 mg/kg/h of maximal infusion rate) for maintenance. • Paediatrics: Not enough literature

(*Contd.*)

Drug	Description and Perioperative Indications	Cautions and Contraindications	Side Effects	IV Dose (Paediatric)
Rocuronium	• Rapidly acting aminosteroid non-depolarising muscle relaxant. Rapid sequence induction (avoiding suxamethonium). • Duration 10–60 min (variable)	Neuromuscular block potentiated by amino-glycosides, loop diuretics, magnesium, lithium, hypothermia acidosis, prior use of suxamethonium and volatile anaesthetic agents	• Mild tachycardia, enhanced effect in myasthenia gravis, effects antagonised by anticholinesterases, e.g., neostigmine. • Monitor response with a peripheral nerve stimulator	• Intubation: IV 0.6–1 mg/kg • Maintenance: IV 0.1–0.15 mg/kg • Infusion: 0.3–0.6 mg/kg/hr
Ropivacaine	Amide-type local anaesthetic agent. Possible less motor block than other agents. Duration similar to bupivacaine but with lower toxicity	Allergy to local anaesthetics	Local anaesthetic systemic toxicity	• 0.2–1% solution • Maximum dose dependent on injection site 3–4 mg/kg/4 hr
Salbutamol	β_2 receptor agonist. Treatment of bronchospasm	Hypokalaemia possible	Tremor, vasodilation and tachycardia	• 4 μg/kg slow IV, then 0.1–1 μg/kg/min • Nebuliser: <5 years 2.5 mg. • >5 years: 2–2.5 mg
Sodium valproate	Acid chemical compound. Sole and adjunctive therapy for complex partial seizure activity	Suspected mitochondrial disorders, urea cycle disorders	Under the age of 2 years increased risk of hepatotoxicity	5 mg/kg 8–12 hr oral, increase if required to max 20 mg/kg. Slow release 15–60 mg/kg
Succinylcholine chloride (suxamethonium chloride)	• Depolarising muscle relaxant • Neuromuscular blockade during surgery	• Hepatic and renal impairment • Hyperkalaemia – burns, trauma, prolonged immobilisation • Neuromuscular disease, myopathies • Raised intraocular pressure • Familial history of pseudo choline esterase deficiency	• Arrythmias • Muscle pain • Trismus • Malignant hyperthermia	• IV (5–10 min of muscle relaxation): – 2 mg/kg, 0–1 year – 1–1.5 mg/kg, 1–17 years • IM (up to 30 minutes): – 5 mg/kg, 0–1 years – 4 mg/kg, 1–17 years
Sufentanil	More potent thiamyl analogue of fentanyl (five times potency). Analgesia. Duration 20–45 min	See fentanyl	See fentanyl	• Analgesia: 10–30 μg IV (0.2–0.6 μg/kg). • Anaesthesia: 0.6–4 μg/kg IV
Sugammadex	Cyclodextrin binds to non-depolarising muscle relaxant (rocuronium)		• Hypersensitive reaction • Mild prolongation of PT and aPTT	IV 2 mg/kg (after spontaneous recovery), 4 mg/kg (if 1–2 post-titanic counts), 16 mg/kg for immediate reversal of rocuronium
Tapentadol	Centrally acting, μ opioid and norepinephrine reuptake inhibitor	Obesity, Seizures, on SSRI drugs	Asthenia, decreased appetite, sleep disorders	• 1–2 mg/kg 4–6 hr oral • Lesser incidence of nausea, vomiting compared with tramadol

(Contd.)

Drug	Description and Perioperative Indications	Cautions and Contraindications	Side Effects	IV Dose (Paediatric)
Terbutaline	Asthma acute and maintenance of acute asthma		Cardiac arrhythmias	• SC 5–10 µg/kg, IV child 3–6 µg/kg/min for 1 hr, then 0.4 µg/kg/min • Inhalation 0.25–0.5 ml diluted in 4 ml 3–6 hr
Tetracaine (amethocaine)	• Ester-type local anaestheticTopical analgesia prior to venepuncture. Ametop® gel contains 4% amethocaine (also available as eye drops, but has a temporary disruptive effect on corneal epithelium). • Duration 4 h	• Apply only to intact skin under occlusive dressing. • Remove after 45 min		As adult. <1 month not recommended
Theophylline	Acute and chronic asthma	Can cause tachycardia arrhythmias	Cautious in patients with acute migraine, peptic ulcer and, convulsive disorders	• 80 mg theophylline = 100 mg aminophylline • Loading dose 8 mg/kg oral. Maintenance: 1st wk of life 2 mg/kg, 2nd wk 3 mg/kg, 3 wk–12 months (0.1 × age in wk) + 2.7 mg/kg 8 hr • 1–9 yr 4 mg/kg 4–6 H, 10–16 yr 3–7 mg/kg
Thiopentone sodium	• Short-acting thiobarbiturate. Induction of anaesthesia, anticonvulsant, cerebral protection. • Recovery due to redistribution	Accumulation repeated doses. Caution in hypovolaemia porphyria	Hypotension	Induction: IV neonate 2–4 mg/kg child 5–6 mg/kg
Tramadol	Opioid analgesics thought to have less respiratory depression, constipation euphoria or abuse potential, than other opioids. Has opioid and non-opioid mechanisms of action	Only 30% antagonised by naloxone. Caution in epilepsy MAOI	Nausea, dizziness and dry mouth. Increased in conjunction with other opioids	Up to 2 mg/kg IV
Tranexamic acid	• Inhibits plasminogen activation reducing fibrin dissolution by plasmin. • Reduced haemorrhage	Avoid in thromboembolic disease and renal impairment	Dizziness and nausea	PO: 15–20 mg/kg tds
Triamcinolone hexacetonide (Lederspan®)	Relatively insoluble corticosteroid for depot injection	Dose depends on the site of injection. Strict asepsis is essential. Dilute 20 mg/mL solution prior to use		Intra-articular or intrasynovial: 2.5–15 mg

(*Contd.*)

Drug	Description and Perioperative Indications	Cautions and Contraindications	Side Effects	IV Dose (Paediatric)
Vasopressin	Extract from the posterior pituitary used in upper GI bleed, diabetes insipidus and septic shock. Available as an aqueous or oily compound	Epilepsy, heart failure, chronic nephritis	Chest pain, gangrene, Headache	• Aqueous IM/SC 2.5–10 U 6–12 hourly, IV, put 2–5 U in 1 L fluid, replace urine output + 10% IV; or 2–10 U IM or SC 8th hourly every 2–4 days; for GI haemorrhage 0.4 U/min IV in an adult • Oily: 2.5–5 U IM every 2–4 days
Vecuronium	Aminosteroid non-depolarising muscle relaxant. Cardiostable and no histamine release. Duration 30–45 min	Neuromuscular block potentiated by aminoglycosides, loop diuretics, magnesium lithium, hypothermia, acidosis, prior use of suxamethonium, volatile anaesthetic agents	• Enhanced effect in myasthenia gravis. • Effects antagonised by anticholinesterases, e.g., neostigmine. Monitor response with the peripheral nerve stimulator	• Intubation 0.08–0.1 mg/kg • 0.01–0.015 mg/kg IV once in 20–45 min
Warfarin	Coumarin derivative, oral anticoagulant AF, mitral valve disease: INR 2.5–3.0 prosthetic heart valve: INR 3.0–4.5		Haemorrhage	PO: 0.2 mg/kg up to 10 mg od for 1 day, then 0.05–0.2 mg/kg od depending on INR

aPTT, activated partial thromboplastin clotting time; ARDS, Acute respiratory distress syndrome; BPD, bronchopulmonary dysplasia; CHF, congestive heart failure; CNS, central nervous system; GERD, gastroesophageal reflux disease; ICP, intracranial pressure; IVH, intraventricular haemorrhage; IVRA, intravenous regional anesthesia; MAOI, monoamine oxidase inhibitor; NSAID, non steroidal anti inflammatory drugs; PDA, patent ductus arteriosus; PONV, post operative nausea and vomiting; SSRI, selective serotonin reuptake inhibitor; SVT, supra ventricular tachycardia.

Appendix 2

Antibiotics

Amar Nandhakumar

Drug	Description and Perioperative Indications	Cautions and Contraindications	Side Effects	IV Dose (Paediatric)
Amikacin	Infections due to susceptible strains of Gram-negative bacteria, including *Pseudomonas* species, *Escherichia coli*, species of indole-positive and indole-negative Proteus, *Providencia* species, *Klebsiella-Enterobacter-Serratia* species and *Acinetobacter* (*Mima-Herellea*) species	Pregnant female, severe asthmaticus, kidney disease, parkinsonism and myasthenia gravis	Neurotoxic, nephrotoxic, skin rash, fever, headache, nausea, arrhythmia and hypotension	Neonate 15 mg/kg stat, then 7.5 mg/kg daily if <30 wk gestation, 10 mg/kg; if 30–35 weeks daily gestation, 1 wk to 10 yr, 25 mg/kg day 1, then 18 mg/kg daily; >10 yr: 20 mg/kg day 1, then 15 mg/kg daily IV
Ampicillin	Broad spectrum penicillin antibiotic	History of allergy	Nausea, diarrhoea and rash	10–25 mg/kg qds IV
Amoxicillin	Broad spectrum penicillin antibiotic	History of allergy	Nausea, diarrhoea and rash	10–25 mg/kg tds, 50 mg/kg in severe infections IV
Azithromycin	Acute bacterial sinusitis, community-acquired pneumonia, patients with cystic fibrosis, patients with nosocomially acquired infections, patients requiring hospitalisation and elderly or debilitated patients	Use with caution in renal failure	Dyspepsia, flatulence, melaena, vaginitis, nephritis, dizziness, somnolence, pruritus and photosensitivity	15 mg/kg on day 1, then 7.5 mg/kg on days 2–5
Benzylpenicillin	Broad-spectrum antibiotic	History of allergy	Nausea, diarrhoea, rash and anaphylaxis	25 mg/kg qds, 50 mg/kg qds for severe infections IV
Cefazolin	First-generation broad-spectrum cephalosporin	History of allergy		25–50 mg/kg
Cefixime	Third-generation, sore throat, otitis media, laryngitis and pneumonia			5 mg/kg, 12–24 hr oral

(*Contd.*)

Drug	Description and Perioperative Indications	Cautions and Contraindications	Side Effects	IV Dose (Paediatric)
Cefotaxime	Third-generation cephalosporin broad spectrum antibiotic	Penicillin sensitivity		25 mg/kg tds, 50 mg/kg qds in severe infections IV
Ceftazidime	As above			15–25 mg/kg 8 hr IV/IM, severe infection or cystic fibrosis: 50 mg/kg 12 hr (1 wk of life), 8 hr (1–4 wk), 6–8 hr (>4 wk)
Cefuroxime	Second-generation cephalosporin broad spectrum antibiotic	10% cross sensitivity with penicillin allergy		20–30 mg/kg tds, IV
Ciprofloxacin	Fluroquinolone	QT prolongation	Arthropathy	IV: 10–20 mg/kg Q8–12 h
Clindamycin	Linomycin antibiotic	Diarrhoea, jaundice, easy bruising and severe skin reaction	• Allergic to drug, kidney disease, liver disease • Antibiotic associated colitis	• 6 mg/kg 6 hr oral/ IV over 30 min • Dilute with NS or 5%D to a concentration not more than 18 mg/ml Infuse slowly: max 20 mg/kg/hour
Erythromycin	Macrolides antibiotic with spectrum similar to penicillin	Arrhythmias with cisapride and terfenadrine	Nausea and diarrhoea	10–25 mg/kg qds PO
Flucloxacillin	Penicillinase resistant antibiotic active agent staphylococci	• Hypotension on rapid • IV administration	Thrombophlebitis	10–25 mg/kg qds IV
Gentamycin	Aminoglycoside	Concurrent and/or sequential systemic or topical use of other potentially neurotoxic and/or nephrotoxic drugs, such as cisplatin, cephaloridine, kanamycin, amikacin, neomycin, polymyxin B, colistin, streptomycin, tobramycin and vancomycin should be avoided	Nephrotoxic and neurotoxic	• IV/IM 1 wk-10 yr 8 mg/kg day 1, then 6 mg/kg daily • >10 yr: 7 mg/kg day 1, then 5 mg/kg daily
Imipenem	• Carbapenem broad-spectrum antibiotic • Administered with cilastatin to reduce renal metabolism	Caution in renal failure	Nausea, vomiting, diarrhoea, convulsions and thrombophlebitis	>3 months 10 mg/kg over 30 min qds IV (25 mg/kg severe infections)

(*Contd.*)

Drug	Description and Perioperative Indications	Cautions and Contraindications	Side Effects	IV Dose (Paediatric)
Meropenem	Broad-spectrum antibiotic	• Caution in renal failure • Administer as IV infusion over about 15–30 minutes or as an IV bolus injection over about 3–5 minutes	• Hypersensitivity, seizures • Clostridium difficile – associated Diarrhoea	• 10–20 mg/kg IV every 8–12 hours • Maximum dose: 1 g/dose
Metronidazole	Antimicrobial drug with high activity against anaerobic bacteria and protozoa		• Unpleasant metallic taste • Abdominal cramps and loss of appetite	• 7.5 mg/kg every 8 hours (max. per dose 400 mg) – 7 days • 10–14 days in Clostridioides difficile infection)
Ofloxacin	As ciprofloxacin	Antibiotic		5 mg/kg 8–12 hr or 10 mg/kg 12 hr oral/ IV over 1 hr
Teicoplanin	• Glycopeptide antibiotic with activity against aerobic and anaerobic. • Gram-positive bacteria		Ototoxicity and nephrotoxicity	IV 10 mg/kg for 3 doses 12 hourly, then 6 mg/kg od
Vancomycin	Glycopeptide antibiotic with activity against aerobic and anaerobic Gram-positive bacteria. Peak level <30 mg/L. Trough level <30 mg/L	Avoid rapid infusion (hypotension, wheezing urticaria, red man syndrome). Reduce dose in renal impairment	Ototoxicity, nephrotoxicity and phlebitis	>1 month 15 mg/kg over 2 h tds IV

Appendix 3

Index of (Some) Syndromes and their Anaesthetic Implications

Venkatesan Thiruvenkatarajan

Name	Description	Anaesthetic Implications
Achondrogenesis Parenti–Fraccaro type	Short neck, short limbs, early death	Difficult intubation
Adrenogenital syndrome	Inability to synthesise hydrocortisone and possibly aldosterone and virilisation of female	Hydrocortisone required even if there is no salt-losing; check electrolytes
Albers–Schönberg disease (marble bone or osteopetrosis)	Brittle bones, pathologic fractures	Anaemia from marrow sclerosis; hepatosplenomegaly; care in positioning and restraint, limited joint mobility
Albright–Butler syndrome	Renal tubular acidosis; hypokalaemia; renal calculi	Correct electrolytes to within normal limits; renal impairment
Albright osteodystrophy (pseudohypoparathyroidism)	Ectopic bone formation; mental retardation	Hypocalcaemia – possible ECG conduction defects, neuromuscular problems; convulsions
Alport syndrome	Progressive renal failure; nerve deafness; ocular abnormalities	Renal failure in second to third decade; care with drugs excreted by the kidney
Alström syndrome	Obesity, blindness by 7 years; hearing loss; diabetes after puberty; glomerulosclerosis	Renal impairment; management of diabetes and obesity
Amyotonia congenita (infantile muscular atrophy)	Anterior horn cell degeneration	Sensitive to thiopental (reduced muscle mass) and respiratory depressants; care with muscle relaxants
Amyotrophic lateral sclerosis	Degeneration of motor neurons	Avoid succinylcholine; possible K^+-release and cardiac arrest; minimal thiopental and curare; avoid respiratory depressants
Analbuminaemia	Almost absent albumin (4–100 mg/dL)	Very sensitive to protein-bound drugs
Andersen disease (glycogen storage disease type IV)	Debranching enzyme deficiency	Possibility of hypoglycaemia during anaesthesia
Apert syndrome (acrocephalosyndactyly)	Craniosynostosis	Syndactyly of hands; difficult intubation; possibly raised intracranial pressure, associated congenital heart disease
Arnold–Chiari syndrome	Stridor by traction of vagus nerve	Airway-related problems
Arthrogryposis multiplex	Multiple congenital contractures; stiffness of joints associated with hypoplasia of attached muscles	10% have congenital heart disease; possible airway problem
Asplenia syndrome	Absent spleen, visceral right-sidedness	Complex cardiovascular anomalies, present with cyanosis and heart failure
Ataxia–telangiectasia	Cerebellar ataxia; skin and conjunctival telangiectasia; decreased serum IgA and IgE; 10% develop reticuloendothelialmalignancy	Defective immunity – recurrent chest and sinus infections; bronchiectasis; maintain strict asepsis

(*Contd.*)

Name	Description	Anaesthetic Implications
Beckwith syndrome (infantile gigantism)	Birth weight > 4000 g; macroglossia and exomphalos; polycythaemia, visceromegaly in infants	Persistent severe neonatal hypoglycaemia; airway problems; older children associated with hepatocellular cancer
Blackfan–Diamond anaemia (syndrome)	Congenital idiopathic red cell aplasia	Liver and spleen enlarged; hypersplenism, thrombocytopenia; steroid therapy required
Bloch–Sulzberger syndrome	Ecto and mesodermal defects, microcephaly, spastic paralysis	Difficult intubation
Bowen syndrome (cerebrohepatorenal syndrome)	Hypotonia, hepatomegaly and neonatal jaundice; polycystic kidneys; associated congenital heart disease	Hypoprothrombinaemia; care with renally excreted drugs and muscle relaxants
Carpenter syndrome	Obesity; cranial synostosis; associated congenital heart disease; mental retardation; peculiar facies; syndactyly of fingers and toes	Hypoplastic mandible; possibly difficult intubation
Central core disease	Muscular dystrophy	• Susceptible to malignant hyperpyrexia, so avoid succinyl choline • Also see Amyotonia Congenita
Cerebrohepatorenal syndrome (Zellweger syndrome)	Jaundice, renal failure, cardiac failure, hypotonia	Multiorgan failure
Chediak–Higashi syndrome	Partial albinism, immunodeficiency; hepatosplenomegaly	Steroid therapy; recurrent chest infection; thrombocytopenia – may require platelets
Cherubism	Tumorous lesions of mandibles and maxillae with intraoral masses; may cause respiratory distress	Intubation may be extremely difficult; may require tracheostomy for acute respiratory distress; profuse bleeding at surgery
Chotzen syndrome	Craniosynostosis	May be difficult intubation; associated renal anomalies and possible impaired renal excretion of drugs
Christ–Siemens–Touraine syndrome (anhidrotic ectodermal dysplasia)	Absent sweating – heat intolerance	Cannot control temperature by sweating; persistent upper respiratory and chest infection due to poor mucus formation
Chronic granulomatous disease	Inherited disorder of leukocyte function; recurrent infection with non-pathogenic organisms	Hepatomegaly in 95%; poor pulmonary function; avoid infection – strict asepsis
Collagen disease; dermatomyositis rheumatoid arthritis, systemic lupus erythematosus, polyarteritis nodosa	Systemic connective disease frequently treated with steroids; osteoporosis and fatty infiltration of muscle; variable systemic involvement	Often have pulmonary infiltration or fibrosis: may have temporomandibular or crico-arytenoid arthritis causing airway and intubation difficulties; anaemia common; risk of fat embolism after osteotomy, fracture or minor trauma; renal involvement common; potential Addisonian crises
Conard syndrome	Chondrodystrophy with contractures, saddle nose, mental retardation; associated congenital heart disease and renal anomalies	Problems are those of associated renal and cardiac disease
Conradi–Hunerman syndrome	Chondrodysplasia, dwarfism, cataracts, difficulty with intubation, poor veins.	Difficult intubation
Costello syndrome	Coarse facies, short neck, macroglossia, hypertrophied tonsil, congenital heart disease and hypertrophic cardiomyopathy, endocrine abnormalities, namely, hypothyroidism, hypopituitarism, hypoadrenalism, seizure disorder	Difficult intubation and post-op respiratory problem, hypoglycaemia, multiple endocrine anomalies
Cretinism (congenital hypothyroidism)	Absent thyroid tissue or defective synthesis of thyroxine and goitre	Airway problems – large tongue, goitre, respiratory centre sensitive to depressants; carbon dioxide retention common; hypoglycaemia, hyponatraemia, hypotension, low cardiac output; transfusion poorly tolerated
Cri-du-chat syndrome (cat cry syndrome)	Chromosome 5-P abnormal; abnormal cry, microcephaly micrognathia; congenital heart disease; hypertelorism exophthalmos; cat-like cry	Airway problems – stridor, laryngomalacia: possibly difficult intubation

(*Contd.*)

Name	Description	Anaesthetic Implications
Crouzon disease	Craniosynostosis; exophthalmos, hypertelorism; hypoplastic mandible	Possibly difficult intubation; severe blood loss with craniofacial operation
Cutis laxa	Elastic fibre degeneration, pendulous skin, frequent hernias; emphysema and cor pulmonale, arterial fragility	Pulmonary infection, emphysema and cor pulmonale; poor tissues – IV difficult to maintain; excess of soft tissues around larynx may lead to respiratory obstruction
Cystic fibrosis	Multisystem involvement	V/Q imbalance resulting in hypoxaemia; bronchial secretions; recurrent infection: cor pulmonale; liver abnormalities; malabsorption; vitamin K deficiency; coagulopathy
Dandy–Walker syndrome	Hydrocephalus, posterior fossa enlargement	Airway, raised ICP-related problems
DiGeorge syndrome (third and fourth arch syndrome)	Absent thymus and parathyroid glands; immune deficiency; susceptibility to fungal and viral infection; treated by foetal thymic transplants	Recurrent chest infections; hypoparathyroidism; low calcium and tetany; stridor; aortic arch abnormalities and reduced cardiac output; donor blood must be irradiated with 3000 rad to prevent graft versus host reaction; strict asepsis to be maintained
Down syndrome (mongolism)	Mental retardation; microcephaly; small nasopharynx; hypotonia; 60% have congenital heart disease; duodenal atresia in some; atlantoaxial instability	Difficult airway – large tongue; risk of airway obstruction; problems of cardiac anomalies; risk of cervical cord injury; radiological evaluation of atlanto-occipital joint to rule out subluxation
Duchenne type muscular dystrophy	Muscular dystrophy with frequent cardiac muscle involvement; usually die in second decade	As for amyotonia congenita plus cardiac involvement; minimal drug dosage; avoid respiratory depressants, muscle relaxants post-op ventilation may be required; risk of MH?
Edward syndrome (trisomy 18)	Congenital heart disease in 95%; micrognathia in 80%; renal malformations 50–80%; usually die in infancy	Possible difficult intubation; care with renally excreted drugs
Ehlers–Danlos syndrome (cutis hyperelastica)	Collagen abnormality with hyperelasticity and fragile tissues; dissecting aneurysm of aorta; fragility of other blood vessels; bleeding diathesis	Cardiovascular system; spontaneous rupture of vessels; angiogram 1% mortality; ECG conduction abnormalities; IV difficult to maintain – haematoma; poor tissues and clotting defect lead to haemorrhage, especially GI tract; spontaneous pneumothorax
Ellis–van Creveld syndrome (chondroectodermal dysplasia)	Ectodermal defects, skeletal anomalies; 50% have congenital heart disease	Chest wall anomalies lead to poor lung function; may have abnormal maxilla and upper lip, hepatosplenomegaly
Epidermolysis bullosa	Erosions and blisters from minor skin trauma	Airway – oral lesions, adhesion of tongue; ketamine is recommended; use small oral tube to avoid laryngeal trauma; avoid skin trauma from tapes; history of steroid therapy; check for porphyria (similar skin lesions)
Fabry disease (diffuse angiokeratoma)	Lysosomal storage disease; corneal opacities; cardiopulmonary involvement; renal failure	Hypertension, myocardial ischaemia (before third or fourth decade); renal failure – care with renally excreted drugs
Familial periodic paralysis	Muscle disease; hypokalaemia, attacks of quadriplegia	Monitor serum K^+; limit use of dextrose; monitor ECG; avoid relaxants; avoid hyperventilation and drugs that shift potassium intracellular like albuterol
Fanconi syndrome (renal tubular acidosis)	Usually secondary to other disease; proximal tubular defect; acidosis, K loss, dehydration	Impaired renal function; treat electrolyte and acid–base abnormalities; look for primary disease (galactosaemia, cystinosis, etc.)
Farber disease (lipogranulomatosis)	Sphingomyelin deposition; widespread visceral lipogranulomas, especially in the central nervous system	Deposits in larynx – careful intubation; generalised systemic involvement leading to cardiac, renal failure
Favism	G-6PD deficiency; haemolytic anaemia	Haemolysis following oxidant drugs (e.g. ASA and sulpha drugs)
Friedreich ataxia	Degeneration of cerebellum, lateral and posterior column of spinal cord; scoliosis; myocardial degeneration and fibrosis	Heart failure and arrhythmias; care with cardiac depressant drugs

(Contd.)

Name	Description	Anaesthetic Implications
Gaucher disease	Cerebroside accumulation in CNS, liver, spleen, etc.	Pulmonary disease from aspiration (pseudo-bulbar palsy); hepatosplenomegaly, hypersplenism; may cause platelet deficiency
Glanzmann disease (thrombasthaenia)	Platelet adenosine diphosphate reduced; abnormal function	No specific therapy for bleeding, platelet transfusion disappointing; history of steroids
Goldenhar syndrome (oculoauriculovertebral dysplasia)	Unilateral facial hypoplasia; congenital heart disease in 20%; 60% mandibular hypoplasia	Difficult airway and intubation; problems of associated cardiac disease
Gorlin–Goltz syndrome (focal dermal hypoplasia)	Hernias, prolapse, etc.; congenital heart disease; renal anomalies	Asymmetry of head – difficult airway
Gorlin–Chaudry–Moss syndrome	Craniofacial dysostosis – difficult intubation; PDA	Difficult intubation
Groenblad–Strandberg (pseudo-xanthoma elasticum)	Degeneration elastic tissue in skin, eye and cardiovascular system	Rupture of arteries, especially GI tract, hypertension, arterial calcification, occlusion cerebral, coronary, arteries; difficult maintenance of IV cannula
Guillain–Barre syndrome (acute idiopathic polyneuritis)	Acute polyneuropathy, progressive peripheral neuritis often involving cranial nerves, bulbar palsy with hypoventilation and hypotension	Avoid succinylcholine for K release, may require tracheostomy, mechanical ventilation, support of blood pressure
Hand–Schüller–Christian disease (histiocytosis X)	Histiocytic granulomas in bones and viscera – larynx, lungs, liver and spleen	Laryngeal fibrosis; pulmonary – diffuse of hilar infiltration; respiratory failure, cor pulmonale; hypersplenism and pancytopenia; liver involvement; diabetes insipidus if sella tursica involved; history of steroids; benign intracranial hypertension; loose teeth
Hanhart syndrome	Hypoglossia/aglossia, micrognathia, limb defects, sixth and seventh cranial nerve palsies	Difficult intubation
Hallermann–Streiff syndrome	Mandibular hypoplasia, microphthalmia, glaucoma	Difficult intubation
Hermansky–Pudlak syndrome	Albinism, bleeding diathesis	Platelet abnormality; try platelet transfusion; no specific treatment
Holt–Oram syndrome (heart–hand syndrome)	Upper limb abnormalities; congenital heart disease – atrioseptal defect; possibly sudden death from pulmonary embolus, coronary occlusion	Problems of cardiac defect
Homocystinuria	Inborn error of metabolism; thromboembolic phenomena; cataract, dislocation of lens, retinal degeneration, optic atrophy and glaucoma	Dextran-70 to reduce viscosity and platelet adhesiveness, increase peripheral perfusion; angiography may precipitate thrombosis
Hunter syndrome (mucopolysaccharidosis II)	Stiff joints, dwarfing, hepatosplenomegaly; pectus excavatum and kyphoscoliosis; valvular and coronary heart disease	Upper airway obstruction due to infiltration of lymphoid tissue and larynx; pneumonias; possible hypersplenism; cardiac failure
Hurler syndrome (mucopolysaccharidosis I)	Pulmonary hypertension; usually die within 10 years from respiratory and cardiac failure	As for Hunter syndrome, but more severe; frequent upper respiratory infection; abnormal respiratory infection; abnormal tracheobronchial cartilages; severe coronary artery disease at early age, valvular and myocardial involvement
Jervell and Lange–Nielsen syndrome (cardiac–auditory syndrome)	Cardiac conduction defects; deafness	Syncope, arrhythmias, ECG – large T waves, prolonged QT interval; may need digoxin or propranolol (or both) or pacemaker
Jeune syndrome (asphyxiating thoracic dystrophy)	Narrow, immobile thorax; respiratory failure; nephritis	Severe restrictive lung disease may require post-op ventilatory support
Johanson–Blizzard syndrome	Dwarfism, a beaked nose, high forehead, micrognathia, associated congenital heart disease, pancreatic dysfunction, hypothyroidism, hypopituitarism	Difficult intubation, delayed gastric emptying, temperature regulation alteration, multiple endocrine dysfunction, cardiac complications, anaemia

(Contd.)

Name	Description	Anaesthetic Implications
Kartagener syndrome (immotile cilia syndrome)	Situs inversus, immotile cilia, deficient mucociliary clearance, sinusitis, otitis media, chronic bronchitis	Chronic respiratory and sinus infection
Kasabach–Merritt syndrome	Haemangioma and thrombocytopenia; average age at death 5 weeks	Haemangioma suddenly increases in size with associated severe thrombocytopenia and haemorrhage; replace blood loss, transfuse platelets; splenectomy; steroids
Kleeblattschadel	Clover leaf skull, facial abnormality, intubation difficulties	Difficult intubation
Klippel–Feil syndrome	Congenital fusion of two or more cervical vertebrae leading to neck rigidity	Difficult airway and intubation
Klippel–Trénaunay syndrome (angio-osteohypertrophy)	Usually unilateral; arteriovenous fistulas, thrombocytopenia	Arteriovenous fistulas and anaemia lead to high cardiac output state; thrombocytopenia; visceral haemangiomas
Langer–Saldingto type	Large head, short limbs, early death	Difficult intubation
Laurence–Moon–Biedl syndrome	Obesity, retinitis pigmentosa; polydactyly; mental retardation	May be associated with cardiac defects, renal disease and occasionally diabetes insipidus
Larsen syndrome	Multiple congenital dislocations; connective tissue defect; poor cartilage in rib cage, epiglottis, arytenoids	Possible difficult intubation; chronic respiratory problems
Leopard syndrome	Multiple large freckles; congenital heart disease, ECG anomalies – aberrant conduction; hypertelorism	95% pulmonary stenosis Cardiomyopathy, long PR interval
Leprechaunism	Failure to thrive, endocrine disorders, severe mental retardation	Hypoglycaemia due to hyperinsulinism from hyperplastic Islet of Langerhans; renal tubular defects – impaired renal function
Lesch–Nyhan syndrome	Hyperuricaemia and mental retardation; renal failure by age 10	High serum uric acid leads to red cell damage and renal stones; care with renally excreted drugs
Letterer–Siwe disease (histiocytois X)	Histiocytosis granulomas in viscera and bones; clinical course similar to acute leukaemia	Pancytopenia – anaemia and purpura haemorrhage; pulmonary infiltration; hepatic involvement; gingival inflammation and necrosis, loss of teeth
Lipodystrophy (total lipoatrophy)	Generalised loss all body fat; fatty, fibrotic liver; portal hypertension and splenomegaly; nephropathy; diabetes	Liver failure – avoid halothane and drugs metabolised by liver; hypersplenism – anaemia and thrombocytopenia; possible renal failure; usual diabetic precautions
Lowe syndrome (oculocerebrorenal syndrome)	Male only; cataract, glaucoma; mental retardation; hypotonia; renal acidosis, proteinuria, osteoporosis and rickets	Check electrolyte and acid–base balance; Check serum Ca^{++} (treated with vitamin D and C^{++}); care with renally excreted drugs
Maffucci syndrome	Enchondromatosis and haemangiomas with malignant change	Pathologic fractures; GI bleeding from haemangiomas; orthostatic hypotension; may be sensitive to vasodilator drugs
Maple syrup urine disease (branched chain ketonuria)	Amino acid disturbance treated by diet only; severe neurologic damage and respiratory disturbances	General supportive measures
Marfan syndrome (arachnodactyly)	Connective tissue disorder; dilated aortic root leads to aortic insufficiency; aortic, thoracic or abdominal aneurysm; pulmonary artery, mitral valve involved; kyphoscoliosis, pectus excavatum, lung cysts; joint instability and dislocation	Care with myocardial depressant drugs; beware of possible dissection of aorta; lung function poor; possible pneumothorax; care in positioning – easily dislocated joints
Maroteaux–Lamy syndrome (mucopolysaccharidosis IV)	Myocardial involvement; kyphoscoliosis and chest infection; hepatosplenomegaly	Heart failure by age 20; care with cardiac depressant drugs; chronic respiratory infection with poor lung reserve; hypersplenism, anaemia, thrombocytopenia
Meckel syndrome	Microcephaly, micrognathia and cleft epiglottis; congenital heart disease; renal dysplasia	Intubation may be difficult Cardiac problems; renal failure in infancy – care with renally excreted drugs

(*Contd.*)

Name	Description	Anaesthetic Implications
Median cleft face syndrome	Varying degrees of cleft face; frontal lipomas, dermoids	Cleft nose, lip and palate may cause intubation difficulties
MELAS (mitochondrial encephalopathy-lactic acidosis-stroke-like episodes syndrome)	Malignant hyperthermia, cardiac arrhythmias, gastrointestinal dysfunction, lactic acidosis, brain injury	Use regional anaesthesia if possible, if general anaesthesia use modified rapid sequence intubation using non-depolarisers (e.g. rocuronium); respiratory and metabolic disturbances are common
Mobius syndrome (congenital facial diplegia)	Associated limb deformities, micrognathia; agenesis of cranial motor nuclei	Feeding difficulties and aspiration may cause chronic pulmonary problems; may be difficult to intubate
Morquio–Ullrich syndrome (mucopolysaccharidosis IV)	Severe dwarfing; aortic incompetence; thoracic deformities; unstable atlantoaxial joint	Cardiorespiratory symptoms by second decade; severe kyphoscoliosis with poor lung function; spinal cord damage from atlantooccipital subluxation
Moschcowitz disease (thrombotic thrombocytopenic purpura)	Haemolytic anaemia and thrombocytopenia; small vessel disease; neurologic damage and renal disease; treatment: splenectomy and steroids	History of steroid therapy; care with renally excreted drugs if kidneys affected
Myasthenia congenita	Similar to adult myasthenia gravis	Avoid respiratory depressants, muscle relaxants; may require post-op ventilation; problems of anticholinesterase therapy pre- and post-op; possibility of cholinergic crisis
Myositis ossificans (fibrodysplasia ossificans)	Bony infiltration of tendons, fascia, aponeuroses and muscle	Airway and intubation problems if neck rigid; thoracic involvement leads to aspiration and asphyxia, lung pathology, and grossly reduced thoracic compliance
Myotonia congenita (Thomsen disease)	Decreased ability to relax muscles after contraction; diffuse hypertrophy of muscle	Avoid relaxants and depressants as for myotonic dystrophy, although this is a more benign disease, non-progressive
Myotonic dystrophy (myotonia dystrophica)	Weakness and myotonia; ptosis, cataracts, partial baldness and gonadal atrophy; cardiac conduction defects and arrhythmias; impaired ventilation	Avoid succinyl choline which causes myotonia in 50% of cases. Non-depolarising drugs do not relax myotonia; use non-depolarising drugs judiciously; neostigmine also induces myotonia; monitor ECG; extremely sensitive to respiratory depressants – use regional or inhalation agents: halothane may cause post-op shivering and myotonia; pulmonary complications due to poor cough
McArdle disease	Glycogen storage disease type V	Muscles affected include cardiac muscle; care with cardiac depressant drugs
McKusick–Kaufman syndrome	Polydactyly, hydrometrocolpos, peripheral cyanosis, tachycardia, tachypnoea, congenital heart diseases, namely, ASD, VSD and other complex congenital anomalies	Gastric decompression, pre-op oxygenation before tracheal intubation, problems due to congenital anomalies
Nager syndrome	facial dysostosis, cleft palate, micrognathia, gastroschisis	Difficult intubation
Nesidioblastosis	Recurrent hypoglycaemia	Metabolic problems
Niemann–Pick disease	Sphingomyelin and cholesterol accumulation in CNS, marrow, liver and spleen; diffuse infiltration of lungs; epilepsy, ataxia and mental retardation	Anaemia and thrombocytopenia due to marrow and spleen involvement; pulmonary insufficiency pneumonia
Noack syndrome	Craniosynostosis and digital anomalies; obesity	May be difficult to intubate because of skull deformity
Noonan syndrome (formerly called male Tuner syndrome)	Short stature, mental retardation, congenital heart disease, micrognathia; hydronephrosis or hypoplasia of kidneys	Usually pulmonary stenosis or patent ductus arteriosus, tetralogy; care with renally excreted drugs if kidneys affected
Ollier disease (enchondromatosis)	Multiple chondromas within bones, usually unilateral; pathologic fractures	With cavernous haemangioma is described as Maffucci syndrome; care with positioning
Orofaciodigital syndrome	Cleft lip and palate, lobed tongue, hypoplastic mandible and maxilla, digital anomalies, hydrocephalus, polycystic kidneys	Difficult airway and intubation, possible renal failure

(Contd.)

Name	Description	Anaesthetic Implications
Osler–Weber–Rendu disease (haemorrhagic telangiectasia)	No coagulation abnormalities; associated pulmonary arteriovenous fistula	Blood loss may be impossible to control; IV may be difficult to maintain due to poor tissues; have recurrent chest infection; dyspnea, cyanosis, and clubbing can occur
Osteogenesis imperfecta (fragilitas ossium)	I: Congenita – stillborn or rapidly fatal II: Tarda – pathologic fractures; osteoporosis leads to kyphoscoliosis	Chest deformity leads to lung pathology; fragile vessels lead to subcutaneous haemorrhage; dentin deficiency causes carious and easily broken teeth; extreme care in positioning as bones are easily fractured
Pallister–Killian syndrome	Characterised by tetrasomy of short arm of chromosome 12p; coarse facies, skin pigment anomalies, cardiovascular disorders, mental retardation	Difficult intubation
Paramyotonia congenita (Eulenburg disease)	Myotonia on exposure to cold; paroxysmal weakness; serum K^+ may be high or low	Anaesthesia as for myotonic dystrophy; also take care of serum K^+ level; avoid succinyl choline
Patau syndrome (trisomy 13)	Mental retardation 100%; microcephaly, micrognathia or dextrocardia (or both); cleft lip or cleft palate; congenital heart disease; usually fatal by 3 years	Difficult intubation; usually ventricular septal defect
Pendred syndrome	Deafness and goitre; incomplete block of thyroxine production	May be euthyroid or hypothyroid; similar to cretinism
Pfeiffer syndrome	Hypertelorism, craniosynostosis, syndactyly	Difficult intubation
Pierre–Robin sequence	Cleft palate, micrognathia, glossoptosis; associated congenital heart disease may occur	Newborn may asphyxiate; may require tongue suture, intubation or tracheostomy; may be difficult to intubate; awake intubation
Polycystic kidneys	One third have associated cysts in liver, pancreas, spleen, lungs, bladder, thyroid; cerebral aneurysm in 15%	Care with renally excreted drugs; beware lung cysts; may lead to pneumothorax; avoid hypertension because of possible cerebral aneurysm
Polycystic liver	Familial – 60% have polycystic kidneys, pancreas and lungs	Usually liver function not impaired until late – fibrosis, splenomegaly, oesophageal varices, etc., possible renal failure, lung cysts
Polysplenia	Bilateral visceral left-sidedness	Complex cardiac anomalies common: artrioseptal defect and endocardial cushion defects; usually not so complex as in asplenia
Pompe disease (glycogen storage II)	Muscle deposits – severe hypotonicity; cardiomegaly; death before 2 years of age	Avoidance of respiratory depressants, muscle relaxants, cardiac depressants, large tongue may cause airway problems
Popliteal pterygium syndrome with syngnathia	Interalveolar syngnathia, face limb and genital anomalies	Difficult intubation
Potter syndrome	Renal agenesis, pulmonary hypoplasia	Renal and respiratory problems are common
Porphyria	Paralyses. Psychiatric disorder; automatic imbalance – hypertension, tachycardia; abdominal pain precipitated by drugs, infections, etc.	Avoid barbiturates (thiopental), sedatives (meprobamate, librium, glutethimide) hydroxydione (steroid anaesthetic), nikethamide, hydantoin derivatives; sulphonamides, antipyretics, hypoglycaemic agents, no harmful effects expected with opiates, phenothiazines, local anaesthetics, N_2O, halothane, isoflurane, muscle relaxants, atropine, neostigmine, pentolinium, corticosteroids
Prader–Willi syndrome	Neonate – hypotonia, poor feeding, absent reflexes; second phase – hyperactive, mental retardation, polyphagia	Obesity of extreme proportions leading to cardiorespiratory failure
Progeria (Hutchinson–Gilford syndrome)	Premature ageing starts at 6 months to 3 years; cardiac disease, ischaemia, hypertension, cardiomegaly	Anaesthesia as for adults with myocardial ischaemia
Prune belly syndrome	Agenisis of abdominal musculature, renal anomalies cryptorchidism	Poor cough – respiratory infections, requires use of accessory muscles; treat as full stomach; intubate and assist or control ventilation; progressive failure

(*Contd.*)

Name	Description	Anaesthetic Implications
Reye syndrome	Liver failure, encephalopathy, respiratory failure	Multiorgan dysfunction
Rieger syndrome	Myotonic dystrophy; hypoplasia of maxilla, abnormal teeth, mental retardation, imperforate anus	Dictated by associated muscle disease
Riley–Day syndrome (familial dysautonomia)	Dopamine hydroxylase deficiency; hyper and hypotensive attacks, absent lacrimation, abnormal sweating, insensitive to pain, poor swallowing and sucking	Emotional lability; recurrent aspiration, pneumonia, chronic lung disease, labile blood pressure; sensitive to adrenergic and cholinergic drugs, respiratory centre insensitive to CO_2, avoid respiratory depressants
Robinow syndrome	Mesomelic brachymelia, short stature, genital hypoplasia, typical facies, developmental delay, congenital heart disease, obstructive uropathy, renal cysts	Airway related, respiratory (thoracic bony anomalies), renal problems, cardiovascular problems
Romano–Ward syndrome	Prolonged QT, sudden heart block	Arrhythmias
Rubella syndrome	Mental retardation, deafness, interstitial pneumonia, cardiac anomalies	Cardiac defects
Rubinstein syndrome	Mental retardation, microcephaly; frequent chest infections; swallowing abnormality, congenital heart disease	Repeated aspiration leads to pneumonia, chronic lung disease
Sanfilippo syndrome (mucopolysaccharidosis III)	Mental retardation and dementia; no hepatosplenomegaly or cardiac problems	No anaesthetic problem described, emotional disturbance, agitation, dementia
Scleroderma	Diffuse cutaneous stiffening; contractures and constrictions	Scarring face and mouth – difficult airway and intubation; chest restriction – poor compliance, diffuse pulmonary fibrosis, difficult veins, cardiac fibrosis or cor pulmonale, history of steroid therapy
Sebaceous nevi (linear)	Linear nevi from forehead to nose, hydrocephalus, mental retardation, coarctation and hypoplasia of aorta	Cardiovascular complications
Short arm deletion syndrome	Typical facies, cleft palate, heart disease, poor prognosis	Cardiovascular complications and difficult intubation
Shy–Drager syndrome	Orthostatic hypotension; degeneration of CNS and autonomic nervous system, decreased sweating; hypersensitive to angiotensin and adrenaline	Labile pulse and blood pressure possibly due to defective baroreceptor response, treat hypotension with IV fluid infusion and henylephrine
Silver syndrome	Short stature; skeletal asymmetry; micrognathia; abnormal sexual development	Difficult intubation
Sipple (multiple endocrine adenomatosis type II)	Phaeochromocytoma and medullary thyroid carcinoma; parathyroid adenoma; CNS tumours, schwannoma of mediastinum associated; Cushing disease	Management of phaeochromocytoma (75% bilateral); problems of multiple endocrine disorders
Smith–Lemli–Opitz syndrome	Mental retardation; micrognathia, thymic hypoplasia Occasional VSD	Airway and intubation problems; pneumonia
Soto (cerebral gigantism) syndrome	Acromegalic features, dilated ventricles, typical facies, prenatal and post-natal overgrowth, mental delay, muscle weakness, prognathism, high arched palate, seizures, congenital heart defects	Possible airway problems due to acromegalic skull; problems due to cardiac anomalies
Stevens–Johnson syndrome	Erythema multiforme, urticarial lesions, and erosions of mouth, eyes, genitalia, possible hypersensitivity to exogenous agents (drugs, infections, etc.)	Oral lesions – avoid intubation, oesophageal stethoscope; monitoring difficult because of skin lesions; fibrillation, myocarditis, pericarditis occurs, febrile episodes, pleural blebs and pneumothorax may occur
Stickler syndrome	Micrognathia, cleft palate	Difficult intubation
Sturge–Weber syndrome	Cavernous angioma over third division of fifth cranial nerve, intracranial calcification, convulsions and may be progressive neurological deficit	No specific anaesthetic problems

(Contd.)

Name	Description	Anaesthetic Implications
Supravalvular aortic stenosis syndrome (idiopathic infantile hypercalcaemia; Williams syndrome)	Hypercalcaemia and mental retardation; abnormal facies; cardiac-dyspnoea, angina; therapy, low calcium diet, steroids; cardiac surgery	Fixed cardiac output and ischaemia; history of steroids; monitor serum calcium or Ca^{++}
Tangier disease (analphalipoproteinaemia)	Low serum cholesterol; orange tonsils and rectal mucosa; splenomegaly; 50% neurologic abnormality; premature coronary disease	Anaemia and thrombocytopenia due to hypersplenism; abnormal EMG – care with muscle relaxants; premature ischaemic heart disease
Tay–Sachs disease	Gangliosidosis; blindness and progressive dementia, degeneration of central nervous system	No described anaesthetic hazard; progressive neurologic loss leads to respiratory complications
Thrombocytopenia with absent radius	Episodic thrombocytopenia precipitated by stress, infection, surgery, etc.; low platelets improve to normal by adulthood; congenital heart disease in 30%	Platelet transfusion for surgery or bleeding (35–40% die in first year of intracranial haemorrhage); avoid elective surgery in first year
Treacher Collins (mandibulofacial dysostosis)	Micrognathia and aplastic zygomatic arches; microstomia, choanal atresia, congenital heart disease may occur	Possible airway and intubation difficulties; gets worse as the child grows older
Trisomy 22	Microcephaly, micrognathia, congenital heart disease, cleft palate	Difficult intubation
Tuberous sclerosis	Adenoma sebaceum of skin, epilepsy and mental retardation, intracranial calcification in 50% hamartomas in lungs, kidneys, heart	Kidneys – pyelolonephritis and renal failure; care with renally excreted drugs, lungs – possible rupture of lung cysts; possible cardiac arrhythmia
Turner syndrome	XO chromosome; micrognathia, coarctation, dissecting aneurysm of aorta or pulmonary stenosis; renal anomalies in more than 50%	Possibly difficult intubation; cardiovascular abnormality; possible renal disease; care with renally excreted drugs
Urbach–Wiethe disease (cutaneous-mucosal hyalinosis)	Type of histiocytosis, hoarseness or aphonia; hyaline deposits in larynx and pharynx	Cautious intubation
VATER syndrome	Vertebral anomalies, VSD, anal atresia, tracheo-oesophageal fistula, radial dysplasia, renal anomalies	Multiple congenital defects
Von Gierke disease	Glycogen storage disease type I; hepatomegaly, enlarged kidneys, severe attacks of hypoglycaemia	Monitor blood sugar and acid base balance (IV glucose infusion); diazoxide for hypoglycaemia
Von Hippel–Lindau disease	Retinal or CNS haemangioblastoma (posterior fossa or spinal cord); associated with phaeochromocytoma; renal, pancreatic and hepatic cysts	Problems associated with phaeochromocytoma, renal and hepatic pathology
Von–Recklinghausen disease (neurofibromatosis)	Café-au-lait spots; tumours in all parts of CNS; peripheral tumours associated with nerve trunks; increased incidence of phaeochromocytoma; 50% kyphoscoliosis; honeycomb cystic lung changes; renal artery dysplasia and hypertension	Screen for phaeochromocytoma, should be investigated for lung function; tumours may occur in larynx and right ventricle outflow tract; care with renally excreted drugs if kidneys involved
Von Willebrand disease (pseudo-haemophilia)	Prolonged bleeding time (decreased factor VIII activity) due to defective platelet adhesiveness; capillary abnormality	Bleeding can be controlled by fresh or fresh frozen plasma, cryoprecipitate; desmopressin may be used for Type I; avoid salicylate therapy (effect on platelets, possible GI bleeding) Avoid regional anaesthesia
Walker–Warburg syndrome	Typical facies with micrognathia, cleft lip and palate, hypotonia, mental retardation, central nervous system malformations, hydronephrosis	Airway difficulties, malignant hyperthermia, exaggerated K^+ release with scoline Use non-MH triggering anaesthesia technique
Weber–Christian disease (chronic non-suppurative panniculitis)	Necrosis of fat, in any situation including retroperitoneal, pericardial, meningeal	Involvement of retroperitoneal tissues may cause acute or chronic adrenal insufficiency, of pericardium leads to restrictive pericarditis, of meninges causes convulsions; avoid trauma to fat by heat, cold or pressure

(*Contd.*)

Name	Description	Anaesthetic Implications
Welander muscular atrophy	Initial involvement peripheral muscles; prognosis good for life, poor for ambulation; cardiac arrhythmias and congestive heart failure may occur	May require spinal fusion; extreme care with thiopental, muscle relaxants, avoid respiratory depressant drugs
Werdnig–Hoffmann disease	Infantile muscular dystrophy feeding difficulties, aspiration, usually death before puberty	Chronic respiratory problems: minimal anaesthesia required; avoid muscle relaxants, ventilatory support may be required and weaning may be difficult
Wermer syndrome (multiple endocrine adenomatosis type I)	Hyperparathyroidism; tumours of pituitary and pancreatic islet cells; occasionally have carcinoid tumours of bronchial tree	Renal failure due to stones; hypoglycaemia from hyperinsulinism
Werner syndrome	Premature ageing, diabetes; early cataracts; mental retardation, bony lesions such as osteomyelitis; cardiac infarction and failure	Anaesthesia as for adult with myocardial ischaemia
Wilson disease (hepatolenticular degeneration)	Decreased ceruloplasmin causes abnormal copper deposits, especially in liver and CNS motor nuclei; renal tubular acidosis	Hepatic failure due to fibrosis
Wiskott–Aldrich syndrome	Immunodeficiency with thrombocytopenia; 100% have low platelets, absent isohaemagglutinins; high IgA, low IgM, eczema, asthma	Blood transfusion and platelets may be required; bone marrow transplantation has been used; all blood products must be irradiated with 3000 rad to prevent graft versus host reaction; avoid contamination – often patients die from generalised herpes or infection from non-pathogenic organisms; strict asepsis to be maintained
Wolff–Parkinson–White syndrome	ECG abnormality – short PR, prolonged QRS with phasic variation in 40%; associated with many cardiac defects; anomalous conduction path between atria and ventricles	Scopolamine preferred to atropine as drying agent; tachycardia due to atropine or apprehension may change ECG with ST segment depression; paroxysmal supraventricular tachycardia on induction of anaesthesia or during cardiac surgery has been reported; should be treated with digitalis, propranolol, pacemaker if necessary; neostigmine may accentuate Wolff–Parkinson–White pattern
Wolman disease (familial xanthomatosis)	Adrenal calcification; resembles Niemann–Pick disease with hepatosplenomegaly and hypersplenism; involvement of other tissues from foam cells, including myocardium	Anaemia, thrombocytopenia; platelet transfusion successful only post-splenectomy

Index

Note: Page numbers followed by *t*, *f*, and *b* indicate table, figure, and box respectively.

B

J

K

L

N

O

Notes